Dickens and Women
Michael Slater

J. M. Dent & Sons Ltd
London, Melbourne and Toronto

First published 1983
© 1983, Michael Slater

All rights reserved. No part of this publication may be reproduced,
stored in a retrieval system, or transmitted, in any form or by any means,
electronic, mechanical, photocopying, recording or otherwise, without the
prior permission of
J. M. Dent & Sons Ltd

This book is set in 11/13 VIP Sabon roman by
Inforum Ltd, Portsmouth
Printed and made in Great Britain by
Richard Clay (The Chaucer Press) Ltd, Bungay, Suffolk for
J. M. Dent & Sons Ltd
Aldine House, 33 Welbeck Street, London W1M 8LX

British Library Cataloguing in Publication Data

Slater, Michael
  Dickens and women.
  1. Dickens, Charles, *1812–1870*—Friends
  and associates
  I. Title
  823'18   PR4582

ISBN 0-460-04248-3

Dickens and Women

Contents

List of Illustrations

To the memory of Leslie C. Staples,
Hon. Editor of *The Dickensian*, 1944–67.

A great friend and a great Dickensian.

Preface

During the writing of this book I have incurred debts of gratitude to many people who, in various ways, have given me valuable help and encouragement. Their faith, maintained throughout eight years, that I would actually finish the book before the Greek Kalends has been no less valuable.

Professor Philip Collins has been prodigal of advice and information at all stages of the book's composition and, most generously of all, found time to read through the entire final draft and to make innumerable, and always very helpful, comments and criticisms. I am deeply grateful to him, as I am also to Professor Barbara Hardy whose close scrutiny, at an earlier stage, of drafts of chapters 11 to 13 stimulated me to much useful re-thinking.

I am also grateful for advice and information on particular points to Miss Nina Burgis, Miss Katharine M. Longley, the late Leslie C. Staples, Mr Graham Storey and Professor Kathleen Tillotson. Both the present Curator of The Dickens House Museum, Dr David Parker, and his predecessor, Miss Marjorie E. Pillers, have been unfailingly helpful and resourceful in guiding me to relevant material and answering queries, as have the staff of the University of London Library, in particular Miss Mavis Oswald.

To my research assistant, Miss Jean Elliott, I owe a very great debt. She has not only been extraordinarily efficient and indefatigable in tracking down information, verifying references, checking quotations and so on, but has also vigilantly monitored my style, massacring otiose adjectives, splitting up interminable sentences and constantly seeking to eliminate such things as repetitiveness, vagueness and unhappy attempts at sprightliness. Another friend, Miss Mary Ford, helped me greatly by locating and summarizing much useful background material during the initial stages of the book's writing.

My thanks go also to Mrs Barbara Brunswick, Miss Sarah Pearsall and Mrs Jean Nunn for their excellent typing work, and I wish to record here my gratitude to the British Academy for a grant from the Small Grants Research Fund in the Humanities towards the costs of the preparation of the final draft of this book.

Various long-suffering friends and relations have kindly submitted to having portions of the book read aloud to them at different times and their comments have often helped me to improve on what I had written. I should particularly like to thank Dr Andrew Sanders, the Hon. Editor of *The Dickensian*, and my sister, Mrs Barbara Parker, in this respect, and above all Q Love whose interest in the book's progress and insistence on being regularly presented with further instalments have been a constant stimulus.

The comments and criticisms of audiences whom I was invited to address on some aspect of Dickens and women have also often proved very helpful, and I remember particularly in this respect audiences at the Free University of West Berlin, the Ohio State University (where also part of the research for this book was carried out during a very pleasant year spent there as a Visiting Professor), the University of Hong Kong and the University of Lódz, Poland; also at meetings of the Dickens Fellowship in London, Nottingham and Holland.

My final and most comprehensive thanks must go to my friend John Grigg without whose regular supportive encouragement, judicious counsel, and remarkable ability to maintain an overall sense of any forest even when most thickly entangled in its trees this book would quite certainly never have been finished.

Birkbeck College, March 1982   Michael Slater

Acknowledgments

I am grateful to Mr Christopher Dickens for permission to quote from unpublished letters and memoranda by Dickens and members of the Dickens family. Quotations from the following volumes are made by permission of the Oxford University Press: *The Speeches of Charles Dickens* (1960), ed. K.J. Fielding; the Pilgrim Edition of *The Letters of Charles Dickens*, vol.1 (1965), edd. M. House and G. Storey; vol.2 (1969), edd. M. House and G. Storey; vol.3 (1974), edd. M. House, G. Storey and K. Tillotson; vol.4 (1977), ed. K. Tillotson; vol.5 (1981), edd. G. Storey and K.J. Fielding; the Clarendon Edition of *Oliver Twist* (1966), ed. K. Tillotson; the Clarendon Edition of *David Copperfield* (1981), ed. N. Burgis.

Introduction

Dickens is the greatest novelist to have written in English as Shakespeare is the greatest poet. Whole libraries have been written in praise of his achievement since Mr Pickwick and Sam Weller first captivated the world in 1837: his mastery of the comic, the grotesque and the macabre; his descriptive, narrative and dramatic powers; his fecundity as a creator of characters who seem definitive embodiments of so many aspects of human nature; his resonant, haunting emblems of social ills and moral corruption; his endlessly inventive and felicitous manipulation of the English language – all these things have exercised leading critics in every generation and many countries. Detailed and illuminating studies have also been made of his response to, and literary presentation of, aspects of the human condition as manifested in the world of early Victorian England: education, religion, city-dwelling, crime, and so on. However, no major study has so far appeared of Dickens's response to, and present-ation of, one of the most fundamental aspects of human existence – femaleness and its myriad interrelationships and interactions with male-ness. Today, with the widespread and ever-growing interest in the history of women in our culture, the time seems particularly ripe for such a study. What did the greatest creative genius in English literature of the last three hundred years have to say about women? What was his perception of female nature and his conception of women's role in life? How did he present female characters in his fiction? These are the questions to which this book addresses itself.

The logical starting-point is a close study of Dickens's own experience of women – as son, brother, lover, husband, father – as it affected the deepest currents of his emotional life, forming in him attitudes towards, and beliefs about, women and female nature that then find expression in his art. This involves considering all the surviving documentary evidence in the form of letters, reminiscences and so on, and also requires a sifting of the mass of legend and doubtful traditions about Dickens's private life that often appear masquerading as biographical fact. In particular, it requires a careful scrutiny of the assertions about Dickens's relations with some of the women in his life, notably Ellen Ternan, assertions made by biographers who are simply reading back from his fiction into his life as though he were an autobiographer rather than a creator of fiction. This is not to say, of course, that no obvious and demonstrable connections exist between the women in his life and characters in his fiction (his mother and Mrs Micawber, for example, or Maria Beadnell and Dora Spenlow or Flora Finching). Clearly there *are* such connections and

Dickens's fictionalization of his emotional experience of particular women must be taken into account when seeking to elucidate that experience.

This study of the most important women in Dickens's life and their effect on him as man and as artist is followed by a more comprehensive and detailed survey of the women in his fiction than has yet been attempted. Three distinct phases in his work emerge from this survey and it can clearly be seen that the middle decade of his career, 1846–56, was the period during which his novelist's imagination was most deeply engaged with women for their own sakes, rather than as 'relative creatures',[1] and with the potentialities of female nature, as he conceived of it, for both good and evil.

The last section of this book switches back from the novelist to the man. It examines Dickens's recorded comments (including relevant authorial commentary in his fictional writings) on women, their nature and their role in life in order to arrive at his basic conception of the womanly ideal, an ideal intimately connected with the Victorian cult of domesticity of which Dickens himself was so celebrated an exponent.

'My father did not understand women',[2] Dickens's younger daughter is reported as having once remarked and, until recently at least, it seems to have been generally assumed that she was absolutely right and that the consequence was a false and feeble presentation of women in his novels. His joke-women like Mrs Nickleby or Mrs Gamp have always been relished but his heroines and other seriously presented female characters have found few admirers. Such cogent modern criticism as Dr Leavis's discussion of Amy Dorrit or Professor Barbara Hardy's of Edith Dombey (both characters having been long regarded as mere stereotypes)[3] has begun to change this situation, however. The present book aims not only to provide a fuller and juster account of Dickens's actual relations with, and ideas about, women than has yet been offered to the world, but also to further the critical rehabilitation of his fictional women, so long unjustly dismissed as the Achilles' heel of our Shakespeare of the novel.

I

Experience into Art

'Being accustomed to observe myself as curiously as if I were another man . . .'
The Uncommercial Traveller, 'A Fly-leaf in a Life'

1

Mother and Son

'Not an orphan in the wide world can be so deserted as the child who is an outcast from a living parent's love.'
Dombey and Son, ch. 24

Elizabeth Barrow, the future mother of Charles Dickens, was born in the fateful year of 1789 when, as her son was later to write, there was an echo in England 'as of a great storm in France with a dreadful sea rising'.[1] It was, no doubt, as a result of the ensuing international tempest that her father, Charles Barrow, a Lambeth music-master, found a new career in 1801. He joined the expanding staff of the Navy Pay Office, soon rising to the important and responsible post of Chief Conductor of Monies in Towns at a salary of £330 a year. He also found, in 1805, a place in the Office for one of his younger sons, Thomas Culliford Barrow, who started work there the same day as another young man called John Dickens. A colleague later recalled John as 'a fascinating rascal who had run away with T.C. Barrow's sister, Elizabeth'[2] which sounds as though the Chief Conductor was not exactly enthusiastic about welcoming his Dickens son-in-law. His consent must have been eventually forthcoming, however, as Elizabeth was still legally a minor when the couple got married in 1809. No doubt John's rapidly improving salary and position in the Pay Office (he was earning £218.15s. p.a. by 1810, having started at £56.15s. five years earlier) helped to recommend him to his father-in-law despite the fact that his mother was 'in service' – fairly exalted service, certainly, as she was housekeeper to Lord Crewe, but service just the same.[3]

Chief Conductor Barrow seems to have lived somewhat beyond his means, bolstering his salary by conducting rather a lot of Government money into his own pocket; when these defalcations were discovered in 1810 the amount involved was well over £5,000 and Barrow soon retreated to the Isle of Man to avoid unpleasant consequences. All this, however, seems not to have affected the positions either of his son, Thomas, or of his son-in-law, John, whose first child, Fanny, was born that year. John and Elizabeth continued to enjoy a modest prosperity for the first ten or eleven years of their married life, first in Portsea, then in

London and eventually in Chatham, where they moved five years after the birth of their first son, Charles (named after his defaulting grandfather), in 1812.

Elizabeth Dickens was at this time a pretty, bright-eyed, vivacious-looking woman with her hair clustered in dark ringlets and a neat wasp waist (of which she was, apparently, 'very vain').[4] The gaiety of her disposition is suggested by her proudly informing one of her granddaughters in later life that she had attended a ball in Portsea only a few hours before giving birth to Charles.[5]* Her marriage to her beloved 'D', as she called him, was evidently a very happy one and continued to be so through all the drastic fluctuations of fortune that befell them: 'Certainly there never was a Man more unselfish', she wrote of him after his death to Samuel Haydon, who had sent her an engraving of his bust of John, 'and ever a Friend to those whom he could serve and a most affectionate kind Husband and Father'. 'To have an affectionate Husband', she added feelingly in a postscript to Mrs Haydon, 'to share pleasures and sorrows is the happiest state in the World.'[6]

All went well in the Dickens household for the first ten years of little Charles's life. Four more children were born of whom two survived, Letitia and Frederick, and Elizabeth employed a nursemaid, Mary Weller, to help her with the growing family. Years later, it was this Mary who – partly perhaps in reaction to the widespread identification of Dickens's mother with the foolish figure of Mrs Nickleby – emphatically described her former mistress as 'a dear good mother and a fine woman'.[7] Mary herself must be said to have played an important part in Dickens's education if indeed it was she and not another servant who stimulated his imagination with those sensational bedtime stories about such 'diabolical' characters as Captain Murderer that he later recalled in his essay 'Nurse's Stories',[8] but it was his mother, he said, who had first encouraged his desire for knowledge and awakened his passion for reading. She 'taught him regularly every day for a long time, and taught him, he was convinced, thoroughly well'. David Copperfield learning his alphabet at his mother's knee, delighting in 'the easy good nature of O and Q and S', is a piece of straight autobiography on Dickens's part, but poor little Mrs Copperfield, the simple ex-nursery governess, would hardly have been able to push David's education as far as Elizabeth Dickens did her son's, shepherding him even so far as the 'rudiments' of Latin.[9]

Apart from this detail about her teaching him in his infancy we glean

---

* Footnote references underlined contain additional information; others are to sources only.

little from Forster's biography about what sort of woman Elizabeth Dickens was and what young Charles's attitude to her was. She figures twice in the fragmentary autobiography written by Dickens in the late 1840s and reprinted in part by Forster – once as comically pathetic in her attempt to help the family finances by starting a school, and once as almost criminally hard-hearted in her anxiety that the twelve-year-old Charles should be sent back to his hated employment in the blacking-factory. Dickens's comments on both these episodes we shall consider in a moment, but first let us look at the most detailed character-sketch of Elizabeth that we have. This appears in a letter to a friend written by Mrs Davey, the wife of the London doctor under whose care Dickens placed his father when John became seriously ill in 1850. John and Elizabeth moved into the Daveys' home in Keppel Street, Bloomsbury, and it was there that John died, after much agony, in 1851. Mrs Davey's letter was written twenty-three years later, after the appearance of the first volume of Forster's biography, and seems to have been intended to vindicate the characters of Dickens's parents and to assert their son's love for them which Forster's readers might well have doubted, especially with regard to Elizabeth. The letter was published in an American journal, *Lippin-cott's Magazine*, as part of a feature called 'Our Monthly Gossip', in June 1874.[10]

'Mrs Dickens', wrote Mrs Davey,

was a little woman, who had been very nice-looking in her youth. She had very bright hazel eyes, and was as thoroughly good-natured, easy-going, companionable a body as one would wish to meet with. The likeness between her and Mrs Nickleby is simply the exaggeration of some slight peculiarities. She possessed an extraordinary sense of the ludicrous, and her power of imitation was something quite astonishing. On entering a room she almost unconsciously took an inventory of its contents, and if anything happened to strike her as out of place or ridiculous, she would afterward describe it in the quaintest possible manner. In like manner she noted the personal peculiarities of her friends and acquaintances. She had also a fine vein of pathos, and could bring tears to the eyes of her listeners when narrating some sad event. She was slightly lame, having injured one of her legs by falling through a trap-door whilst acting in some private theatricals at the Soho Theatre, London. I am of opinion that a great deal of Dickens's genius was inherited from his mother. He possessed from her a keen appreciation of the droll and of the pathetic, as also considerable dramatic talent. Mrs Dickens has often sent my sisters and myself into uncontrollable fits of laughter by her funny sayings and inimitable mimicry. Charles was decidedly fond of her, and always treated her respectfully and kindly.

We get only one glimpse, in Dickens's fragment of autobiography, of those things in Elizabeth's character which Mrs Davey stresses so much, her powers of observation and her talent for amusing reportage. When John's improvidence had at last landed him in the Marshalsea Prison, there to be joined by his wife and younger children, little Charles, who was boarded out, would visit them in the evenings; at such times, he recalled, 'I was always delighted to hear from my mother what she knew about the histories of the different debtors in the prison'.[11] But it is noticeable that he writes, a moment before, of his 'early interest in observing people' without at all considering the obvious thought that this vital basis of his art might have been inherited from his mother or at least strongly developed in him by her example.

About Elizabeth's treatment of her eldest son in the idyllic Chatham days before Camden Town and the Marshalsea darkened his boyhood we learn nothing at all (apart from the account of her early teaching of him already quoted) from the autobiographical fragment. But Forster does quote Dickens's description of himself to Washington Irving in 1841 as having been 'a very small and not-over-particularly-taken-care-of boy'[12] which seems to cast a rather undeserved slur on his mother: it is hard to reconcile, for example, with his own recollection of her daily concern for his early education.

What Dickens would have regarded as having been properly taken care of as a child Elizabeth, who impressed a young acquaintance in 1841 as having 'a good stock of common sense',[13] might have seen as over-indulgence. In the letter to Samuel Haydon quoted earlier she adds a postscript to Mrs Haydon referring to the couple's son, apparently an only child: 'I . . . beg you also *not* to *spoil* the *Young Artist*, I'm fearful the chances are against such advice, with *One* it is rather difficult and requires more firmness than affectionate Mamas possess'. This suggests that, even had she realized in the Chatham days that she was the mother of a budding genius, she would have resisted any temptation to take 'particular' care of him for fear that he might become spoiled. The adult Dickens, however, looking back with pity and anger on his earlier self, 'a child of singular abilities, quick, eager, delicate, and soon hurt',[14] clearly regretted that his exceptional quality had been so unrecognized by his mother — his father had at least taken a pride in his precocious talent for singing comic songs and encouraged him, in their walks together, with the idea of growing up to be somebody, even, perhaps, master of a fine house like Gad's Hill Place. 'Mrs Dickens', wrote Mrs Davey, 'does not seem to have foreseen the future celebrity of her son in his childhood' and it is, we must feel, much to her credit that she did not claim, during the years of her son's stupendous fame, that she had had maternal presentiments on the subject. She did, however, remember 'many little circumstances afterwards which she was very fond of relating'. The example Mrs Davey gives is particularly interesting because Dickens himself used it in *Great Expectations*:

> Once, when Charles was a tiny boy, and the family were staying down in Chatham, the nurse had a great deal of trouble in inducing him to follow her when out for his daily walk. When they returned home, Mrs Dickens said to her, 'Well, how have the children behaved?' 'Very nicely indeed, ma'am – all but Master Charley.' 'What has he done?' 'Why, ma'am, he will persist in always going the same road every day.' 'Charley, Charley, how is this?' 'Why, mamma,' answered the urchin, 'does not the Bible say we must walk in the same path all the days of our life?'

Here, surely, we have the source for that passage at the beginning of chapter 7 of *Great Expectations* when Pip confesses to the inaccuracy of his ideas about the 'theological positions' to which his Catechism bound him:

> . . . I have a lively remembrance that I supposed my declaration that I was to 'walk in the same all the days of my life,' laid me under an obligation always to go through the village from our house in one particular direction, and never to vary it by turning down by the wheelwright's or up by the mill.

When we seek to match Elizabeth's reminiscences about herself and her son in the Chatham days with Dickens's own, however, the only material we can find for the latter, apart from what Forster tells us, seems to be an anecdote recorded by Marcus Stone, the young artist whom Dickens befriended for the sake of his father, Frank Stone, and who illustrated Dickens's last completed novel, *Our Mutual Friend*. Walking with Stone in Chatham one day in the 1860s Dickens pointed out a low wall and said, 'I remember . . . my poor Mother, God forgive her, put me up on the edge of that wall, so that I might wave my hat and cheer George 4th – then Prince Regent – who was driving by'.[15] This has the same disconcerting tone of amusement tinged with contempt that pervades the famous account, in the autobiographical fragment, of Elizabeth's attempt in 1823 to retrieve the family fortunes by starting a school. With her husband's finances getting into a worse and worse state after the move back to London and five children now to feed, the time had come, she felt, 'to exert herself'. Relying on a family friend, Christopher Huffam, Dickens's godfather, Elizabeth determined to start a school. She seemed, after all, to have a natural gift for teaching, according to Dickens himself. Huffam was a ship's chandler, rigger and naval contractor, living 'in a substantial handsome sort of way' at Limehouse.[16] He naturally knew many people engaged in the East India trade and it was surely reasonable enough to expect that he might be able to help find pupils for 'Mrs Dickens's Establishment' by recommending it to families living in India who wanted their small children cared for and educated in England. But, as Charlotte Brontë was later to lament, 'people often think they can do great things in that way till they have tried – but getting pupils is unlike getting any other sort of goods'.[17] Moreover, Huffam himself unfortunately got into difficulties just at this time (he went bankrupt in 1824) and so he had other things to worry about besides poor Elizabeth's project. In the autobiographical fragment Dickens mentions the affixing of a large brass plate announcing the school to the front-door of the specially hired premises in Gower Street North and then describes the collapse of the enterprise in three withering sentences:

> I left, at a great many other doors, a great many circulars calling attention to the merits of the establishment. Yet nobody ever came to the school, nor do I recollect that anybody ever proposed to come, or that the least preparation was made to receive anybody. But I know that we got on very badly with the butcher and baker; that very often we had not too much for dinner; and that at last my father was arrested.[18]

Angus Wilson perceptively notes that 'the details of this attack on his mother's ill-thought-out scheme [not *so* 'ill-thought-out' either] deserve careful attention, for he directly connects it to the failure of household management (which is only partly logical) and to the imprisonment of his father (which is quite illogical)'.[19] There is indeed something more here than contemptuous amusement. And what that something is blazes forth in Dickens's next reference to his mother in the autobiographical fragment.

Young James Lamert, stepson of Mrs Dickens's sister, had taken an interest in Charles, making a toy theatre for him whilst lodging with the family in Camden Town, before their move to Gower Street. Now he suggested to Charles's beleaguered parents that the boy should come and work, pasting labels on bottles, in a newly launched blacking-factory where he himself was a sort of manager. The wages would be six or seven shillings a week. It is hardly surprising that John and Elizabeth accepted this proposal 'very willingly'. Of the shock and outrage it caused their son they perhaps never had any idea although their later silence on the subject is suggestive. 'From that hour, until this,' Dickens wrote, 'my father and my mother have been stricken dumb upon it. I have never heard the least

8

allusion to it, however far off and remote, from either of them.'[20]

In the autobiographical fragment Dickens leaves no doubt as to the degree of the psychological and emotional earthquake suffered by his twelve-year-old self:

> It is wonderful to me how I could have been so easily cast away at such an age . . .

> No advice, no counsel, no encouragement, no consolation, no support, from any one that I can call to mind, so help me God.

> . . . I might easily have been, for any care that was taken of me, a little robber or a little vagabond.[21]

'A little robber' is precisely what Fagin seeks to make the orphan Oliver Twist (whose parents had failed him in the most basic way by dying, one before and one just after his birth, leaving him branded with illegitimacy); and it is to this strange second novel of Dickens's, where public satire merges into private nightmare, that we must look, I believe, as well as to the autobiographical fragment, if we want to register the full horror of the blacking-factory episode for Dickens – to this book rather than to the more consciously autobiographical early chapters of *Copperfield*.

The actual factory, Dickens wrote, was 'a crazy, tumble-down old house, abutting . . . on the river, and literally overrun with rats'. So is Fagin's den and so, admittedly, is Murdstone and Grinby's wine-bottle depository in which little David endures his 'secret agony'. But Murdstone's manager, the shallow Mr Quinion, has no designs on David's immortal soul comparable to Fagin's devilish plan to 'blacken' Oliver's and 'change its hue for ever'.[22] Oliver is thrust into a kind of hell where he is tempted and menaced by the Devil himself, David suffers only a terrible loss of caste. The very name of Fagin is fraught with significance in regard to Dickens's biography, as John Bayley has pointed out,[23] for it was the name of the boy who befriended and protected the child Dickens in the blacking-factory. For this presumption and for the appalling danger his kindliness represented, that the child might be lulled into some sort of acceptance of the outrage that had been perpetrated against him, Bob Fagin was punished by the extraordinary artist that his little protégé grew up to be. Dickens's off-hand comment on the matter, 'I took the liberty of using his name, long afterwards, in *Oliver Twist*' (as though Fagin were just any character) is tantalizing; just how aware was he of what it was in him that was generating the imaginative power manifested in *Oliver*? In *Copperfield* where he consciously distances the horror of the whole blacking-factory episode he clearly knows very well what he is doing; and nowhere is this distancing more evident, as we shall see, than in his treatment in that novel of the role played by his mother.

But before looking at what Dickens the novelist made of Elizabeth let us return to Dickens the remembering man writing his autobiography. No reader of the passages from it published by Forster can fail to notice, as Dickens's wife noticed,[24] his greater harshness towards Elizabeth than towards John Dickens so that, as Wilson has pointed out in the passage quoted above, even his father's imprisonment is made to seem the direct result of her incompetence. Some of this extra harshness towards his mother may be explained, I think, by recalling Dickens's acknowledgment that she was the first person to stimulate his intellectual curiosity. This it was, perhaps, that led to those 'dreams of growing up to be a learned and distinguished man' that, he later wrote, were so cruelly crushed in his breast during the blacking-factory time when he was in a situation with which both John and Elizabeth seemed to be 'quite satisfied'. 'They could hardly have been more so', Dickens wrote, 'if I had been twenty years of age, distinguished at a grammar-school, and going to Cambridge.' Elizabeth visited Lamert at the factory 'many times' whilst her son was employed there (John went there 'not more than once or twice') and it must have been heart-sickening for the little boy she had once taught to see her apparent indifference to his degraded state.[25]

We may be sure that Elizabeth was not indifferent to her son, however – it is most probable, in fact, that her attentiveness to Lamert involving frequent visits to the factory was the result of concern for Charles and his future. A family connection of hers had given the boy a position in what might become a flourishing business. The position was indeed a lowly one but Elizabeth's optimistic outlook on life no doubt persuaded her that this was but the first necessary step on a ladder (one recalls Matthew Arnold's 'vivacity' on the subject of 'Mrs Gooch's Golden Rule', the mother who said every day to her son, the future Chairman of the Great Western Railway, when he was a boy going to work, 'Ever remember, my dear Dan, that you should look forward to being some day manager of that concern!').[26] But little Charles was dreaming of becoming 'a learned and distinguished man', not a manager of a rat-infested blacking-factory.

His release from the place came after some months through his father's falling out with Lamert and abruptly withdrawing him from employment there. With 'a relief so strange it was like oppression' the child emerged from Fagin's den. And then, to his incredulous horror, he found his mother trying to push him back into it:

My mother set herself to accommodate the quarrel, and did so next day. She brought home a request for me to return next morning . . . My father said I should go back no more, and should go to school. I do not write resentfully or angrily: for I know how all these things have worked together to make me what I am: but I never afterwards forgot, I never shall forget, I never can forget, that my mother was warm for my being sent back.[27]

'Resentment' and 'anger' are indeed terms too mild for the emotions that must lie behind such rhetoric as this. An enduring sense of horrified dismay and ultimate betrayal – such feelings as these must, at the deepest level, have been those of Dickens towards his mother for the rest of his life. They surface in the characterization of the almost criminally irresponsible Mrs Nickleby and a whole subsequent line of 'bad mother' figures in his novels like Mrs Joe in *Great Expectations* with the bib of her apron symbolically bristling with pins and needles, culminating in the horrific virago-mother of 'George Silverman's Explanation' (1867).

Happily oblivious of the catastrophic maternal failure her son had registered so bitterly, Elizabeth continued to do her best to get her eldest son a good job. When he finally finished his interrupted schooling it was Elizabeth not John who bestirred herself to help him 'begin the world' as the Victorian phrase had it. Her aunt kept a boarding-house in Berners Street where lodged Edward Blackmore, partner in the legal firm of Ellis and Blackmore. Elizabeth, Blackmore recalled later, often visited Berners Street with her children and 'expressed a great wish to get [Charles] employment in my office and the boy's manners were so prepossessing that I agreed to take him as a clerk'.[28] (That this first employment gave Dickens a lifelong dislike and distrust of the legal profession is irrelevant: at least working in an office, even that of Dodson and Fogg, was preferable to being lost for ever in Fagin's lair.) Later on, it was on *The Mirror of Parliament*, a paper run by one of Elizabeth's brothers, that Dickens began his highly successful career as a journalist.

Nor was it only in helping him find work that Elizabeth made herself useful to her son. Although the autobiographical fragment creates the impression, as we have seen, that she was altogether inept on the domestic front Dickens's letters in the later 1830s and early 1840s tell a different story. We can see from these that he regarded Elizabeth as a shrewd and efficient household manager, with a talent for bringing about that state of domestic affairs generally referred to by him as 'comfortable' (always a powerful and important word for Dickens in this context). Evidently she helped greatly in preparing his bachelor chambers in Furnival's Inn for occupation by him and his bride. Later on, he trusted her to go and vet possible new homes for them. Down in Devon in 1839, arranging for his parents' occupancy of a cottage there, Dickens asked his mother to come down a few days ahead of his father; if she would do this, he wrote, 'the house will be *perfect* by the Saturday Night, and I shall be saved – not only a world of uneasiness, but a great deal of money, for the people will take me in and I can't help it'. To his friend and solicitor, Mitton, he wrote, 'There are so many things she can make comfortable at a much less expense than I could . . . .'.[29]

We might note also that one of the reasons Dickens gives in a letter to his wife (5 March 1839) for asking his mother to come down to Devon earlier than she was expecting was that he thought 'the suddenness of the call would break the force of the separation, and spare much of the pain of coming away'. There is other evidence that he did indeed treat her 'respectfully and kindly', as Mrs Davey claimed, and that he did, on one level at least, have, in Thomas Powell's words, 'a deep affection for her'. When his father died in 1851 Dickens's conduct, Mrs Davey recalled, was 'noble':

> I remember he took her in his arms, and they both wept bitterly together. He told her that she must rely on him for the future. He immediately paid whatever his father owed, and relieved his mother's mind on that score.[30]

Elizabeth wrote, in the letter to the Haydons already quoted, of her resolution not to live with any of her children after John's death, 'thinking it better to be independent as my beloved Charles made me immediately on the death of his Father' (she jokes about being 'rather profitable' to her landlady since she is so seldom at home because of 'the kindness of all my Friends' and adds a charming postcript to the whole letter – 'What an Egotistical Note'). 'It is something to know how nobly Charles has behaved in this trial', her third son Alfred wrote to her, adding, 'but although we are not all in a position to shew such substantial proofs of affection for the memory of our dear father you may rest assured there is not one of us who is not ready to show you how great and deep our affection for you is.'[31]

Evidently, neither Elizabeth herself nor anyone in the immediate family saw Charles as anything but an exemplary devoted son. True, he did become exasperated with her when she backed up John in complaints about their enforced Devon retirement, sending him 'an unsatisfactory epistle' soon after they had been settled there and, shortly after that, another letter which moved him to declare, 'I am sick at heart with both her and father too'.[32] Also, he sometimes became annoyed – rather priggishly, we might think – by her reluctance in middle age to behave in what he considered a becomingly matronly manner. Young Eleanor Picken, later Eleanor Christian, who was privileged to consort with the Dickens family during a holiday at Broadstairs in 1841, recalled that 'old Mrs Dickens', whom she found 'very agreeable', 'entered into youthful amusements with much enjoyment'; in particular, she showed a great love for dancing but 'never indulged in it with any other partner than her son-in-law, or with some relation'. Nevertheless, whenever she did dance 'Charles always looked as sulky as a bear the whole time'.[33] 'My mother', Dickens wrote to his old flame, Maria Winter, in 1855, 'has a strong objection to being considered in the least old, and usually appears here on Christmas Day in a juvenile cap which takes an immense time in the putting on.'[34] Her excitability would also exasperate him sometimes: 'I suppose Letitia really has had a Miscarriage?' he inquired from abroad about his younger sister in 1845. 'She ha[d one before that] existed only in my Mother's brain, and led to the dilution of more gu[shing floods of] tears, than any failure of that kind, being real, has probably ever do[ne in the whole history of] the World.'[35]

But we find little direct evidence in his surviving letters, or in reminiscences of him by others, of that undying bitterness he felt towards her which emerges so unmistakably in the autobiographical fragment. Some interesting indirect evidence exists, however, in a letter he wrote to his fiancée, Catherine Hogarth, in the autumn of 1835. He was sending her a book – not the romantic novel, Ainsworth's *Rookwood*, for which she was waiting but a volume of Dr Johnson's *Lives of the English Poets*. The life to which he drew her particular notice by turning down the leaf on which it began was that of Richard Savage, the early eighteenth-century poet and dramatist. 'Now *do* read it attentively,' he exhorted her, 'if you do, I know from your excellent understanding you will be delighted. If you slur it, you will think it dry.'[36] The *Life of Savage* is a story of maternal rejection and cruelty which, in certain details, Dickens surely identified with his own story. Savage was, so he himself claimed (and Johnson does not question this) the illegitimate son of a Mrs Brett, formerly Countess of Macclesfield. She had disposed of her inconvenient offspring 'by committing him to the care of a poor woman whom she enjoined to educate as her own'.[37] Through the charity of Mrs Brett's mother he was placed at a grammar school where, since he always spoke respectfully of his master, Johnson thought it 'probable that the mean rank in which he then appeared did not hinder his genius from being distinguished, or his industry from being rewarded'. This schooling was abruptly broken off, however, and an attempt was made – instigated, Johnson asserts, by Mrs Brett – to ship the boy off to the American plantations. When this was foiled Mrs Brett resolved to bury him in 'poverty and obscurity in his own country' by apprenticing him to a shoemaker in Holborn. Savage, discovering his true relationship to her, previously concealed from him, rejected his lowly trade and sought help from her to rise in the world but 'all his assiduity and tenderness were without effect, for he could neither soften her heart nor open her hand, and was reduced to the utmost miseries of want, whilst he was endeavouring to awaken the affection of a mother'. Despite her hostility he did succeed, however, in making a name for himself by his literary genius.

One can hardly doubt that Dickens's intense response to this story, and his eagerness to have Catherine read and react to it, stemmed from the feelings of injury he continued to nurse against his own mother and her being 'warm' for permanently suspending his schooling and sending him back to a degradingly menial occupation. (His empathy with Savage was no doubt further stimulated by the praise bestowed by Johnson on his subject's writings which was just such as that which reviewers were giving to the brilliant young author of *Sketches by Boz*: Savage was, says Johnson, extraordinarily *observant*; 'he easily received impressions from objects and very forcibly transmitted them to others'.)[38]

Catherine, of course, at this stage ignorant of Dickens's early history, could not have suspected the bitter memories that underlay his directing her to this biography of a minor poet of the last century. And, on the face of things, Dickens continued all his mother's life to care 'nobly' for her. She began to lapse into senility some eight or nine years after her husband's death and Dickens did not skimp his duty to her. We find him writing to Wills, his sub-editor on *Household Words*, in March 1860:

> When I got home last night, I found a note from the lady with whom my mother lives, who is terrified by the responsibility of her charge and utterly relinquishes it. Consequently I must at once devote myself to the difficult task of finding good hands for my mother, and getting her into them without alarming her . . .

He is hopeful the next month that she 'will become no worse, but will go on very gently'. By August, however, with the harassment of his brother Alfred's sudden death and the responsibility of looking after the widow and her five children, exasperation is beginning to overcome filial concern and we get a glimpse of that essential hard-heartedness towards his mother that had inspired the creation of Mrs Nickleby twenty-odd years earlier. He writes to a friend:

> My mother, who was also left to me when my father died (I never had anything left to me but relations), is in the strangest state of mind from

14

senile decay; and the impossibility of getting her to understand what is
the matter, combined with her desire to be got up in sables like a female
Hamlet, illumines the dreary scene with a ghastly absurdity that is the
chief relief I can find in it.

Three months later Dickens reported on another visit to his mother in a
letter to his beloved 'little housekeeper', his sister-in-law, Georgina
Hogarth. Elizabeth was 'much better than I had supposed' he wrote:

> She was not in bed, but down-stairs. Helen and Letitia [her daughter-in-
> law and younger daughter] were poulticing her poor head, and, the
> instant she saw me, she plucked up a spirit and asked me for 'a pound'![39]

Immediately following this, as Walter Dexter notes in his Nonesuch
edition of Dickens's letters, a passage of about five lines has been cut out
of the letter by Georgina when preparing it for inclusion in her edition of
Dickens's collected correspondence. Georgina, 'Guardian of the Beloved
Memory', would, of course, be anxious that nothing unfitting – such as
mockery of his mother – should be revealed and the letter perhaps went
on to some remarks rather notably lacking in filial tenderness. Elizabeth's
senile demand for some money (horribly reminiscent of Grandmother
Smallweed in *Bleak House*) must have seemed all too symbolically
appropriate to her son. Not only had she once sacrificed him, as he saw it,
for the few shillings a week he could earn as a child but she had aided and
abetted her improvident husband in constant assaults on his purse, or in
complaints about his provision for them, during his years of fame and
prosperity. When she finally died in 1863 his private epitaph on her was
terse: 'My poor mother died quite suddenly at last. Her condition was
frightful.'[40]

Forster records that 'on one occasion' after Dickens had revealed to
him the miseries of his childhood the novelist ruminated about how he
could have been so neglected in those years by so kind and good a father.
He gave Forster this sketch of John's character:

> I know my father to be as kind hearted and generous a man as ever lived
> in the world. Everything that I can remember of his conduct to his wife,
> or children, or friends, in sickness or affliction, is beyond all praise. By
> me, as a sick child, he has watched night and day, unweariedly and
> patiently, many nights and days. He never undertook any business,
> charge or trust, that he did not zealously, conscientiously, punctually,
> honourably discharge. His industry has always been untiring. He was
> proud of me, in his way, and had a great admiration of the comic singing.
> But, in the ease of his temper, and the straitness of his means, he appeared
> to have utterly lost at this time the idea of educating me at all . . .'[41]

Later he said that the longer he lived the better man he thought his father to have been.[42] But we shall search Forster in vain for any comparable testimony to his mother or even any such half-excusing of her as this. There is perhaps an oblique tribute to her in his description, in *A Child's History of England*, of how King Alfred was encouraged to learn to read by his mother ('he had – as most men who grow up to be great and good are generally found to have had – an excellent mother') but we cannot even be certain of that.

*

Elizabeth certainly had a profound general effect on something that we shall be considering in a later chapter, Dickens's presentation of woman in her maternal role. But, besides this, there are two major characters in his novels for whom she provided some direct inspiration, Mrs Nickleby and Mrs Micawber.

On the face of it Mrs Nickleby seems, in her character and actions, very unlike the woman we have been looking at. Admittedly, one of Elizabeth's grandsons, Alfred Tennyson Dickens, said in 1910 that he remembered her well on a visit to Gad's Hill in 1863 and that, 'She was a gentle, quiet, simple lady whose character undoubtedly inspired to no small degree that of Mrs Nickleby'.[43] But, apart from the apparent contradiction here ('quiet' is hardly the first adjective that comes to mind when we think of Mrs Nickleby), we should note that he is referring to the last year of Elizabeth's life when she was far gone in senile decay. A fairer testimony to consider would be that of Eleanor Christian, who remembered that in 1841 she could detect 'no resemblance' in Elizabeth to her alleged fictional counterpart. And Mrs Davey, as we have seen, declared that such likeness as there may have been was 'simply the exaggeration of some slight peculiarities'.

Mrs Nickleby is absurdly vain and garrulous, grotesquely self-centred and self-satisfied, with the brain, as Gissing put it, 'of a Somerset ewe'. She ruins her husband by imprudent advice and this causes him to die of a broken heart. Although she loves her children, her gullible vanity and snobbery and her general helplessness contribute to bringing them both into desperate situations. She all but pushes her frightened young daughter into the arms of a wicked seducing baronet and is comically punished when she herself is wooed by a lunatic whose madness everyone but she recognizes, and also at the end of the novel when she is 'disgusted' by the marriage of Miss La Creevey to Tim Linkinwater, a disgust that clearly stems from wounded vanity (Miss La Creevey, she asserts, is 'half as old again as I am'). Her zany ramblings provide us with wonderful entertainment throughout the book and Dickens occasionally half-excuses her ('a well-meaning woman enough, but weak withal') on the grounds that her sudden poverty has brought out the worst in her. But the fact remains that she is at best a serious embarrassment to her heroic son's struggle to win a place in the world for himself and his family and at worst a positive hindrance. It is no wonder that Elizabeth failed to see any connection between herself and this character, even asking Dickens, to his secret delight, whether he 'really believed there ever was such a woman'.[44]

In the light of all this we must feel that Forster is rather blandly undiscriminating when, excusing Dickens's portrayal of his parents in Mr Micawber and Mrs Nickleby, he writes that the 'foibles' of these two characters 'however laughable, make neither of them . . . less lovable'.[45] We do indeed love Micawber for his *joie de vivre* (and especially *de parler*), for his resilience, his optimism and his ability to create pleasure for himself and everyone around him out of the most unpromising materials. He brings warmth and delight into little David's dreary life and in the end 'explodes' the evil genius of the book, Uriah Heep. The affectionate laughter that he evokes in us is very different from the satirical laughter that we direct at Mrs Nickleby.

In so far as Mrs Nickleby is a portrait of Elizabeth she is a harsh caricature of some aspects of the real woman's character – her ebullience, her little vanities and worldlinesses and her often ill-grounded optimism (that school again). No doubt traits were added from other originals, as Georgina Hogarth suggested when she instanced Mrs Nickleby as an example of 'several people in a single character'.[46] But, portraiture apart, she is undoubtedly Dickens the novelist's first judgment on his mother, a judgment none the less severe for being presented with such rich comic detail. I have argued elsewhere that Nicholas Nickleby is an idealized self-portrait by the young Dickens.[47] His sister Fanny is complimented in Kate Nickleby, though the name, of course, is a compliment to his wife. But by far the most vital character in the Nickleby family, from a literary point of view, is the mother; it is with her that the imagination of Dickens the great comic artist is most deeply engaged, and this gives us, I think, a clear indication of the importance of Elizabeth to his fictional world at the time. *Oliver Twist* and *Nicholas Nickleby* together point us to that nightmare 'memory' which underlies so much of all his fiction, the memory of a Mrs Nickleby-like figure thrusting little Oliver into Fagin's den, the horror of this being intensified by the fact that Oliver is, after all, no orphan but her own acknowledged son.

The year after completing *Nickleby* Dickens launched a weekly miscellany called *Master Humphrey's Clock*. In his introduction of the character of Master Humphrey in the first number we can see, I believe, some remarkable wish-fulfilment fantasizing about his own childhood and his mother's attitude towards him. Master Humphrey, a cripple from his childhood, remembers his mother as a great fount of pity and love:

> I was but a very young creature when my poor mother died, and yet I remember that often when I hung around her neck, and oftener still when I played about the room before her, she would catch me to her bosom, and bursting into tears, would soothe me with every term of fondness and affection. God knows I was a happy child at those times, – happy to nestle in her breast, – happy to weep when she did, – happy in not knowing why.

When his hour of trial comes and, with a sudden shock, he realizes that he is set apart from other children by his deformity, 'the old sorrow came into my dear mother's mild and tender look . . . and I knew . . . how keenly she had felt for her poor crippled boy'. 'Now', continues Humphrey, 'my heart aches for that child as if I had never been he, when I think how often he awoke from some fairy change to his own old form, and sobbed himself to sleep again.' So must 'the little labouring hind' at Warren's Blacking have dreamed of some 'fairy change' back to his Chatham self but, far from being comforted by a mother's 'mild and tender look' when he awoke, the loving parent he had once known seemed to have died and been replaced by one who wanted to prolong his woe.

Dickens's underlying attitude towards his mother had clearly not softened by the time he came to write the autobiographical fragment in the late 1840s and the flash of bitterness revealed in his Christmas Book for 1848, *The Haunted Man*, has been noted by previous commentators. The hero Redlaw's evil spirit broods, 'I am he, neglected in my youth, and miserably poor, who strove and suffered . . . No mother's self-denying love . . . no father's counsel, aided *me*.' His parents

> at the best, were of that sort whose care soon ends, and whose duty is soon done; who cast their offspring loose, early, as birds do theirs; and, if they do well, claim the merit; and, if ill, the pity.

But *The Haunted Man* is a strange, confused little book in which Dickens's personal preoccupations do not mesh easily with that combination of social purpose, celebration of domestic joys, and supernatural interventions which is the essence of his Christmas fiction. He was now wanting, it seems, to consider his past in a fuller, more conscious

18

and more deliberate way than he had so far done and so moved towards the writing of his great quasi-autobiographical story, *David Copperfield*, involving what he called some 'very complicated interweaving of truth and fiction'.[48]

Once he had determined to put his own story into fiction he had naturally to decide as a basic step how to handle the matter of his parents. As regards his father he had already given himself a clue as to how to do this in *The Haunted Man*: 'A stranger came into my father's place when I was but a child, and I was easily an alien from my mother's heart'. So David's father is dead when the novel opens and soon the cruel figure of Mr Murdstone steps into his place. John Dickens is then free to enter the novel in the radiant figure of Mr Micawber who becomes a sort of foster-father to David during the grim warehouse-labourer period. And he brings with him Mrs Micawber in whom Dickens can portray his mother's 'foibles' and many of her good qualities with an affection untrammeled by bitterness.[49] Although she is almost a parody figure of maternity with one of her twins always at her breast 'taking refreshment', she is not *David*'s mother and indeed treats him as though he were a sympathetic adult rather than a little boy. Having distanced her from David by having no blood-relationship between them Dickens can make a benign joke of what had been so long a source of bitter wonder to him, how his mother could have precipitated him into the cold adult world – and into a singularly bleak corner of it at that – when he was still 'such a little fellow'. In the novel he writes after Mrs Micawber's first burst of confidence to David about Mr Micawber's difficulties:

I never can quite understand whether my precocious self-dependence confused Mrs Micawber in reference to my age, or whether she was so full of the subject that she would have talked about it to the very twins if there had been nobody else to communicate with, but this was the strain in which she began, and she went on accordingly all the time I knew her.[50]

David's real mother in the novel is a roseate vision of Dickens's earliest experience of his own pretty, vivacious and loving mother with her fondness for dancing and gaiety:

We are playing in the winter twilight, dancing about the parlour. When my mother is out of breath and rests herself in an elbow chair, I watch her winding her bright curls round her fingers, and straightening her waist, and nobody knows better than I do that she likes to look so well, and is proud of being so pretty.[51]

Not only the little boy's father but all his siblings too have vanished in this fictional intensification of the real-life emotional situation as Dickens remembered it; David and his mother are blissfully alone in their Edenic world where the fruit in the garden clusters 'riper and richer than fruit has ever been since', guarded and protected by the devoted Peggotty whose comfortable domesticity completes the vision of an ideally mothered infancy.

Dickens manages the shift from this idyll to Murdstone and Grinby's warehouse, alias Warren's blacking-factory, and yet preserves the vision unsullied, by the introduction of the 'wicked parent' figures of Mr and Miss Murdstone who in effect kill off his mother and then dismiss Peggotty. Miss Murdstone tells David that he will not be going back to school, and, after a period of neglect, the child is informed that he is to be sent to work in the warehouse. 'In short, you are provided for', says Miss Murdstone, 'and will please to do your duty.'

Miss Murdstone is not, of course, in any sense a *portrait* of Elizabeth but she does surely represent what Dickens thought of as his mother's hard-heartedness towards him (it is interesting to see that Elizabeth recommends maternal 'firmness' in her letter to Mrs Haydon and firmness is, of course, the great watchword of the Murdstones). Clara Copperfield and Jane Murdstone are, in fact, the light and dark of Dickens's childhood memories of his mother. Their creation frees him to present Elizabeth more objectively in the figure of Emma Micawber. Again, as in the case of Mrs Nickleby, it is a caricature rather than a portrait but the harshness has now gone from the drawing.

We can see this clearly in one detail common to the characterization of both Mrs Nickleby and Mrs Micawber, a proneness to lament the social glories of a former state of existence in contrast with the poverty of the present one. This, it seems highly probable, was based on lamentations the young Dickens must often have heard uttered by Elizabeth herself who had had to sacrifice many little luxury objects as John's 'difficulties' became ever more pressing. Here is Mrs Nickleby lamenting the loss of her jewelry:

> 'Dear, dear,' cried Mrs Nickleby . . . 'if I had but those unfortunate amethysts of mine – you recollect them, Kate, my love – how they used to sparkle, you know – but your papa, your poor dear papa – ah! there never was anything so cruelly sacrificed as those jewels were, never!'[52]

And here is Mrs Micawber:

> 'The pearl necklace and bracelets which I inherited from mama, have been disposed of for less than half their value; and the set of coral, which was the wedding gift of my papa, has actually been thrown away for

nothing. But I will never desert Mr Micawber. No!' cried Mrs Micawber, more affected than before, 'I will never do it! It's of no use asking me!'[53]

The difference is that Mrs Nickleby, although she has not the faintest notion of it, was actually the cause of her husband's ruin (and, indeed, his death) yet blames him entirely for it, whereas Mrs Micawber blames anyone and everyone — creditors, her family, the country at large — *except* her husband for his 'pecuniary embarrassments' and supports him with a loyalty that has become a familiar quotation.

Many things about the Micawbers, as has long been noted, closely resemble the personalities of John and Elizabeth Dickens and their situation during the early 1820s. The unsympathetic attitude of Mrs Micawber's family towards her husband's difficulties clearly echoes the irritation of Elizabeth's brothers whose names John used to raise money (Thomas Barrow eventually refused to have him in his house). Elizabeth's ill-fated school ('The centre of the street-door was perfectly covered with a great brass plate, on which was engraved "Mrs Micawber's Boarding Establishment for Young Ladies" ') makes the first of its two appearances in Dickens's fiction.[54] And the 'matter-of-fact manner' which Eleanor Christian noted in Elizabeth may well be reflected in Mrs Micawber's 'logical air', so much in evidence when she is reviewing the family's situation or expounding some astonishing plan — she 'prided herself', Dickens writes, 'on taking a clear view of things, and keeping Mr Micawber straight by her woman's wisdom'.

But there are two very significant points in the story when Mrs Micawber is made to act not as Elizabeth had done but as Dickens must have wished she had. Instead of taking little David's bitterly-earned shillings to help keep the family afloat Mrs Micawber actually refuses them:

> I had two or three shillings of my week's money in my pocket . . . and with heart felt emotion begged Mrs Micawber to accept of them as a loan. But that lady, kissing me, and making me put them back in my pocket, replied that she couldn't think of it.[55]

This is the first motherly kiss that she gives to David. The second is made still more telling. Released from the King's Bench and about to leave London by stage-coach, the Micawbers are being seen off by David who will then be quite alone in the world:

> I think, as Mrs Micawber sat at the back of the coach, with the children, and I stood in the road looking wistfully at them, a mist cleared from her eyes, and she saw what a little creature I really was. I think so, because she

beckoned me to climb up, with quite a new and motherly expression in her face, and put her arm round my neck, and gave me just such a kiss as she might have given to her own boy.[56]

In real life it had been John and not Elizabeth, as it seemed to Dickens, who had suddenly glimpsed their suffering little son through the 'mist' in which he felt they had lost him – not only glimpsed him but actually did something to help his forlorn condition. When the family went into the Marshalsea lodgings had been found for Charles with a 'reduced old lady' in Camden Town on whom he later modelled the grim figure of Mrs Pipchin in *Dombey and Son*.[57] He was very miserable there, so far from his parents, and remonstrated with his father about it one Sunday night 'so pathetically and with so many tears' that John's 'kind nature gave way. He began to think that it was not quite right.'[58] He quickly arranged pleasanter lodgings for his son, closer to the Marshalsea, lodgings that Dickens thought 'a Paradise'. But for the coming into Elizabeth's face of 'quite a new and motherly expression' as she flitted about the blacking-factory little Charles felt that he looked in vain.

Mrs Micawber, then, bears quite a complicated relationship to Elizabeth Dickens. She is partly an amused, but not contemptuous, view of the real woman by the adult Dickens, carefully distanced from the child David who is re-enacting his author's childhood sufferings, and partly a 'wish-fulfilment' rewriting of the role played by Elizabeth during the blacking-factory time. The 'mist' of anger and resentment that covered his memory of her and that had inspired the creation of Mrs Nickleby lifted enough in the writing of *Copperfield* for him to see her more truly as she had really been in his later boyhood – harassed and perhaps comically unrealistic in many ways but also courageous, devotedly loyal to her feckless husband, socially delightful and truly concerned to 'exert herself' for the sake of her family.

It has been plausibly suggested recently that another Emma occurring later in Dickens's fiction, the garrulous good-hearted Emma Lirriper, who is the main narrator of two of his Christmas Stories, also reflects a more benign judgment on Elizabeth. Deborah Thomas notes that the character was created within a few months of Elizabeth's death and was partly inspired by 'his complex response to this event'.[59] Mrs Lirriper's garrulity certainly links her with Mrs Nickleby and her name and devotion to an easy-going, convivial, improvident husband (who died 'behindhand with the world') link her with Mrs Micawber, but her flow of speech reveals shrewd good sense and practicality as well as generosity and motherly warm-heartedness and she is shown to have 'exerted herself' to some purpose in paying off all her husband's debts through her lodging-house enterprise. It would be pleasant to think that she represented a benevolent valediction to his mother by Dickens the story-teller, but four years later he wrote a very different story, startlingly bleak in tone, which clearly shows that neither Emma Micawber nor Emma Lirriper had finally exorcised his 'bad mother' memories.

'George Silverman's Explanation', published in *The Atlantic Monthly* in 1868, is Dickens's most lurid exploitation since writing *Oliver Twist*, thirty-odd years before, of his own private legend, that undying memory ('. . . I never shall forget, I never can forget') of an exceptionally gifted and sensitive child, fired with glorious ambition, being nearly ruined for life by a mother transformed by poverty. Silverman, who narrates his own story, recalls that his parents were 'in a miserable condition of life' living in a Preston cellar:

> Mother had the gripe and clutch of poverty upon her face, upon her figure, and not least of all upon her voice. Her sharp and high-pitched words were squeezed out of her, as by the compression of bony fingers on a leathern bag; and she had a way of rolling her eyes about and about the cellar, as she scolded, that was gaunt and hungry. Father, with his shoulders rounded, would sit quiet on a three-legged stool, looking at the empty grate, until she would pluck the stool from under him, and bid him go bring some money home. Then he would dismally ascend the steps; and I, holding my ragged shirt and trousers together with a hand (my only braces), would feint and dodge from mother's pursuing grasp at my hair.
>
> A worldly little devil was mother's usual name for me. Whether I cried for that I was in the dark, or for that it was cold, or for that I was hungry, or whether I squeezed myself into a warm corner when there was a fire, or ate voraciously when there was food, she would still say, 'O you worldly little devil!' And the sting of it was, that I quite well knew myself to be a worldly little devil. Worldly as to wanting to be housed and warmed, worldly as to wanting to be fed, worldly as to the greed with which I inwardly compared how much I got of those good things with how much father and mother got, when, rarely, those good things were going.[60]

This nightmare passage presents us with Dickens's final fictional version of his childhood suffering. The mother even has prosperous relations who will not help, a situation which was a rich source for comedy in the Micawbers. Ironically, Silverman, despite his horrendous childhood, does grow up to be a learned man as the young Dickens (according to the adult Dickens) had dreamed of becoming; he wins a scholarship to a grammar school and goes from there to Cambridge University. That he goes to Cambridge rather than Oxford is significant, as we realize when we recall Dickens's bitter words in the autobiographical fragment about his parents' being almost as contented when he entered the blacking-factory as they could have been had he 'been twenty years of age, distinguished at a grammar-school, and going to Cambridge'. Despite these academic triumphs, however, Silverman's life has been irretrievably ruined because of the paralysing sense of guilt about his 'worldliness' first planted in him by his ferocious starving mother in that dark cellar of his childhood.

2
Brother and Sister

'There was once a child, and he strolled about a good deal, and thought of a number of things. He had a sister, who was a child too, and his constant companion. These two used to wonder all day long. They wondered at the beauty of the flowers; they wondered at the height and blueness of the sky; they wondered at the depth of the bright water; they wondered at the goodness and power of GOD who made the lovely world.'

Reprinted Pieces, 'A Child's Dream of a Star'

One of Dickens's earliest memories, Forster tells us, was of a 'small front garden' where, 'watched by a nurse through a low kitchen-window almost level with the gravel-walk, he trotted about with something to eat, and his little elder sister with him'.[1] Fanny was, indeed, his 'constant companion' in the happy years of his childhood: together they braved 'that baleful Pug' with 'a certain radiating way . . . of snapping at our undefended legs' who skirmished with them every morning in the door-way to their preparatory dayschool;[2] together they shared the mysterious adventure of the wooden-legged man in the coal-cellar;[3] together they 'used to wander at night about a churchyard near their house, looking up at the stars';[4] together, 'mounted on a dining table for a stage', they entertained their convivial father's boon companions at the Mitre Inn in Chatham by singing a comic duet between a sailor and his sweetheart.[5]

In 'The Holly Tree', a Christmas Story written seven years after Fanny's untimely death at the age of thirty-eight, Dickens recalled the old Mitre where 'I was cried over by my rosy little sister, because I had acquired a black eye in a fight' but does not say whether she was in the secret of his 'loving the landlord's youngest daughter to distraction'. A later involvement of Fanny's in her brother's affairs of the heart proved, as we shall see, not too happy. But in childhood she seems to have supplied perfectly (and by so doing no doubt helped to form Charles's lifelong need for) the 'other woman' sister-figure so necessary for a happy Dickens ménage whether in life or literature: David Copperfield needs his beautiful good angel-sister, Agnes, as well as his pretty little wife Dora. So young Charles must have depended very much on the emotional continuity of his relationship with Fanny, whilst he was busy losing his

25

juvenile heart to 'some peach-faced creature in a blue sash, and shoes to correspond'[6] or to the golden-haired little Lucy Stroughill next door but one.

The treatment accorded to Fanny when the family fell on hard times after the move to London must, then, have produced a complex reaction in her twelve-year-old brother, consigned as a 'poor little drudge' to the blacking-factory. She was sent as a piano pupil and boarder to the newly opened Royal Academy of Music at a fee of thirty-eight guineas a year and Forster records that Dickens told him 'what a stab to his heart it was, thinking of his own disregarded condition, to see her go away to begin her education, amid the tearful good wishes of everybody in the house'.[7] The likely reason why John and Elizabeth, hard pressed as they were, yet determined to invest money in Fanny's education whilst they had nothing to spare for Charles's has been well expressed by the late Mr W.J. Carlton: 'although Charles had given promise of a precocious literary bent . . . Fanny's talent as a pianist and her possession of a good soprano voice were deemed to be a surer guarantee of potential earning power'.[8]

Fanny did well at the Royal Academy, where she was for some time taught the piano by Ignaz Moscheles, a former pupil of Beethoven's.[9] She made friends among her fellow-pupils and won golden opinions from all her teachers (arithmetic, English grammar and elementary Italian also featured in the Academy's curriculum besides moral and religious education, 'to which the directors attached great importance'). All this Charles heard about on Sundays when he would leave his lodgings in Camden Town to call for Fanny at the Academy in Tenterden Street at 9 a.m. and then go with her to spend the day with their parents in the Marshalsea, walking back again with her at night, a round distance of some twelve miles. What he was missing 'most sorely' at this time, he afterwards told Forster, was 'the companionship of boys of his own age, with whom he might share in the advantages of school, and contend for its prizes'.[10] From this we can easily imagine the emotions with which he must have listened to Fanny's story of her week and are unlikely to be surprised by his description, years later, of his reaction to the occasion in June 1824 (after he had been some months in the blacking-factory) when Fanny was publicly presented, by one of the King's sisters 'before a numerous and fashionable audience', with the Academy's silver medal:

> I could not bear to think of myself — beyond the reach of all such honourable emulation and success. The tears ran down my face. I felt as if my heart were rent. I prayed, when I went to bed that night, to be lifted out of the humiliation and neglect in which I was. I never had suffered so much before.[11]

He immediately adds, 'There was no envy in this', and it is certainly true that his deep emotional attachment to Fanny was not consciously affected by all this in the way that his feelings towards his mother evidently were. But, as I shall suggest later, we do find in one of his later novels an oblique reflection of this whole episode which may be seen as, among other things, a belated 'revenge' on Fanny for her greater good fortune in those early years.

It seems to have been very shortly after the Academy prize-giving that Charles was finally released from the blacking-factory and returned to school – not a very satisfactory school as we can gather from the use he later made of it in portraying Salem House in *Copperfield* but at least a school. Fanny, meanwhile, continued to do well at the Academy although her staying there was a precarious matter because of her father's difficulties in keeping up payment of her fees. Numerous orotund letters on the subject were addressed by him to the Committee of the Academy ('A circumstance of great moment to me will be decided in the ensuing term which I confidently hope will place me in comparative affluence ...') but on 22 November 1826 the Committee's secretary recorded in the minutes of that day's meeting: '*Dickens* – The quarterly payments must be secured or to withdraw his daughter'.[12] Apparently, the payments could not be secured and Fanny left the Academy the following June but returned as a sub-professor (she was now aged seventeen) in September and remained another five years at the institution, teaching the piano and later, taking singing lessons from Domenico Crivelli, son of the famous tenor, Gaetano Crivelli.

As Fanny steadily pursued her musical career, Charles left school, tried the law, and opted finally for journalism. Having fallen desperately in love with Maria, the pretty youngest daughter of prosperous Mr George Beadnell, a senior clerk in one of the City banks, he was determined to make himself more desirable, economically speaking, as a potential son-in-law: 'I bought an approved scheme of the noble art and mystery of stenography ... and plunged into a sea of perplexity that brought me, in a few weeks, to the confines of distraction'.[13] Like his own David Copperfield, however, he 'tamed the savage stenographic mystery' at last and began work as a freelance reporter in the now vanished courts of Doctors' Commons. That Fanny was close to him in all his plans and feelings at this time is suggested by her being 'in the secret' of his application to the stage-manager of Covent Garden Theatre for a job as a professional actor (this, he felt, might offer a quicker path to fame and fortune than his hard-won stenographic skill); she was to go with him to an audition and play the musical accompaniment to the comic songs he intended to present.[14] In fact, 'a terrible bad cold' prevented his going and, soon afterwards, his greatly improved prospects in the world of journalism, in the shape of permanent employment on *The Morning Chronicle*, made him forget about the stage as a way of earning a living. He did not forget it as a way of enjoying himself, however: he and Fanny were the principals in getting up a private production of the opera *Clari: or the Maid of Milan* (now only remembered for the abducted Maid's song, 'Home Sweet Home!') at their parents' home in Bentinck Street on 27 April 1833, Fanny singing the title role and Dickens taking the part of her father.

Whilst he was busy staging amateur theatricals in his parents' drawing-room, young Charles was being forced to act what seemed to him an increasingly confusing and humiliating role in a little real-life drama got up by Maria, his coquettish beloved, and her bosom friend, Mary Anne (or Marianne) Leigh. This seems all to have centred on whether or not Dickens had ever made a confidante of Mary Anne. She, apparently, claimed that he had done and Maria either really was vexed or just pretended to be so. Fanny knew what Mary Anne was saying but said nothing to her brother so that the first intimations about the matter that he had came in a reproachful note from Maria herself. In his reply Dickens declared, 'no consideration on earth shall induce me ever to forget or forgive Fanny's not telling me of it before'. Responding, Maria seems to have attempted some defence of Fanny for in his next letter Charles wrote:

> With regard to Fanny if she owed a duty to you she owed a greater one to me – and for this reason *because she knew* what Marianne Leigh had said of *you*; she heard from you what she had said of *me* and yet she had not the fairness the candour the feeling to let me know it – and if I were to live a hundred years I never would forgive it.[15]

Obviously, there was a serious quarrel – Dickens was frantically in earnest in his love for Maria and, quite unreasonably, felt himself to have been badly betrayed by his gentle sister's not telling tales. But his angry words in the letters to Maria just quoted, words scribbled in the heat of the moment, are a very different matter, I think, from that famous deliberate, unforgiving sentence about his mother – '. . . I never afterwards forgot, I never shall forget, I never can forget, that [she] was warm for my being sent back'. That was written not in the dishevelled immediacy of a hasty letter but in a fragment of formal autobiography some twenty years after the event and should be weighed accordingly: Dickens himself is reported to have said, 'We should always remember . . . that

28

letters are but ephemeral: we must not be affected too much either by those which praise us or by others written in the heat of the moment'.[16] In general, anyway, Dickens seems to have felt that Fanny always showed a proper sisterly response to the (for him) very special nature of his love for Maria: 'I think she always knew I never could bear to hear of you as of any common person',[17] he wrote to Maria when his old flame re-entered his life many years later.

The professional careers of both Fanny and Charles were now prospering and the ace young political reporter on *The Morning Chronicle*, whose brilliant 'Sketches of London Life' in the same paper were also attracting such attention, must have been gratified to read in his paper on 30 May 1835 a highly eulogistic notice of 'Miss Dickens's Soirée Musicale' at the Academy's rooms the previous evening:

> Miss Dickens sang Haydn's unrivalled ballad, 'My Mother Bids me Bind my Hair'; and . . . we have no hesitation in saying we never before heard it sung in so pure and simple a style, or with a more true and touching expression. It was encored with expressions of the warmest delight . . .[18]

Within two-and-a-half years both brother and sister were married, Charles to Catherine Hogarth, eldest daughter of the *Chronicle*'s music critic (the author, no doubt, of the eulogy on Fanny's singing), and Fanny to Henry Burnett, a fellow-student of hers at the Academy, who had begun to carve out a career for himself as an opera singer – he was performing in Dickens's operetta, *The Village Coquettes*, at the St James's Theatre a few months before his marriage. (It was Fanny, incidentally, who had brought together Dickens and John Hullah, the composer of the music for the *Coquettes*. Hullah was another of her Academy fellow-students; he recorded that Fanny was 'an excellent musician, *one who knew the sound of what she saw*, and could reproduce it by voice or hand readily and correctly'.)[19]

Clearly, the fact that they were both now married somewhat altered the relationship between Dickens and his elder sister. For one thing he had found a perfect successor for her in her domestic, sisterly role in his young sister-in-law Mary[20] (and later in the next youngest of the Hogarth girls, Georgina) and, for another, he does not seem to have found Henry Burnett altogether congenial. Fanny's handsome husband – who later claimed to have been the artist's model for the original portrayal of Nicholas Nickleby[21] – was definitely a serious young man and Dickens's letters suggest that Dickens was inclined to poke fun at him. Writing to his brother Frederick in 1842 and describing the secretary he has hired on his American tour, Dickens says:

He is sentimental certainly – has a languishing air – and is a cross between Burnett and Hartland [an early acquaintance of Dickens's]. He sings too – and tells marvellous lies concerning his past life – in both of which aspects of his character, you will detect a resemblance to one of the gentlemen I have likened him to.

Two years later, in a letter to his wife, he refers ironically to him as 'the great Burnett' and in 1861 finds him 'the express embodiment of Imbecility' at a family funeral. A few weeks later Burnett (Fanny being long dead and himself remarried) turned up at one of Dickens's public Readings and 'went behind' afterwards to chat with his former brother-in-law: 'His imbecility,' Dickens wrote home to Georgina, 'was overwhelming'.[22]

We may suspect, I think, that Dickens's inclination to mock Burnett was provoked at least in part by the latter's somewhat ostentatious Nonconformist piety. As a result of his early upbringing,[23] Burnett grew up a deeply religious man and, soon after marrying Fanny, became uneasy about the morality of earning his living on the stage and, indeed, about his and Fanny's London life-style generally. A Congregational minister in Manchester, James Griffin, who was subsequently the Burnetts' pastor for many years, has recorded that at this period of their life Sunday evenings were spent by the young couple (after fulfilling their duties as professional singers at the Church of the Sardinian Ambassador) with Dickens and his family 'in a manner which, though strictly moral, was not congenial with his [Burnett's] feelings'.[24] Eventually, he decided to leave the stage, something for which he believed Dickens never forgave him,[25] and he and Fanny moved to Manchester to become teachers of music and members of Mr Griffin's congregation at Rusholme Road Chapel. In his *Memories of the Past* Griffin quotes a letter he received from Fanny soon after their arrival in Manchester, a letter that shows she was wholly in sympathy with her husband:

I was brought up in the Established Church, but I regret to say, without any serious ideas of religion. I attended Divine worship as a duty, not as a high privilege. . . . I was thrown very much into society, and seemed to live as if this world were to be my home for ever, entirely forgetting that I was merely a pilgrim wending my way to eternity. . . . I seemed gradually to lose my relish for the pleasures of the world, but I was still wholly ignorant of gospel truths.

She goes on to refer to having been brought to a sense of her sinfulness by Griffin's preaching, 'my utter worthlessness in the sight of God', and to express with joy her conviction of God's grace now working in her – 'I feel great pleasure in mixing with God's people. I feel anxious to be spiritually-minded and to devote myself entirely to the service of Christ'. Sundays never seemed long enough for her, recalled Griffin:

> Frequently she would say at the close of the evening service, 'May we go home with you, and stop with you a little?' Our house was more than a mile from the chapel, and hers a considerable distance on its opposite side; but all that was nothing in her account, if she could but have a little more savour of Sabbath enjoyments. So, after supper and family prayer, she would say, 'Can't we have a hymn?'[26]

We have no direct comment by Dickens on his sister's new-found religion and can only surmise what strain, if any, it put on their relationship. The creator of such vehement caricatures of Dissenters as the red-nosed Mr Stiggins in *Pickwick* or the Rev. Melchisedech Howler in *Dombey* is unlikely to have been greatly in sympathy with Fanny's conversion. It was only a few years before that he had caused old Tony Weller in *Pickwick* to complain to his son about Mrs Weller's becoming 'Methodistical' and 'uncommon pious': 'She's got hold o' some inwention for grown-up people being born again, Sammy; the new birth, I think they calls it'.[27] The 'new-born' Fanny, Griffin records,

> When visiting, or receiving at her house, her former friends whose sentiments and feelings with regard to religious matters she knew differed widely from her own, and well aware how her supposed fanaticism might be the object of their pity or contempt . . . unequivocally persisted in all she would have thought it right to do if they had not been present.

She refused to suspend the custom of morning or evening family prayers when her parents came to stay in Manchester for some while (they 'appeared to be much interested in the new character and new associations of their daughter', Griffin blandly tells us)[28] and, presumably, did the same when Dickens himself made a much briefer stay there in 1843. He makes no mention of this aspect of the household, however, but continued to show that 'utmost pride', stressed by Forster, in the acclamations won by Fanny's talent. She and her husband gave a public concert in Manchester in 1842 and Dickens wrote to his brother, 'I need not say what delight it gives me to hear that Fanny is doing so well, nor how sure I feel that she will yet do much better' (he cannot resist adding a jocose reference to Burnett, however: 'I suppose Burnett has become quite an aristocrat – and that he rides to give lessons on a thorough-bred Hunter?').[29] The whole tone of a letter to her 'dearest Fan', written from America in January 1842 by Dickens's wife, suggests that a closely affectionate relationship existed between the two families.[30] The

31

previous year they had holidayed together at Broadstairs. Fanny was, Eleanor Christian recalled later, 'very sweet and amiable' but also 'in delicate health'.[31] Five years later, after she had collapsed whilst singing at a private party, Dickens was 'deeply, deeply grieved' to learn that she was consumptive. He exerted himself to get the best medical advice for her but, two years later, on a visit to her sister in London, she became ill again, this time fatally so. Dickens sent to Forster a detailed account of one of the long talks he had with her as she lay wasting away (he didn't know why he wrote it, he said, but felt 'in the very pity and grief of my heart . . . as if it were doing something'). He dwelt on her 'extraordinary sweetness and constancy', her faith and her over-riding concern for others: 'Such an affecting exhibition of strength and tenderness, in all that early decay, is quite indescribable. I need not tell you how it moved me.'[32]

A month or two later Dickens was at work on his fifth and last Christmas Book, *The Haunted Man*, and smuggled into it a celebration of Fanny and her sisterly love. The book's hero, a scientist called Redlaw, 'learned and distinguished' as Dickens believed his own younger self had dreamed of becoming, broods continually on past sorrows and wrongs. Alienated from his mother's heart, such 'glimpses of the light of home' as he had ever known 'streamed' from his sister: 'How young she was, how fair, how loving! I took her to the first poor roof that I was master of, and made it rich. She came into the darkness of my life and made it bright.' This image of a brother and sister living together in a sort of sexless marriage, supporting each other against the world, is a persistent one in Dickens's fiction, beginning with Nicholas and Kate Nickleby (Ruth and Tom Pinch in *Martin Chuzzlewit* are another example). As we have seen, he and Fanny never did, in fact, live like this but he seems to have projected the image forward, so to speak, from their childhood companionship, which her dying had made both him and her recall in vivid detail. A day or two before her death, for example, she told him that

> in the night, the smell of the fallen leaves in the woods where we had habitually walked as very young children, had come upon her with such strength of reality that she had moved her weak head to look for strewn leaves on the floor at her bedside.[33]

'On the day of her funeral, which we passed together,' Forster recalls, 'I had most affecting proof of his tender and grateful memory of her in . . . childish days.'[34]

Fanny's error (as Dickens saw it) over Maria Beadnell is quietly suppressed in this Christmas Story: whilst Redlaw strove to 'climb' so that he could marry the girl he loved, his 'sweet companion' sister shared with him 'the expiring embers and the cooling hearth' as he worked late into the night. But then his friend – who was, of course, to have married his sister – betrayed both him and her by walking off with Redlaw's beloved, after which:

> My sister, doubly dear, doubly devoted, doubly cheerful in my home, lived on to see me famous, and my old ambition so rewarded when its spring was broken, and then . . . Died, gentle as ever, happy, and with no concern but for her brother.[35]

Fanny is acquitted, as it were, not only of having contributed to difficulties with Maria but also of having 'left' her brother for a husband. Like a good sister she had 'no concern but for her brother'. Thus Dickens the artist gives her her quietus.

Whilst still alive Fanny had made an interesting appearance in the first and best of her brother's Christmas Books, *A Christmas Carol* (1843). When the Ghost of Christmas Past takes Scrooge back into his childhood Dickens gets the best opportunity he has had since conceiving *Oliver Twist* to once again 'tell' his thousands of sympathetic readers about the great horror of his own boyhood. The longed-for school and the dreadful blacking-factory are deftly merged (with considerable assistance from Tennyson's 'Mariana')[36] into one house of desolation, where 'Scrooge sat down upon a form, and wept to see his poor forgotten self as he used to be'. He is 'forgotten', because all the other boys in the place have gone home for the Christmas holidays but Scrooge's father never lets him come home. The boy has to remain alone in the rather spectacularly decaying mansion where 'fragments of plaster fell out of the ceiling, and the naked laths were shown instead'.

One Christmas, however, the door opens:

> . . . and a little girl, much younger than the boy, came darting in, and putting her arms about his neck, and often kissing him, addressed him as her 'Dear, dear brother'.
>
> 'I have come to bring you home, dear brother!' said the child, clapping her tiny hands . . .
>
> 'Home, little Fan?' returned the boy.
>
> 'Yes!' said the child, brimful of glee. 'Home, for good and all . . . Father is so much kinder than he used to be, that home's like Heaven! He spoke so gently to me one dear night when I was going to bed, that I was not afraid to ask him once more if you might come home; and he said Yes, you should; and sent me in a coach to bring you. And you're to be a man!' said the child, opening her eyes, 'and are never to come back here;

but first, we're to be together all the Christmas long, and have the merriest time in all the world.'

'You are quite a woman, little Fan!' exclaimed the boy.[37]

We can, of course, only speculate about the relationship of this passage to Dickens's recollection of his own emotions during the blacking-factory months. No doubt the company of the tender-hearted Fanny, who had wept over his black eye at the Mitre years before, consoled him on those Sunday walks to and from the Marshalsea, even if he was careful to conceal from her just how wretched he was, and we can well imagine how he might have elaborated some fantasy about her suddenly arriving at the factory one day to release him ('[you] are never to come back here') with the news that their father was no longer imprisoned ('so much kinder than he used to be') and had summoned him home. I am not sure why 'little Fan' is made 'much younger' than her brother in the *Carol*, though. Perhaps it is to heighten the 'little woman' effect that Scrooge is made to comment on: a female child managing and organizing domestic affairs in a loving, protecting, 'womanly' way is always irresistibly charming to Dickens's imagination and it may well be that this originally stems from his early observation of Fanny helping her mother or the nurse, Mary Weller, with the younger children – Letitia, Frederick and Alfred (John and Elizabeth Dickens's last child, Augustus, was not born until after Fanny had left home).

The adult Fanny had two children of her own, the eldest of whom, Harry, born in 1839, was deformed and sickly. His mother, whom he did not long survive, nursed him with tender devotion, observing with joy, no doubt, his precocious spirituality. When Harry was seven years old, Dickens began creating the figure of little Paul, the 'son' of *Dombey and Son*. In Paul, Dickens fused his own forlorn earlier self and his little nephew who had, like Paul, been taken to Brighton for his health and

> had there, for hours lying on the beach with his books, given utterance to thoughts quite as remarkable for a child as those which are put into the lips of Paul Dombey. But little Harry loved his Bible, and evidently loved Jesus. The child seemed never tired of reading his Bible and his hymns, and other good books suited to his age.[38]

It may be that Mr Griffin exaggerates here as part of his general effort to confer a kind of Congregationalist sainthood on Fanny; certainly, in portraying Paul, Dickens substitutes for his nephew's biblical fervour a more diluted spirituality:

> Very often afterwards, in the midst of their talk, he would break off, to

try to understand what it was that the waves were always saying; and would rise up in his couch to look towards that invisible region, far away.[39]

This represents little Harry Burnett's intimations of immortality, of course, but it is also a spiritualization of that passionate yearning (stimulated not by the Bible, however, but by novels and romances) for 'something beyond that place and time' that David Copperfield recalls as characterizing his neglected childhood in a passage which, Forster tells us, is literally autobiographical on Dickens's part. Paul Dombey is, in fact, like Oliver Twist and Little Nell and the young Scrooge in the deserted schoolroom, one more astonishing variant on the highly personal 'deprived-child' theme so central to Dickens's fiction. One of the figures most closely associated in Dickens's mind with the darkest period of his childhood was a Mrs Elizabeth Roylance, 'a reduced old lady, long known to our family, in Little-college-street, Camden-town, who took children in to board, and had once done so at Brighton'.[40] It was to her that he was sent to lodge when his parents entered the Marshalsea and he now summoned her from out of the shadows of his past to model, 'with a few alterations and embellishments',[41] for that redoubtable 'ogress and child-queller', Mrs Pipchin, to whose steely care little Paul is confided. 'I hope you will like Mrs Pipchin's establishment', he wrote to Forster. 'It is from the life, and I was there – I don't suppose I was eight years old . . .'[42] In fact, he was twelve but his memory was faithful to the emotional situation as he so vividly recalled it rather than to the actual facts ('I was so young and childish . . .', 'I was such a little fellow').[43]

In Mrs Pipchin's grim 'castle' little Paul is lovingly ministered to by his devoted elder sister, Florence, just as little Charles had been emotionally sustained and supported by the love and concern of Fanny on those Sundays when they trudged down to the Marshalsea in the morning and back again at night. The closeness to the actual biographical facts in this respect becomes more marked when Paul is removed to the even more formidable castle of Dr Blimber. Then he can see Florence only at weekends. Running through the details of those weekends, which relate of course to the imagined story and its setting, there is undoubtedly a strong current of Dickens's memory of those weekly reunions with Fanny and what they had meant to him:

Oh Saturdays! Oh happy Saturdays, when Florence always came at noon, and never would, in any weather, stay away, though Mrs Pipchin snarled and growled, and worried her bitterly. Those Saturdays were Sabbaths for at least two little Christians among all the Jews, and did the holy Sabbath work of strengthening and knitting up a brother's and a sister's love.

Not even Sunday nights – the heavy Sunday nights, whose shadow darkened the first waking burst of light on Sunday mornings – could mar those precious Saturdays. Whether it was the great sea-shore, where they sat, and strolled together; or whether it was only Mrs Pipchin's dull back room, in which she sang to him so softly, with his drowsy head upon her arm; Paul never cared. It was Florence. That was all he thought of. So, on Sunday nights, when the Doctor's dark door stood agape to swallow him up for another week, the time was come for taking leave of Florence; no one else.[44]

The whole presentation of Florence in her loving, protecting relationship to Paul is, in fact, a double tribute to Fanny. It reflects her sisterly devotion to Charles, especially in those difficult early years, and also her maternal care for her own little Harry. It seems less certain to me that a strange paper entitled 'A Child's Dream of a Star', hastily written by Dickens two years after Fanny's death, to supply 'something tender' for the second issue of his new weekly journal, *Household Words*, is also the tribute to her alone that Forster has led us to believe.[45] The inspiration, if that is the right word, for this embarrassing mixture of *fausse naïveté* and would-be Scriptural solemnity has, I believe, quite as much to do with his dead sister-in-law Mary Hogarth, his 'better Angel in Heaven' as he called her, as with Fanny, despite the clear opening allusion to her quoted as an epigraph to this chapter; I shall, therefore, reserve discussion of it until we come to consider Mary and her role in his life and art.

Just as his memories of Fanny blend with his memories of Mary Hogarth to form the ultimate sisterly ideal in the 'Star' so they seem to blend with his memories of his first love, Maria Beadnell, in a piece in similar vein, 'The Child's Story', written for the Christmas 1852 number of *Household Words*. The child supposedly narrating the story by the family's Christmas fireside is also the hero, 'the traveller', because the story is an allegory of life as a journey. The traveller meets himself as a child, then as a boy (in both cases the details of the episodes point very much towards *Dickens*'s childhood and *Dickens*'s boyhood – with the blacking-factory episode excised, of course), then as a young man and so on. When he meets the young man (who says 'I am always in love. Come and love with me') he goes with him,

and presently they came to one of the prettiest girls that ever was seen – just like Fanny in the corner there – and she had eyes like Fanny, and hair like Fanny, and dimples like Fanny's, and she laughed and coloured just as Fanny does while I am talking about her. So, the young man fell in love directly – just as Somebody I won't mention, the first time he came here, did with Fanny. Well! he was teased sometimes – just as Somebody used to be by Fanny; and they quarrelled sometimes – just as Somebody and Fanny used to quarrel; and they made it up. . . .

Jack Lindsay in his very psychoanalytical biography of Dickens comments interestingly on this passage:

> Here, partly through the coy style and partly through the splitting of character in the dream-method, it is difficult to make out exactly what [Dickens] is talking about; but the excited, evasive stimulus of the name Fanny is not in doubt. He cannot bear to use any other name to express the lost love, the lost relationship which constituted happiness.[46]

It does not, in fact, need a psychoanalytical approach to Dickens's fiction to perceive that one of the dominating influences in his attitude to women, and thus his presentation of them in his fiction, was a yearning to unite beloved sister and beloved sweetheart or wife in the same figure. Clearly, his childhood relationship with Fanny must have been a decisive factor in forming this attitude but this particular passage is one of the few places where he seems almost consciously to be recognizing this.

His next use of the name Fanny in his writings points us in a very different direction, however. Four years after writing 'A Child's Story' he was at work on his eleventh novel, *Little Dorrit*. In this predominantly sombre book (tinged even with sourness in places), which disconcerted many of his admirers, Dickens returned to the debtors' prison of his childhood to take another voyage round his feckless father. Instead of the affectionate caricature of him he made in the delightful Mr Micawber we have the ruthless analysis of the pathetic William Dorrit, 'Father of the Marshalsea', keeping up a mean and shabby pretence of gentlemanly dignity during the long debilitating years of imprisonment. His wife is dead before the action of the novel opens and the family – Dorrit, his ne'er-do-well son, and his haughty elder daughter – depend, morally, and to a large extent financially, on the youngest child, Little Dorrit, whose small stature causes her to be regarded as a child although she is a grown woman of two-and-twenty. Born in the prison, she is the only member of the family not poisoned by the long-standing fiction of their social superiority. Quietly and selflessly, she ministers to them all. She persuades a dancing-master, also in the prison, to teach her pretty sister who then gets an engagement at a cheap theatre. Little Dorrit herself goes out to work as a needlewoman in the grim old mansion of Mrs Clennam and this 'degrading' occupation cannot be acknowledged to exist by her father though he takes and spends her earnings complacently enough.

Now, clearly, Little Dorrit in the Marshalsea is not autobiographical in the direct way that Little Copperfield in the blacking-factory is, but she can be seen as a purification, as it were, of that 'poor little drudge', his younger self, who so haunted Dickens's imagination. Mrs Clennam's decaying house by the river with its 'gaunt rooms, deserted for years upon years' and 'not one straight floor, from the foundation to the roof', with its ceilings 'so fantastically clouded by smoke and dust, that old women might have told fortunes in them',[47] is, essentially, the blacking-factory where the 'Child of the Marshalsea' comes to labour for her few shillings a week to support her spineless family. But, instead of the despair and bitter resentment that the young Dickens had felt, and portrayed in David Copperfield, she is all goodness, sweet and uncomplaining. Her very name, Amy, means love.

The bitter sense of social degradation and resentment that Dickens, and David, felt is transferred from her to her sister who excuses her bad temper by talking of the other dancers at the theatre just as Dickens had earlier written of 'the common labouring men and boys' at the factory.

> If I am ever a little provoking, I am sure you'll consider what a thing it is to occupy my position and feel a consciousness of being superior to it. I shouldn't care . . . if the others were not so common. None of them have come down in the world as we have. They are all on their own level. Common.[48]

This discontented sister is called Fanny. Why, we ask ourselves, should Dickens have picked, out of all the female names at his disposal, the name of his beloved dead sister for this character? Surely what must have gone on in his mind – who can say how consciously? – must have been similar to what went on when he named Fagin in *Oliver Twist*.[49] The sister who had – in all innocence – caused him such exquisite suffering by her scholastic triumphs at the Royal Academy of Music is similarly 'punished' by the use of her name for Little Dorrit's selfish, shallow sister and the Royal Academy itself is degraded to a tawdry theatre putting on 'leg-shows' for the delectation of such vacuous young men as Fanny's admirer, Mr Sparkler.

Unlike an earlier Fanny in Dickens's fiction, Mr Squeers's grotesquely vain and spiteful daughter in *Nicholas Nickleby*, Fanny Dorrit is by no means a wholly unsympathetic character, but of course she is not to be seen as in any sense a portrayal of the young Fanny Dickens. What is significant here is simply the use of the latter's name for this particular character in this particular context.

This is the only clue we get, in Dickens's fiction, to feelings of resentment and hostility towards his elder sister which may have lain buried deep in him, beneath his conscious love and gratitude, ever since those fateful years of 1823 and 1824. In general, his work strenuously celebrates the sisterly relationship by showing us, for example, a long procession of gentle, devoted, self-effacing (not to say self-sacrificing) sisters, from Kate Nickleby to Lizzie Hexam in *Our Mutual Friend* (Helena Landless in the last novel, *Edwin Drood*, is rather a special case). Elsewhere in this book there will be more to say about Dickens's fascination with Woman in her sisterly aspect, and about his heroine-sisters; I am here concerned only to trace the biographical basis of all this in his relationship with Fanny and the direct or indirect allusions to her in his fiction. His marriage into a family of sisters, and the characters of Mary and Georgina Hogarth, probably intensified the existing predilection but its roots certainly lie deep in his childhood, in those idyllic days when he and Fanny 'trotted about' together, 'with something to eat', and found their world 'Paradise enow'.

3

Lucy

The second five years of his life, those passed at Chatham, 'the birthplace of his fancy', always glowed in Dickens's memory as his Edenic period. That solitary stage-coach journey that terminated them, when he followed his parents to London in 1822, took on the proportions of a dismal rite of passage from innocence to experience:

> Through all the years that have since passed, have I ever lost the smell of the damp straw in which I was packed – like game – and forwarded, carriage paid, to the Cross Keys, Wood-street, Cheapside, London? There was no other inside passenger, and I consumed my sandwiches in solitude and dreariness, and it rained hard all the way, and I thought life sloppier than I had expected to find it.[1]

Nor did Forster fail to point up the epoch-forming significance of this childhood journey when he came to write Dickens's life: 'Kentish woods and fields, Cobham park and hall, Rochester cathedral and castle, and all the wonderful romance together, including a red-cheeked baby he had been wildly in love with, were to vanish like a dream'.[2] Forster does not reveal, perhaps did not know, the identity of the 'red-cheeked baby' but it was made public a few years later in Robert Langton's *Childhood and Youth of Dickens*. The aged Mary Gibson, née Weller, told Langton that 'the especial favourite and little sweetheart of Charles at this time' was one Lucy Stroughill, daughter of the Dickenses' next-door neighbours in Ordnance Terrace. Mrs Gibson remembered Lucy as a 'blue-eyed, golden-haired fairy', and asserted that little Charles was her 'constant companion'.[3] Whether or not Lucy was also, as Edgar Johnson implies,[4] the 'peach-faced creature in a blue sash' whose birthday party Charles attended at a very early age (assuming this event really to have happened and not to have been a piece of fanciful invention by 'the Uncommercial Traveller') we do not know. It is, I think, unlikely. Dickens describes the party as follows:

At so early a stage of my travels did I assist at the anniversary of her nativity (and become enamoured of her), that I had not yet acquired the recondite knowledge that a birthday is the common property of all who are born, but supposed it to be a special gift bestowed by the favouring Heavens on that one distinguished infant. There was no other company, and we sat in a shady bower – under a table, as my better (or worse) knowledge leads me to believe – and were regaled with saccharine substances and liquids, until it was time to part.[5]

This surely sounds as though he is recalling something that happened when he was less than five and so before he became friends with Lucy (whose brother, Dickens's great friend, George, 'a frank, open and somewhat daring boy',[6] would surely also have been at the party, one assumes). Moreover, the combination of adult amusement and a touch of wistful nostalgia that characterizes this passage tones towards anti-women satire at the end of the paragraph:

A bitter powder was administered to me next morning, and I was wretched. On the whole, a pretty accurate foreshadowing of my more mature experiences in such wise!

Dickens is here thinking of the subject of our next chapter, the flirtatious Maria Beadnell, and of the anguish she caused him in his late teens and early twenties, rather than of little Lucy Stroughill. The phrases, 'peach-faced creature' and 'distinguished infant' and her association with cloying 'saccharine substances' make this little girl into a comic, even a satiric, object. The presentation of 'Lucy Green' in an earlier *Uncommercial Traveller* essay, 'Dullborough Town' (1860), is not at all like this and here, we can be sure, prompted by the Christian name, that he *is* remembering Lucy. Dickens is revisiting Chatham and Rochester and looking at the site of a former playing-field:

Here, in the haymaking time, had I been delivered from the dungeons of Seringapatam, an immense pile (of haycock), by my own countrymen, the victorious British (boy next door and his two cousins), and had been recognized with ecstasy by my affianced one (Miss Green), who had come all the way from England (second house in the terrace) to ransom me, and marry me.

Later in the essay he describes how he encountered 'Joe Specks',[7] an old schoolfellow, now a busy doctor in the town, and found that he had married 'Lucy Green':

So I saw her, and she was fat, and if all the hay in the world had been heaped upon her, it could scarcely have altered her face more than Time had altered it from my remembrance of the face that had once looked down upon me into the fragrant dungeons of Seringapatam. But when her youngest child came in. . . . I saw again, in that little daughter, the little face of the hayfield, unchanged, and it quite touched my foolish heart.

Whether Dickens really did re-encounter Lucy Stroughill as the matronly 'Mrs Specks' or whether, with his experience of seeing Maria Beadnell again in middle age, the stout mother of a pretty young daughter, he is only imagining how it would have been if he had done so, we cannot be sure. But what is clear enough is that Lucy stands for all the innocent romance of his happy childhood. Excusing the lack of interest in him shown by the phlegmatic greengrocer whom he also meets and remembers as having always been exactly the same, Dickens writes, 'I was nothing to him: whereas he was the town, the cathedral, the bridge, the river, my childhood, and a large slice of my life, to me.' Lucy was all this and something more; she was the young Dickens's first experience of romance, the Eve of his childhood Eden, but one to whom no subsequent blame attached for it was not through her that he had had to leave that place. She was the flesh-and-blood successor to his 'first love', Little Red Riding-Hood, and the little Fairy of the pantomime, 'with the wand like a celestial Barber's Pole', on whom he had doted and with whom he had pined to share 'a Fairy immortality'.[8] Above all, she was the childish embodiment of a love-relationship for which he yearned but which, of course, could never be realized in the post-pubertal world.

Because there could be, he assumed, no thought of a sexual reward in such childish love Dickens seems to have regarded it as morally superior to adolescent or adult love. So David Copperfield asserts that as a child he loved Little Em'ly 'with greater purity and more disinterestedness, than can enter into the best love of a later time of life'.[9] Dickens's experience of Lucy and the way in which she was all entangled with his golden memory of the days before the Fall moves him, in his minor writings, to pen many passages that must appear to modern readers to be the most sugary sentimentality. An early example occurs in *Sketches of Young Couples* (1840) when, in describing a wedding very much in his smart 'Boz' vein, he devotes a different-toned paragraph to two young children who are among the bridal company:

Of these, one is a little fellow of six or eight years old, brother to the bride, — and the other a girl of the same age, or something younger, whom he calls 'his wife'. The real bride and bridegroom are not more devoted than they: he all love and attention, and she all blushes and fondness, toying with a little bouquet which he gave her this morning, and placing the scattered rose-leaves in her bosom with nature's own coquettishness. They have dreamt of each other in their quiet dreams, these children, and their little hearts have been nearly broken when the absent one has been dispraised in jest. When will there come in after-life a passion so earnest, generous, and true as theirs; what, even in its gentlest realities, can have the grace and charm that hover round such fairy lovers!

In the last sketch of the volume Dickens pictures the young couple whose marriage he describes in the first sketch as 'The Old Couple' and rounds up also all the characters who attended their wedding to see what has become of them:

Where are the fairy lovers of that happy day whose annual return comes upon the old man and his wife, like the echo of some village bell which has long been silent? Let yonder peevish bachelor, racked by rheumatic pains, and quarrelling with the world, let him answer the question. He recollects something of a favourite playmate; her name was Lucy – so they tell him. He is not sure whether she was married, or went abroad, or died. It is a long while ago, and he don't remember.[10]

It is a grim picture of the fate that befalls the man whose imagination loses touch with his childhood Eden and the purity of his first experience of love. By using the name Lucy for the little girl now only half-remembered by the peevish old bachelor Dickens shows, in one of those deeply significant but entirely esoteric autobiographical allusions that one finds everywhere in his work, that he himself has avoided this fate. Lucy Stroughill and what he felt for her as a child is still very much a part of the world of his imagination and a moral force in his life. And all one can say, with regard to charges of sentimentality brought against such passages as the description of the 'fairy lovers' at the wedding is that, if sentimentality is to be defined as expression of feeling disproportionate to the object towards which that feeling is directed, such writing as this was far from sentimental for Dickens himself as he re-created in these 'tiny lovers' himself and Lucy as they had been in those blissful Chatham days which had 'sported by [them], as if Time had not grown up himself yet, but were a child too, and always at play'.[11]

This startling and beautiful image, suddenly making us credit the stooping, grey-bearded figure of Old Father Time with having had a carefree, sportive childhood, is a specimen of the far richer poetic prose of the early chapters of *Copperfield* in which the idyll of David and Little Em'ly is presented to us. Here Dickens, instead of simply relying, as he

does in the *Young Couples* sketch, on the mere mention of childhood
sweethearts, accompanied by a few rhetorical flourishes, to evoke in the
reader the same intense response as he himself feels, is skilfully using all
his 'inimitable' poetic gifts to make us share his nostalgia. The picturesque setting of Mr Peggotty's house that was once a boat, the comedy of
Mrs Gummidge, and the seemingly effortless evocation of a child's
delight in novelty, exploration and freedom with security all help us to
feel a sense of magic or enchantment about David's holiday with the
Peggottys. His response to Em'ly is presented, 'innocent kisses' under the
lee of the lobster-outhouse notwithstanding, as primarily a great en-
riching of the child's life of the imagination, and at the same time Dickens
strikes that elegiac note which is to sound so movingly throughout
Copperfield as David relates to us just how the ceremony of innocence
was drowned:

> Of course I was in love with little Em'ly. I am sure I loved that baby quite
> as truly, quite as tenderly, with greater purity and more disinterestedness,
> than can enter into the best love of a later time of life, high and ennobling
> as it is. I am sure my fancy raised up something round that blue-eyed mite
> of a child, which etherealized, and made a very angel of her. If, any sunny
> forenoon, she had spread a little pair of wings, and flown away before my
> eyes, I don't think I should have regarded it as much more than I had had
> reason to expect.[12]

Any tendency on the reader's part to consider *this* passage sentimental is
quickly deflected by his being made to smile at the Peggotty household's
admiring enthusiasm for the child-sweethearts: 'They had something of
the sort of pleasure in us, I suppose, that they might have had in a pretty
toy, or a pocket model of the Colosseum'. Even in this joke, however,
which releases the embarrassment some readers might have been beginning to feel, there is a suggestion of that sense of fragility and fairy-tale
unreality which underlies the whole of the chapter. The broad hint we are
given in the course of it that Em'ly is not going to have a sunny angelic
existence and our consciousness that little David himself is on the verge of
a dramatic and very miserable change in his life combine to make us feel
the poignancy of this childhood idyll in a way that no amount of mere
authorial comment could.

Dickens's presentation of childhood sweethearts after *Copperfield* is
rather less happy. The runaway children in the 1855 Christmas Story,
'The Holly Tree', eight-year-old Harry Walmers and his seven-year-old
'bride', Norah, are presented to us exclusively through the doting voice of
the Boots at the Holly-Tree Inn and we quickly become aware that this is
mere ventriloquism on the part of Dickens himself with a few collo-

quialisms adopted to express a heart-warming, forelock-tugging old retainer, a sort of deliquescent Sam Weller ('. . . it was better than a picter, and equal to a play, to see them babies, with their long, bright, curling hair, their sparkling eyes, and their beautiful light tread, a rambling about the garden, deep in love'). Dickens is writing out a private fantasy which he yearns to make even more fantastic: 'he wished with all his heart that there was any impossible place where those two babies could make an impossible marriage, and live impossibly happy ever afterwards'. But as fantasies about 'impossible', in the sense of 'innocent' (i.e. sexless), marriages were by no means confined to Dickens in the Victorian period we should not be surprised that this embarrassing effusion proved to be one of the most popular of his public readings.[13]

Lucy Stroughill, the memory of whom undoubtedly lay behind all this fascination with childhood sweethearts, was recalled more specifically in Dickens's next Christmas Story, 'The Wreck of the Golden Mary' (1856), but here she is more of a property than a character. On board the doomed ship is a young wife with a three-year-old daughter called Lucy, 'a most engaging child' with 'a quantity of shining fair hair, clustering in curls all about her face'. The child's business in the story is mainly to intensify the pathos by dying of exposure in the open long-boat after the shipwreck and to illustrate her mother's heroism; Dickens is simply using the Lucy of his childhood as a model here,[14] not drawing on that experience of her that had been part of his inspiration for the third chapter of *Copperfield*.

Dickens's reversions to the childhood-sweetheart theme after 'The Holly Tree' tend, with one exception, to be devoid of the intense feeling invested in its manifestations up to that point. In the story about his fighting a duel at the age of ten with his rival for the favours of 'the youngest Miss Clickitt but one' (aged nine) and in another about loving a little girl in sage green whom he adored so much that he was 'obliged to get out of [his] little bed in the night, expressly to exclaim to Solitude, "O, Olympia Squires!" ',[15] the dominant tone is jocose rather than nostalgic. The same applies to the stories purportedly written by children that compose *A Holiday Romance* (1868) — at least with regard to the childhood-sweethearts theme.

The one piece that does evoke for us as successfully as the third chapter of *Copperfield* (though in a very different way) both the charm and the poignancy of the subject as Dickens felt it is a section of his Christmas Story for 1859, 'The Haunted House'. The idea of the story is that Dickens and a group of friends have taken up residence in an allegedly haunted house. Dickens sleeps in 'Master B's Room' and dreams that a schoolboy ghost appears to him. It is, in fact, the ghost of his own childhood and he finds himself changing back into an earlier shape:

> I was myself, yet not myself. I was conscious of something within me, which has been the same all through my life, and which I have always recognized under all its phases and varieties as never altering, and yet I was not the I who had gone to bed in Master B's room. I had the smoothest of faces and the shortest of legs, and I had taken another creature like myself, also with the smoothest of faces and the shortest of legs, behind a door, and was confiding to him a proposition of the most astounding nature.
>
> This proposition was, that we should have a Seraglio.

There is a fascinating blending of fact and fiction going on here. As a child at Chatham Dickens had indeed been enthralled by *The Arabian Nights* with its wondrous tales of caliphs, genii, magicians, houris and so on[16] and it is entirely likely that he, either alone or with other children, acted out in play some of the adventures related by Scheherazade. He had not, however, been at a school with only one other boy and eight little girls as he pretends in this piece to have been (also, the school is located in Hampstead not Chatham)[17] and there is, one suspects, something a bit *voulu* about the description of the children's deciding to play at seraglios, the school with eight little girls and two little boys having been invented expressly for this purpose. Dickens is bent on asserting the total purity and innocence of childhood love, its utter freedom from all notion of sexuality, by having these children pitch on what to the adolescent or adult must be a decidedly erotic element in *The Arabian Nights* and make that the very basis of their 'innocent' game – which to them is no game but a fairy reality. Miss Bule, 'whom I judge to have attained the ripe age of eight or nine', becomes the Caliph's Favourite and her particular friend, Miss Pipson, becomes 'a Fair Circassian' who must be 'inveigled by a Merchant, brought to [the Caliph] veiled, and purchased as a slave':

> 'Shall I not be jealous?' Miss Bule inquired, casting down her eyes.
> 'Zobeide, no,' I replied; 'you will ever be the favourite Sultana; the first place in my heart, and on my throne, will be ever yours.'

Much of the comic effect of this story depends on the tension between the adult reader's ideas about seraglios and the innocence of the children's make-believe, an innocence that the reader is, Dickens assumes, going to be as delighted to believe in as is Dickens himself.[18]

The story ends with the child's experiencing a sudden and brutal transition from the innocent world of childish love-making to a bleak world of bitter experience. News comes to the school that his father has died:

> Haroun Alraschid took to flight at the words; the Seraglio vanished; from that moment, I never again saw one of the eight of the fairest of the daughters of men.
>
> I was taken home, and there was Debt at home as well as Death, and we had a sale there. My own little bed was so superciliously looked upon by a Power unknown to me, hazily called 'The Trade,' that a brass coal-scuttle, a roasting-jack, and a birdcage, were obliged to be put into it to make a Lot of it, and then it went for a song. So I heard mentioned, and I wondered what song, and thought what a dismal song it must have been to sing!

As in *David Copperfield*, and as in Dickens's own life, there is an abrupt and sudden shift from the world of childhood romance to a much darker world of pain, betrayal and distress. In every case the childhood world is centred on a little sweetheart and in the real-life situation this was that 'blue-eyed, golden-haired fairy' remembered so vividly by old Mrs Gibson.

Although Lucy Stroughill inevitably emerges as the shadowiest of all the figures we are looking at in this section of the book, the importance of the part she played in the development of Dickens's attitude towards women, and hence his presentation of them in his writings, can hardly be overestimated. She was central to the haunting of him by 'the ghost of my own childhood, the ghost of my own innocence, the ghost of my own airy belief',[19] and she imprinted on his heart a certain type of feminine beauty not only as supremely desirable but also as having a sort of redemptive or restoring-to-grace potentiality. Lucie Manette in *A Tale of Two Cities* is perhaps the most obvious expression of this and it is curious to note that while her name and her golden hair recall Lucy Stroughill another aspect of her physical being was apparently drawn from Ellen Ternan.[20] Dickens's first and last loves touch in one fictional woman.

Above all, the unforgettable apparition of little Lucy and the dramatic way in which she vanished from his young life along with all its 'wonderful romance together' set up in Dickens's heart certain expectations about love and women which life refused to fulfil and which could therefore only be gratified in fiction. Neither Maria Beadnell nor Catherine Hogarth could be a 'fairy' figure able to restore Dickens's 'lost innocence' to him. Quite apart from their own characters and personalities, there was consciously present in Dickens's relationships with them a strong sexual element which had not been there, so he believed, in the case of Lucy Stroughill. Lucy, I suggested earlier, was a real-life successor to the beautiful Fairy in the pantomime in little Charles's romantic affections; of that fairy he wrote in 1850:

> Ah, she comes back, in shapes, as my eye wanders down the branches of my Christmas Tree [i.e., as I review my life to date], and goes as often, and has never yet stayed by me.[21]

Seven years later he was to meet a 'small fair-haired rather pretty actress',[22] eighteen-year-old Ellen, who did, in fact, stay by him. But whether she was a sort of Lucy *rediviva*, romantically but 'innocently' adored, or whether she was something rather different, a seraglio of one, is a matter of much debate and one that must be considered in its place. Meanwhile, Dickens's abiding tribute to little Lucy Stroughill and all that she meant to him endures for us in that wonderful third chapter of *Copperfield* with its picture of the two little sweethearts delightedly rambling about together 'like two young mavishes', as Mr Peggotty says, and 'glowing with health and pleasure'.

4
Maria

'I broke my heart into the smallest pieces, many times between thirteen
and three and twenty. Twice, I was very horribly in earnest, and once I
really set upon the cast for six or seven long years, all the energy and
determination of which I am owner.'
Dickens to Thomas Powell, 1845[1]

'. . . such a past is always present to a man; such a passion once felt forms
a part of his whole being, and cannot be separated from it.'
W.M. Thackeray, *Henry Esmond*, Book III, ch. 6

Some time during the latter half of 1831 a certain City banker and his
wife, Mr and Mrs George Beadnell, gave a dinner-party at their home in
Lombard Street for a dozen or so friends of their own and of their
daughters. Among the guests was the nineteen-year-old Dickens who was
just beginning to develop his career as a reporter of Parliamentary
debates for the newspapers. It is not known how he first became
acquainted with the Beadnells – possibly through a young bank clerk
called Henry Kolle who was engaged to the second Beadnell daughter,
Anne – but by 1831 he was well established as a member of the circle of
young people who surrounded Maria, the third and youngest daughter of
the family. In fact, he was devotedly, obsessively in love with her and had
been for at least one year and more probably two. She was thirteen
months older than he, small in stature and very pretty, a 'pocket Venus' as
she was later to be called.[2] As she sat playing the harp 'in a sort of
raspberry coloured dress' Dickens's 'boyish heart', he recalled years later,
was 'pinned like a captured butterfly' on every one of the little black
velvet vandykes with which the top of the dress was trimmed.[3] She was
the driving force of his ambition to better himself so that he might be
favourably regarded as a prospective son-in-law by Mr Beadnell. For he
was painfully conscious that Maria's parents were most unlikely to
welcome a struggling young newspaper reporter into their family. Their
eldest daughter, Margaret, had just married a partner in a flourishing tea
and coffee business,[4] and this was the safe kind of match they would
certainly have wanted for all their girls. Young 'Mr Dickin', as Mrs

Beadnell always called him, was simply not in the running.

But the idea of Maria 'pervaded every chink and crevice' of his mind. Perhaps if he could impress the Beadnells with the extraordinarily earnest nature of his love and also with his literary talents, giving promise of future prosperity, they might look more favourably on him? His comic reminiscing (in an essay of 1863 entitled 'Birthday Celebrations') about writing never-posted letters, 'more in number than Horace Walpole's', to his beloved's mother, 'soliciting her daughter's hand in marriage' may well be only a slight exaggeration of what he actually did:

> Sometimes, I had begun 'Honoured Madam. I think that a lady gifted with those powers of observation which I know you to possess, and endowed with those womanly sympathies with the young and ardent which it were more than heresy to doubt, can scarcely have failed to discover that I love your adorable daughter, deeply, devotedly.' In less buoyant states of mind I had begun, 'Bear with me, Dear Madam, bear with a daring wretch who is about to make a surprising confession to you, wholly unanticipated by yourself, and which he beseeches you to commit to the flames as soon as you have become aware to what a towering height his mad ambition soars.'[5]

But at the time this would have been no joking matter to him. Although as far as we know he was discreet enough not to actually send any such letters to Mrs Beadnell he still longed to convey to her and her husband, in some striking way, the state of his emotions with regard to their youngest daughter. The dinner-party must have seemed to offer an ideal opportunity. He would make up some doggerel verses descriptive of all the company which should gratify the host and hostess and their family, agreeably tease their friends, and, at the same time, make very clear, though in the lightest possible manner, his passion for Maria.

He found a model for his verses in his beloved Goldsmith who in a poem called 'Retaliation' had described his friends as though they were dishes at a banquet and had then proceeded to write a series of mock-epitaphs for them. So Dickens in his verses (entitled 'The Bill of Fare') hails Mr Beadnell as 'a good fine sirloin of beef' and his wife as 'an excellent *Rib* of the same'. Then follows much flattering unction for their souls. Mr Beadnell is 'An excellent man, and a good politician . . . most hospitable, friendly and kind' and Mrs Beadnell 'Can be summ'd up in one word – *perfection*'.[6] Of himself Dickens wrote that he was

> . . . a young Summer Cabbage, without any heart; –
> Not that he's *heartless*, but because, as folks say,
> He lost his a twelve month ago, from last May.

Maria's 'epitaph' makes it clear that it was to her that he lost his heart:

> My bright hopes and fond wishes were all centred here;
> Their brightness has vanished, they're now dark and drear.

He rhymes about her little lapdog, Daphne, and makes a roguish joke about its being folded to her breast in a last sleep:

> . . . I'd resign all my natural graces,
> E'en now, if I could with 'Daphne' change places;

and reverts to Maria in the last lines of the poem, describing his own 'death':

> His death wasn't sudden; he had long been ill,
> Slowly he languished, and got worse, until
> No mortal means could the poor young fellow save,
> And a sweet pair of eyes sent him home to his grave.

After hearing all this the Beadnells could hardly have been left in doubt that this smart young fellow was deeply in love with Maria and it was unfortunate for him that, before the year ended, his father's name appeared in *The London Gazette* as being sued in the Insolvent Debtors Court. Mr and Mrs Beadnell may possibly have taken steps, about this time, to discourage the young suitor as we find in 1832 that he is having to communicate surreptitiously with Maria by using Kolle – now offici-ally engaged to Anne Beadnell – as a go-between. But I shall suggest later that this clandestine correspondence may have been more of a whim of Maria's than a result of intervention by her parents.

The received version of this episode has Maria being sent away at this point (the winter of 1831/2), to Madame Martinez's finishing school in Paris, to distance her from this undesirable suitor. From Paris, so this version runs, she returned 'strangely altered', prone to 'coldnesses, quarrels, caprices', her feeling for Dickens 'apparently cooled', and so on.[7]

Two things seem wrong here. First, we have no evidence at all that Maria was at Madame Martinez's during 1831/2 but we do know that she was there much earlier, in April 1830.[8] Now, when Dickens later told her that he remembered his existence being 'entirely uprooted' and his 'whole Being blighted' by her ('the Angel of my soul') being sent away to Paris, he recalled that she had gone there 'to finish her education'.[9] Surely it is much more likely that she would have been sent to a finishing-school in 1829 or 1830, when she was eighteen or just into her nineteenth year, than in 1831 or 1832, after coming of age? If Dickens's allusion in 'The

Bill of Fare' to having lost his heart 'twelve month ago from last May' refers to May 1830, as seems most probable, this might suggest that it was just after Maria returned from Paris (May would be a very likely time for Madame Martinez's term to end) that he declared himself to her and perhaps received some encouragement. It was in 1830, we note, that he was first permitted to write something in her sumptuous album. He composed a laboured acrostic on her name which ended:

> Life has no charms, no happiness, no pleasures, now for me
> Like those I feel, when 'tis my lot Maria, to gaze on thee.[10]

Dora Spenlow, we might recall, has just returned 'from finishing her education at Paris' when David Copperfield 'falls into captivity'.[11] Dickens is there surely dramatizing and intensifying what happened in real life by making this the first time that David had ever actually set eyes on Dora.

The second thing that seems wrong about the received version is that it apparently supposes a period during which Maria was consistently kind and encouraging to Dickens; and that it was only during the last few months of the affair that she became capricious and difficult; such evidence as we have does not seem to bear this out. Maria's album clearly shows that she encouraged many young men to pay court to her, among her versifying admirers (French as well as English) being Henry Austin, who was later to marry Dickens's younger sister, Letitia. Perhaps most revealing of Maria's character and coquettish ways are the verses contributed by a young man identifiable only by his initials, 'T.E.R.'. His first entry, 'To Maria', is dated February 1832 and seems to be a response to some doubt she had expressed about the genuineness of his passion:

> Art thou not dear unto my heart?
> Ah! search that heart and see
> And from my bosom tear the part
> That beats not true to thee! . . .

His next offering, 'The Envy of Love', seems to have been inspired by Maria's teasing him about being attracted to some other young lady and by her pretended jealousy:

> Yes, Maria, I freely grant —
> The charm of —'s eyes I see
> But when you gaze I something want
> I want *thine* eyes to gaze on me . . .

Below his verses T.E.R. wrote, severely, '*Il y a dans la jalousie plus d'amour propre, que de propre amour'*. His last contribution, a few pages later, reads like a bitter farewell to a cold-hearted flirt:

> Say what is she, who steals the heart away
> Speaks to deceive and smiles but to betray
> Who strives – nor vainly strives – the soul to move
> And then deserts him she allured to love?

While Maria was driving 'T.E.R.', among others, to these pleadings and reproaches she was also keeping Dickens dangling. He composed two long poems for her album in November 1831, one satirical and one solemn and both pretty clearly penned with an eye on her political Papa. In the first, 'The Devil's Walk', the Devil visits the House of Lords where he sees 'a few Nobles rich and proud/War 'gainst the people and Prince' and he also exults in some riots that have just taken place in Bristol stirred up by the presence there of his 'old friend', Sir Charles Wetherell (who, like the Lords, was a strong opponent of the Reform Bill). All this might be expected to gratify a keen Reform Bill supporter like Mr Beadnell. But Maria herself is not forgotten. The Devil glimpses 'not far from Lombard Street'

> a face so fair
> That it made him start and weep
> For a passing thought rushed over his brain
> Of days now beyond recall
> He thought of the bright angelic train
> And of his own wretched fall.

There is no such direct compliment to Maria in the second poem, 'The Churchyard', but no doubt Dickens trusted that both she and her parents would be suitably impressed by the scorn he pours on a 'Roué' who has broken the heart of a young girl so that 'Death was to her a glad relief':

> In truth it is a manly deed
> With woman's heart to trifle,
> To break the bent and bruised reed
> And with neglect to stifle
> The feelings man himself has raised
> Which he can't prize too high –
> To leave the object he has praised
> Alone to weep and die.

There is something touchingly ironic in the young man's seeking in this album to show what a serious and responsible lover he is whilst its other pages testify so amply to Maria's frivolity in this respect. She herself transcribed (or maybe composed) a couple of poems for her own book and both of them breathe the very spirit of coquetry. One trills away about which season of the year is the best one for lovers and the second is a mock-warning to men:

Till he beheld a Woman's face
Adam was in a happy state.
For in the sex you'll see appear
Hypocrisy, deceit, and pride,
Truth, darling of a heart sincere,
In women never can reside.
Destruction take the men, I say,
Who make a woman their delight.

Dickens was in no condition to heed a serious warning let alone one like this that was simply a disguised come-on. He was in the helpless condition he later recalled so vividly when describing David Copperfield in love with Dora:

She was more than human to me. She was a Fairy, a Sylph, I don't know what she was – anything that no one ever saw, and everything that everybody ever wanted. I was swallowed up in an abyss of love. . . .[12]

In *Copperfield* he gives us what we might call his '*pièce rose*' version of his love for Maria; in *Great Expectations* it is very much a '*pièce noire*'. There Estella repeatedly warns Pip, in all earnestness, to conquer his passion for her but he is powerless to do so: 'I never had one hour's happiness in her society, and yet my mind all round the four-and-twenty hours was harping on the happiness of having her with me unto death'.[13]

A revealing letter written to Maria by Dickens in 1831 has only recently come to light.[14] It seems to suggest that Dickens's own family were not too happy about his liaison with Maria (his sister Fanny would know her very well) but it was clearly also written before Dickens was discouraged (if indeed he *was* ever discouraged) from visiting in Lombard Street. He has had the privilege of being set a little task by Maria – no doubt she was adept at finding errands for her knights – but she is being generally difficult. She demurs about accepting a present he is trying to give her and she is making it hard for him to see her:

My dear Maria. – (I fear I ought to say 'Miss Beadnell' but I hope you will pardon my adhering to the manner in which I have been accustomed to address you.) I have taken the opportunity of returning your sister's Album to write these few hurried lines for the purpose of saying that my Glover has made some stupid mistake about your gloves, and I shall therefore be much obliged if you will have the kindness to inclose me one of those I had before in an envelope addressed to me here.[15] – Pray do not think this wrong *under existing circumstances*. You need not fear the fact of your writing being known to any one here for I shall be very busy at home and alone all day tomorrow as my mother and sister will be in town. I have another favour to ask: it is that you will tell me when you think would be a good opportunity for me to bring the Gloves. I am most anxious indeed to see you as I wish much to speak to you particularly about the Annual. – Surely, surely you will not refuse so trivial a present: a mere common place trifle; a common present even among the merest 'friends'. Do not misunderstand me: I am not desirous by making presents or by doing any other act to influence your thoughts, wishes, or feelings in the slightest degree. – I do not think I do: – I cannot hope I ever shall: but let me entreat of you do not refuse so slight a token of regard from me.

I cannot unless you will grant me an opportunity speak to you either on this, or any other subject; – I hope and trust you will not refuse: consider how long it is since I have seen you.

Trusting you will excuse haste and most anxiously waiting to hear from you which I hope and trust I shall in the course of tomorrow.

I remain

My dear – Miss Beadnell

Ever Yours Sincerely

C.D.

I hope you will like the Lines. I do not *think* what I *write* you know. – I allude particularly to the *last four lines* of the *Third Verse*.

The 'lines' Dickens refers to in his postscript are 'The Bill of Fare' which he has transcribed into Anne Beadnell's album. In that poem verse three ends:

> I think what I say – *I feel it*, that's better,
> Or I'd scorn to write of these lines one letter.

His postscript is, in fact, urging Maria to take him seriously (he really *feels* what he *writes*) when she reads what he has said about her and his feelings for her in 'The Bill'; she must not take it as a mere *jeu d'esprit*. But, as poor 'T.E.R.' was to discover a few months later, Maria was very good at pretending not to believe in her lovers.

So adept was she, in fact, at playing games with her many admirers that we need not suppose her parents thought it necessary to warn off young Dickens in particular. Their attitude towards him is well suggested by a little episode of which, years later, he reminded Maria:

55

... I found you three [i.e., Maria and her sisters] on Cornhill with your poor mother, going to St. Mary Axe to order mysterious dresses – which afterwards turned out to be wedding garments [for the eldest girl's marriage to David Lloyd in April 1831] ... I escorted you with native gallantry to the Dress Maker's door, and your mother, seized with an apprehension ... that I might come in, said emphatically, 'And now, Mr Dicken' – which she always used to call me – 'We'll wish *you* good morning.[16]

He was tolerated, perhaps even encouraged for his talent to amuse, but kept within pretty firm limits.[17] Always he was somewhat nervous about his standing with the family. 'With our friends the Beadnell's [*sic*]', he wrote to Kolle when beseeching him to take over the organization of some projected pleasure-jaunt, '... *you* can do no wrong; *I* am not so sure of coming off well.'[18] It is hard to believe that Mr and Mrs Beadnell took him seriously enough to forbid him the house, still less that they felt Maria (who can hardly have given the impression of being infatuated with him) had to be whisked away to Paris, out of his reach.[19]

The explanation for the period during 1832 when he had to communicate with Maria by surreptitious notes carried by Kolle may lie as much in some little drama got up by Maria herself as in any intervention by Mr Beadnell. Dickens was evidently not prevented from meeting her as he apologizes in one letter to Kolle for troubling him with another note for Maria, saying he would have 'communicated it's [*sic*] contents verbally' to her the previous evening but had 'lost the opportunity by keeping the old gentleman [i.e. Mr Beadnell] out of the way [of Kolle and his fiancée, Anne] as long as possible'.[20] Maria would no doubt have greatly relished receiving smuggled *billets doux* to keep with her album and perhaps show to her confidantes. Such trophies would have been preferable to poor Dickens's attempted 'verbal communications' and she may well have contrived a situation whereby he was forced into this clandestine correspondence. Kolle does not seem to have been the only channel for this, incidentally. Some sympathetic friend or relative of the Beadnells who aided and abetted the intrigue must have lived in Finsbury Place about this time. Writing to Maria from Paris some twenty-odd years later Dickens said,

I reply by return of post – with a general idea that Sarah [presumably a servant of the Beadnells'] will come to Finsbury Place with a basket and a face of good-humoured compassion, and carry the letter away, and leave me desolate as she used to do.[21]

'Desolate' was what poor Dickens seems to have been during most of his three or four years of infatuation with Maria. Sometimes she gave him encouragement but mostly she made him suffer. In a 'burst of low-spirited madness' he once appealed to Anne to tell him where he really stood in Maria's affections. She replied, 'My Dear Charles, I really cannot understand Maria, or venture to take the responsibility of saying what the state of her affection is. . . '.[22] She concluded with 'a long quotation about Patience and Time' which Dickens must surely have been remembering when he later composed the hilarious entries for Dora's confidante Julia Mills's journal, so eagerly scanned by young David: 'Must not D.C. confide himself to the broad pinions of Time?'.[23]

In February 1833 Dickens came of age, still besotted with Maria. His mother issued invitations for a party to celebrate the event ('Quadrilles. 8 o'clock'). In the 'Birthday Celebrations' essay thirty years later he describes the occasion with all those little comic imaginative touches that make his ostensibly autobiographical essays slippery guides to the actual biographical truth:

> I gave a party . . . She was there . . . She was older than I, and had pervaded every chink and crevice of my mind for three or four years . . . Behind a door, in the crumby part of the night when wine-glasses were to be found in unexpected spots, I spoke to Her – spoke out to Her. What passed, I cannot as a man of honour reveal. She was all angelical gentleness, but a word was mentioned – a short and dreadful word of three letters, beginning with a B – which, as I remarked at the moment, 'scorched my brain'. She went away soon afterwards.

Written for comic effect though this clearly is, I would take it as evidence that Maria was present at his birthday party – as indeed one would have expected her to be. Whether she, just entered into her twenty-third year, did actually tease him there about his still being a mere 'boy' we cannot be sure, but it is perhaps worth noting that one of the things that really stings young Pip in his first dealings with Estella is the contemptuous way in which she constantly addresses him as 'boy' ('. . . she was of about my own age' but 'seemed much older than I, of course, being a girl, and beautiful and self-possessed').[24]

A few weeks after his twenty-first birthday party when, as he said, his meetings with Maria had become 'little more than so many displays of heartless indifference' on her part whilst being for him 'a fertile source of wretchedness and misery', Dickens could stand it no longer. Humiliated at hearing himself discussed as an object of pity by Maria's friends, he sent her an agonized letter (which she was careful to take a copy of before returning it to him). In its quivering pride, its furious self-vindication and its general vehemence of tone it is a characteristic Dickens effusion. He perceives, he writes, that he has been 'engaged in a pursuit which has long since been worse than hopeless'. To persevere in it any longer would merely expose him to 'deserved ridicule' so he is returning to her a 'little present' she once gave him, a present 'which I have always prized as I still do far beyond anything I ever possessed'. He does not wish to hurt her feelings but must speak his mind as 'this is neither a matter nor a time for cold deliberate calculating trifling' (did the galled jade wince, one wonders?). His feelings towards her ('to you a matter of very little moment still I *have* feelings in common with other people') have, on the other hand, 'perhaps . . . been as strong and as good as ever warmed the human heart' and so, he somewhat curiously concludes, he feels it would be 'mean and contemptible' of him to keep 'one single line or word of remembrance or affection' from her.[25] It is a remarkable instance of covertly transferred epithets.

The second half of the letter implicitly contrasts Maria's coquettish behaviour with his own steadfast love. Maria was stung into an immediate reproachful reply, accusing Dickens of unkindness and bitterness. This was enough to bring him to heel and he at once wrote again, a declaration of undying love. But when she sent that letter back to him, '*by hand wrapped in a small loose piece of paper without even the formality of an envelope*',[26] he realized he had only exposed himself to further hurt and humiliation. The Mary Anne Leigh imbroglio[27] twisted the knife in the wound still more as Dickens sought desperately to extricate himself with as much dignity as possible from this sad wreck of all his 'happy hopes', but it did also give him an opportunity to keep corresponding with Maria, through the good offices of Kolle. As the date of Kolle's marriage to Anne Beadnell (22 May) approached, however, Dickens, who was to be Kolle's best man, realized that he would soon have 'no postman' and resolved to make one last attempt to change Maria's heart. He sent her what he described to Kolle as 'a very conciliatory note sans pride, sans reserve sans anything but an evident wish to be reconciled'.[28] The letter is not exactly 'sans pride' – it would hardly be a Dickens letter if it were – as we realize when we come across a phrase like 'all that any one can do to raise himself by his own exertions and unceasing assiduity I have done', but it is almost wholly free from the bitter undertones and veiled reproaches of his earlier letters. 'I never have loved and I never can love any human creature breathing but yourself', he tells Maria and begs her to answer him seriously and soon. She replied, however, 'very coldly and reproachfully' and Dickens, despairing of her at last, 'went [his] way'.[29]

It is true to say, I believe, that Dickens never loved any other woman as he loved Maria. He wrote later that he had been 'horribly in earnest' about one other girl between the ages of thirteen and twenty-three, but implied that even that was not comparable to his passion for Maria which had exercised 'for six or seven long years [actually, three or four] all the energy and determination of which I am owner'.[30] We do not even know this other girl's name though she is usually identified as Georgina Ross, a sister of one of Dickens's fellow-journalists (another sister, Janet, married one of his maternal uncles). The only evidence for this, however, is a Ross family tradition that Dickens had admired Georgina and had even become engaged to her but that her formidable old father 'wouldn't have it, as he thought Dickens was a "dissolute young man" '.[31] Dickens's writing a poem, 'The Ivy Green' (later used in *Pickwick Papers*) in Georgina's album in May 1836 proves nothing – by then he was married to Catherine Hogarth. But Georgina's being nine years older than Dickens is perhaps more relevant; it surely seems unlikely that such a dominating character as he would be attracted to the idea of a wife so much his senior. In any case, unless we believe with Thomas Wright that Georgina may have inspired the entertaining episode of the eldest Miss Larkins in *David Copperfield*, chapter 18,[32] she is of little moment to us here, concerned as we are with what Dickens the artist made of Dickens the man's experience of women.

What he at first made, artistically, of Maria and her friends was the spirited caricature of middle-class young ladyhood drawn in his earliest fiction. Whilst lay figures such as Rose Maylie and Kate Nickleby show what, in young Dickens's view, the ideal young lady *should* be, the general rule is shown to be very different. Vanity, snobbery, sentimental or romantic affectation, tittering silliness, petty spitefulness and mutual competitiveness ('. . . young ladies . . . will jostle each other in the race to the altar, and will avail themselves of all opportunities of displaying their own attractions to the best advantage')[33] – these are the things presented as typical of young ladyhood. Here are the girls at Minerva House, Hammersmith, a very genteel school, preparing for a ball:

> The smaller girls managed to be in everybody's way, and were pushed about accordingly; and the elder ones dressed, and tied, and flattered, and envied one another, as earnestly and sincerely as if they had actually *come out.*
>
> 'How do I look, dear?' inquired Miss Emily Smithers, the belle of the house, of Miss Caroline Wilson, who was her bosom friend, because she was the ugliest girl in Hammersmith, or out of it.
>
> 'Oh! charming, dear. How do I?'[34]

'Delightful! you never looked so handsome,' returned the belle, adjusting her own dress, and not bestowing a glance on her poor companion.[35]

Even in the lower depths of Madame Mantalini's work-room the same characteristics appear:

... all the young ladies suspending their operations for the moment, whispered to each other sundry criticisms upon the make and texture of Miss Nickleby's dress, her complexion, cast of features, and personal appearance, with as much good-breeding as could have been displayed by the very best society in a crowded ball-room.[36]

One suspects that Nicholas Nickleby's habitual facetious gallantry towards the young ladies he encounters is a pretty faithful reflection of the young Dickens's own behaviour in mixed company; and I feel sure that locating the enchanting Miss Snevellicci's Portsmouth lodgings 'in a place called Lombard Street' is one of those private jokes with himself of which Dickens was so fond. His readers would, of course, have no idea how highly charged with emotional memories this address was for him. The little impromptu that Miss Snevellicci and her bosom friend, Miss Ledrook, act out so charmingly on first being introduced to Nicholas faithfully conveys to us what must have been the very essence of social life in Maria's set:

'Oh! you men are such vain creatures!' cried Miss Snevellicci. Whereupon, she became charmingly confused, and, pulling out her pocket-handkerchief from a faded pink silk reticule with a gilt clasp, called to Miss Ledrook —
'Led, my dear,' said Miss Snevellicci.
'Well, what is the matter?' said Miss Ledrook.
'It's not the same.'
'Not the same what?'
'Canterbury — you know what I mean. Come here! I want to speak to you.'
But Miss Ledrook wouldn't come to Miss Snevellicci, so Miss Snevellicci was obliged to go to Miss Ledrook, which she did, in a skipping manner that was quite fascinating; and Miss Ledrook evidently joked Miss Snevellicci about being struck with Nicholas; for, after some playful whispering, Miss Snevellicci hit Miss Ledrook very hard on the backs of her hands, and retired up [i.e. upstage], in a state of pleasing confusion.[37]

It is usually assumed by Dickens's biographers that after 1833 he lost sight of Maria completely until she suddenly re-entered his life as Mrs

Winter twenty-two years later and released in him a great flood of emotion about their earlier association. The truth seems not to have been quite as dramatic as this. There survive nine letters from Dickens to Maria's father written between 1837 and 1854, two of them long letters of condolence on family bereavements, which show that the Beadnell family did maintain some contact with Dickens in his fame. Some time during 1838 or 1839, for example, Dickens wrote to Mr Beadnell, 'Mrs D and I have much pleasure in accepting your invite' and sent his and Catherine's 'best regards' to Mrs Beadnell and Maria.[38] It is difficult to imagine that, even though he was living abroad at the time, he did not get to hear of Maria's marriage, in February 1845, to Henry Winter, a saw-mill manager in Finsbury. He does not, however, mention it in a letter written to Mr Beadnell on New Year's Day 1846 when he sent 'earnest' good wishes 'for you and yours in the years to come – for the love and remembrance of the years that are gone'.[39] But, according to a rather confused memorandum made by Georgina Hogarth in 1906 Dickens took her and Catherine 'to have Tea and Supper with Mr and Mrs Winter who were living in Finsbury Crescent soon after their marriage' and laughed about his former love for her, in the carriage driving home ('*I could not see a trace even of the prettiness which seemed to have been her only attraction*', Georgina remarks).[40] Dickens himself, however, makes no reference to such a visit in his 1855 letters to Maria. In them he does indeed convey the impression that he had never set eyes on her since 1833. 'I could not,' he tells her,

> at any time within these nineteen years, have been so unmindful of my old truth, and have so set my old passion aside, as to talk to you like a person in any ordinary relation towards me. And this I think is the main reason on my side why the few opportunities that there have been of ever seeing one another again have died out.[41]

He also, however, 'begs to be remembered' to Mr Winter, which surely suggests that he had met him at least once. And what conceivable reason could Georgina have had to invent this anecdote about Dickens, Catherine and herself visiting the Winters after their marriage?[42] I believe, therefore, that the visit did take place but that, for all his merriment on the homeward journey, Dickens found purely social contact with this woman who had so strongly bewitched his younger self just too disturbing and so allowed it to 'die out'.

She would not die out of his mind and heart, however. Or rather, the memory of how ardently he had loved her would not. As he entered early middle age he thought of the Maria years of his youth as the time when he had been truly among the pure in heart even though he was no longer the child that had been so 'innocently' in love with Lucy Stroughill: 'I have never been so good a man since . . . I shall never be half so good a fellow any more'. She belonged to 'the most innocent, the most ardent, and the most disinterested days' of his adult life for she had been 'their Sun'; and in that beautiful sunlight 'the qualities that have done me most good since, were growing in my boyish heart'. 'I know', he told her in 1855, 'that the Dream I lived in did me good, refined my heart, and made me patient and persevering.' But the suffering this fickle sun had caused him in his purity had been so intense that, when he set himself to recall those days on paper (in a projected autobiography), he 'lost courage' as he approached the subject and abandoned the attempt.[43] Once he had conceived the story of *David Copperfield*, however, a *Bildungsroman* in which he could dramatize his understanding of 'how all these things have worked together to make me what I am'[44] through depicting the emotional and moral history of an invented character, he found a way he could write about himself and Maria that was not only emotionally tolerable but even positively exhilarating.

David is presented as a pure-hearted innocent, bruised but not corrupted by the Murdstones' cruelty, who must outgrow both 'Daisy' and 'Doady' (the pet-names given him by Steerforth and Dora respectively) to become Trotwood Copperfield, 'a fine, firm fellow with a will of [his] own', a worthy mate for Agnes. His heart is disciplined not, as in Dickens's case, by being devoted to one girl who proves to be unworthy of such love but by being devoted to two people: an idolized friend, Steerforth, who betrays him through a cold-hearted sexual conquest; and a pretty little child-wife who adores but disappoints him. All of what had been really agonizing in Dickens's disillusionment with Maria is, I believe, concentrated in the figure of Steerforth — handsome and captivating, entrancing company, yet ultimately shallow, selfish and cruelly frivolous. Dickens makes David exclaim, after a particularly triumphant exhibition of charm on Steerforth's part:

> If any one had told me, then, that all this was a brilliant game, played for the excitement of the moment, for the employment of high spirits, in the thoughtless love of superiority, in a mere careless course of winning what was worthless to him, and next minute thrown away: I say, if any one had told me such a lie that night, I wonder in what manner of receiving it my indignation would have found a vent![45]

Just so, one imagines, would young Dickens have reacted in 1831 or 1832 to such an attack on Maria's truthfulness after some occasion on which she had bathed him in bliss by her graciousness. But now, older, wiser, sadder, he too 'cried when he read about Steerforth'.[46]

The invention of Steerforth enables Dickens to create David's Maria-figure, Dora Spenlow, untouched by unhappy memories of the way in which her real-life original had tormented and ultimately failed him. When, years later, he wrote to Maria, '. . . you may have seen . . . in little bits of "Dora" touches of your old self sometimes . . .'[47] he was presumably referring to such external details as Dora's diminutive stature, her abundant curls, her little lapdog and her sweet singing, perhaps also to what David calls her 'prettily pettish manner'. But, apart from these things, Dora is not physically presented in any solidly-realized way. She enters the novel as a faery vision of loveliness, a vision fixed for the reader by that unforgettable image of 'a straw hat and blue ribbons, and a quantity of curls, and a little black dog being held up, in two slender arms, against a bank of blossoms and bright leaves'. For Dickens is not concerned to evoke Maria as she actually was but as the 'Sun' that she had once been for him. She must seem to the reader as to David 'everything that everybody ever wanted' and to particularize her too closely would work against this. Maria's eyebrows had had a tendency to join together, Dickens fondly remembered,[48] but to give this feature to Dora could only distance her from the reader who would, of course, have his own taste in eyebrows. So Dickens tactfully concentrates on vague evocative phrases ('What a form she had, what a face she had, what a graceful, variable, enchanting manner!') leaving the reader's imagination and own personal memories to do the rest.

Maria's knowingly provocative flirtatiousness which had caused Dickens such agonies of sexual jealousy is converted into the innocently provocative playfulness of Dora with her little dog, Jip, David's only 'rival':

> He was mortally jealous of me, and persisted in barking at me. She took him up in her arms – oh my goodness! – and caressed him, but he insisted upon barking still. . . . It increased my sufferings greatly to see the pats she gave him for punishment on the bridge of his blunt nose, while he winked his eyes, and licked her hand, and still growled within himself like a little double-bass. At length he was quiet – well he might be with her dimpled chin upon his head! – and we walked away to look at a greenhouse.[49]

Remembering Maria's little dog, Daphne, Dickens hits upon a way of establishing Dora as a sexual presence without detracting from his depiction of her as a vision of innocence as well as of loveliness. Daphne becomes Jip winking lazily as Dora kisses 'his ball of a head' (and sharing all his female original's taste for mutton chops).⁵⁰

Dora's innocence is seen to stem from an immaturity that will wring David's heart but it is not a culpable immaturity. She has had no mother to guide her towards womanhood, her schooling, we can assume, has been of the highly inadequate kind provided by establishments like Minerva House, Hammersmith, or Miss Monflathers's academy, and her pompous ass of a father has given her the repellent Miss Murdstone for a companion ('We are not going to confide in such cross people, Jip and I'). She fails David but not as Maria had failed Dickens. In her artless innocence she is incapable of the coquettish behaviour that had made Lombard Street such a purgatory for Maria's ardent young lover; on the contrary, she responds to David's passion with a childlike directness and trustfulness and never fails him in love. In their unsatisfactory marriage she is shown to be as much a sufferer as he is and the delicate art with which Dickens presents her character and her love will be discussed in a later chapter. From the biographical-critical viewpoint she may be said to represent the same sort of comic forgiveness of Maria that Mrs Micawber does of Dickens's mother; all his darker memories of his early love are concentrated in Steerforth just as his darker memories of Elizabeth are concentrated in Miss Murdstone.

Whatever emotional equilibrium Dickens may have achieved through the writing of *Copperfield* did not survive long into the 1850s, however. By the winter of 1854/5 he was in a highly restless state and had begun making hints to Forster about the unsatisfactoriness of his private life. 'I have had dreadful thoughts of getting away somewhere altogether by myself', he wrote, '. . . of living for half a year or so, in all sorts of inaccessible places, and opening a new book therein':

> *Restlessness*, you will say. Whatever it is, it is always driving me, and I cannot help it. I have rested nine or ten weeks, and sometimes feel as if it had been a year – though I had the strangest nervous miseries before I stopped. If I couldn't walk fast and far, I should just explode and perish.

A few months after this outburst Forster received another:

> Am altogether in a dishevelled state of mind – motes of new books in the dirty air, miseries of older growth threatening to close upon me. Why is it, that as with poor David, a sense comes always crushing on me now, when I fall into low spirits, as of one happiness I have missed in life, and one friend and companion I have never made?⁵¹

As if pat on cue, Maria, unseen for at least ten years, chose this moment to re-enter his life. She wrote to him in February 1855, apparently just a chatty letter giving news of herself, her family (she had two small daughters by then) and friends and containing some tender allusions to the old days in Lombard Street. Dickens received her letter on the eve of rushing off to Paris with Wilkie Collins for a short break but responded immediately with a warmth that must have gratified yet also somewhat startled Maria. The very sight of her handwriting had, he told her, 'curiously disturbed' him even before he realized whom the letter was from and then —

> suddenly the remembrance of your hand came upon me with an influence that I cannot express to you. Three or four and twenty years vanished like a dream, and I opened it [i.e. Maria's letter] with the touch of my young friend David Copperfield when he was in love. . . .
>
> Believe me, you cannot more tenderly remember our old days and our old friends than I do. I hardly ever go into the City but I walk up an odd little court at the back of the Mansion House and come out by the corner of Lombard Street . . . I forget nothing of those times. . . .
>
> Your letter is more touching to me . . . than I could tell you if I tried for a week . . .
>
> My Dear Mrs Winter, I have been much moved by your letter. . . . The associations my memory has with you made your letter more – I want a word – invest it with a more immediate address to me than such a letter could have from anybody else. Mr Winter will not mind that. . . .[52]

In response to his asking her if he could 'discharge any little commission' for her in Paris Maria requested the purchase of some jewellery. This little bit of business seems to have been a mere pretext, on both sides, for continued correspondence. Encouraged, no doubt, by the warm tone of Dickens's reply to her first note, Maria, writing back, seems to have adopted a more intimate tone, assuring Dickens that no one but she would read whatever he wrote to her. He, by now in Paris, at once replied with a letter full of tender reminiscences of the 'old days'. The tenderness, we should note, however, is primarily directed towards his younger self and towards Maria only in so far as she had been the inspirer of that self. Dickens manages both to flatter Maria and also to blame her, in a veiled way, for not having properly appreciated him and 'the most extraordinary earnestness' of his love:

> I have always believed since . . . that there never was such a faithful and devoted poor fellow as I was. Whatever of fancy, romance, energy, passion, aspiration and determination belong to me, I never have separated and never shall separate from the hard-hearted little woman – you –

whom it is nothing to say I would have died for, with the greatest alacrity! . . .

. . . The sound of [your name] has always filled me with a kind of pity and respect for the deep truth that I had, in my silly hobbledehoyhood, to bestow upon one creature who represented the whole world to me. . . .

. . . perhaps you have once or twice laid down that book [i.e., *David Copperfield*], and thought, 'How dearly that boy must have loved me, and how vividly this man remembers it!'[53]

He ends by urging her to write to him again before he leaves Paris and meanwhile busies himself about her jewellery commission. We get some clue, I think, to his state of mind during these days in an episode in chapter 18 of Book II of *Little Dorrit*, a chapter written just two years afterwards. There he describes Mr Dorrit busy building his castle in the air, a principal foundation-stone of which is the marriage he is contemplating offering to Mrs General. He enters a jeweller's shop in Paris to buy her a present (and also to speak some of Dickens's extraordinary Franglais):

> For example, then, said the little woman [i.e., the shopkeeper], what species of gift did Monsieur desire? A love-gift?
> Mr Dorrit smiled, and said, Eh, well! Perhaps. What did he know? It was always possible; the sex being so charming. Would she show him some?

Having bought some superb jewels Mr Dorrit strolls back to his hotel with his head high, 'having plainly got up his castle, now, to a much loftier altitude than the two square towers of Notre Dame'.

Dickens is surely looking wryly back here to the airy castle-building he himself had indulged in as he eagerly anticipated the coming reunion with his old love. The decision he and Collins made to abandon a projected trip to Bordeaux and to return instead to London may have owed as much to his impatience to see Maria again as to the severe weather he mentions in his letters home. He took great care that the letter he was expecting from Maria should be forwarded quickly after him and duly received it the morning after his return home to Tavistock House. He replied at once, addressing her no longer as 'Mrs Winter' but as 'Maria'.

Evidently, she now told him that she had, in fact, loved him and that the obstacles to their love had not been of her making, also that she had thought much of him at important moments in her life since then. She seems to have proposed the establishment of some special confidential relationship with him, a sort of *amitié amoureuse*. She was back, in other words, at her flirtatious tricks – Georgina had thought her, ten years earlier, 'a kind good natured woman but *fearfully silly*!!'[54] – and Dickens reacted with as much vehemence as he had done in those far-off Lombard Street days:

> Ah! Though it is so late to read in the old hand what I never read before, I have read it with great emotion, and with the old tenderness softened to a more sorrowful remembrance than I could easily tell you . . . if you had ever told me then what you tell me now, I know myself well enough to be thoroughly assured that the simple truth and energy which were in my love would have overcome everything. . . .
>
> . . . nobody can ever know with what a sad heart I resigned you . . .
>
> All this . . . you have changed and set right – at once so courageously, so delicately and gently, that you open the way to a confidence between us which still once more, in perfect innocence and good faith, may be between ourselves alone. All that you propose, I accept with my whole heart. Whom can you ever trust if it be not your old lover?

Who knows what airy castles were building in Dickens's mind? That 'one friend and companion I have never made', was she at last about to enter his life in the shape of his old love? Was she to give him now a sweet companionship, as blameless as Mary Hogarth's had been during the first months of his marriage but with the added excitement of shared romantic memories? He scorned forty-five-year-old Maria's nervous archness about herself being now 'toothless, fat, old and ugly'. 'You are always the same in my remembrance,' he told her, and his feelings for her had never died or changed: 'You ask me to treasure what you tell me, in my heart of hearts. O see what I have cherished there, through all this time and all these changes!'[55]

He could not bear the thought of their reunion taking place in the presence of other people and so towards the end of his letter (written on a Thursday) he proposes that the following Sunday Maria should call at Tavistock House, 'asking first for Catherine and then for me? It is almost a positive certainty that there will be none here but I, between 3 and 4.' But if she does not like that idea then he will come and call on her. The letter ends, 'Remember, I accept all with my whole soul, and reciprocate all. – Ever your affectionate friend.'

Maria must have preferred to receive her old lover on her home ground in Finsbury, because, when Dickens writes to her again on the Saturday, he addresses her in such a totally different way that it is clear he must have seen her in the interim. This letter (which begins 'My dear Mrs Winter' and ends 'Very faithfully yours') has exactly the same jokey tone as his ordinary familiar letters to friends. He is amusing about the jeweller from whom he bought the brooches he is sending her and also about the hideous toys on sale in Paris; and he tells her that Catherine will come and arrange a Tavistock House dinner-date with her and Mr Winter, a dinner to which Maria must be sure to bring her niece, Margaret's daughter.

The change in tone and style from Thursday's letter, 'accepting and reciprocating all with his whole soul', is certainly startling and may well have disconcerted poor Maria. It seems to have taken her a little while to realize, however, that the special relationship she and Dickens had canvassed so eagerly before their reunion was, after all, a non-starter. She and her husband dined at Tavistock House, under the candid eyes of Georgina (who later recalled, 'By that time poor Dora had become *very* fat! and quite common place')[56] and Dickens sent her some tickets for a theatre with a vague half-promise to join her there. When he did not appear she wrote a somewhat reproachful letter and got back a lecture:

> A necessity is upon me now – as at most times – of wandering about in my own wild way, to think. . . . I hold my inventive capacity on the stern condition that it must master my whole life, often have complete possession of me, make its own demands upon me, and sometimes for months together put everything else away from me. . . . All this I can hardly expect you to understand – or the restlessness or waywardness of an author's mind. You have never seen it before you, or lived with it or had occasion to think or care about it. . . . I am grieved if you suspect me of not wanting to see you, but I can't help it; I must go my way, whether or no.

He ends by telling her that he is 'going off, I don't know where or how far, to ponder about I don't know what':

> Once upon a time I didn't do such things, you say. No, but I have done them through a good many years now, and they have become myself and my life.[57]

If poor Maria still did not get the message it was rather brutally spelled out for her in *Little Dorrit* a year later. In that book the depressed middle-aged bachelor hero, Arthur Clennam, returns to London after an absence abroad of nearly twenty-five years and re-encounters Flora whom he had adored in his youth but whom his stern mother had prevented him from marrying. Flora is now a buxom widow, the relict of someone she refers to as 'Mr F.' (Maria, it seems, was given to referring to her husband as 'dear Mr W.').[58] Dickens describes the former lovers' reunion as follows:

Clennam's eyes no sooner fell upon the subject of his old passion, than it shivered and broke to pieces.

Most men will be found sufficiently true to themselves to be true to an old idea. It is no proof of an inconstant mind, but exactly the opposite, when the idea will not bear close comparison with the reality, and the contrast is a fatal shock to it. Such was Clennam's case. In his youth he had ardently loved this woman, and had heaped upon her all the locked-up wealth of his affection and imagination. That wealth had been, in his desert home, like Robinson Crusoe's money; exchangeable with no one, lying idle in the dark to rust, until he poured it out for her. Ever since that memorable time . . . he had kept the old fancy of the Past unchanged, in its old sacred place. . . .

Flora, always tall, had grown to be very broad too, and short of breath; but that was not much. Flora, whom he had left a lily, had become a peony; but that was not much. Flora, who had seemed enchanting in all she said and thought, was diffuse and silly. That was much. Flora, who had been spoiled and artless long ago, was determined to be spoiled and artless now. That was a fatal blow.[59]

What is remarkable here is the way in which Dickens, instead of presenting Clennam's sudden disillusionment comically (and the idea of a man's expecting a girl he had loved to be still the same twenty-five years later is undoubtedly matter for comedy), casts over it an air of almost tragic nobility. What might be called romantic folly in Clennam is presented as a fine constancy of mind, as being true to himself. The comedy that develops in the scene following is directed wholly against the woman and the reader is meant to feel, even while he laughs at her extravagances, the pain of Clennam in witnessing such a grotesque travesty of that 'old fancy of the Past' which had been the chief nourisher of his imagination in his bleak youth:

'I am sure,' giggled Flora, tossing her head with a caricature of her girlish manner, such as a mummer might have presented at her own funeral, if she had lived and died in classical antiquity, 'I am ashamed to see Mr Clennam, I am a mere fright . . .'

When Clennam considerately tries to reassure her she responds with distressing archness:

'Oh Mr Clennam you insincerest of creatures,' said Flora, 'I perceive already you have not lost your old way of paying compliments, your old way when you used to pretend to be so sentimentally struck you know — at least I don't mean that, I — oh I don't know what I mean!' Here Flora tittered confusedly, and gave him one of her old glances.

Although Dickens calls Clennam's dismay 'ludicrous' and his distress 'ridiculous' he does not mock Clennam himself: on the contrary, the reader is clearly meant to admire the man's gentleness, tact and forbearance with Flora in the present as much as his romantic devotion of the past.[60]

In fact, of course, Clennam was not so vulnerable to mockery as Dickens himself had been in February 1855. Clennam had not written tender and passionate letters to Flora immediately prior to their reunion and his devastating disillusionment. But while it is possible, as I have suggested, that Dickens may be laughing at his own behaviour at that time in the episode of Mr Dorrit castle-building in Paris it is very unlikely that it ever struck him, as it might strike a modern reader, that the long letters of tender reminiscence mingled with reproach that he had written to Maria, are gloriously parodied in the headlong monologues Flora addresses to Clennam:

> . . . you must be very well aware that there was Paul and Virginia which had to be returned and which was returned without note or comment, not that I mean to say you could have written to me watched as I was but if it had only come back with a red wafer on the cover I should have known it meant Come to Pekin Nankeen and What's the third place barefoot.

Not having any of the letters Maria wrote to him at the time of their reunion, nor any records of what she actually said to him, we have to believe that Flora's outpourings are an exaggeration and wonderfully inventive fantastication of Maria's own speech. ('She was always romantic', recalled Georgina Hogarth, 'and used to talk a great deal about her early love.')[61] Within the novel itself, esoteric reminiscing about former times is carried to its ultimate absurdity by Flora's companion, Mr F.'s aunt. This grim old lady, left to Flora by Mr F. as a legacy, terrifies Clennam by such sudden and inscrutable allusions to the past as 'When we lived at Henley, Barnes's gander was stole by tinkers', or '. . . the Great Fire of London was not the fire in which your uncle George's workshops was burned down'. She also plays a part in the grotesque travesty of Flora and Clennam's long-ago love-affair that Flora insists on staging 'now, when the stage was dusty, when the scenery was faded, when the youthful actors were dead, when the orchestra was empty, when the lights were out'. Appropriately for such a travesty, Mr F.'s aunt take the role of a threatener of the lovers' hopes, showing an implacable hostility towards Clennam at every encounter.

It says much for the good humour of Flora's original that she seems not to have resented Dickens's caricature. He was always 'dear Charles Dickens' for her.[62] The unkindest aspect of the thing is the emphasis Dickens places on Flora's Gamp-like fondness for strong liquors (according to Thomas Wright, 'Further acquaintance with Mrs Winter increased [Dickens's] disillusionment. She drank brandy in her tea!').[63] Apart from this, however, it is a benignly comic portrait, quite different from the savage lampooning of Leigh Hunt as Mr Skimpole in *Bleak House*, and so Maria was perhaps more flattered than hurt. Dickens himself was delighted when his readers found Flora a particularly sympathetic character. To one eminent admirer, the Duke of Devonshire, he wrote:

> I am so glad you like Flora. It came into my head one day that we have all had our Floras (mine is living, and extremely fat), and that it was a half serious half ridiculous truth which had never been told. It is a wonderful gratification to find that everybody knows her. Indeed some people seem to think I have done them a personal injury, and that their individual Floras (God knows where they are, or who) are each and all Little Dorrits![64]

His gratitude to Maria for having inspired him to portray so satisfactorily this 'half serious half ridiculous truth' about life did not prevent him from keeping her in her place in his busy life, however. He wrote charmingly to her little daughter, Ella, and found a significance in the child's responsiveness to him ('No man ever really loved a woman,' he was later to declare, 'lost her, and knew her with a blameless though an unchanged mind, when she was a wife and a mother, but her children had a strange sympathy with him – an instinctive delicacy of pity for him').[65] But we find him warning Maria in June 1855 that he will be 'out of town that Sunday, and for several Sundays in succession' – she had evidently written suggesting that she might call. A few days later he heard that her baby, Ella's younger sister, had died and wrote a tenderly sympathetic letter of Christian consolation but was clearly apprehensive of the results of visiting her at such an emotional time ('It is better that I should not come to see you. I feel quite sure of that, and will think of you instead'). The next year, when he was working in Paris on *Little Dorrit*, he replied belatedly and very briefly to a 'little letter' Maria had written him: 'My own writing so absorbs my time and attention, and my business is so very large, that the letters I write for pleasure are miraculously few. That they are also laudably short, let this sheet of paper witness'.[66] Ironically, the writing that was so absorbing his time at that particular moment was the very instalment of the novel that introduces Flora to the reader.

It was Georgina not Dickens who wrote to Maria in May 1858 to break the news of the impending separation from Catherine and, later in the year, Dickens excused himself from meeting Maria in Liverpool (she was, apparently, going to be there just at the time he was due to give one of his public Readings in the town). Just at this time Henry Winter got into serious financial difficulties and Maria, unable to see Dickens, wrote to ask him if he could help her husband to a 'new opening in life'. He wrote back sympathetically, enclosing a friendly letter to Winter, but saying that he had no contacts in the commercial world and so was not in a position to assist. Surely, Dickens suggested, there was a more obvious and appropriate source of help than himself: 'I really think that your Father who could do so much in such a case, without drawing at all heavily upon his purse, might be induced to do what – I may say to you, Maria – it is no great stretch of sentiment to call his duty'.[67]

Winter became officially bankrupt a few months later (March 1859) and evidently decided that there was a world elsewhere than in commercial London. He was admitted as a Fellow Commoner at Queens' College, Cambridge, in February 1860 and began reading for Holy Orders. Maria and their daughter remained in London and we get a rather sad picture of her as a Flora untransfigured by Dickens's comic art in the reminiscences (published in the *Daily Chronicle*, 18 March 1912) of a nursemaid she employed at the time. This maid, who later married and became a Mrs Warren, claimed that she had become 'friendly and extremely intimate' with Mrs Winter and recalled that the allowance made to her by her husband was inadequate owing to her intemperate habits. 'Her father called once a month at Artillery Place, and left a bag of money' but, Mrs Warren asserted, she more than once kept this from Mrs Winter in that lady's own interest:

> She would be sweet and kindly in the early part of the day, but after, and often before luncheon, her addiction to nips of drinking would render her like another woman. All her refinement and restraint seemed then to break down, and it would be during these times, induced, I think, by the recollection of the past, that she would refer to Dickens. She had a tremendous collection of his books by that time. They were to be found all about the house. When excited she would take them from the shelves and run through their pages, commenting on their contents, interspersing them with references to the author. At other times she would lie on her couch, and say 'Nurse, it was here that he used to sit'; and I have seen her, in one of these moods, actually kiss the place on the couch, and recall something that Charles Dickens had said to her . . . while I was in her service I was satisfied that her heart was still upon the 'poor reporter' whom her father would not tolerate.

72

Well might Dickens cry, 'O, Angelica, what has become of you . . .?' when the sight of a pair of lovers one Sunday morning in 1863 in an old City of London church moves him to remember a happy incident of the Lombard Street days:

> . . . I mind when I, turned of eighteen, went with my Angelica to a City church on account of a shower (by this special coincidence that it was in Huggin-Lane), and when I said to my Angelica, 'Let the blessed event, Angelica, occur at no altar but this!' and when my Angelica consented that it should occur at no other – which it certainly never did, for it never occurred anywhere. And O, Angelica, what has become of you, this present Sunday morning when I can't attend to the sermon; and, more difficult question than that, what has become of Me as I was when I sat by your side?[68]

What had become of 'Angelica' was, as Dickens knew only too well, Mrs Henry Winter. But enough of the lost girl's appearance and demeanour survived, however altered, in the mature woman to move Dickens profoundly every time he set eyes on her. Seeking to convince a sceptical Forster of the extraordinary intensity of his youthful passion for Maria, and of how vivid the memory of it still was for him, Dickens wrote:

> And so I suffered, and so worked, and so beat and hammered away at the maddest romances that ever got into any boy's head and stayed there, that to see the mere cause of it all, now, loosens my hold upon myself. Without for a moment sincerely believing that it would have been better if we had never got separated, I cannot see the occasion of so much emotion as I should see any one else. No one can imagine in the most distant degree what pain the recollection gave me in *Copperfield*. And, just as I can never open that book as I open any other book, I cannot see the face (even at four-and-forty), or hear the voice, without going wandering away over the ashes of all that youth and hope in the wildest manner.[69]

It was surely inevitable that when, a few years later, Dickens turned for the second time to the form of a first-person, *Bildungsroman*-type novel, the main love-interest should be drawn, as it had been in *Copperfield*, from his own extraordinary, character-forming experience of passion ('I have stood positively amazed at myself ever since!' he said to Forster). Biographers have long associated Estella in *Great Expectations* exclusively with the great love of Dickens's last years, Ellen Ternan, and Pip's unhappy passion for her with Dickens's supposed miseries in loving Ellen. This is mere speculation, however, impure but simple, as I hope will be clearly seen in a later chapter. It is not, I believe, to Ellen that we owe the powerful vision of frustrated love that Dickens gives us in the most perfectly achieved of all his novels but to Maria, making her last and most haunting appearance on the Dickens stage. This time, however, she appears neither as a radiant vision of her younger self (Dora) nor as a comic version of her mature self (Flora) but as an ice-maiden, Estella, who is, as her name suggests, as cold and as beautiful and as desolatingly unattainable as a star.

For Estella Pip suffers all the love-torments that his creator so feelingly remembered from his own youth. They begin during Pip's childhood visits, as a hired 'entertainer', to Miss Havisham's weird mansion. There he 'falls into captivity', as David Copperfield had done before him, but Pip's captivity is emphatically not of the 'blissful' kind. The beautiful, self-possessed little girl whom he adores behaves towards him like a cruel princess in a witch's castle: adept at humiliating him, she knows how to lacerate his feelings in their most sensitive part; and she does it with a cold, contemptuous carelessness which is worst of all. She harps on his being 'a common labouring-boy', reduces him to tears of bitterness and then mocks him for crying.

As he grows up Pip cannot stop loving her and hopelessly longs to become a gentleman so that he might dream of one day marrying her, though knowing that she could only bring him unhappiness. Then, as if by magic, he suddenly finds himself made into a gentleman and thrown much into Estella's society. She is as tormenting as ever but Pip goes on loving her 'against promise, against peace, against hope, against happiness, against all discouragement that could be'. Just as the young Dickens, besotted by Maria, had 'hammered away at the maddest romances that ever got into any boy's head and stayed there', so Pip believes that Miss Havisham plans to marry him to Estella at last: 'She reserved it for me to . . . do all the shining deeds of the young Knight of romance, and marry the Princess'. But whenever he finds himself actually with Estella, even when she seems to be treating him with intimacy, he is wretched: 'Whatever her tone with me happened to be, I could put no trust in it, and build no hope on it; and yet I went on against trust and against hope'.[70] Always, too, he is in terror lest she might somehow discover the disgraceful secret of his childhood, his involuntary connection with jail-birds and prison-ships; just so must the young Dickens have been constantly apprehensive that Maria might somehow chance on knowledge of his father's having once been in prison.

When Estella comes to London to stay with friends of Miss Havisham and make her entrée into society Pip's agonies become extreme:

I suffered every kind and degree of torture that Estella could cause me.
. . . She made use of me to tease other admirers, and she turned the very
familiarity between herself and me, to the account of putting a constant
slight on my devotion to her. If I had been her secretary, steward,
half-brother, poor relation . . . I could not have seemed to myself further
from my hopes when I was nearest to her. The privilege of calling her by
her name and hearing her call me by mine, became under the circumstances an aggravation of my trials; and while I think it likely that it
almost maddened her other lovers, I knew too certainly that it almost
maddened me.[71]

Who, except those bemused by their own imaginings about Dickens's
relations with Ellen Ternan, can doubt what unforgettable experience he
was drawing on to evoke so powerfully the bleakness of Pip's hopeless,
tormenting love? It is instructive in this respect to juxtapose with the
passage just quoted the following words from his bitter letter to Maria of
March 1833, in which he speaks of his feelings of 'utter desolation and
wretchedness':

Thank God! I can claim for myself and feel that I deserve the merit of
having ever throughout our intercourse acted fairly, intelligibly and
honorably. Under kindness and encouragement one day and a total
change of conduct the next I have ever been the same. I have ever acted
without reserve. I have never held out encouragement which I knew I
never meant; I have never indirectly sanctioned hopes which I well knew I
did not intend to fulfil. I have never made a mock confidante to whom to
entrust a garbled story for my own purposes, and I think I never should
. . . encourage one dangler as a useful shield for — an excellent set off
against — others more fortunate and doubtless more deserving. I have
done nothing that I could say would be very likely to hurt you.[72]

Some words from Dickens's brief preface to *A Tale of Two Cities*
might be applied to the story of Pip and Estella with a much more literal
truth than they are intended to bear in their place: 'I have so far verified
what is done and suffered in these pages, as that I have certainly done and
suffered it all myself'.

*

We have seen how the invention of Steerforth enabled Dickens to create a
pièce rose version of his experience of loving Maria: now, in *Great
Expectations*, the invention of Miss Havisham and her crazy vengeful-
ness against men enables him to create his *pièce noire*. All Pip's dreaming
love, all his passion and romance, is thrown away upon a beautiful
monster, an utterly heartless woman trained from her babyhood to

entrap and torture men. Maria becomes at last fully mythologized and thereafter appears no more in Dickens's fiction.[73] In his life, however, she continued to haunt him as a comic Flora-figure. In Newcastle in 1866 to give a reading, Dickens wrote to Georgina, 'No news yet of the Winter family. I live in a tremble' (Henry Winter's parish at Alnmouth was very close to Newcastle), and, a few days later, he reported from Leeds, 'Thank heaven, there have been no signs, either of Mrs Winter or "dear Mr W." '.[74]

'Mr W.' died the year after Dickens but Maria lived on for another sixteen years, keeping in touch with Georgina Hogarth and treasuring always her memories of those days when she had been so beloved by the great novelist. One wonders whether her romantic heart would have been pleased or otherwise could she have foreseen that Dickens's last love, Ellen, would come one day to lie in the same Southsea cemetery where Maria herself lay, in an unmarked grave.[75]

5
Mary

'The heart of this fair girl bounded with joy and gladness. Devoted attachment to her sisters, and a fervent love of all beautiful things in nature, were its pure affections. Her gleesome voice and merry laugh were the sweetest music of their home. She was its very light and life . . .'
Nicholas Nickleby, ch. 6

In March 1836 Dickens wrote to his maternal uncle, Thomas Barrow, announcing his imminent marriage. He told Barrow that he was about to wed 'Miss Hogarth — the daughter of a gentleman who has recently distinguished himself by a celebrated work on Music, who was the most intimate friend and companion of Sir Walter Scott, and one of the most eminent among the Literati of Edinburgh'.[1] The Hogarths were, indeed, as well endowed culturally as the Beadnells had been financially and the exultation with which Dickens describes his future father-in-law is understandable. He who felt that he had been so cruelly stinted of education, so hampered in his early social ambitions, was now the accepted son-in-law of a friend of Scott's, a man who had been a leading light of the cultural scene in 'the Athens of the North'.

George Hogarth had, in fact, left the Scottish capital four years before Dickens first met him. He had abandoned his legal career there as insufficiently remunerative to support his large family, and had turned instead to full-time journalism.[2] After brief spells of provincial-weekly editing in Devon and Yorkshire he had joined the London *Morning Chronicle* as music and drama editor in August 1834, the same month that the young Dickens was taken on to the paper's reporting staff. Hogarth's 'guileless simplicity of character and never-failing geniality of temper',[3] together with his admiration for his young colleague's 'various and extraordinary intellectual gifts' (to quote a phrase from his glowing review of Dickens's first book),[4] no doubt encouraged the rapid development of a friendship between the two men. This was further consolidated after Hogarth had been appointed the first editor of the *Evening Chronicle* at the end of 1834. He encouraged Dickens to write a series of sketches of London life for the paper (later collected, with others, as *Sketches by Boz*) and the young man became a welcome visitor at the Hogarth family's Brompton home. Here he met the three daughters, Catherine, Mary and Georgina, who, with one other, were destined to be the most important women of his adult life. Catherine was nineteen, Mary fourteen and Georgina only seven. Dickens himself was still smarting from the collapse of his hopes of winning Maria Beadnell but his career, both as a journalist and as a writer, was beginning to prosper. His easy reception into the Hogarth household, connected as it was with the cultural establishment, showed that he was beginning to make his mark. The gentle, voluptuously attractive Catherine with her evident favourable disposition towards himself ('Mr Dickens improves very much on acquaintance he is very gentlemanly and pleasant', she wrote to a cousin after attending Dickens's twenty-third birthday party)[5] must have made a refreshing and soothing contrast to the vivacious, tormenting Maria, and the kind of background that she offered – artistic and literary-professional – must have been more congenial to Dickens than the hard, purse-proud City background of Maria. It was not long before he was in love with Catherine, though not, to be sure, as he had been with Maria – '*les amours qui suivent sont moins involontaires*' – and very soon they were officially engaged, some time during the earlier part of 1835.

Dickens's relations with Catherine will be the subject of the next two chapters. Here, I want to focus on a relationship which, it seems, soon became for him more intense than anything he felt for Catherine. His young sister-in-law, Mary Scott Hogarth, had been Catherine's constant companion and chaperone during the courtship period ('tell [Mary] I rely on her characteristic kind-heartedness and good nature to accompany you',[6] Dickens wrote to his fiancée on one occasion when inviting her to breakfast with him in his bachelor chambers), and was presumably a bridesmaid at the quiet family wedding in April 1836. She did not, as one Dickens biographer has written, 'tag ecstatically along' on the modest week's honeymoon in a little Kentish village,[7] although it was quite normal at this period for bridesmaids to accompany honeymooning couples – Fanny Squeers, we recall, travelled to London with the newly married Browdies in *Nicholas Nickleby*. Mary's month-long visit to Charles and Catherine on their return to start housekeeping in a three-roomed flat in Furnival's Inn may well have been a substitute for the honeymoon jaunt she might reasonably have been hoping for. She thoroughly enjoyed herself, as she reported in a long gossipy letter[8] to her cousin and best friend, another Mary Scott Hogarth:

I have just returned home from spending a most delightfully happy month with dearest Catherine in her own house! I only wish you could see her in it . . . she makes a capital housekeeper and is as happy as the day is long – I think they are more devoted than ever since their Marriage if that be possible – I am sure you would be delighted with him if you knew him he is such a nice creature and so clever he is courted and made up to by all the literary Gentlemen, and has more to do in that way than he can well manage . . .

Clearly she is impressed – as well she might be – by her handsome, brilliant young brother-in-law but she seems hardly to have been in the trance of rapturous adoration which Dickens's biographers have fixed her in (though, one suspects, Dickens's own memory did this long before his biographers did). After a brief description of Furnival's Inn and the Dickens's apartments ('. . . they have furnished them most tastefully and elegantly, the drawing-room with Rose-wood the dining room with Mahagony [*sic*] furniture – I hope you are fully satisfied with *this* discription!'), Mary goes on to gossip with equal zest about other friends, relatives and acquaintances. It is gossip noticeably lacking in spite or malice though not devoid of mischievous mockery: 'Mrs Lawrance and her sisters are just as pedantic and Eliza Rose as wonderful (in their eyes at least) as before'. A delightfully good-hearted *joie de vivre* breathes through the whole letter, as well as a genuine warmth of affection for the person to whom it is addressed.[9]

Mary appears to have been a frequent visitor at Furnival's Inn, though not the permanent inmate of the Dickens household that many biographers have supposed, and was certainly there in the New Year of 1837 when Catherine was confined with her first child. On 6 January 1838, eight months after Mary's devastating sudden death, Dickens mournfully recorded in his diary:

This day last year, Mary and I wandered up and down Holborn and the streets about, for hours, looking after a little table for Kate's bedroom which we bought at last at the very first Broker's we had looked into, and which we had passed half a dozen times because I *didn't like* to ask the price. . . . She came back again next day to keep house for me, and stopped nearly the rest of the month.[10]

Mary's loving concern for her sister emerges very strongly in the letter she wrote, again to her cousin, just after returning home from this visit:

. . . I know your kind heart will be anxious to hear of my dearest Kate, who I am sorry indeed to say has not gone on so well as her first week made us hope she would. After we thought she was getting quite well and strong it was discovered she was not able to nurse her Baby so she was obliged with great reluctance as you may suppose to give him up to a stranger. Poor Kate! it has been a dreadful trial for her . . . it is really dreadful to see her suffer. I am quite sure I never suffered so much sorrow for any one or any thing before . . . Every time she sees her Baby she has a fit of crying and keeps constantly saying she is sure he will not care for her now she is not able to nurse him.[11]

She goes on to praise Dickens's kindness to his wife ('constantly studying her comfort in every thing') and to tell Mary that

his literary career gets more and more prosperous every day and he is courted and flattered on every side by all the great folks of this great City – his time is so completely taken up that it is quite a favour for the Literary Gentlemen to get him to write for them. He is going to begin a Novel very soon.

Here again, the way Mary reports this – amusedly rather than in tones of hushed reverence or dazzled admiration – seems to indicate that her attitude towards Dickens and his rocketing reputation was far less intense and more normal than has generally been supposed.

Part of the legend that has grown up around Mary is that she was really, both physically and mentally, an unremarkable girl, who was posthumously transformed into a shining Ideal of Maidenhood by Dickens's fervent imagination. But the letters I have been quoting (the second of which did not come to light until 1967) are surely those of quite an exceptional sixteen- or seventeen-year-old, with a lively and affectionate disposition, a keen and sympathetic interest in people and a delightful appetite for social experience. She packs an astonishing amount of information and comment into the letters, which remind one of Mrs Gaskell's – they have the same rather breathless style, the same warmth of personality, the same directness and feeling of being actually spoken to by a living voice. Evidently impatient of pen and paper as a medium of communication, Mary breaks out towards the end of her second letter with:

And now my own dear Mary I must bring this very personal letter to a close, but not without telling you dear Mary how much I love you and how often I think of you and wish I had you here to *speak* to, I have never met and shall never meet I am sure any body so completely to my mind as your own dear self – Now Mary you must not think these words of course; I say them from my heart I assure you – .

Mary's affectionate words here should not, I think, be dismissed as mere schoolgirl gush to a 'best friend', especially as the rest of the letter has not been like this but has all been news about other people, rejoicing in the good reports her brother George has been getting from 'his Master', in the prettiness of her baby sister, and so on. She ends by joking about the illegibility of her letter: 'George has just looked over my shoulder and remarks he pities whoever this Epistle is to and as I cannot help agreeing I think I had better stop at once'.[12]

Besides what he called 'abilities far beyond her years' Dickens also credited Mary with 'every attraction of youth and beauty'. 'Conscious as she must have been of everybody's admiration,' he wrote, 'she had not a single fault, and was in life almost as far above the foibles and vanity of her sex and age as she is now in Heaven.'[13] Unfortunately, the only image we have of her today is an engraving of a painting done for Dickens after her death by his illustrator H.K. Browne ('Phiz'). This shows an insipid young creature with rather a bulging forehead, rather a large nose, a little rosebud mouth and a rounded receding chin – in other words, a standardized beauty of the day. Apparently, there did exist another portrait of her, done from life, a copy of which was sent to Dickens by her mother on the sixth anniversary of her death. 'It has no interest in my eyes', Dickens wrote to Mrs Hogarth, 'beyond being something which she sat near in its progress, full of life and beauty . . . As any record of that dear face, it is utterly worthless.'[14] Nonetheless, he kept it, or perhaps the Phiz painting, 'in the place of honour in his study', according to Mrs Christian.[15] That he was not, in fact, exaggerating Mary's charms is confirmed by independent witnesses. John Strang, a Glaswegian worthy who saw her on a visit to London in 1836, later wrote to his friend Macrone, one of Dickens's publishers:

How does [Boz's] pretty little sister-in-law get on. She is a sweet interesting creature. I wonder some *two-legged* monster does not carry her off. It might save many a younker losing his night's rest![16]

Another publisher, Richard Bentley, remembered how Mary's charm persuaded him to stay a little longer at one of Dickens's parties: 'Towards midnight . . . I rose to leave, but D. stopped [me] & pressed me to take another glass of Brandy & water. This I wd. gladly have avoided, but he begged Miss Hogarth to give it me. At the hand of the fair Hebe I did not decline it.'[17] For Robert Story, a Northumbrian poet who visited the Hogarths in 1836, Mary stayed in his mind as 'a beautiful and light-hearted girl', a 'fine young woman', and the shocking news of her sudden death moved him to write the following elegy for her:

I saw her in the violet time,
　　When bees are on the wing,
And then she stood in maiden prime –
　　The fairest flower of spring!
Her glances, as the falcon's bright,
　　Had archness in their play;
Her motion and her heart were light
　　As linnet's on the spray!
'Tis come again, the violet time,
　　When flits the mountain bee;
And others stand in maiden prime,
　　But where – O! where is *She*?
Alas! the linnet now may sing
　　Beside her early tomb!
Alas! the fairest flower of spring
　　Hath perished in its bloom! . . .[18]

Mary died at Dickens's new home in Doughty Street on 7 May 1837. On the 6th she had accompanied him and Catherine to the theatre (where the programme had included a farce written by Dickens); after the party had returned home, wrote Dickens to a friend,

> she went up stairs to bed at about one o'Clock in perfect health and her usual delightful spirits; was taken ill before she had undressed; and died in my arms next afternoon at 3 o'Clock. Everything that could possibly be done *was* done but nothing could save her. The medical men imagine it was a disease of the heart.[19]

Dickens was shattered. The agonizing pain in his side that had sometimes incapacitated him during the blacking-factory months returned;[20] he was quite unable to continue with the writing of *Pickwick* and *Oliver Twist*; and in letter after letter he strove to express the catastrophe that it was for him to lose this 'dear girl whom I loved, after my wife, more deeply and fervently than anyone on earth'. The 'grace and life' of his home had gone, the angel on his hearth had been brutally snatched away. 'I solemnly believe', he wrote to his intimate friend Thomas Beard, 'that so perfect a creature never breathed. I knew her inmost heart, and her real worth and value. She had not a fault.' Apart from the one instance I have just quoted he did not except his wife when declaring that he had lost 'the dearest friend I ever had'. Indeed, in his diary seven months later he recalled Mary as 'sympathizing with all my thoughts and feelings more than any one I knew ever did or will'; and the public announcement explaining the non-appearance of the June instalments of his two novels informed his readers that he had lost 'a very dear young relative to whom he was most affectionately attached, and whose society has been, for a long time, the chief solace of his labours' (no concessions to wedded bliss there!). 'That pleasant smile and those sweet words which [were] bestowed upon an evening's work in our merry banterings round the fire were more precious to me', he later wrote to Mary's mother, 'than the applause of a whole world would be.' In his diary he stated, 'I shall never be so happy again as in those Chambers three Stories high [in Furnival's Inn] – never if I roll in wealth and fame. I would hire them, to keep empty, if I could afford it.'[21]

When he began indeed to roll in wealth and fame, a very few years later, he found, I believe, a better way of immortalizing the Eden of his adult years than by the museum-fantasy he had confided to his diary. He appears to be recreating it in his enduring fictional world, first in *Martin Chuzzlewit* (1844), where it is (to the pure at least) purely a brother/sister idyll. Ruth Pinch, that 'blooming little busy creature', keeps gleeful house for her child-like brother, Tom, in a 'triangular parlour and two small bedrooms' in Islington:

> As she sat opposite to Tom at supper, fingering one of Tom's pet tunes upon the table-cloth, and smiling in his face, he had never been so happy in his life.[22]

Then, at the end of *David Copperfield* (1850) Dickens seems to come closer to the actual facts. David's friend, Tommy Traddles, and his newly wedded bride live in three rooms on the top storey of a building in Gray's Inn and here receive joyous visits from the bride's sisters. It requires, we notice, no less than *five* visiting sisters-in-law to represent Mary here – I am not suggesting, of course, that Dickens is attempting actually to portray Mary herself in any or all of them, any more than he means Traddles to be his younger self; but that it is an emotional *situation* that he is recreating, and the galaxy of sisters-in-law, 'a perfect nest of roses', who play romping children's games with Traddles are simply his attempt to find in art what T.S. Eliot calls an 'objective correlative' for the intensity of delight and joy that Mary's presence had given him in Furnival's Inn. This was so important a part of his emotional history that it surely demanded a place in this, the most personal of his novels to date.

Dickens's loftier feelings about Mary – what we might call his spiritual experiences of her – may be enshrined in the central figure of Agnes, but somewhere in *Copperfield*, I believe, he had to record, too, the human delightfulness and charm of his innocent lost love. Agnes, clearly, could not be allowed to play at Puss in the Corner with David at any point in the book – it is not easy to play *any* game, after all, when you are obliged to keep 'pointing upward'. But the Crewler girls, Traddles's sisters-in-law, meant nothing to Dickens and so could happily be used to set up the emotional situation he wants to evoke. The reader, who cannot be expected to meet the author more than half-way since he does not share Dickens's particular memories (to each his own Eden) is yet made to feel surprised by the joy through art with which the scene is evoked. Even if he holds out against Dickens throughout the actual description of the Traddles ménage he will surely be seduced by the 'clinching' paragraph which invests the whole episode with glamour in a very Dickensian way:

> If I had beheld a thousand roses blowing in a top set of chambers, in that withered Gray's Inn, they could not have brightened it half so much. The idea of those Devonshire girls, among the dry law-stationers and the attorneys' offices; and of the tea and toast, and children's songs, in that grim atmosphere of pounce and parchment . . . seemed almost as pleasantly fanciful as if I had dreamed that the Sultan's famous family had been admitted on the roll of attorneys, and had brought the talking bird, the singing tree, and the golden water into Gray's Inn Hall.[23]

We respond with delight to the powerful sensuous contrast Dickens achieves here between the blooming young country lasses, who have the fresh beauty and fragrance of a whole field of roses, and their incongruous setting, the musty old chambers of Gray's Inn. Their innocent feast and child-like pleasures contrast dramatically with the Inn's grim legal atmosphere with all its connotations of sophisticated coldness, formality and remorseless logic. The *Arabian Nights* allusion, so characteristic of Dickens when he is seeking to evoke a sense of wonder and romance, suggests that there has been a kind of benign infiltration and subversion of the heartless world of Dodson and Fogg by the powers of human imagination and feeling.

Time had to pass before Dickens was able to convert his piercing nostalgia for Mary's presence into such writing as this – if, indeed, my theory is correct, that Mary's ghost is hovering over and inspiring this passage. The first literary effort demanded by her death was very different, the bleak necessity of composing an epitaph for her tombstone in Kensal Green Cemetery: 'Young, beautiful and Good. God in His mercy numbered her with His angels at the early age of seventeen'. He also composed a three-stanza elegy which he published anonymously (August 1837) in the 'Songs of the Month' series he was featuring in his journal, *Bentley's Miscellany*:

> I stood by a young girl's grave last night,
> Beautiful, innocent, pure, and bright,
> Who, in the bloom of her summer's pride
> And all its loveliness, drooped and died.[24]

He set his heart on eventually sharing her grave and went through fresh agonies four years later when her brother George was buried there instead – 'I cannot bear the thought of being excluded from her dust. . . . It seems like losing her a second time.'[25] He clung pathetically to everything that had been hers – keeping her dresses, for example, and watching them moulder away 'in their secret places',[26] wearing the ring he took from her finger after she died and a locket he had himself given her. It is not surprising that rumours flew around which heightened the already sufficiently dramatic circumstances of Mary's death and assumed, not unreasonably, that she must have been Dickens's sister, not merely his sister-in-law. Mary Howitt, not yet personally acquainted with the novelist, wrote to a friend on 3 March 1839:

> You heard, perhaps, of the sudden death of Dickens's favourite sister – a very lovely and every way amiable and charming girl – it was awfully melancholy. Mr Dickens gave her and a young friend of hers a note in these words, 'Admit two Angels to Paradise' – meaning to the Theatre – the note was addressed to the Manager, I suppose. The two young ladies had scarcely entered the box and taken their seats when Miss Dickens died suddenly. The shock was terrible, as you may believe. Poor Charles Dickens was taken ill from his extreme distress. It was while he was in the midst of the Pickwick Papers, and as you may remember, the publication of one number was suspended in consequence. Those who know him say he has not yet thoroughly recovered his former spirits.[27]

Certainly Dickens himself grieved for Mary as for a sister: on the mourning-locket he had made for himself to enclose a lock of her hair were inscribed the words, 'In memory of my dear Sister M.S.H. May 7th 1837 C.D.';[28] and to an American correspondent in 1842 he wrote that, although Mary had not actually been his sister, 'God knows that no tie of blood could have bound her closer to me, or endeared her to me more . . . my constant affectionate, and chosen companion'.[29]

His chief consolation was a fervent belief that her 'constant affection' had not ceased with death. He found a passage in Scott's diary written after the death of Scott's wife which seemed wonderfully to express his own feelings:

> She is sentient and conscious of my emotions *somewhere*; where we cannot tell – how we cannot tell; yet would I not at this moment renounce the mysterious yet certain hope that I shall see her in a better world, for all that this world can give me.

Mary appeared to him in dreams and he distinctly sensed her presence at times of exaltation in his waking life – for example, during his rapturous reception in America in 1842:

> I feel, in the best aspects of this welcome, something of the presence and influence of that spirit which directs my life, and through a heavy sorrow has pointed upward with unchanging finger for more than four years past.

Standing by the majesty of Niagara Falls he feels himself to be in a sacred place, close to God. It is natural for him then to suppose that it was a favourite haunt of Mary's, that she had been there 'many times, I doubt not, since her sweet face faded from my earthly sight'.[30]

For months after her death he dreamed of her every night, 'sometimes as a spirit, sometimes as a living creature, never with any of the bitterness of my real sorrow, but always with a kind of quiet happiness'.[31] As soon as he told his wife about these dreams they stopped abruptly, however, and he did not dream of her again until one night in Genoa in 1844 when she appeared to him not in her own person but like a Raphael Madonna:

> . . . I knew it was poor Mary's spirit. I was not at all afraid, but in a great delight, so that I wept very much, and stretching out my arms to it called it 'Dear'. At this, I thought it recoiled; and I felt immediately, that not being of my gross nature, I ought not to have addressed it so familiarly.

He entreated this vision to tell him which was 'the True religion'. Was it Roman Catholicism? ' "For *you*," said the Spirit, full of such heavenly tenderness for me, that I felt as if my heart would break; "for *you*, it is the best!" '[32] (This, considering Dickens's virulent anti-Catholicism, so marked in his *Pictures from Italy*, published a couple of years later, is sufficiently astonishing and offers a rich enough subject for the psychoanalysts.)[33]

These dreams evidently formed, like the days in Furnival's Inn, one of Dickens's sweetest memories (he shared the Genoa dream with his public in his Christmas Story for 1855, 'The Holly Tree' where he refers to Mary as 'a very near and dear friend', a 'dear lost one') and perhaps explain his excited reaction many years later to a very stilted narrative poem by Bulwer Lytton. Bulwer's poem, 'The Secret Way', was the first in a volume called *The Lost Tales of Miletus* (1866): it described the heroic readiness of a young daughter, Argiope, to sacrifice herself for the sake of her father, a subject which would certainly have touched Dickens to the heart. But this alone, even given his inexplicably high general estimate of Bulwer's work, does not, I think, account for the intensity of his reaction.

'The extraordinary beauty, picturesqueness and completeness' of the poem so fascinated him, he wrote to Bulwer, that he read it again and again:

> Argiope holds her place in my heart against all her rivals ... she is peerless against all the world of women. But the narrative itself, the painting in it, the distinctness attained, the glowing force of it, the imagination in it ... these *astonish* me! I declare to you that I have never read any story, whatsoever the manner of its telling, so perfectly amazing to me in these respects quite apart from its winning tenderness and grace.[34]

This is something more than routine praise or even a determination to gratify a beloved and honoured friend. Bulwer's poem has evidently touched something deep in Dickens's personal life and that something was, it seems clear, his undying love for the young girl who had died in his arms nearly thirty years before.

In the poem Argiope, 'Sweet with unconscious charm,/And modest as the youngest of the Graces', begins suddenly to droop and pine and King Omartes, her father, is told by his wise counsellor that he must find her a husband, for woman is like a climbing plant, the woodbine that 'From its own birthplace drinking in delight' yet needs the support of something to climb and grow:

> Its lot obeys its yearning to entwine;
> Around the oak it weaves a world of flowers;
>   Or, listless drooping, trails
>   Dejected tendrils lost mid weed and briar.

The king is initially dismayed:

> Sharp is a father's pang when comes the hour
> In which his love contents his child no more,
>   And the sweet wonted smile
>   Fades from his hearthstone to rejoice a stranger's.

But, Bulwer happily asserts, 'soon from parent love dies thought of self'.

It seems to me that Dickens reading this poem would inevitably have filled out Bulwer's hollow description of his ideally lovely young heroine with Mary's unforgotten figure and would, moreover, have been prompted to identify strongly with the father Omartes. Mary was for him a daughter as well as a sister figure, someone in whom he said he had 'the fondest father's pride'[35] and he must often have speculated on what his feelings would have been if she had survived only to leave him for a husband. Having had his private 'Mariolatry' thus activated by the poem,

Dickens must have been shaken indeed to come upon verses that seemed to describe his long-ago dream-experiences of Mary. The young hero of the poem, Prince Zariades, dreams of Argiope before he knows who she is:

> Know that each night (thro' three revolving moons)
> An image comes before me in a dream;
>> Ever the same sweet face,
>>> Lovely as that which blest the Carian's slumber.
>
> . . .
>
> But never yet so clearly visible,
> Nor with such joy in its celestial smile
>> Hath come the visitant,
>>> Making a temple of the soul it hallows,
>
> As in the last night's vision; there it stooped
> Over my brow, with tresses that I touched,
>> With love in bashful eyes,
>>> With breath whose fragrance lingered yet in waking.

At this point Dickens would surely be powerfully identifying with the young dreamer as he had earlier identified with Argiope's father. The distinct erotic overtones of Zariades' dream no doubt disturbed him (though they are no stronger than in his own depiction of the brother/sister housekeeping of the Pinches that I have also associated with his feelings about Mary), inviting his imagination to play once more what Professor Guerard has called his 'fondest forbidden game', that of marrying a virginal young sister.[36] As to the overall effect of the poem on him, when we register just what Mary and his memories and dreams of her meant to him we can hardly be surprised at the extravagant terms in which he praises Bulwer.

But it was not only in dreams that Mary continued to live for Dickens. In February 1844 he had a considerable shock when he met a beautiful eighteen-year-old girl, Christiana Weller, who, it would appear, seemed to him to be Mary come alive again. Dickens was presiding at a soirée of the Liverpool Mechanics' Institution and had to introduce Miss Weller who was to play 'a fantasia upon the piano'. The audience, thinking of the immortal Wellers in *Pickwick*, roared with laughter and Dickens had to help the girl over her momentary embarrassment. Next day he visited her father and composed some comic flirtatious lines for her album:

> I love her dear name which has won me some fame
> But, Great Heaven how gladly I'd change it!

But his real feelings lay much deeper than this sort of facetious gallantry, however. To his friend, T.J. Thompson, who had also met Christiana he wrote:

> I cannot joke about Miss Weller; she is too good; and interest in her (spiritual young creature that she is, and destined to an early death, I fear) has become a sentiment with me. Good God what a madman I should seem, if the incredible feeling I have conceived for that girl could be made plain to anyone![37]

The strangely gloomy touch about the girl's being 'destined to an early death' (in the event she outlived Dickens) gives us a strong clue, I think, that he is associating Christiana with Mary. Nor was he the only person to make the connection; when Christiana became acquainted with Mary's family a year later she was in 'ecstasies' after being told by Mrs Hogarth that the family thought she resembled Mary – 'a charming compliment', wrote Christiana in her diary, 'for she must have been an angel'.[38]

Back in London Dickens fired off to Christiana's father a letter accompanying two volumes of Tennyson's poetry specially marked up for the girl's perusal. He impressed upon Mr Weller who, proud parent though he was, must have been a little taken aback, the warmth and depth of his interest in the girl: '. . . I read such high and such unusual matter in every look and gesture of the spiritual creature who is naturally the delight of your heart and very dear to you, that she started out alone from the whole crowd the instant I saw her. . .'. A few days later he received a letter from Thompson who had remained in Liverpool announcing that he had fallen carnally in love with the 'spiritual young creature'. The effect on Dickens was dramatic. 'I swear to you,' he wrote to his friend, 'that . . . I felt the blood go from my face to I don't know where, and my very lips turn white. I never in my life was so surprised, or had the whole current of my life so stopped, for the instant, as when I felt, at a glance, what your letter said.'[39] Just so, we may imagine, would he have reacted to a declaration by a lover of Mary's had she lived to be courted in marriage.

Thompson was, significantly enough, just thirty-two, the same age as Dickens himself. The shock that for the moment 'stopped the whole current' of Dickens's life was surely a sudden vision of Christiana, that angelic reincarnation of Mary, not simply as a matrimonial object but as such for a man of his own age. Small wonder that he threw himself so ardently into promoting the marriage: here his Mary-haunted imagination had real people to play with, not just fictional characters.

Thompson was, in fact, almost as unencumbered a character as any novelist could have created; he was a widower (with two small children) and very comfortably off, having been left a fortune by his grandfather on the agreeable condition that he should never adopt any profession. There being thus no external obstacles, on Thompson's side, anyway, to his courtship of Christiana, Dickens masterfully set himself to sweep away any vague scruples that might trouble his friend: 'I would answer it to myself', he told Thompson, 'if my world's breath whispered me that I had known her but a few days, that hours of hers are years in the lives of common women'.

Moreover, marriage with Thompson and escape from Liverpool to Italy, where Dickens himself was about to go, was, Dickens insisted, the only hope of saving Christiana from that early death his imagination had marked her for:

> I saw an angel's message in her face that day that smote me to the heart
> ... Repose, change, a mind at rest, a foreign climate would be, in a
> springtime like hers, the dawning of a new existence. I believe, I do
> believe and hope, that this would save her. . . .[40]

Once in Italy, 'all of us together, in some delicious nook', Dickens and his family and Thompson and Christiana could settle down to enjoy 'quiet happiness' together. Dickens seems here to be excitedly envisaging a re-creation of that idyllic time in those 'chambers three stories high' in Furnival's Inn with Christiana in the role of Mary. He continued to stiffen Thompson's resolve, Christiana's father's consent was won, and Dickens sent his ecstatic congratulations – 'I swear, my dear Thompson, that I am as well pleased as yourself'. He writes not like a well-wishing friend but as though he and Thompson were some kind of Siamese-twin lovers:

> Good Heaven what a Dream it appears! Shall we ever forget that night
> when she came up to THE Piano – that morning when Dick, the energetic
> Dick, devised the visit! Shall we ever cease to have a huge and infinite
> delight in talking about the whole Romance from end to end – in
> dwelling upon it, exaggerating it; recalling it in every possible way, form,
> shape, and kaleidoscopic variety![41]

We notice the words 'Dream' and 'Romance': it is for Dickens as though real life were now imitating his fantasies. When a sudden hitch occurred – hesitation on Christiana's part on account of a prior attachment ('other footprints in the field') – Dickens again rushed to Thompson's rescue and wrote the girl a wonderful letter, both passionate and funny, pleading his friend's cause. It is also a declaration of his own impossible love for her:

I had that amount of sympathy with his condition, which, but that I am beyond the reach – the lawful reach – of the Wings that fanned *his* fire, would have rendered it the greatest happiness and pleasure of my life to have run him through the body. In no poetical or tender sense, I assure you, but with good sharp Steel. . . .

. . . Whatever happens in this case, of this I am quite sure – that it will all happen Wrong, and cannot happen otherwise but Wrong; the undersigned being excluded from all chance of competition, and only throwing up his cap for other men, instead of cutting it up into Favors for himself.[42]

But the game his imagination was playing could not go on for ever. Christiana soon stepped out of her passive Mary-role. She came to London with her family and set about trying to get herself launched as a concert pianist. Dickens's aid was enlisted; he got his father-in-law and other cognoscenti to hear her play, he wrote to theatre managers on her behalf and no doubt used his press contacts to get maximum publicity for her concerts. Meanwhile, to his perturbation, his unsteady young brother, Fred, was falling in love with Christiana's fifteen-year-old sister, Anna. Amidst all these complications it would hardly have been possible to preserve that initial intense excitement caused by Christiana's resemblance, real or fancied, to Mary and we should not, I think, read too much into Dickens's determination to 'eclipse the bridegroom' at the Thompson/Weller wedding in October 1845 by appearing in a particularly dazzling waistcoat. Only a few days before he had written to Fred seeking to dissuade him from committing himself to Anna. The whole Weller family are 'amiable', he tells his brother, but also 'feverish, restless, flighty, excitable, uncontrollable, wrong-headed; under no sort of wholesome self-restraint; and bred to think the absence of it a very intellectual and brilliant thing'.[43] Christiana is not excepted from this description and we may see from it how far she has now become separated in Dickens's mind from that young girl, ever alive in his heart and mind, who 'had not a single fault'.

Final disillusionment seems to have come when Dickens re-encountered Christiana in Switzerland in the summer of 1846, ten months after her marriage to Thompson:

Mrs Thompson disappoints me very much. She is a mere spoiled child, I think, and doesn't turn out half as well as I expected. Matrimony has improved him, and certainly has not improved her. She is to be confined here. I wish her well through it, – but upon my Soul, I feel as if her husband would have the worst, even of that.[44]

*

Mary had been to some extent a successor to Dickens's sister Fanny in his emotional history[45] and it is natural, I think, to suppose that when Fanny lay dying (her lingering painful death a dramatic contrast to Mary's sudden painless one) Dickens's thoughts should have dwelt on Mary and that, after Fanny's death, the two women who had been such ideal sisters to him perhaps tended to merge in his imagination. Seeking in 1850 to inject a little 'Household tenderness' into the second issue of his weekly magazine *Household Words* Dickens composed a peculiar fantasy which he called 'A Child's Dream of a Star'.[46] It begins with the sanctified version of his childhood memories of Fanny quoted as an epigraph to chapter 2, above. The child and his little sister wonder at all the 'lovely world' and in particular at 'one clear shining star that used to come out in the sky before the rest, near the church spire, above the graves'. This, we have Forster's word for it, is literally accurate reminiscence.[47] But then the sister, while still a child, dies a lingering but gentle death, and the brother sees that she becomes an angel dwelling on the star where she waits for him to join her. I believe that Dickens here mingles Fanny's slow death ('the patient pale face on the bed'), minus the agony, with Mary's tragically early one ('very young, oh very very young') but for the rest of the fantasy, which describes how the angelic sister watched eagerly for the coming of her brother and received him into the star at last, Mary alone seems to have been the inspiration. Dickens had told Longfellow in 1842 that Mary had been his 'better Angel six long years' and we have seen how he felt convinced that he would one day be joyously reunited with her. This sketch, though it begins with Fanny, develops into an intense expression of his feelings for Mary. The child in it grows up to be a father and has to suffer the death of his 'maiden daughter'. She goes, of course, straight to the star and the bereaved man is granted an ecstatic vision: 'My daughter's head is on my sister's bosom'. Mary doubled, as it were, appearing simultaneously in both her aspects for Dickens.

Dickens's lifelong mourning and yearning for his lost love is in its strength and intensity certainly worthy to set beside those two other famous Victorian griefs, Tennyson's for his friend, Arthur Hallam, and the Queen's own for her beloved Albert. Unfortunately, it cannot be said to have resulted in anything as beautiful as *In Memoriam*, nor anything as useful as the Albert Hall. Mary Hogarth certainly had a profound influence on Dickens's art but it was not a happy one. His experience of her hugely intensified his response to the sisterly, 'sexless' aspect of women, and, for much of his writing career, the young women of his fiction seem only to have any life or passion about them when they are presented in a sisterly relationship (I can think of only one major exception to this rule among his earlier heroines – Dolly Varden in *Barnaby Rudge*).

The first such sister-heroine, and the one closest to Mary Hogarth, is Rose Maylie in *Oliver Twist*. She first appeared in the April 1838 instalment of the serialization of the novel in *Bentley's Miscellany*, very nearly one year after Mary's death.[48] Dickens introduces her to the reader thus:

> . . .[she] was in the lovely bloom and spring-time of womanhood; at that age, when, if ever angels be for God's good purposes enthroned in mortal forms, they may be, without impiety, supposed to abide in such as hers.
> She was not past seventeen. Cast in so slight and exquisite a mould; so mild and gentle; so pure and beautiful; that earth seemed not her element, nor its rough creatures her fit companions. The very intelligence that shone in her deep blue eye, and was stamped upon her noble head, seemed scarcely of her age, or of the world; and yet the changing expression of sweetness and good humour, the thousand lights that played about the face, and left no shadow there; above all, the smile, the cheerful, happy smile, were made for Home, for fireside peace and happiness.[49]

If we should be in any doubt as to whether Dickens is here labouring to describe Mary we can find certainty by looking at the passage in the manuscript where, we see, the following sentence originally appeared at the end of the first paragraph: 'Oh! Where are the hearts which following some halting description of youth and beauty, do not recal [*sic*] a loved original that Time has sadly changed, or Death resolved to dust.'[50] Rose's main business in the novel is to become very ill, suddenly and mysteriously, soon after Oliver has been taken into the Maylie household and become her devoted, adoring brother. One beautiful summer evening old Mrs Maylie (Rose's aunt), Rose herself and Oliver take a delicious walk together with Rose in 'high spirits'. Shortly after returning home she collapses at the piano and Dickens forces himself to re-live in fiction that devastating May night of the previous year:

> . . . when candles were brought, they saw that in the very short time which had elapsed since their return home, the hue of her countenance had changed to a marble whiteness. Its expression had lost nothing of its beauty; but it was changed; and there was an anxious, haggard look about the gentle face, which it had never worn before. Another minute, and it was suffused with a crimson flush: and a heavy wildness came over the soft blue eye. Again this disappeared, like the shadow thrown by a passing cloud; and she was once more deadly pale.

Oliver, desperately seeking to argue away Mrs Maylie's fears for Rose's life is Dickens pleading with God for Mary's life:

> Oh! consider how young and good she is, and what pleasure and comfort she gives to all about her. I am sure – certain – quite certain – that, for your sake, who are so good yourself; and for her own; and for the sake of all she makes so happy; she will not die. Heaven will never let her die so young.[51]

The godlike novelist can answer his own prayers, of course, and so, after a night of 'fearful, acute suspense' (in a powerfully written paragraph Dickens, remembering, describes the terrible feeling of helplessness we experience 'while the life of one we dearly love, is trembling in the balance'), Dr Losberne emerges from Rose's room to announce that 'as [God] is good and merciful' she will 'live to bless [them] all, for years to come'. Poetry can indeed deliver a golden world – for the poet, anyway, if not always for his readers.

There is just one other thing Dickens wants to do with Rose, having thus 'saved' Mary through her. She must be shown to be blood-related to Oliver just as Mary would, in an ideal world, have been blood-related to Dickens. It is beyond the ingenuity even of the astounding plot of *Oliver Twist* to bring Rose out at last as Oliver's long-lost sister but she can at least turn out to be his aunt and Oliver can then firmly reject this miserable compromise with plausibility in favour of what *ought* to be:

> 'Not aunt,' cried Oliver, throwing his arms about her neck; 'I'll never call her aunt – sister, my own dear sister, that something taught my heart to love so dearly from the first! Rose, dear, darling Rose!'[52]

Rose has now served her purpose in the book for Dickens and can be perfunctorily married off to the colourless Harry Maylie (Dickens was so irritated by Cruikshank's introducing Harry and his mother into the final illustration for the novel, entitled 'Rose Maylie and Oliver', that he caused the plate to be cancelled and a new one substituted showing Rose and Oliver alone). But in a strange elegiac-sounding paragraph, the antepenultimate one of the whole novel, Dickens says how much he would like to 'show Rose Maylie in all the bloom and grace of early womanhood . . . the life and joy of the fireside circle and the lively summer group. . .' . The paragraph ends:

> I would recall the tones of that clear laugh, and conjure up the sympathizing tear that glistened in the soft blue eye. These, and a thousand looks and smiles, and turns of thought and speech – I would fain recall them every one.

It is, in fact, a kind of confession of the limitations of pure wish-fulfilment art. Dickens can imagine how joyful he would have been if Mary had recovered and lived; he can even imagine something which had never been even a possibility in real life, that she should suddenly turn out to be of his own blood; but he cannot for all his art imagine her as she would have been after her recovery – cannot keep her alive and growing in his fictional world, in other words. The thin device of the fictional character Rose gradually disappears in the course of the paragraph and in the two final sentences Dickens seems to forget the novel altogether and to be writing as directly about his treasuring of Mary's memory as if he were writing about it, as he so often did, in a private letter to Mrs Hogarth.

The heroine of his next novel, Kate Nickleby, is the hero's inspiring young sister and also a 'very beautiful girl of about seventeen', but manages to get a little further away from the 'loved original' than does Rose Maylie – not sufficiently far, however, to be able to flicker into much independent life. But near the beginning of the novel, Dickens seizes on a good opportunity to recall Mary very simply and directly when he retells the legend of the Five Sisters of York. Alice, the heroine of this lugubrious piece of Protestant propaganda, is 'a fair creature of sixteen'. She has a gentle face, eyes, like Rose Maylie's of 'deep blue', and 'clusters of rich brown hair'. In his description of her, quoted at the head of this chapter, Dickens echoes some of the very phrases he had used in his grief-stricken letters about Mary. With credentials like these Alice's early death is, of course, guaranteed in the world of Dickens's imagination.

It is Little Nell, the heroine of his fourth novel, who is generally associated with Mary by Dickens's biographers, mainly because of a comment in one of Dickens's letters to Forster, written in January 1841 just as he was finishing the novel and approaching the description he would have to write of Nell's death:

> It is such a very painful thing to me, that I really cannot express my sorrow. Old wounds bleed afresh when I only think of the way of doing it: what the actual doing it will be God knows ... Dear Mary died yesterday, when I think of this sad story.[53]

What Dickens is saying here is that his grief for Mary is brought freshly back to him when he sets his mind to writing about Nell's death. Perhaps, even, as the Editors of the Pilgrim Edition of Dickens's letters suggest,[54] he deliberately brought thoughts of Mary's death into his mind in order to get himself into the right emotional state for describing Nell's. But this early death is really the only thing that links Nell with Mary Hogarth.[55]

Though the phrase 'young beautiful and good' applies to both the fictional heroine and the dead Mary, one is a child and the other was a young woman. The difference for Dickens was a crucial one as we can see from a strange passage in one of his later novels where Little Dorrit is kissed in the street by a prostitute who takes her for a child. Finding that Little Dorrit is, in fact, a young woman, the prostitute recoils in dismay and, when Little Dorrit pleads with her, 'Let me speak to you as if I really were a child', she answers, 'You can't do it. You are kind and innocent; but can't look at me out of a child's eyes. I never should have touched you but I thought you were a child.'[56]

The difference between Rose Maylie and Little Nell in relation to Mary Hogarth is that in the first instance the longing to bring Mary back to life and 'save' her seems to be the sole *raison d'être* for the fictional character whereas in the second Dickens is exploiting his deliberately recollected experience of intense grief for Mary for the sake of his story. Nell is not a projection of Mary but of Dickens himself. Like Oliver Twist, she represents the child-Dickens of his own intense private mythology – a beautiful, delicate, sensitive little creature, threatened, plotted against, betrayed, isolated, but ever strong in faith and love.

Dickens may well have concentrated his mind upon thoughts of Mary's death in order to help him create that atmosphere of combined sadness and soothing apotheosis with which he wanted to surround the death of Little Nell; but Mary herself does not impinge upon his fictional world again until she serves as a model for the gentle, beautiful Mary Graham (in *Martin Chuzzlewit*) who is described as 'apparently no more than seventeen'. Like Rose Maylie, Mary Graham is an embodiment of that youthful sweetness and purity that Dickens identified with Mary Hogarth but she is an altogether calmer recollection of her original; she is not made to re-enact Mary's sudden illness and she marries her morally reformed lover at the end without any of the excited authorial commentary that attends Rose in the closing pages of *Oliver Twist*.

Dickens's yearning memories and dreams of his dead young sister-in-law find fuller and more complex expression in his fourth Christmas Book, *The Battle of Life* (1846). The writing of this little book cost him much agony as he struggled to complete it whilst at the same time getting his next great novel, *Dombey*, under way: yet it has to be said that the story, considered as literature, is, after its first five paragraphs, simply a disaster. Considered, however, as a map of an important part of his emotional landscape, his relationship not only to Mary but to her sisters too, it is a fascinating document. Dickens wanted to tell a story which should show in high relief the way in which ordinary human beings fought every day 'bloodless battles' of moral courage and self-sacrificing love triumphing over personal considerations. The effect was to be obtained by setting his story on the site of an ancient battle 'where thousands upon thousands had been killed', the kind of battle famous in history though actually a shame and disgrace to humanity, a manifestation of 'the evil passions of men'.

Once he had further decided that the 'bloodless' modern battle of the story was to take the form of a striking instance of *sisterly* self-sacrifice, that theme so perennially dear to his heart, it was perhaps inevitable that his mind should turn to thoughts of Mary, his lost perfect sister, and that her replacement in his household, her younger sister, Georgina, should also come into the picture. On the sixth anniversary of Mary's death, in May 1843, when sixteen-year-old Georgina had been nearly a year resident under his roof, Dickens had written to her mother:

> I trace in many respects a strong resemblance between [Mary's] mental features and Georgina's — so strange a one, at times, that when she and Kate and I are sitting together, I seem to think that what has happened is a melancholy dream from which I am just awakening. The perfect like of what she was, will never be again, but so much of her spirit shines out in this sister, that the old time comes back again at some seasons, and I can hardly separate it from the present.[57]

The leading characters in *The Battle of Life* are two sisters called Grace and Marion — an example, Steven Marcus observes, of Dickens beginning, 'surely unconsciously', to play 'what in the interests of brevity I will call the alphabet game'.[58] For so closely does the characterization of the two girls relate to the characters of Georgina and Mary Hogarth that it can hardly be purely fortuitous that the fictional names begin in each case with the same initial letter as the names of their respective originals. The ages of the originals are reversed, however, Grace being the elder but only by 'four years at most'. Georgina was, at the time Dickens was writing *The Battle*, three-quarters of the way through her nineteenth year, and death had frozen Mary in Dickens's mind at the age of seventeen.

Georgina, whom Dickens was to come to refer to as his 'little housekeeper', is reflected in the 'quiet household figure' of Grace with her 'home-adorning, self-denying qualities ... and her sweet temper, so gentle and retiring' and Mary in the more beautiful younger sister Marion, who becomes invested, during the course of the story, with an exalted spiritual quality. This manifests itself in a certain expression of face that Dickens confesses himself unable to put a name to, 'a something shining more and more through all the rest of its expression':

> It was not exultation, triumph, proud enthusiasm. They are not so calmly shown. It was not love and gratitude alone, though love and gratitude were part of it. It emanated from no sordid thought, for sordid thoughts do not light up the brow, and hover on the lips, and move the spirit like a fluttered light, until the sympathetic figure trembles.[59]

Both the sisters love the same young man, Alfred Heathfield. He is as near to being their brother as is compatible with decency for he is their father's ward and has been brought up with them. Grace suppresses her feelings for the sake of her beloved Marion whom Alfred has asked to marry him when he shall return from a three-year absence required by his career. Marion can read her sister's heart, however, and in her great love for her, determines to sacrifice her own love for Alfred and to vanish mysteriously on the day of his return; she is certain that, if she stays away long enough, his heart will turn to Grace. It costs her much agony to do this not only because of her own love for Alfred but also because of the pain it will cause her father (the girls' mother, of course, is dead) and the pain of separation from her adored sister, but she heroically carries out her resolution and, as she had foreseen, Grace and Alfred do eventually marry. They have a little daughter whom they name after her, just as Dickens and Catherine had named their first daughter after Mary. Six years after Marion's disappearance Alfred and his wife are sitting in the garden of their home and Dickens mingles, in his description of how Marion is still a presence among them, the way in which he himself thought constantly of Mary, 'unchanging, youthful, radiant', and the way in which Georgina seemed to him to recall her, as he had written to Mrs Hogarth. Where was Marion, the narrator asks:

> Not there. Not there. She would have been a stranger sight in her old home now, even than that home had been at first, without her. But a lady sat in the familiar place, from whose heart she had never passed away; in whose true memory she lived, unchanging, youthful, radiant with all promise and all hope; in whose affection . . . she had no rival, no successor; upon whose gentle lips her name was trembling then.
>
> The spirit of the lost girl looked out of those eyes. Those eyes of Grace, her sister, sitting with her husband in the orchard, on their wedding-day [i.e., the anniversary of that day], and his and Marion's birth-day.

It is at this point that 'the lost girl' is restored to them. She appears like one coming back from the dead, a vision of a 'figure, with its white garments rustling in the evening air' but –

It was no dream, no phantom conjured up by hope and fear, but Marion, sweet Marion! So beautiful, so happy, so unalloyed by care and trial, so elevated and exalted in her loveliness, that as the setting sun shone brightly on her upturned face, she might have been a spirit visiting the earth upon some healing mission.[60]

She is, she tells Grace, 'still your maiden sister, unmarried, unbetrothed: your own loving old Marion . . .' and she addresses Alfred now as her 'kind brother'. Dickens's imagination, dwelling on Mary, has taken him one stage further than it did in *Oliver Twist*. In that novel he had rewritten Mary's history to give it a different ending (Rose survives her sudden terrible illness); in the *Battle* she does 'die' so that her sister may become the wife of the man they both love but she is miraculously resurrected, as it were, to take her place as loving sister to them both. Alfred, we notice, has not seen her for nine years, exactly the period of time that had elapsed between Mary's death and the writing of this story (the only one he ever wrote in which, for no obvious reason, Dickens was moved to tell his readers his age).[61]

With Mary thus fixed in her sisterly role – the role that Georgina was carrying on in real life – and Georgina herself blended with Catherine in the wife-figure of Grace, Dickens, disguised as the featureless Alfred Heathfield, 'possesses all the [Hogarth] sisters now', as Marcus says, 'and everything they do has reference to him' ('Dickens's story is really saying that Mary's death was in some way a sacrifice made out of love for him').[62] One feels that the element of fantasy, at whatever level of consciousness or subconsciousness it was operating, has got decidedly out of hand in this story, resulting in a preposterously artificial plot and characters to match. This strains the reader's imagination in a way that contemporary reviewers were not slow to point out.[63] Dickens himself seems to have realized that he had failed to accomplish what he had hoped and blamed the small space into which he had to cram the tale owing to the Christmas Book format: 'What an affecting story I could have made of it in one octavo volume', he lamented to Forster.[64] But whether he could, in fact, have succeeded in gaining the requisite artistic control over the 'day-dreaming' (to use Marcus's word) that lay at the heart of the story's conception must be a matter of doubt.

For it *was* day-dreaming, and similar to the use made of his memories of Fanny in the next Christmas Book, *The Haunted Man*.[65] He clearly was at this time (the late 1840s) much preoccupied with his past, brooding over it and reshaping it in various fictional patterns as well as embarking on an actual autobiography.[66] All this was working towards his great personal novel, *David Copperfield*, which he began writing in 1849. We have looked at the way in which he used his mother and Maria Beadnell in that book and how the ambiguity of his feelings towards them resulted in the creation of the pathos of David's mother, the comedy of Mrs Micawber and the delicately mingled pathos and comedy of Dora. But his feelings towards Mary seem to have been less complex — at least on the conscious level at which he was working in *Copperfield* — and to have excluded all hint of criticism ('she had not a single fault') and hence all possibility of comedy in any fictional presentation of her. But Dickens was essentially a comic genius and the total exclusion of comedy tended to cripple his art. Hence it is that Agnes Wickfield in *Copperfield* is a major embarrassment for Dickens's readers. Mary Hogarth's sanctified shadow falls on her just as heavily as it did on Rose Maylie. But whereas Rose is not at all important in *Oliver Twist* (David Lean sensibly cut the Maylies out altogether from his classic film version) Agnes, the book's 'true heroine', can no more be ignored in *Copperfield* than can another idealized Victorian heroine, Dinah Morris in George Eliot's *Adam Bede*.

Because Mary was transfixed as a sort of young household saint in Dickens's mind so Agnes is transfixed too. She is the same at all ages, David's angelic inspiring 'sister', who has stepped down from a stained-glass window[67] with her 'bright calm face', her 'placid smile', her 'cheerful cordial voice', her 'clear calm eyes and gentle face', etc., etc. Dead adjective is piled on dead adjective and inert phrases repeated again and again as Dickens strives to incarnate for himself and for his readers all that Mary Hogarth means to him.[68] David is made to feel that even when he is married to someone else (for he does not love Agnes 'in that way') his adopted sister will be a necessary presence in his home:

> I remember . . . cherishing a general fancy as if Agnes were one of the elements of my natural home. As if, in the retirement of the house made almost sacred by her presence, Dora and I must be happier than anywhere.[69]

Agnes and Dora enter into a sort of instant, intense sisterhood, to David's ecstatic joy ('I never was so happy. I never was so pleased as when I saw those two sit down together, side by side'), but we do not have any picture of a Furnival's Inn type ménage after the marriage (as has been noted above, the celebration of that joyous period of Dickens's life seems to appear in another place in the book). For Agnes has business elsewhere, required by her credentials as the most exalted of Dickens's heroines to date: she must devote herself to her hapless old father whose weakness is involving him ever deeper in the toils of Uriah Heep. She does eventually visit her 'brother' and his 'child-wife' but that is in her 'Angel of Death' capacity.[70] She comes to preside benignly over Dora's death and to receive the latter's blessing as her destined successor as David's wife. Instead of the Mary-figure dying so that the Dickens-figure can marry her sister as had happened (using 'dying' in a metaphorical sense) in *The Battle of Life*, here the situation is reversed and Agnes is the one who survives and, again after a decent interval, becomes David's second wife.

All the intensity in the novel's last chapter, however, is directed not towards the presentation of Agnes as a wife and mother (a brief 'my domestic joy was perfect' takes care of that) but towards her as the sort of continuing spiritual presence that Mary was for Dickens — 'one face, shining on me like a Heavenly light by which I see all other objects'. The novel ends with a prayer:

> Oh Agnes, Oh my soul, so may thy face be by me when I close my life indeed; so may I, when realities are melting from me like the shadows which I now dismiss, still find thee near me, pointing upward!

It was eight years earlier that Dickens had written to Forster about 'that spirit which directs my life, and . . . has pointed upwards with unchanging finger for more than four years past'. Agnes is his attempt to make a novel-heroine out of that spirit. But novel readers prefer the company of flesh and blood and few indeed have been the enthusiasts for Agnes, even among the most devoted Dickensians. The passages in which she figures are, for the most part, quite as strained as anything in *The Battle of Life* and one can only be thankful that after *Copperfield* Dickens did not again try to draw directly on Mary and his feelings about her for his fiction. He did, however, continue to make private allusions to her in his writings — for example, the heroine of his Christmas Story for 1857 is called Marion Maryon (a sort of intensification of Mary) and lives with her sister and brother-in-law on the Island of Silver-store where 'it was easy to see she was the light and spirit of the Island' (we recall the phrases in Dickens's 1837 letters about Mary's being 'the grace and life of our home', etc.). But Marion Maryon is simply, like Mary Graham, a passing tribute to Mary Hogarth, a loving recollection of her, not an attempt to fictionalize Dickens's experience of her. Agnes was his last essay along these lines. Ironically, at least one of Dickens's friends, Hans Christian Andersen, convinced himself that the character was modelled on Catherine, Dickens's wife.[71] This amiable misinterpretation points us towards a remarkable fact that will pervade the two chapters following this one, namely, that the woman whom the young Dickens loved not as a brother but as a lover, the woman he married and lived with for twenty-two years, fathering a large family by her, appears to have had less impact upon his deepest imagination and on his art than any of the other women who hold an important place in his emotional history.

6
Catherine

'The grand affair of your life will be to gain and preserve the esteem of your husband. Neither good-nature nor virtue will suffer him to *esteem* you against his judgment; and although he is not capable of using you ill, yet you will in time grow a thing indifferent and perhaps contemptible; unless you can supply the loss of youth and beauty with more durable qualities. You have but a very few years to be young and handsome in the eyes of the world; and as few months to be so in the eyes of a husband who is not a fool; for I hope you do not still dream of charms and raptures, which marriage ever did, and ever will, put a sudden end to.'

Sketches of Young Gentlemen, 'Conclusion'[1]

Once we know how a story ends we can never again read its beginning with an open mind. So it is with the story of Dickens's marriage. We know that in May 1858, after twenty-two years of wedded life and the bearing of ten children, that 'poor matron', as Thackeray called Catherine Dickens, was exiled for ever from her husband's home; we know that Dickens himself, taking arms against the sea of slanders that surged about him, directly addressed his startled public about this 'domestic trouble of mine' ('Household Words' indeed!); and we, like that startled public, have read the famous 'Violated Letter' in which Dickens writes of himself and Catherine, 'I suppose that no two people, not vicious in themselves, were ever joined together, who had a greater difficulty in understanding one another, or who had less in common'.[2] For us, therefore, these things inevitably cast their shadows back to the 1830s, to Dickens's earliest association with Catherine; but we should be careful not to find too luxuriant a crop of disaster-seeds sprouting in that shade. The surviving letters written by Dickens to Catherine before their marriage do indeed have some ominous undertones but Kate Perugini, the younger daughter of that marriage, was surely overstating the case when she told Shaw that they clearly demonstrated that 'even before his marriage' her father 'had given up all hope of finding adequate companionship in his wife's limited sensibilities and outlook'.[3]

These letters all date from the period of Dickens and Catherine's official engagement. They are not the letters of a desperate young wooer, and their calm firmness should not be significantly contrasted with the tremulous, passionate urgency of the letter to Maria Beadnell quoted earlier. Their writer was an earnest, hard-working young fiancé address-ing his wife-to-be, and they were mostly scribbled under great pressure of time and business – this, no doubt, accounts for the repeated adjurations to Catherine to be punctual at their various rendezvous. Dickens was at this time a crack newspaper reporter, working long irregular hours in the Commons press-gallery and liable to be sent off at a moment's notice to cover a provincial by-election or some such non-political newsworthy event as the accidental incineration of a Marchioness.[4] Simultaneously, he was struggling to establish the names both of 'Boz' and of Dickens in the literary world; his much-praised sketches of 'every-day life and every-day people' were appearing in newspapers and magazines and he was also hard at work on two other literary projects, an operetta and a farce.

As the eldest daughter in a not over-prosperous family of nine children, the twenty-year-old Catherine no doubt had plenty of domestic duties to keep her busy. We know little about her mother, Georgina Thomson Hogarth, daughter of a distinguished Scottish musicologist, but what little we do know suggests that she was an excitable, not to say somewhat hysterical, lady and Catherine may often have found herself having to help her gentle father cope with crises as sudden as those that disrupt the Varden household in *Barnaby Rudge*. But she still had time to notice aggrievedly what a preoccupied and absentee fiancé Dickens tended to be. In these letters Dickens repeatedly deprecates what they mutually refer to as her 'cossness': 'my pursuits and labours such as they are,' he told her, 'are not more selfish than my pleasures . . . your future advancement and happiness is the main-spring of them all'.[5] Was he, perhaps, teasingly reminding Catherine of this situation years later when he makes Dora reproach her 'Doady' (David Copperfield) who is work-ing phenomenally long hours in order to make himself sufficiently solvent to marry her?

'Now don't get up at five o'clock, you naughty boy. It's so non-sensical!'
'My love,' said I, 'I have work to do.'
'But don't do it!' returned Dora. 'Why should you?'
It was impossible to say to that sweet little surprised face, otherwise than lightly and playfully, that we must work to live.[6]

In real life, however, Dickens did not treat his wife as a charmingly silly child, despite the snatches of baby-talk ('dearest Titmouse', etc.) in his notes to her. In general, he addresses her as a sensible and sensitive girl who has only to get the better of what he saw as a certain tendency to self-indulgent pettishness to be an ideal wife:

> With regard to your note my love, I will only say, that it displays all that amiable and excellent feeling which I know you possess, and for which I believe from my heart, you are unrivalled; – if you would only determine to *shew* the same affection and kindness to me, when you feel disposed to be ill-tempered, I declare unaffectedly; I should have no one solitary fault to find with you. Your asking me to love you 'once more' is quite unnecessary – *I have never ceased to love you for one moment, since I knew you; nor shall I.*[7]

This may strike us today as more cool and distant than it actually was because of the greater formality of epistolary English, even in familiar letters, a century and a half ago. That it is egocentric is undeniable, however. Catherine, who was, we learn from another source, 'prone to the immediate expression of her feelings',[8] is to control her moods for his comfort. But again, we must remember that marriage was not generally seen as a partnership of equals until our own day (if, indeed, it is generally so regarded even now). At least Dickens here is, very humanly, asking for demonstrations of the love that he knows Catherine has for him rather than simply insisting, God-like, on obedience as Carlyle did when he wrote to his Jane before their marriage in 1826, 'The man should bear rule in the house and not the woman. This is . . . the Law of Nature herself which no mortal departs from unpunished.'[9]

Language and social changes apart, however, it remains true that these love-letters (or fiancé's letters, as it would be less misleading to call them) contain strikingly little about the state of their writer's emotions. Like the vast majority of all the letters written by Dickens they are more about what he has seen, done, heard and said than about what he has felt – unless a sort of 'public' emotion is in question, like the indignation inspired by the Tories' rowdy behaviour at a Northamptonshire by-election he was reporting. Catherine, it seems, found the letter in which he expressed the indignation 'stiff and formal' – and no doubt it was disconcerting for her to find her lover saying at the outset of the letter 'what on earth I am to write about I know not' – so he tried to make his next one more humorous and anecdotal ('sweet nothings' he could not write,[10] except facetiously, so he tries to compensate for their absence by humorous 'somethings'). Still, he does not omit to comment on her not yet having subdued her 'distrustful feelings and want of confidence'.[11]

Confidence begets confidence, though, and in these letters Dickens seems to confide nothing. I say 'seems' because Catherine did receive one communication from him which, had she understood it – not that she could possibly have done so – would have bared for her some strange places in her fiancé's heart. This was the volume of Johnson's *Lives of the Poets* containing the life of Savage, the keen personal significance of which for Dickens has been noted in chapter 1 above. Knowing what we know now of Dickens's 'hard experiences in boyhood', and of the feelings implanted in him by them, we can form some idea, I think, of just how deeply Dr Johnson's narrative involving an unnatural mother and also debtors' prisons must have stirred him, and also of how important for him it must have been that his fiancée should respond strongly to it. On the conscious level, no doubt, he wanted to bring home to Catherine the necessity for his hard and regular work and to disabuse her of any notions she might have imbibed in her artistic home that genius could dispense with prudence and industry; but, on a deeper level, he was surely 'telling' her all that bitterness and shame he could not bring himself to talk directly about, whether to her or to anyone else. It is just such an oblique confession as we might expect from a nature in which, as Forster put it, 'a stern and even cold isolation of self-reliance [existed] side by side with a susceptivity almost feminine and the most eager craving for sympathy'.[12] These qualities are clearly seen in a letter of January 1836 in which, after invoking Catherine's sympathy by describing the 'exquisite torture' a pain in his side has been giving him and how his head aches so much that he can hardly hold it up, he cuts all this off with the words: 'Don't mind on my account: I am so used to suffer from this cause that it never alarms me'.[13]

However secretive and oblique Dickens may have been with Catherine about the darker side of his emotional history, he certainly shared his literary preoccupations with her in a way that makes it hard to understand how Kate Perugini could have thought the pre-marriage letters showed he had 'given up all hope of finding adequate companionship' in her.[14] He seems to have been eager to show his work to her regularly and on at least one occasion that we know of he derived practical benefit from discussing it with her – 'I am going to begin the second act of *The Village Coquettes* [the operetta he was writing] with a Scene founded on your suggestion', he tells her, and later he reports, 'I . . . like the second act very much – I think it will tell'. He is keen to take her with him to the St James's Theatre where the operetta was to be performed 'as I should very much like you to see a place and a set of people in which we are likely to be so much interested'. In February 1836 he joyfully announces the *Pickwick* commission to her ('The work will be no joke, but the emolument is too tempting to resist') and a later letter tells her how the work is developing and what he thinks about it. He will, he says, 'speak rationally about what I have been doing, as I hope I shall always be able to do, to my own Wife'. That 'rationally' means that Dickens is hoping he will not have to continue coping with Catherine's recurrent feeling that he is neglecting her:

> If the representations I have so often made to you, about my working as a duty, and not as a pleasure, be not sufficient to keep you in the good humour, which you, of all people in the World should preserve – why then, my dear, you must be out of temper and there is no help for it.[15]

Great prominence has usually been given by omen-finding biographers to this sort of remark but we must remember that this one, for example, occurs in a letter beginning 'My Dearest Life' and ending with the postscript, 'I wish you were a fixture here – I should like to have you by me – *so* much'.[16] We must remember, too, that Dickens is writing fairly lightheartedly, expecting, he says, that his words will make Catherine smile. Certainly, it is a far cry from that much-quoted stiff letter to 'My dear Catherine' of several months earlier, gravely reproving her for treating him to a sudden fit of the sulks. He is, he tells her, deeply hurt 'because I feel for you far more than I have ever professed' and he begs her to strive against whatever it is that gives rise to such displays:

> If a *hasty* temper produce this strange behaviour, acknowledge it when I give you the opportunity – not once or twice, but again and again. If a feeling of you know not what – a capricious restlessness of you can't tell what, and a desire to teaze, you don't know why, give rise to it – overcome it; it will never make you more amiable, I more fond, or either of us, more happy. . . . [If she is really tired of him, he says, he will leave her however hard this may be for him.] Depend upon it . . . that what you do not take the trouble to conceal from a Lover's eyes, will be frequently acted before those of a husband.[17]

It is very much the letter of a young man on his dignity but it is also, I think, in its way a passionate letter. Knowing from his experience with Maria just how lacerating it could be to love a girl who indulged herself in changes of mood, Dickens is desperate to avoid a renewal of that agony with Catherine where it would be all the more terrible because she can offer him so much more than Maria of what he needs and craves – not only physical beauty, but also gentleness and a loving companionship based on a community of tastes and interests. The Johnsonian cadences of his language here betray not, I think, any chilly sense of superiority but an effort to rise to the 'heighth of his great argument', to impress upon

Catherine the gravity, the desperate importance for them both, of what he is talking about.

These letters of the engagement period leave one in no doubt of the eagerness with which Dickens looked forward to their living together as husband and wife. He adored Catherine to come, chaperoned by Mary, and preside, at his bachelor breakfast table by way of anticipating the time when this would be one of her wifely functions and one November evening, toiling away at one of his sketches, he pauses to write to his 'dearest Girl':

> If you knew how eagerly I long for your society this evening, or how much delight it would afford me to be able to turn round to you at our own fireside when my work is done, and seek in your kind looks and gentle manner the recreation and happiness which the moping solitude of chambers can never afford, you would believe me sincere in saying that necessity and necessity alone, induces me to forego the pleasure of your companionship for one evening in the week even. You will never do me the justice of believing it however . . .[18]

It is a revealing glimpse of how Dickens envisaged marriage and the wife's role – hardly distinguishable, really, from that of a kind and loving sister, but there are surely worse ways (many of them vividly dramatized by Dickens later in his novels) of approaching one's future wife than that of thinking of her in these terms. It was unfortunate, however, that Catherine was going to be so very seldom in a position of being the sole provider of sympathetic female friendship in Dickens's home but had nearly always to share this important role with one of her sisters, first Mary and later Georgina.

These early letters certainly give the impression that Dickens expected and intended that his wife should share very fully in his literary career and the social life connected with it whilst he himself shared very fully in the organization of their domestic life – the two spheres 'work' and 'home' were not to be sexually segregated as in so many Victorian marriages. Thus he busies himself with purchasing items for their home:

> I have bought today, a pair of quart Decanters, and a pair of pints, a chrystal [*sic*] Jug, & three brown dittos with plated tops, for beer and hot water, a pair of Lustres, and two *magnificent* china Jars – all, I flatter myself, slight bargains.[19]

And, on the other hand, he relies on her to tell him 'all the news about Braham', the famous tenor and impresario who was going to stage Dickens's farce *The Strange Gentleman* and also his operetta *The Village Coquettes*.[20]

The marriage to which the young couple had so eagerly looked forward took place at St Luke's Church, Chelsea on 2 April, with Catherine 'a bright, pleasant bride, dressed in the simplest and neatest manner', according to Henry Burnett, recalling the scene many years later.[21] The young bridegroom had every reason to feel proud of his choice. Not only was Catherine 'a pretty little woman' with her 'heavy-lidded large blue eyes', retroussé nose and 'small, round, and red-lipped' mouth with its 'pleasant smiling expression',[22] she was also everything that the age demanded a young lady should be – gentle and amiable in manner, possessed of some proficiency in music and in French (a recently published letter of hers, written in 1856, shows that she certainly had a good command at least of the written language).[23] She was also an excellent needlewoman, 'very clever with her fingers, point-lace being among her accomplishments'[24] and evidently a worthy recipient of that sandalwood work-box presented to her by her admiring husband on their wedding day. And, of course, she was an individual, too, not a mere type of ideal young ladyhood. One aspect of her individuality seems to have been a decided sense of fun, a fondness for 'perpetrating the most absurd puns, which she did with a charming expression of innocence and deprecation of her husband's wrath'. Dickens would pretend to be disgusted, writhing and tearing his hair, but 'could neither resist laughter at the puns nor at the pretty comic *moue* she made (with eyes turned up till little of the whites were visible) after launching forth one of these absurdities'.[25] The young Catherine seems, too, to have had something of a taste for satirical gossip. To a cousin she writes:

The interesting Miss Frampton came here . . . to dress for the ball – her dress really looked well – but instead of a wreath she stuck a great vulgar white flower with her usual taste on the front of her bow which quite spoilt [it]. . . .

Equally sharp is a comment in another letter on the mother of a friend of hers supposed to be at death's door – 'The old Mother is always dying but never dies'.[26]

Catherine apparently also had a good line in Scottish jokes and comic anecdotes, later to be much relished by the little daughters of Dickens's friend Mark Lemon, the Editor of *Punch*, as well as by her own children. Years after her death one of her sons, visiting his sister Kate, reminded her of one of their mother's stories:

It concerned a Scottish woman who, after listening at great length and with much patience to a religious friend discoursing about Eve and the sin of falling for the temptation of the apple in the Garden of Eden, confidently remarked: 'Weel – all I can say is that it wouldna be nae temptation tae me to go rinnin' aboot a gairden stairk naked, 'ating green apples!'[27]

Angus Wilson is surely right in suggesting that there was 'a bond of humorous vision of life' between Catherine and her genius-husband;[28] it was, in fact, commented on by contemporaries.[29] Evidence of it exists in the highly entertaining letters he regularly wrote to her whenever they were apart from one another during their married life. Their joyous spontaneity of comic description may be contrasted with the determined jocularity or elaborate facetiousness so often characteristic of his letters to his friends. Here he is writing to her from Yorkshire in 1838, for example, about one of his travelling companions on the stage-coach:

> We had . . . a most delicious lady's maid for twenty miles who implored us to keep a sharp look-out at the coach windows as she expected her carriage was coming to meet her and she was afraid of missing it. We had many delightful vauntings of the same kind; and in the end it is scarcely necessary to say that the Coach did not come, and a very dirty girl did.[30]

And, seventeen years later, here he is reporting from Manchester his publisher's wife's 'wonderful' account of her discovery of her husband's having accidentally set fire to their bed in her absence:

> It seems that . . . he kept the secret of what had happened until she came home. Then, on composing that luxuriant and gorgeous figure of hers between the sheets, she started and said, 'William, where his me bed? – *this* is not me bed – wot has append William – wot ave you dun with me bed – I know the feelin of me bed, and *this* is not me bed.' Upon which he confessed all.[31]

Less than two years after writing this last letter, however, Dickens had persuaded himself that there had never been any true compatibility between himself and Catherine and that she was somehow essentially to blame, living as she did 'in some fatal atmosphere which slays everyone to whom she should be dearest'. In support of this astonishing assertion he invoked the (for him) most powerful conceivable witness, the long-dead Mary Hogarth, the guiding-spirit of his life. Mary, he claimed, had understood this terrible thing about Catherine 'in the first months of our marriage'.[32] But, as we have seen, Mary's intimate letters to her cousin, written during those months, contain not the slightest hint of such a thing; the marriage was, in her view, utterly idyllic ('I think they are more devoted than ever since their marriage if that be possible') and her very sympathetic report of Catherine's distress at not being able to feed her baby hardly sounds as though she is writing about a woman as unnatural as Dickens later asserted his wife to be.

Biographers have, of course, speculated about unhappiness which might have been caused in the newly-weds' home by Catherine's becoming jealous of her husband's affection for her beautiful and vivacious young sister or by her resenting the passion with which he mourned for the girl after her death. Contemporary observers detected no sign of such feelings, however. Catherine, remarked Mrs Christian, quoting an unnamed friend 'who had every opportunity of knowing the real state of affairs with regard to [Dickens's] domestic difficulties',

> must have been a most amiable woman, free from all mean jealousy, to have borne so sweetly his preference for her sister . . . one cannot doubt that his romantic love was given to [Mary], and he never hesitated to speak of her as his ideal, in his wife's hearing.[33]

The truth was, I think, almost the opposite. Treasuring the memory of Mary and of what she had been to them was a great bond between Dickens and Catherine – as it was also, for a time, between him and his difficult mother-in-law. A letter from Catherine to her cousin, just a few days after Mary's death, shows how perfectly in accord with Dickens's were her feelings about her dead sister:

> Oh Mary is it not dreadful to think she has left us for ever, although it is a blessed change for her, for if ever there was an angel she is one. She was only too good for this world. Since my marriage she had been almost constantly with us and my dear Husband loved her as much as I did. She died in his arms. We have both lost a dear and most affectionate sister and we have often said we had too much happiness to last, for she was included in all our little schemes and pleasures, and now every thing about us, brings her before our eyes.

Catherine strongly urges her cousin to come and spend 'a few months' visiting Dickens and herself 'and then we could talk of the time when we were *all* together. Dear dear Mary often spoke of you with the greatest affection.' We notice too, that, in spite of her sisterly grief, her joyous happiness as young wife and mother shines through the letter:

> . . . how proud I shall be to make you acquainted with Charles. The fame of his talents are now known over all the world, but his kind affectionate heart is dearer to me than all. . . . My darling boy grows sweeter and lovelier every day. Although he is my own I must say I never saw a dearer child.[34]

Later in this year Dickens took Catherine to Belgium on their first trip abroad (accompanied by his illustrator, H.K. Browne, better known as 'Phiz') and they afterwards spent the late summer and early autumn by the sea, first at Broadstairs and then at Brighton. There they were joined by John Forster, with whom a very close friendship was rapidly developing. Forster, like Mary Hogarth, has been blamed for coming between Dickens and Catherine ('You are a part, and an essential part, of our home, dear friend' Dickens told him in 1842[35]) and the almost total absence of reference to Catherine in Forster's biography of Dickens has been seen as indicating dislike or contempt for her on his part. The explanation for this is surely that Catherine was still alive when Forster wrote the book and he no doubt felt that to feature her at all prominently would simply revive all the painful public discussion of 1858; as the Pilgrim Editors point out, 'To have praised her even as a young wife would have reflected on Dickens's later conduct towards her'.[36] Nor could he really consult with her about the matter as they had been estranged since the separation; Dickens tried vehemently to force all his friends to take sides at the time of his separation from Catherine and there was no way that Forster could have remained a friend to both parties though he had evidently tried hard to counteract Dickens's complaints about her in the period before the separation and had got somewhat snubbed for his pains: 'You are not so tolerant as perhaps you might be,' Dickens wrote to him, 'of the wayward and unsettled feeling which is part (I suppose) of the tenure on which one holds an imaginative life . . .'.[37] It was about this time that Forster, on the eve of marriage himself, wrote to Catherine:

> My dearest Mrs Dickens,
>   Many, many most happy returns to you, and to us all on this day which for so many years we have passed together. I do not know how it is that I associate you so much with the change that is about to befall me – and that I have never felt so strongly as within the last few months how much of the happiness of past years I owe to you.[38]

Such evidence as we have about the early years of Dickens's marriage, in fact, points towards the existence of a genuinely happy, mutually pleasing quartet of Dickens, Catherine and two close friends, Forster and the dashing young painter Daniel Maclise. The latter seems to have been a particular favourite of Catherine's, so much so that she once insisted on commandeering him for her partner at a dance even though he was engaged to someone else.[39] She wrote – no doubt in consultation with Dickens – at least one joky letter to him from America, and he sent her when she was in Italy a heart-warming account of Dickens's highly successful reading of *The Chimes* to a group of friends in London.[40] Both Maclise and Forster had intended to see the Dickenses off at Liverpool on their voyage to America in 1842 but Maclise was prevented from going and Dickens and Forster wrote to him jointly from the hotel after seeing the absurdly tiny cabin the Dickenses were to live in on board ship. Dickens had at first been put out by this, Forster reports, but he had soon recovered:

> And the greatest source of recovery with him, from this and all other little annoyances of the hour, has been, I should not omit to say, in Mrs D's cheerfulness about the whole thing. Never saw anything better. She deserves to be what you know she is so emphatically called – the Beloved. Even the toothache [from which Catherine was suffering], in admiration, moderates his fangs.[41]

How can we reconcile this sort of evidence with what Dickens wrote to this same witness some twenty-odd years later, when his marriage was heading towards breakdown: 'What is now befalling me I have seen steadily coming, ever since the days you remember when Mary was born'?[42] Mary, or 'Mamie' as she was always called, was born in March 1838 and as with her first child, born the previous year, Catherine seems to have suffered badly from some post-natal illness.[43] It may have been that Dickens was less sympathetic with her on this occasion and that this created difficulties, or there may have been some other cause of marital friction at this time; we simply do not know. Later evidence, such as Forster's letter just quoted indicates, however, that the marriage continued to work well, even though Dickens later dated its deterioration from this period. He was, of course, a supreme dramatizer of his own past, adept at organizing its incidents into a coherent plot ('I know how all these things have worked together to make me what I am'). It is natural, therefore, that he should have sought in the misery of 1857 to find a definite point of origin for the domestic catastrophe that he felt was approaching: 'Pause you who read this', he makes Pip say in *Great Expectations*, 'and think for a moment of the long chain of iron or gold, of thorns or flowers, that would never have bound you, but for the formation of the first link on one memorable day'.[44] So in real life, it would seem, Pip's creator looked back to some trouble of those far-off days 'when Mary was born' and convinced himself that that was the forging of the first link in the iron chain that now galls him ('WE, fettered together').[45]

Professor Edgar Johnson, author of the now-standard modern bio-

graphy of Dickens, seems to accept without reserve Dickens's own 'plot'
for the story of the marriage. Thus Johnson writes of 'rifts' that appeared
in it 'from the time of Mary's birth' but produces no evidence, apart from
Dickens's own later words, to support this statement.[46] He does point to
one or two examples in the early novels of wives turning out disagreeably
different from what they had seemed before marriage (he cites Mrs
Corney and Miss Petowker) but such characters are, as Johnson himself
admits, part of the stock-in-trade of traditional farcical humour and I can
see no reason to assume a personal element in Dickens's use of them. We
must, I think, regret that Dickens's most thorough and scholarly modern
biographer should have so uncritically accepted his subject's own version
of the history of the marriage because it leads to the misinterpretation of
evidence[47] and the gradual building-up of what I believe to be a seriously
distorted picture of poor Catherine as some kind of marital incubus from
the earliest days of her union with Dickens.

Rather than looking at Dickens's fairly perfunctory use of stock
comic types like Mrs Corney we might, when considering what suggest-
ions about the novelist's own marital relations may be gleaned from his
early fiction, contemplate the figure of Quilp, the anarchic, super-
energetic dwarf who capers through *The Old Curiosity Shop* with such
grotesque vigour. This novel engaged Dickens's imagination more deeply
than anything he had written since *Oliver Twist* and it has long been
recognized that in Quilp, of whom Dickens said that he had 'heaped
together in him all possible hideousness',[48] the novelist was joyously (but
who can tell how consciously?) embodying all his own aggression. Quilp
has a wife, a 'pretty little mild-spoken, blue-eyed woman', over whom he
maintains an impish reign of terror. She is kept in a perpetual flutter by
his bizarre antics, such as drinking boiling tea or pulling hideous faces,
and her arms are 'seldom free from impressions of his fingers in black or
blue colours'. Nevertheless, she is infatuated with him and makes clear to
her scandalized neighbours how conscious she is of his sexual magnet-
ism:

> 'Very well,' said Mrs Quilp, nodding her head, 'as I said just now, it's
> very easy to talk, but I say again that I know – that I'm sure – Quilp has
> such a way with him, when he likes, that the best-looking woman here
> couldn't refuse him if I was dead, and she was free, and he chose to make
> love to her. Come!'[49]

There was, one suspects, a definite element of Quilpishness in the bond
between Dickens and Catherine. Her softness and mildness, especially if
accompanied by an air of 'bashful sensuality',[50] must have been de-

liciously provocative to a man like Dickens. Some jokes in Dickens's letters suggest he was well aware of his own Quilpishness: on one occasion he refers to himself and Catherine as 'Bully and Meek', on another to his having exerted 'despotic conjugal influence' to prevent her from attending a wedding, and on another to keeping a strict watch over her housekeeping, 'concerning which we hold solemn weekly councils when I consider it my bounden duty to break a chair or so, as a frugal demonstration'.[51]

That Dickens did sometimes positively enjoy putting young women in bodily fear is suggested by the famous anecdote related by Mrs Christian in her reminiscences of a summer holiday she had spent at Broadstairs in 1841 with some relatives who were close friends of Dickens's.[52] Dickens and his family spent a lot of time with these friends and on one occasion when the whole party was taking an evening stroll on the pier

> Dickens seemed suddenly to be possessed with the demon of mischief; he threw his arm around me and ran me down the inclined plane to the end of the jetty till we reached the tall post. He put his other arm round this, and exclaimed in theatrical tones that he intended to hold me there till 'the sad sea waves' should submerge us. . . . I implored him to let me go, and struggled hard to release myself.
>
> 'Let your mind dwell on the column in the *Times* wherein will be vividly described the pathetic fate of the lovely E.P., drowned by Dickens in a fit of dementia! Don't struggle, poor little bird; you are powerless in the claws of such a kite as this child!'
>
> By this time the gleam of light had faded out, and the water close to us looked uncomfortably black. The tide was coming up rapidly and surged over my feet. I gave a loud shriek and tried to bring him back to common sense by reminding him that 'My dress, my best dress, my *only* silk dress, would be ruined.' Even this climax did not soften him; he still went on with his serio-comic nonsense, shaking with laughter all the time, and panting with his struggles to hold me.
>
> 'Mrs Dickens!' a frantic shriek this time, for now the waves rushed up to my knees; 'help me! make Mr Dickens let me go – the waves are up to my knees!'
>
> 'Charles!' cried Mrs Dickens, echoing my wild scream, 'how can you be so silly? You will both be carried off by the tide' (tragically, but immediately sinking from pathos to bathos), 'and you'll spoil the poor girl's silk dress!'

Dickens still refusing to release the unfortunate girl, she managed to wrestle free but with her beautiful dress ruined. Catherine, evidently not at this stage of their marriage so afraid of Dickens that she dared not express an opinion, said, 'It was too bad of you, Charles; remember poor E. cannot afford to have her dress destroyed. Of course you'll give her another?' only to receive the answer, 'Never! I have sacrificed her finery and my boots to the infernal gods. Kismet! It is finished! . . . etc.' Well might poor Eleanor Christian, looking back, remark that 'Dickens was rather reckless in his fun sometimes' for on the same holiday he ruined two of her bonnets by merrily pushing her underneath waterfalls.

He certainly seems to be at his most Quilpish in Mrs Christian's reminiscences. It was an aspect of himself that his readers did not encounter in print, of course, except indirectly through his fictional characters. Only once does he give a glimpse of it but, interestingly enough, that glimpse is related to Catherine. In *American Notes* he describes the extraordinary lassitude that he experienced in place of sea-sickness during the voyage out and adds:

> . . . I think I can remember, in this universal indifference, having a kind of lazy joy – of fiendish delight, if anything so lethargic can be dignified with the title – in the fact of my wife being too ill to talk to me.[53]

As to Catherine herself in Mrs Christian's reminiscences, she there emerges as an extraordinarily nice, kind and sensible woman, quite unperturbed by the mock-flirtations her strenuously relaxing husband carried on with young Eleanor (playfully pulling her 'long yellow curls', etc.) and also with Eleanor's friend, Milly, 'a charming woman of a certain age'. Indeed, far from being made sulky or uneasy by this, Catherine, so Mrs Christian tells us, 'entered into the fun with great gusto and good humour'.

Earlier in the year she had accompanied Dickens to her native Scotland where he was granted the freedom of the city of Edinburgh. She seems to have managed the role of celebrity's wife very well, endearing herself to many of the distinguished men who flocked to do honour to Dickens (Lord Jeffrey referred to her as 'your true-hearted and affectionate Kate' and 'that true-hearted Kate' in his letters to Dickens)[54] and she repeated this success on a much larger scale during their punishing six months' tour of America the following year.

Her achievement in America seems all the more admirable in that she had not wanted to go there at all, crying 'dismally' whenever the project was mentioned because of the very long separation it would mean from her children (now four in number). Dickens was determined to go, however, and organized all his friends to bear down her resistance. The great Macready wrote to her pledging himself and his wife to watch over the children during her absence, and was clearly touched by her gratitude. 'Pray tell your good wife,' he wrote to Dickens, 'that she made me very happy in the sweet & amiable letter she sent me, and that she cannot gratify me more than by calling, and believing me her true friend'. Forster and Maclise also played a part in persuading Catherine to make the journey and Maclise gladly undertook to make a sketch of the children for her to take with her: '*With all my heart* I will do what you wish. . . '.[55]

We have noted Forster's report of how Catherine's cheerful behaviour on the eve of the transatlantic crossing helped Dickens to survive all the 'annoyances of the hour'. Clearly, once she had reconciled herself to the expedition, Catherine proved to be an admirable helpmate to her husband on his triumphant, exhausting progress. She seems to have begun her work as a sort of public relations officer on the voyage out, compensating the passengers on the SS *Britannia* for Dickens's self-preserving stand-offishness. One of them, Pierre Morand, recalling the voyage nearly fifty years later, still remembered with pleasure Catherine's presiding over 'informal after-dinner levées over a glass of punch or sherry':

> . . . this maritally much unappreciated lady was not insensible to such polite attentions as her simple hospitalities called forth, and conscientiously strove to carry out the information of her liege lord to make herself as agreeable as possible, while he sought fresh air in another direction.[56]

Whether Dickens had, as Morand here suggests, actually ordered Catherine to make herself agreeable to their fellow-passengers or whether her instinctive good manners (she was 'a lady born' her younger daughter said) and natural amiability moved her to it, the result must have been highly satisfactory for Dickens. And, once they were ashore, there must have been many occasions like this one in Boston when Catherine was able to cover his retreat from intrusive bores:

> . . . a man inquired for him at the Tremont House [hotel], and, in spite of Dickens's repeated refusals to see him, contrived to make his way into his parlour, where the poor man was extended on the sofa; he remained an hour, and then requested Mr D. to allow him to bring up his wife, who was waiting below. Dickens told him he really must excuse him, he was too ill to remain up any longer, and went to his room and threw himself on the bed. In spite of this, the man brought up his wife and passed another hour with Mrs Dickens.[57]

The very presence of Catherine with him at least ensured him some privacy – 'But for her,' he wrote to one of his friends, 'they never would

117

leave me alone by day or night'. And in her company he could relax in a way that he found possible with only very few of his American acquaintances. They could marvel together at American prodigality ('One day . . . dining alone together, in our own room, we counted sixteen dishes on the table at the same time') or swap anecdotes of their respective sufferings in the gruelling 'levées' at which they were continually obliged to appear, like (Dickens said) 'a kind of Queen and Albert'. Catherine, for example, would make him laugh over the St Louis lady who complimented her on her accent, saying 'she would have taken her for an American, anywhere: which she (Kate) was no doubt aware was a very great compliment, as the Americans were admitted on all hands to have greatly refined upon the English language!' and Dickens in turn would cap this with some droll conversation that *he* had found himself involved in.[58]

Above all, they could talk about home together: 'Mr and Mrs Dickens', recalled Dickens's American secretary many years later, 'talked constantly of their children and seemed to derive great comfort from the pictured presence of their little ones'. No wonder that Catherine exclaimed to Maclise when reporting to him the ineffable N.P. Willis's request that she should give him Maclise's picture of the children, 'imagine such impudence! and audacity!' They evidently grew more and more homesick as the weeks passed by, and by the time they were travelling in Canada (late May) Catherine was, according to the *Quebec Gazette*, unable to conceal the eagerness with which she looked forward to the approaching reunion with her children, 'those fond objects of her maternal solicitude'.[59]

That Catherine was a great credit to Dickens during his American tour, as well as a helper and a comforter, is clear from the many enthusiastic descriptions of her, ranging from the New York press ('Mrs Dickens is a fine-looking Englishwoman, and appeared much to enjoy the honours given her husband') to innumerable privately recorded opinions in letters and journals. Longfellow thought her 'a good-natured – mild, rosy young woman – not beautiful, but amiable', a Pittsburgh lawyer praised her gracious smile and 'modest and diffident demeanour', a Boston lady found her 'simply a pleasant nice looking woman' with a 'kind and self possessed manner'. 'She was aware,' this last-named witness wrote, 'that they were Lions, but recognized it I think only as a *fact*, and sincerely wished to give satisfaction to all who came to do them honour.' This was also the impression of R.H. Dana, then a Harvard student: 'She is natural in her manners, seems not at all elated by her new position, but rests upon a foundation of good sense and good feeling'. A Southern Senator thought her 'amiable and sensible, of which I think she gave proof by continuing at her needle all the time, when I visited them in the morning, except when she took part in the conversation'. And the former President, John Quincy Adams, was even inspired to 'drop into verse' to greet her, evidently for her own sake as he cared not at all for Dickens's novels. Above all, she seems to have enraptured Putnam, Dickens's secretary, who recalled her beauty years later – 'the high, full forehead, the brown hair gracefully arranged, the look of English health-fulness in the warm glow of color in her cheeks, the blue eyes with a tinge of violet, well-arched brow, a well-shaped nose, and a mouth small and of uncommon beauty'. 'She had', he said, 'a quiet dignity mingled with great sweetness of manner; her calm quietness differing much from the quick, earnest, always cheerful, but keen and nervous temperament of her husband.' If it was true that, as Dickens told his brother, Catherine didn't like Putnam (and he was rather a solemn ass) then she must have controlled her feelings very well for him to retain such idyllic memories of her.[60]

A great part of her charm, it seems, was the evident relief with which she put aside the role of 'lioness' to have a quiet talk 'concerning the best shops in Oxford Street, and other such homely and familiar matters'. But it is her 'amiability' and general complaisance which are mentioned again and again. It is difficult to reconcile with all this the tradition preserved in the Barrow and Macready families that Catherine was 'a complaining woman', 'a whiney woman'.[61] The Dickenses were exposed to fierce and unremitting scrutiny throughout the American tour but never once is Catherine reported as being other than perfectly serene and pleasant. Nor is there the slightest hint that the marital relationship showed any signs of strain. Elizabeth Latimer, the Bostonian lady with whom Catherine chatted about shops in Oxford Street, later wrote in her 'A Girl's Recollections of Dickens':

> There was no sign then of any disagreement or incompatibility between husband and wife. . . . After their return to England I saw several amusing and familiar letters written by Dickens to his Boston friends, – letters in which repeated and affectionate allusions were made to 'Kate', – and it struck me with the greatest surprise when several years after-wards I learned that conjugal difficulties in the Dickens household had led to estrangement and separation.[62]

We saw earlier that Morand, the Dickenses' fellow-passenger on the *Britannia*, described Catherine as a 'maritally much unappreciated lady' but he, of course, was writing with hindsight, not describing something that struck him at the time. In fact, Forster, for all his understandable reluctance to feature Catherine prominently in his biography of her husband, quotes one letter from Dickens which shows considerable – and evidently richly deserved – 'marital appreciation':

> She really has, however, since we got over the first trial of being among circumstances so new and fatiguing, made a *most admirable* traveller in every respect. She has never screamed or expressed alarm under circumstances that would have fully justified her in doing so, even in my eyes; has never given way to despondency or fatigue, though we have now been travelling incessantly, through a very rough country, for more than a month, and have been at times, as you may readily suppose, most thoroughly tired; has always accommodated herself, well and cheerfully, to everything; and has pleased me very much, and proved herself perfectly game.[63]

This passage comes immediately after a joking couple of sentences, 'plainly affectionate', as the Pilgrim Editors say, about Catherine's 'propensity' for stumbling and falling over and bruising herself.[64] Catherine earned herself, in fact, exactly the sort of encomium that Dickens later caused his Inspector Bucket to bestow on the gentle but courageous Esther Summerson:

> 'My dear . . . when a young lady is as mild as she's game, and as game as she's mild, that's all I ask, and more than I expect. She then becomes a Queen, and that's about what you are yourself.'[65]

But no husbandly praises of Dickens's can be taken at face value by modern readers, it seems. His enthusiastic comments to Forster about Catherine's debut as an amateur actress in Montreal ('But only think of Kate playing! and playing devilish well, I assure you!') were solemnly exhibited, nearly a century later, in a *Times* leading article, as 'a tragic little sentence' – 'That MRS DICKENS should do anything well was the unexpected. . . '.[66] But the reason for Dickens's exclamation marks is surely the opposite of this: they emphasize that his gentle little wife, with her modest demeanour, having nerved herself to act on a stage, has actually acquitted herself with astonishing ability. Like her tourist intrepidity on the sulphurous slopes of Mount Vesuvius a couple of years later, it is yet another example of her proving herself to be 'perfectly game'.

*

The most severe test of Catherine's 'gameness' in her marriage was not any foreign adventure, however, but the frequency of her pregnancies – ten children and at least two miscarriages in sixteen years. This was by no means an extraordinary tally by Victorian standards – the Barretts of Wimpole Street numbered twelve, Matthew Arnold mocked at the typical 'Philistine' presenting himself proudly at the gate of Heaven as the father of just that number, and Queen Victoria herself was the mother of nine – but Catherine does seem to have had more than her share of pain in childbirth. Dickens's facetious and apparently heartless jokes about Catherine's pregnancies in letters to friends (jokes which don't begin, incidentally, until after his fourth child has been born) have often been quoted but we should not be misled by them. They are far outnumbered in his letters by expressions of great concern and sympathy, e.g. 'She had a very hard trial indeed'; 'she suffered very much'; 'I was horribly alarmed last Sunday'; 'of course my dear Kate suffered terribly'. 'Men never think:' lamented Queen Victoria, 'at least seldom think, what a hard task it is for us women to go through this *very often*.'[67] Dickens not only thought about this, however, he also – with characteristic determination – took some practical steps to ameliorate the situation. In January 1849 he insisted that, for the birth of her eighth child, Catherine be given chloroform although this anaesthetic was very much a newcomer to English midwifery (first used in November 1847). 'The doctors were dead against it,' he told Macready, 'but I stood my ground, and (thank God) triumphantly. It spared her all pain. . . .'[68] His anxious concern for Catherine when pregnant was evident again the following year. She stayed in London whilst Dickens and her sister Georgina were settling the family in at their traditional holiday quarters in Broadstairs and Dickens wrote to her with affectionate tenderness: 'without you we shall be quite incomplete and a great blank everywhere'. He sought to divert her with comic anecdotes about the latest fortunes of local characters known to her and ended one letter, 'I think of you all day . . . God bless you my darling'.[69]

Facetiousness apart, I have only once found Dickens sounding less than fully sympathetic to his wife in her pre-natal trials and that was in January 1844, just before the birth of the fifth child, when he wrote to an American friend that she was 'nervous and dull' and added, 'But her health is perfectly good, and I am sure she might rally, if she would'.[70]

Why did Dickens not avail himself of contraceptive devices to avert these frequent pregnancies of Catherine's? Mainly, I suspect, because the intrusion of prudential considerations into the intimate expression of connubial love would have been even more deeply repugnant to a man of his temperament than the 'moral restraint' propaganda directed towards the teeming poor of Victorian England by the followers of Malthus.[71] Catherine's fecundity just had to be accepted as part of God's will. Wryly,

Dickens wrote to his friend and fellow-novelist, Mrs Gore, in 1852 that he thought of 'interceding with the Bishop of London to have a little service in St Paul's beseeching that I may be considered to have done enough towards my country's population'.[72]

*

However sympathetic Dickens may have been to his wife in her maternity trials, he seems to have been rather less sensitive in another important respect. He delighted in adopting an archly flirtatious attitude towards congenial girls and women of his acquaintance and this must sometimes have jarred on Catherine. Mostly, however, she seems to have reacted well to this. Eleanor Christian, we have noted, recalled that she 'entered into the fun with great gusto and good humour' when Dickens pretended to be madly in love with both Eleanor and her older friend on a Broadstairs holiday. No doubt Catherine responded similarly to a pretended infatuation with the young Queen Victoria which Dickens, Forster and Maclise made a long-running joke of among themselves during the first few years of the Queen's reign (for example, Dickens writes to Maclise about the agony it is for him to pass on the road pubs called the Queen's Arms — 'what visions of Albert in the Queen's arms calling for what he liked and having it. The thought is madness').[73] And we may suppose that she also smiled benignly on Dickens's exuberant mock-flirtation with Frances Colden, a lady fourteen years his senior and the wife of one of his American friends. The following bit of doggerel, one verse of three, typifies the tone of Dickens's 'love-letters' to Mrs Colden:

> Sweet Woman is of many kinds;
>   She sometimes is propi-tious;
> She sometimes has a Thousand minds;
>   Sometimes is rayther wi-cious.
> Above her sex, my love doth shine,
>   Though by no means a bold 'un,
> 'I'd crowns resign, to call her mine'
>   — Her name is Missis. . . .[74]

Very different from this sort of thing, however, was Dickens's relationship with the English wife of Emile de la Rue, a Swiss banker, who became Dickens's neighbour when the entire Dickens household moved to Genoa in the summer of 1844 for a year's stay there. Madame de la Rue, an attractive little woman who reminded Christiana Weller of Dickens's sister Fanny, suffered from some nervous disorder which produced 'convulsions, distortions of the limbs, aching headaches, insomnia, and a plague of neurasthenic symptoms'.[75] Dickens believed he could help her by the mesmeric powers he knew himself to possess (he had first exercised them, with astonishing success, on Catherine during their American tour: 'Kate sat down, laughing, for me to try my hand upon her . . . In six minutes, I magnetized her into hysterics, and then into the magnetic sleep . . . I can wake her with perfect ease').[76] With M. de la Rue's wholehearted consent Dickens undertook the 'case' in December 1844, having, as he said, 'the truest interest in her, and her sufferings',[77] and for the next few months his intense therapeutic relationship with Madame de la Rue seems to have been the dominant, not to say the obsessive, interest of his life. Writing about the episode, twenty-four years later, to Sheridan Le Fanu, Dickens said:

> She then [i.e. after the treatment had begun] disclosed to me that she was, and had long been, pursued by myriads of bloody phantoms of the most frightful aspect, and that, after becoming paler, they had all *veiled their faces*. From that time, wheresoever I travelled in Italy, she and her husband travelled with me, and every day I magnetized her; sometimes under olive trees, sometimes in vineyards, sometimes in the travelling carriage, sometimes at wayside inns during the mid-day halt. Her husband called me up to her, one night at Rome, when she was rolled into an apparently impossible ball, by tic in the brain, and I only knew where her head was by following her long hair to its source. Such a fit had always held her before at least 30 hours, and it was so alarming to see that I had hardly any belief in myself with reference to it. But in half an hour she was peacefully and naturally asleep. . . .[78]

In fact, the de la Rues did not travel *everywhere* in Italy with Dickens and Catherine (who, of course, has disappeared from view in the letter to Le Fanu, written eleven years after Dickens had decreed, 'That figure is out of my life for evermore').[79] For a few weeks early in 1845 Dickens and his wife, joined at Naples by Georgina, travelled about, ending up at Rome where the de la Rues came to meet them. But life on the road was still dominated by his distant 'patient'. M. de la Rue sent Dickens regular bulletins about her condition, she wrote to him herself (one of her letters Dickens described to de la Rue as 'full of interest, patience, the most winning confidence, strong hope, and the best side of the best nature that belongs to a woman'),[80] and the Dickenses' itinerary was to be determined entirely by the news from Genoa. Moreover, every morning at eleven o'clock Dickens abstracted himself from his surroundings and concentrated for an hour on trying to mesmerize Madame de la Rue long-distance as he had arranged with her to do before leaving Genoa.

That Dickens was strongly stimulated by all this, moved by Madame de la Rue herself and 'this gentle Trust of hers in my power to help her' and excited by the apparently very effective exercise of his mesmeric powers, all this is evident. Kathleen Tillotson sees the intensity of his involvement in the matter as 'an overflow of creative energy at a time when this had no other outlet'[81] and, certainly, in his letters to M. de la Rue he creates a fine melodrama out of his battle with the chief and most terrifying of Madame's phantoms, the one she called her 'bad spirit': 'I see, af[ar] off, how *essential it is that this Phantom should not regain its power* for an instant. And we can hardly expect, yet, that she will very long be able to combat it, successfully, alone.'[82]

Catherine, surely understandably, refused to accept the role of a mere cheering onlooker in this drama in which her husband galloped, a psychological knight, to the rescue of another gentle little woman. We learn from a letter Dickens wrote her nearly ten years later that she became so unhappy in Genoa about his relationship with the de la Rues that he was at last 'constrained' to make a 'painful declaration of [her] state of mind' to them[83] and she refused to consider returning to Genoa when Dickens proposed moving abroad again in 1846.

Whilst accepting Professor Tillotson's contention that what fascinated Dickens most in his relations with Madame de la Rue at this time 'was the successful exertion of his own powers as an amateur mesmerist', we may also legitimately bear in mind Fred Kaplan's drawing attention to 'the potential sexual basis of the power relationship between a male operator and a female subject in Victorian mesmerism'.[84] A story that Dickens wrote a few years later was clearly based on the de la Rue episode and certainly seems somewhat revealing in this respect. The story appears in 'To Be Read at Dusk', a contribution to *The Keepsake* for 1852, a literary annual.[85] The piece presents a series of reports of weird but not ghostly experiences related to one another by various couriers chatting outside that same convent on the Great St Bernard that later figured so memorably in *Little Dorrit*. One courier, a Genoese, tells a story about a young English bride sojourning with her husband in a dreary old palazzo near Genoa. She is haunted by the memory of a face seen in a dream, the face of 'a dark, remarkable-looking man . . . a handsome man except for a reserved and secret air . . . looking at her fixedly, out of darkness'. She has a dread of encountering this watchful face in real-life and faints with terror when she at last does so – a certain Signor Dellombra, introduced to her husband, proving to be the very man of whom she had dreamed. The husband, determined to cure her of her 'fanciful terror', insists on her becoming well acquainted with Dellombra, a man of great artistic accomplishments whose society 'in any grim palazzo, would have been welcome'. The poor woman, however, 'would cast down her eyes and droop her head, before the Signor Dellombra, or would look at him with a terrified and fascinated glance, as if his presence had some evil influence or power upon her'. They all go to Rome for Holy Week, just as the Dickenses and the de la Rues had done, and then, suddenly, the lady is found to be missing. The husband and his Genoese courier set out to look for her 'across the desolate Campagna' but, the courier recalls,

> When it was day, and we stopped at a miserable post-house, all the horses had been hired twelve hours ago, and sent away in different directions. Mark me! by the Signor Dellombra, who had passed there in a carriage, with a frightened English lady crouching in one corner.

She 'vanished into infamous oblivion, with the dreaded face beside her that she had seen in her dream'.

In refashioning the de la Rue episode for literary purposes Dickens seems to have produced rather a revealing fantasy. The evil Phantom and the benevolent mesmerist ('looking fixedly at her, out of darkness') have merged into one sinister but irresistible figure and the power-relationship with the frightened woman has become explicitly sexual. Catherine presumably read the story and must have recognized its source. It was hardly calculated to make her think that she had been wrong to feel so uneasy during that Genoa time.

Apart from the problem created by his relations with Madame de la Rue, we have no evidence of any serious difficulties between Dickens and Catherine before the mid-1850s. 'I will warrant my Wife to be as gentle a little woman, and as free from affectation or formality of any kind, as ever breathed',[86] Dickens wrote to Douglas Jerrold in 1844, and his mother is reported to have said often of Catherine in the late 1840s that 'there was not another woman in all England so well suited to her son'.[87] True, there has recently come to light a description of Catherine as she was about 1845/6 which paints a different picture but this was written in 1895, with the dubious wisdom of hindsight, and its author, J.T. Danson, who was employed on the *Daily News* during Dickens's brief editorship of the paper, had hardly been on terms of sufficient intimacy with the Dickenses to warrant our attaching much weight to his reminiscences in this respect; he would certainly not have been in a position to observe 'a constant sense of incompatibility in the daily lives of husband & wife' and his contention that the society Dickens cultivated (which Danson calls 'his literary followers & parasites') 'quite rejected' Catherine is manifestly untrue.[88] The affection in which she was held by such intimate friends as Maclise, Forster and Lord Jeffery has already been noted, and against Charles Kingsley's sharp comment after meeting her at a dinner in 1855 ('Oh the fat vulgar vacancy!')[89] we should set the very different response of one who saw much more of her, the waspish old banker-poet, Samuel Rogers. His letters, Kathleen Tillotson observes, show a very warm regard for her, one of 17 December 1843 saying, 'every hour brings me something to awaken my gratitude – my admiration!'[90]

Catherine was remembered by the actress Emmeline Compton, who participated in Dickens's amateur theatricals in 1848 and 1851 as a 'delightful hostess',[91] and we have a pleasing record of her fulfilling this role at Tavistock House in 1851. It was written by the young Henry Morley, a new recruit to Dickens's journal *Household Words*. After observing that 'Literary people do not marry learned ladies' he goes on to say:

> Dickens has evidently made a comfortable choice. Mrs Dickens is stout, with a round, very round, rather pretty, very pleasant face, and ringlets on each side of it. One sees in five minutes that she loves her husband and her children, and has a warm heart for anybody who won't be satirical, but meet her on her own good-natured footing. We were capital friends at once, and had abundant talk together. She meant to know me, and once, after a little talk when she went to receive a new guest, she came back to find me when I had moved off to chatter somewhere else. Afterwards, when I was talking French politics on a sofa, she came and sat down by me, and thereupon we rattled away; and I liked her, and felt that she liked me, and that we could be good friends together. . . .[92]

With one or two honourable exceptions, however, modern biographers, and most damagingly Professor Johnson, have tended to bear hard on Catherine and in the absence of much comment on her by Forster there has been little to redress the balance until now when successive volumes of the great Pilgrim Edition of Dickens's letters are providing new evidence. As Philip Collins has recently remarked, what is emerging about Catherine from that source is 'generally very creditable'.[93]

Two of the chief charges brought against Catherine by way of explaining the eventual collapse of the marriage concern her alleged physical clumsiness and her supposed domestic incompetence. Both of these things, we are told, galled Dickens over a period of many years ('Daily contact with her clumsiness, lassitude, and inefficiency set his teeth on edge').[94] It is worth looking in some detail at some of the evidence adduced to support this view.

As regards the 'clumsiness', the one and only time Dickens makes any reference to such a thing is in the letter to Forster from America quoted above and, as already suggested, the tone of that can hardly be called one of irritation. Most biographers link this 1842 letter, however, with a bad fall Catherine had in 1850 when rehearsing for some amateur dramatics to be held at Bulwer Lytton's Knebworth, so as to give an impression of years of nerve-jangling stumbling around on Catherine's part. Professor Johnson, first specifying that Catherine's role in the play under rehearsal was a negligible one, writes that she 'managed to fall through a trap door on the stage' (neatly 'managing' to suggest, by his very phraseology, that she was indulging in irritatingly perverse behaviour). He continues, 'With the course of years, in fact, the clumsiness Dickens had noted in America seemed to be growing more marked'.[95] As evidence for Catherine's alleged clumsiness becoming ever more 'marked', Johnson quotes [96] an anecdote told to him by Shaw, who had it from R.H. Horne, about Catherine's bracelets sliding off her arms at dinner and falling into her soup (Professor Johnson skilfully contrives to suggest that this was a recurrent party-trick of Catherine's but Horne's anecdote presumably referred to one occasion only). Dickens, according to Horne, laughed 'uproariously, his eyes streaming with mirth'. To Johnson this laughter sounds like 'the hilarity with which we hide a secret irritation from ourselves'; to me, however, it sounds like simple, if somewhat insensitive, amusement.

No sign of irritation, nor of insensitive hilarity, is to be found in Dickens's letter to Bulwer reporting Catherine's accident in 1850. He merely says that the injury is indeed an incapacitating one as regards her being able to act, and, at the end of the letter, says:

> My unfortunate other half (lying in bed) is very anxious that I should let you know that she means to break her heart, if she should be prevented from coming as one of the audience – and that she has been devising means, all day, of being brought down in the Brougham, with her foot upon a T.[97]

The legend of Catherine's domestic and general incompetence also seems based on distorted interpretations of certain letters and other documents. One such letter is that written by Dickens to his friend, the Hon. Richard Watson, in October 1851 when he is describing the trials of moving to a new house (Tavistock House). A 'tremendous cold', Dickens says, has 'reduced [his] mental condition . . . to one of mere drivel and imbecility'. He continues:

> Catherine is here with me and sends her kind love. She is all over paint, and seems to think that it is somehow being immensely useful to get into that condition. We sit in our new house all day, trying to touch the hearts

of the workmen by our melancholy looks and are patched with oil and lime and haggard with white lead. We sit upon a ladder. All the doors are always open; and there is no repose or privacy, as Irish labourers stare in through the very slates.[98]

Clearly, Dickens is going in for comic extravagance here and to say, as Johnson does, that he is remarking 'only half jestingly' that Catherine's part 'was limited to wandering about getting herself "all over paint" '[99] is surely to misrepresent the matter (that 'wandering about', which has no source in the letter being paraphrased, introduces an idea of mooning vacancy that helps in building up such a negative picture of Catherine in the minds of Johnson's readers).[100]

Another piece of evidence cited by Johnson[101] for Catherine's hopelessness on the domestic front is some gossip at a London dinner-party in the summer of 1856, recorded in his diary by Nathaniel Hawthorne, then American consul in Liverpool. When we actually turn to Hawthorne's *English Notebooks*, however, the passage seems to show the opposite of what Johnson leads us to believe it does:

> Speaking of Dickens, last evening, Mrs [Monckton] Milnes mentioned his domestic tastes, how he preferred home-enjoyments to all others, and did not willingly go much into society. Mrs Bennoch, too, the other day, told us how careful he was of his wife, taking on himself all possible trouble as regards his domestic affairs, making bargains at butchers and bakers, and doing, as far as he could, whatever duty pertains to an English wife.[102]

As Hawthorne does not indicate any ironic tone here on Mrs Bennoch's part we have no more grounds for assuming that she was really hinting at Catherine's domestic incompetence than for assuming that she was really laughing at Dickens's fussy uxoriousness; she was simply praising, in a wondering sort of way perhaps, Dickens's remarkable solicitude for his wife which she, like many others, saw – and delighted to see – as part of his essentially home-loving nature and his very knowledgeable domesticity.

That Dickens would have insisted on running his domestic affairs in this highly personal fashion whatever the character or competence of his wife might have been is not to be questioned. Johnson observes that 'Dickens was not incapable of delegating power', pointing out how he left 'routine details' of the running of *Household Words* to Wills and then says, of his domestic affairs, 'His egoism was not of a kind that needed to assert itself over every roast of meat or scuttle of coal'.[103] But he ignores, in arguing thus, the crucial difference that Dickens would certainly have made (and which he immortalized in the two worlds of Wemmick in *Great Expectations)* between the office and Home. Some comments of Forster's in his summing-up of his friend's 'personal characteristics' are very relevant here:

> If it is the property of a domestic nature to be personally interested in every detail, the smallest as the greatest, of the four walls within which one lives, then no man had it so essentially as Dickens. No man was so inclined naturally to derive his happiness from home concerns. *Even the kind of interest in a house which is commonly confined to women, he was full of* [my italics]. . . . there was not an additional hook put up wherever he inhabited, without his knowledge, or otherwise than as part of some small ingenuity of his own. Nothing was too minute for his personal superintendence. Whatever might be in hand, theatricals for the little children, entertainments for those of larger growth, cricket matches, dinners . . . he was the centre and soul of it. . . . The usual result followed, in all his homes, of an absolute reliance on him for everything.[104]

As regards shopping, Dickens plainly delighted in 'making bargains at butchers and bakers' quite as much as he had enjoyed buying glassware and china jars ('all, I flatter myself, slight bargains') for his first home before he married Catherine. Planning a venison dinner in 1842, for example, he writes to his old friend, Thomas Beard, as follows:

> I have consulted Mr Groves of Charing Cross [a fishmonger and venison dealer]. His suggestive mind gave birth to this remarkable expression – 'then why not consider this here breast o' wenson, off – and let me git another prime 'un in good eatin' order for you, for Sunday week? What' – continued Mr Groves – 'is the hodds to a day?'[105]

Even as late as January 1857 we find Dickens writing to Wills that he is 'going to Newgate Market with Mrs Dickens after breakfast to shew her where to buy fowls'.[106] Evidently, he had spotted a bargain on one of his famous perambulations of the city streets and is making sure that Catherine will take advantage of it. It is worth noting, by the way, that it is Catherine and not Georgina, apparently, who is still responsible for the family provisions; most Dickens biographers have her giving up all pretence of housekeeping years before 1857, 'surrender[ing] such responsibilities to more capable hands during her constant child-bearing'.[107]

There was, in fact, a period of some months during 1851 when Catherine's state of health clearly required that she should be altogether relieved of domestic responsibilities but this was nothing to do with any basic inefficiency. She had developed, Dickens wrote to Mrs Watson, 'an alarming disposition of blood to the head, attended with giddiness and dimness of sight' and he added, 'I am inclined to believe that it is not at all a new disorder with her'.[108] Her case, he wrote to a doctor, was 'a nervous one and of a peculiar kind'.[109] As she was only thirty-five, and was anyway to bear her tenth and last child the following year, we can rule out the menopause as the cause of her trouble. But how much of it was due to purely physical causes and how much to emotional or psychological strain we cannot know. It is likely that fifteen years of marriage to a man like Dickens were taking their toll. The energetic tourism and frequent *déménagements,* the elaborate amateur theatricals, the endless dinner-parties and other convivialities, the arrival of child after child – even given the devoted help and support of a sister such as Georgina, this would have been a formidably demanding life-style for any woman, however 'game'.

Whether he thought of this or no, Dickens's attitude towards Catherine at this time was everything one could expect of an affectionate and concerned husband. He arranged for her to go to Malvern, having been advised by Dr Southwood Smith that she might be helped by the famous water-cure there. Knowing that Catherine would be uneasy staying in someone else's house and anxious that she 'should begin with a favourable impression of Malvern', he resolved to set up a temporary home there. Accordingly, he wrote to Dr Wilson who was to treat Mrs Dickens at Malvern: 'I purpose sending down a trusty female servant [Anne Cornelius], who has been with her many years and accompanied her in all our travels . . . to take some cheerful cottage or house for us in your neighbourhood'.[110] For the next six or seven weeks he spent most of his time, as did Georgina, with Catherine at Malvern, only dashing up to London for various business engagements. His old father suddenly becoming seriously ill, he had to remain up in town at the end of March, writing sympathetically to Catherine, 'I am afraid you have had but a dull time of it this week – with no amusement but baths – and little to look at but bad weather'.[111] John Dickens died on 31 March and Dickens was still reeling from that blow when there followed a still more grievous one for him and especially for Catherine – the sudden and wholly unexpected death of their infant child Dora on 14 April. The letter in which Dickens gently prepares his sick wife down at Malvern for this shock G.M. Young has called – I think with justice – 'a touching example of the native delicacy which Bagehot singled out as one of Dickens's most attractive characteristics as a writer':[112]

My Dearest Kate,

Now observe. You must read this letter, very slowly and carefully. If you have hurried on thus far without quite understanding (apprehending some bad news), I rely on your turning back, and reading again.

Little Dora, without being in the least pain, is suddenly stricken ill. She awoke out of a sleep, and was seen, in one moment, to be very ill. Mind! I will not deceive you. I think her *very* ill.

There is nothing in her appearance but perfect rest. You would suppose her quietly asleep. But I am sure she is very ill, and I cannot encourage myself with much hope of her recovery. I do not – why should I say I do, to you my dear! – I do not think her recovery at all likely.

I do not like to leave home. I can do nothing here, but I think it right to stay here. You will not like to be away, I know, and I cannot reconcile it to myself to keep you away. Forster with his usual affection for us comes down to bring you this letter and to bring you home. But I cannot close it without putting the strongest entreaty and injunction upon you to come home with perfect composure – to remember what I have often told you, that we never can expect to be exempt, as to our many children, from the afflictions of other parents – and that if – *if* – when you come, I should even have to say to you 'our little baby is dead,' you are to do your duty to the rest, and to shew yourself worthy of the great trust you hold in them.

If you will only read this, steadily, I have a perfect confidence in your doing what is right.

Ever affectionately
CHARLES DICKENS[113]

His confidence was evidently not misplaced. A few days later he writes to Bulwer Lytton:

Kate is as well as I could hope. I do not yet know what the effect of such a shock may be on her nervous condition, but she is quite resigned to what has happened and can speak of it tranquilly. She is so good and amiable that I hope it may not hurt her.

Their home in Devonshire Terrace, where Dora had passed her cruelly short little life, must have been a sad place for both parents so Dickens determined to let it and take 'the dear old Fort at Broadstairs' for the whole of the summer. Meanwhile, he wrote to Wills, his sub-editor on *Household Words*, 'I am taking Mrs Dickens out, under a variety of pretences'.[114]

Later in the year he sought to involve her as much as possible in the move to their new London home, Tavistock House. She is to decide which room shall be their bedroom, she is to come up to London and 'choose the paperings', and so on. The family moved in in November and

Dickens almost immediately had to rush off to perform in a play at Clifton. Catherine evidently wrote him progress reports on how they were all settling in. 'I . . . am quite delighted', he wrote back, 'to find that all is going on so vigorously, and that you are in such a methodical, business-like, and energetic state.' He ends the letter by saying, 'I am continually thinking of the House in the midst of all the bustle, but I trust it with such confidence to you that I am quite at my ease about it'. He then adds a characteristic postscript about a friend:

> I forgot to say that Topham has suddenly come out as a Juggler, and swallows candles, and does wonderful things with the poker – very well indeed, but with a bashfulness and embarrassment extraordinarily ludicrous.[115]

The letters of this period seem to me to breathe a tender concern for his wife and one can imagine that such expressions of approbation and confidence as those that I have quoted (representative, no doubt, of many more communicated verbally) must have helped enormously in re-establishing Catherine's equilibrium and self-confidence. I believe, too, that some such motive on Dickens's part lay behind the production by his publishers, Bradbury and Evans, of Catherine's one and only venture into authorship.

What Shall we have for Dinner? Satisfactorily answered by numerous bills of fare for from two to eighteen persons. By Lady Maria Clutterbuck, appeared towards the end of 1851 and went into a second edition the next year. Mrs Beeton was to make it clear a few years later (her *Book of Household Management* began appearing in monthly parts in 1859) that for the Victorian middle-class housewife, 'The great event of the day was dinner. Careful preparations for this must be made, especially if there were to be guests . . .'. Catherine had been called upon to stage dinner-parties from the earliest days of their marriage, including some very grand ones like the one in 1849 attended by Mrs Gaskell, Samuel Rogers, the Carlyles and other literary celebrities. Both Mrs Carlyle and Mrs Gaskell wrote accounts of this occasion in private letters and, though the former disliked the lavish profusion – 'such an overloaded dessert! pyramids of figs raisins oranges – ach!'[116] – neither hints the slightest criticism of Catherine as a hostess. It may well be that Dickens, wishing both to flatter and distract her at this time, suggested that she publish a collection of her menus for the benefit of other women. The pen-name 'Lady Maria Clutterbuck' was derived from the part she had played in a little farce *Used Up* at Rockingham Castle at the beginning of the year. Dickens, I am sure, wrote the joky preface for her:

Catherine

The late Sir Jonas Clutterbuck had, in addition to a host of other virtues, a very good appetite and an excellent digestion; to those endowments I was indebted (though some years the junior of my revered husband) for many hours of connubial happiness. . . .

My experience in the confidences of many of my female friends tells me, alas! that others are not so happy in their domestic relations as I was. That their daily life is embittered by the consciousness that a delicacy forgotten or misapplied; a surplusage of cold mutton or a redundancy of chops; are gradually making the Club more attractive than the Home . . . while the ever-recurring inquiry of

WHAT SHALL WE HAVE FOR DINNER?

makes the matutinal meal a time to dread, only exceeded in its terrors by the more awful hour of dinner!

Modern commentators have marvelled at the heaviness, richness and elaborateness of Catherine's menus: 'more meals than one would have thought possible end with bloaters', observes Margaret Lane (to find them 'recommended again and again for a "dinner for four or five people"', at the end of a substantial meal and following, say, apple fritters or a boiled batter pudding, suggests almost an obsession').[117] But, remembering Mrs Carlyle's expressive 'ach!', we cannot doubt that Catherine kept the kind of (groaning) table Dickens wanted. He was, after all, the man who had given the English public this ecstatic vision of Christmas fare in his *Carol*:

Heaped up on the floor . . . were turkeys, geese, game, poultry, brawn, great joints of meat, sucking-pigs, long wreaths of sausages, mince-pies, plum-puddings, barrels of oysters, red-hot chestnuts, cherry-cheeked apples, juicy oranges, luscious pears, immense twelfth-cakes, and seething bowls of punch, that made the chamber dim with their delicious steam.

'Muddled, inept and unhelpful'[118] as *What Shall we have for Dinner?* may be when set against Mrs Beeton's classic work, it can also be considered, I think, as a monument to Dickens's tender concern for his wife as she emerged from a very sad time, and perhaps also to his pride in her as the 'delightful hostess' of Devonshire Terrace.

Catherine seems to have suffered no recurrence of her nervous illness. She resumed her role as mother, housewife and hostess (Henry Morley's glowing account of her in the latter capacity was written in December 1851). And the wonderful series of letters Dickens wrote to her in the autumn of 1853, when he was holidaying in Europe with Wilkie Collins and Augustus Egg, shows that the bond of humour was still strong between them. 'Nowhere else', Angus Wilson observes, does Dickens

> provide such a lively, gossipy account of people as he does to her of the
> English residents of Genoa, Naples and Rome – slightly malicious,
> slightly censorious, but, above all, enjoying the fun of people. And in
> letters to Georgina he often adds pieces of such gossip specifically for
> Catherine . . . considering how vital to Dickens's art his continuous sense
> of the absurdity of human behaviour is, we may think that he found some
> stimulation in his wife's company that was invaluable to him.[119]

But it is soon after this, in January 1854, that we find, for the first time in
his surviving correspondence, an expression of serious dissatisfaction
with her. Writing about his eldest son, Charley, to the millionaire philanthropist Miss Coutts, who stood in a quasi-godmotherly relationship
towards the boy, Dickens says, 'With all the tenderer and better qualities
which he inherits from his mother, he inherits an indescribable lassitude
of character – a very serious thing in a man'.[120] Dickens was, as we shall
see in the next chapter, entering a phase of his life marked by an intensification even of his own phenomenal restlessness, and his wife's gentle
passivity, which had previously so well complemented his own active and
energetic nature, was now beginning to seem irksome, although he still
pays tribute to her 'tenderer and better qualities'. During the next four
years the marriage was inevitably destined to come under increasing
strain, and to culminate at last in the kind of state that Dickens himself
would have called a 'total smash'.

7

Catherine: The End of the Marriage

'Grant that . . . we may . . . be held together in a bond of affection and mutual love which no change or lapse of time can weaken.'

From a prayer written by Dickens for use by himself and Catherine[1]

When Forster came to write what was bound to be the most difficult and delicate chapter of his great Dickens biography, he entitled it, with massive tact, 'What Happened at This Time', and began as follows:

> An unsettled feeling greatly in excess of what was usual with Dickens, more or less observable since his first residence at Boulogne [i.e., the summer of 1853], became at this time almost habitual, and the satisfactions which home should have supplied, and which indeed were essential requirements of his nature, he had failed to find in his home.[2]

He goes on to speak of Dickens's imaginative world as having always kept him in balance by exercising and gratifying that side of his nature which tended towards Romantic idealism ('those eager, impetuous, somewhat overbearing natures, that rush at existence without heeding the cost of it'). But during the writing of *Little Dorrit,* begun in late 1855, and even earlier during the completion of *Bleak House* in 1853, Dickens, Forster believes, 'first felt a certain strain upon his invention which brought with it other misgivings'.[3]

During the period of 1853-7, in fact, many things combined to darken Dickens's sturdily optimistic outlook and he plunged into ever more frenetic activity, 'to get by some means at some change that should make existence easier'. The despairing disgust with which he viewed the state of the nation, intensified as the fearful mismanagement of the Crimean War became more and more apparent, is already reflected in the political satire in *Bleak House*; it is further seen in *Hard Times* where Parliament is 'the national cinder-heap' in which Mr Gradgrind and his fellow MPs throw the dust about in 'a great many noisy little fights among themselves'; and it culminates in the great Circumlocution Office satire in *Dorrit*. But the sad undertow to be felt in these three books is not wholly a matter of public affairs. About such central characters as Mr Jarndyce, Louisa Gradgrind and Arthur Clennam there hangs a wistful yearning air of 'might-have-been' that is quite different from the atmosphere surrounding David Copperfield's emotional growing pains. Dickens creates these wan figures (for wan Mr Jarndyce is in essence, despite various devices Dickens uses to try and liven him up), who find they can only achieve emotional fulfilment at the expense of others and therefore resign themselves to an unfulfilled life, at a time when he himself is living more strenuously than ever before. Some of the activities into which he plunges are new, such as his work for the Administrative Reform Association; some are intenser developments of previous activities – amateur dramatics or charity readings from his own works. The Dickens household shifts from Boulogne to London, back to Boulogne again, to Folkestone, to Paris, and Dickens himself is perpetually rushing away from it, usually in company with Wilkie Collins. Collins, twelve years his junior, and a thorough-going hedonist leading a complex and unorthodox love life, seemed able to give Dickens something at this time that neither his home nor his older friends could supply – an excitement that had previously been fully provided by his art. He delighted to write jocular notes to Collins proposing wild debaucheries:

> The interval I propose to pass in a career of amiable dissipation and unbounded license in the metropolis. If you will come and breakfast with me about midnight – anywhere – any day, and go to bed no more until we fly to these pastoral retreats [Boulogne], I shall be delighted to have so vicious an associate.

It is with Collins in 1855 that he intends, he says, to throw himself '*en garçon* on the festive *diableries de Paris*' and even in London, he tells him two years later, 'if the mind can devise anything sufficiently in the style of sybarite Rome in the days of its culminating voluptuousness, I am your man'.[4]

This was not a world in which Catherine could play any role of the kind that she had earlier played in her husband's friendship with Maclise, for example. The self-conscious 'naughtiness' of Dickens's revellings with Collins (it is disconcerting and significant to find him making a cheap joke to this friend about French procuresses in relation to his beloved and hitherto sacrosanct *Arabian Nights*)[5] would hardly have been congenial to such 'a lady born' as Catherine was, and it is not impossible that Collins indulged in some mockery of her behind her back.[6]

Other members of the Dickens circle were to claim later that they had noticed at the time the difficult atmosphere that seemed to be developing between husband and wife. It was obvious to visitors to the household in 1857, wrote Edmund Yates, one of 'Dickens's Young men' (i.e., his journalistic protégés),

> that, for some time, the relations between host and hostess had been somewhat strained; but this state of affairs was generally ascribed to the irritability of literary temperament on Dickens's part, and on Mrs Dickens's side to a little love of indolence and ease, such as, however provoking to their husbands, is not uncommon among middle-aged matrons with large families.[7]

Hans Christian Andersen, on a five-week visit to Gad's Hill in the summer of 1857, seems to have been quite as unaware of any friction between Dickens and Catherine (who was evidently very kind and sympathetic towards him, unlike Georgina) as he was that he was seriously outstaying his welcome. With the benefit of hindsight, however, he remembered some significant details:

> Mrs Dickens was a beautiful, though plump woman, rather indolent. He had occasionally met her crying, and he had also seen her come out of a room together with her mother with her eyes full of tears. Her sister was piquante, lively and gifted, but not kind.[8]

The most dramatic account of the Dickenses' marital discord at this time is to be found in a letter of Harriet Martineau's, written to her friend, Fanny Wedgwood, on 20 October 1860. Miss Martineau's source was Dickens's ex-publisher Frederick Evans of Bradbury and Evans, who had just been visiting her. He told her that he and even W.H. Wills, Dickens's 'worshipper',

> had for 2 years declined their annual visit to D's country house, because they 'could not stand his cruelty to his wife'. I asked what 'cruelty' meant; and he said 'Swearing at her in the presence of guests, children and servants;' – swearing often and fiercely. He is downright 'ferocious' now, and has quarreled with almost every friend he had. Next to him, Forster behaved worst, – aggravating his discontent with his wife, who 'is not the sort of woman they say', Mr E declares. Dickens had terrified and depressed her into a dull condition; and she never *was* very clever. ...[9]

We should hesitate to accept the details of this undoubtedly prejudiced testimony without any corroboration from other sources.[10] Both Miss Martineau and Evans had plenty of reason, Evans especially, to feel hostility towards Dickens and Forster; and it is hard to reconcile such a foul-mouthed Dickens with the strong abhorrence for bad language that

he expresses in one of his *Uncommercial Traveller* essays (where he
describes how he actually went out of his way to get a girl arrested, tried
and convicted for swearing in the streets).[11] But the essential fact that the
strains of the marriage were now publicly obvious may well have been
true.

Whether Dickens's marital unhappiness during the last four years or
so before the separation was the essential cause or only, as I think, a
major *symptom* of his basically disturbed state it is impossible to say.
However that may have been, by January 1855 he was, he told Forster,
'altogether in a dishevelled state of mind – motes of new books in the
dirty air, miseries of older growth threatening to close upon me'.[12] Here
he certainly seems to be suggesting that his domestic unhappiness is of
long standing but, as I have argued, there appears to be little evidence for
this. Although it is humanly understandable that Dickens, having felt
himself to be an unhappily married man for perhaps two years or so,
should persuade himself that he had actually been so much longer, the
first concrete evidence that we have of his feelings for Catherine being
anything other than those of an affectionate, if demanding, husband is
that reference to her 'indescribable lassitude of character' in the letter to
Miss Coutts of January 1854 (and even here he is careful to mention her
'tenderer and better qualities' too). His ceasing to address her in letters as
'My dearest Kate' and switching to 'My dearest Catherine', or even just
'Dear Catherine', from late 1853 onwards may be another tiny clue to
what is going on but, the salutation apart, the letters themselves are just
the same in tone – gossipy, affectionate, humorous – as they have always
been.

The fact surely is that more and more of Dickens's general sense of
dissatisfaction and disillusionment (which the sudden excitement and
devastating anti-climax of Maria Beadnell's reappearance early in 1855
must have helped to heighten) focused – inevitably, perhaps – on his wife
as she sank into comfortable middle age; whilst her family, Georgina
excepted of course, became quite intolerable to him in their 'imbecility'.
A feeling with which many men entering their forties are familiar, that life
is no longer so satisfying as once it was, Dickens seems to have linked
closely with his relationship to Catherine: 'The old days – the old days!'
he wrote to Forster in 1856, 'Shall I ever, I wonder, get the frame of mind
back as it used to be then?'. Then, almost immediately, he adds, 'I find
that the skeleton in my domestic closet is becoming a pretty big one'.[13]

Seven of the nine surviving Dickens children were over ten years old,
and four of them over fifteen, by 1857, the year in which the marriage
seems to have become finally intolerable to Dickens. The baby, Edward,

nicknamed 'Plorn', was five and still basking in that delighted adoration that Dickens lavished on his children in their infancy. He and his nearest brother (Henry, aged eight) might perhaps have held the marriage together for a little longer – at least in appearance – but Dickens was not a man to live long with a skeleton in any of life's cupboards, let alone in his 'domestic closet'. The forsaken little boy and the betrayed young lover, former Dickenses whom he cherished in his heart to the great profit of his work, were one thing; but a jarring, distracting contemporary skeleton was another matter altogether – he could draw no Philoctetan strength from that.[14] It could, however, inspire him on occasion to strike out a fine image of a failed but still dismally persisting relationship: describing the progress of Fanny Dorrit's wedding-coach after it left the church in Rome, Dickens writes (this passage, by the way, would have been written in January or February 1857):

> So, the Bride had mounted into her handsome chariot . . . and after rolling for a few minutes smoothly over a fair pavement, had begun to jolt through a Slough of Despond, and through a long, long avenue of wrack and ruin. Other nuptial carriages are said to have gone the same road, before and since.[15]

Journey's end for the badly jolting Dickens nuptial carriage was foreshadowed by the appearance in his life, in the summer of 1857, of a pretty, charming and intelligent girl of seventeen called Ellen Ternan. Dickens in his role of amateur actor-manager was about to take Collins's melodrama, *The Frozen Deep*, to Manchester. It had been staged at his home the previous January with Georgina and his daughters in the women's roles. But for the great Free Trade Hall in Manchester professional actresses, used to projecting their voices in large auditoria, were needed; and Dickens, acting on the advice of a theatre-manager friend, engaged a distinguished member of the profession, Mrs Frances Ternan, and two of her three daughters, Maria, and Ellen, the youngest.

Dickens's relations with Ellen will be the subject of a later chapter. As will be seen there, it is (and is likely to remain) an aspect of Dickensian biographical studies in which speculation triumphs over knowledge but there can be no doubt whatever, from the evidence we have, that she had a very powerful effect on him, that summer of 1857. How aware of this Catherine was, and whether it had anything to do with an illness she suffered in August, we do not know. If we are to believe her daughter Kate Perugini's reminiscences as transmitted to us by the latter's friend, Gladys Storey, 'In the early stages of their married life Dickens made a compact with his wife that if either of them fell in love with anybody else, they were to tell one another'. Dickens, Miss Storey reports, now not only told Catherine his feelings about Ellen but even insisted that she go to 'call upon the girl with whom he had fallen in love', hence the well-known anecdote about Katey's discovery of her mother 'seated at the dressing-table in the act of putting on her bonnet, with tears rolling down her cheeks', sobbing, 'Your father has asked me to go and see Ellen Ternan', and not having the courage to refuse to go as her daughter angrily insisted that she should.[16]

This seems such monstrously cruel behaviour on Dickens's part that one instinctively seeks some less romantic, more understandable, explanation of it than a strange 'compact' made twenty years before – always assuming, of course, that some such incident did actually take place. Miss Storey does not indicate exactly when the scene occurred. It could have been at any time between July 1857 and April 1858 but more likely it was some months after Dickens's first acquaintance with Ellen. Scandal's tongue may have been already wagging and Dickens, infatuated with Ellen but also vividly conscious of the technical 'innocence' of the relationship, may have hoped to silence it by demonstrating to the world a 'friendship' between his wife and Ellen.

Once the excitement of acting *The Frozen Deep* was over Dickens found it impossible to resume normal domestic life. 'I want to escape from myself', he wrote to Collins, ' . . . my blankness is inconceivable – indescribable – my misery amazing.'[17] On the pretext of getting copy for some articles in *Household Words* he persuaded Collins to join him on a twelve-day ramble into Cumberland and other 'out-of-the-way places' (these included the not so out-of-the-way Doncaster where Ellen and her mother had an engagement during Race Week). Meanwhile, to Forster he expounded his despair about his relations with Catherine. She and he were 'not made for each other', he told his friend, 'and there is no help for it':

> It is not only that she makes me uneasy and unhappy, but that I make her so too – and much more so. She is exactly what you know, in the way of being amiable and complying; but we are strangely ill-assorted for the bond there is between us. . . . I am often cut to the heart by thinking what a pity it is, for her own sake, that I ever fell in her way; and if I were sick or disabled to-morrow, I know how sorry she would be, and how deeply grieved myself, to think how we had lost each other. But exactly the same incompatibility would arise, the moment I was well again; and nothing on earth could make her understand me, or suit us to each other. Her temperament will not go with mine. It mattered not so much when we had only ourselves to consider, but reasons have been growing since

which make it all but hopeless that we should even try to struggle on. What is now befalling me I have seen steadily coming, ever since the days you remember when Mary was born; and I know too well that you cannot, and no one can, help me.[18]

Before we are tempted to laugh unsympathetically at Dickens's anticipation here of the stock modern joke-line, 'My wife doesn't understand me', we should recall that he was no ordinary straying husband but an 'uncanny genius', as his younger daughter put it,[19] and that he had a curious, almost objective, appreciation of his own uniqueness. Regarding himself as the phenomenon that he indeed was, he can feel a genuine pity – sentimentalizing as it may look to us – for his wife. 'I think,' he wrote later to Miss Coutts about Catherine, 'she has always felt herself to be at the disadvantage of groping blindly about me, and never touching me'; she had certainly been sometimes mentally confused, he added.[20] Readers insufficiently alert to Dickens's extraordinary ability to compartmentalize might almost imagine that he was looking back in laughter on all this in *Edwin Drood* where the pompous 'jackass' Mr Sapsea talks about his late wife, the 'reverential' Ethelinda:

> When I made my proposal, she did me the honour to be so overshadowed with a species of Awe, as to be able to articulate only the two words, 'Oh Thou!' meaning myself. . . . we became as nearly one as could be expected under the circumstances. But she never could, and she never did, find a phrase satisfactory to her perhaps-too-favourable estimate of my intellect. To the very last (feeble action of liver) she addressed me in the same unfinished terms. . . . I have been since a solitary mourner . . . I will not say that I have reproached myself; but there have been times when I have asked myself the question: What if her husband had been nearer on a level with her? If she had not had to look up quite so high, what might the stimulating action have been upon the liver?[21]

But there was, unfortunately, no road open in Dickens between the supreme comic artist who was to write this and the self-consciously tragic figure who wrote that letter to Forster with a heart bleeding so nobly for poor hapless Catherine. Both comic artist and self-conscious tragic figure create fictions, however: as suggested earlier, that reference to 'the days you remember when Mary was born' indicates that Dickens is busy recasting the story of his married life into that of a doomed-almost-from-the-start relationship.

Evidently, Forster tried to reconcile Dickens to the situation but only succeeded in intensifying the tragic role in which his friend was now lost: 'the years have not made it easier to bear for either of us; and, for her sake

141

as well as mine, the wish will force itself upon me that something might be done. I know too well it is impossible.' Forster is not to imagine that Dickens thinks the blame to be all Catherine's: 'There is plenty of fault on my side, I dare say, in the way of a thousand uncertainties, caprices, and difficulties of disposition'. But this 'wayward and unsettled feeling', he has been careful to explain, is a necessary concomitant of 'the imaginative life'. In other words, Catherine's contributions to their marital difficulties stem from her inadequacy, his own from his genius.[22]

To M. de la Rue he felt he could write even more frankly than to Forster, it seems (of course, much of his correspondence with Forster has disappeared, so this can only be surmise). De la Rue had witnessed just how difficult Catherine could be back in Genoa during the winter of 1844/5 when she suspected that Dickens was taking a more than purely therapeutic interest in his phantom-haunted 'patient'. Just as Dickens had then felt such suspicions to be offensively irrelevant and brutally insensitive so, I feel sure, he now felt about Catherine's attitude towards his new protégée, Ellen. 'Between ourselves', Dickens wrote to de la Rue on 23 October 1857,

> I don't get on better in these later times with a certain poor lady you know of, than I did in the earlier Peschiere days. Much worse. Much worse! Neither do the children, elder or younger. Neither can she get on with herself, or be anything but unhappy. (She has been excruciatingly jealous of, and has obtained positive proof of my being on the most intimate terms with, at least fifteen thousand women of various conditions of life, since we left Genoa. Please to respect me for this vast experience.)[23]

It is noticeable here how instead of the general complaints about Catherine's temperament of the letters to Forster we have a very specific reference to her proneness to jealousy – although, Madame de la Rue apart, Catherine seems to have been remarkably free of any such thing until Ellen came on the scene. Behind the wild exaggeration of Dickens's parenthetical remark lies his fury about this particularly jarring – but to anyone other than Dickens surely very understandable – reappearance of jealousy in his normally placid wife.

It is curious to read, bearing in mind Dickens's emotional state at the time, a weird short story that he wrote and published in *Household Words* on 24 October (it appears in the fourth instalment of *The Lazy Tour of Two Idle Apprentices* in which he and Wilkie Collins wrote up their September jaunt together). The central and most intensely imagined scene of the tale shows a husband killing his wife by a kind of diabolic mesmerism. He simply orders her to die. The 'poor fool' is 'soft white wax' in his hands.

> She was not worth hating; he felt nothing but contempt for her. But, she had long been in the way, and he had long been weary . . .
>
> He sat before her . . . day after day, night after night, looking the word at her when he did not utter it. As often as her large unmeaning eyes were raised from the hands in which she rocked her head, to the stern figure, sitting with crossed arms and knitted forehead, in the chair, they read in it, 'Die!' . . . When she fell upon her old entreaty to be pardoned, she was answered, 'Die!' When she had out-watched and out-suffered the long night, and the rising sun flamed into the sombre room, she heard it hailed with, 'Another day and not dead? – Die!'[24]

Gone, clearly, are the days when Catherine's meek submissiveness could help to inspire, as I believe it did, the superlative comedy of Quilp and his wife. Now it can move him only to gloomy fantasies that read like the work of a talented imitator of Poe.[25] Fortunately for literature, it was not to be long before Dickens would be (to paraphrase a chapter-heading from *Nickleby*) 'relieved, by a very expeditious Process, from all Commerce with' his wife and her relations other than Georgina.

A week or so before the story about the wife ordered to die was published Dickens arranged for the doorway between his dressing-room and the bedroom he had so long shared with Catherine to be closed up with shelves and 'a plain light deal door, painted white', and for a bed for himself to be put into the dressing-room.[26] And it was perhaps about this time, or soon after, that he began to hint at what Catherine's aunt, Helen Thomson, was to describe as 'absurd' or 'insulting' proposals:

> of her going abroad to live alone, or keeping to her own apartment in his house in daily life, at the same time to appear at his parties still as mistress of the house, to do the honors, and to visit their friends in turn with him, and at another time proposing that when he and his family lived in the town house, she should occupy with a servant the country house or vice versa.[27]

Miss Thomson's letter flatly contradicts Dickens's claim in the 'Violated Letter', also made by Georgina in a letter to Maria Winter, that 'for some years past Mrs Dickens has been in the habit of representing to me that it would be better for her to go away and live apart'. Catherine 'had no desire to leave her home or children so long as that home was endurable to her', Miss Thomson claims. There is, of course, no way that we can now get at the truth in studying all these evidently biased statements. But it seems likely that Dickens, anxious to avoid any kind of scandal before

143

embarking on his new career of giving public readings from his own works – he made his domestic unhappiness one of the reasons for embarking on this ('I must do *something*, or I shall wear my heart away') – did try to get Catherine to agree to some arrangement whereby appearances would be kept up. This perhaps is what he is referring to when later on he writes to his American friend, Felton, to announce the separation. 'We have tried all other things, and they have all broken down under us . . . '.[28]

Clearly, the situation was becoming intolerable. Dickens was behaving 'like a madman'[29] and Catherine could do nothing without provoking a ferocious reaction, it seems. In February 1858 Dickens discovered that Catherine had applied to Miss Coutts for help in finding a new situation for one of her brothers, unaware that Dickens himself had already heard from Miss Coutts about the matter. He was, he told Miss Coutts,

> inexpressibly vexed to find that Mrs Dickens, in my absence and without my knowledge, wrote to you yesterday about her brother. I had not told her of the contents of your last kind note to me, concerning him. That is her only excuse; and I hope you will forgive her more freely and more readily than I do.

It is ironic that poor Catherine was here behaving like a true Dickens heroine in her sisterly concern – almost as though she had modelled herself on that devoted daughter and sister, Little Dorrit, trying to procure some decent work for her feckless brother, Tip (' . . . my Father,' Catherine had written to Miss Coutts, 'is not able to do much for him, and it is a serious and anxious thing for him, that my Brother should be unemployed').[30]

To Forster Dickens wrote in March that all was 'despairingly over' with his married life: 'A dismal failure has to be borne, and there an end'. Something, however, happened in late April or early May that brought matters to a head. What it was, exactly, is not known though some gossip about a present of jewellery designed for Ellen somehow coming to Catherine's notice has been widely credited as the cause of the final rupture.[31] Catherine's parents became involved and it seems to have been quickly settled that she should live separately. On 9 May Dickens broke the news to Miss Coutts, taking very much the same line about things as he had done when writing to Forster the previous autumn: both Catherine and he were to be pitied as 'she is the only person I have ever known with whom I could not get on somehow or other'; he himself admittedly had 'many impulsive faults' connected with being an artist ('but I am very patient and considerate at heart', he adds); both Georgina and the dead Mary Hogarth are invoked as witnesses against their sister and how she lives 'in some fatal atmosphere which slays every one to whom she should be dearest'. Catherine's mother is at Tavistock House trying to get her away, with Forster's help, 'to some happier mode of existence if possible'. 'They all know', Dickens adds, 'that I will do anything for her Comfort, and spend anything upon her.'

All this was distressing enough coming from a man like Dickens, a combination of boasting and whining which can hardly have gone down well with a woman as clear-headed as Miss Coutts. But it is in this letter that Dickens first begins that attack on Catherine for her alleged failure as a mother which he was later to make so public:

> . . . she has never attached one of them to herself, never played with them in their infancy, never attracted their confidence as they have grown older, never presented herself before them in the aspect of a mother . . . Mary and Katey (whose dispositions are of the gentlest and most affectionate conceivable) harden into stone figures of girls when they can be got to go near her, and have their hearts shut up in her presence as if they were closed by some horrid spring.[32]

It is instructive to juxtapose this with just one of Dickens's 1850 letters from Broadstairs to Catherine, confined in London. He writes:

> Having no news, I must tell you a story of Sydney [their seventh child, three years old in 1850]. The children, Georgy, and I, were out in the garden on Sunday evening . . . when I asked Sydney if he would go to the Railroad and see if Forster was coming. As he answered very boldly, Yes, I opened the garden gate. Upon which he set off, alone, as fast as his legs would carry him; and being pursued, was not overtaken until he was through the Lawn House Archway . . . Being brought back in triumph, he made a number of fictitious starts, for the sake of being overtaken again, and we made a regular game of it. At last when he and Ally [the sixth child, aged four] had run away – instead of running after them, we came into the garden, shut the gate, and crouched down on the ground. Presently, we heard them come back and say to each other with some alarm, 'Why, the gate's shut, and they are all gone!' Ally began in a dismayed way to cry out, but the Phenomenon, shouting 'open the gate!' sent an enormous stone flying into the garden (among our heads) by way of alarming the establishment. I thought it a wonderful piece of character, shewing great readiness of resource. . . .
>
> They are all in great force, and send their loves. They are all much excited with the expectation of receiving you on Friday – and would start me off to fetch you, now, if I would go.[33]

Whatever Dickens had convinced himself of by May 1858, the man

who wrote this letter certainly does not sound like a man who thought the wife to whom he was writing was a woman who took no interest in her children and inspired no affection in them. A great mass of evidence could be heaped up showing that Catherine was a loving mother (she evidently liked children generally as she gave many children's parties even after her separation from Dickens) and that she was loved by her children (Alfred, the 'Ally' of the anecdote in the letter just quoted, said of his parents 'we, their children, always loved them both equally')[34] but it is hardly necessary. It will be sufficient to quote a passage from Catherine's letter to her aunt[35] very shortly after the separation when 'she had a visit of a few days from her youngest boys during their holidays':

> I need hardly tell you, dearest Aunt, how very happy I have been with my dear boys, although they were not allowed to remain with me so long as I wished . . . I cannot tell you how good and affectionate they were to me. One of them, little Sydney, was full of solicitude and anxiety about me, always asking what I should do when they were gone, and if I would not be very dull and lonely without them; he should so like to stay.[36] Upon the whole their visit has done me much good, and dear Charlie is so kind and gentle, and tried to cheer me. I trust by God's assistance to be able to resign myself to His will, and to lead a contented if not a happy life, but my position is a sad one.

This all sounds perfectly genuine and just what one would have expected from the woman who had wept so inconsolably at having to leave her children behind when she accompanied Dickens to America in 1842. So why should Dickens suddenly begin, in May 1858, to call her a bad mother so insistently? The charge appears in the 'Violated Letter'[37] (which Dickens may or may not have intended to make public): 'In the manly consideration toward Mrs Dickens which I owe to my wife, I will merely remark of her that the peculiarity of her character has thrown all the children on someone else'. And he repeats it, vehemently, to Miss Coutts in August: 'She does not – and she never did – care for the children; and the children do not – and they never did – care for her'.[38] It seems a gratuitous piece of cruelty and quite at odds with the pity Dickens was expressing for his wife up to the time he first calls her a bad mother to Miss Coutts.

It was not gratuitous cruelty, I believe, but something that Dickens *had* to get himself to believe so that he could the more freely pity himself in the image of his own children, a psychological trick that he had shown himself perfectly understanding of when he had created Dombey ('It may have been characteristic of Mr Dombey's pride, that he pitied himself through the child. Not poor me . . . but poor little fellow!').[39] He was, at the age of forty-six, going through the most agonizing time of his life since his sojourn in the blacking-factory thirty-four years earlier. As he had then, he felt, been deserted by his mother – how could she have loved him when she was 'warm for [his] being sent back' to the blacking-factory? – so now his misery was caused by a woman who should have loved and cherished him. But the situation was complicated by the fact that the woman was his wife, a wife he had freely chosen, not a mother he had been born to; moreover, he could hardly claim, even to himself, that she had failed in love towards him. So, I believe, this strange shift occurs and it is in her maternal aspect that Catherine must be arraigned so that Dickens can present his children as re-enacting his own childhood loss of mother-love. Just as Nancy in *Oliver Twist* pities her former and her present self through little Oliver so Dickens pities his former and present self through his children 'rejected' by their mother. He makes an explicit link between the blacking-factory and the breakdown of his marriage and its aftermath when he writes to Forster in 1862, 'The never to be forgotten misery of that old time, bred a certain shrinking sensitiveness in a certain ill-clad ill-fed child, that I have found come back in the never to be forgotten misery of this later time' (he is referring to 'the last five years').[40] My suggested reason for Dickens's insistence that Catherine was a bad mother is one that would have been peculiar to him and his emotional history; but we should also remember how sadly common it is for couples whose marriage is breaking up to attack each other through their children. No doubt this factor played its part, too, in Dickens's distasteful advertising of Catherine's alleged maternal shortcomings.

Painful as it all was, however, arrangements for the separation seemed in early May to be proceeding fairly smoothly. On the 14th Mark Lemon, acting for Catherine, told Forster, acting for Dickens, that 'Mrs Dickens thankfully accepts the proposal – as made by you on May 7th'.[41] But then Mrs Hogarth and her youngest daughter, Helen, must have begun to talk about Dickens's relationship with Ellen and perhaps even to speculate whether Catherine might not have grounds for suing for divorce under the new Act of 1857.[42] This, by establishing a regular Divorce Court, made it simpler and cheaper to sue for a divorce (previously, those wishing to do so had first to win a case in the ecclesiastical courts and then take the matter to the House of Lords).[43] A woman, however, could still not obtain a divorce on the grounds of adultery alone as a man could; she had to prove that the adultery was compounded by some aggravating circumstances such as cruelty or incest. Mrs Hogarth and Helen perhaps urged Catherine to accuse Dickens of adultery with Ellen and allege also cruelty on his part. Excitable as Mrs Hogarth seems to have been, we can surely rule out the idea that she would have invoked incest with respect to Dickens's relations with Georgina (a liaison between a brother and a sister-in-law would still have been, technically, incestuous in 1858). But Dickens clearly saw the danger that whispers about this might well arise if it were known that his wife were contemplating an action for divorce. As soon as he heard about Mrs Hogarth's scandalmongering Dickens's tone about her changed abruptly. 'If you have seen Mrs Dickens in company with her wicked mother', he wrote to Miss Coutts on 19 May, I can not enter – no, not even with you – upon any question that was discussed in that woman's presence.'[44] Mark Lemon received on 20 May a letter from Catherine, perhaps hinting at a divorce action, which he refused to forward to Dickens but sent to Forster saying, 'Of course I shall never refuse to see Mrs Dickens, but whatever she may do for the future must be without my interference'.[45]

Once it became known that Georgina intended, much to the grief and indignation of her family, to remain in her brother-in-law's home, she became a prime target for gossip, gossip which Dickens seems to have seen as largely originating with Mrs Hogarth. Her chatter about Ellen was no doubt reported by others as relating to Georgina who was, after all, a well-known figure in Dickens's life whereas his newly formed friendship with Ellen would have been known to very few.

Lashed into fury, Dickens refused to proceed any further with the settlement arrangements for Catherine until his mother-in-law and her youngest daughter signed a statement saying that they disbelieved all rumours of his having liaisons with other women. Not only did Mrs Hogarth refuse to sign but she apparently continued to talk publicly about Ellen. Dickens wrote to his lawyer on 26 May that he had heard 'from a very honorable and intelligent gentleman, information of Mrs Hogarth's having repeated these smashing slanders to him in a concert Room, *since our negociations have been pending*'. This showed, he said, 'the stern necessity of being relentless with her'.[46] On the previous day he had written the 'Violated Letter' which speaks of 'Two wicked persons who should have spoken very differently of me, in consideration of earned respect and gratitude' dragging into the discussion of the Dickenses' separation the name of 'a young lady for whom I have a great attachment and regard'. 'Upon my soul and honor,' he continues

> there is not on this earth a more virtuous and spotless creature than that young lady. I know her to be innocent and pure, and as good as my own dear daughters. Further, I am quite sure that Mrs Dickens, having received this assurance from me, must now believe it, in the respect I

know her to have for me, and in the perfect confidence I know her in her better moments to repose in my truthfulness.

(That reference to Catherine's 'better moments' looks back to an earlier passage in the letter about 'a mental disorder under which she sometimes labors'.)[47]

What poor Catherine believed about Dickens's relations with Ellen at this time we do not know. According to Miss Thomson (a very prejudiced witness we must remember) he 'wrote to his elder children [that] their mother had not character to appreciate' the nature of his 'platonic attachment' to Ellen – just as earlier, he no doubt reminded himself, she had not had the character to appreciate his special relationship with Madame de la Rue.

But still his attitude towards Catherine at this stage of the separation procedure was one of pitying impatience, as for a chronic invalid, rather than one of anger or bitterness. In that letter to his lawyer, quoted earlier, about Mrs Hogarth's continued scandalmongering, he wrote

> Pray do me the kindness to detach Mrs Dickens from these wrongdoings, *now*. I do not in the least suspect her of them, and I should wish her to know it. She has a great tenderness for me, and I sincerely believe would be glad to shew it. I would not therefore add to her pain by a hair's breadth. It would be a pleasure to her (I think) to know that I had begun to trust her so far; and I believe that it would do her lasting good if you could convey that assurance to her.

On 29 May he at last obtained the signatures of Mrs Hogarth and Helen to the statement he had drawn up: they 'solemnly declared' their disbelief in any of the rumours about scandalous causes for the Dickenses' separation and stated their knowledge that such rumours were not believed by Catherine. That evening he wrote to Mary Boyle, a platonic friend of longer standing than Ellen:

> Mrs Dickens (really, generously indignant at the baseless scandals she hears, whatever her weakness may once have done circuitously, towards originating them) has hastened to declare in writing that there is no other cause for our separation than our having lived unhappily together for some time.[48]

But the rumours did not die out, of course, just because Dickens had bullied his mother-in-law into signing a statement. Juicy gossip about his supposed incestuous relationship with Georgina was the talk of the London Clubs in the summer of 1858 and pursued him about the country when he set out on his first nationwide Reading tour: a Glaswegian admirer of his felt constrained to report to him that a local newspaper editor had told him Dickens 'was the outcry of London, and enquired if I knew that Mr Dickens's sister-in-law had three children by him'.[49]

With such very damaging rumours as this flying around (as well as absurd ones such as the one relayed later to Ruskin by Dr John Brown, that one of Dickens's professed reasons for 'turning the mother of his children out of his house & never seeing her again [was] that she had a cutaneous eruption!')[50] we can well understand, I think, why Dickens felt it necessary to make a public announcement in the national press and in his own journal *Household Words* about his personal affairs. Not only were Georgina and, to a lesser extent, Ellen in danger of becoming public by-words but his own new career of public Readings, begun in April, might be jeopardized. Hence an announcement appeared in *The Times* and other papers on 7 June and in *Household Words* on the 12th. In it, after some preamble about his relations with his public, Dickens wrote:

> Some domestic trouble of mine, of long-standing, on which I will make no further remark than that it claims to be respected, as being of a sacredly private nature, has lately been brought to an arrangement, which involves no anger or ill-will of any kind, and the whole origin, progress, and surrounding circumstances of which have been, through-out, within the knowledge of my children. It is amicably composed, and its details have now but to be forgotten by those concerned in it.
>
> By some means, arising out of wickedness, or out of folly, or out of inconceivable wild chance, or out of all three, this trouble has been made the occasion of misrepresentations, most grossly false, most monstrous, and most cruel – involving, not only me, but innocent persons dear to my heart, and innocent persons of whom I have no knowledge, if indeed, they have any existence – and so widely spread, that I doubt if one reader in a thousand will peruse these lines, by whom some touch of the breath of these slanders will not have passed, like an unwholesome air.
>
> Those who know me and my nature, need no assurance under my hand that such calumnies are irreconcilable with me, as they are, in their frantic incoherence, with one another. But, there is a great multitude who know me through my writings, and who do not know me otherwise; and I cannot bear that one of them should be left in doubt, or hazard of doubt, through my poorly shrinking from taking the unusual means to which I now resort, of circulating the Truth.
>
> I most solemnly declare, then – and this I do, both in my own name and in my wife's name – that all the lately whispered rumours touching the trouble at which I have glanced, are abominably false. And that whosoever repeats one of them after this denial, will lie as wilfully and as foully as it is possible for any false witness to lie, before Heaven and earth.

Dickens sent a copy of this purposefully vague vehemence to Catherine before its publication with a covering letter:

> Dear Catherine,
>   I will not write a word as to any *causes* that have made it necessary for me to publish the enclosed in Household Words. Whoever there may be among the living, whom I will never forgive alive or dead, I earnestly hope all unkindness is over between you and me.
>   But as you are referred to in the article, I think you ought to see it. You have only to say . . . that you do not object to the allusion.
>   CHARLES DICKENS [51]

This letter seems to suggest that Dickens, all the details of the separation having been settled (Catherine's agreed allowance of £600 a year was a generous one – as Professor Wagenknecht points out, it was greater than the yearly salary of Dickens's sub-editor on *Household Words*, W.H. Wills),[52] felt that some sort of road might be left open between Catherine and himself. Her solicitors had put into the Deed of Separation a clause stating that she should have access to the children except at Tavistock House but Dickens struck it out because, he told Charley, the 'exception seemed to me to convey an unnecessary slight upon her, and I said she should see them there or anywhere'.[53] He may even have contemplated meeting her socially from time to time – certainly somebody gave Catherine this impression. Having confessed to her aunt that she still loved Dickens and thought about him 'too much for my peace of mind' she went on,

> I have been told that he has expressed a wish that we should meet in society, and be at least on friendly terms. Surely he cannot mean it, as I feel that if I were ever to see him by chance it would almost kill me. . . .[54]

Catherine need not have feared. During the summer she either did or said something, or was reported to Dickens as having said or done something, that he found so heinous as to be literally unforgivable. On 23 August he wrote to Miss Coutts that Catherine had caused him 'unspeakable agony of mind' since he had last spoken of her to Miss Coutts:

> As to Mrs Dickens's simplicity in speaking of me and my doings, O my dear Miss Coutts do I not know that the weak hand that could never help or serve my name in the least, has struck at it – in conjunction with the wickedest people whom I have loaded with benefits. I want to communicate with her no more.[55]

Was it that Catherine, having preserved a dignified – or a stunned –

151

silence throughout May whilst her mother and sister Helen were filling everyone's ears with Ellen's name had at last begun to talk herself? If so, and if what she said at all resembled what the American John Bigelow was told at a dinner-party given by Thackeray in 1860 at which she was present, then Dickens's new-found bitterness towards her may be accounted for. Bigelow noted in his diary:

> Mrs Caulfield told me that a Miss Teman – I think that is the name – was the source of the difficulty between Mrs Dickens and her husband. She played in private theatricals with Dickens, and he sent her a portrait in a brooch, which met with an accident requiring it to be sent to the jeweller's to be mended. The jeweller, noticing Mr Dickens's initials, sent it to his house. Mrs Dickens's sister, who had always been in love with him and was jealous of Miss Teman, told Mrs Dickens of the brooch, and she mounted her husband with comb and brush. This, no doubt, was Mrs Dickens's version in the main.[56]

The detail about Catherine's physical assault on her husband must, one imagines, be a fanciful bit of embroidery by Mrs Caulfield but, otherwise, what Bigelow heard might well have been the sort of thing that Catherine was beginning to say in the summer of 1858, just when Dickens was hoping that everything would settle down. The suggestion that Georgina was in love with him and maliciously jealous of Ellen would naturally have been especially upsetting to him if this particular scandalous rumour reached his ears.

Whether or not the cause of Dickens's revulsion from Catherine in the period between early June and late August 1858 can be explained in these terms, revulsion there certainly was, and Catherine was henceforth cast in the role Dickens's mother had so long been burdened with, that of a woman who had emotionally betrayed him in the most serious way. His bitterness against her lasted for the rest of his life.

Miss Coutts, who was amongst Catherine's 'kindest and warmest friends' at the time of the separation, even inviting her (according to Miss Thomson) to share her home 'before matters were settled', evidently tried several times to bring about a reconcilement. An occasion offered in 1860 when Dickens's younger daughter, Katey, was about to get married. It seems that Miss Coutts suggested Catherine might join her husband for the wedding but Dickens would not even pretend to consider this:

> In the last two years, I have been stabbed too often and too deep, not to have a settled knowledge of the wounded place.
>
> It is simply impossible that such a thing can be. That figure is out of my life for evermore (except to darken it) and my desire is, Never to see it again.[57]

A tendency to blame Catherine for everything that displeased Dickens in his family life after the separation is noticeable. In 1861 Charley married, to his father's intense disapproval, the daughter of Dickens's former publisher, Frederick Evans. Dickens wrote to Miss Coutts,

> . . . the dear fellow does what is unavoidable – his foolish mother would have effectually committed him if nothing else had; chiefly I suppose because her hatred of the bride and all belonging to her, used to know no bounds, and was quite unappeasable.[58]

Here, it seems, he is again busy rewriting the past and changing people's roles. Nothing we can learn about Catherine suggests that she was a person given to violent, persisting hatreds of anyone – quite the opposite, in fact.

The final reference to her in Dickens's correspondence with Miss Coutts occurs in 1864, when he is answering a letter of condolence on the death of his second son, Walter. Clearly she had taken the opportunity to urge yet again reconcilement and forgiveness, but Dickens has by this stage made Catherine virtually a non-person in his life:

> Do not think me unimpressed by certain words in your letter concerning forgiveness and tenderness when I say that I do not claim to have anything to forgive – that if I had, I hope and believe I would forgive freely – but that a page in my life which once had writing on it, has become absolutely blank, and that it is not in my power to pretend that it has a solitary word upon it.[59]

This domestic anticipation of the methods of Orwell's historians in *1984* is chilling indeed and gives us a measure of the depth of the bitterness Dickens must have come to feel towards his wife. The previous year he had had to write to her on a sufficiently poignant business matter, her mother's death and wish to be buried in her daughter Mary's grave. Even to Catherine herself, we notice, he writes as though she had had no part in his earlier life. He begins the brief letter thus: 'When I went to America (or to Italy: I cannot positively say which, but I think on the former occasion) I gave your mother the paper which established the right in perpetuity to the grave at Kensal Green'.[60] The use at the beginning of the sentence of the first person singular instead of the plural must have been deeply wounding.

Dickens communicated directly with Catherine only twice more before his death, both times in response to letters from her. She wrote to express concern after he had been involved in a terrible railway accident in the summer of 1865 and received an almost impersonal four-sentence

153

note of acknowledgment, its tone somewhat redeemed by the fact that Dickens was able to bring himself to sign it 'Affectionately'. She wrote again in November 1867 when he was about to leave for his American Reading tour and received the following reply, the last words she had from him:

> My dear Catherine
>   I am glad to receive your letter, and to accept and reciprocate your good wishes. Severely hard work lies before me; but that is not a new thing in my life, and I am content to go my way and do it.
>
> Affectionately yours
Charles Dickens[61]

One can see that it would not have been possible for Dickens, feeling as he now did, to make any softening reference to his previous visit to America when Catherine was by his side and helping him so much; but one may wish that he had made no allusion at all to the past rather than one which seems like only a harsh echo of their engagement time, that period when Catherine was so often admonished about the necessity for Dickens's working so hard and was called on to lovingly admire his tenacious courage whilst still being kept, herself, at a certain emotional distance from him.

Shakespeare's famous second-best bed bequest to Anne Hathaway has led many an earnest scholar to infer from it a whole history of marital troubles for the Bard. Dickens's sole reference to Catherine in *his* will, however, is pretty unequivocal. Even if he did not abide our question and we knew no more about his married life than we do about Shakespeare's, we would hardly be able to mistake the resentful tone. After solemnly enjoining his children 'never to be wanting in grateful and affectionate attachment to [Georgina Hogarth] for they know well that she has been, through all the stages of their growth and progress, their ever useful self-denying and devoted friend', Dickens continues:

> AND I DESIRE here simply to record the fact that my wife, since our separation by consent, has been in the receipt from me of an annual income of £600, while all the great charges of a numerous and expensive family have devolved wholly upon myself.[62]

That a man as generous-natured as Dickens should feel impelled to show his rankling twelve-year-old sense of resentment against his wife in this public way, as part of his last will and testament, should make us realize how terribly he must have felt himself wounded by her in the summer of 1858. He was, of course, in a very disturbed state then and thus likely to over-react, even beyond his customary vehemence, to anything touching the deepest currents of his emotional life. But it is sad indeed that he remained so unsoftened towards her as the years passed and a kind of normalcy returned to his existence.

*

Long before Dickens's actual death in June 1870 Catherine had become inured to widowed status; and the fact of Dickens dead to all the world was perhaps easier for her than Dickens dead to her in particular. 'Poor dear,' her daughter-in-law wrote after she had heard the news,

> she is better than I dared to hope she would be, and I am sure that in a little time she will be more settled, and even happier than she has been for years, for she says what is true that she has already lived 12 years of widowhood and she feels [now, presumably] that there is nobody nearer to him than she is.[63]

For she had never ceased to love him though she could not have borne to see him in their estranged circumstances. She continued to follow his public career and to read his work, and there is a touching eye-witness account of her emotion at the first night of a dramatization of *Dombey and Son* at the Globe Theatre in 1873.[64] She seems to have harboured no resentment against Georgina, indeed Mrs Panton (daughter of Frith the painter) 'often heard Mrs Dickens say that [Georgina's] presence among "the children" was her one comfort and consolation, and that she wished people who did not know all would not talk'.[65] The two sisters were able to meet again after Dickens's death and Georgina's letters about Catherine's painful final illness in 1879 are full of affectionate solicitude although earlier she seems to have been inclined to keep up Dickens's 1858 line about her sister: when Sydney Dickens died at sea in 1872 she wrote to her American friend, Mrs Fields, that Catherine had felt the shock of his death 'as much as she can feel anything, but she is a very curious person – unlike anyone else in the world . . . We dined with her on Saturday. She was very well, and seemed to be in very good spirits again.'[66]

When the separation became public in 1858 Harriet Martineau, pitying Catherine, had written to Henry Arthur Bright,

> No, – she [Catherine] does not drink . . .[67] but if she does not now take to the bottle or to suicide, she will show that she has some strength.[68]

In fact, Catherine behaved with both dignity and spirit in her post-separation life. She continued to go into society and to maintain established friendships with many eminent people and members of 'the Dickens circle' such as John Leech (as we have noted, Bigelow met her at a dinner-party at Thackeray's in 1860 and, a few months earlier, Millais had dined with her and a select party at Leech's: she 'desired her best remembrances to you,' he wrote to his wife, and 'hopes you will call and bring the children to see her').[69] She remained a keen theatregoer, one passion at least that she had fully shared with Dickens.[70] And she kept in close touch with all her children,[71] except for Mamie whose life seems to have been so wholly consecrated to Dickens. About a month after Dickens's death Mrs Shirley Brooks, wife of Mark Lemon's successor as Editor of *Punch*, called on Catherine and described her, according to Brooks's diary,

> as looking well, being calm, and speaking of matters with a certain becoming dignity. Is resolved not to allow Forster, or any other biographer, to allege that she did not make D. a happy husband, having letters after the birth of her ninth child in which D. writes like a lover. Her eldest daughter visited her and declared that the separation between *them* had resulted solely from her, Mary's, own self-will. Miss H. [i.e. Georgina] has also visited her – I will not write about this, but the affair is to the honour of Mrs D.'s heart.[72]

After 1870, of course, Catherine was able to revisit her former home, Gad's Hill, spending several Christmases there with Charley Dickens and his family, and enjoying her grandchildren.[73] She refrained from public comment on Forster's *Life of Dickens* but authorized Charley to put on record after her death, if a suitable occasion should arise, one very important fact. This was that Dickens had shared with her, 'in strict confidence', the autobiographical fragment narrating his childhood sufferings which was later printed by Forster. Readers of Forster's volume would certainly derive from it the impression that Forster alone was Dickens's confidant in this matter and that Catherine had been admitted to no such intimacy. 'I have never', Forster quotes Dickens as writing, 'until I now impart it to this paper, in any burst of confidence with any one, my own wife not excepted, raised the curtain I then dropped, thank God.' Writing an introduction to a Macmillan reprint of *Copperfield* in 1892 gave Charley an appropriate opportunity to carry out his mother's wishes:

> I have my mother's authority for saying . . . that the story was eventually read to her . . . by my father, who at the time intimated his intention of publishing it by and by as a portion of his autobiography. From this purpose she endeavoured to dissuade him: on the ground that he had

spoken with undue harshness of his father, and, especially of his mother: and with so much success that he eventually decided that he would be satisfied with working it into *David Copperfield*, and would give up the idea of publishing it as it stood . . . That Mr Forster did not know what had passed between my father and mother as to this matter I think most probable. That he did not take any steps to find out I know to be a fact.

There seems no reason to doubt the truth of this. One could argue that Catherine brooded on the past during the twenty years she lived after the separation, and nursed a pathetic desire to convince the world post-humously that she and Dickens had been closer and happier during their married life than all the painful publicity of 1858 had indicated (the almost total ignoring of her in Forster's biography must have been hard to bear). She would naturally, the argument might run, want to assert her importance in Dickens's life, including his artistic life, through such information as this, given to her eldest son and intended for eventual publication. In so doing, she could well exaggerate or misrepresent certain matters, more out of wishful thinking than out of conscious distortion of the truth. Everything we know about her, however, suggests that she was not prone to fantasize but was, on the contrary, rather literal-minded; also, that she was a kind and compassionate woman with a strong sense of family loyalty. She would have been greatly shocked by what Dickens had written about his parents (she seems to have enjoyed a particularly affectionate relationship with her mother-in-law)[74] and would have expressed this to Dickens. It is noticeable that she does not claim to have inspired him to use the material in *Copperfield*, only to have persuaded him never to publish it as it stood. It must have been upsetting for her, then, to find Forster publishing, only two years after Dickens's death, these same harsh words written by him about his mother.

Charley thought it 'most probable' that Forster knew nothing of the husband-and-wife discussion of the autobiographical fragment. Forster, we might note, seems to have liked assuming that he was as much in Dickens's confidence as Catherine was: writing to her from Paris in June 1850, Dickens describes his social activities and then adds, 'I suppose when you compare notes with Forster he will tell you that he knows all this – but he don't . . .'. It seems clear from letters that Dickens and Catherine enjoyed laughing together at Forster's pompous eccentricities and self-importance: 'I never heard him *half so loud* (!)' Dickens writes to her on one occasion, and in an 1856 letter to Georgina we see Dickens hugging himself at the prospect of comically startling Catherine – in Paris with Georgina and the children – with the news of Forster's impending marriage:

157

> Tell Catherine that I have the most prodigious, overwhelming, crushing, astounding, blinding, deafening, pulverizing, scarifying secret of which Forster is the hero, imaginable by the united efforts of the whole British population.[75]

This giggling together, however affectionately, at the man who was probably – and who certainly considered himself to be – Dickens's most intimate friend suggests that there was a higher degree of intimacy between Dickens and Catherine than is often recognized and inclines me to accept as true the latter's recollections of what took place between them regarding the autobiographical fragment.

*

Catherine died at her home in Gloucester Crescent on 21 November 1879 after a lingering and painful illness. She had been failing since sustaining a bad fall in the street on her way home from church one Sunday morning about eighteen months earlier. (The anecdote Miss Storey relates about this incident nicely illustrates that amiability and tactful kindness for which so many people praised Catherine: a passer-by who helped her to rise 'was struck by her so grateful appreciation . . . and modestly said: "I am only a working man, madam." "You could not be anything better," returned Mrs Dickens.')[76] Soon the cancer from which she was suffering declared itself and it became obvious that she was dying. Only then, apparently, did she protest against the usage she had experienced from Dickens.[77] Her younger daughter, Katey, was with her and later told Shaw,

> During every day almost of that time she spoke to me, whenever I was alone with her, of my father. All her grievances against him came out. Fortunately for myself I had heard *from his own lips* the worst she had to tell me. Of course I did what any daughter would do. I tried to soften her remembrance of him. In a way I succeeded. . . .[78]

Catherine's will is certainly not marred by any touch of the aggressive self-vindication that we saw in Dickens's. It is mainly concerned with a lovingly careful portioning-out of all her treasures among her children (it is noticeable how anxious she is for them to have photographs of each other) and is a moving document to read, remembering Dickens's bitter words of 1858, 'she is glad to be rid of [the children], and they are glad to be rid of her'. A typical passage reads as follows:

> To my daughter Katherine Perugini my turquoise snake bracelet pearl brooch and earrings The story card basket brought to me by my Charles from China The Sketch by Maclise of Charles, Mary,

Katherine and Walter when children   The case of various stuffed birds given to me by Sydney and my Tortoise shell card case   To my son Frank the gold watch and chain with locket attached which formerly belonged to Sydney   The photograph of Katherine in red velvet and gilt frame ...   To my son Alfred my silver sugar basin with lid and spoon, the small agate vase with cupids ...   To my son Edward the gold locket formerly worn by his father containing portraits of Mary and Katherine, the pair of small silver Candlesticks given to me by Sydney. . . .[79]

Much has been made of her bequest to Georgina (along with a photograph of her dead son, Walter) of 'the blue enamel snake ring given to me by the late Count D'Orsay'; it has been asserted that she was thus covertly accusing her sister of having been a snake in the grass. But this is mere 'second-best-bedding', as it were, the fashionable snake design of the ring being no more significant than that of the snake bracelet left to her daughter Katey. If we want to read things into the will, beyond the obvious, then we might pause at the bequest to her other sister, Helen Roney, of 'My favourite picture which hangs always in my bedroom of a copy of the Magdalene brought from Rome by my said son Sydney', not so much because of the legatee's identity but because of the object itself. The Magdalene was one of the great images of Sorrowing Woman for Victorian England – how often, we might think, did Catherine in her widowed bedroom find a sad comfort in contemplating this 'favourite' picture?

As she lay dying Catherine gave to Katey her collection of letters from Dickens, saying 'with great earnestness', 'Give these to the British Museum – that the world may know he loved me once'.[80] The world has generally preferred, however, to believe that the marriage was doomed from the start, that Dickens understandably soon ceased to love a wife who was (to quote the latest judgment) 'a weak and self-pitying woman who found it difficult to make the best of life, and was certainly unsuited for the strains of the part in which her marriage had cast her', a woman 'unable to enjoy motherhood', who bore 'all the vagaries of her husband's difficult temperament without sharing in his fun and good humour' and whose 'negative state of mind had done much to bring her marriage to breaking point'.[81] Physical clumsiness, domestic and maternal incompetence, social nullity, constant fretfulness and general dullness – these are the faults with which Catherine is traditionally charged but when all the available evidence about her is assembled and balanced against Dickens's excited statements of 1857/8 a very different picture emerges. There must have been considerable strength in Catherine's sweetness and gentleness and in her love for her 'uncanny genius' of a husband for her to have survived twenty years of marriage with him with the equanimity that she did. Dickens may have jested about the 'sudden outbursts of causeless rage and demoniacal gloom'[82] to which he was prone when in the throes of writing but they cannot have been such a joke for his wife.

Moreover, Catherine had to cope with being the wife of a great celebrity who, although he might often be withdrawn and abstracted in his home ('I very often sit a long time without saying anything at all – when I am thinking, or when I am thinking I am thinking – and . . . [Catherine] is well used to it'),[83] was nevertheless extremely gregarious and hospitable, delighting in organizing large social events. 'You will form some idea of the number of people who were continually in the house [during preparations for some amateur theatricals in January 1857]', wrote Charley Dickens,

> when I tell you that the butcher called in person on my mother one day, to point out that he was supplying such an abnormal quantity of joints that he thought it his duty to mention it to her, in order to be sure that there was no mistake.[84]

If Catherine herself, or her housekeeping, had borne much resemblance to Dora after her marriage to David Copperfield, as is often alleged by modern biographers,[85] it is certain that the Dickenses' marriage would have collapsed long before it actually did. All the evidence points not to a Dora-like ineptitude on Catherine's part (imagine Dora compiling a cookery-book instead of teaching her little dog to balance on one) but to a most un-David-like domestic masterfulness on Dickens's. What he wanted from his wife was not the depriving him of the joys of shopping, interior decoration, furniture arrangement, etc., but co-operation in creating a certain kind of home atmosphere, one in which, as Forster points out, there would be 'an absolute reliance on him for everything'. At the same time he required the sort of protection from unwelcome social pressures that Catherine clearly provided, notably in America but also elsewhere (he writes to Maclise from Italy in 1845, 'I very much resort to my old habit of bolting from callers, and leaving their reception to Kate')[86] and the maintenance of a tender slave demeanour on the domestic hearth. Harriet Martineau commented scornfully on all this after the failure of the marriage:

> I always . . . distrust such an amount of *sentimentality,* combined with self-love in the husband, as has always existed in the D. household. Moreover, amidst it all, he openly & thoroughly regarded his wife as '*his* woman' . . . chose her to dress in black velvet, & sit at her embroidery, at leisure *for him* , & so on.[87]

160

But Miss Martineau, like everyone else, had had a very different impression a few years earlier. In her autobiography, written in 1855 when she thought she was dying, she had said of Dickens: 'He is a virtuous and happy family man, in the first place. His glowing and generous heart is kept steady by the best domestic influences'.[88] This sounds as though she saw Catherine as an Agnes figure rather than a Dora one and I feel pretty sure that this is how most people who met the Dickenses and who speculated on possible autobiographical elements in *Copperfield* would have interpreted Agnes. Indeed, Hans Christian Andersen 'had frequently heard it remarked that Agnes in *David Copperfield* was a likeness of Mrs Dickens' before his 1857 visit to Gad's Hill when Dickens, preoccupied with raising money for Douglas Jerrold's widow and children, largely left the entertaining of his somewhat awkward guest to Catherine. Andersen found that 'no other character in all [Dickens's] writings resembles her so much for her kindness and amiability as this very Agnes'. He

> found in Mrs Dickens a calm, feminine, and retiring nature, but when she spoke, her large gentle eyes assumed a peculiar brilliancy, a good-humoured smile played around her mouth and in the sound of her voice was something so attractive, that, since the meeting M. Andersen has always imagined Agnes to himself as possessed of these attributes.[89]

Agnes in her more spiritual aspect as David's 'good angel', ever pointing upward, probably relates, as suggested earlier, more to the dead Mary Hogarth than to any living original among Dickens's womenfolk; but in her personality and *physical* presence (in so far as she can be said to have one), in her sweet patience, gentleness, calmness and amiability, it seems to me distinctly arguable that she is indeed a husbandly tribute to Catherine, just as Andersen and others supposed. And this may partly account for her nullity as a character when compared with Dora, based on Maria whom Dickens had loved not with a steady and grateful affection but with a raging passion, or even compared with Little Em'ly as a child, probably based on the golden-haired little Lucy Stroughill of Dickens's childhood adoration. David himself is aware of a distinction: 'I love little Em'ly, and I don't love Agnes – no, not at all in that way – but I feel there are goodness, peace and truth, wherever Agnes is'. 'Goodness, peace and truth', however, are not what inspire Dickens's greatest artistry. All his 'fancy, romance, energy, passion, aspiration and determination', he told Maria in 1855, he had never separated, and never could separate, from one 'hard-hearted little woman – you'. Philip Collins has observed that this implicitly defines how little impact, at any

161

deep emotional level, Catherine had had on him, but we must make a distinction here between the artist and the man, I think. As a great Romantic artist Dickens needed to have experienced people who caused him to suffer agonies and ecstasies; as a man inside whom still shivered a hungry, homeless child, 'forsaken and neglected', he needed the uncritical love and admiration, the secure domesticity, that a model Victorian wife was supposed to give her husband, those 'home comforts and fireside virtues' for which England was, according to Mrs Sarah Ellis, author of *The Women of England* , 'so justly celebrated'. All this Catherine seems, both by training and nature, to have been well able to provide – quite unlike David's 'child-wife' who could provide only uncritical love and admiration.

For upwards of seventeen years Catherine Dickens satisfied a very important part of her genius-husband's nature, played a vital role in his domestic and social existence, and participated fully in many of the enjoyments of his life. Although the very things that made her such a good wife for him may have militated against her being a source of inspiration for his greatest artistic achievements, she deserves better of Dickens scholarship than to be dismissed as a colourless and futile nonentity, a mere drag on his triumphal chariot.

8
Georgina

'. . . let his home be made more comfortable, let his peculiarities of habit and temper be studiously consulted, and social and familiar gratifications provided for his daily use; and . . . he will be sure to regard the source from whence his comforts flow with extreme complacency, and not unfrequently with affection . . .'

Mrs Ellis, *The Women of England*, ch. 8 (advice to sisters keeping house for their brothers)

'The best and truest friend man ever had.' Richly did Dickens's sister-in-law, Georgina Hogarth, deserve this tribute in his will. For nearly thirty years she had devoted herself to him and his family, having become a permanent member of the household when she was only fifteen. Dickens and Catherine, when they returned from America in 1842, may have been impressed by the affectionate concern she had shown for their temporarily orphaned children;[1] or they may have been moved by memories of Mary and felt that Georgina might now fill that still-aching gap in their family circle. Whatever the reason for her establishment in the Dickens home, once she was there she seems to have fulfilled many functions: she was a companion for Catherine and sometimes also deputized for her on social occasions when Catherine was not well enough to appear; she was a companion, too, for Dickens, being one of the few people who could keep up with his pace on his formidable daily walks. Above all, she assisted with the children, playing with them and helping with their nursery education. When the marriage at last broke down (she had tried hard, as we shall see, to keep it going), she elected to stay loyal to Dickens. Her mother's vehement dissuasions notwithstanding, she remained in his home when her sister left it, outfacing scandal. For the last twelve years of Dickens's life Georgina ran his household at Gad's Hill (nominally in conjunction with his elder daughter, Mary, or 'Mamie' as she was always called in the family, but we may suspect that it was Georgina who kept everything running whilst

Mamie perfected her flower arrangements for the dining-table and visited her county friends). She became practically and emotionally indispensable to him. After his death – his last conscious breath was drawn in her arms – Georgina lived on for over forty 'widowed' years, her existence deriving its point and purpose from her long, intimate association with the great man. She fretted over the depressing lives of his unsatisfactory children, consoling herself by drawing closer to the one indubitable success among them, the sixth son, Henry Fielding Dickens; and she worked to keep 'the Beloved Memory' properly venerated and untarnished before the world. The story of these later years has been fully and sympathetically told by Professor Adrian in his *Georgina Hogarth and the Dickens Circle* and need not be retold here. I am concerned with Dickens's attitude towards Georgina, rather than Georgina herself, and also what (if anything) Dickens the artist made out of his feelings for her.

At first he seems to have treated his petite sister-in-law, although he was only fifteen years older than she, like a favourite young daughter, his 'little Pet'.[2] Stimulated by the exciting new people she was meeting – people like the famous novelist, Bulwer Lytton, who must have seemed to her like some romantic wizard[3] – and by the wonderful new places she was seeing, in Italy and elsewhere, young Georgina was full of high spirits. One evening, for example, she made Dickens 'weak with laughter' by mimicking a comic family acquaintance 'in a manner quite inconceivable'. She had to learn discretion, however; when she made fun of a tiresome relative of Dickens's beloved (and very touchy) friend, Macready, she found herself sharply rebuked, along with Catherine, by Dickens for 'glaringly foolish and unnecessary silliness'. Not that his anger lasted long. Within a month or so we find him writing anxiously to Catherine about some plans which would involve leaving Georgina on her own with the children for a couple of weeks in the Dickenses' Genoese palazzo. Will that be all right? he asks Catherine. 'For I love her too dearly, to think of any project, which would involve her being uncomfortable for that space of time'.[4]

It was her relationship to Catherine, however, rather than any 'daughterly' relationship to himself that was, I believe, most deeply important to Dickens during these years. All his fiction shows that, for him, an essential quality of true 'womanliness' is the capacity to form close, emotional, 'sisterly' relationships with other women. Nearly every major Dickens heroine has a beloved sister-figure in her life sooner or later. But in his own home there had been no one to fulfil this role for Catherine since Mary's death five years before. Now Georgina, happily, was the right age to do so and she seemed, moreover, uniquely fitted to take Mary's place. As we have seen, Dickens perceived so strong a resemblance between her 'mental features' and Mary's that it brought 'the old time' back again 'at some seasons'.[5] The joyous days of Furnival's Inn seemed revived by her presence and in his letters Dickens loved to make exuberant references to Georgina and Catherine together — 'my two Venuses', 'my pair of petticoats', 'my woman-kind', and so on.

As the years passed, however, Dickens felt twinges of uneasiness about the continued spinsterhood of 'his Miss Hogarth'.[6] She still graced his home, 'a lively young damsel of twenty or twenty-four, rather good-looking'[7] and showed no signs of choosing a husband. She 'is not yet married', Dickens wrote to one of his Swiss friends in 1852, 'and not in the least likely to be. She seems unaccountably hard to please.'[8] One suitor favoured by Dickens was the painter Augustus Egg with whom he and Collins went on an Italian jaunt in the autumn of 1853. Dickens was intensely home-conscious on this tour, as is shown by his several long affectionate letters to Catherine, and no doubt reflected much on the little figure of Georgina who contributed so much to making his 'commodious family mansion look natural and home-like'.[9] Should she not really have a home of her own? He made a joke of the subject in a letter to Catherine: 'A general sentiment expressed this morning, that Georgina ought to be married. Perhaps you'll mention it to her! — .'[10] And in a letter to Georgina herself he contrives to introduce some rather artless praise of Egg, 'an excellent fellow and full of good qualities . . . He is not above the average, intellectually; but I believe he is, in a good and honourable nature.'[11] On the same day he wrote to Miss Coutts about the marriage that might have been:

> It would have been a good thing for her, as he is an excellent fellow, and is well off, over and above his professional reputation which stands high. But she said No, though they are very good friends. I took no other part in the matter than urging her to be quite sure that she knew her own mind.
>
> He is very far her inferior intellectually; but five men would be out of six, for she has one of the most remarkable capacities I have ever known. Not to mention her being one of the most amiable and affectionate of girls. Whether it is, or is not a pity that she is all she is to me and mine instead of brightening up a good little man's house where she would still have the artist kind of life she is used to, about her, is a knotty point I never can settle to my satisfaction. And I have been trying to untwist it in my mind on the road here, until it will persist in ravelling itself out on this paper.[12]

This letter to Miss Coutts was not the first time he had tried to ravel out this 'knotty point' on paper. In the great novel he had just completed,

Bleak House, he had depicted a young heroine, Esther Summerson, whose character, behaviour and situation resembled in many ways the character, behaviour and situation of Georgina; whose very conception had perhaps been largely inspired by her. Esther is presented as a modest, sensible, cheerful, attractive young woman with a great aptitude for housekeeping and a passionate desire to devote herself lovingly to the service of others.[13] She is taken into the family of the benevolent old bachelor, Mr Jarndyce, whom she comes to venerate as almost a saint, and becomes his 'little housekeeper' and the loving companion of his two young wards, Richard and Ada. She forms a bond of intense sisterly affection with Ada, her 'darling', and in her devotion to Jarndyce and Ada hardly allows herself to become conscious of the possibility that she may be loved by someone outside the family circle, someone to whom she herself is attracted, the young doctor, Allan Woodcourt. When, eventually, Jarndyce asks her, in the gentlest and most considerate way, if she could bring herself to marry him and become the mistress of Bleak House, she is both exalted and yet also obscurely saddened, 'as if something for which there was no name, or distinct idea were indefinitely lost to me'.[14] Ceremoniously, she burns the 'dried remains' of the flowers that Woodcourt had once given her, thinking, 'It would be better not to keep them now'. Part of the ceremony is the putting of them to the sleeping Ada's lips before burning them, weeping as she does so though, she asserts, 'I could have no reason for crying'. Later, Woodcourt declares his love to her and she has to tell him that she is not free to entertain it. After speaking of the 'pride and joy' she will always have in having been loved by him she says,

> From my childhood I have been . . . the object of the untiring goodness of the best of human beings; to whom I am so bound by every tie of attachment, gratitude, and love, that nothing I could do in the compass of a life could express the feelings of a single day.[15]

She can, she tells him, conceive of no higher or happier destiny than to devote herself to this wonderful man and her 'first wild thought' (of passionate regret that Woodcourt has proposed to her too late) dies away. Though she is blinded by tears as she stands at the dark window, watching the street after he has left her, the tears, she asserts to us, her readers, were ones of joy and exaltation, not of 'regret and sorrow'.

Jarndyce is not easy in his mind about her, however. Becoming gradually convinced of her buried love for Woodcourt, he perceives, as he tells Woodcourt's mother, that she will sacrifice it 'to a sense of duty and affection, and will sacrifice it so completely, so entirely, so religiously, that you should never suspect it, though you watched her night and day'. Like some benign deity, therefore, he arranges a happy dénouement. He takes Esther to inspect the house he has bought, in a remote Yorkshire town, for Allan Woodcourt. Then, angelically transfigured by the setting sun, he explains to her that *this* is the Bleak House she is to become mistress of and that Woodcourt, not he, is to be her husband. Esther reports for us the speech in which Jarndyce presents her to her lover:

> 'Allan', said my guardian, 'take from me a willing gift, the best wife that ever man had . . . Take with her the little home she brings you. You know what she will make it, Allan; you know what she has made its namesake. Let me share its felicity sometimes, and what do I sacrifice? Nothing, nothing.'[16]

The whole affair seems very odd and strained and readers who are made uncomfortable by it are surely right in such a response. Dickens's personal preoccupations can, I believe, here be seen warping his art into some peculiar shapes. Esther is damaged as a character because she is ultimately denied the freedom to choose whom she will marry; she seems to be entirely manipulated, along with her lover, by the masterfully paternal figure of Mr Jarndyce. There is absolutely no reason why Dickens could not have shown Jarndyce perceiving the growing mutual love of Esther and Woodcourt and encouraging it by all the means in his power. Why introduce the crisis of his improbable offer of marriage to Esther? Is this not an attempt to dramatize what Dickens felt was now happening in Georgina's life? She was twenty-five years old and had rejected at least one very eligible suitor; unless she married soon she would be seen as having embraced a spinsterhood dedicated to Dickens for life. In his story Dickens can present this dedication as a consciously made decision at a particular moment by the dramatic device of having Jarndyce propose marriage to her. This is not to suggest that Dickens himself had any desire to marry Georgina – there is not the slightest evidence that his feelings towards her were anything but fatherly or brotherly – but by arranging the plot in this way he can show not only the heroine's willing self-sacrifice but also, more importantly, he can intervene to save her from her own noble resolution. He can, in the person of Jarndyce, who plots, like the novelist, alone, give her what he knows will be better for her, a 'good little man' whose home she can 'brighten'. Jarndyce will 'sacrifice nothing' of Esther's devotion to him in giving her to Woodcourt because Woodcourt fully shares Esther's feelings of veneration towards him and, evidently, Jarndyce will be more than welcome to visit the new Bleak House as often and for as long as he likes whenever he feels the lack of Esther's incense. So, one imagines, might Dickens have envisaged his visits to Ivy Cottage, Eastbourne, after Egg, its 'good little' owner and a true Dickens devotee, should have made Georgina mistress of it.

What, one wonders, did Georgina privately think of the way in which Mr Jarndyce settled Esther's fate and did she at all connect it in her mind with Dickens's vigorous praise to her of Egg, her rejected suitor, in that letter written only a few months later? All we can say is that, whether consciously or unconsciously, she firmly rejected an Esther-ending for herself and continued to make herself useful to Dickens and his family as she had been doing for a decade already. And as Dickens's relations with the Hogarths, especially with his mother-in-law, became more strained she inevitably became more distanced from her own family. Dickens evidently felt quite free to vent to her his exasperation with Mrs Hogarth ('I never in my days beheld anything like your mother's letter, for the desperation of its imbecility')[17] during one of the Hogarths' recurrent financial crises which he was wearily helping to sort out. Nor, after the autumn of 1853, do we find him expressing any more uneasiness about Georgina's unmarried state. He can even permit himself, in his next major novel, *Little Dorrit*, to let a comic light fall on the sacred theme of sisterly/daughterly self-sacrifice. When Little Dorrit gently refuses the courtship of 'good little' John Chivery his mother, bewailing the fact to Arthur Clennam, represents her as having said,

> No, John, I cannot have you, I cannot have any husband, it is not my intentions ever to become a wife, it is my intentions to be always a sacrifice, farewell, find another worthy of you and forget me![18]

Little Dorrit, we should note, may be another Georgina-like heroine but the personal preoccupations which lie behind the conception of her character and help to shape her story go much further back in Dickens's life, to a time well before Georgina entered it.[19] Her resemblance to Georgina is not significant for Dickens's plot in the way that Esther Summerson's is.

*

So Georgina continued as a member of the Dickens household. As to the role she played in it, modern scholars have perhaps tended to credit too unreservedly the assertions made by Dickens in 1858 and later about her compensating for Catherine's alleged maternal deficiencies ('she has', he told Macready in 1862, 'supplied an empty place and an ever widening gap, since the girls were mere dolls').[20] As we have seen, there is scant evidence to back up these assertions and there may well, in any case, have been a deep-seated psychological reason for Dickens's wanting to see Catherine as a failed mother whatever the facts of the situation. Nor is there any real evidence, before 1856 at least,[21] to support the view that Georgina took over all housekeeping and family management duties from an increasingly supine and incompetent Catherine. 'She was useful to my mother, of course,' Kate Perugini is reported as having once said, 'but that was all. My poor, poor mother.'[22] Mrs Perugini's expression of pity for her mother perhaps related to the really formidable task that housekeeping and family management must have presented to Catherine and, clearly, there was every opportunity for Georgina to make herself useful, to earn her keep, as it were. She would have had to be a very extraordinary sort of young woman to have lived in such a busy house and such a teeming family *without* helping her sister; and what Dickens would have thought of such behaviour is sufficiently indicated by his description (all the more acid in that it is spoken so innocently by Traddles) of Sophy Crewler's idle, selfish sisters in *David Copperfield*. [23]

What, therefore, was entirely natural and appropriate behaviour on Georgina's part became, it seems, increasingly inflated in Dickens's eyes, as his feelings towards Catherine changed, into a splendid example of domestic heroism, and he began to attribute to Georgina the very preservation of his home and family. Referring to his children in the 'Violated Letter' he says:

> I do not know – I cannot by any stretch of fancy imagine – what would have become of them but for this aunt, who has grown up with them, to whom they are devoted, and who has sacrificed the best part of her youth and life to them.[24]

Against this we should set Catherine's aunt's assessment of Georgina's role in the Dickens household:

> While during the 22 or 23 years of her married life, Catharine [*sic*] was having her family fast, ten children . . . and frequently made slow and tedious recoveries, reducing her bodily strength, was it not natural that she should lean upon the assistance of a sister in the care of her children; nor was [Catherine] at all insensible to her services. But again, ought it not to be felt a natural duty for that sister living under her roof, sharing all the indulgences which she herself had, all her wants liberally supplied, etc., to give in her turn her time and attention to lighten her sister's domestic duties when she herself was laid aside and unable to attend to them. All that Georgina did was to teach the little boys to read and write until they went to school at the age of seven; in turn at that age the girls

always had a daily governess. Catharine, when well, had no light task to manage the household affairs of an establishment where constant company was kept, to receive the many guests her husband's popularity brought to the house, to travel and visit about with him. Georgina made herself occasionally useful, I believe, as a sort of amanuensis to Dickens,[25] and this was all very right and creditable (within proper bounds) but in no way ought to have eclipsed the more sacred claims of a wife in her husband's esteem and affection; but he has proved a spoiled child of fortune, dazzled by his popularity, and given up to selfish egotism.[26]

This account is obviously biased against Dickens but nevertheless reads, in all its indignant detail, more convincingly than the dramatic vehemence of Dickens's own statements. But we may well credit his assertion (also in the 'Violated Letter') that Georgina had 'remonstrated, reasoned, suffered and toiled, again and again to prevent a separation between Mrs Dickens and me'.[27] For Georgina had nothing to gain by such a separation which was bound to pose her with a terrible dilemma. If she were to stay with her adored brother-in-law and to continue sharing in his glamorous and exciting existence she would bitterly offend her own family and become also a target for public scandal. If, on the other hand, she were to go off with her sister she would alienate the glittering hero of her life and abandon her three youngest nephews (aged eleven, nine and six in 1858) just when they would be needing her most. Moreover, she would be launching herself into a financially very uncertain future, one in which she might well have to turn governess to keep herself afloat. It is hardly surprising that, for her own sake as much as for the rest of the family's, she should have 'suffered and toiled' to prevent the breach happening. At last, however, she became *'perfectly convinced'*, as she wrote to Maria Winter (*née* Beadnell), that the arrangement of Catherine's going away would be best for all concerned: 'I worked hard to prevent it as long as I saw any possibility, but lately I have come to the conviction that there was no other way out of the domestic misery of this house'. By the time she wrote this letter to Maria (perhaps one of several that she wrote at this time to closer friends of the family, to help Dickens in getting the news to them before it became public knowledge) she had made up her mind to stay with him, and with the children, and clearly felt that the blame for the breakdown of the marriage should be laid more at Catherine's door than at Dickens's, maintaining, as we shall see, that 'a man of genius ought not to be judged with the common herd of men'. In the letter to Maria she says of Catherine:

Unhappily . . . by some constitutional misfortune & incapacity, my sister

always from their infancy, threw her children upon other people, consequently as they grew up, there was not the usual strong tie between them
and her – in short, for many years, although we have put a good face
upon it, we have been very miserable at home.[28]

As I have argued in the previous chapter, it is hard to reconcile such
allegations as these about Catherine's maternal shortcomings with other
evidence concerning Catherine's attitude to her children and theirs to her.
Still, while Georgina cannot be regarded as an unprejudiced witness, due
weight should be given to her testimony nevertheless.

Dickens's feelings of love, gratitude and admiration towards Georgina must have soared to new heights during the agonies of 1858. She
provided vital domestic continuity for him in the family upheavals and,
by the very fact of staying in his house, seemed strongly to witness to his
being the one who was in the right, the one who should most be sym-
pathized with, in the breakdown of the marriage. How maddened he
must have been, therefore, to find that all this precious loyalty was being
vilely misinterpreted by the gossips such as those whom Thackeray encountered when going into the Garrick Club and who told him that
Dickens was separating from his wife 'on account of an intrigue with his
sister in law'.[29] This story, Thackeray thought, had 'not got to Dickens's
ears' but apparently it had in fact done so, and it seems to have been his
belief that Mrs Hogarth and her youngest daughter were responsible. His
solicitor, Frederic Ouvry, spurred on by a letter from Dickens, quickly
obtained a written denial of the scandal from Mr Hogarth whose
statement ended:

> It is of course a matter of grief to us that after the unfortunate differences
> which have arisen between my daughter Mrs Chas. Dickens and her
> husband, my daughter Georgiana [*sic*] should remain with his family but
> while we regret what we regard as a mistaken sense of duty we have never
> for one instant imputed to her any improper motive for so doing.

This was not enough for Dickens, however, and, as we have seen, he
insisted on a statement signed by Mrs Hogarth and Helen, one which
repudiated in general terms *all* the rumours flying around (which would
include the ones about Ellen Ternan as well as the ones about Georgina):
'with reference to the disgusting and horrible nature of that charge [i.e.,
the one of impropriety with Georgina]', Ouvry wrote to Hogarth, 'I
cannot think it desirable that it should be distinctly written down even for
the purpose of denial'.[30]

Whatever she may have been saying about Ellen Ternan, it is scarcely
credible that Mrs Hogarth would have spread such rumours about her

own daughter. And if she had thought that there was something going on between Dickens and Georgina surely we should have found some hint of this in her sister Miss Thomson's letter to Mrs Stark from which I quoted earlier. Miss Thomson is evidently reporting all she has heard from Mrs Hogarth about the separation. She is highly critical of Georgina but the worst she says of her is this:

> Georgina is an enthusiast, and worships [Dickens] as a man of genius, and has quarrelled with all her relatives because they dared to find fault with him, saying, 'a man of genius ought not to be judged with the common herd of men'. She must bitterly repent, when she recovers from her delusion, her folly; her vanity is no doubt flattered by his praise, but she has disappointed us all, as we thought her affectionate and disinterested.

Had Miss Thomson thought that there was any question of something worse than deluded vanity on Georgina's part she would, one feels, have at least hinted at the matter in writing a full account of the separation – as seen from the Hogarths' angle – to an intimate family friend.

But whether or not Mrs Hogarth's loose talk was in fact the source of the scandalous gossip about Dickens and Georgina, the point to note here is that Dickens *believed* it to have been so. 'The question', he wrote to Macready on 7 June,

> was not I myself; but others. Foremost among them – of all people in the world – Georgina! Mrs Dickens's weakness, and her mother's and her youngest sister's wickedness, drifted to that, without seeing what they would strike against – though I warned them in the strongest terms.[31]

Given his obsession with bad mothers, his conviction that Georgina was being vilely traduced by her own mother must have given him a very deep and special bond of sympathy with her at this time.

The evil rumours certainly spread far afield. In October 1858 Dickens received, as we have seen, a letter telling him that Colin Rae Brown, the editor of one of Glasgow's newspapers, was going about asserting that 'Mr Dickens's sister in law had three children by him'.[32] Dickens had ignored the scurrilous innuendoes of the cheap London press[33] but felt he could not overlook this incident and prepared to prosecute Brown (it was perhaps in connection with this that a doctor's certificate of virginity may have been obtained for Georgina)[34] and desisted only when he received from Brown a vigorous and circumstantial denial that he had said what had been attributed to him.

Though this kind of brutal scandalmongering gradually died down Georgina still had her crosses to bear — an awareness, for example, of the bitter feelings with which her own family regarded her. Catherine was later reported as having frequently said that she was comforted by Georgina's remaining among the children but, initially at least, she seems to have felt much resentment, even to the extent of blaming her sister for the marriage breakdown. Thackeray talked with her in February 1859 and evidently came away with the impression that it was Georgina not Ellen who had been the cause of the trouble. He reported to his mother:

> The row appears to be [about] not the actress, but the sister in law — nothing against Miss H — except that she is the cleverer & better woman of the two, has got the affections of the children & the father.[35]

No doubt it was better to be thought of in this light rather than as incestuous but it cannot have been very comfortable for Georgina all the same. Was it at her prompting, perhaps, that, many years later, Kate Perugini wrote, when depositing in the British Museum Dickens's letters to her mother, 'As it has been erroneously suggested, I believe, that . . . Miss Georgina Hogarth, was in some way responsible for [the] separation, I take the present opportunity of entirely exonerating my aunt from any blame in the matter'?[36]

Even to her well-wishers, however, Georgina's position as Dickens's beloved domestic companion, unofficial hostess of Gad's Hill, was an embarrassing one. Visitors found her gracious and agreeable: 'a really delightful person' wrote one in 1862, 'plain, unassuming, totally unaffected and of singularly pleasant and easy manner'.[37] But they did not know how to talk about her in the outside world. On one occasion in 1870 Dickens's actor friend, Fechter, was chatting to Longfellow in Boston, deploring Dickens's paternal woes: 'all his fame goes for nothing since he has not the one thing. He is very unhappy in his children.' Annie Fields, the wife of Dickens's American publisher and an ardent devotee of the novelist's, recorded the conversation in her journal and thought back to her own visit to Gad's Hill the previous year and her impressions of Georgina:

> Poor Miss Hogarth spends her life hoping to comfort and care for him. I never felt more keenly her anomalous and unnatural position in the household. Not one mentioned her name. They could not dare, I suppose (lest they might do her wrong).

A few months later, after Dickens's death, Mrs Fields received a letter in which Georgina herself reflected on her own past history. 'My life has been a curious one', she wrote, ' – and not the ideal of a happy woman's existence. And I have often felt it hard – and wondered whether it was *all* a mistake – and a *waste*!' Dickens's death had put a total stop to such doubts, however: '*Now* I feel that with all its difficulties and drawbacks, I would not change it – I would not have it altered for the brightest and most prosperous existence any woman could have had'.[38]

What Georgina was rejoicing in was the thought that for over a dozen years she had been a great and beloved genius's chief sustainer in his fiercely lived life. No one else could have served Dickens as she had done. 'No man', his daughter Mary wrote of him, 'was so inclined naturally to derive his happiness from home affairs',[39] and Gad's Hill Place, of which he was so proud and which Georgina managed so efficiently for him, was a very special home for it was the fulfilment of a dream and the reward of virtue. When he had been a 'very queer small boy' his father had indulged his passion for coming to look at the house and had thrilled him by saying, 'If you were to be very persevering and were to work hard, you might some day come to live in it'. It was not simply his home that Georgina maintained for him but his House Beautiful, the goal of his earthly pilgrimage.

Since Mary Dickens, who was nominally the châtelaine of Gad's Hill, seems often to have been away, enjoying the social whirl of London[40] or visiting her county friends in Hampshire (where she even took to canvassing for the Tories – 'Imagine my feelings as a Radical parent!' Dickens wrote), it was Georgina who regularly coped with everything, from the tribe of troublesome relatives that swarmed after Dickens all his life to the stream of distinguished visitors who came to stay at his country house. She dealt with all the household bills, as far as we can tell from surviving letters, and Mary seems only to have been given financial instructions when Dickens had forgotten to give them in a previous communication to Georgina. Well used as she was to Dickens's ways, Georgina was able to anticipate what he would want done, even to the smallest domestic detail. When, in early 1861, the family was about to occupy a temporarily rented London house he wrote to her:

> Some envelope-case &c should be brought, I think, for the library table in the back dining-room. Perhaps you have thought of this, as you think of everything.[41]

But it was not only in practical matters that Georgina gave Dickens such uniquely invaluable service. She gave him a domestic companionship that was both comforting and stimulating[42] (as we have seen, he had a very high regard for her mental capacities); he could share with her as with no one else his family worries, especially those about his children; and her ardent sympathy with his work must have constantly been a strong source of encouragement and happiness. Condemning modern novels as 'morbid, unhealthy, and uninteresting', Georgina told a London news-paper reporter in 1909, 'I think it should be the purpose of the novel to touch one's better nature, and to leave us better and morally healthier for the reading of it. . . . and that is what the books of Dickens do in my opinion'. 'Almost invariably', she said, Dickens read to her 'in the evening what he had written during the day'.[43]

'Miss Hogarth, always Miss Hogarth', wrote Dickens to his Swiss friend de Cerjat in 1860, when sending all the family news, 'is the guide, philosopher, and friend of all the party . . . I doubt if she will ever marry. I don't know whether to be glad of it or sorry for it.'[44] This momentary return to the subject of Georgina's resolute spinsterhood seems very different in tone from the letter to Miss Coutts of autumn 1853 – not off-hand exactly, but far from the troubled brooding of that earlier letter. For Georgina's happiness in, and deep satisfaction with, her lot, uncon-ventional as it was, must have become abundantly clear to Dickens by 1860. He chose to attribute it chiefly to her devotion to his children just as he tends to transfer to them the intensity of his affection and gratitude towards her (compare the way he transferred to them his stirred-up 'orphan' feelings at the time of his marriage's collapse). She was, he proclaimed to the world, the ideal aunt, utterly and happily lost in her aunt-ish functions. He sketched in his Memorandum Book some time between 1855 and 1865 an idea for a character of which, says Forster, 'the most part was applicable to his sister-in-law, if the whole was not suggested by her':

> She – sacrificed to children, and sufficiently rewarded. From a child herself, always 'the children' (of somebody else) to engross her. And so it comes to pass that she is never married; never herself has a child; is always devoted 'to the children' (of somebody else): and they love her; and she has always youth dependent on her till her death – and dies quite happily.[45]

It is interesting to speculate on how Dickens might have depicted that 'somebody else' had he written this character's story, and what the heroine's relationship (if any) to that 'somebody else' might have been. A clue is given us by that word 'sacrificed' perhaps. Something or someone would have been responsible for denying the heroine the fulfilment of normal marital and maternal love so that she becomes a loving aunt instead. This was standard aunt-mythology in Victorian England (and no doubt actually true in thousands and thousands of cases) as we can see from the most famous aunt in Dickens's own fiction, Betsey Trotwood,[46] and from an article celebrating aunts by Andrew Halliday that Dickens published in his magazine, *All The Year Round,* on 19 August 1865.[47] The writer muses on aunts as 'the fairy good godmothers of society, the supplementary mothers who are often more kind and indulgent to the children, than their parents are'. Imagining many of them as women 'passed over in life', who have 'toiled hard' and 'suffered much', never tasting 'the joys of maternity', he marvels that 'the fire of love should not have been quenched in their lonely hearts'. In fact, however, he argues, celibacy is likely to make that fire burn brighter and even to preserve women from downright cold-heartedness: ' . . . women are never *naturally* vain, heartless, and unloving. They are made so.' And often made so, he seems to suggest, by marriage – a woman 'is apt to think that she has fulfilled her mission, so far as her heart is concerned, when she drives away from the church door'. He ends with a personal reminiscence of his own great-aunt whose 'sailor-boy' lover was lost at sea when she was only seventeen:

> 'And what did you do, aunty,' I said, 'when you heard the news?'
> 'What did I do, laddie? I criet and criet until my heart was dry and my een were sair. I think I should ha' deet if your mother hadna' come; but when she came I took up wi' her. She had bonny black een just like my laddie's, and I loved her and nursed her for his sake. And when they had ower mony o' them at hame I took her to live with me, and she was my lassie until your father married her. And then I was lonely again until your father had ower mony o' them, when I took your sister, and now I've got you . . .

But Georgina did not fit into this quasi-tragic conception of aunt-hood. She had rejected at least one eligible suitor; she had lost no lover by sudden death; quite freely had she chosen the lot of an 'old maid'. Nor had she done so because she nourished a secret hopeless passion for the man who had become her brother-in-law when she was still a child.[48] Her utter freedom from any touch of jealousy regarding such old-established *amitiés amoureuses* as Dickens's with Mary Boyle or such new ones as those with Annie Fields or Ellen Ternan (in the latter case perhaps more than *amitié*) is proof enough of this if proof is needed. Far from being jealous, she welcomed both Annie and Ellen to Gad's Hill and kept up a warm friendship with them both long after Dickens's death. And there is some evidence that she was responsible for summoning Ellen to the dying Dickens's side although jealousy or hidden resentment (not to mention prudence) could have found plenty of plausible and respectable reasons at such a time for keeping away the younger woman he had loved so deeply.[49] It was not Dickens the dream-lover, the husband-in-fantasy, that Georgina devoted herself to but the beloved brother-in-law who had given meaning, colour and excitement to her life and who was also a great genius, whose work she saw as a benefit to the whole human race.

This was Georgina's chosen role and in playing it she was 'sufficiently rewarded'. She had every reason to be grateful to Dickens not only for all the drama and interest he had brought into her life but also for the very comfortable existence he had provided for her since she was in her teens; and she certainly felt great affection and concern for the children she had helped to bring up (she was, her niece Mary claimed, 'the aunt *par excellence'*).[50] And after 1870 her conviction of Dickens's great genius and her Agnes-like veneration for the noble work he had done for humanity provided further motivation for her dedication of the rest of her long life (she lived until 1916) to 'the Beloved Memory'.

When we consider her role in Dickens's art, as opposed to his life, however, the same paradox manifests itself as in the case of Catherine. Unlike his mother, unlike his sister Fanny, unlike Maria Beadnell and unlike her own sister Mary, Georgina had never caused him anguish and suffering as, in their very different ways, all those women had, and so she did not stir his deepest imaginative faculties. The type of domestic heroine she (in his eyes) represented was already established in his fiction with Ruth Pinch in *Martin Chuzzlewit*, written just after she had joined the Dickens household, and was further developed over the next five or six years in Harriet Carker and in Agnes Wickfield. It has been customary to see Georgina as an 'original' for Agnes and it may well be that she was responsible for a touch or two in Dickens's portrayal of Agnes's 'little housekeeper' ways. But the essential inspiration for David's 'good angel' was, as I have argued earlier, surely Mary Hogarth rather than Georgina. That Georgina herself realized this is suggested, I believe, by her vehement reaction to an innocent young Dickensian's asking her in her old age if she 'was' Agnes;[51] to her this must have been an almost sacrilegious idea, knowing what she did of Dickens's feelings about Mary. She conceded, however, that she might have served for a model for Esther and, in a certain superficial way, this is no doubt true; also, as we have seen, Dickens's concern about her probably affected the way in which he finally disposes of Esther. But all that is most interesting and vital in Dickens's conception of this character really has nothing at all to do with Georgina. The same applies to Little Dorrit, the last of the domestic heroines usually associated with her. The biographical approach to these two characters lies through Dickens's own turbulent central self and not

177

through the placid figure of his sister-in-law, obvious though that route may seem. So, if Georgina cannot be said to have enriched his art in the way that certain other women did, neither can she fairly be blamed for those blemishes in it that have sometimes been laid at her door.[52]

9

Father and Daughters

'Bella was more delightful than any other item in the festival; drawing Pa out in the gayest manner . . . and in short causing Pa to be quite enraptured with the consideration that he *was* the Pa of such a charming daughter.'

Our Mutual Friend, Book II, ch. 8

Dickens had three daughters: Mary ('Mamie') born in 1838; Catherine, born in 1839 and always called Katey by her father until he eventually adopted his sons' name for her, Kitty;[1] and Dora who, as we have seen, died in infancy in 1851. Like most fathers, perhaps, Dickens seems to have been able to remain closer, emotionally, to his daughters than to his sons as his children grew up and the bond with Katey was a particularly close one. Mamie, noting that she herself had sometimes been called her father's 'favourite daughter', commented, 'If he had a favourite daughter . . . my dear sister must claim that honor'.[2] There was no 'if' about the matter, in fact. Even from their infancy, that time in their lives when all his children were adored by Dickens, Katey seems to have been his especial pet. Aware of this, her sisters and brothers generally 'pushed' her into their father's study ('rather a mysterious and awe-inspiring chamber' to them) when any favour was to be asked and she 'always returned triumphant'.[3] She it was whose pleas could obtain one of those delicious paternal treats such as, on summer evenings, 'driving up to Hampstead in the open carriage with him . . . and getting out for a long walk through the lovely country lanes, picking wild roses and other flowers, or walking hand in hand with him listening to some story'.[4]

Both the little girls naturally adored their dazzling father who would sing them such irresistible comic songs[5] as he sat in his American rocking-chair of an evening; who gave such marvellous 'shining' parties for his children[6]; who made them 'scream with laughter' when dressed as a magician and performing wonderful conjuring tricks; who took them on a great toyshop expedition every Christmas Eve; who insisted on bright pretty colours for their clothing and bedroom decorations; and who took them on long jolly seaside holidays or to live for a while in an old, romantic Italian palazzo. He was also the best of tender nurses when they were sick: and when the six-year-old Katey had a serious illness soon after the family's move to Genoa she 'would let nobody touch her; in the way of dressing her neck or giving her physic . . . but her Papa'.[7] (Many years later, after her marriage, she still found, when laid low by a bad fever, that her father had a unique power to comfort her: 'his very coming', she told Thackeray's daughter, 'seemed to bring healing and peace to her as she lay, and to quiet the raging fever'.)[8]

Katey was a passionate little girl, inheriting all her father's vehemence of temperament as well as his good looks.[9] She took an intense dislike to Gower Street, for example, telling Shaw later on, 'when I was particularly naughty as a child, it was always after a walk up or down that – to me – hideously dull and eminently respectable thoroughfare' – it was, she added, the street's 'respectability' which made it so dreadful to her.[10] She was equally impulsive in her benevolent actions as when she rushed over to her quiet little sister at a neighbour's party to ask, 'Are you enjoying yourself, Mamie?'. When Mamie said yes Katey said, 'Then so am I' and gave her sister's hand 'a reassuring little squeeze before running away to escape being "caught" in the game of blind man's buff'.[11] Dickens who loved to invent appropriate nicknames for his children called Katey 'Lucifer Box' and the more docile Mamie 'Mild Glo'ster'.

Fond parent though Dickens was, his two girls were quite strictly disciplined, like their brothers. They could decorate their attic room at Devonshire Terrace to their own taste but it had to be kept tidy and neat, this neatness applying also to their drawers and cupboards which Dickens regularly inspected:

> Remonstrances were frequently consigned to notepaper, folded neatly and left by him on their pincushion, which they called 'pincushion notes'. 'Oh dear! – what's up now?' Katie would remark, observing the third in a week! His punctuality was almost painful – Katie being the only one in the family who dared be five minutes late at breakfast-time, when it was noted and remarked upon, [Dickens receiving] in response a light kiss upon the forehead, and a lighter, 'Yes, Pa,' to his observation that it was the third time that week she had been late for breakfast.[12]

She also dared to protest about the vexatious pincushion notes; 'Possessed of more courage than the others, she decided to tackle her father and beg him not to send any more . . . but to *tell* them in future when they displeased him, which had the desired effect'.[13]

180

Elizabeth Dickens photographed in later life.

Elizabeth Dickens. Watercolour by Clarkson Stanfield (undated).

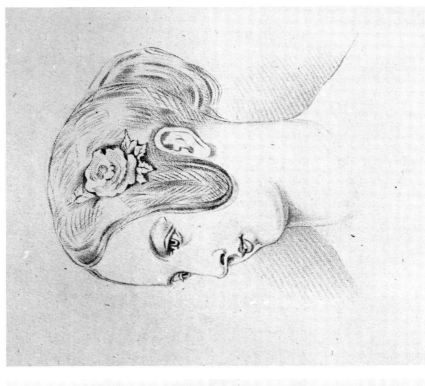

Mary Hogarth. Engraving after a painting by 'Phiz' (H.K. Browne). The portrait was painted from memory after her death in 1837.

Dickens's sister, Fanny Burnett, by Samuel Laurence (1836).

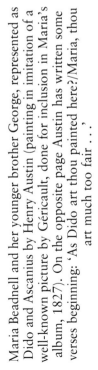

Maria Beadnell and her younger brother George, represented as Dido and Ascanius by Henry Austin (painting in imitation of a well-known picture by Géricault, done for inclusion in Maria's album, 1827). On the opposite page Austin has written some verses beginning: 'As Dido art thou painted here?/Maria, thou art much too fair . . .'

Maria Winter (*née* Beadnell), *c.* 1855.

Catherine Dickens photographed in later life.

Catherine Dickens painted by Maclise in 1846.

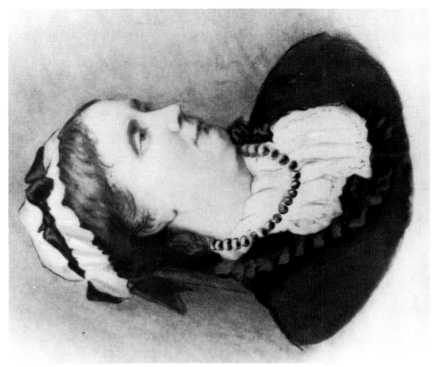

'A Girl at a Waterfall' by Daniel Maclise (1842). Georgina Hogarth (then aged fifteen) modelled for this picture and Dickens bought it from Maclise.

Georgina Hogarth in middle age.

Mary Dickens ('Mamie').

Katey Dickens as seen by her second husband, Carlo Perugini.
The painting is entitled 'A Labour of Love'.

Dickens photographed by Mason at Gad's Hill with Mamie (*left*)
and Katey (*c*. 1865).

Ellen Ternan photographed *c*. 1867.

As to the girls' education, Dickens seems never to have considered sending them to school. If we assume that his novels reflect his general attitudes this is hardly surprising for, from the Misses Crumpton in *Boz* to Miss Twinkleton in *Drood*, the schoolmistresses who appear in his books are all uniformly foolish old maids. They may sometimes be benign but they are always snobbish, absurdly prudish and prim, and wholly unintellectual. For them superficial appearances are all-important: the terrestrial and celestial globes in Miss Twinkleton's 'dainty' parlour, for example, are only there to suggest to her charges' parents and guardians that 'even when [she] retires into the bosom of privacy, duty may at any moment compel her to become a sort of Wandering Jewess, scouring the earth and soaring through the skies in search of knowledge for her pupils'.[14] Of such important new developments in middle-class girls' education as the work being done from 1850 onwards at her North London Collegiate School by Frances Buss (whose father had featured briefly and not very happily as *Pickwick Papers'* illustrator some years earlier) Dickens seems, sadly, to have been unaware. He gave his daughters an almost ostentatiously conventional upper-middle-class 'education'[15] — governesses both English and French, music lessons, and a period of 'polishing' in Paris during the winter and spring of 1855/6. Not that they were sent away to any finishing-school establishment like that of Madame Martinez who had 'polished' Maria Beadnell twenty years earlier: the whole Dickens family moved with them to Paris to assist at the polishing process and Dickens perhaps was turning the experience to good comic account a few months later when he created that accomplished varnisher, Mrs General, hired by Mr Dorrit to help *his* two daughters in 'forming a surface'. In Paris Mamie and Katey were taught Italian by no less a personage than Daniele Manin, the refugee President of the Venetian Republic, and Katey was encouraged to pursue her interest in art. She had early shown a definite talent in this respect and Dickens happily fostered it, arranging for her to attend a drawing class at the newly founded Ladies' College in Bedford Square.[16] Now in Paris she shared with Thackeray's daughters tuition by a master recommended by the fashionable portrait-painter, Ary Scheffer, and earnestly laboured on sketches of 'gigantic ears and classic profiles'.[17] Also studying under Scheffer at this time was a young Neapolitan, Carlo Perugini, who was destined to play a very important part in her life later on, but she did not actually meet him then.[18]

Mamie cultivated music rather than art but said later:

> . . . if I pleased my father in dancing, I am afraid I was a great disap-

pointment to him as regards my music. I never could be persuaded to play at any of our musical parties. For one thing, my extreme nervousness came in the way; and for another, my powers as a pianist never came up to my ideal. As a child, on the other hand, I used to sing to my father a great deal, and in after years I used to play and sing to him constantly.[19]

Mamie's 'extreme nervousness' seems to have inhibited only her piano-playing. She was evidently able to throw herself happily into the private theatricals so energetically got up by Dickens in the summer of 1855 and the winter of 1856/7. On the first occasion she played the *jeune première* in Wilkie Collins's melodrama, *The Lighthouse,* and earned a bouquet from the *Illustrated Times* (which reviewed, on 21 July, the Campden House production of the play). She acted, said this critic, 'with charming freshness and naiveté', and 'sang a new and exceedingly pretty ballad, by Mr Linley, with a sweetness, simplicity, and expression which deservedly gained her the warm applause of the audience'. Eighteen months later came a second Collins melodrama expressly written for Dickens and his amateurs, *The Frozen Deep*, and Mamie played the leading female part. It was not a taxing role but still required more of the actress than the part she had played in *The Lighthouse*, especially in supporting the self-sacrificing hero's great death-scene which climaxes the play (this hero was played by Dickens himself, of course – evidently with stupendous effect). Dickens exacted a high standard from his amateurs but Mamie seems to have passed with flying colours. After watching her at a rehearsal he wrote to Miss Coutts that it made him 'quite unhappy' to think that she might not come to see Mamie's acting, 'something that seems so fresh and wholesome to me'.[20]

Pleased as he was with his elder daughter's histrionic triumphs, Dickens would certainly not have encouraged her, even had she wished it, to become a professional actress as he encouraged Katey to become a professional painter. Quite apart from the disreputable air that still clung to the name of actress, the fact was (as Katey told a Dickens Fellowship audience many years later, long after she had become Mrs Perugini) that for a middle-class woman in mid-Victorian England, 'to undertake an occupation or profession other than literature or painting was to run the risk of being considered "masculine" or "unladylike" '. And Dickens very much wanted his daughters to be considered as young ladies. The kind of life that this involved for them was described by Mrs Perugini in that same Dickens Fellowship speech: it was a 'pleasant if uneventful' one of 'peace and plenty':

... plenty of rather monotonous amusement such as garden parties, croquet, long walks, drives and rides, and in the evening occasional rather dull dinner parties, dances, and the always popular opera and theatre parties. [Women's] mornings were occupied with the usual small domestic worries, and very often in looking after the interests of their poorer neighbours. Business disposed of, they managed to get through a large amount of letter-writing, embroidery and reading – novel reading and reading of a more serious character, for many of them were thoughtful in those days, and greatly given to introspection, a fault, no doubt, of too much leisure. Their manners were gentle and unobtrusive, their voices held the low music that Shakespeare loved, now raised to shriller tones, and as a rule, they were careful in their consideration for the feelings of those surrounding them; but they certainly had too much spare time on their hands.[21]

Katey herself clearly determined to fill her time with the purposeful pursuit of art and did not greatly care how much the Mrs Generals of the world threw up their hands in horror at the way that 'the fast Miss Kate Dickens'[22] ordered her life. She also took a part in the Dickens theatricals and doubtless relished one of her speeches in *The Frozen Deep* which ran, 'I must have my father near me, or I can never enjoy myself as I ought', but seems rather to have played second fiddle to Mamie in this branch of the family's activities. These were very intermittent, however, compared with her constant artistic interests: it does not appear that Mamie had any continuing preoccupation, equivalent to Katey's painting, other than her adored father and her little white Pomeranian dog, 'Mrs Bouncer'.

It was a foregone conclusion that Mamie would stay with Dickens when her parents separated. This was determined not only by her hero-worship of him[23] but also by the fact that it would be natural for his elder daughter to become mistress of his household, her mother being gone. Moreover, Georgina in her very anomalous situation was kept in some sort of countenance by her niece's remaining in the house and, ostensibly, running it. It would have been equally natural, of course, for the second daughter to take up residence with her mother yet Katey did not do this (Harriet Martineau, commenting on the harshness of Catherine's fate exclaimed, 'And not a daughter has she with her! only that weak son . . .').[24] Gladys Storey tells us that Katey 'took her mother's part in-so-far as it was possible for her to do so' and relates the anecdote about her angrily protesting against Catherine's going, at Dickens's orders, to call on Ellen Ternan.[25] She may have done so (clearly she was always a brave woman), because some later words of hers, recorded by Miss Storey, sound as though they could have been prompted by memories of some terrible 'scene' which had been provoked by her attempting to remonstrate with Dickens on his treatment of Catherine:

> My father was like a madman when my mother left home . . . this affair brought out all that was worst – all that was weakest in him. He did not care a damn what happened to any of us. Nothing could surpass the misery and unhappiness of our home.[26]

Still, there is no hint in Helen Thomson's letter to Mrs Stark that either of her great-nieces had protested at all at the way their mother was being treated; rather, she writes of them as though they were utterly under their father's spell:

> . . . they, poor girls, have also been flattered as being taken notice of as the daughters of a popular author. He, too, is a carressing [*sic*] father and indulgent in trifles, and they in their ignorance of the world, look no further nor are aware of the injury he does them.[27]

What Miss Thomson means by the 'injury' that Dickens was causing to his daughters is illustrated by a maliciously gossiping letter written in January 1859 by the critic and reviewer, Eneas Sweetland Dallas (who was later to please Dickens so much by his *Times* review of *Our Mutual Friend* that he was given the manuscript of the novel). Dallas wrote to the Edinburgh publisher, John Blackwood:

> [Dickens's] daughters – now under the benign wing of their aunt, Miss Hogarth – are not received into society. You would be excessively amused if you heard all the gigantic efforts the family make to keep their foot in the world – how they call upon people that they never called on before & that they have treated with the most dire contempt. Fancy Dickens & his family going to call on that worthy couple – Mr and Mrs Pecksniff [i.e., Samuel Carter Hall the original of Pecksniff, and his wife], & informing these people upon whom they never called before that they would be happy to see them at Tavistock House. But still better – fancy Pecksniff and his wife in a high moral transport and religious spite informing Miss Hogarth & the Misses Dickens, that it was with Mrs Dickens they were acquainted, that if Mrs Dickens were at Tavistock House they should be happy to call, but otherwise – afraid – very sorry – but etc., etc.[28]

Whether it was because she could not tolerate such social snubs as these or whether it was because of unhappiness at home, Katey lost little time, after her mother's departure, in arranging to leave home herself. In July 1860, just three months before her twenty-first birthday, she married Wilkie Collins's brother, Charles Allston Collins. Eleven years older than Katey, Charles Collins was an artist of Pre-Raphaelite convictions who had exhibited at the Royal Academy between 1847 and 1855. His 'modest and sensitive nature' having caused him to become dissatisfied with his painting, which, he felt, fell far too short of his ideals,[29] he was turning to literature instead. He had published some travel writings in 1859 and was contributing a series of papers called 'The Eye-Witness' to Dickens's journal *All The Year Round*. Since Katey was, in physical appearance, very much what the Pre-Raphaelites would have called a 'stunner'[30] it is not surprising that Collins was attracted by her. (He had earlier been greatly enamoured of one of the Rossetti sisters, Maria, but she had chosen to become an Anglican nun.) He proposed and was accepted. According to Gladys Storey (who purports to be simply recording what she was later told by Katey):

> Katie . . . although she respected him and considered him the kindest and most sweet-tempered of men, was not in the least in love with him. Dickens did not desire the marriage, but Katie saw in it an escape from 'an unhappy home', away from which, as a married woman, she considered she could more or less do as she liked, and for these reasons only she accepted Mr Collins.

Miss Storey also records an anecdote of Dickens's being found by Mamie sobbing into Katey's wedding-dress on the evening of the wedding-day and saying brokenly, 'But for me, Katey would not have left home'.[31] But, apart from Miss Storey's book, there is no other evidence that Dickens 'did not desire the marriage' or that he knew Katey was not marrying for love. It could be said, however, that his tone in writing about his future son-in-law does not suggest great enthusiasm. Writing to De Cerjat in May 1860 Dickens says of Collins: 'He was bred an artist; is a writer, too, and does the Eye Witness, in All The Year Round. He is a gentleman, accomplished, and amiable.' And the capital letters he uses, when writing about the wedding, just after the event, to a close woman friend, would seem to indicate some doubts about the satisfactoriness of the match: '. . . the whole thing was a great success – SO FAR'.[32]

We get, in fact, a bright and happy picture of the first year of the marriage (spent mainly in France and Belgium) from surviving letters of the newly weds' written to Collins's mother.[33] Katey 'enjoys every kind of housewifely employment prodigiously', Collins wrote from Calais on 23 July and, a few days later, he describes how she 'puts a huge basket on her arm and goes forth to market and we carp at fowls as if we knew something about it . . .'. Katey adds a postscript which indicates the establishment of a warmly affectionate relationship with her mother-in-law:

My dearest Mrs Collins. Have you forgiven me yet for going away in black? The fact is I thought you were too much occupied with your flirtations to notice what I went away in. I really think your conduct was disgraceful, and *my respect for you is gone for ever*. I am very, very happy, and hope to become some day a good wife. . . .

They settled in Paris in September where Collins began work on his *Cruise upon Wheels*, based on their journeying in a cab from Calais, driving themselves. In another postscript to one of his letters home Katey tells Mrs Collins,

Charlie says I may say I am such a dear little thing. My *temper* is unbearable, he spoils me so, and lets me do whatever I like. He is very good to me and I am very happy. He is such a good man isn't he, no wonder you love him so. . . .

In a later letter she exclaims, 'Oh! he is so good and so dear. I never knew anyone so unselfish.' This all seems consistent enough with Miss Storey's report of Katey's attitude towards her first husband: respect, admiration, gratitude, affection, all those things are present but no passion such as, apparently, she had felt for the already-married Edmund Yates, one of 'Dickens's young men', as the group of journalists he attached to *Household Words* were called.[34]

Katey evidently delighted in her new housewifely role and was proud of the economical way in which she and Collins contrived to live:

We cook our own food, no one in the world could cook a chop better than Charlie does, and I am very great indeed at boiled rice. In the morning Charlie lights the fire and I lay the cloth while he fries the bacon I make the tea. After breakfast I clear away, put his writing materials on the table, and he sits down to work while I wash up the breakfast cups in the kitchen, put away everything sweep up the crumbs, and the hearth and get the room neat. Then Charlie goes on working all the morning till about two, and I darn, or mend, or write letters. At two we have our lunch, then a little more work & then we go out for a walk, get what things we want for dinner, come in, cook our dinner and eat it. As soon as dinner is over . . . we get out the Account book. . . . Then comes tea, and then another great tidying of the room, and sweeping up of crumbs, and putting away of things. Then we put on our things & go out for a long walk, and look at all the beautiful things in the shop windows, and enjoy ourselves as much as we can.

Anxiously she assures Mrs Collins that they are living in this way because they like it and 'could keep a servant if we liked' and begs her not to divulge any details of their domestic economy to Dickens or to 'Mama' lest they 'should fancy we were really frightfully badly off'. Charlie is never happier than when he is cooking, she insists, and 'As for me I have given up reading, hardly ever sit down, and am happier than I have ever been'.[35]

The exhilarating novelty of being a careful, busy housekeeper perhaps compensated Katey for whatever of romance may have been missing from the marriage. She might have been expecting, too, that it would soon be succeeded by the even greater novelty of motherhood but this she was not to experience until her second marriage. And, however stimulating it may have been in the first year or so of marriage and living abroad to rise to the challenge of the need for economical housekeeping, this must have become somewhat frustrating after the couple's return to London and their settling down to regular married life. For Collins's literary career did not prosper like his brother Wilkie's. Although *A Cruise upon Wheels* met with some success, his delicate health prevented him from capitalizing on it and developing further the whimsical vein of travel writing for which he seems to have had a gift. He turned instead to novel writing ('I don't want him to write a novel', Katey had written to her mother-in-law in one of those early letters, 'He would not do it nearly so well, and everybody writes novels') but made very little mark in that line.[36]

Collins was suffering from cancer of the stomach and his condition grew steadily worse as the years passed: his last years 'were little less than martyrdom when "paroxysms of anguish were followed by profound prostration" '.[37] Katey would have had to be as much the breadwinner as he. Gladys Storey records that, 'They were far from being well-off, and life was becoming increasingly difficult for them' (medical expenses alone, one imagines, must have been considerable). Katey 'went on with her painting, selling her work now and again, which helped the financial position', and was even considering an invitation to turn professional actress until Dickens dissuaded her. She would have been eager not to rely financially on her father as so many of his nearest and dearest did (he had been very generous to her at the time of her marriage, giving her upwards of £500 in the few months preceding it)[38] and he was probably trying to help in the most delicate way possible by getting Collins the commission to illustrate his new novel, *Edwin Drood*, but Collins had to abandon this project too because of his health.

Dickens was naturally much concerned about his favourite daughter's marriage to a man who was turning out to be such a desperate invalid. Writing to De Cerjat again in October 1864 he confessed to 'strong apprehensions' that Collins would never recover and that Katey would be left 'a young widow'. Four years later he writes to his American friend, James Fields, 'Charley Collins – *I* say emphatically dying'. But Collins, like Tiny Tim, 'did *not* die' and Dickens seems to have given the impression that he resented this. His actor friend Charles Fechter may have been right in tracing this resentment to Dickens's inability to understand 'the prolonged endurance of such an existence' ('in his passionate nature . . . it produced disgust') but it was surely the predicament in which it placed his beloved daughter that distressed him most: 'Charles Collins continues in the same state', he told Fields in December 1868, 'and his pretty young wife's life is indeed a weary one'.[39]

The 'strange dislike' that Fechter and others thought Dickens had taken to his son-in-law may have been resentment at something deeper than chronic sickliness on Collins's part, however. Gladys Storey told Walter Dexter in 1939 that she had learned from Katey that Collins 'ought never to have married' being not only a sick man but also an impotent one. Katey, asserted Miss Storey, 'once complained to her father on this account and said how her marriage was a complete failure and wrecking her life; she wanted to get a separation as she could have done – but C.D. would not hear of it'.[40] Before we condemn him too harshly for taking this attitude (always assuming, of course, that Miss Storey was accurate in this matter) we should consider what a great resurgence of potentially damaging gossip and scandal would have taken place had there been a *second* separation crisis in Dickens's immediate family. Not that scandal was left unprovoked by Katey anyway. Frederick Lehmann, reporting to his wife in 1866 on a London dinnerparty given by Dickens's eccentric friend, the music critic, H.F. Chorley, described Katey as looking like 'a spectacle of woe . . . quite distracted'. Mamie, who was also at the dinner, seems to have been behaving rather indiscreetly, 'darting distressed and furious glances and shaping her mouth all the time for the word "beast" whenever Chorley looked away from her', and Katey startled Lehmann by dropping dramatic hints about her sister's way of life at Gad's Hill. She herself 'could not lead such a life', Katey told Lehmann, adding mysteriously, 'she takes her happiness when she can, and a few visits to town lately have given her all she cares for'. Then Katey said, 'Of course, it will come out. Sure to.' One is inclined to feel that Lehmann was perhaps reacting a bit too solemnly to Katey's provocative chatter but clearly the two girls, especially Mamie, *were* behaving rather indiscreetly. Lehmann's letter continues:

> My dear, these two girls are going to the devil as fast as can be. From what I hear from third parties who don't know how intimate we are with them, society is beginning to fight very shy of them, especially of Kitty C.

... Mamie may blaze up in a firework any day. Kitty is burning away both character and I fear health slowly but steadily.[41]

Whether or not it was a bad year for her reputation, 1866 clearly was a bad one for Katey as regards her health. Dickens told Macready in February that she was in a delicate state and 'could not maintain the family reputation in some Scotch reels', and in December he wrote to his sister, Letitia, that she was suffering from 'a nervous fever' and, though slowly progressing, was 'a bad subject for illness, having long been in an unsatisfactory and declining state'.[42]

By the time James Fields's wife, Annie, met Katey in her London home in 1869, however, she seems fully to have recovered her bloom. Mrs Fields confided an elaborate impressed description to her journal:

> She is like a piece of old china with a picture by Sir Joshua Reynolds painted upon it and with manners as piquant peculiar and taking as such a painting come to life ought to have. She wore at our first dinner with her a kind of paradise coloured dress ... with an antique lace and muslin cape just drawn over her beautiful shoulders and coming down in straight lines in front leaving her throat and neck uncovered. She has red hair which she wears very high on the top of her head worn with pearls in a loose coil. Altogether the effect is like some rare strange thing, which does not quite wear away in spite of her piquancy; for she is clever enough to be a match for the best of us I am sure.[43]

Just a couple of years earlier Thackeray, who was very fond of both Dickens's girls but especially of Katey, had published a poem in honour of her beauty in his *Cornhill Magazine*, 'Mrs Katherine's Lantern' (actually written in 1862). He pretends to be someone in the next century who has bought an old lantern with the initials K and E on its panes (Katey's second name was Elizabeth):

> Full a hundred years are gone
> Since the little beacon shone
> From a Venice balcony:
> There, on summer nights, it hung,
> And her lovers came and sung
> To their beautiful K E.[44]

It is hardly surprising that Dickens was so adoringly proud of his striking younger daughter and he must have been distressed indeed to find that she had entered a marriage which had proved so depressing. When she remarried after her father's death (Collins died in 1873) Georgina Hogarth wrote to Mrs Fields:

For many years [Dickens] had been much concerned and troubled about the dreary unfortunate fate of his bright handsome younger daughter and he had been especially occupied in mind about her – and had been speaking of her a good deal the two or three last days of his life. This blessed change in her existence [i.e., her marriage to Carlo Perugini in 1874] would have greatly eased and brightened *him*, I know.[45]

Katey's unsatisfactory marriage did not deter Dickens, it seems, from hoping that Mamie would marry too. He particularly favoured one of his 'young men' on *All The Year Round*, Percy Fitzgerald, whom he thought 'a very clever fellow' with 'charming sisters [an important point for Dickens] and an excellent position'. 'Between ourselves', he continued in this 1866 letter to Bulwer Lytton, 'I am grievously disappointed that Mary can by no means be induced to think as highly of him as I do.'[46]

Mamie is a more difficult figure than Katey to bring into focus now. 'Mild Glo'ster' she may have been to her father but she evidently had a wilful side too, as Percy Fitzgerald testifies:

Decidedly pretty she was, but her power lay in her interesting character – its curious spirit of *independence* and haughty refusal of submission, which made one think some Petruchio might arrive and confront this imperious being. From this spirit of hers I confess I suffered a good deal, as she never spared me. Many a hard knock I received. At one moment I was in favour, presently quite out of it.[47]

She seems to have been prone to intense emotional relationships with her friends (Nina Lehmann wrote to her husband after visiting Mamie once, 'I was received as a lover might be by a loving and beloved mistress')[48] and was especially attached to a certain county family in Hampshire. This was the family of a sporting Tory MP William Humphery, son-in-law and successor as MP for Andover of the builder William Cubitt. Mamie frequently visited the Humpherys at Penton Lodge and in July 1865, to Dickens's mock-horror, went canvassing there on behalf of her friend. 'My daughter', Dickens warned Fitzgerald when inviting him down to Gad's Hill,

has been decoyed to Andover for the election week, in the Conservative interest; think of my feelings as a Radical parent! The wrong-headed member and his wife are the friends with whom she hunts, and she helps to receive (and *de*ceive) the voters, which is very awful![49]

Mamie seems to have had a great appetite for social life in London as well as the provinces and it was for her sake that Dickens would take a London house for the season during the 1860s. But she would often dash off somewhere else even from there: Dickens wrote to his friend Mrs Elliott in December 1869, 'On Mary's account (as she will probably go somewhere else, the moment we take possession!) I have hired Milner Gibson's house, opposite the Marble Arch, until the 1st of June'.[50]

All of this is a bit hard to reconcile with the 'Mild Glo'ster' idea of Mamie as is her persistence in not ever visiting her exiled mother until the month after Dickens's death when she remorsefully declared to Catherine 'that the separation between *them* had resulted solely from her, Mary's, own self-will'.[51] If Mamie was rightly characterized by Fitzgerald as showing always a 'haughty refusal of submission' can it be true that she docilely accepted Dickens's veto on a love-affair?[52] And if she was that docile why did she not marry Fitzgerald to please her father? And what about Katey's sensational hints to Lehmann about Mamie's private life? (Katey continued to enjoy hinting at things about her sister: 'Some day', she wrote to Shaw in 1897, 'I will tell you about Mamie and myself — it will help you to a better understanding of our old home life'.)[53]

What the evidence seems to point to is that Mamie was, in fact, as spirited as her sister, though not so gifted, but that her love for her father, the dominant passion of her life, made her struggle to be always in her demeanour at home the kind of young lady he approved of: soft, gentle, modest, ministering to her father by playing and singing to him in his hours of relaxation, adding grace and elegance to the domestic surroundings as in her daily floral decorations for the family dining-table. When all this became too much of a strain for her she would rush off to London or to Hampshire and plunge into a social whirl before returning to be that 'mild quiet and attentive' presence at Gad's Hill, 'very lady-like and pretty', that Mrs Fields observed in 1869. She continued to resist all matrimonial lures and a certain Major Lynch, much favoured as a suitor to her by Dickens and Georgina, fared no better than Percy Fitzgerald had done. To be Dickens's daughter was enough for her: 'It is a glorious inheritance to have such blood flowing in one's veins', she wrote later to Annie Fields, adding, 'I am so glad I never changed my name'.[54]

Her life after Dickens's death seems to have been wholly dedicated to his memory in various different ways. She laboured with her aunt on an edition of his letters, she composed a little children's book about him which she hoped might be the means of making 'boys and girls love and venerate the Man — before they can know and love and venerate the Author and Genius', and later wrote *My Father as I Recall Him,* in similar vein, for a more general readership. She denied her former self in so far as it now seemed unworthy of Dickens, telling a journalist who interviewed her in 1895 that 'she never really liked London life, with its social

excitement and gaiety'; and she devoted herself to good works, 'ministering under the guidance of a dear friend, a devoted and enthusiastic
clergyman of the Church of England, to the sick and poor', first in rural
areas and later on the dismal outskirts of Manchester and Birmingham.[55]
She could not bear to hear anyone, even her own elder brother, give
public readings of the texts Dickens himself had read, but was happy to
read 'A Child's Dream of a Star' publicly herself.[56] She quotes this piece *in
extenso* in her children's book and was evidently much attached to it. It is
easy to understand why this pinchbeck item (as we would now think it)
chosen from among the great Aladdin's Cave of her father's works should
have appealed to her so strongly and why she should have wished to
publicize it. It has a prettily religious sound to it and it is clearly intended
to be very pathetic yet also 'uplifting': only a very good, loving, Christian
man of great literary genius could have written it, Mamie would surely
have argued, so what could be a better vehicle to convey the essence of
him to those who had never known him? And no doubt the idea of one's
dead loved one sitting on a star eagerly awaiting a rapturous reunion after
one's own death would have moved her with regard to her own situation.
When she died in July 1896 she was exactly the same age (58 years and 4
months) as Dickens had been when he died: a curious fact which almost
makes one feel that she must have decided that that was the appropriate
time for her to die and to go at last to her adored father on that bright
distant star.

*

Katey survived until 1929 and led a very different sort of life. Her
second marriage seems to have been a very happy one, saddened though it
was after only two years by the death in infancy of their only child,
Leonard. Her career developed too. She began exhibiting at the Royal
Academy in 1877 and became a member of the Society of Women Artists
in 1886. She specialized in painting children and her pictures have titles
like 'Little Nell', 'Mollie's Ball Dress', and so on. Perugini, like her first
husband, suffered illness and Katey raged in 1906 about doctors who
talked 'in a very learned manner about sensory and motory nerves and
appear[ed] to be quite satisfied with their knowledge of the complaint'
whilst doing 'absolutely nothing to relieve his sufferings'.[57] But he lived
on until 1918 so that they had over forty years together. Katey continued
to fascinate all who met her including, of course, the members of the
Dickens Fellowship (formed in 1902): 'Hers was a strong and delightful
personality like that of a great actress', Leslie C. Staples recalled in 1977.
'It filled any room she entered and everyone fell before her charm.'[58]

Among her friends were W.S. Gilbert and George Bernard Shaw and, as her surviving letters to the latter show, she was more than able to hold her own in witty exchanges with him, e.g.,

> . . . I also imagine a Socialist . . . to have rather ungracious manners, and to wear creaky boots . . . The only Socialist I know is indeed very unlike this, he has a pretty house, gives charming dinners – and rumour has it, that he rides in the Row every morning on a very handsome horse – but I suppose *my* Socialist has not the courage of his opinions – or he would live on a crust, would he not? And cut up his horse into mincemeat to divide among his poorer friends?

Nor were even Dickens idolaters spared her vivacity in this correspondence. F.G. Kitton, one of the founders of the Fellowship and an indefatigable researcher into everything Dickensian, is judged 'as kind and inoffensive as he is weak and credulous' but, just after writing that, Katey received from Kitton a letter 'so amiable so kind', she told Shaw, that she felt 'extremely wicked to wish even for a moment that he had been drowned at birth'. But, she added, 'that is what I do wish nevertheless'.[59]

In one of Mamie's little books we get a charming glimpse of Katey affectionately exercising her wit on Dickens himself. Mamie is describing a special bond between her sister and her father that related to Dickens's beloved Gad's Hill:

> There were always 'improvements' – as my father used to call his alterations – being made at 'Gad's Hill,' and each improvement was supposed to be the last. As each was completed, my sister – who was always a constant visitor, and an exceptionally dear one to my father – would have to come down and inspect, and as each was displayed, my father would say to her most solemnly: 'Now, Katie, you behold your parent's latest and last achievement.' These 'last improvements' became quite a joke between them. I remember so well, on one such occasion, after the walls and doors of the drawing-room had been lined with mirrors, my sister's laughing speech to 'the master': 'I believe papa, that when you become an angel your wings will be made of looking-glass and your crown of scarlet geraniums'.

Dickens, Mamie also records, was at his 'most delightful' when alone with his family sitting over dessert after dinner and this was especially the case when Katey was present 'for she had great power in "drawing him out" '.[60] A distinguished American visitor to Gad's Hill in 1868, the critic Charles Eliot Norton, observed that none of Dickens's family 'seemed to enjoy his *humour* as much as Katie, and in her quick perception of it she was more like him than the others'.[61]

In the pages of the *Pall Mall Magazine* in June 1906, Katey herself recalled, in moving detail, her last visit to Gad's Hill, only a day or two before her father's death:

There was a matter of some little importance to myself that I wished to consult him upon. This I told him, and he said that later in the evening, when my aunt and sister went to bed, we would talk of it together. My sister then played and sang, and her voice, which was very sweet and thrilling, reached us from the drawing-room, where she sat alone. My father enjoyed her music, as he always did, and was quite happy, although silent now, and looking very pale, I thought. At about eleven o'clock my sister and aunt retired; the servants were dismissed, and my father and I remained seated at the table: the lamps which had been placed in the conservatory were now turned down, but the windows that led into it were still open. It was a very warm, quiet night, and there was not a breath of air: the sweet scent of the flowers came in through the open door, and my father and I might have been the only creatures alive in the place, so still it was.

I told him of what was on my mind, and for a long time he gave his close attention to it, helping and advising me to come to a decision. It was very late when I at last rose from my seat and said that I thought it was time for him to rest, as he looked so tired; but he bade me stay with him for a little, as he had much to say. He was silent, however, for some minutes after this, resting his head upon his hand, and then he began talking of his own affairs, telling me exactly how he stood in the world, and speaking, among other things, of 'Edwin Drood,' and how he hoped that it might prove a success – 'if, please God, I live to finish it.'

I must have turned to him, startled by his grave voice, for he put his hand upon my arm and repeated, 'I say *if*, because you know, my dear child, I have not been strong lately.' Again he was silent, gazing wistfully through the darkened windows; and then in a low voice spoke of his own life, and many things that he had scarcely ever mentioned to me before. I was not surprised, nor did it seem strange at the time, that he should be speaking thus; but what greatly troubled me was the manner in which he dwelt upon those years that were gone by, and never, beyond the one mention of 'Edwin Drood,' looked to the future. He spoke as though his life were over and there was nothing left. And so we sat on, he talking, and I only interrupting him now and then to give him a word of sympathy and love. The early summer dawn was creeping into the conservatory before we went upstairs together, and I left him at his bedroom door.

Katey recalled this last evening with her father again in private conversation many years later. She then revealed what the matter was on which she had consulted him: an offer she had received from a theatrical manager to go on the stage professionally 'as a means of earning a little extra money':

> With great earnestness my father dissuaded me. . . . 'You are pretty and no doubt would do well, but you are too sensitive a nature to bear the brunt of much you would encounter. Although there are nice people on the stage, there are some who would make your hair stand on end. You are clever enough to do something else.' He finally dismissed the subject by saying, 'I will make it up to you.'

He then went on to talk with sadness of other things:

> He wished, he said, that he had been 'a better father – a better man.' He talked and talked, *how* he talked, until three o'clock in the morning, when we parted for bed. I know things about my father's character . . . that no one else ever knew; he was not a good man, but he was not a fast man, but he was wonderful! He fell in love with this girl, I did not blame *her* – it is never one person's fault.[62]

In late 1897 and early 1898 Katey had also written much about her father, in correspondence with Shaw whom she had consulted about the disposition of the batch of her father's letters to her mother that the dying Catherine had entrusted to her 'asking her to read them when she was dead and consider whether they could not be published, to show the world that Dickens once loved her'. Katey felt, however, that the letters proved no such thing and asked Shaw if he did not think they had therefore best be burned. He 'energetically dissented', persuading her instead that they should be placed in the British Museum[63] (they were eventually published, edited by Walter Dexter, in 1935).

In the course of their correspondence Katey seems to have enjoyed dropping dramatic hints about some great secret in her father's life which would 'take [Shaw's] breath away' if he were told it:

> . . . his heart and soul are not in these letters [to Catherine] as you suppose, but some of his Sunday clothes are; and then – here comes the truth at last – there may be other letters in which the real man *is* revealed, minus his Sunday clothes and all shams, and with his heart and soul burning like jewels in a dark place! I say there *may* be such letters and they may be one day given to the world; in which case how should I be helping my mother or what good should I be doing to future generations by leaving these letters in the tin box to the British Museum, these letters which might have been written to anyone? I am assured that these other letters of which I speak have all been burnt, but as little Paul said to Mrs Pipchin, 'I don't believe that story'.[64]

We can be pretty certain that it is Dickens's letters to Ellen that Katey is so
sensationally referring to here but it seems unlikely that she would ever
have actually seen them.[65] Despite her characterization of her father
elsewhere in the correspondence as 'most extraordinarily reticent for a
man who was supposed to be so full of frankness and geniality',[66] she
romantically imagines that he bared his soul in his letters to Ellen, 'his
heart and mind burning like jewels in a dark place' (that 'dark place'
sufficiently indicates the view Katey took of her father's relationship with
Ellen). I doubt very much, in fact, that Dickens's letters to Ellen, if ever
they should come to light, would prove to be very different in kind, or
even in tone, from other known letters of his written to beloved intimates
– we might appositely recall what he wrote to Maria Winter in 1855
when he attributed to his youthful affair with her 'a habit of suppression
which now belongs to me, which I know is no part of my original nature,
but which makes me chary of showing my affections, even to my children,
except when they are very young'.[67]

It is unfortunate that all the excitement over Katey's dark utterances
about her father and Ellen as made public by Miss Storey ten years after
Katey's death should have deflected Dickens scholars' attention away
from Katey herself and her evident great importance in her father's
emotional life. Otherwise, they might have reflected that the spirited and
beautiful girl who is arguably the most successful of his later heroines,
Bella Wilfer in *Our Mutual Friend* (written 1864/5), might well have
been modelled to a considerable extent upon his favourite child. Biographers have generally preferred to see in Bella a portrait of Ellen and to
deduce from that and from her immediate predecessor in the line of
Dickens's fictional heroines, Estella, that Dickens's 'dear girl' was not
only sexually cold towards him but also something of a tormenting little
gold-digger and that he, to his sorrow, clearly perceived this.

Bella, of course, is no more a 'portrait' of any individual than
any other of Dickens's major female characters. The conception of a
beautiful, good-hearted girl, born into genteel poverty but hungry for the
good things of life, who determines to be 'a mercenary little wretch' and
who is shamed out of such an attitude by some good people who love her
was no doubt central to his overall conception of a novel which sets out to
show a whole society thoroughly corrupted by mercenary values. But
when he began to 'fill in' the character, as it were, to bring her alive, he
would, it seems natural to assume, have found some inspiration in
contemplating his 'bright handsome' daughter, struggling so bravely for
financial independence for herself and her ailing husband (Mrs Fields
noted how determined Katey was not to be dependent for money upon

her father).⁶⁸ It is even possible, I suppose, that Bella's peculiar situation at the beginning of the novel, which she deplores so vehemently ('. . . I am a most unfortunate girl. The idea of being a kind of widow, and never having been married!')⁶⁹ may be an oblique reflection of Katey's real-life situation, married as she apparently was to an impotent and (as Dickens believed) dying husband.

If I am right in thinking that Katey was, to some extent, Dickens's model for his wilful young heroine, it surely follows that we can see him delightedly creating, in Bella's teasingly affectionate relationship with her shabby, 'cherubic' little father, Rumty Wilfer, a charmingly comic version of Katey's real-life relationship with himself. Bella's prettily playful domineering over Rumty is also, of course, a benign variant on one of his favourite and perennial themes, that of devoted daughters looking after inadequate fathers (contrast, in the same novel, the shrewish behaviour of Jenny Wren to her 'bad child', her alcoholic wreck of a father) but it is so fresh and different, and treated in such loving detail, that a peculiarly personal element strongly suggests itself.

The scene in which Bella's relationship with her father is most intensely presented is found in the chapter entitled 'In Which an Innocent Elopement Occurs'. Bella, now the indulged protégée of the 'Golden Dustman' and his wife, impetuously descends on Rumty Wilfer toiling away in the dusty offices of Chicksey, Veneering and Stobbles, and carries him off for a tête-à-tête dinner. 'I like to have you all to myself today,' she tells him, 'I was always your little favourite at home, and you were always mine.' They go by river to dine at Greenwich (which was a favourite jaunt of Dickens's in real life):

> Everything was delightful. The park was delightful, the punch was delightful, the dishes of fish were delightful, the wine was delightful. Bella was more delightful than any other item in the festival; drawing Pa out in the gayest manner; making a point of always mentioning herself as the lovely woman [this being what her father has called her]; stimulating Pa to order things, by declaring that the lovely woman insisted on being treated with them; and in short causing Pa to be quite enraptured with the consideration that he *was* the Pa of such a charming daughter.

After dinner they sit watching the ships going by down to the sea and Bella elaborates all sorts of fantasies about them, relating to herself and her father ('. . . now, Pa was going to China in that handsome three-masted ship . . . to bring home silks and shawls without end for the decoration of his charming daughter'), in which visions of a future husband for 'the lovely woman' play a very dim and secondary part.

When, eventually, Bella does fall in love and marry a poor man (as she thinks) it is all described as a sort of delightful conspiracy between her father and herself. She and John Harmon (perhaps the shadowiest of all Dickens's heroes) announce their engagement to Rumty at his office and all three then share in an impromptu picnic there which was 'as Bella gaily said, like the supper provided for the three nursery hobgoblins at their house in the forest, without their thunderous low growlings of the alarming discovery, "Somebody's been drinking *my* milk!" '. The fairy-tale allusion is a characteristic Dickensian device for evoking a sense of innocent glamour and romance in the midst of mundaneness. The engagement is concealed from the rest of the Wilfer family, and Bella and her father 'elope' again to Greenwich early one morning for the actual marriage. This, in great contrast to Katey's splendid wedding at Gad's Hill, is a very simple affair, though surrounded with 'an ethereal air of happiness' which so powerfully affects 'a gruff and glum old pensioner' with two wooden legs, who sees Rumty and Bella disembarking, that he follows them to the church 'to see it out'. The fear that Bella's gloomily majestic mother might arrive at Greenwich 'in a car and griffins, like the spiteful Fairy at the christenings of the Princesses, to do something dreadful to the marriage service' proves groundless and soon Bella, her father and her new husband are enjoying an enchanted wedding feast:

> What a dinner! Specimens of all the fishes that swim in the sea, surely had swum their way to it, and if samples of the fishes of divers colours that made a speech in the Arabian Nights . . . were not to be recognized, it was only because they had all become of one hue by being cooked in batter among the whitebait.

Bella reassures her father that their relationship will not be changed, only enhanced:

> 'You know that you have only made a new relation who will be as fond of you and as thankful to you – for my sake and your own sake both – as I am; don't you, dear little Pa? Look here, Pa!' Bella put her finger on her own lip, and then on Pa's, then on her own lip again, and then on her husband's. 'Now we are a partnership of three, dear Pa.'[70]

Of course it is part of the whole scheme of the novel that Bella's definitive rejection of mercenary ideas by marrying the man she loves despite his apparent poverty should be a high point of celebration in the book and Dickens pulls out every stop (including his favourite *Arabian Nights* one) to achieve the required effect. But the biographical critic may well be justified in believing that an element of overcompensation is helping in the process. I have already alluded to the anecdote concerning

Dickens's stricken behaviour after Katey's wedding, an anecdote that originated, presumably, in what Mamie had told Katey herself:

> After the last of the guests not staying in the house had departed, Mamie went up to her sister's bedroom. Opening the door, she beheld her father upon his knees with his head buried in Katie's wedding-gown, sobbing. She stood for some moments before he became aware of her presence; when at last he got up and saw her, he said in a broken voice:
> 'But for me, Katey would not have left home', and walked out of the room.[71]

Instead of being, like Rumty Wilfer, a beloved father whose relationship with his favourite daughter had been such that he could play a vital role in promoting her marriage to the man she loved, Dickens had been a beloved father whose great personal crisis had had the effect of driving his favourite daughter into marriage with a man for whom she felt affection and respect but no love.

Once the connection between Katey and Bella is admitted it is possible to see in the idyllic presentation of Bella's wedding and of all her happiness in married life thereafter a sort of fictional making up to both himself and his daughter for the dreariness of the marriage she had entered. All Katey's apparent delight in her new role of housewife during 1860/1 is perhaps reflected in Bella's transformation from a much-admired young lady of leisure to busy little mistress of the modest cottage on Blackheath:

> Such weighing and mixing and chopping and grating, such dusting and washing and polishing, such snipping and weeding and trowelling and other small gardening, such making and mending and folding and airing. . . .[72]

But where Katey's initiation had led only to a life of nursing an invalid husband and striving to make ends meet, Bella's quickly leads to the joys of motherhood (she soon acquires a beautiful baby 'of wonderful intelligence') and a life of wealth and ease, for her husband turns out not to be the poor man she had supposed but the rightful inheritor of the Harmon fortune.

I would not want to press this point very far since Bella's role, her marriage and her fortunate destiny are all essential both to the plot and to certain major themes in *Our Mutual Friend*; they are unlikely to have been influenced by Dickens's private emotions about a particular person in the way that I have suggested Esther Summerson's story was influenced at one point by his anxieties about Georgina. But that a greater *intensity* may be present in his descriptions of Bella's happiness because of his awareness of Katey's unhappiness seems to me entirely plausible.

*

As Bella Wilfer is, most readers would agree, the most fascinating and attractive young woman that Dickens ever created, so Katey is surely the most remarkable and attractive of all the women in his life who were privileged to know him intimately. She seems to have been the one who understood him best both as man and as artist, recognizing him for the 'uncanny genius' that he was.[73] The only other woman who was sufficiently undazzled by the love and admiration she felt for him to see more deeply than others into the complexities of Dickens's character and personality was the beloved American friend of his last years, Annie Fields. She it was who recorded the following perceptive and haunting comment on him in her diary: 'wonderful, the flow of spirits C.D. has for a sad man'.[74] But Katey, with her special relationship with her father and her intimate domestic experience of him over thirty years and through such dramatic changes in his life, knew him as no friend could have done. Gladys Storey gives us a remarkable summing-up by Katey, towards the end of her life, of her attitude towards Dickens:

> 'I loved my father better than any man in the world – in a different way of course. . . . I loved him for his faults.' Rising from her chair and walking towards the door, she added: 'My father was a wicked man – a very wicked man'.[75]

'An uncanny genius', 'a wicked man': these are certainly startling judgments coming from the favourite daughter of Charles Dickens, even when we remember that the 'wickedness' to which she was referring relates specifically (as the context in Miss Storey's book makes clear) to his treatment of his wife in 1858. She wrote a book about him, 'clearing her mother of false accusations', but burned the manuscript:

> 'I told only half the truth about my father,' she said, 'and a half truth is worse than a lie, for this reason I destroyed what I had written. But the truth *must be told* when the time comes – after my death.'[76]

Her decision to destroy the manuscript is all the more admirable when one considers how much money she might have made by publishing it. But the idea that she could be seen as 'giving away my father and mother for pounds shillings and pence' was clearly repugnant to her and she had already decided to postpone the book's publication until after her death before she finally resolved to destroy it.[77] Acutely aware that her father was a far greater, far more richly human man than the figure created by the public's image of him, she once wrote, in comical exasperation, to Shaw:

> If you could make the public understand that my father was not a joyous, jocose gentleman walking about the world with a plum pudding and a bowl of punch you would greatly oblige me.[78]

Although we may today still have got many things about Dickens 'all wrong', as she feared would be the case, we have at least emancipated ourselves from this sort of travesty of the greatest novelist in our language. And the fact that we have done so is owing in no small measure to the courageous testimony to the complexity of his nature borne by that child of his who was, in more senses than one, the closest to his heart.

10

Ellen

'I wish I had been born in the days of Ogres and Dragon-guarded Castles. I wish an Ogre with seven heads (and no particular evidence of brains in the whole lot of them) had taken the Princess whom I adore – you have no idea how intensely I love her! – to his stronghold on the top of a high series of mountains, and there tied her up by the hair. Nothing would suit me half so well this day, as climbing after her, sword in hand, and either winning her or being killed. – *There's* a state of mind for you, in 1857.'

Dickens to the Hon. Mrs Watson, 7 December 1857[1]

On 13 April 1857 an eighteen-year-old girl 'with a pretty face and well-developed figure'[2] made her London debut on the stage of the Haymarket Theatre. She was playing the role of the young prince Hippomenes in a burlesque version of the legend of Atalanta, written by the son of Dickens's old friend Thomas Talfourd. Her name was Ellen Lawless Ternan and she came of good theatrical stock. Her mother, herself the daughter of a noted actress, had been on the stage for over forty years and had early established a reputation for herself not only as an actress but as a lady who was a model of virtue in her private life.[3] Her last major role in London had been in April 1856 as Paulina in Charles Kean's spectacular production of *The Winter's Tale* (the production in which another young Ellen, Ellen Terry, had made *her* debut, as the child Mamilius) and she was really now in semi-retirement, devoting herself to the education and careers of her three talented daughters, Fanny, Maria and Ellen. Her husband, an Irish actor called Thomas Ternan (once described by the great but irascible Macready as 'opinionated, jealous, and of course little-minded')[4] had died in a lunatic asylum at Bethnal Green in 1846. With Ellen's Haymarket appearance that April all three girls were now firmly launched upon a theatrical career. Fanny was also in Kean's company but was really seeking opportunities to pursue an operatic career; Maria, too, was engaged at the Princess's but had so far been restricted to minor roles, mainly rather romping parts in the farces which preceded or followed the main piece of the evening.

In the summer of 1857 Mrs Ternan, Maria and Ellen were all disengaged until the autumn when the two girls were due to appear with the Princess's company at the Theatre Royal, Doncaster, which was reopening for Races Week. Dickens was seeking some professional actresses to play in *The Frozen Deep* in Manchester for a couple of nights in August following its great success in London private performances (one of which had been attended by a well pleased Queen Victoria). The Ternans were recommended to him by Alfred Wigan, manager of the Olympic Theatre where Fanny had once been engaged, and Dickens, who must have seen Mrs Ternan act many times and who claimed to remember seeing Maria on the stage as 'a little child', was delighted to secure their services. Dickens himself played the hero, Richard Wardour, Mrs Ternan took the part of Nurse Esther, a character given to spine-chilling bouts of clairvoyance, and Maria was cast as the leading lady, Clara Burnham. The less experienced Ellen was given the minor role of Lucy Crayford and took also the not very demanding ingénue part of Eliza Comfort in Buckstone's farce, *Uncle John,* given as an after-piece to the main drama. In this she played opposite to Dickens, who acted the title role.

Some biographers seem to have let their imaginations run away with them in writing of Dickens's first contacts with Ellen during the rehearsals for the Manchester performances.[5] (Indeed, some have preferred to imagine that he had met her even earlier, during her playing in *Atalanta* at the Haymarket, when he had comforted her behind the scenes having found her weeping with embarrassment over the scantiness of her costume.[6] There is, however, no direct evidence whatever about Ellen's behaviour at the rehearsals or about Dickens's initial response to her. The nearest we can get to it is in Katey's remarks as posthumously reported by Gladys Storey: Ellen, Katey is alleged to have said,

> came like a breath of spring into the hard-working life of Charles Dickens
> – and enslaved him. She flattered him – he was ever appreciative of praise
> and though 'she was not a good actress she had brains, which she used to
> educate herself, to bring her mind more on a level with his own. Who
> could blame her? . . . He had the world at his feet. She was a young girl of
> eighteen, elated and proud to be noticed by him.'[7]

It is clear from what followed that Dickens did become infatuated with Ellen this summer and we can reasonably assume that Catherine became miserably aware of this, whether or not there is any truth in the story about the misdirected present of jewellery discussed in chapter 5; but how aware Ellen herself was of what was happening and how she responded to the situation we can only guess.

The Manchester performances were a tremendous success with Dickens 'literally electrifying the audience', according to Wilkie Collins (who played Dickens's favoured rival in love, the man whom Wardour saves for his beloved at the cost of his own life). Dickens's state of frenzied depression after the performances were over was partly a natural reaction but no doubt had also something to do with the feelings Ellen had aroused in him. To resume his strained domestic relations with Catherine with this added complication was simply impossible. 'I want to escape from myself', he wrote to Collins on 29 August. 'For when I *do* start up and stare myself seedily in the face, as happens to be my case at present, my blankness is inconceivable – indescribable – my misery amazing.' He urged Collins to accompany him on some expedition 'anywhere', to some 'out-of-the-way places': 'Have you any idea tending to any place in the world?' he asked him.[8] By 7 September it was apparently settled that they should go first to the Cumberland fells and then proceed to visit Doncaster to see the town in Races Week. It was not the races that drew Dickens to Doncaster, however: the 'loadstone rock' in this case was undoubtedly that 'small fair-haired rather pretty actress'[9] by whom he had now become fascinated.

Dickens and Collins arrived in Doncaster in time to attend the opening (14 September) of the Theatre Royal, their presence being duly recorded by the *Doncaster Gazette*.[10] The Ternan girls did not appear that night but made their debut on the following evening. Although we have no evidence that Dickens attended again on that second evening it seems improbable that he would not have done so and his outburst in *The Lazy Tour of Two Idle Apprentices*[11] about drunken and obscene-minded playgoers in the Doncaster theatre may derive much of its hysterical tone from the fact that he saw Ellen exposed to such loutish-ness, leading him momentarily to doubt 'whether it *is* a wholesome Art which sets women apart on a high floor before such a thing as this [i.e., a tipsy young "gent" whose drawling "slang criticisms on the representation" had particularly incensed Dickens]'.

We do not know how much, if at all, Dickens confided in Collins about his emotions whilst they were on their anything but 'lazy' tour. As Collins himself was notoriously irregular in his private life Dickens certainly did not need to fear any censoriousness from his friend but he may well have shrunk from exposing himself to Collins's light-hearted cynicism about affairs of the heart. The desperate intensity of 'Mr Good-child's' (i.e., Dickens's) emotional and physical existence contrasted with the relaxed and easy-going disposition of 'Mr Idle' (Collins) is, in fact, a running theme throughout the whole of the *Lazy Tour*. With respect to love-affairs it comes up especially in the Doncaster races section when Idle teases Goodchild about having 'fallen into a dreadful state concerning a pair of little lilac gloves and a little bonnet' that he has seen at the St Leger. Dickens then launches into a loving parody of what, it seems, was his own romantic state of mind as he makes Goodchild rhapsodize:

> O little lilac gloves! And O winning little bonnet, making in conjunction with her golden hair quite a Glory in the sunlight round the pretty head, why anything in the world but you and me! Why may not this day's running – of horses, to all the rest: of precious sands of life to me – be prolonged through an everlasting autumn – sunshine, without a sunset! Slave of the Lamp, or Ring, strike me yonder gallant equestrian Clerk of the Course, in the scarlet coat, motionless on the green grass for ages! . . . Arab drums, powerful of old to summon Genii in the desert, sound of yourselves and raise a troop for me in the desert of my heart, which shall so enchant this dusty barouche . . . that I, within it, loving the little lilac gloves, the winning little bonnet, and the dear unknown wearer with the golden hair, may wait by her side for ever, to see a Great St. Leger that shall never be run!

As always with Dickens the *Arabian Nights* allusions are a sure sign that his emotions are deeply stirred; they are a guarantee of the genuineness of his romantic feelings. And under the lightest of fictional guises he enjoys yet again that pleasure, so exquisitely dear to him, of exposing his deepest feelings to his beloved public without that public's at all suspecting what it is that he is doing.

I think it most likely that Dickens would have concealed from Collins the true depth of his feelings about Ellen. His own natural reticence and Collins's likely attitude towards the affair would surely incline him to disguise the matter by discussing it only in terms of comic fantasy as in the passage just quoted. To another friend not actually present and able to observe matters for himself, however, Dickens evidently felt able to drop arch hints of the truth, sure of not being understood. To his sub-editor W.H. Wills he wrote from Doncaster, 'But Lord bless you, the strongest parts of your present correspondent's heart are made up of weaknesses, and he just come to be here at all (if you knew it) along of his Richard Wardour! Guess *that* riddle, Mr. Wills!'. And two days after sending this mysterious intimation that his presence in Doncaster resulted directly from the *Frozen Deep* theatricals he announced to Wills, 'I am going to take the little – riddle – into the country this morning; and I answer your letter briefly, before starting . . . So let the riddle and the riddler go their own wild way, and no harm come of it!'.[12] This sounds as though Wills had guessed the 'riddle' (or perhaps Dickens had told him something more directly about his feelings for Ellen) and had remonstrated with his chief, warning him that great 'harm' might be done both to his reputation and his personal life (and he was by now nationally recognizable) by his publicly escorting a young actress.

Dickens, it seems pretty clear, was in a state of emotional confusion. Not the least disconcerting aspect of the situation for him may have been the realization that he was now in a predicament that only eighteen months or so before he had been vividly imagining for the wan hero of his last book, *Little Dorrit*. In Book I, chapter 14, of that novel Arthur Clennam debates with himself 'whether he should allow himself to fall in love with Pet [Meagles]':

> He was twice her age. Well! He was young in appearance, young in health and strength, young in heart. A man was certainly not old at forty ... On the other hand, the question was, not what he thought of the point, but what she thought of it.

The perplexity is resolved for Arthur by his discovering that Pet's love has already been bestowed on another. Dickens himself had a difficulty far more formidable than Arthur's diffidence to wrestle with, however. He was very much a married man, a paterfamilias indeed, and very famous. There was no likelihood whatever of his adoring public, let alone his wife, letting him and Ellen 'go their own wild way' without harm coming of it. But all such prudential considerations were opposed by his intense rest-lessness and dissatisfaction at this time, a dissatisfaction which, perhaps inevitably, was most strongly focused on his domestic life. He was haunted by visions of what might have been in this respect, and the tragi-comic vaporization of one such vision by poor Mrs Winter two years before had probably only intensified other, vaguer ones. Now as a focus for all such visions here was a real substantial young woman – charming, pretty, intelligent and (if Katey's testimony as transmitted by Miss Storey can be trusted) admiring and flattering him. It is small wonder that he was emotionally confused by his 'little riddle'.

Several years later we can, I believe, find him making effective artistic use of these emotional experiences of the summer and autumn of 1857. Eugene Wrayburn, the secondary and far more interesting hero of *Our Mutual Friend*, finds himself powerfully attracted by Lizzie Hexam, a Thames boatman's daughter. There is no great disparity in their ages, nor is Eugene already married, but for him marriage across such a great class-barrier as that between himself and Lizzie is socially almost unthinkable. He goes off on a pre-arranged boating vacation with his friend, Mortimer Lightwood, but is so distracted during it and afterwards that Lightwood at last taxes him with concealing something. Eugene replies that he can't tell his friend what is happening to him because he doesn't understand himself: '. . . how can I possibly give you the answer that I have not discovered? The old nursery form runs, "Riddle-me-riddle-me-ree, p'raps you can't tell me what this may be?" My reply runs, "No. Upon my life, I can't." ' An irruption at this point by Lizzie's brother and the schoolmaster, Bradley Headstone, reveals to Lightwood who Lizzie is and how Eugene has been preoccupying himself about her. After the visitors have gone the worried Lightwood interrogates his friend:

'Eugene, do you design to capture and desert this girl?'
'My dear fellow, no.'
'Do you design to marry her?'
'My dear fellow, no.'
'Do you design to pursue her?'
'My dear fellow, I don't design anything.'

Throughout the conversation Eugene has referred mockingly to 'the domestic virtues' that he is trying to cultivate in himself by surrounding himself with household implements ('miniature flour-barrel, rolling-pin', etc.) so that they may exert a 'moral influence' upon him. The chapter, which is entitled 'A Riddle without an Answer', ends with him still brooding on the 'troublesome conundrum' of his relations with Lizzie.

Dickens the plot-master eventually finds a way for Eugene to reconcile his passion for Lizzie with 'the domestic virtues', the sneers of the Podsnappian world notwithstanding. But as he contemplated his own 'little riddle' in the autumn of 1857 and wondered about the future, no amount of masterful plotting seemed likely to promise *him* such a happy deliverance. Meanwhile he could not linger in Doncaster for ever. He left on 21 or 22 September, before the Ternan girls' highly successful benefit night at the theatre (at which their mother, who had been chaperoning them during their time in the town, also appeared), returning to London and an increasingly unhappy Catherine. There he exerted himself to promote Ellen's career, writing (13 October) to Buckstone, manager of the Haymarket Theatre, to express his pleasure in the fact that Ellen had been re-engaged by him, perhaps at Dickens's instigation:

I need hardly tell you that my interest in the young lady does not cease with the effecting of this arrangement, and that I shall always regard your taking of her and remembering her, as an act of personal friendship to me. On the termination of her present engagement, I hope you will tell me, before you tell her, what you see for her, 'coming in the future'.[13]

He was, it would seem, publicly adopting an *in loco parentis* role[14] (a hardened theatrical manager like Buckstone is very unlikely to have been deceived by it, one must add) and Catherine's suspicions that this was but a thin disguise for very different feelings towards Ellen must have been maddening to him – especially since even a man as adept as Dickens at self-deception could hardly have helped recognizing how well founded those suspicions were. We noticed earlier the letter he wrote to Emile de la Rue on 23 October 1857 in which he complained of Catherine's 'excruciating' jealousy: '[she] has obtained proof positive of my being on the most intimate terms with, at least fifteen thousand women . . . since we left Genoa'.[15] He could feel sure of a sympathetic understanding from a friend who had seen for himself just how difficult Catherine could be when she felt she had cause for jealousy. There is, of course, no mention of, or allusion to, Ellen in this letter; and the grotesque exaggeration of 'fifteen thousand women' implicitly denies that there has ever been, or that there is now, any one woman whose presence in his life might give Catherine reasonable grounds for her Mrs Snagsby-like behaviour.

Even as he angrily rejected what he saw as Catherine's hysterical insinuations about the relationship, however, Dickens apparently continued to see his attachment to Ellen, represented to his friends as so paternal in character, in wildly romantic terms. This is clear from the passage from a letter to his dear friend, the Hon. Mrs Watson, châtelaine of Rockingham Castle, quoted as an epigraph to this chapter. And the fantasy therein developed about either rescuing an adored princess from a horrible imprisonment or perishing in the attempt[16] had already, by the time he wrote to Mrs Watson, helped to mould a bizarre ghost-story he had written for inclusion in the *Lazy Tour*. In this tale, as we saw in chapter 7, he developed another fantasy about a 'safe' wife-killing but he also contrived to work in one about trying to rescue a beleaguered girl. After the bride has been driven to her death her husband discovers a 'slender youth . . . with long light brown hair' has been spying on his nefarious activities and communing with the imprisoned girl from the branches of a tree outside her window. Powerless to save her, the gallant boy is determined to bring her psychological-murderer husband to justice and indeed proves eventually to be the means of doing so, but at the cost of his own life (the discovery of his corpse buried in the garden leads, after many years, to the husband's arrest, trial and execution). The girl is the only named character in the story. She is called Ellen.[17]

*

In real life Dickens's relations with Ellen Ternan were to have no such melodramatic dénouement. But just what those relations were and how they may have changed or developed during the last twelve years of Dickens's life has been, ever since a biographer called Thomas Wright first made the matter public in a 1934 newspaper article, a matter of intense controversy.[18] Hard evidence in the shape of letters from Dickens to Ellen, or from her to him, is still lacking,[19] and the few references made to her in his surviving letters to other people are for the most part rather ambiguous.[20] When, however, he was in America on his Reading tour during the winter of 1867/8 he enclosed his letters to Ellen in the business ones he was constantly sending to Wills and his references to these enclosures can leave us in little doubt about his feelings towards her:

> (December 10) Enclosed is another letter to my dear girl, to your usual care and exactness. . . . my spirits flutter woefully towards a certain place at which you dined one day not long before I left, with the present writer and a third (most drearily missed) person.

> (Xmas Eve) Enclosed, another letter as before, to your protection and dispatch. I would give £3,000 down (and think it cheap) if you could forward *me,* for four and twenty hours only, instead of the letter.

> (December 30) Another letter for my Darling, enclosed.

> (February 21, 1868) You will have seen too (I hope) my dear Patient, and will have achieved in so doing what I would joyfully give a Thousand Guineas to achieve myself at this present moment![21]

'The Patient' evidently became an affectionate nickname for Ellen between Dickens and Wills after her involvement in the Staplehurst railway accident in 1865 when she, and perhaps her mother also,[22] were travelling with Dickens on the boat-train (or 'tidal train' as it was then called) from Folkestone to London. We do not know if she was physically injured but she must, one imagines, have suffered badly from shock, like Dickens himself. He was certainly solicitous about her, sending from Gad's Hill the following instructions to his servant in London:

> Take Miss Ellen tomorrow morning, a little basket of fresh fruit, a jar of clotted cream from Tuckers, and a chicken, a pair of pigeons, or some nice little bird. Also on Wednesday morning, and on Friday morning, take her some things of the same sort – making a little variety each day. . . .[23]

Whether or not Ellen had by this time become Dickens's mistress and whether or not she also bore him a child (as alleged by various commentators citing hearsay and circumstantial evidence) must still be regarded as an open question. What is certain is that she became a major focus of his emotional life from 1858 onwards, that he spent much time with her whenever and wherever he could, and that he pined for her when they were separated for almost half a year by his American tour. The prospect of such a separation had nearly deterred him from undertaking the tour at all: 'The Patient I acknowledge to be the gigantic difficulty', he wrote to Wills in June 1867 when trying to make up his mind whether to go.[24] He made tentative arrangements for Ellen to visit America[25] (where she had relatives) whilst he himself was there but the plan was abandoned, no doubt because of the realization of the tremendous scandal that would ensue if his old enemy, the American press, should get hold of the story. In England, too, maximum discretion was necessary, of course, because, even if his relationship with Ellen was, in fact, an 'innocent' one, it was clearly susceptible of a scandalous interpretation by malicious observers such as the wife of the proprietor of *The Morning Post* (a snobbish newspaper always hostile to Dickens) who later wrote:

> Charles Dickens was once by chance my fellow-traveller on the Boulogne packet; traveling with him was a lady not his wife, nor his sister-in-law, yet he strutted about the deck with the air of a man bristling with self-importance, every line of his face and every gesture of his limbs seemed haughtily to say – 'Look at me; make the most of your chance. I am the great, the *only* Charles Dickens; whatever I may choose to do is justified by that fact.'[26]

If it had been widely known that Ellen's financial situation had changed in such a way after the beginning of her friendship with Dickens that she was able to retire from the stage, acquire property and become a young lady of leisure,[27] this would no doubt have fanned the flames of gossip. But we shall look in vain in the records of Dickens's bank-account at Coutts's for clear evidence that Ellen's improved circumstances resulted from his generosity.[28] It could equally well have been the case, after all, that upon attaining her majority in March 1860 (the month in which she became official leaseholder of the substantial London house in which her family were living) Ellen came into some inheritance which had been being held in trust for her.

Ellen was, as we can see from photographs of her, an attractive young woman. In certain of these photographs her facial expression strongly recalls, it seems to me, Dickens's oddly elaborate description of Lucie Manette's forehead in *A Tale of Two Cities*. At her first appearance in the novel Lucie, 'a short, slight, pretty figure' with 'a quantity of golden hair' and blue eyes is described as having

a forehead with a singular capacity (remembering how young and

smooth it was), of lifting and knitting itself into an expression that was
not quite one of perplexity, or wonder, or alarm, or merely of bright fixed
attention though it included all the four expressions[29]

and this particular expression of hers is often referred to thereafter. None
of Dickens's other heroines are given such a very individualizing physical
trait. Their characters and personalities are suggested far more through
speech and actions than through physical appearance (Bella Wilfer's
'petulant' shoulders being the only exception I can think of and these are
at once described as typical of her age and sex), and this makes me think it
highly likely that it was Ellen's face that was in Dickens's mind when he
came to describe the first heroine he had created since he began to love
her.

Our impressions of Ellen's actual character and personality must be
derived mainly from materials relating to her life after her marriage in
1876 because nearly all the surviving documentary evidence dates from
then. Her husband was George Wharton Robinson, a 'serious young
man', twelve years her junior, whom she had met when he was an Oxford
undergraduate reading for Holy Orders, and she was staying with her
sister Maria, married to an Oxford brewer since 1863. George went up to
Queen's College in October 1869 and graduated B.A. in 1873, taking his
M.A. two years later.[30] Ellen persuaded him to abandon the idea of
becoming a 'full-blown clergyman' and to concentrate on schoolmastering
instead. He took over a school at Margate and Ellen 'helped materially,
teaching in some of the classes, Elocution and French being her particular
subjects'. She also became friends with a local clergyman, Canon Benham,
an enthusiastic Dickensian, and joined him in giving recitals of Dickens's
work.[31] Dickens remained in her life in other ways too: she kept up a close
and warm friendship with Georgina Hogarth in particular but also with
Mamie and other members of the family.[32]

She had two children, Geoffrey, born 1879, and Gladys, born 1884.
Both of them seem to have grown up devoted to her. They reacted rather
differently, however, to Wright's allegations about the nature of their
mother's friendship with Dickens. Geoffrey preserved an outraged silence
on the subject until his death in 1959 but Gladys, who became Mrs
Reece, was stung into protest and gave J.W.T. Ley, Secretary of the
Dickens Fellowship, all the help she could to refute Wright's allegations.
She was particularly distressed by his portraying Ellen as cold-hearted,
capricious and mercenary in her dealings with Dickens and wrote heated-
ly to Ley that her mother was, on the contrary, warm, sympathetic, and
affectionate. Her generosity was attested by the fact that, despite her own
straitened circumstances in later life, she was always willing to help

friends less fortunate than herself. If there had been a liaison between her
mother and Dickens, she added, it could only have been because her love
for him was so strong that it swept aside all other considerations.[33]

This certainly sounds more like the kind of woman who would have
been Dickens's 'dear girl' than the figure portrayed by Thomas Wright
and copied by later biographers. Another aspect of her can be glimpsed in
some rather difficult business correspondence she engaged in (on behalf
of the Poet Laureate, Alfred Austin) with the publisher George Smith in
1872, and published by Leslie Staples in 1965.[34] She conducts her side
of the correspondence with admirable clear-headedness, business-like
conciseness and dignity, all qualities which we know Dickens esteemed
very highly.

Wright's version of the relationship, based on what he claimed to
have been told him by Canon Benham nearly forty years earlier, was that
Dickens 'prevailed upon' Ellen to become his mistress shortly after
his separation from Catherine and that 'she gave herself reluctantly',
influenced by 'vanity combined with a desire for a competence'. The
result was wretchedness for both of them. Dickens, wrote Wright,

> could not be happy (how could he!) knowing that Miss Ternan was
> assailing herself with reproaches and drawing daily further and further
> from him. They were both of them latterly miserable, and Dickens's
> unhappiness is reflected in his later books, which can only be understood
> in the light of this knowledge.[35]

This sentence first appeared in Wright's *Daily Express* article in April
1934 and inspired Hugh Kingsmill in his hostile biography of Dickens
published later that year to identify some of Dickens's later heroines
with Ellen. Estella's 'insolence and capriciousness no doubt reflect Miss
Ternan's contempt for her middle-aged lover and resentment against
him'; 'It is clear that . . . Bella declaiming against her poverty, and Miss
Ternan accepting jewellery from Dickens, are the same person'; and
the description of Helena Landless with her 'indefinable kind of pause
coming and going on [her] whole expression . . . which might be equally
likened to the pause before a crouch or a bound' 'probably sum[s] up
Ellen Ternan in her relation to Dickens' ('When she was frightened of
offending him past repair she crouched; when she was exasperated
beyond control she bounded'). Supporting evidence for these identifications could be found, Kingsmill believed, in the echoes of Ellen's two
first names in the names of these characters.[36] Wright repeated these
identifications in his own biography of Dickens published the following
year and, though prudently eschewed by Una Pope-Hennessy in her 1945

biography, they reappeared in Hesketh Pearson's *Dickens* (1949) and, in a slightly more tentative form, in Edgar Johnson's more substantial work in 1952. By now they seemed established and accepted as definite 'facts' and Dickens's 'dear girl' condemned as a result to live in literary history as a hard-hearted little gold-digger.[37]

What seems to me so extremely unsound about all this is that, firstly, it depends on assumptions about Ellen's relations with, and attitude towards, Dickens for which we have no direct evidence whatever and, secondly, it ignores some important continuities in Dickens's art, continuities which will be studied in more detail in the chapters following this one. Estella and Bella, for example, are clearly developments or modifications of a certain type of female character which Dickens began to explore in Edith Dombey,[38] long before Ellen entered his life. The type is that of the outwardly cold, haughty beauty who is torn by an inner conflict in which gentler, more loving aspects of her nature seek to assert themselves. As to possible biographical aspects of these two heroines, it seems to me, as I have argued in earlier chapters, that Maria Beadnell and Katey, Dickens's younger daughter (who was Ellen's age), are more likely than Ellen to have provided inspiration for creating Estella and Bella respectively. As to Helena Landless, her name may indeed echo Ellen's, but we should note that the surname has an obvious appropriateness to her and her brother as disinherited orphans. True, it may have been *suggested* to Dickens's mind by Ellen's middle name 'Lawless' just as Helena may be a toned-down version (suggested by thinking of 'Ellen') of 'Olympia', the exotic name with Grecian connotations that Dickens first intended to give to the girl.[39] But this is a very different thing from arguing that the character's name clearly shows that she was based upon the real-life girl whose name hers echoes. Helena is, in fact, no more an altogether new type of female character for Dickens than is Estella or Bella. He had created dark passionate types before, for example, Rosa Dartle and Hortense, and Helena is surely a softened-down, more sympathetic, version of these.

It is not, I would suggest, to Dickens's portrayal of his later heroines that we should look for evidence of the impact which his love for Ellen and his relationship with her had on his art, but to the intensity with which he depicts the love-passions of some of his later male protagonists, notably Bradley Headstone and Jasper, and his evident fascination with the themes of guilt and double lives. The biographical origins of this fascination would seem to be self-evident. His involvement with Ellen had resulted in his having to lead two lives, the one centred on Gad's Hill and known to the public, and the second centred on Ellen which it was imperative to keep strictly private both for his own sake and for hers.[40] Whether or not she was his mistress, their association still had to remain a secret because, of course, were it to become a matter of public knowledge it would generally be interpreted as an affair. Whilst this situation in itself may not have induced any deep-seated sense of guilt in Dickens, especially if the later allegations were untrue, he must surely have been concerned about the situation of gifted young Ellen herself and the effect on her life of her close friendship with him. Very suggestive in this respect is his strong reaction to a Parisian production of Gounod's *Faust* in January 1863. In this production, he wrote to Macready, there were 'some admirable, and really poetical, effects of light':

> In the more striking situations, Mephistopheles surrounded by an infernal red atmosphere of his own. Marguerite by a pale blue mournful light. The two never blending. After Marguerite has taken the jewels placed in her way in the garden, a weird evening draws on, and the bloom fades from the flowers, and the leaves of the trees droop and lose their fresh green, and mournful shadows overhang her chamber window, which was innocently bright and gay at first. I couldn't bear it, and gave in completely.[41]

To Georgina he wrote, more revealingly: 'I could hardly bear the thing; it affected me so, and sounded in my ears so like a mournful echo of things that lie in my own heart.'[42]

Four-and-a-half years later Dickens and Ellen were still in the same situation and its tensions were being highlighted by the 'gigantic difficulty' of facing up to the period of separation which would result if he decided to go on the projected American Reading tour. It was just at this time that he wrote 'George Silverman's Explanation', actually finishing it on 26 June 1867 in Ellen's Peckham home.[43] The latter part of this story is unquestionably, I believe, fantasizing about his relationship with Ellen. The clergyman Silverman finds himself acting as the tutor of a very beautiful and outstandingly intelligent young woman, Adelina Fareway. Looking back on his life, Silverman writes of this episode:

> I will not expatiate upon her beauty; I will not expatiate upon her intelligence, her quickness of perception, her powers of memory, her sweet consideration, from the first moment, for the slow-paced tutor who ministered to her wonderful gifts. . . .
>
> When I discovered that I loved her, how can I say? In the first day? in the first week? in the first month? Impossible to trace. . . .
>
> Whensoever I made the discovery, it laid a heavy burden on me. And yet, comparing with it the far heavier burden that I afterwards took up, it

does not seem to me now to have been very hard to bear. In the knowledge that I did love her, and that I should love her while my life lasted,
and that I was ever to hide my secret deep in my own breast, and she was
never to find it, there was a kind of sustaining joy or pride, or comfort,
mingled with my pain.

The 'far heavier burden' that he had soon to bear after his realization that
he loved Adelina was the realization that she loved him:

She may have enhanced my knowledge, and loved me for that; she may
have over-valued my discharge of duty to her, and loved me for that; she
may have refined upon a playful compassion which she would sometimes
show for what she called my want of wisdom, according to the light of
the world's dark lanterns, and loved me for that . . . but she loved me at
that time, and she made me know it.

Adelina has her own fortune and there is no external barrier to her union
with Silverman, but he, a psychologically crippled man, feels he has no
right to take 'advantage of her noble trustfulness' and bind her 'in the
zenith of her beauty and genius . . . to poor rusty, plodding me'. After
brooding for 'many and many a bitter night' he resolves to suppress his
love for her and to pretend not to recognize hers for him; instead, he sets
about diverting her affections to his other pupil, Granville Wharton, a
young man who is poor but of good family and 'well-looking, clever,
energetic, enthusiastic, bold; in the best sense of the term, a thorough
young Anglo-Saxon'. Silverman grooms Wharton for Adelina and takes
himself out of the running, as it were:

. . . I counterfeited to be older than I was in all respects (Heaven knows!
my heart being all too young the while) . . . and gradually set up more
and more of a fatherly manner towards Adelina. . . .

As I depressed myself with one hand, so did I labour to raise Mr
Granville with the other . . . fashioning him (do not deride or miscon-
strue the expression, unknown reader of this writing; for I have suffered!)
into a greater resemblance to myself in my solitary one strong aspect.

Wharton and Adelina obediently fall in love with each other and one
glorious summer morning, after indulging in some exalted meditations
on the seashore, Silverman marries them. For this he is reviled, dismissed
and persecuted by Adelina's mother but the young couple stand by him
and he eventually finds a sort of peace as a clergyman 'in a sequestered
place' where he composes his 'Explanation' which, he says, he writes 'for
the relief of [his] own mind, not foreseeing whether or not it will ever
have a reader'.[44]

Now the immediate occasion for Dickens's writing 'Silverman' was the acceptance of an American commission to write a short story for a substantial fee but, certainly, the work was not for him merely a pot-boiler: 'Upon myself', he told Wills, 'it has made the strangest impression of reality and originality!! And I feel as if I had read something (by somebody else) which I should never get out of my head!!'[45] What he had done, in fact, was to create a fiction which turned on him, its creator, sounding in his ears 'so like a mournful echo of things that lie in my own heart'. As I have suggested earlier, Silverman's horrific childhood and his emotionally devastating encounter with the pretty well-to-do farmer's daughter, Sylvia, can be seen as the latest echoes in Dickens's art of that searing boyhood suffering for which he blamed his mother and the later, almost equally searing, suffering caused him by Maria. In the story's final episode, about Adelina, it is difficult not to see a similar echo of Dickens's preoccupation with Ellen. Whether or not he and she were actually lovers, was he not keeping her in a situation which held no emotional future for her? She was already twenty-eight years old by 1867; ought he not to 'release' her so that she could marry and become the happy wife and mother he so fervently believed every woman ought to be?

When he was baffled by Georgina's quietly stubborn persistence in her dedicated spinsterhood Dickens was able, I have suggested, to console himself by solving the problem in his imaginative life by manipulating the ending of *Bleak House*. Now, I think, we see him doing a similar thing in this strange story. Just as Jarndyce plots against himself to wed Esther to young Woodcourt so does Silverman plot against himself to wed Adelina to young Granville Wharton.[46] But a much greater impression of agony on the part of the plotter is conveyed in 'Silverman', of course – inevitably so in that the plotter here is also the narrator whereas we glimpse Jarndyce's pain only through Esther's half-comprehending eyes, but surely also as a result of the great difference in Dickens's feelings towards Georgina and towards Ellen.

*

Dickens earned £1,000 by writing 'Silverman' and this was also the amount of the legacy that he left to Ellen in his will, made in May 1869 and published by Forster at the end of the last volume of his *Life of Dickens*. This legacy has been seen by some as confirmation that Ellen was indeed Dickens's mistress, by others as strong evidence against this supposition. A thousand pounds would certainly seem to be a remarkably ungenerous legacy to leave, out of an estate of £93,000, to a woman who had been one's mistress for upwards of ten years. Moreover, if Dickens's association with Ellen had been a guilty one he would hardly have named her so prominently (her legacy is the first item dealt with in the will) in a public document but would surely have made separate and private provision for her. In the absence of any clue as to his motivation in making this bequest and in fixing its amount we are reduced to pure (or impure) speculation. My own view is that the naming of Ellen in his will was a gesture of defiance by Dickens, a preparation for a sort of posthumous outfacing of scandal. People might be convinced of the innocence of his friendship with Ellen by the very fact that he made no secret of it in this place and left her the kind of legacy appropriate to a dear friend.

The debate about the history and precise nature of Dickens's relationship with his dear 'Patient' will doubtless continue indefinitely, in the absence of any first-hand, unambiguous evidence for or against the belief that Wright's assertions and Katey's reported comments are correct. But I venture to hope that students of Dickens's life may, as a result of this chapter, be a little less ready to accept as evidence of any real value the highly questionable reconstruction, based on the later fiction, of Dickens's relations with Ellen which was first put forward by Kingsmill in 1934 and later given the stamp of authority through the use made of it by Edmund Wilson in his epoch-making essay, 'Dickens: the Two Scrooges'.[47] Dickens's later novels may indeed exhibit features which seem likely to have derived from the impact of Ellen on his emotional life but they are, I have suggested, rather to be found in his portrayal of certain of his leading male figures than in his heroines.

*

So far in the book we have been examining Dickens's female characters in the light of his biography. The aim has been to explore some of the ways in which the presentation of women in his fiction can be shown to have resulted from the impact of certain individual women on his emotional life. The business of the next three chapters will be to consider his women characters from a more purely critical standpoint. To what extent can he be said to have created convincing representatives of female nature? This has generally been regarded as an area of his art best passed over quickly (at least until Estella in *Great Expectations* is reached) although Mrs Nickleby and Mrs Gamp have always been celebrated as wonderful examples of grotesque characterization. It is to the great women novelists of the mid-Victorian period, and to Trollope, that critics have turned to find non-stereotyped women characters, not to Dickens. The following survey aims to test the justice of this and, it is hoped, to show that this aspect of Dickens's art will bear closer scrutiny than has yet been accorded to it.

217

II

The Women of the Novels

'One blockhead talked of [Dickens's] deficiency in the female character – the very thing in which he and Shakespeare most excel.'
W.S. Landor to Lady Blessington, 1841

'All *his* women are dots, or drolls, and when he attempts to change the construction, he turns us into Lady Macbeths!'
Anna Maria Hall, *A Woman's Story*, 1857

11

'Sketches by Boz' to 'Martin Chuzzlewit'

In 1872 Wilkie Collins noted in his copy of Forster's *Life of Dickens*:

> The character of 'Nancy' is the finest thing he ever did. He never after-wards saw all sides of a woman's character – saw all round her. That the same man who could create 'Nancy' created the second Mrs Dombey is the most incomprehensible anomaly that I know of in literature.[1]

There is more to be said for 'the second Mrs Dombey' and for her successors in Dickens's fiction than Collins here allows but few would disagree with the assertion that, in the earlier fiction at least, Nancy does shine among all the female characters as a bright particular star.[2] She is the only character in whose portrayal Dickens seems to be seeking to explore a conception of female nature itself rather than simply pre-senting aspects of it, no matter how vividly, as perceived by men. It is undeniable that Nancy's speech, appearance and general demeanour lack the kind of social verisimilitude that Thackeray condemned Dickens for glossing over (Nancy, he declared, was 'no more like a thief's mistress than one of Gesner's shepherdesses resembles a real country wench').[3] But, as Dickens portrays her, with her resourcefulness and quick-witted cleverness, her various moods, her fears and her courage, she emerges as a far more complete embodiment of his conception of woman's nature than any of his other early female characters. This greater complexity is enhanced by her sudden pity for the little kidnapped boy, the passionate violence of her bitter outburst against Fagin, her swift capitulation to Rose Maylie's gentleness, and her strong assertion of her own values of personal loyalty against Mr Brownlow's reasoned exhortations to her to abandon her criminal associates and begin a decent new life far away.

For Nancy personal relations take precedence over most other con-siderations and her horrible death is the direct result of efforts to save the child she pities and yet to stay loyal to the man she loves. The mystery of her unswerving devotion to the brutish man who is in every way her inferior, and the paradoxical strength and dignity that this devotion gives her, 'fallen woman' though she is, fascinate Dickens and inspire him to develop her into the only one of his early female characters that can be taken at all seriously. Although she is often made to speak, especially at climactic moments, in high-flown and melodramatic terms, as in her last appeal to Sikes, there is more than one point in the book where Dickens makes her *sound* and behave in a movingly natural fashion. For example, there is her dialogue with Sikes when they hear a church-clock striking eight of the evening as they pass near Newgate with the recaptured Oliver:

> 'Eight o'clock, Bill,' said Nancy, when the bell ceased.
>
> 'What's the good of telling me that; I can hear it, can't I!' replied Sikes.
>
> 'I wonder whether *they* can hear it,' said Nancy.
>
> 'Of course they can,' replied Sikes. 'It was Bartlemy time when I was shopped; and there warn't a penny trumpet in the fair, as I couldn't hear the squeaking on. Arter I was locked up for the night, the row and din outside made the thundering old jail so silent, that I could almost have beat my brains out against the iron plates of the door.'
>
> 'Poor fellows!' said Nancy, who still had her face turned towards the quarter in which the bell had sounded. 'Oh, Bill, such fine young chaps as them!'
>
> 'Yes; that's all you women think of,' answered Sikes. 'Fine young chaps! Well, they're as good as dead, so it don't much matter.'
>
> With this consolation, Mr Sikes appeared to repress a rising tendency to jealousy, and, clasping Oliver's wrist more firmly, told him to step out again.
>
> 'Wait a minute!' said the girl: 'I wouldn't hurry by, if it was you that was coming out to be hung, the next time eight o'clock struck, Bill. I'd walk round and round the place till I dropped, if the snow was on the ground, and I hadn't a shawl to cover me.'
>
> 'And what good would that do?' inquired the unsentimental Mr Sikes. 'Unless you could pitch over a file and twenty yards of good stout rope, you might as well be walking fifty miles off, or not walking at all, for all the good it would do me. Come on, and don't stand preaching there.'
>
> The girl burst into a laugh; drew her shawl more closely round her; and they walked away. But Oliver felt her hand tremble, and, looking up in her face as they passed a gas-lamp, saw that it had turned a deadly white.[4]

There is an effective contrast here between, on the one hand, Nancy's quick imaginative sympathy with the condemned men and her horror at humanity's helping death to triumph over life in this way ('such fine young chaps as them!') and, on the other, Sikes's thoroughly masculine indifference to them and to their fate. Convincing, too, is the way in which, prompted by Sikes's surly reminiscences of his own time in Newgate, Nancy swiftly translates the situation into personal terms, vividly imagining how she herself would feel and act if *he* were one of the men awaiting execution. Out of context, the imagery in which she proceeds to express her tenderness and her fear for him might sound like melodramatic cliché but, given the strong emotion under which she is labouring, it seems entirely natural and appropriate. And her shocked reaction to Sikes's 'unsentimental' rebuff is most convincingly conveyed to the reader through the strung-up senses of the frightened child she is clutching. It is one of several places in the book where Dickens succeeds very well in dramatizing Nancy, at the level of speech and gesture as well as at a deeper level, as a figure of genuine emotional complexity. She is, of course, greatly helped in this particular passage by a momentary freedom from the twin burdens of the novel's intensely melodramatic plot and of Dickens's urgent social message, burdens which topple her speech towards implausibility on other occasions such as her interview with Rose in chapter 40 ('Oh, lady, lady! . . . if there was more like you, there would be fewer like me, – there would – there would!').

When we turn from Nancy, however, there are only three other female figures in Dickens's early fiction who can be included in the ranks of 'famous Dickens characters', three only who have achieved the same mythic status in our culture as a whole crowd of male figures (Pickwick, Pecksniff, Scrooge, and the rest) from the same period of the novelist's creativity. These are Little Nell, Mrs Nickleby and Mrs Gamp.

Little Nell is, like Oliver Twist, a symbolic figure, a bright Blakean innocent menaced and hunted through a dark world by the demon-figure of Quilp as Oliver is by Fagin; what is important is their age and vulnerability not their sex.[5] The femaleness of Mrs Nickleby and Mrs Gamp, on the other hand, is central to their comic vitality. For all that, however, we cannot discuss them as great comic types of female nature, characters who, like Chaucer's Wife of Bath or Shakespeare's Mistress Quickly, or indeed Dickens's own Flora Finching, have been imagined from the inside, as it were. They are not so much women as endlessly entertaining embodiments of certain traditional masculine attitudes towards women. In the case of Mrs Nickleby, Dickens pours into his creation of her all the time-honoured causes of men's serio-comic exasperation with women – their supposed butterfly-mindedness, illogicality, vanity, garrulousness, preoccupation with petty things, impracticality, sentimentality, proneness to romantic daydreaming, exaggerated respect for social rank and social conventions, and a complacent pride in the superiority of 'feminine intuition' over reason and common sense. As she happily stupefies all around her with her endless inconsequential chatter, or falls an easy victim to the flattery of titled scoundrels whilst

223

congratulating herself on her own 'womanly' perceptiveness, or simper-
ingly flirts with someone whom everyone but she sees to be a raving
madman, Mrs Nickleby is revealed as a huge anti-woman joke on
Dickens's part, originating, as we have seen, in feelings of hostility
towards his unforgiven mother. The point of departure for the whole
story is the financial ruin and subsequent death of her husband which
was the direct result of his following her advice against his better judgment, and she comes near to producing a second catastrophe during the
story by playing into the hands of her daughter's would-be seducers; it is
appropriate, therefore, that she should experience a little comic catastrophe of her own at the end of the story when her vanity is outraged by
old Tim Linkinwater's marrying Miss La Creevy, the little spinster whom
she as a widow has patronized so grandly throughout the story: 'That he
should have gone and offered himself to a woman who must be – ah, half
as old again as I am – and that she should have dared to accept him! . . .
I'm disgusted with her!'

If Mrs Nickleby is an anti-woman joke developed out of masculine
exasperation, Mrs Gamp is one developed out of masculine fears. Like
the ubiquitous Femme Fatale, Sairey Gamp is a clear literary expression
of a dread of the female. She is, in her 'highest walk of art', a midwife, also
'a nurse, and watcher, and performer of nameless offices about the
persons of the dead'. Her ample form presides, with tipsy gusto, over the
great twin mysteries of our existence, birth and death, and she overflows
with arcane female wisdom on these matters, a wisdom dauntingly
inaccessible to men. It is impressively displayed in her frequent reports of
thrilling dialogues she claims to have held with her mysterious friend,
Mrs Harris. Here she is about to set out on a journey and speaking to her
admiring little landlord:

> 'Says Mrs Harris, with a woman's and a mother's art a-beatin in her
> human breast, she says to me, "You're not a-goin, Sairey, Lord forgive
> you!" "Why am I not a-goin, Mrs Harris?" I replies. "Mrs Gill," I says,
> "wos never wrong with six; and is it likely, ma'am – I ast you as a mother
> – that she will begin to be unreg'lar now? Often and often have I heerd
> him say," I says to Mrs Harris, meaning Mr Gill, "that he would back his
> wife agen Moore's almanack, to name the very day and hour, for nine-
> pence farden. *Is* it likely, ma'am," I says, "as she will fail this once?" Says
> Mrs Harris, "No, ma'am, not in the course of nater. But," she says, the
> tears a-fillin in her eyes, "you knows much betterer than me, with
> your experienge, how little puts us out. A Punch's show," she says, "a
> chimbley sweep, a newfundlandog, or a drunkin man a-comin round the
> corner sharp, may do it." So it may, Mr Sweedlepipes,' said Mrs Gamp,

'there's no denigning of it; and though my books is clear for a full week, I takes a anxious art along with me, I do assure you, sir.'[6]

Mrs Gamp, Dickens tells us, took very kindly to her profession 'in so much that, setting aside her natural predilections as a woman, she went to a lying-in or a laying-out with equal zest and relish'. And it is precisely this indiscriminate 'zest and relish' that make her both so funny and so frightening. She is at her most sinister when, on first inspecting a fever-ridden young man she has come to nurse, she bends down and pins his arms against his sides 'to see how he would look if laid out as a dead man' ('Ah!', she exclaims, 'he'd make a lovely corpse!'); and she is at her most comic in the next few paragraphs as she greedily enjoys her assorted beverages and carefully ordered tasty supper ('I don't believe a finer cowcumber was ever grow'd') before taking her patient's pillow to make herself more comfortable in the 'extemporaneous bed' she constructs for the night. Her 'natural predilections as a woman', among which Dickens and his readers would have numbered gentleness, sympathy and self-sacrificing devotion to the care of the sick, have been 'set aside' with a vengeance and she appears as a monstrous travesty of that 'Angel of Death' aspect of Victorian woman that, as Alexander Welsh has shown,[7] was so dear to the Victorian male imagination, and especially to Dickens's.

Another most exalted and venerated female role for the Victorians was that of Niobe or the bereaved mother. We might recall those mothers who had 'daughters as was dead' encountered by Mr Peggotty in his search for Em'ly and his exclamation, 'God only knows how good them mothers was to me!'; also the joy of the women in one of Dickens's later Christmas Stories, 'The Perils of Certain English Prisoners', over the discovery that a certain child was not dead as had been feared: 'The joy of the women was beautiful; the joy of those women who had lost their own children was quite sacred and divine'. Yet in his huge Gamp joke against women Dickens contrives to turn even maternal bereavement into comedy (Mrs Gamp is reporting yet another of her alleged conversations with Mrs Harris to Ruth Pinch):

' "Our calcilations, ma'am," I says, "respectin' wot the number of a family will be, comes most times within one, and oftener than you would suppoge, exact." "Sairey," says Mrs Harris, in a awful way, "Tell me wot is my indiwidgle number." "No, Mrs Harris," I says to her, "ex-cuge me, if you please. My own," I says, "has fallen out of three-pair backs, and had damp doorsteps settled on their lungs, and one was turned up smilin' in a bedstead, unbeknown. Therefore, ma'am," I says, "seek not to proticipate, but take 'em as they come and as they go." Mine,' said Mrs Gamp, 'mine is all gone, my dear young chick.'[8]

And later we hear about a stillborn child of Mrs Harris's sister which was 'kep in spirits in a bottle':

> . . . and that sweet babe [Mrs Harris] see at Greenwich Fair a-travelling in company with the pink-eyed lady, Prooshan dwarf, and livin' skelinton, which judge her feelins when the barrel organ played, and she was shown her own dear sister's child, the same not bein' expected from the outside picter, where it was painted quite contrairy in a livin' state, a many sizes larger, and performing beautiful upon the Arp, which never did that dear child know or do: since breathe it never did, to. speak on, in this wale![9]

It is as though, in portraying Mrs Gamp, Dickens decided to make the gruel of her boozy ramblings thick and slab with all those things which were held to be pre-eminently female concerns, aspects of life very much in the female domain – childbirth, babies, sustaining food and drink, nursing the sick, deathbeds – and so turned them all into grotesqueness, matter for laughter. His drunken old midwife is, like Mrs Nickleby, a great anti-woman joke rather than a serious attempt, like Nancy, at creating an actual woman character; only this time the joke has a decided undercurrent of fear – and is all the better for it.

*

Mrs Nickleby and Mrs Gamp both 'surprise us by a fine excess', as Keats said great poetry should: they are wonderful triumphs of Dickens's popular art. But besides them, in his early fiction, we find a whole host of other comic female figures – mostly having very limited and minor roles to play – that Dickens adopted more or less straight from established stock types of traditional farce. Foremost among them is the figure of the nagging, tyrannical wife, a figure whose ancestry stretches all the way back to the Mrs Noah of medieval miracle plays and beyond. Mrs Tibbs in *Sketches by Boz* is a comparatively mild specimen but her shrew-successors, Mrs Pott, Mrs Raddle, Mrs Sowerberry and Mrs Bumble, are formidable viragos. They keep their hapless husbands under a perpetual reign of terror through the power of hysterics, or, in the case of Mrs Bumble (who is the most fearsome of them all, having already broken one husband before taking Bumble in hand), by actual physical violence:

> . . . the expert lady, clasping him tightly round the throat with one hand, inflicted a shower of blows (dealt with singular vigour and dexterity) upon it with the other. This done, she created a little variety by scratching

his face, and tearing his hair; and, having, by this time, inflicted as much punishment as she deemed necessary for the offence, she pushed him over a chair . . . and defied him to talk about his prerogative again, if he dared.[10]

Other virago-figures in the early fiction are Mrs Mann (also in *Oliver Twist*), Mrs Squeers and Sally Brass, but these are shown as tyrannizing over children rather than over husbands, as nightmare mothers rather than as nightmare wives. Mrs Squeers and Sally Brass do have male partners, in fact, but these function as accomplices rather than victims. In the case of Sally and her brother Dickens emphasizes the element of role-reversal – Sampson is soft and gentle in his villainy whereas Sally is bold and harsh; she has, moreover, a 'gaunt and bony figure', a deep voice and 'upon her upper lip certain reddish demonstrations, which . . . might have been mistaken for a beard'. And she 'delighted in nothing so much as irritating her brother' who was 'at heart in great fear' of her.

Sally's physical violence is directed not towards Sampson, however, but towards their diminutive servant, nicknamed 'The Marchioness' by Dick Swiveller; nor is it presented as straightforward virago-brutality like Mrs Squeers's conduct towards Smike and the other boys but as something more complex. Swiveller secretly observes her rationing out and supervising the child's meagre dinner:

> It was plain that some extraordinary grudge was working in Miss Brass's gentle breast, and that it was that which impelled her, without the smallest present cause, to rap the child with the blade of the knife, now on her hand, now on her head, and now on her back, as if she found it quite impossible to stand so close to her without administering a few slight knocks. But Mr Swiveller was not a little surprised to see [her], after walking slowly backwards towards the door . . . dart suddenly forward, and falling on the small servant give her some hard blows with her clenched hand. The victim cried, but in a subdued manner as if she feared to raise her voice . . .[11]

The surviving proofs and manuscript of *The Old Curiosity Shop* reveal that Dickens originally intended to make it clear that the Marchioness was Sally's natural child and to hint strongly that the father was Quilp.[12] But then, realizing the difficulties readers would have in accepting that a child of such hideous heredity should turn out a heroine, he suppressed the passage in which Sally explicitly asserts the Marchioness to be her child and leaves in the text only such mysterious hints at the truth as the above description and one or two other passages like Quilp's mock-gallantry towards Sally in chapter 33:

'There she is,' said Quilp . . . 'there is the woman I ought to have married
– there is the beautiful Sarah – there is the female who has all the charms
of her sex and none of their weaknesses. Oh, Sally, Sally!'
To this amorous address Miss Brass briefly responded 'Bother!'

It seems, in fact, that in his original conception of Sally Brass Dickens
was aiming at something a little more complex than the standard virago,
man-woman figure he had already portrayed so effectively in Mrs
Bumble or Mrs Squeers. In Sally he was seeking to depict, though still
comically (that is, unsympathetically), a woman who had not been as
successful as she had wanted in suppressing all 'normal' female feelings.
The child would be a constant, resented reminder to her of this failure, as
would Quilp's facetiousness, and so her cruelty to the Marchioness
would be understandable to the reader if not to Dick Swiveller.

Besides the virago-figures we find in Dickens's early fiction another
kind of misery-causing wife. These are women like Mrs Weller and Mrs
Varden, whose buxom charms proclaim that they ought by nature to be
kind and comfortable Good Providers but who have been spoiled by
becoming addicted to a sensational brand of religion, some form of
hell-fire Protestantism. Dickens noted in Boston in 1842 that one of the
chief occupations of the ladies was going 'in crowds' to some Evangelical
church or chapel and he comments,

> . . . wherever religion is resorted to, as a strong drink, and as an escape
> from the dull monotonous round of home, those of its ministers who
> pepper the highest will be the surest to please. They who strew the Eternal
> Path with the greatest amount of brimstone . . . will be voted the most
> righteous.[13]

It seems as if he regarded Evangelical religion as a noxious addiction to
which women were particularly prone, with dismal consequences for
their nearest and dearest. In the midst of denouncing this tendency, we
notice, he points very clearly to one of the main social reasons for it, the
confinement of women to 'the dull monotonous round of home', but this
is done very much *en passant*. In the novels female addiction to Evan-
gelicalism is always presented as the result either of simple-minded
gullibility or of sheer perversity in the women themselves.

Mrs Nubbles is one of the least culpable of these religion-infected
women, but Kit still has to beseech her to give up her going to Little Bethel
lest he should see her 'good-humoured face that has always made home
cheerful, turned into a grievous one, and the baby trained to look
grievous too, and to call itself a young sinner . . .'. Under the ministration
of the Reverend Mr Stiggins, Mrs Weller makes her easy-going husband's

domestic life a trial which only his 'philosophy' enables him to support.[14] One of the most trying aspects of the situation for him is to see the perversion of her 'Good Provider' qualities in the service of Stiggins on whom she lavishes unlimited quantities of pineapple rum and hot buttered toast, as well as joining with other, similarly deluded, ladies in the Brick Lane Branch of the United Grand Junction Ebenezer Temperance Association to provide huge quantites of ham and muffin for the delectation of another 'shepherd', 'a fat chap in black, with a great white face, a smilin' away like clockwork'. Mrs Varden in *Rudge* is rather less farcically presented than Mrs Weller, but she is essentially the same type: a zealous supporter of Lord George Gordon's Protestant Association (she is a member of the Clerkenwell Branch), she is at her most disagreeable domestically when at her most Protestant and vice versa ('Whenever she and her husband were at unusual variance, then the Protestant Manual was in high feather').

Once the spell of their high-spiced religion has been broken such women as Mrs Weller and Mrs Varden naturally revert to their true wholesome 'comfortable' selves; Mrs Weller is made to point the moral – implausibly enough – on her deathbed:

> 'I begin to see now,' she says, 'ven it's too late, that if a married 'ooman vishes to be religious, she should begin vith dischargin' her dooties at home, and makin' them as is about her cheerful and happy, and that vile she goes to church, or chapel, or wot not, at all proper times, she should be wery careful not to con-wert this sort o' thing into a excuse for idleness or self-indulgence.'[15]

Mrs Varden's being made to see the error of her ways comes about more credibly as she gradually realizes what appalling results the fanaticism of the Protestant Association is leading to. During the Gordon Riots, 'too much scared . . . to have recourse to her usual matrimonial policy', she begins obeying her husband 'quite amiably and meekly' and when we see her again, after the Riots are over, she has become the comfortable Good Provider Nature meant her to be, presiding over a family feast of 'clear, transparent, juicy ham, garnished with cool green lettuce-leaves and fragrant cucumber' and divers other eatables, 'all set forth in rich profusion'; and, as is Dickens's custom in such cases, the woman herself is made to figure as the choicest delicacy in the whole feast – 'buxom in bodice, ruddy in cheek and lip, faultless in ankle, laughing in face and mood, in all respects delicious to behold'.[16] She retains what Dickens evidently regarded – however much he guyed it in Mrs Nickleby – as a charming feminine failing, a confidence in her own 'penetration and extreme sagacity' in the matter of personal relationships, but her firm rebuff to Miggs shows that she has definitely renounced her really vicious faults, those which Dickens so strongly associated with her attachment to a fanatical sectarianism.

*

The tyrannical wives who feature so prominently in Dickens's early fiction show him exploiting one time-honoured vein of anti-woman comedy. Another such vein is worked in his frequent presentation of various kinds of social competitiveness, something which seems traditionally to have been regarded as a form of behaviour almost exclusively feminine – men being, presumably, concerned with other, more serious and important forms of competition. The Wife of Bath's rage against those of her neighbours who dared to take precedence of her at church is, rather mutedly, echoed in some of the earliest-written of the *Sketches by Boz* such as 'The Steam Excursion' or 'Mrs Joseph Porter'. In the former, the absurd rivalry between Mrs Briggs and her daughters and Mrs Taunton and hers becomes one of the basic running jokes of the piece after the fact of its existence has been established with great verve:

> If Mrs Taunton appeared in a cap of all the hues of the rainbow, Mrs Briggs forthwith mounted a toque, with all the patterns of the kaleido-scope. If Miss Sophia Taunton learnt a new song, two of the Miss Briggses came out with a new duet. The Tauntons had once gained a temporary triumph with the assistance of a harp, but the Briggses brought three guitars into the field, and effectually routed the enemy.

In 'Mrs Joseph Porter' the Gattletons' ostentation and presumption in staging some elaborate amateur theatricals offends their Clapham neighbour, Mrs Porter, who promptly sets herself to spoil their triumph.[17] In another sketch, 'Ladies' Societies', Dickens turns his attention to the way in which the setting up of charitable organizations can be merely one form taken by the endless suburban or parochial warfare waged against each other by women: the Misses Brown's 'child's examination society' is counteracted by Mrs Johnson Parker's Bible and prayer-book distribution society, and so on.

In the novels that follow *Sketches*, however, Dickens does not much exploit the comic potential of this particular aspect of middle and lower-middle class female behaviour though it is touched on in his presentation of Mrs Kenwigs, bursting with pride at the thought of her children's having private tuition in French and ensuring that the neighbours will hear all about it:

'And when you go out in the streets, or elsewhere, I desire that you don't boast of it to the other children,' said Mrs Kenwigs; 'and that if you must say anything about it, you don't say no more than "We've got a private master comes to teach us at home, but we ain't proud, because ma says it's sinful".'[18]

More richly mined is another traditional vein of anti-woman humour (the 'bluestocking' gibe, one might call it), in which any female manifestation of interest in art and culture or in things of the mind generally is found to be irresistibly laughable. Mrs Leo Hunter and her 'Ode to an Expiring Frog' and Mrs Wititterly for whom Shakespeare is 'such a delicious creature' are excelled in absurdity only by the American Transcendentalist Mrs Hominy, 'writer of reviews and analytical disquisitions', who 'went headlong into moral philosophy at breakfast' and 'not only talked, as the saying is, like a book, but actually did talk her own books, word for word'; and by the two 'Literary Ladies' (Miss Toppit and Miss Codger) whom Mrs Hominy presents to Elijah Pogram in chapter 34 of Martin Chuzzlewit. Schoolmistresses are, of course, ridiculous ex officio, like the Misses Crumpton of Minerva House, Miss Tomkins, the 'lady abbess' of Westgate House Establishment for Young Ladies, or Miss Monflathers who berates Little Nell for being 'a waxwork child': intense snobbery and hysterical prudishness seem to be their characteristic qualities rather than any interest in matters educational.

The assumption seems to be that all schoolmistresses must be frustrated spinsters who would have married if they could have done so. Indeed, virtually all the single women, whether maids or widows, in Dickens's early fiction are presented primarily as husband-hunters of one sort or another. The longer they are unsuccessful the more bitter and spiteful do the maiden ladies become, like Miss Knag or the 'divers unmarried ladies past their grand climacteric' whom Mr Pickwick sees in the Assembly Rooms at Bath, sitting on the back benches 'not dancing because there were no partners for them, and not playing cards lest they should be set down as irretrievably single' but 'in the favourable situation of being able to abuse everybody without reflecting on themselves'.

Miss La Creevy seems to be young Dickens's one concession to the argument that prolonged spinsterhood does not necessarily turn every woman into a sour old maid,[19] and she is duly rewarded with a 'comfortable' old husband at the end of the story. Otherwise, the main exceptions to this husband-hunting rule fall into three groups: innocent young heroines like Rose Maylie, Kate Nickleby, Madeline Bray, Mary Graham (also one such secondary heroine, Ruth Pinch), who are devoted to the

231

care of elderly relatives and/or a beloved brother and whose husbands come to them unsought; grotesque men-women like Sally Brass and Betsey Prig; and those two supreme solipsists, Mrs Nickleby and Mrs Gamp.

Dickens is, of course, doing no more than reflecting the social realities of contemporary middle and lower-middle class life when he portrays match-making mothers like Mrs Maplesone and Mrs Malderton in *Sketches* or Mrs Colonel Wugsby in *Pickwick*. He sees, and presents, the comic side of their activities and is conventionally critical of the mercenariness involved but there is, at this stage in his writing, no deeper investigation of the effect upon the young women themselves of this maternal manipulation. By the time he comes to create Edith Dombey and Annie Strong it will have ceased to be a matter for easy laughter, but in these earlier writings he simply sees the young women as being quite as comic as their mothers in their efforts to attract a husband:

> One of [Mrs Maplesone's daughters] was twenty-five; the other, three years younger. They had been at different watering-places, for four seasons; they had gambled at libraries, read books in balconies, sold at fancy fairs, danced at assemblies, talked sentiment – in short, they had done all that industrious girls could do – but, as yet, to no purpose.[20]

There are hints here for a comic character that might have been developed into a Dickensian forerunner of Thackeray's Becky Sharp.[21] But Dickens seems to have found more attractive as a subject for comedy (perhaps because he did, after all, have some feeling that young women like the Miss Maplesones could also be seen as victims of social conventions) the older woman possessed of property and a romantic temperament who yearns for a dashing young husband. Such a type, for example, is Miss Julia Manners in *Sketches*, 'a buxom richly-dressed female of about forty', who plans to elope with a silly young lord in a post-chaise to Gretna Green. When another man is put into the chaise by mistake, however, she happily reconciles herself to the situation since the stranger 'was a young man, had highly promising whiskers, an undeniable tailor, and an insinuating address . . .'. Her successors include the spinster aunt in *Pickwick*, Rachel Wardle, who falls such an easy victim to Jingle's gallantry, and Madame Mantalini whom we see repenting at leisure, and at considerable expense, her infatuation with her much younger, magnificently bewhiskered, spouse.

The blooming widows who abound in Dickens's early fiction – usually landladies of one sort or another and emphatically Good Providers (the 'comely' Mrs Bardell's 'natural genius for cooking', for example, has been 'improved by study and long practice into an exquisite talent') – tend not to share the romantic weaknesses of the middle-aged spinsters, but rather to be concerned with the comfort and security that a second husband might provide. It is not Mark Tapley's youthfulness nor any 'dashing' qualities about him that inspire Mrs Lupin's affection but his sturdy dependability and good-heartedness – much the same qualities, in fact, that lead Mrs Jarley to prefer her prosaic George before the 'poetic' Mr Slum. This kind of 'comfortable' middle-aged marrying has Dickens's wholehearted approval, and we should note that Mrs Bardell is not ridiculed for longing to marry Mr Pickwick but only for jumping the gun, as it were, and for subsequently allowing herself to be manipulated by a pair of rascally lawyers.

*

Presentable young ladies on the marriage market, middle-aged spinsters yielding to romance, buxom widows yearning for a 'comfortable' man – none of these types are exposed to quite such harsh mockery in Dickens's early fiction as unattractive young women – 'frights', to use the Victorians' own word – who presume to aspire to matrimony. Miss Squeers doting on Nicholas's straight legs or Miss Miggs vainly sharing Sim Tappertit's adoration of his own legs ('perfect curiosities of littleness', according to the author) stimulate Dickens to ecstacies of masculine jeering. In Miss Miggs's case her intense sexual frustration and its relation to the sharpness of her temper is made quite clear, but all possibility of feeling sympathy for this character is rigidly excluded (we might contrast the very different way in which Dickens portrays Rosa Dartle a few years later). Miggs, hungering for ravishment, is simply a figure of fun. Hearing Sim's 'stealthy footsteps' outside her bedroom door, she

> turned pale and shuddered, as mistrusting his intentions; and more than once exclaimed, below her breath, 'Oh! what a Providence it is, as I am bolted in!' – which, owing doubtless to her alarm, was a confusion of ideas on her part between a bolt and its use; for though there was one on the door, it was not fastened.[22]

Charity Pecksniff is another example of this sort of jeering at 'frights', though her attraction to her unprepossessing cousin, Jonas, seems to be not so much sexual as financial. Her subsequent fastening on the hapless young Moddle, too, is mainly a matter of scoring off her sister by securing as quickly as possible a more satisfactory (i.e. more docile) husband than she (Mercy) has got, as well as of triumphing over her unmarried female cousins and their 'strong-minded' mother. When she is jilted at the last minute it is not the loss of Moddle himself (bound in desperation for Van Diemen's Land) that makes her swoon but 'the bitterness of knowing that the strong-minded woman and the red-nosed daughters towered triumphant in this hour of their anticipated overthrow'.

'Frights' apart, the young women in Dickens's early fiction mostly belong to one of two groups, either to the 'Marys' or to the 'Marias' (to label them by the great names from the emotional life of his young manhood). The 'Marys' – Rose Maylie, Kate Nickleby, Madeline Bray, Mary Graham – are beautiful, sympathetic, devoted, self-sacrificing seventeen-year-olds, a succession of stained-glass memorials to Mary Hogarth as she had become angelically transformed in Dickens's mind. Not, of course, that this type of angel-heroine was an invention of Dickens's; she had passed into the fiction of his day from the Gothic novel of the late eighteenth century. There, her main business had been to suffer various startling vicissitudes in some romantic setting such as Udolpho's castle, to be sexually threatened and yet to remain steadfastly true in love to the hero. Rose Maylie, the first of the 'Marys', escapes the sexual threat because the pretty little child, Oliver, undergoes this for her (Fagin's attempted seduction of him is not sexual in nature, of course, only in atmosphere) but Kate, Madeline and Mary Graham all have to endure the hot breath, and hot hands, of evil men, like true Gothic heroines but without the exotic setting. Dickens seems to be acknowledging the literary provenance of Madeline, his secondary heroine in *Nickleby*, when, commenting on Nicholas's dazzled sight of her shining away in a slum setting, he writes: 'And yet Nicholas was in the Rules of the King's Bench Prison! If he had been in Italy indeed, and the time had been sunset, and the scene a stately terrace! . . . '.[23]

Kate, Madeline and Mary Graham are all the subject of their creator's strong moral approval but this is not enough for him to be able to breathe life into them; they remain one-dimensional. This, I believe, is because they cannot show real fear, as distinct from shrinking modesty; they must be strong and resolute in love, whether for brother or father or fiancé, and Dickens, however much he might consciously endorse and approve this resoluteness, was not really happy with its manifestation in a woman, even when caused by love. 'Strong-minded women' we know he feared and disliked; 'strong-souled' ones he professed to admire, even venerate, but imaginatively they left him cold. Another 'Mary' heroine, Little Nell, is more successful as a character because, being still a child, she can be permitted to be afraid, even terrified, and this stimulates Dickens's imagination to good effect as in the scene in which Quilp leeringly asks the child how she would like to become his 'number two', or the later scene where she wakes to find a robber in her bedroom. Nell also has an advantage over the other 'Mary' figures, from the point of view of coming to life as a character, in that she has to act whereas they only react to events. The mingled fear and courage, innocence and cunning, trusting-ness and suspicion, with which Nell pursues her naive determination to save her grandfather from Quilp by flight into the depths of the country is, I think, quite convincingly evoked by Dickens, as is the child's crushing sense of isolation and loneliness. What damages Nell's credibility with the reader is surely not Dickens's portrayal of the child herself but the fantastic improbability of a beautiful fourteen-year-old girl's being able to take to a tramping life in the England of 1840, with no more protection than a senile old man, and experience nothing worse than anxiety and exhaustion. It is this that forces us to take her as a symbolic rather than a 'real' girl.

Dickens was able to make his 'Maria' figures, those whom we may think of as having been generally inspired by Maria Beadnell, a good deal livelier than his 'Mary' ones since they are not required to be 'strong-souled' and their business is to provoke action rather than just to react. They are pretty, flirtatious girls, frivolous in their behaviour but essenti-ally good-hearted, sometimes only faintly sketched in like Arabella Allen in *Pickwick* ('one black-eyed young lady in a very nice little pair of boots with fur round the top') or poor Sophy Wackles, left by Dick Swiveller 'sorry – in the possession of a Cheggs'; sometimes given a little more character and individuality like 'Tilda Price or Miss Snevellicci. The most developed 'Maria' type, one whom Dickens tries to render with some complexity, is Dolly Varden. In the scene when her lover Joe Willet, to whom she is by no means indifferent, comes to take leave of her before despairingly enlisting in the army, he appeals for 'one word of comfort from her'. Dolly is affronted that he is going away, considering that he professes to love her so much: 'Here he was, talking like a gentleman at large who was free to come and go and roam about the world at pleasure, when that gallant coach-maker had vowed but the night before that Miss Varden held him bound in adamantine chains'. Having treated him coldly, she lets him go but

> waited a little while, thinking he would return, peeped out at the door . . . came in again, waited a little longer, went up-stairs humming a tune, bolted herself in, laid her head down on her bed, and cried as if her heart would break. And yet such natures are made up of so many contradictions, that if Joe Willet had come back that night, next day, next week, next month, the odds are a hundred to one she would have treated

him in the very same manner, and have wept for it afterwards with the very same distress.[24]

Although here and elsewhere Dickens seems genuinely concerned to explore Dolly's nature his basic attitude towards her is jovially and archly patronizing: 'When and where was there ever such a plump, roguish, comely, bright-eyed, enticing, bewitching, captivating, maddening little puss in all this world, as Dolly!' This sort of authorial intervention constantly dissipates our interest in the character so that we overlook the real subtlety with which it is being portrayed. Dickens's own excitement about Dolly does, however, enable him to make her a more intense sexual presence than any other female character in his early fiction. Like the 'Gothic' heroines, she is sexually threatened but, unlike them, she can show passionate terror as when she is assaulted in the woods by the satyr-like Hugh or later when she is abducted, with Emma Haredale, by the rioters. For Dickens her attractiveness is greatly heightened by her being in a state of terror, with 'her hair dishevelled, her dress torn, her dark eye-lashes wet with tears, her bosom heaving', and when she knelt down to comfort Emma

and laid her cheek to hers, and put her arms about her, what mortal eyes could have avoided wandering to the delicate bodice, the streaming hair, the neglected dress, the perfect abandonment and unconsciousness of the blooming little beauty? Who could look on and see her lavish caresses and endearments, and not desire to be in Emma Haredale's place; to be either her or Dolly; either the hugging or the hugged?[25]

The reader may not find this scene as erotically stimulating as Dickens himself evidently does (its combination of feminine terror and demonstrative 'sisterly' affection being just what would excite him most) but that dishevelled hair and torn dress do help enormously in establishing Dolly as a sexual presence.

An interesting attempt on Dickens's part to combine the 'Mary' and 'Maria' types in one character occurs in *Chuzzlewit*, the novel that concluded the first major phase of his artistic career. In little Ruth Pinch he tries to combine the 'Mary' qualities of selfless dedication to a beloved brother, domesticity, passivity and gentle sweetness with the greater liveliness and 'sex-appeal' of the 'Maria' type, a mixture he tried again a few months later with Dot Peerybingle in *The Cricket on the Hearth* (in Dot's case the male to whose happiness and domestic comfort she is so dedicated is not a brother but a middle-aged husband). The essence of Dickens's 'Maria' type, however, is a charming, but not very serious, vanity and a fondness for flirtation, qualities quite irreconcilable with the angelic ones of the 'Marys'. To bring them in at all Dickens has to 'domesticate' them very thoroughly and himself as author flirt with the character, as it were. Here is Dot filling her husband's pipe for him:

> She was, out and out, the very best filler of a pipe, I should say, in the four quarters of the globe. To see her put that chubby little finger in the bowl, and then blow down the pipe to clear the tube, and, when she had done so, affect to think that there was really something in the tube, and blow a dozen times, and hold it to her eye like a telescope, with a most provoking twist in her capital little face, as she looked down it, was quite a brilliant thing.[26]

And here is Ruth preparing to make a beef-steak pudding for her brother:

> When all the materials were collected, she was horrified to find she had no apron on, and so ran *up*-stairs, by way of variety to fetch it. She didn't put it on up-stairs but came dancing down with it in her hand; and being one of those little women to whom an apron is a most becoming little vanity, it took an immense time to arrange; having to be carefully smoothed down beneath – Oh, heaven, what a wicked little stomacher! and to be gathered up into little plaits by the strings before it could be tied, and to be tapped, rebuked, and wheedled, at the pockets, before it would set right, which at last it did, and when it did – but never mind; this is a sober chronicle. And then, there were her cuffs to be tucked up, for fear of flour; and she had a little ring to pull off her finger, which wouldn't come off (foolish little ring!); and during the whole of these preparations she looked demurely every now and then at Tom, from under her dark eye-lashes, as if they were all a part of the pudding and indispensable to its composition.[27]

Tom Pinch's friend, John Westlock, is duly captivated by all this flirtatious housewifery and begins to court Ruth, thereby throwing her into a state of delicious panic which, of course, increases her attractiveness for her creator:

> The brown hair that had fallen down beneath her bonnet, and had one impertinent imp of a false flower clinging to it, boastful of its license before all men, *that* could not have been the cause [of her running away from Westlock's approach], for it looked charming. Oh! foolish, panting, frightened little heart, why did she run away!
> Merrily the tiny fountain played, and merrily the dimples sparkled on its sunny face. John Westlock hurried after her. Softly the whispering water broke and fell; and roguishly the dimples twinkled, as he stole upon her footsteps.
> Oh, foolish, panting, timid little heart, why did she feign to be

unconscious of his coming! Why wish herself so far away, yet be so flutteringly happy there![28]

The Temple Fountain does all the flirtation for Ruth in this embarrassing passage. This leaves her free to be, simply and innocently, in that childlike state of pleasing alarm that Dickens most heartily approves of for nice women who are about to receive honourable proposals of marriage.

The Dot Peerybingle/Ruth Pinch type is too obviously the result of masculine wish-fulfilment (a variant of the standard mother/mistress fantasy) to find much favour with today's readers, but we have to recognize that Dickens himself believed in the possibility of such women, and continued to do so (witness Bella Wilfer after her marriage), and that for him they represented the feminine ideal more truly satisfactorily, perhaps, than the pure 'Mary' figures. He confessed that Ruth Pinch was one of his favourite characters[29] and there is a marked reluctance to lose sight of Dot ('I . . . turn . . for one last glimpse of a little figure very pleasant to me') at the end of *The Cricket on the Hearth*.

Ruth, with her substantial admixture of 'Mary' qualities, is certainly the 'Maria' type at her most innocent. Mercy Pecksniff, on the other hand, is the type at her most culpable.[30] She is introduced with some emphatic irony:

> Miss Pecksniff sat upon a stool because of her simplicity and innocence, which were very great: very great. Miss Pecksniff sat upon a stool because she was all girlishness, and playfulness, and wildness, and kittenish buoyancy. She was the most arch and at the same time the most artless creature . . . that you can possibly imagine. It was her great charm. She was too fresh and guileless, and too full of child-like vivacity . . . to wear combs in her hair, or to turn it up, or to frizzle it, or braid it. She wore it in a crop, a loosely flowing crop, which had so many rows of curls in it, that the top row was only one curl. Moderately buxom was her shape, and quite womanly too [i.e., she had noticeable breasts]; but sometimes – yes, sometimes – she even wore a pinafore; and how charming *that* was![31]

Mercy assiduously keeps up this charade of innocent girlishness and it enables her to make many 'conquests', among them Jonas, a particularly sweet one to her because he had been supposed to be an admirer of her sister's. His ugliness and uncouthness make him a ripe subject for torment and ridicule (she nicknames him 'Griffin') and, promising herself a lifetime of such enjoyments, she consents to marry him, disregarding the sombre warnings of Old Martin. But after only a few weeks of marriage she is 'sadly, strangely altered! So careworn and dejected, so faltering and full of fear; so fallen, humbled, broken; that to have seen her quiet in her coffin would have been a less surprise.' Jonas punishes her heavily, even with blows ('Stern truth against the base-souled villain,' Dickens excitedly exclaims when reporting this), for her 'Maria' behaviour, and for the rest of the novel she becomes an object of melodramatic pathos. She implores Jonas's forgiveness, and everyone else's, for her previous self and tries vainly to win his love, 'turn[ing] a little fragment of a song he used to say he liked' and being humble, devoted and submissive.

Dickens, we may suspect, is here getting a fictional revenge on Maria, such is the relish with which he describes Jonas's brutalization of his wife. The whole episode certainly makes an interesting comparison with his later presentation of Estella's humbling through marriage to the brutal Drummle in *Great Expectations*. There Dickens carefully keeps off-stage any scenes from Estella's married life; we learn merely that it was 'most unhappy' and that she had been 'used . . . with great cruelty' and do not actually see her until the very end when, a widow, she meets Pip in the ruined garden of Satis House and begs for his forgiveness. Moreover, she alludes to some 'determined resistance' that she made to Drummle (they were, in fact, eventually separated before his death). The melodrama is, in other words, so subdued and covered with 'realistic' surface that the reader feels none of the uneasiness that he experiences in the sections of *Chuzzlewit* to which I have been referring.

Dickens's preoccupation with devoted women – wives, mothers, sisters – who are rewarded for their devotion by ill-usage yet who go on loving and trying to care for their brutish men, is very marked in the early fiction, and Mercy as Jonas's wife is only one of the most developed examples. The type appears several times in *Sketches by Boz*: in the poor mother of his rêverie in Monmouth Street whose beloved son grows up into a mere lout ('We beheld the look of patience with which she bore the brutish threat, nay, even the drunken blow'); in the devoted and hard-working wife whose husband is arraigned in the pawnbroker's shop by his neighbour for savagely beating her, and 'his own child too, to make her more miserable';[32] in the 'Hospital Patient', a young Nancy actually dying of the wounds she has received but steadfastly refusing to incriminate her brutal lover; and in the wife and daughter in 'The Drunkard's Death'. She appears, too, in some of the gloomier of the inset tales in *Pickwick*, notably in the figure of Mrs Edmunds in 'The Convict's Return'. Edmunds is a 'morose, savage-hearted, bad man; idle and dissolute in his habits' who treats his wife and son with persistent cruelty, both physical and mental,

... but she bore it all for her child's sake, and, however strange it may seem to many, for his father's too; for brute as he was and cruelly as he had treated her, she had loved him once; and the recollection of what he had been to her, awakened feelings of forbearance and meekness under suffering in her bosom, to which all God's creatures, but women, are strangers.[33]

This perception of a certain kind of female behaviour that clearly fascinated him Dickens later dramatizes very effectively in Betsey Trotwood's inability to wholly abandon her worthless husband, even though she has separated herself from him (a course of action hardly available to the poor abused working-class women in the *Sketches*), and he might perhaps have made Barnaby Rudge's mother a more convincing character by giving her more complexity in this respect. She, however, is confined in the moral straitjacket of melodrama; knowing her husband has committed an atrocious double murder, she can only show terror and horror towards him whilst focusing all her love on the child she was carrying at the time of the murder and whose idiocy she sees as God's punishment on the murderer. She cannot be allowed to have any other feeling for Rudge unless and until he confesses and repents. 'From that hour', she tells him in his prison-cell, 'I will love and cherish you as I did of old, and watch you night and day in the short interval that will remain to us, and soothe you with my truest love and duty' ('Begone!' he appropriately responds). Part of the strength of Nancy's portrayal as opposed to Mrs Rudge's is that she continues to love Sikes *despite* his criminality (but it should be noted that this does not apparently include the crime of murder until, of course, he murders *her*).

*

In summing up Dickens's presentation of women in his early fiction, it seems fair to say that at this stage of his development as a writer he shows a strong emotional response towards certain female stereotypes but is, for the most part, not concerned to explore through his imagination female nature as a whole. He sees women only as they have been typecast by men – as angelic ministers of grace and inspiration (the 'Marys'), as tormenting charmers (the 'Marias'), as threateners of male liberty (the husband-hunters), as trying partners (the viragos), as gloriously absurd in their distinct femaleness (Mrs Nickleby, Mrs Gamp), or as singularly capable of dog-like devotion to men they love even when they meet with nothing but cruelty and brutality in return. Nancy, although she belongs in this latter group, transcends her typecasting, above all through asserting an independence of action, both implicitly against Sikes by seeking to save Oliver and explicitly against Brownlow by refusing to betray or abandon Sikes. The only other female character who takes such an independent line is the little Marchioness when she boldly decamps from the Brasses' to go and nurse Dick Swiveller through his fever[34] (her flight, in contrast to Nell's, is not desperately embarked upon but one with a positive object in view). By this very act, however, she immediately forfeits her just-won independence; she has, in effect, put herself under Swiveller's protection and he eventually arranges for, and supervises, her transformation into a model young Victorian lady, 'good-looking, clever and good-humoured', and, when she has achieved this, he marries her and she becomes 'ever a most cheerful, affectionate and provident wife to him'. (The reader feels naturally somewhat disappointed that the vital, highly individualized figure of the Marchioness has 'dwindled into a wife' in this conventional way, and it is worth noting how much better Dickens manages the transformation of Susan Nipper into Mrs Toots at the end of *Dombey.)*

Truly independent, in the sense of financially independent, women hardly appear in Dickens's early fiction. Mrs Gamp is in more ways than one a substantial exception here and one cannot but admire the skilful way in which she makes her professional terms clear to Mr Pecksniff on her way to the job he has come to fetch her to; it is, of course, done through the medium of a reported conversation with Mrs Harris:

> ' "Mrs Gamp" [Mrs Harris] says, in answer, "if ever there was a sober creetur to be got at eighteen pence a day for working people, and three and six for gentlefolks – night watching," ' said Mrs Gamp, with emphasis, ' "being a extra charge – you are that inwallable person." '[35]

Apart from her and her grim colleague, Mrs Prig, however, the only other working women that we are shown are those whom John Carey terms 'woebegone strugglers-for-a-living',[36] such as Miss La Creevy and Mrs Todgers, comic figures of pathos (one might include Miss Snevellicci and her single female colleagues here, though they are anything but 'woebegone'), and the fiercely caricatured schoolmistresses. Madame Mantalini is, apparently, a successful businesswoman but she is fatally undermined by her emotional dependence on her spendthrift husband. Other women who run businesses such as Mrs Jarley, proprietress of a travelling waxworks, or Mrs Lupin, landlady of the Blue Dragon, are more fortunate in the men on whom, emotionally and psychologically, they depend and it is quite natural that they should eventually marry them since they have really been in a situation of wifely dependence on the men all along. As to financially independent, even wealthy, women

241

who do not have to work, such as Betsey Trotwood or Miss Havisham, such characters do not appear in the early novels at all.

*

A gap of two years separated the end of Dickens's writing of *Chuzzlewit* from the beginning of his next novel, *Dombey and Son*, in the summer of 1846. This novel represents, as has long been recognized, a major new departure in his art. Kathleen Tillotson writes that it

> stands out from among Dickens's novels as the earliest example of responsible and successful planning; it has unity not only of action, but of design and feeling. It is also the first in which a pervasive uneasiness about contemporary society takes the place of an intermittent concern with specific social wrongs.[37]

It should also stand out as the first novel in which Dickens's presentation of women rises above the level of stereotype and caricature and the first of a series of novels in which the interest attaches predominantly to women and their nature.

12

'Dombey and Son' to 'Little Dorrit'

In Dickens's first six novels only 85 out of a total of 280 characters, or less than one-third, are female (*Nickleby* with its troupe of actresses, all but two of them very minor in importance, is the only one in which women begin to approach the half-way mark). In the next five books – *Dombey, Copperfield, Bleak House, Hard Times* and *Dorrit* – women account for 99 characters out of 214, or just under a half. In the last four novels he wrote the proportion of female characters sinks again to less than a third (46 out of 127).[1]

Dickens not only brings more women on to his stage in the middle five novels, however; three of the five centre on a heroine rather than a hero and in the case of one of the exceptions, *Copperfield*, a whole series of major female characters plays a dominant role in the story's development. Many of the central concerns of these books, moreover, relate to dangers, frustrations and humiliations experienced by women in the male-orientated world of Victorian England. In *Dombey* Dickens makes us feel the painfulness of Florence's position as a daughter in the house of a great dynastic capitalist ('. . . such a child was merely a piece of base coin that couldn't be invested – a bad Boy – nothing more'); and he wants us to feel also the degradation of Edith, a woman who must catch a rich husband to ensure her social survival ('There is no slave in a market; there is no horse in a fair; so shown and offered and examined and paraded, mother, as I have been for ten shameful years'). In *Copperfield* Dora's story, with its mingled comedy and pathos, dramatizes the plight of a motherless middle-class girl whose expensive 'education' trains her for a purely decorative, 'fascinating' role but whom the mere fact of being married is supposed to change into a competent and responsible wife and housekeeper, providing her husband with both inspiration and practical support as he struggles to make his way in the world. This novel also features several other women who are the subjects of exploitation and betrayal – David's mother, Rosa Dartle, Little Em'ly, Martha, Annie Strong, even the redoubtable Betsey Trotwood herself. Half of *Bleak House* is the story, told by herself, of an illegitimate orphan girl, Esther Summerson, who must find some role for herself in the world, a role which will involve suppression of her own desires and a determination to 'win love' by living for others; meanwhile, her mother, a great society lady with a guilty secret, lives her frozen life under that Damoclean sword which threatened all women in Victorian society whose history contained the slightest 'irregularity'. In *Hard Times* we have Louisa Gradgrind whose joyless existence in her Benthamite father's 'deadly statistical' household affords her no nourishment for either heart or mind; she lavishes her love on her spineless brother who responds by exploiting her, encouraging her to enter into a hideous marriage for his benefit, a marriage that leaves her vulnerable to the first attractive philanderer that comes along. Finally, *Little Dorrit* presents us with another girl exploited by her family, especially by its male members, and who, like Agnes and Esther, loves a man but cannot tell him so until, by confessing his own late-realized love for her, he at last releases her from her dumb modesty.[2]

All this should not be taken as evidence that in these middle novels Dickens can be seen as anticipating Kate Millett and other modern feminist critics of the patriarchal society. Millett herself indicates the difficulty of seeing him in this light:

> Dickens . . . achieved a nearly perfect indictment of both patriarchy and capitalism in *Dombey and Son*, a novel virtually inspired by the phenomenon of prenatal preference, and a superb illustration of Engels' statements on the subordination of women within the system of property. Yet Dickens did this without ever relinquishing the sentimental version of women which is the whole spirit of Ruskin's 'Of Queens' Gardens'. It is one of the most disheartening flaws in the master's work that nearly all the 'serious' women in Dickens' fiction, with the exception of Nancy and a handful of her criminal sisters are insipid goodies carved from the same soap as Ruskin's Queens.[3]

This oversimplifies Dickens's presentation of his female characters and his whole attitude towards the womanly, an attitude in which Ruskinian 'sentimentality' was only one strand, but it does point us towards a strange feature of these middle novels. Here is Dickens apparently preoccupied with women as the insulted and injured of mid-Victorian England yet voicing no general condemnation of prevailing patriarchal beliefs and attitudes; rather, he seems to see the social and sexual trials of his heroines as a sort of tragic nurture which serves to bring them to their full 'womanly' (or spiritually superior) potential. Even Dora achieves a sad wisdom about herself and David during the difficulties of their marriage; and by the time she is on her death-bed she has become quite angelic in this respect, soothing and comforting David by telling him, 'It is better as it is', and by taking all the blame for their trials on herself ('I was such a silly little creature!') and safeguarding his spiritual future by 'bequeathing' him to Agnes (who has been of angelic status since childhood).

But, however little Dickens's basic beliefs about and attitudes towards women had changed, it seems clear that by 1846, the year in which he began writing *Dombey* – also the year in which he wrote that strange apology for a Christmas Book, *The Battle of Life*, all about sisterly love and female heroism – Dickens's imagination was more deeply engaged with women, their nature and their social role, than it had been since creating Nancy. True, during the next ten years he continues happily to use the stock comic female types that had populated his earlier fiction, witness the virago Mrs MacStinger or the shrewish Mrs Snagsby (to whom Chadband is as Stiggins was to Mrs Weller). And he also creates some memorable new ones such as that fearsome old eccentric, Mr F.'s Aunt, given to startling and peremptory announcements and inexplicable hostilities and grudges; or the querulous old widow who so amused Carlyle, Mrs Gummidge, constantly lamenting in the midst of all the love and comfort Mr Peggotty provides for her, how 'lone and lorn' she is and declaring that she had better 'go into the house [i.e. workhouse] and die and be a riddance'. But Mrs Gummidge also demonstrates how Dickens is seldom content, in this phase of his work, to rest in a mere caricature of a female type. When catastrophe strikes the Peggotty household Mrs Gummidge totally ceases to complain and devotes herself to being useful and to taking tender care of Mr Peggotty, becoming 'the prop and staff of [his] affliction'; and at the end, when Mr Peggotty is about to emigrate to Australia with the reclaimed Em'ly, Mrs Gummidge insists on accompanying them despite the many hardships that will have to be faced:

> 'My good soul,' said Mr Peggotty, shaking his head, 'you doen't know what a long voyage, and what a hard life 'tis!'
>
> 'Yes, I do, Dan'l! I can guess!' cried Mrs Gummidge. 'But my parting words under this roof is, I shall go into the house and die, if I am not took. I can dig, Dan'l. I can work. I can live hard. I can be loving and patient now – more than you think, Dan'l, if you'll on'y try me. I wouldn't touch the 'lowance [Mr Peggotty has proposed to make her an allowance so that she can live independently after his departure], not if I was dying of want, Dan'l Peggotty; but I'll go with you and Em'ly, if you'll on'y let me, to the world's end! I know how 'tis; I know you think that I am lone and lorn; but, deary love, 'tan't so no more!'[4]

This is a moving and convincing speech, all the more so because Mrs Gummidge retains her comic idiom and does not start speaking that lofty 'good' English that Dickens's comic characters so disconcertingly tend to break into when required to transact 'serious' business (contrast Miss Mowcher in chapter 32, for example).

A more elaborate example of Dickens no longer resting in caricature for minor female characters is Miss Tox. This character is first presented as an absurdly romantic spinster who, unprepossessing as she is with her 'stupendously aquiline' nose and straggling attire, yet fondly dreams of becoming the second Mrs Dombey. At first we laugh at her, but, as the novel progresses, Dickens forces us to consider her more deeply and she eventually becomes a figure commanding the reader's affection and admiration without losing anything of her comic appeal. (That Dickens himself respects the creature he has made is shown, I think, by his not marrying her off, as a kind of reward, to the nearest suitable single male at the end of the novel, as he had married off Miss La Creevy at the end of *Nickleby*. To have done so would have devalued or undermined the one great passion of Miss Tox's mild existence, a love that, though it is quite as comically hopeless when Mr Dombey becomes a broken man as it ever was in the days of his pride, is nevertheless to be respected by the reader.)

Our experience of Flora Finching is another case in point. A silly fat middle-aged woman, endlessly babbling sentimental nonsense about the past and indulging in girlish behaviour would seem to be merely a variant on the great anti-woman joke perpetrated in the portrayal of Mrs Nickleby; but the more we see (and hear) of Flora, and of the genuine kindness and shrewd common sense that lies beneath her foolish manner, the more we come to accept her as a complex and sympathetic human being.

The inspired invention of Mr F.'s aunt helps provide Dickens with the means of developing Flora into such a character instead of leaving her simply as a devastating lampoon of poor Maria Winter. Just as Betsey Trotwood, who might otherwise have been no more than a particularly amusing variant on a stock comic type, the frumpy anti-male spinster, is humanized, individualized and dignified for us through Dickens's delicate presentation of her loving care for Mr Dick and pride in him, so Flora is humanized for us through her devotion to this very difficult old woman whose senile aggressiveness she copes with beautifully by a mixture of tactful firmness, good-humoured patience and delighted pride in the old lady's 'spirit' and 'liveliness'. This prepares us, too, for Flora's sensitivity and kindness towards Little Dorrit. Moreover, Dickens allows the reader to glimpse, through the comic cascade of Flora's disjointed chatter, a story not lacking in poignancy. Abruptly separated from the boy she loved by the interference of others ('when your Mama came and made a scene of it with my Papa and when I was called down into the little

246

breakfast-room where they were looking at one another with your Mama's parasol between them seated on two chairs like mad bulls what was I to do?') and later ardently wooed by Mr F. ('you will be surprised to hear that he proposed seven times once in a hackney-coach once in a boat once in a pew once on a donkey at Tunbridge Wells and the rest on his knees'), she marries him out of kindness – '. . . in giving my hand to Mr F. I know I did so with my eyes open but he was so very unsettled and in such low spirits that he had distractedly alluded to the river if not oil of something from the chemist's and I did it for the best'. Mr F. proved an indulgent if rather prosy husband (' . . . only necessary to mention Asparagus and it appeared or to hint at any little delicate thing to drink and it came like magic in a pint bottle it was not ecstasy but it was comfort') but the marriage was short-lived – 'ere we had yet fully detected the housemaid in selling feathers out of the spare bed Gout flying upwards soared with Mr F. to another sphere'.

Flora's chief legacy from the marriage is Mr F.'s aunt and she returns to her father's dead-alive house to live 'secluded if not happy', caring for this weird old woman, until suddenly excitement at long last re-enters her life with the return of the only man she had ever loved. Brief as this excitement is doomed to be, Flora's good nature and basic good sense is such that, at the end of the novel, she can frankly and cheerfully congratulate Little Dorrit on her approaching marriage with Clennam:

> . . . I heartily wish well to both and find no fault with either not the least, it may be withering to know that ere the hand of Time had made me much less slim than formerly and dreadfully red on the slightest exertion particularly after eating . . . it might have been and was not through the interruption of parents and mental torpor succeeded until the mysterious clue was held by Mr F. still I would not be ungenerous to either and I heartily wish well to both.

Flora is splendid, but it is Dora Spenlow, that other avatar of Maria Beadnell, who gives us the best example of Dickens's deepening presentation of a comic female type in these five novels. Unlike Mrs Gummidge, Miss Tox and Flora, however, Dora is a major character, central to the structure of the novel in which she appears. The character from the earlier fiction with whom she should be compared is Dolly Varden, Dickens's first presentation in a leading role of a pretty, comfortably circumstanced young girl, full of innocent vanity and playfulness, and one into whom, as I claimed in the previous chapter, he succeeded in infusing considerable vitality. In one particular way, indeed, Dolly may seem more credible to the modern reader than Dora does; being lower down on the social scale she is much less insulated from the real workaday world. We can hardly conceive of the sugar-candy unreality of the world that genteel young Victorian misses were supposed to inhabit and Dora, clinging desperately to this pretty world as she receives shock after shock from the real one (her father's death, the sudden change in David's fortunes, the responsibilities of housekeeping), is likely to seem merely idiotic to us if we make no effort of historical imagination. But on the other hand, Dickens's lip-smacking authorial commentary on Dolly works against his portrayal of her as a character worthy of serious attention, whereas the presentation of Dora entirely through the senses of David, as he moves from rapturous enchantment with her to feelings of disquiet and eventually to recognition and acceptance of her as she really is, greatly helps the reader to respond to her as a complex and developing character. (The fact that David's perception of Agnes's nature never changes from the moment in his childhood when he first sees her, also a child, and at once thinks of a figure in a stained-glass window has much to do with the reader's inability to credit her with more than the single dimension such a figure has.)

An important aspect of Dora, one that gives her weight as a character, is Dickens's dramatization through her of the traditional belief, which he fully endorsed, that women tend to be instinctively wiser, more perceptive and sensitive about human relations, especially love relations, than men are. In the process of dramatizing this he also makes Dora utter some implicit social criticism of a feminist kind which in its very implicitness is more powerful than all the rhetorical diatribes of Edith Dombey. In chapter 42 of *Copperfield* Dora, now engaged to David, faces the ordeal of meeting Agnes, the wonderful 'sister' she has heard so much of from David and on whose opinion she knows that David so much relies. Though Agnes soon puts her at her ease (as usual, Dickens fails to dramatize Agnes here and falls back on clichés about her 'gentle cheerfulness', 'pleasant way', 'modest grace and ease' and so on) Dora is made unusually thoughtful by this encounter with the first young woman she has ever met (so far as we are told) who is both beautiful and sensible and also very capable. She knows, too, that there is a strong emotional bond between David and Agnes. When she is saying goodnight to David she tries to probe the problem of why he loves her and not the perfect Agnes. Her first question implies a dawning awareness that her own upbringing and social conditioning, though it has been everything that is considered fitting for a young lady, has nevertheless stunted her in some very damaging way:

'Don't you think, if I had her for a friend a long time ago, Doady,' said

Dora, her bright eyes shining very brightly, and her little right hand idly busying itself with one of the buttons of my coat, 'I might have been more clever perhaps?'

'My love!' said I, 'what nonsense!'

'Do you think it is nonsense?' returned Dora, without looking at me. 'Are you sure it is?'

'Of course I am!'

'I have forgotten,' said Dora, still turning the button round and round, 'what relation Agnes is to you, you dear bad boy.'

'No blood-relation,' I replied; 'but we were brought up together, like brother and sister.'

'I wonder why you ever fell in love with me?' said Dora, beginning on another button of my coat.

'Perhaps because I couldn't see you, and not love you, Dora!'

'Suppose you had never seen me at all,' said Dora, going to another button.

'Suppose we had never been born!' said I, gaily.

I wondered what she was thinking about, as I glanced in admiring silence at the little soft hand travelling up the row of buttons on my coat, and at the clustering hair that lay against my breast, and at the lashes of her downcast eyes, slightly rising as they followed her idle fingers. At length her eyes were lifted up to mine, and she stood on tiptoe to give me, more thoughtfully than usual, that precious little kiss – once, twice, three times – and went out of the room.

This is exquisitely done both as regards Dora's searching questions and David's obtuseness. Fixated in true masculine fashion on Dora's physical beauty, so flatteringly and excitingly leaning on his breast, David sees merely the same pretty 'idleness' in Dora's questions as in the movement of her fingers. Yet only in the previous chapter he had confessed his intermittent worry that 'Dora seemed by one consent to be regarded like a pretty toy or plaything', and how he himself 'sometimes awoke, as it were, wondering to find that I had fallen into the general fault, and treated her like a plaything too – but not often'. Alerted by this, the reader is then confronted with the dialogue in which the depth and complexity is all on Dora's side and the superficiality all on David's. It can be said to mark the beginning of a more complex response to Dora on our part. She realizes before David does, despite his intermittent worries, that something will be missing from their marriage, something that she knows he will feel the need of and that she will not be able to supply, though she might have been able to do so had her social conditioning, her 'education' so-called, been different. All she can do in these circumstances is to hope that her beauty and love will compensate for what she cannot give him. Her anxiety about this lies behind the apparently playful question as she and David drive away together from the church, 'Are you happy now, you foolish boy . . . and sure you don't repent?'

Her domestic incompetence soon becomes very evident and causes their 'first little quarrel' after which Dora tries to make David see (what he has already been told by clear-sighted Aunt Betsey) that he must love her for what she is and not risk their love by demanding that she become what she cannot be:

> When you are going to be angry with me, say to yourself, 'it's only my child-wife!' When I am very disappointing, say, 'I knew, a long time ago, that she would make but a child-wife!' When you miss what I should like to be, and I think can never be, say, 'still my foolish child-wife loves me!' For indeed I do.[6]

This speech made 'a strong impression' on him, David tells us, but several chapters later we find him still trying to change his wife, 'forming her mind' by reading Shakespeare (whom she clearly thinks 'a terrible fellow') to her and exploding 'little scraps of useful information' on her, like crackers. This makes them both so miserable that he eventually desists and confesses to her what he has been trying to do. She reminds him of her 'child-wife' speech and wistfully asks, 'It's better for me to be stupid than uncomfortable, isn't it?' David answers, 'Better to be naturally Dora than anything else in the world', and one wonders if Dickens intended us to notice here David's persistence in attributing to Dora's (female) nature that which, as the reader has clearly seen, has quite as much to do with her nurture or social conditioning. And Dora's reply 'In the world! Ah, Doady, it's a large place!',[7] reminds us that, for all her inability to run a household, she has a deeper insight into the truth about life and love than David does.

Whether she be considered primarily as an individual character or as the embodiment of a critique of women's position in Victorian society, Dora is one of the most impressive achievements of this middle period of Dickens's work. She is not, however, the heroine of *David Copperfield*. That is Agnes and it would be a bold critic indeed who would claim this character to be a success. Orwell's jeer ('the real legless angel of Victorian romance') is only one of the most memorable dismissals of her; even Forster complains of her 'too unfailing wisdom and self-sacrificing goodness'.[8] Dickens's failure to vivify Agnes satisfactorily for his readers relates closely, I am convinced, to her association in his mind with Mary Hogarth – or rather with Dickens's sanctified memory of the dead girl ('that spirit which directs my life, and through a heavy sorrow has

250

pointed upward with unchanging finger . . .'). Mary's shade, that of a secular Madonna, invariably inhibited Dickens's prodigious powers as a creator of character, powers which were essentially comic ones, just as memories of all-too-worldly Maria liberated them, notably in the case of Dora. Agnes is very much a religious ikon, an inert figure. She has, Philip Collins observes, 'nothing to do except wait around, good and patient and wise'[9] whereas the other three heroines of this period (Florence, Esther, Amy Dorrit) act and react to people and events in a way that Agnes doesn't.

Agnes, although she gets more and more uneasy about Uriah Heep's growing power over her alcoholic old father, apparently does little to counteract this development; indeed, she persists, against all the evidence, in trying to think the best of Uriah which makes her appear almost stupid (and is hardly consistent with her clear perception of the inner rottenness of Steerforth). She assures David she will never marry Uriah but apart from that one negative resolve, forms no plan, confiding instead, as a saint might, in the prevalence of 'simple love and truth'. (In the end she is rescued from Uriah, the 'red-headed animal', not by David but by that unlikely St George, Mr Micawber.) Towards David himself she is equally passive. As he repeatedly calls her his beloved sister and his good angel ('I never think of you in any other light,' he tells her) Dickens limits her reaction to a 'distressful shadow' passing across her face, or writes of her giving David a 'momentary look' which David can interpret only negatively – 'not wondering, not accusing, not regretting'.[10] Even at the end when David desperately needs to be released from his loving-brother attitude so that he can declare a very different (and, from the reader's viewpoint, scarcely credible) love for her, Agnes can only weep and drop, in all innocence, some distracted hints – quite unlike Florence Dombey, whom Dickens had shown taking the initiative in releasing herself and her lover from *their* brother/sister bind.

We long for Agnes to give way to one bout of nervous irritation or a burst of tears of frustration[11] that would be as startlingly mysterious to 'blind, blind' David as Rosa Dartle's 'wild-cat' outburst in chapter 29. But Agnes, trailing clouds of Mary Hogarth as she does, is sanctified for her creator as well as for David and so, by her very nature, will show no such signs of human weakness (nor will she make fun of herself as, in their very different ways, Dora and Betsey Trotwood do). She is shown as breaking down at one point only before the end of the story, but then the effect is not to humanize her but the very reverse; the episode only intensifies David's sense of her superhuman saintliness. She is blaming herself for her father's degeneration:

. . . I almost feel as if I had been papa's enemy, instead of his loving child. For I know how he has altered, in his devotion to me. I know how he has narrowed the circle of his sympathies and duties, in the concentration of his whole mind upon me. I know what a multitude of things he has shut out for my sake, and how his anxious thoughts of me have shadowed his life, and weakened his strength and energy, by turning them always upon one idea.[12]

The elaborate diction and rhetorical structure of this speech, after the first sentence which is direct and potentially moving, signals to us that Dickens is less concerned here to show an actual loving daughter breaking down into grief than to remind us through Agnes's words of the moral point about Mr Wickfield and also of his place in the spectrum of parent/child relationships examined in the novel. The voice of individual feeling is absent. Agnes is being tormented by the results of her father's obsessive love for her, just as Little Nell was by her doting grandfather's, and she is tormented too by David's blindness to her real feelings for him ('Pray, Agnes, don't! Don't, my dear sister!' he beseeches her); but even in this supposedly passionate outburst she utters no hint of reproach or resentment towards either her father or David. No shade of self must sully the secular Madonna whose only concern is to redeem ('If I could ever set this right! If I could ever work out his restoration, as I have so innocently been the cause of his decline!').

Besides the character's association in Dickens's mind with Mary Hogarth there is one other reason, a formal one, for his failure with Agnes. Of David's three great loves she is the only one with respect to whom our response is meant always to coincide with David's own (i.e. David-in-the-story, not David as retrospective narrator, though the coincidence of response applies there too in this case). True, we realize long before David-in-the-story does that Agnes loves him in a more than sisterly sense but our perception of her essential character is always identical with his whereas, with Steerforth and with Dora, there is for a long time a clear gap between what 'Daisy' or 'Doady' (their respective, and very significant, nicknames for David) believes them to be and what the reader, nudged by David the narrator, sees them really to be. This double focus helps to give a sense of complexity to the characters. But Agnes is a fixed quantity in the story and, although such rigidity is a source of joyful strength for the great drolls in Dickens's work, it is almost always severely disabling for his non-comic characters and is certainly so in her case. She never has a chance to stir our imagination from the moment she first appears complete with 'her keys and her adjectives – *placid, sweet, tranquil, bright, happy, quiet, good, calm, grave* — and with her religiose associations'.[13]

Most of these transfixing adjectives appear, though less profusely, in descriptions of Dickens's three other major heroines of this middle period, Florence Dombey, Esther Summerson and Amy Dorrit, but none of the three seems as lifeless as Agnes. We may find a clue to one of the things that damagingly distinguishes her from them in the definition of female heroism offered to Esther by Inspector Bucket when he is praising her endurance of discomfort and distress during the nocturnal pursuit of her fugitive mother: '. . . when a young lady is as mild as she's game, and as game as she's mild . . . she then becomes a Queen, and that's about what you are yourself'.[14] The 'mildness' or gentle, passive sweetness that Dickens and his age regarded as an ideal quality in a young lady needs to be joined with the more active virtue of 'gameness', or courageous readiness to affront dangers and difficulties, if the literary presentation of such characters is to hold the reader's interest. Agnes is not 'game' in this way, has no great confrontation scene with the villainous Uriah, for in such a scene she would have to become self-assertive. Such behaviour on her part, however virtuously motivated, would be a moral impossibility for her as her character is conceived by Dickens.

There is another, higher, form of 'gameness', one that Dickens associates especially with women and loudly celebrates in *The Battle of Life*. Its triumphs are those victories of self-denial and self-sacrifice 'gained every day, in struggling hearts, to which the fields of battle [are] nothing',[15] but while the narrative in *Copperfield* strongly implies that Agnes is constantly achieving such victories, the form of the novel militates against the direct dramatization of them. We are restricted to David's point of view, and the secrets of Agnes's heart are sealed from his sight; we cannot become involved in that heart's struggles or even gauge their intensity. In *Dombey* and *Dorrit*, on the other hand, the omniscient narrator has access to his heroine's heart and can either tell us directly about its trials as in the chapter of *Dombey* entitled 'The Study of a Loving Heart', or (more satisfactorily from an artistic point of view) *show* them to us through such devices as Little Dorrit's story about the Princess and the 'poor little tiny woman' (i.e. herself).[16] And in *Bleak House*, Esther tells her own story, revealing in the process (as Dickens skilfully makes it appear) much more than she realizes of the emotional conflicts she has undergone and perhaps not even yet fully resolved.

If Dickens had written *Copperfield* in the omniscient-author mode or had had Agnes telling her own story we should certainly have learned more directly about the 'victories gained' in her 'struggling heart'. We should have registered the pain they caused her but also seen how

253

unfalteringly she followed the path of selfless devotion. She would not have retreated into dreamy fantasy as does Florence Dombey when she begins to think of her father 'rather as some dear one who had been, or who might have been, than as the hard reality before her eyes', nor would her heart have so disconcertingly betrayed her at critical moments as Esther Summerson's does ('I was very happy, very thankful, very hopeful; but I cried very much').[17] Agnes can feel pain and she can shed tears but she cannot experience Florence's near-despair, or Esther's emotional confusion, or even the conscious wistfulness of Little Dorrit. And it is precisely by this Madonna-like presentation of her, like the figure in his dream of Mary Hogarth in Genoa, that Dickens kills the thing he loves.

In creating the other middle-period heroines Dickens was in each case writing out of his own still-bleeding heart in a way that he was also doing in portraying the young David Copperfield. The deepest powers of his imagination were always released, in one way or another, for the portrayal of a rejected, abused or exploited child, and Florence, Esther and Little Dorrit are all just such children. Florence experiences the bitterness of feeling that 'not an orphan in the wide world can be so deserted as the child who is an outcast from a living parent's love'. Esther is sternly told on one of her childhood birthdays that she was her mother's 'disgrace' and that she had better never have been born. And Little Dorrit is first presented to the reader as a child-like figure going out from the prison where her feckless family languish to earn a few shillings for their support by monotonous toil in Mrs Clennam's dark decaying house, just as little Charles had once gone to earn for *his* family in that 'crazy tumble-down house', the blacking-factory. But, although Little Dorrit's situation was the one that most obviously recalled those actual circumstances of Dickens's own childhood, it was in describing a certain trick of Florence's psychology that the novelist came closest, I think, to his own inner life. In chapter 30 he describes how, just before her father's marriage to Edith, Florence 'thought of her late self as if it were some other poor deserted girl who was to be pitied for her sorrow; and in her pity, sobbed herself to sleep'. This strangely objective pity for the sufferings of his earlier self was a prominent feature of Dickens's own psychology and a major source of his imaginative power.

Perhaps because of the very intensity of the autobiographical pressures, Florence is less well realized than Esther or Little Dorrit. She is sensitively portrayed as a child, in her sisterly devotion to Paul and in her bewilderment and fear at her domestic isolation after his death. The growth of her dismal conviction that there must be something wrong with her, differentiating her from all other children and making it impossible for her father to love her, is credibly and movingly dramatized, despite the cardboard quality of the exemplary and allegorical extras who occasionally appear to emphasize what is happening, as in chapter 24, for example. What strains our credulity is the stasis of her passionate yearning for her father's love. It undergoes no change as she grows into womanhood; as in her childhood, it is unsullied by any touch of impatience, resentment or reproach towards Dombey and is all compact of what Agnes would call 'simple love and truth'. Her marriage to Walter Gay, like Cordelia's marriage in *Lear*, seems there primarily to give her a base from which to return in order to forgive and redeem her broken father. Florence's character and behaviour in the latter part of the novel surely have more to do with certain self-exalting, retrospective fantasies of Dickens's about his younger self and his father (fantasies that achieve an apparent objectivity by the deliberate echoing of *Lear*) than with any concern to develop a distinctive individuality in the character of his heroine.

Although Esther in *Bleak House* shares with Florence the status of rejected child, she seems, for most of the novel, freer from her creator's personal fantasies, just as she is uncoloured by Mary Hogarth's stained-glass shade. Moreover, Dickens boldly decided to make this heroine tell her own story; he would for the first time write in the character of a woman, an enterprise which, he confessed to a young American lady whilst he was composing the novel, 'cost him no little labor and anxiety' ('Is it quite natural', he asked her, 'quite girlish? . . .').[18] He has generally been judged to have failed artistically in his rendering of Esther's self-portrait by those who take the character straight and consider her to be narrating her life from the same standpoint of emotional stability and maturity as David Copperfield. Charlotte Brontë, for example, thought Esther's narrative 'too often weak and twaddling; an amiable nature is caricatured, not faithfully rendered . . .'.[19] For many she has simply been an exasperating paragon of female virtue: the *Spectator*'s reviewer was provoked into wishing that 'she would either do something "spicy" or confine herself to superintending the jam-pots at Bleak House'.[20] In recent years, however, it has become widely recognized that Esther as a narrator may not be comparable with David Copperfield or Jane Eyre and should perhaps rather be classed with that much lesser-known Dickens narrator, George Silverman, or with Charlotte Brontë's Lucy Snowe, as a character who has been severely damaged psychologically by a loveless childhood and whose narration is marked by emotional and psychological peculiarities which show the abiding scars.[21] Esther's constant self-deprecation, her apparently desperate desire to be incessantly busy and useful to others, her idolization of Ada, her willing acceptance of the Dame Durden little-old-woman role in Jarndyce's household, her fierce reaction to Guppy's coarse nuptial overtures, her total confusion over her attraction to Alan Woodcourt and his to her, her strange hallucinations when dangerously ill, the complexity of her response to Jarndyce's sexless marriage-proposal, all these things, and many other touches in the narrative, may be seen as creating a coherent and convincing impression of a neurotic personality. What is objected to as intolerable coyness on Esther's part – her self-deprecating flutterings about any compliment paid to her, or any expressions of love and gratitude of which she is the subject, her painfully contorted references to Woodcourt – can be taken as very authentic-sounding mimicry of the accents of a certain kind of neurosis, the kind in which the sufferer is always struggling with a crushing sense of his or her own total worthlessness and is virtually paralysed with regard to any conscious assertion of personal needs, desires, beliefs and feelings.

There is, however, undoubtedly a problem with Esther in that Dickens seems to be wanting to do incompatible things with her. He wants in the first place to present her as one of life's walking wounded, like George Silverman. More particularly, she is to appear as a victim of that whole dead-locked system of institutionalized muddle, prejudice and injustice that is the England we see in *Bleak House*; and it was certainly a brilliant notion to have her tell her own story in her own highly personal, hesitant way in counterpoint to the scorching satirical tones of the impersonal third-person narrator. But Dickens also wants Esther to end happily, to take her leave of the reader as a fulfilled, emotionally well-balanced woman who has been, as she tells us, for 'full seven happy years' the mistress of Bleak House – not as housekeeper/companion to old Jarndyce but as wife to the young man whom she had timidly, secretly and sacrificially loved with a very different sort of love from that she bore to Jarndyce, but whom she had persuaded herself it was her duty to renounce. She has borne her husband two beautiful children ('my dearest little pets') and has at last a clearly defined and congenial social role as a village doctor's wife. Even though she still writes rather feverishly about her 'darling' (the new-widowed Ada) and is as compulsive as ever in her self-effacement ('The people even praise Me as the doctor's wife. The people even like Me as I go about, and make so much of me that I am quite abashed. I owe it all to him [i.e., to her husband]'), we are surely intended to see her as finally released from the psychological and emotional straitjacket into which her early experience had forced her. And yet there have been no indications throughout her narrative that she is writing from such a standpoint of serenity, able to take a clear view of her own earlier self and of the people and events that have figured in her life and of the events that have shaped it. Rather, as I have suggested, the impression built up is one of a woman with a distinctly compulsive personality whose gushes of confidence are mixed with strange hesitancies and reticences, making us feel a constant need to interpret or gloss her narration.

Dickens seems, in fact, to be trying to make Esther function both as an unreliable and as a reliable narrator at the same time and the result is, not surprisingly, unsatisfactory. If he had followed through his conception of her character as an illustration of the damage done to individuals in the 'Chancery World' of *Bleak House* he would have ended the novel with her entering into a self-sacrificing, essentially sterile, marriage with Jarndyce. Instead, he suddenly turns Jarndyce into a sort of *deus ex machina* ('I felt as if the brightness on him must be like the brightness of the Angels', Esther tells us) who ensures that Esther is saved from herself to achieve the happiness in love that marriage with him would have denied her.

Dickens presents the last of his middle-period heroines, Little Dorrit, as a young woman who, unlike Esther, is not inhibited from allowing herself to be fully aware of her own emotions. She is conscious of the shame intermingled with the love and pity she feels so strongly for her father; and she cherishes, with a kind of gentle pride, her secret and seemingly hopeless love for Arthur Clennam, witness the touching autobiographical fable about the 'poor tiny woman' and the shadow which she tells to her poor idiot 'child', Maggy.[22] Her strong sense of her own identity is shaken only when she is suddenly transported from the only world she has ever known, that of the Marshalsea prison, a world of which she early came to have a deep and compassionate understanding, to the bewildering unreality of the newly wealthy Dorrits' life in Italy. There superficiality seems to be the be-all and the end-all and the values of that arch-varnisher Mrs General, 'ignorant of the existence of anything that is not perfectly proper, placid and pleasant', reign supreme. In the Marshalsea world Little Dorrit had had her chosen and necessary function, to protect and care for her broken father and to try to counteract the deteriorating effect on her shallow brother and sister of self-deception and tawdry class pride. But in Italy her occupation's gone and she is 'quite displaced even from the last point of the old standing ground in life on which her feet had lingered'.[23] Only through her continuing love for Clennam and her befriending of the woman he had loved and lost, now painfully learning the true nature of the man she married, can Little

Dorrit maintain any sense of selfhood.

Her devotion to her father, stemming originally from her childish pity for his apparent life-sentence to prison, seems more realistic than Florence Dombey's in that it includes a clear and painful recognition of his moral failings. And whilst she willingly and lovingly supports the self-deception which is his strategy for survival so long as only she is the sufferer by it ('I could never have been of any use, if I had not pretended a little', she tells Clennam'),[24] it is not in her nature to connive at the harmful deception of others, even for her father's sake. Perhaps the most harrowing scene in all Dickens's work is the one in which Mr Dorrit hints with clumsy artifice to his perfectly comprehending daughter that she should help to make his situation more comfortable by pretending to be responsive to the honest love felt for her by young John Chivery, the head turnkey's son:

> His voice died away, as if she could not bear the pain of hearing him, and her hand gradually crept to his lips. For a little while, there was a dead silence and stillness; and he remained shrunk in his chair, and she remained with her arm round his neck, and her head bowed down upon his shoulder.[25]

Here, as in a later scene in Italy when her father again exposes himself to her in his very worst and meanest light, she shows her goodness and its strength in a totally believable way. As Dr Leavis puts it 'merely by continuing to be what unselfconsciously she is, [she] brings him to a halt and an unwilling self-realization'.[26] That gentle yet strong passivity which Dickens saw as the noblest aspect of the truly womanly seems merely inert in Agnes or in Florence but in Little Dorrit it becomes a positive force for good in the world, all the more convincing in that it is not all-powerful (she cannot finally redeem her father, nor prevent her sister's loveless marriage to a rich booby, nor convert Mrs Clennam from her vindictive perversion of Christian values). Dickens for once manages to breathe life into his feminine ideal and give it a credible place in this imperfect world where 'the noisy and the eager, and the arrogant and the froward and the vain, [fret] and [chafe] and [make] their usual uproar'.[27]

*

Hard Times is the one novel of this middle period that does not present us with a heroine to love and admire. It is a very schematic novel and Gradgrind, Sleary, Bounderby and the rest are essentially exemplary. Their function is to bring out the social and educational message of the story, not to interest us in them as individuals. But *Hard Times* does show itself to be very much a product of this period of Dickens's work in that the most complexly rendered character in the book is a woman. Louisa Gradgrind is no successor to Florence, Agnes and Esther, however; the supposedly pre-eminently female virtues these heroines exhibit are in *Hard Times* located in the shadowy forms of two secondary characters, Sissy Jupe and Rachel. These two, like Agnes, have virtually nothing to do except to radiate 'simple love and truth', albeit in a much darker world than the world of *David Copperfield*. Sissy has to be turned up to full strength for her scene with Louisa's would-be seducer, Harthouse, and imposes her influence on him through her 'modest fearlessness, her truthfulness . . . her entire forgetfulness of herself in her earnest quiet holding to the object with which she had come'. Because she herself is not threatened she can go on to the offensive against villainy without appearing self-assertive, but Dickens is significantly careful to qualify both her fearlessness and her earnestness as 'modest' and 'quiet'. Rachel's big moment comes when she inadvertently saves Stephen from, in effect, committing murder ('. . . he went down on his knees . . . and put the end of her shawl to his lips. "Thou art an Angel. Bless thee, bless thee!" '). But though she and Sissy each have one 'heroic' scene, neither of them occupies the central position in the book that Louisa does.

The female type to which Louisa belongs is one that makes its debut in Dickens's fiction during this period of his career, though it had been foreshadowed in his portrayal of Nancy. This type is characterized by a passionate nature and a strong intelligence − not the intuitive heart-wisdom of the heroines but an intellectual ability to analyse and generalize her own particular predicament. Nancy alone in the earlier fiction had been allowed to manifest this sort of intelligence − not very happily, perhaps (I am thinking primarily of her interview with Rose Maylie),[28] and, alone amongst the non-comic women, had been allowed to show strong feelings. Apart from her, female manifestations of passion were confined to the viragos and related comic types and the passions involved were those childish 'angry' ones so deplored by the Victorians' favourite moralizer of the nursery, Dr Watts, such as greed, spite, jealousy, vanity, love of dominance − all things eminently suitable for farcical treatment. And in so far as these comic women were supposed to have any mental processes these were entirely identified with the expression of their passions, as is made clear by Dickens's use of the term 'strong-minded woman' to describe Mrs Ned Chuzzlewit:

> . . . being almost supernaturally disagreeable, and having a dreary face and a bony figure and a masculine voice, [she] was, in right of these qualities, what is commonly called a strong-minded woman; and . . . if

she could, would have . . . shown herself, mentally speaking, a perfect Samson, by shutting up her [wealthy] brother-in-law in a private mad-house, until he proved his complete sanity by loving her very much.[29]

If they were not 'strong-minded' like this then the comic women were utterly feeble-minded like Mrs Nickleby. As to the heroines and other non-comic women they were, apart from Nancy, all gentle, of course, and endowed with that wisdom of the heart which is supposed to transcend mere 'masculine' ratiocination.

But the middle novels confront us with a substantial number of non-comic women characters, often in prominent roles, who show both passion and analytic intelligence. Sometimes, as in the cases of Mrs Clennam and Miss Wade (forerunners of Miss Havisham), they may show thought-processes perverted by passion, but still they are given minds even if diseased ones. Sometimes, as in the case of the murderess Hortense, passion has overmastered the reasoning faculty altogether, leaving only a furious cunning at work. But in many other cases, such as Edith Dombey, Alice Marwood, Annie Strong and Louisa, Dickens is creating women who know passion and suffering but who can also reflect justly on their predicament and articulate it with precision and energy. I am not claiming that all of these characters are realized by Dickens with equal success, (Alice Marwood and Annie Strong, for example, are tedious puppets vainly proffered to us as tragic flesh and blood), only that, collectively, they do represent a remarkable new development in Dickens's presentation of women.

The first example of this new type of woman in Dickens's fiction is the young widow, Edith Granger, who becomes Dombey's second wife. As she has already been the subject of much critical discussion[30] I want only to note one thing about her here. This is how closely the conception of her character, situation and actions relates to that of Nancy. Like Nancy, Edith has been corrupted and exploited as a child and, like Nancy again, she is moved to an active compassion (essentially a compassion for her younger self) by the spectacle of an innocent child threatened with the same fate. As Nancy tries to save Oliver from Fagin so Edith determines to save Florence from the worldly designs of the Hon. Mrs Skewton: 'I will have no guileless nature undermined, corrupted, and perverted, to amuse the leisure of a world of mothers. . . . Florence must go home'.[31] We remember the kidnapping of the child Florence by Mrs Skewton's *doppelgänger*, 'Good Mrs Brown', and our memory of the physical terror and humiliation to which the witch-like old creature submitted the little girl powerfully evokes for us the potential moral and spiritual consequences for Florence of now being delivered over to Mrs Skewton for 'the formation of her mind'. Nancy, inspired by contact with the shining goodness of Oliver, and of Rose Maylie, appealed vainly to the furious Sikes to join with her in reforming their lives, and Edith, similarly moved by Florence's goodness and concerned for her, appeals, equally vainly, to the icily-affronted Mr Dombey: 'We are a most unhappy pair . . . but in the course of time, some friendship, or some fitness for each other may arise between us. I will try to hope so, if you will make the endeavour too . . .'.[32] Dombey's response ('Madam . . . I cannot entertain any proposal of this extraordinary nature') balks her of her one hope of salvaging something positive from the wreck of her life, and soon afterwards she begins devoting herself to a reckless and elaborate revenge, planning the threefold repayment of her humiliation.[33]

Edith's immediate successor in Dickens's fiction is Lady Dedlock in *Bleak House*.[34] The 'Bought Bride' is succeeded by the Great Lady with a Guilty Secret, a figure belonging more to the world of melodrama (Miss Braddon was to give Victorian readers a definitive embodiment of the role in her *Lady Audley's Secret* ten years later) than the Bought Bride, who was so much closer to contemporary social realities. Yet Lady Dedlock seems, on the whole, less jarringly melodramatic than Edith, even in her 'big scenes' such as her declaration of herself to Esther, her illegitimate child, in chapter 36, or her confrontation with the threatening Tulkinghorn in chapters 41 and 48. This is so partly, I think, because she generally speaks a terser, tenser language than Edith and is not required by Dickens, as Edith is, to provide a scornful running moral commentary on her own situation nor so much elaborate explanation to others of her own feelings and motivations. The satiric commentary is provided by the author himself, and Lady Dedlock with her class-pride and fashionable 'boredom' is a major focus for it instead of having awkwardly to be, like Edith, both the satirist and the satirized. (This double role as scourge and victim produces such absurdities as the description of her 'spurning from her' her own 'broad white bosom' which John Carey rightly finds so risible.)[35] And whereas Edith, carefully protected by Dickens from any breath of his own life-giving comic genius,[36] stiffens into rather a pasteboard creature, Lady Dedlock is spiritedly caricatured for us at her first appearance as a beautiful, clever and ambitious woman who, marrying into the aristocracy, has successfully set herself to beat her new peers at their own game:

> How Alexander wept when he had no more worlds to conquer, everybody knows . . . My Lady Dedlock, having conquered *her* world, fell, not into the melting but rather into the freezing mood. An exhausted com-

posure, a worn-out placidity, an equanimity of fatigue not to be ruffled by interest or satisfaction, are the trophies of her victory. She is perfectly well-bred. If she could be translated to Heaven to-morrow, she might be expected to ascend without any rapture.[37]

We gain another perspective on this role-playing talent when we see Lady Dedlock having to deploy it not just to dazzle the fashionable world but to baffle the 'young man of the name of Guppy' as he innocently blunders near to her shameful secret and, more desperately, to defend herself against the subtle and relentless Tulkinghorn both before and after he discovers the truth. So, too, we come to interpret more sympathetically her general moodiness and actions like her sudden favouring of the pretty young maidservant, Rosa, which might otherwise seem like mere *grande-dame* whims, when we learn that she believes the only child she has ever had, a girl born out of wedlock, to have died at birth nineteen years before. Yet she remains distanced from us by the very form of the narration both in the satiric third-person section and in Esther's narrative. We get only glimpses of her pain, her pride, her concern for her stately old fool of a husband, her gracious charm, her iron self-control and her terror at the end when she believes herself about to be accused of Tulkinghorn's murder (with strong evidence against her) and 'shudders as if the hangman's hands were already at her neck'. Dickens is not constantly presenting her in melodramatic encounters as he is Edith — when, for example, the latter is fleeing from the Dombey mansion to 'elope' with Carker and meets Florence on the stairs ('shuddering through all her form, and crouching down against the wall, [Edith] crawled by her like some lower animal'). This keeping of Lady Dedlock out of the limelight (the end of chapter 29 and her meeting with Esther in chapter 36 are two of the few places when she is in its full glare, centre stage) greatly helps us to suspend our disbelief as far as she is concerned, whereas Edith's tirades and gestures remind us all too forcibly that we are viewing her across the footlights in the Dickens theatre.

Edith is firmly rooted in the kind of Victorian melodrama that points a strident social moral. She is a victim (however despairingly co-operative in her own doom) of the corrupt social values embodied by her mother. Lady Dedlock, on the other hand, breathes the larger air of tragedy. She is no victim of social evils but of her own passionate nature and of occasions conspiring against her — the false report of her lover's death, her sister's outraged puritanism, the malignity of Tulkinghorn, the vindictiveness of Hortense. What Angus Wilson sees as a 'defect' in Dickens's plan for *Bleak House*, that Lady Dedlock's catastrophe (unlike that of Miss Flite's sister) does not stem from the great source of evil in the novel, the Chancery suit of Jarndyce v. Jarndyce, actually works to her advantage as a character commanding the reader's interest and sympathy. In her big scene with Esther the purely personal nature of her predicament does not require her to become the voice of Victimized Womanhood and begin spouting the kind of rhetoric that Edith immediately launches into when we first see her alone with her mother (' "What childhood did you ever leave to me? I was a woman – artful, designing, mercenary, laying snares for men – before I knew myself . . .". And as she spoke, she struck her hand upon her beautiful bosom . . .').[38] Indeed, there is very little rhetoric of any kind in Lady Dedlock's scene with Esther – most of her account of herself is rendered to us in indirect speech, and also through a letter she gives Esther to read. Neither during this scene nor anywhere else in the book does Lady Dedlock 'repent' as a fallen woman in the melodramatic mode must always do (for example, Steerforth's victim, Em'ly, in *Copperfield*). She is tortured by a passionate regret but consistently affronts her destiny until she feels those 'hangman's hands' closing round her neck and breaks down at last into a panic-stricken flight.

Louisa Gradgrind is the next creation after Lady Dedlock in this new line of Dickens women. Louisa clearly reverts to the Edith type of social victim, though the nature of her victimization is not peculiar to her sex as Edith's was. Louisa's father embodies what Dickens sees as a pernicious theory of education, one that concentrates entirely upon facts and figures, on developing the intellect at the expense of all other faculties, just as Edith's mother had embodied the ethos of the marriage-market; and Louisa herself is eventually made to declaim against her victimization with the same sort of rhetoric as Edith's (even more flowery in places) and with identical gestures:

'How could you give me life, and take from me all the inappreciable things that raise it from the state of conscious death? Where are the graces of my soul? Where are the sentiments of my heart? What have you done, O father, what have you done, with the garden that should have bloomed once, in this great wilderness here?'
She struck herself with both her hands upon her bosom.[39]

But whereas Edith comes into her novel as an adult fully conscious of, and articulate about, her victimization, Louisa first enters hers as a child on the verge of womanhood, only confusedly aware that something has gone badly wrong in her upbringing. She tries to express this to her father after a truant expedition to the circus: 'I was tired, father. I have been tired a long time'. When he amazedly asks, 'Tired! Of what?', she answers, 'I don't know of what – of everything, I think', only to be sternly reproved for being 'childish'. We see her gradually becoming clearer about just what it is that has gone wrong (through observation of, and talks with, her discontented brother and also with Sissy Jupe, a girl from a very different background), and we witness one telling little private act of rebellion when she rubs the spot in her cheek that Bounderby has kissed until it is 'burning red' and tells her brother, 'You may cut the piece out with your penknife if you like, Tom, I wouldn't cry!'.

All this builds up her character and her predicament ready for her first big scene when her father puts Bounderby's marriage proposal to her, whereas with Edith and Dombey's proposal we are plunged *in medias res*. And even in this scene between Louisa and her father the moral message, although it comes across loud and clear to the reader, is not conveyed by declamatory speeches from Louisa but through the dry reticence of her answers and the laconic but searching penetration of her questions. Only towards the end does she wax rhetorical and even then it is still in 'her quiet manner' so that her father, happily misinterpreting her tone, completely misses the point and the scene's powerful dramatic irony is sustained. After all Edith's withering speeches to her mother about mercenary marriage her acceptance of Dombey may seem uncomfortably paradoxical; but Louisa's acceptance of Bounderby in the poignant hope that only so, apparently, can she give any meaning or direction to her life (she may be able to help her brother, Bounderby's employee, and love of him is the only positive emotion she knows, the only thing that seems to make her life worth living) is entirely plausible and consistent with her character and situation as they have been developed by Dickens.

Since Louisa's marriage is incidental to the main anti-Utilitarian theme of *Hard Times*, rather than absolutely central to it as the Edith/ Dombey marriage is to the theme of pride in *Dombey*, Dickens does not need to keep the spotlight on her after the event. The atmosphere of the marriage is sketched in by one or two telling glimpses of it – for example, the breakfast-table altercation in Book II, chapter 9 – and her gradual entanglement with Harthouse is convincingly dramatized (with acceptable heightening from Mrs Sparsit's melodramatic imaginings).

Like her predecessors, Edith Dombey and Lady Dedlock, Louisa eventually seeks refuge in flight. As in Edith's case the flight is accompanied by the thrilling implication that she is about to become an adulteress, but whereas Edith's flight is high melodrama, full of plot and counter-plot, sensational reversals, brandished knives and pistols tucked into bodices, together with an exotic and suggestive setting, Louisa's is altogether more low-key and the reader's attention is brilliantly deflected on to the comically vindictive figure of the pursuing Mrs Sparsit 'with a rash of rain upon her classical visage' and her soaked-through bonnet 'like an over-ripe fig'. We quickly discover that Louisa has fled not to the waiting Harthouse but to her father and it is only upon her arrival in his study that Dickens abandons his naturalistic presentation of her and makes her launch into Edith-like speechifying. *Hard Times* being a much more compressed novel than *Dombey*, the passionate woman's great *éclaircissement* scene is in this case swiftly followed by her absolution scene, when she lays her head upon the loving bosom of a pure young girl, whereas in *Dombey* six chapters separate the two episodes. Once this second scene has been achieved Dickens has really no more to say about his passionate-woman type, no more action for her to perform. 'When you leave me in this dark room, think that you have left me in the grave,' Edith, melodramatic to the last, tells Florence at the end of *her* absolution scene. In Louisa's case, however, he manages to modulate the character back into a subdued sort of ordinary life as a kind of spiritual protégée of Sissy's, all passion spent (she has 'a gentler and humbler face'), devoting herself quietly to a life of good works.

*

A frozen life, a premature death, a life selflessly devoted to the service of others: such are the fates of Edith Dombey, Lady Dedlock and Louisa Gradgrind. When we note that one or other of these fates is also allotted to nearly all Dickens's women characters who are endowed with passion we can register just how disturbed he was by this quality in the opposite sex; he seems compelled to show it as finally punished or at least neutralized. It is also to be noted, however, that these characters chiefly express their passionate natures through resentment; their most powerful speeches, like Nancy's, are fierce protests against their situations and against those who have exploited, betrayed or injured them. This would seem to suggest a latent, uneasy awareness in Dickens that the world he was reflecting in his novels was one that dealt harshly with women who could not or would not conform to socially approved patterns of feeling and behaviour.

Foremost among those secondary female characters in these middle novels who vehemently reject the practice of the conventional feminine virtues of meekness, gentleness, mercy, long-suffering and self-abnegation are Rosa Dartle, Miss Wade and Mrs Clennam. In all three the pattern of passionate resentment punished is very clear.

Rosa Dartle is called by John Carey 'Dickens's only extended portrait of a cultured, intellectual woman . . . significantly a diabolic amalgam of

envy, hatred and malice'.[40] Whilst it would not be easy to find much
evidence in the text of *Copperfield* to support the idea that Rosa is a
cultured intellectual (she plays the harp but does this make her any more
cultured than Dora with her guitar?) she is certainly convincingly presented as the owner of a sharp piercing intelligence. This she uses to
attack or undermine the pride and complacency of Steerforth and
his mother in whose house she lives as a semi-dependant. When, for
example, Steerforth off-handedly refers to the lowly Peggottys as 'that
sort of people' Rosa at once catches his tone and adopts her favourite
oblique method of attack:

> 'Oh, but really? Do tell me. Are they, though?' she said.
> 'Are they what? And are who what?' said Steerforth.
> 'That sort of people. Are they really animals and clods, and beings of
> another order? I want to know *so* much.'
> 'Why, there's a pretty wide separation between them and us,' said
> Steerforth, with indifference. 'They are not to be expected to be as
> sensitive as we are . . . they have not very fine natures, and they may be
> thankful that, like their coarse rough skins, they are not easily wounded.'
> 'Really!' said Miss Dartle. 'Well, I don't know, now, when I have
> been better pleased than to hear that. It's so consoling! It's such a delight
> to know that, when they suffer, they don't feel! Sometimes I have been
> quite uneasy for that sort of people; but now I shall just dismiss the idea
> of them altogether.'[41]

Dickens here endows Rosa with his own powers of irony. She functions as the satirist within the novel, the critic of society, 'quite uneasy for
that sort of people'. But at the same time he enhances her psychological
realism. Herself a victim of Steerforth's brutal insensitivity, she derives a
masochistic pleasure from provoking him to exhibit so blatantly this
aspect of his nature. 'She brings everything, herself included, to a grind-
stone', Steerforth tells David, 'and sharpens it. . . . She has worn herself
away by constant sharpening. She is all edge.' Later he confesses that he is
'half afraid of her. She's like a goblin to me.' Even the least sophisticated
reader can hardly miss the symbolic significance of the disfiguring scar on
her face caused by Steerforth's throwing a hammer at her when he was
a boy (and the more sophisticated can, I suppose, read what phallic
meaning they wish into the detail). Steerforth has damaged her for life
and she makes clear just how he did so in her savage outburst of grief to
his mother after the news of his death:

> 'I attracted him. When he was freshest and truest, he loved *me*. Yes,
> he did! Many a time, when you were put off with a slight word, he has
> taken Me to his heart!'

She said it with a taunting pride in the midst of her frenzy – for it was little less – yet with an eager remembrance of it, in which the smouldering embers of a gentler feeling kindled for the moment.

'I descended – as I might have known I should, but that he fascinated me with his boyish courtship – into a doll, a trifle for the occupation of an idle hour, to be dropped, and taken up, and trifled with, as the inconstant humour took him. When he grew weary, I grew weary. As his fancy died out, I would no more have tried to strengthen any power I had, than I would have married him on his being forced to take me for his wife. We fell away from one another without a word. Perhaps you saw it, and were not sorry. Since then, I have been a mere disfigured piece of furniture between you both . . .'[42]

But if her pride has prevented her from struggling to keep his love, she cannot quench her own passionate love for him, that 'wasting fire within her' that David senses when he first meets her. The sexual tension between Steerforth and Rosa is powerfully dramatized in the harp-playing scene in chapter 29 when Steerforth has set out to charm her (David innocently attributes her attempt to resist him as the result of being 'sometimes jaundiced and perverse'), and has eventually succeeded in softening her and recreating the atmosphere of their childhood love. He persuades her to sing to him and David, accompanying herself on the harp, and she proceeds to pour out her yearning passion for him through the medium of the song.[43] David is stupefied by the power of her performance but –

A minute more, and this had roused me from my trance: – Steerforth had left his seat, and gone to her, and had put his arm laughingly about her, and had said, 'Come, Rosa, for the future we will love each other very much!' And she had struck him, and thrown him off with the fury of a wild cat, and had burst out of the room.

Rosa suddenly realizes that she has been deliberately seduced by Steerforth all over again, once more made to become 'a trifle for the occupation of an idle hour'. Her unwary exposure of her deepest feelings towards him is met with a frivolous response and her self-control snaps with shockingly violent results. Mrs Leavis justly observes of this episode:

This and the other passages of arms between Steerforth and Rosa cannot be dismissed or relegated as theatrical and rhetorical: if such scenes, thus written, had appeared in a tale by D.H. Lawrence, who would have failed to recognize them as in the genuine mode and style of Lawrence, and as exhibiting his characteristic insight into the relations between a man and a woman in such a case?[44]

Dickens is less happy in rendering Rosa's ecstasy of jealous rage against Emily after she has learned of Steerforth's elopement with the girl ('I would have her branded on the face, drest in rags, and cast out in the streets to starve. . . . If I could hunt her to the grave, I would'). The feeling is by no means too intense for the situation[45] but Dickens has failed to preserve Rosa's individual voice and style as he preserves Mrs Gummidge's or Flora's at moments when these characters are required to transcend their normal selves. He falls back here on the conventionalized eloquence of melodrama. Worse still, he determines, despite the great implausibility involved, to have David overhear the tremendous tongue-lashing that Rosa administers to Em'ly after hunting her down. The scene is evidently irresistible to Dickens as a particularly hideous distortion of female nature as he conceives it (a concept involving belief in the 'natural' sisterhood of all women), but the dialogue is slack and banal:

> 'I have deserved this,' said Emily, 'but it's dreadful! Dear, dear lady, think what I have suffered, and how I am fallen!'

To which Rosa replies:

> Listen to what I say! . . . and reserve your false arts for your dupes. Do you hope to move *me* by your tears? No more than you can charm me by your smiles, you purchased slave.[46]

Yet even this scene that Dickens could neither resist writing nor redeem from melodrama is only a local flaw in a remarkable characterization. The authentically tragic quality that Dickens succeeds in imparting to the story of Steerforth owes a great deal to the power and the truthfulness of his conception and rendering of this unhappy woman's nature and of the forces that have warped it.

Miss Wade is, like Rosa Dartle, both passionate and intelligent (her autobiographical narrative opens with the words, 'I have the misfortune of not being a fool') and, again like Rosa, she is an orphan brought up in someone else's family. We understand from her narration that her perverted intelligence has always interpreted proferred love and kindness – from her schoolfellows, her employers when she becomes a governess, the rich young man who wants to marry her – as pitying condescension or as some form of exploitation. This fills her with indignation and resentment. Believing that everyone around her is false, she falls an easy prey to the cynical Gowan whose mistress she becomes 'as long as it suited his inclinations'. Her pride forbids her to try and keep him when he tires of her ('[he] reminded me that we were both people of the world . . . that we both knew there was no such thing as romance. . . . So he said, and I did not contradict him') but she has loved him and bitterly hates the woman he subsequently marries. The only consolation of her sterile after-life is to make a protégée of the orphan maidservant, Tattycoram, and set herself to strengthen the latter's rejection of affectionate gratitude as the proper response for an orphan dependent on the kindness of the more fortunate members of society.

Dickens clearly intends us to see Miss Wade as a pathological case, a 'self-tormentor'. We are meant to identify with the well-meaning folk who pity her for her 'unhappy temper' (thus fuelling the fires of her resentment still further). But, as so often with him, there seems to be a secret bond of sympathy between his imagination and the creature he is ostensibly encouraging us to view with hatred, fear or repulsion. Quilp is perhaps the most celebrated and obvious example of this, and although Miss Wade is no female Quilp she is still a very vital creation, who stays in the reader's mind long after the minor role she plays in the novel's intricate plot has been forgotten. The power of the tightly controlled satirical prose of her narrative forces us to see how the world and the ideals of conduct and feeling it sets before women might appear to someone of a fiercely independent spirit, strong passions and a keen mind who finds herself to be, successively, an orphan child, a governess, the poor fiancée of a young man of wealth and family, and the discarded mistress of an emotionally brutal flâneur. Her description of the latter is probably the best example in her narrative of Dickens's endowing Miss Wade with his own linguistic vitality:

> He made me feel more and more resentful, and more and more contempt-ible, by always presenting to me everything that surrounded me, with some new hateful light upon it, while he pretended to exhibit it in its best aspect for my admiration and his own. He was like the dressed-up Death in the Dutch series; whatever figure he took upon his arm, whether it was youth or age, beauty or ugliness, whether he danced with it, sang with it, played with it, or prayed with it, he made it ghastly.

Miss Wade's frozen-life punishment evokes equally vital language from Dickens as he describes the place of her retreat:

> A dead sort of house, with a dead wall over the way and a dead gateway at the side, where a pendant bell-handle produced two dead tinkles, and a knocker produced a dead, flat, surface-tapping, that seemed not to have depth enough in it to penetrate even the cracked door. However, the door jarred open on a dead sort of spring; and [Clennam] closed it behind him as he entered a dull yard, soon to be brought to a close at the back by another dead wall, where an attempt had been made to train some creeping shrubs, which were dead; and to make a little fountain in a

grotto, which was dry; and to decorate that with a little statue, which was gone.[47]

Here is a remarkable and compelling concentration of images of stasis, barrenness and sterility, with the word 'dead' tolling through the whole passage. And Clennam's coming to the place is to result in Miss Wade's losing the only still-vital thing in her existence, her intense relationship with Tattycoram. Even Rosa is not left quite so desolate at the end of her story for she has Mrs Steerforth whom she alternately caresses and rages against ('thus I always find them;' writes David Copperfield, 'thus they wear their time away from year to year').

The most heavily punished of all the passionate women of these middle novels, however, is Mrs Clennam. She was morally outraged and personally humiliated to discover that the husband her father had arranged for her already had a 'wife', a young singer, whom he loved and who had borne him a child, Arthur. Mrs Clennam uses her harsh Calvinist religion to justify to herself her long and vindictive revenge but acknowledges, in her confession to Little Dorrit, that there was an emotional reason too, psychologically a very plausible one:

> She [Arthur's mother] not only sinned grievously against the Lord, but she wronged me. What Arthur's father was to me, she made him. From our marriage day I was his dread, and that she made me. I was the scourge of both, and that is referable to her.

Rejecting mercy and forgiveness of those who have wronged her, Mrs Clennam works out a terrible scheme of vengeance which blights the lives of the innocent Dorrits as well as those of the guilty lovers, and for years feeds on her resentment in the dark airless chamber to which she confines herself. Matters are suddenly brought to a crisis by Rigaud's blackmailing, and the shock of witnessing the physical collapse of her house following hard upon this effectively kills her:

> . . . she never from that hour moved so much as a finger again, or had the power to speak one word. For upwards of three years . . . the rigid silence she had so long held was evermore enforced upon her, and, except that she could move her eyes and faintly express a negative and affirmative with her head, she lived and died a statue.[48]

Mrs Clennam, Miss Wade and Rosa Dartle, the three most formidable passionate women among the secondary characters of these middle novels, are thus strongly punished by their creator. Of the others Alice Marwood is granted a peaceful and repentant death in the arms of the saintly Harriet Carker, and Tattycoram saves herself by repenting and conforming, but Miss Barbary dies of a stroke, Hortense ends on the gallows and Fanny Dorrit, a more trivial character (excellently realized), ends up in a comic version of the frozen life, warring daily with her mother-in-law 'in a genteel little temple of inconvenience to which the smell of the day before yesterday's soup and coach-horses was as constant as death to man'.

Apart from the complex case of Betsey Trotwood, to be considered in a moment, the nearest Dickens comes to allowing a woman's resentment to lead to a positive outcome is in his portrayal of Caddy Jellyby, that ink-stained slave to her mother's philanthropic African enterprises. Caddy's sullen resentment at her own condition ('I wish Africa was dead!') is aggravated by the appearance in her dirty, chaotic home of two such elegant and accomplished young ladies as Esther and Ada. Later she tells Esther:

> I felt I was so awkward . . . that I made up my mind to be improved in that respect, at all events, and to learn to dance. I told Ma I was ashamed of myself, and I must be taught to dance. Ma looked at me in that provoking way of hers as if I wasn't in sight; but I was quite determined to be taught to dance, and so I went to Mr Turveydrop's Academy in Newman Street.[49]

There she falls in love with young Prince Turveydrop who with his diminutive stature, blue eyes, flaxen hair and 'little innocent, feminine manner', 'timid tenderness' and so on seems ideally to complement Caddy's stronger nature. In bestowing her love and care on him Caddy is, in fact, championing oppressed womanhood, which strangely manifests itself in Prince. Esther recalls that his manner 'made this singular effect upon me: that I received the impression that he was like his mother, and that his mother had not been much considered or well used', and later she learns that such was indeed the case – Prince's mother, an 'affectionate little dancing-mistress', had 'worked herself to death' in order to maintain her extravagant dandy of a husband, to whom she was devoted. Caddy talks of Prince as though she were the husband and he the wife: he is only semi-literate but 'she could write letters enough for both . . . and it was far better for him to be amiable than learned'. Dickens certainly intends us to be sympathetic to these characters, but at the same time we are to register a sense of unease about them. Their marriage is made to reflect the way in which both Caddy and Prince have been exploited and abused by their mother and father respectively. So when they have a baby it is 'a tiny old-faced mite . . . quite a piteous sight' with (a very telling detail) 'curious little dark veins in its face, and curious little dark marks under its eyes, like faint remembrances of poor Caddy's inky days'.[50] It proves to be a deaf mute. Caddy, no longer resentful, ends up as a good mother to her little husband, poor child, and broken father. Also dependent on her is her selfish old father-in-law whom she implausibly reveres (an instance of Dickens arbitrarily denying intelligence to one of his best minor female characters in the interest of keeping her 'womanly' and loving). It seems grossly inappropriate to say that Caddy is punished for her earlier passionate resentment against her grotesque mother; but our perception, through Esther's sympathizing eyes, of the sadness that underlies her cheerfully busy life encourages the notion, enforced by the other examples we have been considering, that in the Dickens world women whose passionate natures move them to feel resentment, no matter how justifiably, must undergo some punishment for this.

The one character to escape this doom is Betsey Trotwood. At first she does seem to be identified, however comically, with bad passions and negative action. She has condemned her favourite nephew's marriage on the grounds that he has married 'a wax doll' though she has never seen his bride, and she angrily rejects the boy-child who arrives in place of the great-niece she confidently expected. We learn that Betsey, like Miss Havisham later, has suffered at the hands of a passionately loved man, but we also discover that unlike Miss Havisham she has not become unbalanced nor frozen in her sympathies. Her adoption of the self-defensive role of a 'grumpy, frumpy' spinster, anti-man and anti-marriage, is accompanied and undermined by a still strong capacity for loving and caring and is kept in check by her shrewd common sense. She rescues Mr Dick, a distant relative whose family sufferings (originating, in true Dickensian vein, in his love for his unhappily married sister) have so weakened his mind that he is about to be consigned to a lunatic asylum, and, by her wise and tender treatment of him, ensures that he can live a normal, though protected, life. As to her maidservants, that series of protégées whom she takes into her service 'expressly to educate in a renouncement of mankind', we gather that since they 'generally completed their abjuration by marrying the baker' her efforts to get them to reject the male species were hardly of a very serious or determined kind.

'Go away!' she tells David when he presents his runaway raggedness at her garden gate, 'Go along! No boys here!' and she makes 'a distant chop in the air' with the gardening-knife she is carrying. But as soon as he begins to cry she hurriedly seizes him and takes him in. Betsey, whose nature is capable of deep tenderness, cannot stand tears; she is shy of showing her own emotions and uses her continual battle with the local donkey-boys as a convenient diversion whenever a situation threatens to become overtly emotional.[51] When David breaks down in defending Peggotty against Betsey's strictures on her for marrying ('I only hope . . . her husband is one of those Poker husbands who abound in the newspapers, and will beat her well with one') she at once relents but seizes on the offending donkeys to stop the scene developing any further:

> 'Well, well!' said my aunt, 'the child is right to stand by those who have stood by him. – Janet! Donkeys!'
> I thoroughly believe that but for those unfortunate donkeys, we should have come to a good understanding; for my aunt had laid her hand on my shoulder, and the impulse was upon me, thus emboldened, to embrace her and beseech her protection.

As she grows fonder and prouder of young David she adopts other stratagems to disguise her emotions, such as the invocation of David's non-existent sister and his dead mother. When David has left school and she is discussing his future with him she says:

> 'Your sister, Betsey Trotwood . . . would have been as natural and rational a girl as ever breathed. You'll be worthy of her, won't you?'
> 'I hope I shall be worthy of *you*, aunt. That will be enough for me.'
> 'It's a mercy that poor dear baby of a mother of yours didn't live,' said my aunt, looking at me approvingly, 'or she'd have been so vain of her boy by this time, that her soft little head would have been completely turned, if there was anything left of it to turn.' (My aunt always excused any weakness of her own in my behalf, by transferring it in this way to my poor mother.) 'Bless me, Trotwood, how you do remind me of her!'[52]

Betsey is a woman who takes her stand on Reason[53] but she is far from being a human Houhynhmn. Her strong intelligence and her warm heart work together to dictate her actions. Clear-sighted and sharp-witted, she is more than a match for the Murdstones, let alone the hypocritical obsequiousness of Mrs Crupp or Uriah Heep (Dickens, we note, carefully avoids a meeting between her and Steerforth). She also sees, for all her love for David, that he has potentially the same character-defects as the father and mother he so greatly resembles, and is anxious to make him 'a fine firm fellow, with a will of his own. . . . with strength of character that is not to be influenced, except on good reason, by anybody, or by anything'. She encourages him to be self-reliant by sending him off on a *Wandermonat* before he tackles the serious business of choosing a career. As regards his emotional development her dearest wish is that he should fall in love with, and eventually marry, Agnes, that perpetual fountain of good sense. When, instead, he 'falls into captivity' at the sight of Dora's ringlets, Betsey schools herself not to interfere, after a little gentle probing has shown her how much in earnest David is (though she cannot refrain from disconcerting him by exclaiming 'blind, blind!'). Betsey regrets her treatment of David's hapless mother – which was all a part of the more obsessive stage of her resentment against men following the break-up of her own marriage – and is tenderly loving towards 'Little Blossom' as she calls Dora. 'I never saw my aunt unbend more systematically to any one', David recalls, noting that she never even 'attacked the Incapables' (the incompetent servants whom David has to suffer because Dora is so hopeless a mistress of the house) 'though the temptation must have been severe'. And she reacts strongly against David's diffident suggestion that she might try to guide Dora a little in housekeeping matters:

> 'Trot,' returned my aunt, with some emotion, 'no! Don't ask me such a thing.'
> Her tone was so very earnest that I raised my eyes in surprise.
> 'I look back on my life, child,' said my aunt, 'and I think of some who are in their graves, with whom I might have been on kinder terms. If I judged harshly of other people's mistakes in marriage, it may have been because I had bitter reason to judge harshly of my own. Let that pass. I have been a grumpy, frumpy, wayward sort of a woman, a good many years. I am still, and I always shall be. But you and I have done one another some good, Trot – at all events, you have done me good, my dear; and division must not come between us, at this time of day.'
> 'Division between *us*!' cried I.
> 'Child, child!' said my aunt, smoothing her dress, 'how soon it might come between us, or how unhappy I might make our Little Blossom, if I meddled in anything, a prophet couldn't say. I want our pet to like me, and be as gay as a butterfly. Remember your own home, in that second marriage; and never do both me and her the injury you have hinted at!'
> I comprehended, at once, that my aunt was right; and I comprehended the full extent of her generous feeling towards my dear wife.[54]

The combination of earnestness and wry self-mockery in this speech characterizes all of Betsey's intimate conversation (other examples occur when she tells David about her disastrous marriage at the end of chapter 47, and about her husband's wretched death in chapter 49) and it excellently complements her public manner of humorous abruptness, so disconcerting to Uriah Heep, among others, ('Don't be galvanic, sir!'). Endowed with such brilliantly appropriate and flexible speech, Betsey can be involved in scenes that hover on the verge of melodrama (or topple into it like the scene of the unmasking of Heep) without being contained and defined by them. So successfully, in fact, does Dickens individualize her that she not only fully humanizes her moral-allegorical role, as Mrs Leavis says, but she also compels us to suspend our disbelief in the existence of real-life fairy godmothers.

Betsey is, I believe, the finest flowering of Dickens's concentration on women in the novels of his mid-career. But she is surrounded, as I have tried to show, by many other remarkable achievements in female characterization. Although one eminent woman of letters could see only a procession of 'dots or drolls' in Dickens's work up to 1857 as far as women characters were concerned ('when he attempts to change the construction', she added, 'he turns us into Lady Macbeths!'),[55] critics of our own age have increasingly recognized a great deal more depth and subtlety in this area of his fiction after *Martin Chuzzlewit*. I would, how-ever, distinguish between the five novels considered in this chapter and those that succeeded them. In these last four novels Dickens's main artistic interest, and consequently his most powerful imaginative effects, seem to shift from women themselves to men as passionate lovers of women. Of course, masculine love had been a chief preoccupation of one middle-period novel, *Copperfield*, the 'disciplining' of David's heart being the main motif of the book, but juxtaposing *Copperfield* with *Great Expectations* shows how much more the later book is concentrated on the hero's passion for a woman (in *Copperfield* the role of Steerforth in David's emotional development is of equal importance with Dora's). Nor is Estella a character with whom the author lovingly makes the reader intimate as he does with Dora; she is there in the book as a necessary, and necessarily disastrous, object for Pip's passion, not there for her own sake. Dickens's imagination is concerned with the effect she has on Pip rather than with how Estella herself lives and moves and has her being.

Little Dorrit, the last 'middle' novel, is clearly a transitional one. The reader is encouraged to take as much interest in Clennam's hopeless love for Pet Meagles, and in the effect on him of seeing his first love again after a lapse of twenty years, as in Little Dorrit's painfully repressed love for Clennam. In this novel, written during a period of great change in his emotional life, Dickens is giving the fullest (and, in many essential ways, the most historically accurate) expression to his nightmare memories of the blacking-factory days through the figures of the heroine and her family. But he is also for the first time giving expression in fiction, through the figure of Clennam, to the second great crisis of his life, the realization that he needed a love-relationship that his wife could no longer provide (or, as he convinced himself, never had been able to provide) but that life seemed determined to deny him. The sudden appearance of Ellen Ternan probably intensified this feeling at first, but she may have helped to assuage it as his relationship with her strength-ened and deepened. However this may have been, the feeling remained a source of literary inspiration for him. Through Florence Dombey, Esther Summerson and Little Dorrit Dickens had explored his old wound in some depth. Arthur Clennam is the forerunner of a series of haunted heroes and haunted villains – Sidney Carton, Pip, Bradley Headstone, John Harmon, Jasper – through whom he will explore, and exploit for fictional purposes, the new trouble, the one that he recognized himself to have foreshadowed years before, in *David Copperfield*, witness his lament to Forster, 'Why is it, that as with poor David, a sense comes always crushing on me now, when I fall into low spirits, as of one happiness I have missed in life, and one friend and companion I have never made?'.[56]

13

'A Tale of Two Cities' to 'Edwin Drood'

It is probably safe to say that the best-known female characters in Dickens's last four novels are two grim older women, Madame Defarge and Miss Havisham, and two beautiful and spirited young ones, Estella and Bella (these two, together with Helena Landless in *Drood*, have been acclaimed as showing a remarkable advance in the psychological realism of Dickens's portrayal of his leading ladies, inspired by his experience of Ellen Ternan). Striking though all these characters may be, however, the dominant, most persistently recurring figure in these last books, the one with which Dickens's imagination seems to be most preoccupied, is not a female one. It is that of a lover who, like the lover on Keats's urn, seems doomed never to have his bliss yet who must endure, unlike that marble youth, the pangs and torments of 'breathing human passion'.

This figure appears many times in Dickens's earlier fiction – for example, Smike, Tom Pinch, Augustus Moddle, Toots, Mr Guppy – but always as more or less of a grotesque, and usually a comic one. This grotesqueness distances these earlier hopeless lovers from the reader, who may pity them, laugh at them or admire them – generally a blend of at least two of these responses is called for – but who cannot empathize with them in the way that is clearly intended with Sydney Carton or, still more, with Pip. Carton and Pip are heroes, while two later, equally love-doomed, characters, Bradley Headstone and Jasper (in *Our Mutual Friend* and *Drood*), become murderous villains, but in every case the reader is made to feel the weight and to understand the nature of these men's emotions. It is not a question simply of contemplating them, pityingly or laughingly, as it is with their predecessors in this particular role.

Arthur Clennam in *Little Dorrit* is the first of Dickens's male hopeless lovers to be brought centre stage and presented straight[1] (he is also neatly juxtaposed in chapters 16-18 of Book II of the novel with the last-but-one of the old-style comic/pathetic hopeless lovers, Young John Chivery).[2] But Clennam's heroic suppression of his love for Pet Meagles and his struggle to behave well towards his triumphing rival are only an episode, albeit a very important one, in his history; he eventually finds compensation, and more than compensation, for abandoning his hopes of Pet in his marriage with his 'poor child', Little Dorrit. It was while Dickens was steering Clennam towards this ending that he himself became passionately involved in acting Richard Wardour, the leading role in Collins's melodrama, *The Frozen Deep*. For Wardour no happy ending was reserved, but an exalted death in the arms of his hopelessly loved Clara after exhausting himself to preserve, amidst Arctic ice and snow, the life of the man whom she does love. Carton's fate in *A Tale of Two Cities*, which was inspired by Collins's play, follows a similar pattern. (More fortunate is Gill Davis, the narrator-hero of a Christmas Story, 'The Perils of Certain English Prisoners', written a few months later. Though he cannot hope to win Marion Maryon, so far above him in social station, Davis is 'sufficiently rewarded' by becoming a retainer of hers, her 'poor, old, faithful, humble soldier', after her marriage to a naval officer.)[3]

Pet Meagles, the object of Clennam's hopeless love, is, one feels, a rather hastily sketched-in character, a standard Dickensian charmer blending something of Mary Hogarth with something of Maria Beadnell:

> A fair girl with rich brown hair hanging free in natural ringlets. A lovely girl, with a frank face, and wonderful eyes; so large, so soft, so bright, set to such perfection in her good kind head. She was round and fresh and dimpled and spoilt, and there was in Pet an air of timidity and dependence which was the best weakness in the world, and gave her the only crowning charm a girl so pretty and pleasant could have been without.[4]

This description might lead us to expect that Pet (the name by which her doting parents call her; her real name is Minnie) will prove to be a reworking of Dora, but in the few scenes in which she appears she behaves with a perfectly Agnes-like sweet gravity. Dickens leaves us wondering how such a girl, so lovingly devoted to her parents, could have wanted to set herself, despite her father's unhappiness on the subject, to marry such an obvious bounder as Gowan. Sexual attraction is presumably the answer, but the nearest Dickens comes to giving us a glimpse of such feelings in Pet is when he resorts to a similar dog-device to that which he used when dramatizing Dora's sexual effect on David; he describes Pet fondling and caressing Gowan's Newfoundland dog as it puts 'his great paws on her arm and [lays] his head against her dear bosom' ('How she caressed the dog, and how the dog knew her! How expressive that heightened colour in her face, that fluttered manner, her downcast eyes, her irresolute happiness!').[5] She begins to discover her husband's true character after marriage, but Dickens is not concerned to explore the effect of this on her. It is simply asserted, through the authoritative voice of Little Dorrit herself, that she (Pet) 'is so true and so devoted, and knows so completely that all her love and duty are his for ever, that you [Little Dorrit is writing to Clennam] may be certain she will love him, admire him, praise him, and conceal all his faults, until she dies'.[6] The pretty, allegedly spoiled, girl becomes, we must believe, a perfect wife to an unworthy husband; and that is really all that Dickens has to tell us about Pet because he seems not to be interested in her for her own sake, as he is in the Dorrit sisters, or Flora, or Miss Wade, but only for the effect she has on Clennam.

He works harder on Lucie Manette in *A Tale of Two Cities*, because here he must convince us that her beauty and character are capable of inspiring such adoration in a man that he would actually die for the sake of her happiness. He wants us to feel, too, not only that Lucie can inspire such self-sacrifice but also that she is fully worthy of it. Inevitably perhaps, what we get is a repetition of the Dickensian feminine ideal already so definitively embodied (if that isn't too strong a word for it) in Agnes, only this time with a few physically individualizing features, the most striking of which may have been borrowed from Ellen Ternan.[7] Like Agnes, Lucie is most strongly characterized as a devoted daughter (on her wedding eve she assures her father that her life will continue to be 'consecrated' to him); like Agnes with David, Lucie exhorts Carton to be worthy of his best self; and like Agnes again, Lucie has a genius for creating and sustaining domestic happiness; she is 'ever busily winding the golden thread that bound them [father, husband, child] all together, weaving the service of her happy influence through the tissue of all their lives, and making it predominate nowhere'.[8] It is only in the early part of the novel, during her first interview with Mr Lorry at Dover and her subsequent reunion with her shattered father, that we feel Dickens's creative imagination is truly engaged with her (in the rendering, for example, of her irrational, but wholly credible, sense of guilt that she had been obliviously living at ease whilst her father rotted in the Bastille). Otherwise, she is very much an emblematic figure. All the power and insight of Dickens's genius for character-creation goes into the presentation of two of the three men (for Darnay is a mere 'walking gentleman') who need and love her. Above all, it goes into the creation of the haunting figure of Dr Manette.

With his next novel, *Great Expectations*, Dickens intensifies the pain and pathos of his hopeless-lover figure by presenting the woman who is the object of the love very differently. Marion Maryon and Lucie Manette, incarnations of the feminine ideal, had been infinitely gracious and tender towards their worshippers. The men had at least that much consolation as well as an exalted satisfaction in being able to consecrate their lives to the service of their *princesses lointaines*. But there is no such softening of Pip's agony. Where Gill Davis or Sydney Carton seemed to derive a holy joy merely from being in the presence of the women they adore, Pip is tortured by being with Estella: ' . . . everything in our intercourse [gave] me pain', he recalls at one point; and at another, 'I never had one hour's happiness in her society'. Pip has, we realize, fallen in love with a beautiful monster, a creature who has been made incapable of feeling love. 'I stole her heart away and put ice in its place,' a remorseful Miss Havisham tells him, and the fairy-tale image is very appropriate since the story of Miss Havisham and Estella is essentially that of a malign spirit (who may once have been human) magically depriving someone of some basic human attribute, as the Phantom in *The Haunted Man* deprives Redlaw of his memory and thus of 'all good imagination'. *Great Expectations*, however, is not a Christmas Book, or moralized fairy-tale, nor even a fiction in the avowedly Gothic mode which can appropriately invoke the supernatural and the demonic. It is ostensibly a novel in the realist tradition of Defoe, who held that the novelist's business was to 'lie like truth'. The characters and events, however strange, should nevertheless be such as could occur in nature. Miss Havisham's monstering of Estella, however, seems to me to be essentially a fantastic conception. When Estella tells Pip, 'very calmly', that she can only understand his meaning in saying that he loves her 'as a form of words' ('You address nothing in my breast, you touch nothing there'), he exclaims, 'Surely it is not in Nature', and the reader who pauses to reflect can only agree with him. Estella's retort, 'It is in *my* nature . . . It is in the nature formed within me',[9] underlines the fact that we must here stretch our understanding of nature to accept the idea of an ice-for-heart transplant if we are to maintain 'that willing suspension of disbelief that constitutes dramatic faith'.

Dickens wishes to place Pip as lover in a situation of extreme, even fantastic, hopelessness, and does not want the reader's attention deflected to the character of Estella herself. She is simply a given entity in the novel, star-like, as her name suggests, in her coldness, beauty and remote indifference to the agony and strife of human hearts. Only as a child does she seem psychologically convincing: the self-possessed little girl's gleeful tormenting of the awkward village boy, so out of his depth in her strange home, is entirely plausible. But the adult Estella must, it seems to me, be considered more as a fictive device than as a character in the mode of psychological realism. We are to accept her as a sort of robot carrying out the Zuleika Dobson-like task for which Miss Havisham has programmed her, and we are to believe her when she tells Pip that she has no heart, 'no softness there – sentiment – nonsense'. Human emotions are as incomprehensible to her as to Swift's Houhynhymns and she can make sense of Miss Havisham's passionate complaint about her coldness only by an elaborate analogy drawn from the physical world:

> 'I begin to think,' said Estella in a musing way, after another moment of calm wonder, 'that I almost understand how this comes about. If you had brought up your adopted daughter wholly in the dark confinement of these rooms, and had never let her know there was such a thing as the daylight by which she has never once seen your face – if you had done that, and then for a purpose, had wanted her to understand the daylight, and know all about it, you would have been disappointed and angry?'[10]

Dickens confuses us by not consistently presenting Estella as thus preternaturally passionless. At various points in the narrative he makes her suddenly display natural emotions, either for the sake of a local effect or for that of the story as a whole. She speaks bitterly to Pip in chapter 33 of the treatment she received as a child from Miss Havisham's jealous relatives and rejoices over their discomfiture. She seems to pity him and wish to save him from the fate of her other victims when, in chapter 38, she earnestly warns him against loving her. And she gives him in chapter 44 an emotional reason (weariness of the life she has been leading in obedience to Miss Havisham) for her decision to marry Bentley Drummle in opposition to her patroness's wishes. Finally, when Pip meets her again after Drummle's death she is presented as a woman who has felt great suffering and now feels strong compassion for her old lover.

Barbara Hardy, sensing, like all alert readers, the necessity for a double response to Estella – ice-maiden most of the time, passionate woman sometimes – finds her a 'puzzling character' and seeks to make psychological sense of her by saying she is 'best explained as another looser and vaguer version of Edith Dombey'.[11] There are certainly points of resemblance between these two characters. Both have been exploited and corrupted by their mothers (mother-by-adoption in Estella's case) and both are cold and haughty in their general demeanour. But while it is psychologically plausible that a child may be pushed into scheming and mercenary behaviour by a mother like Mrs Skewton, what Miss Havisham is supposed to have done to Estella surely belongs more to the realm of moral fable or fantasy than to that of psychological realism. Edith's coldness is an understandable defence mechanism, Estella's is that of a fairy-tale ice maiden. It is not a question of more or less 'looseness and vagueness' in psychological realism but of a basic difference in literary mode.

*

Great Expectations is a novel without a heroine to love and admire (for the sturdily virtuous Biddy's role, though an important one, is too minor to entitle her to be considered as the novel's heroine in this respect). As if in compensation for this, Dickens's next novel, *Our Mutual Friend*, features two heroines, Bella Wilfer and Lizzie Hexam, and is, from the point of view of a student of Dickens's women characters, undoubtedly the most rewarding of his last four novels – apart from the characterization of Helena Landless in *Drood*. The male hopeless-lover figure reappears, it is true, both in the book's nominal hero, John Harmon, and in Bradley Headstone but the role is not, in this book any more than in *Little Dorrit*, a masculine monopoly since Lizzie too enacts it. Harmon is, in any case, a relatively individualized figure: the bizarre situation he is in for most of the novel, pretending to be someone else,[12] strains our credulity without helping to establish in our minds any sense of him as an individual, and he is altogether eclipsed in interest by the object of his love, Bella Wilfer.

Bella, introduced as 'exceedingly pretty . . . but with an impatience and petulant expression both in her face and her shoulders', makes an immediate and vivid impression on the reader. Her dialogue is refreshingly acerbic. She grumbles about her family's genteel poverty, declaring, 'I love money, and want money – want it dreadfully', and roundly snubs her younger sister: 'You are a chit and a little idiot . . . Wait till you are a woman, and don't talk about what you don't understand. You only show your ignorance!' Old Harmon, she complains, left her to his son in his will 'like a dozen of spoons' and Dickens shows her keenly alert to the way in which her peculiar situation, 'widowed' before even being married, exposes her to sexist humour: 'When the Harmon murder was all over town, and people were speculating on its being suicide, I dare say those impudent wretches at the clubs and places made jokes about the wretched creature's having preferred a watery grave to me'.[13] Her consciousness of herself as an attractive young woman is well dramatized in the haughty air she puts on when a personable young man suddenly appears seeking lodgings in her parents' house, and she is further established as a sexual presence by the way Dickens presents her relationship with her 'cherubic' little father as a sort of innocent mock-flirtation combined with a mock-mothering. She is always fussing with his hair or his clothes, or showering him with kisses (at one point she actually kisses his hat off), or getting him to place one of his feet alongside one of hers to show she means to keep him 'up to the mark'. Dora's fondling of her lap-dog had helped to endow her with sexuality and Bella's father serves a similar purpose here – yet another (and very Dickensian) way of solving the problem of how to make a young woman sexually attractive and attracting whilst preserving her virginal innocence. Chapter 8 of Book II, in which Bella, referring to herself as 'the lovely woman', entices her father into a trip to Greenwich for a secret feast, is entitled 'In Which an Innocent Elopement Occurs'.

We do not share Dickens's intense preoccupation with uniting in one fictional character the irreconcilable qualities of flirtatious Maria Beadnell and virginal Mary Hogarth and so may soon become embarrassed by the zest with which he dwells on the physical manifestations of Bella's love for her father. But we should not therefore overlook the skill with which he is depicting her as having a plausible emotional immaturity. She is shown as confused about her own feelings (except in relation to her father) and as painfully aware of this. She is made to recognize helplessly that she wants 'contradictory things', and she is constantly surprised by her own reactions to people and events, especially with regard to young Rokesmith, alias Harmon. She realizes that she attracts him but her feelings about him are 'dark to her own heart'. She tries to keep up a careless indifference towards him but cannot resist his influence; 'how do I come to mind him when I don't care for him?' she asks herself. Dickens excellently dramatizes her confusion in all her dialogues with Harmon, especially the one in chapter 13 of Book II when she resolves to put him in his place and veers between would-be haughtiness and genuine embarrassment in a very convincing way, ending up thoroughly dissatisfied with herself and as confused as ever.

Unlike Estella, who defines and explains her own nature with such preternatural detachment and lucidity,[14] Bella does not understand herself, though eventually, as happened with Jane Austen's Emma, 'a few minutes were sufficient for making her acquainted with her own heart' and she chooses to follow Rokesmith into exile from the Boffin mansion rather than to remain in luxury with her 'great expectations'. This is plausibly prepared for through Bella's increasingly uneasy witnessing of Boffin's apparent moral degeneration under the influence of wealth and her experience of Lizzie which makes her view love in quite a new light:

> Bella sat enchained by the deep, unselfish passion of this girl or woman of her own age, courageously revealing itself in the confidence of her sympathetic perception of its truth. And yet she had never experienced anything like it, or thought of the existence of anything like it.[15]

As a newly wedded bride in 'the charm-ingest of dolls' houses' on Blackheath, Bella is made to declare that she wants to be 'something so much worthier than the doll in the doll's house'. But the imagery that Dickens uses in describing her in her new role encourages us to see her as a pretty toy, 'a sort of dimpled little charming Dresden-china clock, by the very best maker', or, at best, as a child playing at being a wife and mother. Her idea of giving her husband intellectual companionship is to memorize the City news in the papers and then try 'to look wise and serious' as she drops bits of it into their evening conversations 'until she would laugh at herself most charmingly'. Her baby is simply a plaything, 'reminding [her father] of the days when she had a pet doll and used to talk to it as she carried it about'.

All this reduces one of Dickens's most believable female characters to the level of Dot Peerybingle in *The Cricket on the Hearth*, his 'fairy tale of home', and undercuts his subsequent depiction of her rising to Dickensian-heroine level as she staunchly affirms total faith in the man she loves, undismayed by mystery and ugly appearances (in this respect she is a successor to that much more one-dimensional character, Rachel in *Hard Times*). Almost immediately after this Dickens showers her with rewards and loving adulation from her husband and the Boffins which produces rather a cloying effect. We can only regret that Dickens, having created such a vital and convincing character as Bella, should in the end smother her with roses as he does.

Harmon, when he is wooing Bella while disguised as a poor secretary, is very much a hopeless lover in the established Dickensian tradition. In the other main plot of the novel, however, the one that revolves round Lizzie Hexam, we find that the hopeless-lover figure is moving into the role of villain and murderer.[16] Bradley Headstone is a powerfully presented newcomer among Dickens's *dramatis personae*, but the object of his hopeless passion is quite as remarkable in her own way, even though at first sight she appears to be a standard Dickens heroine in every respect except that of social class. Lizzie Hexam is beautiful, gentle and modest, a devoted and self-sacrificing daughter and sister. Her quick flow of sympathy towards all sister-women (Jenny Wren, Bella, old Betty Higden) is a sure sign of grace in a female Dickens character, and the novelist's readiness to violate probability by making her, an uneducated girl from the lower depths of the dark city that is the London of *Our Mutual Friend*, talk in good standard English[17] is a further indication that Lizzie is indeed to be seen as a heroine. Like Oliver Twist she is an embodiment of 'the principle of good'. Like Agnes and Little Dorrit before her, Lizzie when she falls in love dreams only of a new form of the self-abnegating, would-be redeeming love she has already shown in her daughterly and sisterly roles. Eugene Wrayburn is so far removed from her socially that she believes she can never be his wife but, if she were 'a lady rich and beautiful', she would say to him:

Only put me in that empty place [the vacancy in his heart caused by his having 'nothing to trust in, and care for'], only try how little I mind myself, only prove what a world of things I will do and bear for you, and I hope that you might even come to be much better than you are, through me who am so much worse, and hardly worth the thinking of beside you.[18]

*

What is new about Lizzie, and this has directly to do with her lowly social status, is that her role is not the traditional passive one. Dickens shows that only she herself, strengthened by a firm sense of personal integrity, can protect herself from the two dangers that threaten her — very similar to the two dangers that threaten Jane Eyre, but Lizzie has to cope with them both at once instead of in sequence. The threat Wrayburn represents is to make her into a 'doll', his plaything-mistress, and it is a powerful threat because Lizzie's own heart is already given to him as Jane's was to Mr Rochester. The threat Bradley Headstone represents is self-sacrificing marriage to a man she finds frighteningly repellent; such a marriage would kill her (marrying a headstone) as surely as marriage to St John Rivers would have killed Jane. What makes the Headstone threat so formidable is her beloved brother's eager desire for it on his own selfish grounds. It is a reworking of the story of Louisa Gradgrind, her brother and Bounderby, but Lizzie is more like Jane Eyre than the despairing Louisa and steadfastly refuses Headstone's passionate offers. The same strong sense of her own integrity with which Dickens has endowed her plausibly moves her to attempt escape from her involvement with Wrayburn, to hide herself away, working in a rural factory, where she trusts he will never find her.

Agnes and Little Dorrit (and Jane Eyre too, for that matter) have only to present themselves to the man they have steadily loved throughout all the vicissitudes of the story at the moment when he is at last ready to love them as they should be loved, for him to be finally redeemed by accepting them. But Lizzie has to take a more active role than that at the end when her quick-wittedness, physical strength and skill in rowing[19] are needed to rescue Wrayburn from drowning after Headstone's murderous tow-path assault on him.[20] She saves his life twice over, in fact, first by pulling him from the river and then by promising to become his wife when he is apparently on his death-bed.

For all the vigour of her actions, however, Lizzie is not a character likely to hold the modern reader's interest for her own sake. The mere mention of Jane Eyre and the recollection of her passionate outbursts, her cool wit and her determination to survive, 'to keep in good health and not

285

die', exposes Lizzie as the idealized character that she is, fatally lacking in any sort of emotional or intellectual complexity. She can be shown as threatened but not as tempted, for she is essentially a melodramatic creation – not, like both the men who, in their different ways, threaten her, a potentially tragic one. The only arresting thing about her, as has been indicated, is that she plays a much more active part, even to the extent of rescuing the hero by her physical prowess, than is at all customary for a melodrama heroine. This may, as Sylvia Manning argues,[21] strongly indicate the way Dickens's conception of femininity has developed to allow the presentation of female characters who, without loss of conventional femininity, display characteristics and attributes hitherto conceived of by him as exclusively masculine; but it does not *of itself* make Lizzie interesting as a character. It is on the characters of the men who love her, Wrayburn and Headstone, and on the presentation of their emotional turmoil, that the reader's attention is fixed.

'George Silverman's Explanation', written two years after the ending of *Our Mutual Friend*, is wholly focused on the psychology and the sufferings of the male narrator, and the objects of his secret love – the farmer's daughter, Sylvia, and the aristocrat, Adelina Fareway – are hardly realized at all (though it is noteworthy that Silverman extols Adelina for intellectual gifts as well as for beauty and goodness). The dominating figure of the novel begun three years later, *The Mystery of Edwin Drood*, is also male, the respectable-seeming cathedral organist and chorister, John Jasper, with his secret drug-addiction and his tormenting hopeless passion for Rosa Bud, the schoolgirl fiancée of Drood, his nephew and ward.

Dickens places Rosa in a situation resembling Bella Wilfer's in that she has been destined by others to a particular husband – although in her case the intention behind this was not malicious but benign and she has familiarly known her fiancé since childhood. This does not prevent her from resenting the situation, however. 'It *is* so ridiculous', she says to Edwin when he visits her at Miss Twinkleton's discreet seminary;

> It *is* so absurd to be an engaged orphan; and it *is* so absurd to have the girls and the servants scuttling about after one, like mice in the wainscot; and it *is* so absurd to be called upon![22]

But if she recalls Bella in her spirited bewailing of her lot she also strongly recalls Dora in being a spoiled and cossetted but essentially good-hearted 'fairy Figure'. She had, Dickens comments,

> grown to be an amiable, giddy, wilful, winning little creature; spoilt, in the sense of counting upon kindness from all around her; but not in the

sense of repaying it with indifference. Possessing an exhaustless well of affection in her nature, its sparkling waters had freshened and brightened the Nuns' House for years, and yet its depths had never yet been moved: what might betide when that came to pass; what developing changes might fall upon the heedless head, and light heart, then; remained to be seen.[23]

The clear suggestion here is that the reader will eventually see Rosa, inspired by love, rising above her own frivolity and, like Bella before her, exhibiting that specially feminine form of heroism in Dickens, steadfast and supportive faith in the man she loves when all occasions seem to be conspiring against him. Exactly how this would have developed must remain a question for those seemingly insatiable speculators, the 'Droodians', who have for the last century been guessing at how Dickens meant to finish the novel, but that Rosa's attainment of true heroic womanhood will essentially follow the pattern set by Bella seems plain enough.

Young and childish as she is shown to be, Rosa, being a Dickensian female, is also shown as instinctively wiser, more perceptive, in the matter of human relationships than her fiancé. After she and he have had yet another of their mutually exacerbating meetings he pleads with her for them to be friends:

> 'Ah!' cries Rosa, shaking her head and bursting into real tears, 'I wish we *could* be friends! It's because we can't be friends, that we try one another so. I am a young little thing, Eddy, to have an old heartache; but I really, really have, sometimes. Don't be angry. I know you have one yourself, too often. We should both of us have done better, if What is to be had been left What might have been. I am quite a little serious thing now, and not teasing you. Let each of us forbear, this one time, on our own account, and on the other's!'[24]

Dickens calls this outburst 'this glimpse of a woman's nature in the spoilt child' and, although he thus over-directs the reader's response and also makes the last of Rosa's sentences sound unnaturally stilted, it seems to me that he here stimulates us to a real complexity of response to the character. It resembles his presentation of Dora's struggles to communicate seriously with David about the problems of their relationship. Yet Rosa does not become a main focus of interest for the reader in the way that Dora does. Dickens describes her shrinking and trembling under Jasper's hypnotic power over her, but it is on the latter rather than on her that our attention is fixed even when he is not present. When we read her words to Helena about how Jasper has 'made a slave of' her with his looks and how he conveys to her in the very sounds of the music he is teaching her 'that he pursues me as a lover, and command[s] me to keep his secret', it is Jasper and his weird power, his repressed passion, that we are concerned with rather than Rosa herself, despite her eloquence about her own reactions:

> . . . to-night when he watched my lips so closely as I was singing, besides feeling terrified I felt ashamed and passionately hurt. It was as if he kissed me, and I couldn't bear it, but cried out.

We may feel that writing this victim's description of a kind of rape is stirring the novelist's imagination but hardly that it is doing so to the extent of prompting him to explore the girl's reactions in any depth or complexity. It is the character to whom Rosa is speaking, Helena Landless, with whom Dickens the experimenting artist is more preoccupied. For Helena, unlike Rosa, is not a skilfully executed variant on an established type but something new, a mingling of elements that have hitherto tended to be strongly opposed to each other in Dickens's characterization of the sexes. It is on Helena that he focuses the reader's attention at the end of the scene in a favourite Dickensian vignette of a beautiful dark woman possessed of inner strength comforting and caressing a weaker, pretty, child-like one:[25]

> The lustrous gipsy-face drooped over the clinging arms and bosom, and the wild black hair fell down protectingly over the childish form. There was a slumbering gleam of fire in the intense dark eyes, though they were then softened with compassion and admiration. Let whomsoever it most concerned look well to it![26]

Helena is, it seems to me, the only female character in *Drood* the conception of whom appears to have exercised Dickens's imagination in the way (though not to the extent) that the conception of Jasper did. It is remarkable that, although she is shown as very passionate by nature, prone to fierce resentments and distinctly 'unfeminine' (i.e., ungentle, independent) in many aspects of her demeanour and attitude to life, she is, unlike such predecessors as Rosa Dartle or Miss Wade, clearly intended to be a wholly sympathetic figure and perhaps even the 'hero' of the novel (in the sense of defeating and unmasking the villain). Mingled with the qualities that link her with Rosa Dartle or Miss Wade are two which, throughout all Dickens's work, as we have seen, have been absolute hallmarks of the author-approved feminine; a quickness to sympathize lovingly with others of her sex, and sisterly devotion to her brother.

Helena and her twin brother, Neville, arrive in Cloisterham after a bitter childhood under the brutal regime of their stepfather in Ceylon. They are introduced, through Crisparkle's first impressions of them, as virtually indistinguishable in manner and appearance:

> An unusually handsome lithe young fellow, and an unusually handsome lithe girl; much alike; both very dark, and very rich in colour; she of almost the gipsy type; something untamed about them both; a certain air upon them of hunter and huntress; yet withal a certain air of being the objects of the chase, rather than the followers. Slender, supple, quick of eye and limb; half shy, half defiant; fierce of look; an indefinable kind of pause coming and going on their whole expression, both of face and form, which might be equally likened to the pause before a crouch or a bound.[27]

Earlier brother/sister pairs in Dickens where there had been such a close and stressed physical and temperamental resemblance between the two had invariably been villainous or downright evil (Samson and Sally Brass, Mr and Miss Murdstone), with particular odium attaching to the masculine traits shown by the woman. In Helena's case, however, Dickens goes out of his way to emphasize, 'to her honour', that she had always played the traditionally masculine role in the brother/sister relationship. Neville tells Mr Crisparkle:

> . . . nothing in our misery ever subdued her, though it often cowed me. When we ran away from it (we ran away four times in six years, to be soon brought back and cruelly punished), the flight was always of her planning and leading. Each time she dressed as a boy, and showed the daring of a man. I take it we were seven years old when we first decamped; but I remember, when I lost the pocket-knife with which she was to have cut her hair short, how desperately she tried to tear it out, or bite it off.[28]

That such masculine qualities are no longer being presented by Dickens as either comically or alarmingly sexually aberrant but rather as fully consonant with what he sees as true 'womanliness' becomes clear in the course of Helena's first intimate dialogue with Rosa (when they sound more like a passionate lover and his coy mistress than two schoolgirls, even two Victorian schoolgirls, making friends). Rosa assures Helena that she can answer for the other girls in the school being all 'good-natured':

> 'I can answer for you,' laughed Helena, searching the lovely little face with her dark fiery eyes, and tenderly caressing the small figure. 'You will be a friend to me, won't you?'

'I hope so. But the idea of my being a friend to you seems too absurd, though.'

'Why?'

'O, I am such a mite of a thing and you are so *womanly* [my italics] and handsome. You seem to have resolution and power enough to crush me. I shrink into nothing by the side of your presence even.'

'I am a neglected creature, my dear, unacquainted with all accomplishments, sensitively conscious that I have everything to learn, and deeply ashamed to own my ignorance.'

'And yet you acknowledge everything to me!' said Rosa.

'My pretty one, can I help it? There is a fascination in you.'

'O! is there though?' pouted Rosa, half in jest and half in earnest. 'What a pity Master Eddy doesn't feel it more!'[29]

Earlier, Dickens had shown Dora paying loving tribute to Agnes, Ada Clare to Esther Summerson, Louisa to Sissy Jupe and Bella to Lizzie Hexam, but the superior womanliness that Dora and the others were acknowledging had not been shown as a matter of 'resolution and power' as it is here with Rosa and Helena. Rather, it related to those qualities of long-suffering goodness, self-denying love and zeal to be of use in the world that Dickens had hitherto regarded, in common with his age, as the proper source of greatness of character in women. Helena is certainly a striking departure from this stereotype.

Dickens's sympathetic portrayal in Helena of an intensely passionate woman is all the more remarkable in that this type had been particularly blackly painted in two of the three novels preceding *Drood. A Tale of Two Cities* and *Great Expectations* feature four cases of women monstered by passion. Madame Defarge is 'a tigress', Mrs Joe a virago, Molly (Estella's criminal mother) 'a wild beast tamed' and Miss Havisham a witch-like creature, a ghastly combination of waxwork and skeleton. In each case the perversion of womanhood that the character represents is stamped on our imaginations by our being shown her apparently enacting some conventionally 'good' female role or performing some conventionally 'good' female activity – but always with some horrible twist given to the thing. Madame Defarge is constantly knitting, an occupation which steadily acquires more and more sinister overtones (Dickens's inspiration here clearly derives from reading about the *tricôteuses* round the guillotine during the Terror):

'You work hard, madame,' said a man near her.

'Yes,' answered Madame Defarge; 'I have a good deal to do.'

'What do you make, madame?'

'Many things.'

'For instance – '

'For instance,' returned Madame Defarge, composedly, 'shrouds.'[30]

Mrs Joe is supplying the place of a mother to her little brother but the bib of her apron is 'stuck full of pins and needles' that get into the bread she gives him to eat. Molly appears as Jaggers's housekeeper, placing food on the table for him and his guests, but she is a very disturbing version of the Good Provider: Pip tells us, 'I had been to see Macbeth at the theatre, a night or two before, and . . . her face looked to one as if it were all disturbed by fiery air, like the faces I had seen rise out of the Witches' caldron'. Jaggers forces her to show her fearsomely powerful wrists and one of them, belonging to the hand with which she had strangled her rival in love, is 'much disfigured – deeply scarred and scarred across and across'.[31] Miss Havisham is arrayed as a young bride but the dress has rotted on her and she herself has withered into hideousness. Dickens's description of Pip's first impression of this eerie figure stamps it indelibly on our minds:

> Once, I had been taken to see some ghastly waxwork at the Fair, representing I know not what impossible personage lying in state. Once, I had been taken to one of our old marsh churches to see a skeleton in the ashes of a rich dress, that had been dug out of a vault under the church pavement. Now, waxwork and skeleton seemed to have dark eyes that moved and looked at me. I should have cried out, if I could.[32]

Most readers of Dickens would agree, I believe, that of these four images of womanhood perverted by passion Miss Havisham is the most compelling and the most haunting. This is not only owing to her having such a central part to play in the plot. Madame Defarge has a central enough role in *A Tale of Two Cities* but she is memorable rather than haunting like Miss Havisham. Madame Defarge is essentially a melo-dramatic creation, like a figure from Jacobean revenge tragedy. Dickens gives her a powerful physical presence but no emotional or psychological complexity. Her vitality derives from one totally dominating passion (her chief companion, when the Revolution gets under way, is a screaming fury, the wife of a starved grocer, called 'The Vengeance'). We know all about her, once we have understood this, and never feel in the way she is presented that there is any transcending of the immediate requirements of the story. The figure of this implacable knitting woman does not come to seem symbolic of some aspect of human experience or the human condition. Madame Defarge's knitting is fateful in a very literal way (it is her 'register' into which she is knitting the names of those who are to be slaughtered when the Revolution comes) and we never feel that Dickens

is intending us to sense in it some wider, more metaphysical significance –
so that we might begin to associate her with the spinning hags who
personify Fate in Classical or in the Norse legend, for example. Miss
Havisham is a different matter, however. As we absorb her image and the
image of Satis House with its windows rustily barred against the light and
its stopped clocks we can hardly fail to become aware of symbolic
overtones, of the immediate story's being transcended. For Chesterton,
indeed, the story here was hardly more than a distracting irritant: 'The
surface of the thing seems more awful than the core of it . . . Something
worse than a common tale of jilting [lies] behind the masquerade and
madness of the awful Miss Havisham.'[33]

As presented to us in the novel Miss Havisham is a fantastic creation,
a being who has once been human[34] but whose life has been frozen as by
some evil enchantment (in terms of the ostensibly realistic plot this was
the 'bad illness' she suffered immediately after the jilting). Even such
good impulses as she may still have now become inevitably perverted and
malign. When the child Estella was first given into her charge she meant
only to love and cherish her but 'gradually did worse' until she had 'stolen
her heart away and put ice in its place'. With her 'wasting hands' Miss
Havisham is like an evil spirit casting a spell over Estella and, through her,
over Pip too. Pip indeed sees Satis House in fairy-tale terms but misinter-
prets Miss Havisham, believing that she is conscious of the evil of the
enchantment she and her house lie under and that she is looking to him to
release her from it:

> She reserved it for me to restore the desolate house, admit the sunshine
> into the dark rooms, set the clocks a going and the cold hearths a blazing,
> tear down the cobwebs, destroy the vermin – in short, do all the shining
> deeds of the young Knight of romance, and marry the Princess.[35]

It is one of the many ironies of this great ironic novel that Pip is indeed
destined finally to exorcise Miss Havisham's evil spirit, to restore her to
humanity (so that she can address him 'with an earnest womanly compassion for [him] in her new affection') by holding up to her a looking-
glass in which she suddenly sees and at once rejects the monstrosity of
what she has done and has become. But the blaze that ensues is fatal to
her and the tearing down of the cobwebs as Pip drags the great cloth off
the table on which the rotting wedding-cake stands is only part of his
desperate attempt to save her life. Once the spell is lifted from her Miss
Havisham with her 'profound unfitness for this earth on which she was
placed'[36] (i.e., her fiercely passionate nature) must die.

*

Just as she is the most haunting, so Miss Havisham is actually the last figure in Dickens's work to illustrate the perversion of womanhood that can be brought about by the passions. *Our Mutual Friend*, appearing four years after *Great Expectations*, features no such character among its dramatis personae. The nearest approach to one is the crippled child, Fanny Cleaver (who has been, surely somewhat extravagantly, hailed as 'the most interesting and complicated of Dickens's women').[37] Fanny, or Jenny Wren as she calls herself, unleashes her rage and frustration against her alcoholic old wreck of a father, her 'bad child', and Dickens comments how 'the dolls' dressmaker had become a quaint little shrew'. But the reader's sympathy is never alienated from her and, despite occasional vicious flourishes with her needle (seeming to prick Bradley Headstone's eyes with it, for example), she never becomes an image of womanhood turned malignant that Madame Defarge, Mrs Joe, Molly and Miss Havisham do. She combines two roles the contemplation of which invariably affects Dickens deeply — the role of heavily disadvantaged child and that of young daughter forced to assume a parental role towards a pathetically inadequate father. Not surprisingly, therefore, she is highly idealized, with her masses of beautiful golden hair and wistful memories of visions of angels coming down to her 'in long bright slanting rows'. Her father is presented as repulsively as possible so that the vivid depiction of Jenny's harsh treatment of him will not turn the reader's sympathies from her to him. She expresses vindictive resentment against ordinary healthy children, masochistically dwelling on their physical freedom ('Always running about and screeching, always playing and fighting, always skip-skip-skipping on the pavement and chalking it for their games!'), but the childish terms in which she expresses her fantasies about punishing those of them that mock her greatly soften down the ugliness of the feelings involved. Also, of course, it keeps us poignantly aware that Jenny *is* still a child in years despite the adult role ('the person of the house') into which she has been prematurely forced:

> There's doors under the church in the Square — black doors, leading into black vaults. Well! I'd open one of those doors, and I'd cram 'em all in, and then I'd lock the door and through the keyhole I'd blow in pepper.[38]

Playfulness is absent, however, from a decidedly more sadistic fantasy in which Jenny indulges when she imagines what she would do to her future, and as yet unknown, husband if he should turn out, like her father, to be a drunkard:

> When he was asleep, I'd make a spoon red hot, and I'd have some boiling liquor bubbling in a saucepan, and I'd take it out hissing, and I'd open his

mouth with the other hand – or perhaps he'd sleep with his mouth ready open – and I'd pour it down his throat, and blister it and choke him.

But this startling vindictiveness is at once exorcised by Lizzie Hexam ('I am sure you would do no such horrible thing') and the reader is then reminded, through dialogue given to Jenny herself, of the overpowering excuses the child has for indulging in this sort of fantasy. 'You', she tells Lizzie, 'haven't always lived among it [i.e., drunkenness] as I have lived – and your back isn't bad and your legs are not queer.' And just in case some readers may still be feeling shocked Dickens adds an authorial comment to guide our response:

> Poor dolls' dressmaker! How often so dragged down by hands that should have raised her up; how often so misdirected when losing her way on the eternal road, and asking guidance! Poor, poor little dolls' dressmaker![39]

The essential difference between Jenny and the four monstered-by-passion women we have been considering is that the strength of her feelings results from the terrible frustrating situation into which she was born – crippled, poor, and the child of a drunkard – and is not indicative of a turbulent passionate nature. Given a kind and loving father like another cripple, Phoebe in 'Mugby Junction' (one of the later Christmas Stories), Jenny would, we may feel sure from Dickens's way of presenting her, be as sweet and saintly as that character is.

Jenny apart, the only other female character in *Our Mutual Friend* who can be said to exhibit passion is the adventuress Sophronia Lammle. She is a more realistic figure than Madame Defarge and Miss Havisham, and is indeed rendered with some convincing complexity, but she is not at all intended to be a sympathetic character despite her occasional fits of conscience.[40] Nothing in this novel any more than in its two predecessors prepares us for the very different presentation of a passionate-natured woman that we find with Helena in *Drood*.

The insistence that we have noted on Helena's masculine qualities of physical boldness, initiative, leadership, and so on forms part of an interesting pattern in Dickens's last novel. The man she is evidently destined to marry, the 'fair and rosy' Minor Canon, Mr Crisparkle, with, on the one hand, his manly vigour and physical prowess and his energetic championship of the just and right and, on the other, his fresh innocence, delicate sensitivity to others, gentleness and sweet goodness, also mingles attributes that are, in the Dickens world, normally the prerogative of one sex or the other. Just as the masculine attributes seem to predominate in Helena's case so do the feminine ones in Crisparkle's. This, together with other things in the novel such as Jasper's love for his nephew, dramatized in terms that combine the maternal and the adoring, suggest that the rigid sexual polarities that had tended up to this point to dominate Dickens's characterization were beginning to give way to a freer and more complex rendering of gender in human beings. Among the principal characters of *Drood* it is only Rosa Bud who seems, in this respect, to continue on the traditional lines of gentle, timid, dependent femininity as opposed to strong, bold, assertive masculinity.

A comic variant on the fusing of the sexes appears in the minor figure of the London landlady whose name 'stated in uncompromising capitals of considerable size on a brass door-plate, and yet not lucidly as to sex or condition, was BILLICKIN'. She explains that the reason for this is to avoid making it public by 'a solitary female statement' that there is no man in the house:

> So long as this 'ouse is known indefinite as Billickin's, and so long as it is a doubt with the riff-raff where Billickin may be hidin', near the street-door or down the airy, and what his weight and size, so long I feel safe.[41]

'The Billickin', as she is always thereafter called, belongs, of course, to the tradition of tyrannical Dickensian landladies, stretching back through Mrs Crupp to Mrs Raddle in *Pickwick* and is linked also to Mrs Gamp and Mrs Lirriper by the marvellous comic inventiveness of her language ('I was put in youth to a very genteel boarding-school . . . and a poorness of blood flowed from the table which has run through my life'). She may serve to remind us here that, whilst various patterns of change and development may be traced in examining chronologically Dickens's major female characters, he never ceased to delight in elaborating many of the comic stereotypes he worked so largely with in the earliest phase of his fiction-writing. Miss Twinkleton is another case in point. By comparison with her the Misses Crumpton of *Sketches by Boz* are crude anti-schoolmistress jokes, but she is very much from the same mould. In the last novels the most entertaining of all such characters is surely Mrs Wilfer, the 'majestic' wife of Bella's 'cherubic' little father. She combines the uncomfortable-wife stereotype with the pretentious-gentility one, and one might think that Dickens had long since exhausted the comic possibilities of both types and would now at best produce a paler version of Mrs Varden with perhaps a dash of Mrs Nickleby added. However, by endowing Mrs Wilfer with a supremely ludicrous pomposity of speech and stateliness of manner, he gives us a character as fresh and funny as the best of his earlier types of female absurdity. Here she is monologizing at the family dinner-table on the occasion of her wedding anniversary, making her husband feel distinctly apologetic for ever having presumed to marry her:

> 'It was one of mamma's cherished hopes that I should become united to a tall member of society. . . . Papa also would remark to me . . . "that a family of whales must not ally themselves with sprats". His company was eagerly sought, as may be supposed, by the wits of the day, and our house was their continual resort. I have known as many as three copper-plate engravers exchanging the most exquisite sallies and retorts there, at one time. . . . Among the most prominent members of that distinguished circle, was a gentleman measuring six feet four in height. . . . This gentleman was so obliging as to honour me with attentions which I could not fail to understand. . . . I immediately announced to both my parents that those attentions were misplaced. . . . They inquired was he too tall? I replied it was not the stature, but the intellect was too lofty. . . . I well remember mamma's clasping her hands, and exclaiming, "This will end in a little man!" . . . Within a month,' said Mrs Wilfer, deepening her voice, as if she were relating a terrible ghost story, 'within a month, I first saw R.W., my husband. Within a year I married him. It is natural for the mind to recall these dark coincidences on the present day.'[42]

Types like Mrs Wilfer, who compose that 'gallery of foolish, ridiculous, or offensive women' that Gissing considered so 'Wonderful as fact, and admirable as art',[43] loom large in our minds when we think of women in Dickens. Apart from them, we tend to have only a generalized impression of angelic heroines, a few dark tragedy queens perhaps, and a host of rosy, cosy, bustling little women cossetting and worshipping their menfolk. The picture is, as the foregoing chapters have sought to show, certainly more complex than this, and distinctions should be made between various stages of Dickens's work. The three distinct phases that, I have argued, can be identified in Dickens's portraiture of women seem to relate pretty clearly to his biography and his general artistic development. The young Dickens, pouring out those 'inimitable' mixtures of farce, melodrama and social satire that constitute his early work, naturally drew on stock types of female characterization already existing in the popular literature with which he was so familiar. His own emotional responses to, on the one hand, his mother and Maria Beadnell and, on the other, his sister Fanny and Mary Hogarth helped to fix women in his early art as either fools or angels. *Dombey and Son*, begun when he was in his middle thirties and after a two-year gap in his novel-writing, marks the beginning of an important new phase in his art, more conscious attention to psychological realism, and more concern for story-development along more naturalistic lines. Inevitably, his presentation of major female characters was affected by this. At the same time experience of life was urging him away from the old fool/angel polarity with regard to women. He had been contentedly married for twelve years to a woman who did not really fit into either category, he had three young women, Georgina and his two daughters, growing up under his roof, he had formed, and was continuing to form, close and enduring friendships with a variety of women – Lady Blessington, the Hon. Mrs Watson, Mary Boyle, Miss Coutts – and friendly acquaintance with many more, including at least one woman of literary genius, Elizabeth Gaskell. Meanwhile, his work for Miss Coutts's home was acquainting him in some depth with female nature at the lowest end of the social scale. The greater range and subtlety of his portraiture of women in the novels of 1846-56 must surely bear some relation to all this experience. Then, in 1857/8 came the greatest crisis of his adult life since Mary Hogarth died in his arms so suddenly. His marriage collapsed and he found himself deeply in love with a young girl whom he could never hope to marry. The shift of focus we have remarked in the last four novels, away from women themselves and on to men as lovers of women, especially as lovers of women they cannot have, seems clearly influenced by this.

*

From the survey of Dickens's women characters that we have been conducting a fairly clear picture emerges of what Dickens loved and admired in women as well as what he disliked, feared and hated. But, as a prominent public figure, a celebrated speech-maker and a leading editor and journalist, he had other channels of communication with the public besides his novels. To complete our picture of Dickens's attitude towards women and the womanly as he conceived of it, we need to look at these other public utterances as well as at the specific generalizations about women and female nature that appear in the novels, and related comments in his surviving private correspondence. It is this material that forms the subject-matter of the next and final section of this book.

III

Dickens and Woman

. . . a nature that is ever, in the mass, better, truer, higher, nobler, quicker to feel, and much more constant to retain, all tenderness and pity, self-denial and devotion, more than the nature of men.

Dombey and Son, chapter 3

'But Wooman, lovely Wooman,' said Mr Turveydrop, with very disagreeable gallantry, 'what a sex you are!'

Bleak House, chapter 14

14
The Womanly Ideal

In the first part of this book we looked at Dickens's response, as man and as artist, to certain individual women who clearly played an important role in his emotional history. In the second we surveyed the presentation of women characters in his fiction. There remains to be considered what he wrote, or is reported to have said, about women in general, about female nature and the role of women both inside the home and in society at large. He wrote no specific treatise on these things but his fictional writings, journalism and letters contain many relevant scattered comments, ranging in tone from the jocose to the solemn, and it is the object of this final chapter to bring together as many of these as possible and group them in a way that may enable us to form some overall impression of Dickens's beliefs about, and attitudes towards, the opposite sex. To a large extent these beliefs and attitudes were typical of the age in which he lived, and this will be readily recognized by anyone who has read at all widely in the period or is even slightly acquainted with the vast scholarly literature that has grown up during the past quarter-century devoted to Victorian Woman and male attitudes towards her. This literature inquires into every aspect of her existence, from morality to menstruation, and often pays detailed attention to the various ways in which she was depicted in the literature of the period – as child, doll, angel, Magdalen, and so on. In Dickens's case it is rather a question of interesting or curious emphases than of any marked idiosyncrasy as regards his ideas about women. The following sections of this chapter will each deal with a particular aspect of his overall attitude towards women and seek to distinguish what is peculiarly Dickensian in emphasis as opposed to what was simply mainline Victorianism. We should bear in mind that during his lifetime he witnessed the gradual evolution of the typical Englishwoman from the meek submissive model of the 1830s to the more self-aware and self-assertive figure of the 1860s, but we shall not discern much change or development in his basic attitude towards her. As Philip Collins has observed, 'most of [Dickens's] ideas lasted a lifetime'.[1]

i

It was for Dickens a fundamental belief, as it was for the great majority of his contemporaries, that man's nature, his psychological and emotional make-up, differed, fundamentally and inherently, from woman's. She was, as Tennyson put it in 1847, 'not undevelopt man,/But diverse'. The adjectives 'manly' and 'womanly' occur very often in Dickens, as in other Victorian writers, and are always used as terms of highest approbation. Behind them lies the assumption that the natural differences – psychological, emotional, moral – between men and women were as clearly known and established as the physical ones. Dickens would not perhaps have been displeased with Virginia Woolf's characterization of him (much as he would have disliked its tone): 'He has to perfection the virtues conventionally ascribed to the male: he is self-assertive, self-reliant, self-assured; energetic in the extreme'. However, these virtues were not for him a matter of 'conventional ascription' to the male sex, but the very essence of 'manliness'.

In J.S. Mill's great essay, *The Subjection of Women* (written 1861 but not published until 1869), Mill protested against this sort of distinction, asserting that nothing could be known about possible natural differences between men and women 'so long as they have only been seen in their present relation to one another', that is, with women subject to men and conditioned to this situation by their whole upbringing and environment. 'What is now called the nature of women', he wrote, 'is an eminently artificial thing – the result of forced repression in some directions, unnatural stimulation in others.'[2] Dickens would certainly have strongly dissented from such views (we have no evidence that he read Mill's essay and it is in fact highly unlikely that he would have done so). For him true 'womanliness' as he understood it was not a matter of nurture but of nature, something timeless and universal. It was complementary to 'manliness' in humanity, and whilst he would have agreed with Tennyson that the two sexes must, for the sake of human advancement, each strive to acquire more of the qualities and virtues inherent in the other, they would always nevertheless remain 'distinct in individualities'. He was critical even of his beloved Defoe for portraying women (he specified Robinson Crusoe's wife) merely as 'terrible dull commonplace fellows without breeches'.[3]

'Mental breadth' was one of those masculine qualities that woman should strive to develop, according to Tennyson (though she would never, of course, be man's equal in this and must take care not to lose 'the childlike in the larger mind')[4] and there was much discussion in journals and elsewhere during the nineteenth century about allegedly inherent intellectual differences between male and female. Charles Kingsley dramatized the question in his first novel, *Yeast* (1844), where the

302

heroine Argemone is forced to discover, when 'matched for the first time with a man who was her own equal in intellect and knowledge', just how different women's minds and mental processes are from men's:

> Again and again she argued with him, and was vanquished. . . . Argemone began . . . to see that her opinions were mere hearsays, picked up at her own will and fancy; while his were living, daily-growing ideas. Her mind was beside his as the vase of cut flowers by the side of the rugged tree, whose roots are feeding deep in the mother earth.

Dickens offers us no such set-piece, however – unsurprisingly because he is very little interested in endowing any of his characters, male or female, with much intellectual life – but he evidently accepts wholeheartedly one popular distinction (that survives strongly still) between the way men's and women's minds work, the belief in 'feminine intuition', especially with regard to matters of love. Writing to his friend de la Rue in 1845 he says:

> It is clear to me that Miss Holdscamp does not love her lover. I am slow to come to the conclusion, for I should have liked her to love him; but in such a case a woman's observation is invariably right — hardly seems to possess the faculty of being wrong; Nature having ordered it otherwise. And you may rely upon it — Madame de la Rue's suspicion in that wise, is the true one. I have no more doubt about it, than I have that I am not standing on my head at this moment . . .

Dickens's novels offer many examples of women 'instinctively' apprehending the emotional truth about other people and their relationships, finding out that someone is in love even before that person is himself or herself aware of it. Mrs Plornish, visiting Arthur Clennam in the Marshalsea, seems instinctively to realize that it is thoughts of Little Dorrit that have been preoccupying him, that he is on the verge of recognizing his true love and need for her. Whereas her husband tries to comfort the prisoner with philosophy ('there was ups you see, and there was downs') Mrs Plornish goes straight to the human heart of the matter which, Dickens comments, 'may have arisen . . . out of her sex's wit, out of a woman's quick association of ideas, or out of a woman's no-association of ideas' but it did happen, 'somehow', that she began to speak about 'the very subject of Arthur's meditations'.[5]

No doubt one of the reasons why Dickens thought a character in Bulwer Lytton's *A Strange Story* was 'a remarkably skilfully done woman' was because in the chapters to which Dickens was referring Bulwer shows the character, Mrs Colonel Poyntz, discovering that the narrator of the story is in love even before he himself is aware of it:

> 'Hush!' she said, lowering her voice; 'you are in love!'
>
> 'In love! – I! Permit me to ask why you think so?'
>
> 'The signs are unmistakeable; you are altered in your manner, even in the expression of your face, since I last saw you; your manner is generally quiet and observant, it is now restless and distracted; your expression of face is generally proud and serene, it is now humbled and troubled. You have something on your mind! . . . an anxiety that is remote from your profession, that touches your heart and is new to it!'
>
> I was startled, almost awed. . . .
>
> 'Profound observer! Subtle analyst! You have convinced me that I must be in love, though I did not suspect it before.'[6]

Moreover, by continuing to observe closely the man's reactions to what she is saying, Mrs Poyntz soon discovers also who it is that is the object of his love.

Female intuition always derives, in Dickens as in Bulwer, from quickness of observation (we may recall Mr Chillip's generalization in *David Copperfield*, 'The ladies are great observers, sir!'). Neither is it confined to matters of the heart, even though it may be most infallible there. Mrs Lammle in *Our Mutual Friend* discovers intuitively the double game that Fledgeby is playing whereas Twemlow cannot see it. 'Men', she says,

> are very wise in their way . . . but they have wisdom to learn. My husband . . . sees this plain thing no more than Mr Twemlow does – because there is no proof. Yet I believe five women out of six, in my place, would see it as clearly as I do.

A woman's instinctive wisdom, based on observation, is again exalted over masculine theorizing about life in the tirade of the landlady of the Break of Day Inn in *Little Dorrit*. Hearing masculine talk about 'philosophical philanthropy' and how it might palliate the crime even of such a monster as Rigaud she bursts in with

> I am a woman, I. I know nothing of philosophical philanthropy. But I know what I have seen, and what I have looked in the face, in this world here, where I find myself. And I tell you . . . there are people . . . who have no good in them – none. . . . who must be dealt with as enemies of the human race.

For Dickens this wisdom born of sharp observation may sometimes go hand in hand with what he presents as feminine susceptibility to fine gentlemanly appearances (the undoing of Madame Mantalini, successful businesswoman though she is). The landlady is so impressed by Rigaud's fine white hands and gentlemanly bearing that she sometimes thinks him a handsome and prepossessing man, whereas her husband has no doubts at all that he is 'an ill-looking fellow'. Dickens is, of course, following a long tradition about female susceptibility here, as we realize when we remember the lament of Shakespeare's Viola, 'How easy it is for the proper-false/In women's waxen hearts to set their forms'.[7]

Yet, even when not undermined by such susceptibility woman's observation may prove fallible. In *Drood* Dickens muses on what happens then:

> ... women have a curious power of divining the characters of men, which would seem to be innate and instinctive. ... But ... this power (fallible, like every other human attribute) is for the most part absolutely incapable of self-revision ... undistinguishable from prejudice, in respect of its determination not to be corrected.

This sort of feminine intuition, wildly off course and deliberately traded upon, is often a source for Dickensian comedy as in the case of Mrs Wilfer who would

> illuminate the family with her remarkable powers as a physiognomist; powers that terrified [her husband] ... as being always fraught with gloom and evil which no inferior prescience was aware of.

Jealousy of the kindly Boffins' wealth moves her to a particularly impressive display of her powers: 'the craft, the secrecy, the dark deep underhanded plotting, written in Mrs Boffin's countenance, make me shudder', she declares.[8]

*

Apart from this matter of feminine intuition Dickens does not show much interest in distinctively female mental processes, for all the rich comedy he derives from the way in which Mrs Nickleby develops her meditations on life. The supposed sexual differences that he constantly stresses are moral and emotional rather than intellectual as, for example, in this passage from one of the interpolated tales in *Pickwick*:

> [Gabriel Grub] saw that women, the tenderest and most fragile of all God's creatures, were the oftenest superior to sorrow, adversity, and distress; and he saw that it was because they bore, in their own hearts, an inexhaustible well-spring of affection and devotion.

Twenty years later this is still an article of faith with him when he writes in his Christmas Story for 1856, 'all men born of women know what great qualities they will show when men will fail'.[9] He is, in fact, like Tennyson, Ruskin, Thackeray and many others, including his beloved Washington

Irving,[10] an exponent of what Mill called 'the tiresome cant' that women are men's spiritual superiors. Deeply believing this, he naturally finds evidence everywhere to support the idea. Observing some English immigrants to Canada on board a boat going to Montreal, he notes 'what gentle ministers of hope and faith the women were' and 'how the men profited by their example'. He contemplates the faces of some American convicts who have been kept in solitary confinement and records that the experience has given the men a haggard look ('as though they had all been secretly terrified') but the women, on the other hand, seem to have been 'humanized and refined' by it. 'Whether', he writes,

> this be because of their better nature, which is elicited in solitude, or because of their being gentler creatures, of greater patience and longer suffering, I do not know; but so it is.

A year or so later he is reporting to the philanthropist Angela Burdett Coutts on children in Ragged Schools (established and run by charitable volunteers to give some basic education to very poor children) and writes that he notices the girls behave better than the boys. This, he adds, is because 'there is much more Good in Women than in Men, however Ragged they are'.[11]

Dickens, conceiving of female nature as 'ever, in the mass . . . quicker to feel, and much more constant to retain, all tenderness and pity, self-denial and devotion, than the nature of men', naturally sees women as born nurses. Their 'delicate fingers', 'beautiful evidence of the Almighty's goodness', are 'formed for sensitiveness and sympathy of touch, and made to minister to pain and grief'. Reading with pleasure about the explorer Mungo Park 'fainting under a tree and succoured by a woman, gratefully [remembering] how his Good Samaritan has always come to him in woman's shape, the wide world over',[12] Dickens would have felt that this was just as it should be. The cottager's wife who, 'being a woman', will not let Nell leave before tending to her blistered foot has 'such a gentle hand – rough-grained and hard though it was, with work' that it makes the child's heart overflow with loving gratitude. Even slovenly Pleasant Riderhood is made to show 'a natural woman's aptitude' for being helpful in a sick chamber as the little Marchioness had also done, even more impressively, when ministering to fever-stricken Dick Swiveller.[13] 'You women,' Tom Pinch tells his sister,

> are so kind, and in your kindness have such nice perception; you know so well how to be affectionate and full of solicitude without appearing to be; your gentleness of feeling is like your touch: so light and easy, that the

one enables you to deal with wounds of the mind as tenderly as the other enables you to deal with wounds of the body.

It is by pausing on such a speech as this that we can register the full 'fascination of repulsion' (to borrow a favourite phrase of his) that must have stimulated Dickens as he elaborated his portrait, in the same novel, of Mrs Gamp and Betsey Prig, those mighty opposites of female tenderness and natural nursing gifts. Confronted with Gampism in real life, of course, he was simply horrified, all the more so when it manifested itself in a wife nursing her husband, one of Dickens's servants:

> . . . that diabolical wife *and her sister*, being left last night to watch him, got blind drunk together on Gin – omitted everything they had undertaken to do – dropped Gin and God knows what over his poor dying figure. . . . I tumbled her out of the sick chamber just now, and will at least . . . have done with that abominable wretch.

He does not, we feel, use the words 'diabolical' and 'abominable' lightly here. 'All good things', Gabriel Varden instructs his wife at the height of the Gordon Riots, 'perverted to evil purposes, are worse than those which are naturally bad. A thoroughly wicked woman, is wicked indeed. When religion goes wrong, she is very wrong, for the same reason.' A more concentrated example of female depravity for Dickens than that of a drunken wife spilling gin over her dying husband would be hard to imagine.[14]

*

Woman in Dickens, and in Victorian ideology generally, has a still more exalted function than that of tender of sick minds and bodies. She is also a sort of natural priest, closer to God than man, and a source for him of spiritual strength and encouragement, especially in the face of death. Alexander Welsh has shown how prevalent in the Victorian age was the notion of woman as the 'Angel of Death', easing through her benign presence by the deathbed the passing of the troubled soul from the earthly life to Heaven and mediating between the human creature and its Maker, and he has drawn attention to the frequency with which she appears in this role in Dickens's work.[15] The great example, of course, is Agnes, to whom David prays at the end of the novel:

> Oh Agnes, oh my soul, so may thy face be by me when I close my life indeed; so may I, when realities are melting from me like the shadows which I now dismiss, still find thee near me, pointing upward!

A rhapsody published in *The Metropolitan* in 1843 suggests how much in tune with his age Dickens was in this conception of Woman as Saviour:

> It is for woman – tender, sympathizing, watching, prayerful woman –
> alone to comprehend those struggles, alone to soothe them, alone to
> invoke mercy and forgiveness for them, alone to feel the blessed assur-
> ance that her prayers are gone up an acceptable sacrifice before
> the throne of the Most High, alone to indulge the hope that him she
> mourneth as dead has awakened to life and immortality in the cloudless
> realms of everlasting light.[16]

Woman becomes, in fact, an embodiment of the grace and mercy of God
('her delicate fingers', we recall, Dickens described as 'beautiful evidence
of the Almighty's goodness'). In *The Old Curiosity Shop* the Single
Gentleman, Nell's great-uncle, says, when reviewing his family's history
for Mr Garland's benefit:

> If you have seen the picture-gallery of any one old family, you will
> remember how the same face and figure – often the fairest and slightest of
> them all – come upon you in different generations; and how you trace the
> same sweet girl through a long line of portraits . . . the Good Angel of the
> race – abiding by them in all reverses – redeeming all their sins.

This is perhaps the most direct general statement in Dickens's fiction
about the spiritually redemptive powers he conceives of as being present
in woman, but of course the belief is central to the characterization and
behaviour of all his major heroines from Florence Dombey to Little
Dorrit. It is also at the heart of his last Christmas Book, *The Haunted
Man* (1849). The evil that Redlaw unwittingly begins to spread when he
has made his bargain with the phantom is dissipated by the unconscious
healing influence of the simple good little woman, Milly – 'the very spirit
of morning, gladness, innocence, hope, love, domesticity, &c &c &c &c'
as Dickens called her when writing to his illustrator, Frank Stone (who
would, said Dickens, 'pictorially, make the little woman whom I love').[17]
We find it again in *Hard Times* where Gradgrind and his daughter are
regenerated spiritually and morally through their contact with Sissy Jupe,
and again in the last but one of the Christmas Stories, 'Mugby Junction'
(1866). Here Jackson, the retired businessman, finds himself at Mugby
Junction void of all happiness, purpose or interest in life, a prey, like
Redlaw before him, to bitter memories of past wrongs and sorrows. His
human identity having become sunk in the uncongenial occupation at
which he toiled for so long, he can only think of himself as 'Barbox
Brothers' even though he has now abandoned the office: other people,
their joys and griefs, are, he glumly tells himself, 'no business' of his. But

then he discovers Phoebe, a beautiful young girl confined to her bed for life by paralysis, and it is through her angelic sweetness and goodness that he is restored to a moral existence, able to forgive and love again those who had wronged him, and participating fully in the human condition 'for he was Barbox Brothers and Co., now, and had taken thousands of partners into the solitary firm'.[18]

ii

This idea of virtuous womanhood as possessed of innate, God-given powers to uplift, regenerate and redeem, which is so ubiquitous in Dickens's writing, is inextricably bound up with his celebrated idealization of the domestic. It was always in terms of personal relationships, especially within a family grouping, that woman, for him as for most Victorians, realized her full moral and spiritual potential. Attempts by her to influence the great world by putting herself forward as the champion of some public cause were always terrible or (depending on the cause and the circumstances) ludicrous aberrations. Dickens presents Joan of Arc in his *Child's History* as a tragic victim of her own disturbed psychology ('She had long been a moping, fanciful girl, and, though she was a very good girl, I dare say she was a little vain, and wishful for notoriety') and of manipulation by bad men:

> Ah! happy had it been for the Maid of Orleans, if she had resumed her rustic dress that day [when she saw the Dauphin crowned], and had gone home . . . and had forgotten all these things, and had been a good man's wife, and had heard no stranger voices than the voices of little children!

Very different is his attitude towards another female warrior, Lady Montford, in Edward III's reign. This 'noble lady' took up arms to rescue her husband after showing her infant son to the people of Brittany with 'many pathetic entreaties to them not to desert her and their young Lord'.

The true source of heroism in woman is always domestic or, if not strictly domestic, then it is a concern personally to save or help individuals. Elizabeth Fry visiting the prisoners in Newgate or Grace Darling, roused to 'generous daring' by the 'peril of a fellow-creature', are true womanly heroines for him, as we see from his essay, 'Sucking Pigs', published in *Household Words* in 1851. This essay sets out to ridicule the hapless Mrs Colonel Bloomer and her campaign, imported into London from the United States, for greater freedom for women. Pretending awe-struck admiration of the 'eminent lady, and the Colonel in whose home she is a well-spring of joy', Dickens writes:

Personally, we admit that our mind would be disturbed, if our own domestic well-spring were to consider it necessary to entrench herself behind a small table ornamented with a water-bottle and tumbler, and from that fortified position to hold forth to the public. Similarly, we should doubt the expediency of her putting up for Marylebone, or being one of the Board of Guardians for St Pancras, or serving on a Grand Jury for Middlesex, or acting as High Sheriff of any county, or taking the chair at a Meeting on the subject of the Income-Tax.

Adopting the name, 'for the sake of argument', of Bellows he asks, 'is our Julia certain that she has a small table and water-bottle Mission round the corner, when here are nine . . . little Bellowses to mend, or mar, at home?'[19]

In a letter to Miss Coutts two years earlier Dickens had poured scorn on an Anglo-Catholic clergyman's project to set up 'Houses of Mercy' for penitent prostitutes which should be run, on a voluntary basis, by 'a little band of self-denying daughters of the Church, of the upper ranks'. He thoroughly shared Miss Coutts's expressed disapproval of 'associations of Females generally' and exclaims,

It would be difficult, to my thinking, to devise any — not wicked — scheme, of a more pernicious and *unnatural* [my italics] nature. As if every home in all this land, were not a World, in which a woman's course of influence and action is marked out by Heaven![20]

Woman's special gift of intuitive insight into the hearts of those around her, her 'natural' timidity, which Dickens saw as a high virtue,[21] her physical gentleness and her role as bearer and nourisher of children clearly pointed, he believed, to the domestic or private circle as her proper sphere. There she could seek to do for individuals what man with his 'larger mind', greater physical stamina and bold enterprise, sought to do for humanity at large in the wider world.

One sure pointer towards her natural role, Dickens would have argued, was what he saw as woman's instinctive fascination with court-ship, weddings, babies. 'It is wonderful', he wrote to Forster about his little daughters in 1846, 'to see how naturally the smallest girls are interested in marriages. Kate and Mamey were as excited as if they were eighteen.'[22] In *Dombey and Son* he writes, 'twenty nursery-maids in Mr Dombey's street alone, have promised twenty families of little women, whose instinctive interest in nuptials dates from their cradles, that they shall go and see the marriage'. He delighted to notice the warm response of the female part of his Readings audiences to the passages about David's courtship of Dora. 'It is very pretty to see the girls and women generally, in the matter of Dora', he writes from Brighton in 1861 and, two years later, he is even more delighted by the response of a fashionable audience in Paris: 'When David proposed to Dora, gorgeous beauties all radiant with diamonds, clasped their fans between their two hands, and rolled about in ecstasy'. When he read the story about the runaway child-sweethearts to American audiences he noticed that 'the women set up a shrill undercurrent of half-pity and half-pleasure that is quite affecting'. In this story, 'Boots at the Holly Tree Inn', there occurs a characteristic aside: as a coach approaches the inn at speed the chamber-maid calls out to the ostler, 'Tom, this is a Gretna job!' and the ostler believes her at once, knowing, says Dickens, 'that her sex instinctively scented a marriage or anything in that direction'.[23]

*

When we consider Dickens's actual presentation in his fiction of wives and mothers in their domestic setting we are struck by the paucity of examples of a woman morally guiding and spiritually inspiring or redeeming a husband or a son. We are to assume, of course, that Florence, Agnes, Esther and Little Dorrit all become such wives and mothers, indeed we are told in the closing pages of *Copperfield* that Agnes has achieved this status, but during the course of the novel we have seen their domestic heroism working itself out entirely in daughterly or sisterly terms. It is perhaps significant that the following description of a noble and uplifting wife is part of a wistful reverie about what might have been rather than what is:

> My dearest and most devoted wife, ever faithful, ever loving, ever helpful and sustaining and consoling, is the priceless blessing of my house; from whom all its other blessings spring. . . . when Christiana sees me, at any time, a little weary or depressed, she steals to the piano and sings a gentle air she used to sing when we were first betrothed.

And it is also worth noting how Dickens the subversive comic genius at one point sends up the whole idea through the voice of Mr Micawber:

> . . . accidents will occur in the best-regulated families; and in families not regulated by that pervading influence which sanctifies while it enhances the – a – I would say, in short, by the influence of Woman, in the lofty character of Wife, they may be expected with confidence, and must be borne with philosophy.[24]

The virtual absence of any serious presentation of Woman in 'the lofty character' of sanctifying wife relates to Dickens's extreme difficulty in reconciling the sexual with the domestic ideal which we shall be

311

considering later. The absence of inspiring angel-mothers has perhaps a more obvious biographical explanation, as has Thackeray's contrasting preoccupation with them.[25] Dickens is only able to present a woman as convincingly noble as wife and mother when she is, in fact, a childless single woman who adopts, sustains and protects a quasi-husband and also a child, so creating a family for herself without any sexual or actual maternal associations. Betsey Trotwood is by far his most persuasive presentation of the domestic ideal of womanhood (the essential formula is repeated later, more sentimentally, in the Mrs Lirriper stories).

Otherwise, Dickens's presentation of admirable wives does not rise much above the level of efficient housewifery with much emphasis on the creation of neatness and order, comfort and the provision of plenty of food. The pattern appears very clearly early on, in *Sketches of Young Couples*, where we meet Mrs Chirrup. She

> is the prettiest of all little women, and has the prettiest little figure conceivable. She has the neatest little foot, and the softest little voice, and the pleasantest little smile, and the tidiest little curls, and the brightest little eyes, and the quietest little manner, and is, in short, altogether one of the most engaging of all little women, dead or alive. She is a condensation of all the domestic virtues, – a pocket edition of the young man's best companion, – a little woman at a very high pressure, with an amazing quantity of goodness and usefulness in an exceedingly small space. Little as she is, Mrs Chirrup might furnish forth matter for the moral equipment of a score of housewives, six feet high in their stockings. . . .
> . . . In all the arts of domestic arrangement and management, in all the mysteries of confectionery-making, pickling, and preserving, never was such a thorough adept as that nice little body. She is, besides, a cunning worker in muslin and fine linen, and a special hand at marketing to the very best advantage. But if there be one branch of housekeeping in which she excels . . . it is in the important one of carving.[26]

It might be the description of a clever, good little girl playing at housewifery and prompts us to register the frequency with which Dickens does present such good wives as he gives us as though they actually were children – Dot Peerybingle in *The Cricket on the Hearth*, for example, and Bella Wilfer after her marriage in *Our Mutual Friend*. And he clearly delighted in portraying a little girl keeping house for her father, as Agnes does for Mr Wickfield ('my little housekeeper', he fondly calls her), ministering to his domestic comfort and cheering his spirits. An elaborate example appears in the chapter of *Dombey* in which Florence wistfully

312

watches the little girl's behaviour with her father in the motherless family opposite:

> It was easy to know when he had gone out and was expected home, for the elder child was always dressed and waiting for him at the drawing-room window . . . and when he appeared, her expectant face lighted up with joy. . . . [She] would come down to the hall, and put her hand in his, and lead him up the stairs; and Florence would see her afterwards sitting by his side, or on his knee, or hanging coaxingly about his neck and talking to him. . . .
>
> [She] remained with her father when the rest had gone away, and made his tea for him – happy little house-keeper she was then! – and sat conversing with him. . . . He made her his companion, though she was some years younger than Florence; and she could be as staid and pleasantly demure, with her little book or work-box, as a woman.[27]

Later, after she has fled for refuge to Captain Cuttle, Florence herself 'comes out amazingly', as Dickens would say, as an instinctive home-maker and man-cosseter, just as the little Marchioness had proved an instinctive nurse. The Captain is delightedly bemused 'at the quiet housewifery of Florence in assisting to clear the table, arrange the parlour, and sweep up the hearth'. Then she gives him his pipe and mixes 'a perfect glass of grog for him, unasked, and set[s] it at his elbow'.[28]

Mrs Bagnet in *Bleak House* is one of Dickens's few examples of a mature woman functioning admirably as wife and mother. Polly Toodle in *Dombey* is another. But both Polly and Mrs Bagnet, we might note, are simple, uneducated working-class women, lacking in the angelical refinement and exquisite sensibility that form part of Dickens's ideal of wifehood as shadowed forth in his middle-class heroines (and Lizzie Hexam) before their marriages. The emphasis tends still to fall, therefore, on these women as creators of comfort and order, Good Providers (Mrs Bagnet is always washing greens ready for a family meal) rather than as moral and spiritual mentors and exemplars in the home. Toodle and Bagnet rely absolutely on their more intelligent wives for guidance and direction in both practical and moral affairs, but this is rather a subject for affectionate humour on Dickens's part than for lofty rhetoric about angels in the house.

In real life, as in his fiction, Dickens seems to have been more ready to celebrate female domestic heroism and nobility when these qualities manifested themselves in a sister or a daughter rather than in a wife. Esther Elton (for whom Esther in *Bleak House* is surely named), the orphaned eldest daughter of a not very successful actor, moved him greatly. He chaired a committee formed to raise funds for her and her younger sisters and wrote about her to Miss Coutts:

> I never in my life saw such gentle perserverance [*sic*] and steady goodness as this girl has displayed, from the first. Going into the establishment [a teachers' training college], a woman grown — with her character already formed, and her habits adapted, as one would have thought, to the easy kind of life she had led, as her poor father's poor housekeeper — she settled herself at once, resolutely, to the discipline and hard-work of the place; and has never turned from it, for one moment, though it has involved her separation from her little sisters, to whom she feels as a mother — her resignation of all her old society — her self-denial in a hundred ways. . . . I regard it really as an instance of patient womanly devotion; a little piece of quiet, unpretending, domestic heroism; of a most affecting and interesting kind.[29]

More bizarre was the case of Caroline Maynard Thompson which he also drew to Miss Coutts's attention. Caroline had lived, unmarried, with a comfortably-off man for nine years and borne him a child. During this time she had brought up and procured some education for her younger sister and younger brother (they had had 'a miserable home' with their parents). She had got her sister a place as a nursery governess and paid the premium to article her brother to an architect. Suddenly her 'protector' deserted her and, in despair of finding means to support herself, her child and her brother (whose articles were cancelled and who had to make a new beginning as a poorly paid clerk) she began working as a part-time prostitute. Her brother was full of gratitude, love and respect for her despite what Dickens called 'the tremendous circumstances of their daily existence' and appealed to the novelist to help him find better employment so that he could release his sister from so terrible a situation. Dickens responded very positively, seeking to arrange for the whole family to be sent abroad, aided by Miss Coutts, to begin a new life overseas. His letters about the matter make it clear that he was much affected by this extraordinary example of sisterly devotion.[30]

The only instances we have of Dickens enthusing over real-life examples of *wifely* heroism and nobility occur when the woman is devotedly nursing a dying husband. 'The beauty of her ministration sank into my heart when I saw him for the last time on earth', he wrote of Clarkson Stanfield's wife in 1867, and sixteen years earlier he had written in almost lyrical terms about Lady de Lancy's account of tending her husband, fatally wounded at Waterloo:

Of all the tender and beautiful passages — the thinking every day how happy and blest she was . . . I say not a word. They are God's own and should be sacred . . . the ground she travelled . . . is holy ground to me from this day. . . .

In the novels, Ada Clare, who devotes herself to caring selflessly for her Chancery-obsessed young husband, grieving to see his steady deterioration, as if under baleful enchantment, but never faltering in her faith and love, is the sole example of this sort of wifely heroism.[31]

iii

Whatever the oddities and idiosyncratic emphases in Dickens's presentation of virtuous woman in her domestic role, what does overwhelmingly emerge from all his writings, both public and private, is a firm central conviction that the home is her proper natural element. Once woman ventures outside the family and seeks to do good on a large and public scale the result, Dickens felt, was bound to be unsatisfactory. Instead of guarding and maintaining the home as a place of healing restfulness and spiritual solace for her menfolk toiling in the cut-throat world outside she brings the clamour and anxieties of that world, its 'telegrams and anger', into the domestic sanctuary. In the essay 'Sucking Pigs' referred to earlier, Dickens asks:

> . . . should we love our Julia better, if she were a Member of Parliament, a Parochial Guardian, a High Sheriff, a Grand Juror, or a woman distinguished for her able conduct in the chair? Do we not, on the contrary, rather seek in the society of our Julia, a haven of refuge from Members of Parliament, Parochial Guardians, High Sheriffs, Grand Jurors, and able chairmen? Is not the home-voice of our Julia as the song of a bird, after considerable bow-wowing out of doors?

Mrs Jellyby, of course, stands as Dickens's great example of woman betraying the home in this way, and it is not surprising that J.S. Mill should have been so angered by this part of *Bleak House* ('That creature Dickens . . . has the vulgar impudence in this thing to ridicule rights of women. It is done too in the very vulgarest way . . .'). She 'devotes herself entirely to the public' and her preoccupation with 'educating the natives of Borrioboola-Gha, on the left bank of the Niger' leads her to neglect her family. The house is dirty and uncomfortable, the servants unruly, the children survive as best they can, and the unfortunate husband sits despairingly in the kitchen with his head against the wall beseeching his eldest daughter never to have 'a Mission'. The clinching image comes in a description of the disorganized family dinner during which Mrs Jellyby

315

imperturbably continues dealing with her business correspondence, receiving so many letters that Richard Carstone, sitting by her, sees 'four envelopes in the gravy at once'. It is an unforgettable emblem of the domestic wrecked by the intrusion of the outer world.[32]

Mrs Jellyby is last heard of campaigning for 'the rights of women to sit in Parliament'. This for Dickens, as for his Queen (who was 'most anxious to enlist every-one who can speak or write to join in checking this mad, wicked folly of "Woman's Rights" '), and for the great majority of his fellow-citizens, represented the height of perverse female heroism, and the horror of the idea contributes strongly to the satire at the end of his spoof retelling of the story of Cinderella in 1853:

> Cinderella, being now a queen, applied herself to the government of the country on enlightened, liberal, and free principles. All the people who ate anything she did not eat, or who drank anything she did not drink, were imprisoned for life. . . . She also threw open the right of voting, and of being elected to public offices, and of making the laws, to the whole of her sex; who thus came to be always gloriously occupied with public life and whom nobody dared to love.[33]

(We can hear in this an echo of Tennyson's fear expressed in *The Princess* that 'Sweet love' would be 'slain' if women were to be made more like men.) Dickens was not unsympathetic towards the demand for extending opportunities of employment for women, and he was prepared to support campaigns against specific legal and social injustices to women.[34] But he never wavered from his conviction that female aspirations to participate in public life were, as Mrs Lynn Lynton put it in 1870, 'a mad rebellion against the natural duties of their sex, and those characteristics known in the mass as womanliness'. Dickens would have agreed with George Eliot in her definition of what actually constitutes this womanliness — 'that exquisite type of gentleness, tenderness, possible maternity suffusing a woman's being with affectionateness, which makes what we mean by the feminine character'. Involvement in public life would inevitably, Dickens firmly believed, be destructive of this. Talking to Whitwell Elwin, editor of *The Quarterly Review*, in 1861 he said,

> The people who write books on the rights of women beg the question. They assume that if women usurped the functions of men it would be a clear gain, – so much added to their present merits. It never occurs to them that it would be destructive of what they have, – a total overthrow of everything in them which is winning and lovable. A male female is repulsive.

Percy Fitzgerald tells us that Dickens 'delighted' in the quip that women's rights 'were usually men's lefts', and one notes the harshness of his satirical vignettes of the 'wiry-faced old damsel who held strong sentiments touching the rights of women, and had diffused the same in lectures' whom Martin Chuzzlewit meets in New York, and of Mrs Jellyby's friend, Miss Wisk, who held 'that the idea of woman's mission lying chiefly in the narrow sphere of Home was an outrageous slander on the part of her Tyrant, Man' (she listens to Caddy's marriage service 'as part of Woman's wrongs, with a disdainful face'). Dickens's beloved American friend, Annie Fields, recorded in her diary how successfully she had once cheered Dickens up by giving him a comic account of a New York women's rights meeting she had attended: 'was able on my return to make Mr Dickens laugh until he declared if anything could make him feel better for the evening that account of the Woman's League would'. Essentially, though, this was no laughing matter for him but a dangerous threat to the happiness and spiritual welfare of humanity.[35]

iv

One socially acceptable way in which certain women, at least, could reach out to a wider world than the domestic was through literature, especially the writing of novels. This was something which had Dickens's wholehearted sympathy. But he, like the Victorian literary establishment generally, would have made a sharp distinction between what George Eliot called 'silly novels by lady novelists', the spate of so-called 'fashionable novels', romantic twaddle about dukes and countesses and so on, produced by women like Lady Stepney (who, he commented, 'could write quite as entertaining a book with the sole of her foot, as ever she did with her head')[36] and the moving dramatizations of the emotional, moral and spiritual life of ordinary people created by the pens of such writers as Mrs Gaskell or George Eliot herself.

By the mid-century there was a general recognition that women had made and were continuing to make an important and distinctive contribution to the contemporary novel. It was, however, a fundamental premise of such recognition that art, of any kind, produced by a woman would always be essentially different from – and ultimately inferior to – art produced by a man. Women's art, a young American journalist writing in *Blackwood's* had declared in 1824, would always be 'less courageous, magnificent, and sublime' but it would be 'more delicate, beautiful, and affecting . . . There would be more tenderness, more delicacy, more timidity in it.' The heart and not the mind being held to 'enshrine the priceless pearl of womanhood', as Kingsley put it, it followed that women would shine most as writers when portraying feelings, nuances of emotion, the subtle fluctuations of personal relationships. Of all literary forms the novel was best suited to such matter, 'the capabilities of that form of literature', as David Masson wrote in 1859, 'being such that we can conceive women conveying most easily through it those views and perceptions which, by presupposition, they were best qualified to contribute'. The result was, however, a somewhat unbalanced presentation of life, the critic W.C. Roscoe had suggested in the *National Review* a year earlier: 'Women indulged their feelings too much' and,

> The justly-celebrated efforts of modern female novelists are all studies and representations of passions and sentiments. Characters are drawn and distinguished with exquisite discrimination and felicity, but only one side of human nature is developed.[37]

Dickens voiced no such reservations about women's writing *per se*, however. He eagerly recruited such prominent women writers as Harriet Martineau, Mrs Marsh and Mrs Gaskell as contributors to *Household Words* and is often to be found praising female authors not only for delicacy and tenderness but also for having a special brand of wit and humour. Mrs Catherine Gore's satires on the *beau monde* delighted him; he was proud, he told her when she dedicated a book to him in 1853, 'to be so esteemed by a writer of such power and humour who knows humanity so well, and dissects it so wittily'. He was enthusiastic, too, about his friend Lady Blessington's *Memoirs of a Femme de Chambre* (1846), telling her that it 'paints Society from a Woman's eye' and adding, 'I think that the height of praise'. And lower down the social scale, he was pleased by 'some very pretty womanly humour, some very good womanly observation' in some sketches of life in a poor country parish sent in to *Household Words* in 1859 by a Mrs Blacker, the wife of a clergyman.[38] Again, writing to Anna Maria Hall about a story she had published called 'The Governess' Dickens commends it as 'delicately and beautifully done; with a womanly touch that cannot be mistaken'.

Only once, so far as we know, did Dickens fail to detect a woman writer's hand – or rather, hesitate to believe that a story could have been written, as it purported to be, by a woman. This was a bizarre ghost story (bizarre chiefly in its hysterical anti-Catholicism, we might think today) submitted for publication in *Household Words* in 1855 by Miss Mulock, whose bestselling *John Halifax, Gentleman* was to appear the following year. It was, Dickens wrote to Miss Coutts, 'the best ghost story . . . that ever was written' but he hesitated to accept it because he felt 'the lady cannot have written it': 'It is so very clever, that I think . . . it must have been written by some wild Frenchman'.[39]

Against this momentary hesitation we must set his celebrated detection of the true sex of 'George Eliot' after reading her first book, *Scenes of Clerical Life*. Writing to congratulate the stories' author on their 'exquisite truth and delicacy', Dickens said he had observed 'such womanly touches, in those moving fictions' that he was strongly inclined to address his correspondent as a woman.[40] In a letter to George Eliot's publisher, Blackwood, he elaborated on his reasons for believing the author of the *Scenes* to be a woman. Blackwood had evidently drawn his attention to certain passages suggestive of masculine authorship and Dickens replies:

> The portions of the narrative to which you refer had not escaped my notice. But their weight is very light in *my* scale, against all the references to children, and against such marvels of description as Mrs Barton sitting up in bed to mend the children's clothes. The selfish young fellow with the heart disease, in 'Mr Gilfil's Love-Story,' is plainly taken from a woman's point of view. Indeed I observe all the women in the book are more alive than the men, and more informed from within. As to Janet, in the last tale, I know nothing in literature done by a man like the frequent references to her grand form, and her eyes and her height and so forth; whereas I do know innumerable things of that kind in books of imagination by women. And I have not the faintest doubt that a woman described her being shut out into the street by her husband, and conceived and executed the whole idea of her following of that clergyman. If I be wrong in this, then I protest that a woman's mind has got into some man's body by a mistake that ought immediately to be corrected.[41]

It is, we notice, small domestic touches and details in the presentation of character, especially female character, that make Dickens so sure the author is a woman. Reading *Adam Bede* a few months later he becomes even more convinced (here it seems that it was above all the portrayal of Hetty Sorrel that persuaded him) and, as he wrote to George Eliot when he eventually learned her identity, he 'warned all men away from Adam Bede, and nailed my colours to the mast with "Eve" upon them'. In the same letter he tells her what a great and special pleasure it would give him if she were ever able and willing to write for *All The Year Round*.[42]

As we might expect, Dickens was less happy with women writers who dealt overtly with the passions rather than with the feelings unless, like Miss Jolly in *The Wife's Story*,[43] the writer showed passion in a woman as an evil force needing to be crushed. He read, Forster tells us, very little of George Sand, despite her immense popularity in England at this time, and 'had no very special liking' for such works of hers as he did know. He experienced a comic relief in meeting her personally: 'Just the kind of woman in appearance whom you might suppose to be the Queen's monthly nurse. Chubby, matronly, swarthy, black-eyed. Nothing of the blue-stocking about her. . . . A singularly ordinary woman in appearance and manner.' As to the Brontës, he declared in 1860, according to an anonymous note-taking guest at Gad's Hill, that he 'had not read *Jane Eyre* and . . . never would as he disapproved of the whole school'. This, the note-taker adds, was 'apropos of Miss Hogarth saying that it was an unhealthy book'. Nor, Dickens said, had he read *Wuthering Heights*. Had he read the Brontës at all it is safe to assume that his views would have coincided closely with Bulwer Lytton's wife's, who wrote of *Shirley* in 1856 that it was

> not only one of the most vulgar, but one of the most disgusting books I ever read (unless indeed I except 'Wuthering Heights'), for in 'Shirley' the young ladies still continue to make all the advances.[44]

No comment of Dickens's has so far come to light on the work of the most famous woman poet of his day, Elizabeth Barrett Browning, but we may imagine that he would have found *Aurora Leigh*, if he ever looked into it, disagreeably coarse and unwomanly in many places. The gentle, not to say vapouring, religiosity of Adelaide Anne Procter, quantities of whose verse he happily published in *Household Words*, was more the sort of poetry appropriate for a woman to produce. The memoir of Miss Procter that he wrote in 1866 to be prefaced to a posthumous collection of her poems entitled *Legends and Lyrics* is interesting as his only extended public tribute to a literary woman. He is at pains to emphasize that this 'finely sympathetic woman' with her 'great accordant heart' looked upon her art as being very secondary in her life to making herself useful in the world, in the absence, presumably, of a family to care for:

> . . . she would far rather have died without seeing a line of her composition in print, than that I should have maundered about her, here, as 'the Poet' or 'the Poetess'. . . .
> Always impelled by an intense conviction that her life must not be dreamed away, and that her indulgence in her favourite pursuits must be balanced by action in the real world around her, she was indefatigable in her endeavours to do some good.[45]

'To do some good': the words recall the childhood resolution of Esther Summerson. We have noted earlier Dickens's speaking of the 'labor and anxiety' he had bestowed on Esther as narrator, endeavouring to write in a 'womanly' way.[46] The timidity, attention to domestic minutiae and the focus on feeling which characterize Esther's narrative represent this endeavour. One womanly touch on which we know Dickens prided himself concerns something reported *to* Esther rather than reported *by* her, however. In one of his facetious/flirtatious letters to Mary Boyle, dated Christmas Day 1852, he wrote:

> . . . O Mary when you come to read the last chapter of the next number of Bleak House I think my ever dear as you will say as him what we knows on as done a pretty womanly thing as the sex will like and as will make a sweet pint for to turn the story on my heart alive for such you are. . . .

And a few days later he alerted another woman friend, Mary Cowden Clarke, to the forthcoming detail: 'You will see a turning point in the two green leaves [referring to the covers of the monthly numbers] this next month, which I hope will not cause you to think less pleasantly and kindly of them'. The incident he is referring to is as follows: Lady Dedlock, on the verge of revealing herself to Esther as her 'unhappy mother', goes incognito to the brickmaker's hovel and surreptitiously takes away, in yearning love for the daughter whom she can never publicly acknowledge, the handkerchief Esther had used to cover the pitiful little corpse of Jenny's baby. This is the sort of 'tender, delicate' touch that Dickens clearly regarded as the hallmark of the best female writing.[47]

*

Literary work, then, provided always that it took second place to whatever domestic responsibilities a woman might have, was quite reconcilable with Victorian public ideals about women. It is, as one novelist remarked, in 1864, 'of all employments the quietest. . . . There is nothing in it which need jar upon the retirement which every woman prizes so dearly.'[48] Another acceptable artistic activity for women was painting, though the number of those who, like Anne Brontë's Helen Huntington, managed to gain an income from such work must have been tiny in comparison with the number of earning female writers: there were no Rosa Bonheurs on the English artistic scene. Dickens sat for at least one professional female portrait-painter, Miss Margaret Gillies, in 1843, and no doubt respected her as an independent working woman. He had scant sympathy, however, as one might expect, for amateur women painters who gave the pursuit of art precedence over their domestic concerns.[49]

We meet with no professional woman writer in Dickens's fiction (one imagines that the splendours of the Den, Eatanswill, were not sustained by royalties from Mrs Leo Hunter's celebrated 'Ode to an Expiring Frog') but he does give us one working female artist, Miss La Creevy, the little miniaturist in *Nickleby* – sometimes claimed to be based on Dickens's miniature-painting aunt, Janet Barrow.[50] Miss La Creevy is a sympathetic, even touching, character as a woman, but her art is simply a joke, part of the satire on social pretensions and hypocrisy that runs through the novel. She specializes in her portrait-miniatures in 'a bright salmon flesh-tint . . . considered by [her] chief friends and patrons to be quite a novelty in art: as indeed it was', and discourses to Kate Nickleby on the anxieties of her profession:

> 'Ah! The difficulties of Art, my dear, are great.'
> 'They must be, I have no doubt,' said Kate. . . .
> 'They are beyond anything you can form the faintest conception of,' replied Miss La Creevy. 'What with bringing out eyes with all one's power, and keeping down noses with all one's force, and adding to heads, and taking away teeth altogether, you have no idea of the trouble one little miniature is.'
> 'The remuneration can scarcely repay you,' said Kate.[51]

At the end of the novel, however, Miss La Creevy is happily rescued into domesticity when Dickens marries her off to Tim Linkinwater.

Miss La Creevy was created in the 1830s and it is an indication of the changing times and Dickens's responsiveness to them (unchanged though his basic views about women were) that we find him twenty years later keen to help secure proper training for aspiring female artists – they are no longer simply a subject for comedy. He writes to W.H. Wills from Gad's Hill in April 1859:

> Hullah's daughter (an artist, who is here), tells me that certain female students have addressed the Royal Academy, entreating them to find a place for *their* education. I think it a capital move, for which I can do something popular and telling, in the Register. Adelaide Procter is active in the business, and has a copy of their letter. Will you write to her for that, and anything else she may have about it: telling her that I strongly approve, and want to help them myself.

No doubt his daughter Katey's growing seriousness about her art helped to influence him and it was sad that she did not begin to achieve recognition and success as an artist until after his death. When one of her paintings was accepted by the Royal Academy in 1877 and sold on the very first day it was exhibited, Georgina wrote to Annie Fields: 'Ah! *how* pleased and proud her dear Father would have been! I don't know anything that could ever have pleased him *more*!'[52]

Dickens might indeed have rejoiced to see his favourite daughter beginning to make her way in the world as a painter but he was, we may recall, adamant that she should not embark on an acting career when, in 1870, she was contemplating this as a means of retrieving her and her husband's finances. For all the respect and adulation accorded to particular actresses in the mid-Victorian period the stage was not an acceptable career for a middle-class young lady – acceptable to her class and family, that is. Dickens's lifelong passion for the theatre brought him into friendly contact with many actresses (most famously and fatefully, of course, with the Ternan family) and his letters contain frequent appreciations of their work. Predictably, what he prized above all was an ability to project 'womanly tenderness' or fresh girlish innocence from the stage[53] (although there is no hint of such qualities among the actresses in the Crummles troupe who are, like Miss La Creevy, written for laughs as far as their being artists is concerned). But his delight in the actress's art was basically in conflict with his feeling that the domestic should really be at the centre of every woman's life, even that of an actress. The resulting ambivalence appears very clearly in an 1851 letter to Bulwer Lytton about one young actress:

> Poor little Anne Romer! I am very sorry she is going to be married so soon. Not that I am otherwise than glad, in the abstract, when young ladies are married, – but I fear her husband will have to refer the baker to the Haymarket Treasury, oftener than is hopeful. Then, she may have children out of number – and that interferes with professional avocations. . . .
>
> I saw her the other night – in a bad part . . . and there was a freshness about her (she sung as if her voice were a sort of bird's, all in bloom) that . . . was, as Mr Pepys says, mighty pretty to see.[54]

Actresses, unlike women novelists or women painters, had actually to practise their art in public and Dickens was torn between his pleasure in seeing aspects of his feminine ideal incarnated on the stage and his fervent concurrence with the age's belief that that ideal could only be realized in the home.

V

One day when the Rev. Patrick Brontë was questioning his children about their beliefs and attitudes to life he asked one of his daughters 'what was the best mode of education for a woman?'. The child's answer, 'That which would make her rule her house well', would certainly have met with Dickens's fullest approval. Woman being clearly destined by

God and Nature for a domestic role, the primary aim of her education should not be academic (she need not be learned, wrote Tennyson, 'save in gracious household ways'), still less the cultivation of elegant 'accomplishments' such as music or sketching, but should focus on training her to become a wise and efficient housekeeper and manager of servants. *Household Words* was barely a month old when it featured an article by Dickens's sub-editor, W.H. Wills, complaining that, whilst 'young ladies of the leisure classes are educated to become uncommonly acute critics of all that pertains to personal blandishment . . . able to tell to a thread when a flounce is too narrow or a tuck too deep', they are totally ignorant of the principles of cookery and so at the mercy of incompetent servants:

> Badly seasoned and ill assimilated soup; fish without any fault of the fishmonger, soft and flabby; meat rapidly roasted before fierce fires — burnt outside and raw within; poultry rendered by the same process tempting to the eye, till dissection reveals red and uncooked joints! These crimes, from their frequency and the ignorance of 'the lady of the house', remain unpunished.

Wills's article appeared only a couple of months before Dickens's hilarious dramatization of the problem in chapter 44 of *Copperfield*, concerning the chaotic housekeeping of the newly wed David and Dora which, as David plaintively remarks 'is not comfortable'. Both the article and the chapter in *Copperfield* were part of Dickens's recurrent satirizing of the inadequacies of middle-class girls' education. From Miss Lillerton in *Sketches by Boz*, who is considered well educated because she 'talks French; plays the piano; knows a good deal about flowers, and shells, and all that sort of thing' to Belinda Pocket in *Great Expectations*, who had 'grown up highly ornamental, but perfectly helpless and useless', and beyond, Dickens repeatedly mocks 'the pursuit of giddy frivolities, and empty nothings' that he sees as characterizing middle-class female education. His criticism of it is not that it fails to develop the girls' mental faculties or train their intellects but that it unfits them 'for that quiet domestic life, in which they show far more beautifully than in the most crowded assembly'.[55]

Dickens's early work features a number of fatuous middle-class schoolmistresses (the Misses Crumpton, the 'Lady Abbess' of Westgate House in *Pickwick*, etc.) including one quite vicious caricature, Miss Monflathers in *The Old Curiosity Shop*, who berates Little Nell for being a 'wax-work child' with Mrs Jarley instead of working in a factory as befits a working-class child. Obsessive gentility, prudery and stupidity characterize all these women, and the only products that could be

expected from the schools they run are girls who, like Dora Spenlow or
Belinda Pocket, may be brimming with fashionable 'accomplishments'[56]
but who are totally ignorant of domestic matters. Mrs General, the
genteel widow employed by Mr Dorrit to 'polish' his daughters, is a
majestic variation on the earlier schoolmistresses, representing another
facet of the so-called 'education' given to middle-class girls (in this case,
of particularly affluent families). Dickens returns to the actual genteel
schoolmistress again in his last novel. It is true that here he makes the
mockery more benign and humanizes the caricature by showing us that
Miss Twinkleton off duty is quite a different person from the prim
school-ma'am, almost skittish indeed; but there is no mitigation of the
underlying criticism of the sort of fatuous education provided by establishments like the Nuns' House where Rosa reluctantly learns some
jumbled ancient history, about 'Isises, and Ibises, and Cheopses, and
Pharaohses', but nothing at all that might help her to cope with running a
home and family.[57]

A *locus classicus* for Dickens's views on women's education may be
found in an article entitled 'My Girls' which appeared in the second
volume of his journal *All The Year Round* (11 February 1860). It is by
Wilkie Collins, not Dickens himself, but obviously must have had his
editorial approval. Collins starts out from the position that women are
'naturally unselfish':

> Women have, or should have, *no identity wholly their own*, no separate
> existence in themselves – this is treating of women in their natural state of
> alliance with men. If a woman (speaking generally) so allied, has any
> thought at all, except for her husband and children, she is nothing.
>
> .   .   .
>
> Now, the whole tendency of a girl's education, as at present con-
> ducted, is to eradicate this natural self-abandonment, and to cultivate
> that quality of selfishness which, barely, and only in the slightest degree,
> excusable in men [who, the writer has said earlier, 'have to hew their way
> to every achievement by mowing down so many obstacles, that they are
> obliged to think of themselves, or they would never get on'], is, in
> women, not only a hideous, but an inconceivably dangerous disfigure-
> ment.

'The excellent Mrs Primways' is ironically praised for teaching the girls at
her school so many accomplishments ('we all know that there is no
gentleman ... who would not prefer a brilliantly executed piece of
Chopin's to a well-served little dinner') and Collins then goes on

humorously to propose a 'Girls' Holiday Occupation Institute' which might make up for the deficiencies in the girls' education:

> I propose that there shall be the following classes: A Physical-Education Class; a Cookery Class; a Household-Bill-auditing Class; a Shirt-button-Supervision Class; and a Mangy-Gossip-Suppression Class.[58]

Only the last of these proposed classes relates to moral, as opposed to domestic-practical, education, but Dickens was as concerned as Mrs Ellis herself that the sort of education provided by a Miss Monflathers or a Miss Twinkleton not only failed to prepare young women for future domestic responsibilities but also failed to prepare them for the more exalted aspect of their destined role as wife and mother, the role of spiritual and moral exemplar and 'humble monitress' (to use Mrs Ellis's phrase). In her book, *The Women of England: Their Social Duties, and Domestic* (1838) Mrs Ellis saw a looming national danger. English-women, she declared, were 'deteriorating in their moral character', corrupted by 'false notions of refinement', and also too much 'mental development':

> When the cultivation of the mental faculties had so far advanced as to take precedence of the moral, by leaving no time for domestic usefulness, and the practice of personal exertion in the way of promoting general happiness, the character of the women of England assumed a different aspect, which is now beginning to tell upon society in the sickly sensibilities, the feeble frames, and the useless habits of the rising generation.

Dickens echoes her two years later, at the end of his *Sketches of Young Couples:*

> How much may depend on the education of daughters and the conduct of mothers; how much of the brightest part of our old national character may be perpetuated by their wisdom or frittered away by their folly – how much of it may have been lost already, and how much more in danger of vanishing every day – are questions too weighty for discussion here, but well deserving a little serious consideration from all young couples nevertheless.[59]

But he nowhere attempts to describe an ideal girls' school, such as might help to remedy the situation, as he attempts to describe an ideal boys' one in Dr Strong's establishment in *Copperfield* (and perhaps it is just as well since his account of Dr Strong's is decidedly woolly).

Had Dickens portrayed his ideal girls' school we may be sure that we would have heard even less, if possible, about actual academic education than we do in his description of Dr Strong's (where it consists of a single

allusion to David's 'growing great in Latin verses'). He would never have
made the connection that George Eliot, reflecting on her Maggie Tulli-
ver's defective education, makes between book-learning and moral or
spiritual development.[60] Indeed, he sometimes wrote as though the pursuit of knowledge in girls' education, especially in humbler schools, were
as big a threat to their all-important domestic training as the emphasis on
accomplishments in middle-class schools. Thus he writes to Miss Coutts
during her preoccupation with the movement for promoting the teaching
of 'Common Things' in elementary schools:

> I thoroughly agree in that interesting part of your note which refers to the
> immense uses, direct and indirect, of needlework. Also as to the great
> difficulty of getting many men to understand them. And I think Shuttle-
> worth [i.e., Sir James Kay-Shuttleworth, first secretary of the Council on
> Education 1839-49 and pioneer of education for the masses] and the like,
> would have gone on to the crack of doom, melting down all the thimbles
> in Great Britain and Ireland, and making medals of them to be given for a
> knowledge of Watersheds and Pre Adamite vegetation (both immensely
> comfortable to a labouring man with a large family and a small income),
> if it hadn't been for you.[61]

In portraying Miss Peecher, the 'small, shining, neat, methodical,
and buxom' elementary schoolteacher in *Our Mutual Friend*, Dickens
delights in emphasizing that true womanliness has been far from crushed
out of her by the learning of facts and figures. She is deeply in love with
her colleague, Bradley Headstone ('The decent hair-guard that went
round his neck and took care of his decent silver watch was an object of
envy to her. So would Miss Peecher have gone round his neck and taken
care of him') and what she occupies herself with in private, after taking
'a refresher of the principal rivers and mountains of the world, their
breadths, depths, and heights', is the making of a dress for her own
personal adornment.[62]

Miss Peecher's dealings with books are made to sound endearingly
comic ('taking a refresher' of the principal rivers, etc.) and this fits in with
an overall tendency in Dickens to present any association of women with
books (other than the Bible, of course) as funny. Mrs Varden and
her addiction when ill-tempered to the study of the Protestant Manual,
Cornelia Blimber 'dry and sandy with working in the graves of deceased
languages', her mother enthusing over Cicero, Julia Mills and her breathless annotations of circulating-library novels ('Entranced here by the
Magician's potent spell. J.M.') and Mrs Tickit with her volume of Dr
Buchan's *Domestic Medicine* are all cases in point.[63] If Annie Strong were
to begin looking into any of those tomes of her learned husband's that she

so assiduously dusts she would at once become a comic character (a consummation, we might feel, devoutly to be wished). The only exceptions to this rule are sisters such as Florence Dombey or Lizzie Hexam who plunge into the world of learning not for their own sakes but for the benefit of their brothers. Only love, it would seem, can provide the right stimulus for a woman to develop her mental powers: Esther Summerson confesses that she has 'not by any means a quick understanding' but adds, 'When I love a person very tenderly indeed, it seems to brighten'.[64] Otherwise, female pursuit of learning is seen by Dickens either as a comic aberration, like Miss Blimber's passion for exhuming dead languages, or as a form of vanity, as in the case of the 'blue' ladies of Boston who 'rather desire to be thought superior than to be so' and the young lady Martin Chuzzlewit meets in New York who was 'distinguished by a talent for metaphysics, the laws of hydraulic pressure, and the rights of human kind . . . and bringing them to bear on any subject from Millinery to the Millennium, both inclusive'. As to the lecture-going ladies in Major Pawkins's New York boarding house ('Philosophy of the Soul' on Wednesdays, 'Philosophy of Vegetables' on Fridays, etc.), they are simply idle, using their cultural activities as an excuse for dispensing with 'family duties at home':

> . . . the chances were a hundred to one that not one of [them] could perform the easiest woman's work for herself, or make the simplest article of dress for any of her children.

When he is faced, even through the medium of print, with a truly intellectual woman Dickens finds himself rather disconcerted. Reading about Madame Roland, he admires 'her brave soul and engaging conversation' but confesses that 'if she had only some more faults, only a few more passionate failings of any kind' he might love her better. He adds, however, with commendable candour, 'I am content to believe that the deficiency is in me, and not in her.'[65]

*

When it came to the question of female employment Dickens's beliefs and attitudes were such as might be expected from someone holding the general attitude towards women that he did. Ideally he believed, of course, that all women should be fully occupied with their own families and domestic duties, but he also recognized that many women who did not marry would have to earn their living and that, in the lower ranks of society, wives and mothers often had to be the breadwinners, the men being unemployed, – the women workers in some East End lead-mills,

328

for example (whom Dickens characteristically sees as looking in their protective clothing like the 'faithful seraglio' of 'some immensely rich old Turk'). He had, his daughter said in 1910, 'the strongest possible sympathy with . . . all women who work in order to gain a livelihood for themselves and those dependent upon their exertions'. This was not how one of the most financially successful women writers of his day saw him, however. Harriet Martineau contributed many articles to *Household Words* during the first four years of the journal's existence, including 'The New School for Wives' (which enthusiastically praised the institution in Birmingham by some volunteer ladies of evening classes in domestic science for women factory workers) but when she was invited to write a series of papers on employment for women she declined, explaining 'rather pertly that her views would seem inconsistent with those which Dickens had previously expressed, also with his general idea that a woman was not to work, but to look pretty'.[66]

This was scarcely fair to Dickens, I think. He certainly condemned the exploitation of female labour by colliery-owners and in 1842 wrote a powerful letter to the *Morning Chronicle* in support of Lord Ashley's Bill to prohibit the employment of women in the mines: it had the effect, he wrote, of blotting out from their sex 'all form and stamp, and character of womanhood', making them 'but so many weaker men, saving in respect of their more rapid and irresistible opportunities of being brutalized themselves, and of brutalizing others'. Nor did he relish the sight of girls towing barges in France, 'sometimes harnessed by the forehead, sometimes by the girdle and the shoulders, not a pleasant sight to see'.[67] But he gave space in *Household Words* to two articles by a clergyman praising the way in which all kinds of jobs (including towing barges) normally thought of as exclusively masculine occupations were open to women in France:

> . . . at Paris the inns are stocked with female waiters, female porters, and female Bootses . . . women conduct all sorts of shops, while their husbands lounge about with their hands in their pockets.
>
> .   .   .
>
> French women have achieved for themselves a standing, an independent position, which is unequalled among civilized nations. They have caused themselves to be made the companions and the friends of the men, as well as their sweethearts and wives; they are not to be put down, or kept in the back-ground.

In the second article, entitled 'More Work for the Ladies', the writer describes some highly professional French female Daguerréotypists and comments,

When I paid for my portrait, I could not help wishing that a few pale-faced, under-fed, thin-clad English girls could see how cheerfully Mademoiselle Lebour was living by the practice of Daguerréotype. She seemed almost as happy and as independent as a first-rate governess at fifty pounds a year; if such a comparison will bear the making.[68]

The miserably underpaid, abused and exploited governess was, of course, a stock figure of pathos in Victorian life and literature and Dickens himself contributed to establishing her as such in his description of the trials undergone as governesses by Madeline Bray and Ruth Pinch (though he also showed, in Miss Wade's embittered autobiography, something of the difficulties an ill-conditioned governess could cause to her employers).[69] He accepted an invitation to speak at a dinner in aid of the Governesses' Benevolent Institution in 1844, telling the wife of the Institution's founder that the governesses' cause had his 'warmest sympathy', and it seems possible that he may have been influenced in his desire to strike a blow for governesses by experiences undergone in that capacity by his younger sister, Letitia. His speech was all about the necessity to elevate 'the moral condition' of governesses (i.e., to treat them with greater respect and consideration, including better pay – their salaries, he said, 'would bear poor comparison with the wages of the butler; they would appear but shabbily with the remuneration of the lady's-maid'). Two articles that he featured in *Household Words*, 'Two-Pence an Hour' by Harriet Parr and 'Only a Governess' by Florence Wilson, also focused attention on the hardships endured by women trying to earn their living in this way. ('There are not many Becky Sharpes amongst us', Harriet Parr remarks, and she praises Ruth Pinch as an authentic portrait of a typical governess).[70]

The Christian Socialists' idea of raising the status of governesses not merely by better pay and according them more respect but also by giving them better education and some sort of professional qualification[71] does not seem to have interested Dickens. As we have seen, he placed actual academic instruction pretty low in his order of priorities for educating girls and would, I believe, have argued that as women were instinctive teachers of children they did not need training for this work. The one trained schoolmistress in his fiction, Miss Peecher, is, as we have seen, presented as a comic figure:

She could write a little essay on any subject, exactly a slate long, beginning at the left-hand top of one side and ending at the right-hand bottom of the other, and the essay should be strictly according to rule.

Otherwise, we have young women like Agnes and Esther who show themselves to be natural teachers (of her little school Agnes says, 'The labour is so pleasant that it is scarcely grateful in me to call it by that name'). The crippled girl, Phoebe, in 'Mugby Junction' is his most elaborate example. After hearing her teaching the children in her voluntary school to sing the multiplication table Barbox Brothers 'hazarded the speculation that she was fond of children, and that she was learned in new systems of teaching them?':

'Very fond of them,' she said . . . 'but I know nothing of teaching, beyond the interest I have in it, and the pleasure it gives me when they learn. Perhaps your overhearing my little scholars sing some of their lessons has led you so far astray as to think me a grand teacher? Ah! I thought so! No, I have only read and been told about that system. It seemed so pretty and pleasant, and to treat them so like the merry Robins they are, that I took up with it in my little way.'[72]

Women were held to be natural nurses as well as natural teachers of children and, as we have noted, Dickens frequently dramatized this belief in his fiction, notably in the Marchioness's nursing of Dick Swiveller. (Mrs Gamp and Betsey Prig are monstrously *un*natural, of course.) Dickens would seem to have favoured women who took up nursing as a profession being trained and qualified in a way that, one feels, he did not really think necessary for women teachers. Florence Nightingale's campaign to establish nursing as a profession received support in the pages both of *Household Words* and *All The Year Round*. In the former Henry Morley, one of Dickens's permanent staff on the journal, declared, 'We English . . . have among us the best nursing for love and the worst nursing for money that can be got in Europe' and he quoted approvingly from a pamphlet by Miss Nightingale describing the training of nurses in Germany. He also praised a Church of England training-school for nurses which had just been opened under the auspices of King's College, London; it was, he said, an excellent effort 'to supplant Mrs Gamp'. Another article in *All The Year Round* (31 March 1860) took the line that nursing was 'a gift, not an acquirement' but warmly recommended Florence Nightingale's *Notes on Nursing* for study by all who had to minister to the sick and concluded with the hope that nursing might become

a matter of scientific training and teaching, and that all professional nurses, at least, may be obliged to go through a regular system of instruction which shall qualify them for their work into something very different from Grimbones [the name given one of the types of incompetent amateur nurses the writer has described] or Mrs Gamp.[73]

Nevertheless, even after Florence Nightingale established nursing as a respectable profession the overwhelming majority of middle-class or lower middle-class girls faced with having to earn their living continued to tread the well-worn paths of teaching, either as governesses or in schools, or of seeking employment in some branch of the clothing industry. 'The tutor, the tailor and the hatter', were, said Harriet Martineau, the only jobs open to them. Dickens acknowledges this restricted choice when he makes Ralph Nickleby say to his niece, 'We must try and get you apprenticed at some boarding-school . . . and if the life is too hard, perhaps dress-making or tambour-work will come lighter', and again when old Martin Chuzzlewit, urged by Pecksniff to 'alter and define' his protégée Mary Graham's position, asks 'How can that be done? Should I make a seamstress of her, or a governess?'

As he had done with governesses so did Dickens seek to rouse his readers' indignation over the way in which women workers in the clothing industry were exploited. Kate Nickleby on her way to start her first day's work at Madame Mantalini's observes

> many sickly girls, whose business, like that of the poor worm, is to produce, with patient toil, the finery that bedecks the thoughtless and luxurious, making towards the scene of their daily labour, and catching, as if by stealth, in their hurried walk, the only gasp of wholesome air and glimpse of sunlight which cheers their monotonous existence during the long train of hours that make a working day [Kate has been told by Madame Mantalini that her hours of work will be from nine to nine 'with extra work when we're very full of business'].[74]

More terrible still is the suffering of the starving sempstresses Meg and Lilian in *The Chimes* (in Trotty's horrific vision of his beloved daughter's likely future). Lilian exclaims:

> Such work, such work! So many hours, so many days, so many long, long nights of hopeless, cheerless, never-ending work – not to heap up riches, not to live grandly or gaily, not to live upon enough, however coarse; but to earn bare bread; to scrape together just enough to toil upon, and want upon, and keep alive in us the consciousness of our hard fate![75]

Later, a number of articles in Dickens's journals also drew attention to the hardships endured by milliner's apprentices, needlewomen and sempstresses and praised, and gave publicity to, attempts to improve their lot.[76]

*

In 1859, responding to the steadily increasing number of single women in the population,[77] the National Association for the Promotion of Social Science set up a committee to consider ways of extending opportunities of employment for women, and this soon evolved into the Society for the Employment of Women. Through its magazine, *The Englishwoman's Journal*, the Society became rapidly aware of the enormous demand for work existing among the female population and began encouraging women, as J.A. and Olive Banks write, 'to become shop assistants, clerks, telegraphists and nurses, all fields of employment which were expanding at this time'. The Bankses note also that the members of the Society

> tried, by their own efforts, to open up new fields, such as hair dressing and printing, and attempted albeit unsuccessfully to persuade the watchmakers' and gilders' trade unions to allow girls to become apprentices. In all this they were more concerned with artisans' daughters than with the middle-class girl but they, nevertheless, gave her far more attention than she received elsewhere, at least in so far as her employment was concerned.[78]

Adelaide Anne Procter, for whom, as we have seen, Dickens felt great admiration, was deeply involved in this movement to widen job opportunities for women and was a member of the committee set up by the Social Science Association. She also edited in 1861 a sumptuous volume entitled *The Victoria Regia*, 'printed and published', as it states on the title-page, 'by Emily Faithfull and Co., Victoria Press, (for the Employment of Women)'. This volume was designed as an impressive demonstration of the skill of Miss Faithfull's women printers and quite a galaxy of literary stars gave support by writing something for it, among them Tennyson, Thackeray, Matthew Arnold and Trollope. John Forster also contributed but Dickens was conspicuous by his absence. It seems hardly conceivable that Miss Procter did not ask him for something but he was doubtless simply too busy with his Reading tours, and with the serialization of *Great Expectations*, to be able to oblige her. He had, however, already taken some notice in print of her work for the employment of women, in the 1859 Christmas Number of *All The Year Round*, a multiple-authorship story called 'The Haunted House'. Miss Procter, a contributor to this story, figures in Dickens's introduction to it as 'Belinda', 'a most intellectual, amiable, and delightful girl':

> She has a fine genius for poetry, combined with real business earnestness, and 'goes in' . . . for Woman's mission, Woman's rights, Woman's wrongs, and everything that is woman's with a capital W, or is not and ought to be, or is and ought not to be. 'Most praiseworthy, my dear, and Heaven prosper you!' I whispered to her . . . 'but don't overdo it. And in

respect of the great necessity there is, my darling, for more employments being within the reach of Woman than our civilisation has as yet assigned to her, don't fly at the unfortunate men, even those men who are at first sight in your way, as if they were the natural oppressors of your sex; for, trust me, Belinda, they do sometimes spend their wages among wives and daughters, sisters, mothers, aunts, and grandmothers; and the play is, really, not *all* Wolf and Red Riding-Hood, but has other parts in it.'[79]

One can imagine few passages more likely to infuriate a modern feminist than this mixture of arch rallying and patronizing patriarchal smugness, but we should nevertheless note that it does concede 'the great necessity' there is for increasing job opportunities for women. Moreover, the kind of fanatic female chauvinism that Dickens is warning 'Belinda' against is indeed something that the Woman's Movement has, at all stages of its history, needed to be on its guard against because of its tendency to alienate public sympathy and to blur the issues with Amazonian emotionalism toppling over into the absurd.

*

Dickens's attitude towards women at work may best be summed up in this way: he was wholly sympathetic towards women whose employment lay in such traditional female domains as primary education, nursing, needlework and the decorative arts. In all these spheres single women, or those who had to become the breadwinners for their families, could be seen as worthily turning to account their womanly talents and aptitudes, the very things that made them good wives and mothers and creators of domestic charm or elegance. For women in this situation Dickens was more than happy to support moves to obtain better conditions of work and helpful training. But he was more uneasy about women working at jobs which were quite unlike domestic activities and, when brought up against an example of such a thing, liked, if possible, to see it as nevertheless leading towards a domestic result. Thus he noticed that 'a large crowd of well-dressed gentlemen' waited every afternoon to meet the female clerks leaving the U.S. Government offices in Washington (he and his Reading Manager, Dolby, had been 'astonished' to find that 'all the clerks employed for copying and official work were ladies') and concluded that the Government was

unconsciously 'running' a matrimonial agency, for he had opportunities of watching the friendly greetings that took place every afternoon, and the little exchanges of love tokens, in the shape of flowers, gloves and sweetmeats.[80]

In Dickens's view, the only really satisfactory destiny for a woman, is a domestic one, and at the end of *Our Mutual Friend* he mocks the notion that a poor girl like Lizzie Hexam might be appropriately rewarded for saving a man's life by being launched on a career of financial independence. The Contractor would have rewarded her by giving her a boat and a small annuity enabling her to set up for herself and the Chairman by 'getting her a berth in an Electric Telegraph Office where young women answer very well' but Eugene does the right thing: he makes her his wife.

vi

While the domestic ideal and a conception of woman as naturally domestic, able to receive and bestow happiness most fully only in a domestic context, is central and basic to Dickens's art, actual presentations or dramatizations of the ideal account for very few pages in his books. He is writing novels not idylls and needs dynamic subject-matter, struggles, stresses and tensions to be worked out and resolved during the course of the story. What he mainly gives us, therefore, are domestic situations where the ideal is somehow perverted or betrayed or prevented from being realized.

In the cases where this situation is the fault of men, it tends to be presented by Dickens in a melodramatic or quasi-tragic way[81] with the woman as a focus for pity, and sometimes terror too if she be driven, as Edith Dombey is, to sheer recklessness and despair. Generally, Dickens will present the situation as eliciting ever more long-suffering, patience, goodness and self-denial from the woman. The old clergyman who tells 'The Tale of the Convict's Return' in *Pickwick* says of a brutal husband and his wife:

> . . . I do firmly and in my soul believe, that the man systematically tried for many years to break her heart; but she bore it all for her child's sake, and, however strange it may seem to many, for his father's too; for brute as he was and cruelly as he had treated her, she had loved him once; and the recollection of what he had been to her, awakened feelings of forbearance and meekness under suffering in her bosom, to which all God's creatures, but women, are strangers.

Dickens's most elaborate dramatization of the brutal husband/suffering wife situation is in *Chuzzlewit*. Jonas Chuzzlewit, Mercy's husband, staggers home drunk late one night and savagely abuses her though, Dickens writes, 'It might have softened him to hear her turn a little

335

fragment of a song he used to say he liked; trying, with a heart so full, to win him back':

> She went up to him . . . and spoke lovingly: saying that she would defer to him in everything, and would consult his wishes and obey them, and they might be very happy if he would be gentle with her. He answered with an imprecation, and –
>
> Not with a blow? Yes. Stern truth against the base-souled villain: with a blow.

The chapter ends with Dickens exclaiming over the sufferings of women (though hardly in terms which would be acceptable to a modern feminist):

> Oh woman, God beloved in old Jerusalem! The best among us need deal lightly with thy faults, if only for the punishment thy nature will endure, in bearing heavy evidence against us on the Day of Judgment![82]

His martyr-wives will find no respite even beyond the grave, it would seem.

In his middle and later fiction wifely suffering tends to be less a matter of physical ill-treatment than of the psychological and emotional suffering inflicted on their wives by such men as Dombey, Murdstone, Bounderby, Gowan or Bentley Drummle. We have also the case of Richard Carstone, where a man who truly loves his wife nevertheless involves her in increasing distress through his own defects of character, the situation that Dickens found so moving in George Eliot's 'Amos Barton'. Ada, as we have noted, stays loyal and devoted to Richard as he makes an ever greater wreck of their lives and their prospects of happiness; she nurses him tenderly during his last illness and mourns for him afterwards. Her sufferings cause her to realize the full spiritual potential of Dickensian womanhood. Esther writes at the close of her narrative:

> The sorrow that has been in her face – for it is not there now – seems to have purified even its innocent expression, and to have given it a diviner quality. Sometimes, when I raise my eyes and see her, in the black dress that she still wears, teaching my Richard, I feel – it is difficult to express – as if it were so good to know that she remembers her dear Esther in her prayers.[83]

*

What is remarkable, however, in Dickens's presentation of women as heroically suffering domestic victims is how few of them are suffering as wives and mothers, in comparison to those who are suffering as sisters, or even more frequently, as daughters. Heroically self-sacrificing mothers are as conspicuous by their absence in Dickens as they are prominent in the work of his great rival, Thackeray, whose Amelia, we read uncomfortably, 'had stealthy and intense raptures of motherly love, such as God's marvellous care has awarded to the female instinct . . . blind, beautiful devotions which only women's hearts know'. There are some solemn allusions to abused but devoted mothers in Dickens's earlier work but the hollow clichés in which he invariably expresses the situation show clearly, I think, that the writing is *voulu*, engaging neither his heart nor his imagination:

> . . . we entered the desolate home, where the mother sat late in the night, alone; we watched her, as she paced the room in feverish anxiety, and every now and then opened the door, looked wistfully into the dark and empty street, and again returned, to be again and again disappointed. We beheld the look of patience with which she bore the brutish threat, nay, even the drunken blow; and we heard the agony of tears that gushed from her very heart, as she sank upon her knees in her solitary and wretched apartment.

When he does present a suffering mother at some length, in Mrs Steerforth, it is certainly not any refinement on, or development of, this sort of thing. In creating this woman with her passionate and pernicious adoration of her gifted son Dickens is mining the same dark vein of human nature that Shakespeare mined for Volumnia in *Coriolanus*. Mrs Steerforth's suffering is a result not of selfless love but of her own pride (she rages against her son's setting 'this wretched fancy [Em'ly], against his mother's claims upon his duty, love, respect, gratitude') and, far from ennobling her, it eventually freezes her into a sort of living death. And there is no comparably detailed portrayal of a 'good' suffering mother to balance the dark figure of Mrs Steerforth anywhere in Dickens's books.[84]

But if he was unstirred (thanks largely, no doubt, to the peculiarities of his attitude towards his own mother) by the sufferings of mothers, he was always warmly responsive to portrayals of daughterly or sisterly suffering as a result of abuse or exploitation. Harry Stone has argued persuasively that Dickens's passionate enthusiasm for Browning's play, *A Blot in the 'Scutcheon*, may be largely attributable to the emphasis placed on the heroine as a sister whose tragedy is precipitated by her impetuous brother; and his warmly expressed admiration for Mrs Marsh's unremarkable novel, *Emilia Wyndham*, had no doubt much to do with its author's belief, elaborately dramatized in the book, that there is not 'a more lovely sight on earth than the devotion of a daughter to an aged, perhaps peevish parent, sinking into a second childhood'. Dickens's own heroines, unless they have the good fortune to be brotherless orphans like Rose Maylie or Esther Summerson, find themselves chiefly occupied not with their lovers but in ministering, or seeking to minister, to selfish, querulous or brutally indifferent fathers and brothers. Madeline Bray, Florence Dombey, Agnes Wickfield, Louisa Gradgrind, Little Dorrit, Clara Barley, Lizzie Hexam (for a time) and Pleasant Riderhood are all cases in point. Even Mrs Lirriper's rival, Miss Wozenham, has, it transpires, been

> out of her small income and her losses doing so much for her poor old father, and keeping a brother that had had the misfortune to soften his brain against the hard mathematics as neat as a new pin in the three pair back represented to lodgers as a lumber-room and consuming a whole shoulder of mutton whenever provided!

Devoted, self-sacrificing daughters and sisters are everywhere in Dickens, in fact, and we may end our list of examples with a particularly concentrated one which appears in 'Gaslight Fairies', an essay he wrote for *Household Words* in 1855. He is sketching the life of an allegedly typical young pantomime actress:

> Miss Fairy is pretty too, makes up very pretty. This is a trying life at the best, but very trying at the worst. And the worst is, that that always beery old Fairy, the father, hovers about the stage-door four or five nights a week, and gets his cronies among the carpenters and footmen to carry in messages to his daughter ... representing the urgent coldness of his stomach and his parental demand for twopence.... A hard life this, I say again, even if John Kemble Fairy, the brother, who sings a good song, and when he gets an engagement always disappears about the second week or so and is seen no more, had not a miraculous property of turning up on a Saturday without any heels to his boots, firmly purposing to commit suicide, unless bought off with half-a-crown. And yet ... through all the narrow ways of such an existence, Miss Fairy never relinquishes the belief that that incorrigible old Fairy, the father, is a wonderful man![85]

It does not require much acquaintance with Dickens's biography to understand why the figure of one delicate, devoted child or young person struggling to support a whole unworthy family should be so omnipresent in his imaginative universe. Making the child invariably female increased both the heroism and the pathos, so providing an adequate fictional representation of Dickens as he essentially saw himself in the domestic aspect of his life from childhood.

vii

Suffering wives and daughters were at least situated in a domestic context, however much it was brutalized or undermined, and this was regarded by the Victorians as the right and natural place for a woman. The prostitute, on the other hand, that preoccupation of so many social reformers of the day, was seen as having for ever forfeited the possibility of becoming a respectable wife and mother. But it was, as we shall see, a distinguishing and important feature of Dickens's attitude towards reclaiming some of 'these melancholy shades of life', 'tarnished and battered images of God', 'Ruined Temples of God',[86] as he at various times called them, that the prospect of eventually realizing a happy domestic destiny should be set before them. Moreover, he was deeply concerned to ensure that the place which should be the setting for their redemption from the life of the streets and for their preparation for decent wifehood should be as domestic in its atmosphere and organization, and as non-institutional, as he could make it.

His earliest allusions to 'the Great Social Evil' (to use the Victorians' phrase for the hordes of prostitutes to be found in the streets of all their great cities, the sight of which so shocked foreign visitors)[87] occur in *Sketches by Boz* where the girls themselves are presented as victims of pure need, driven to 'a last dreadful resource' after struggling hopelessly to earn some sort of respectable living or, worse still, prostituted from childhood by their own needy families, like the two girls in the 'Prisoner's Van' sketch who 'had been thrown upon London streets, their vices and debauchery, by a sordid and rapacious mother'. His most detached sketch of a 'fallen woman' appears in 'The Pawnbroker's Shop':

> . . . a young female, whose attire, miserably poor but extremely gaudy, wretchedly cold but extravagantly fine, too plainly bespeaks her station. The rich satin gown with its faded trimmings, the worn-out thin shoes, and pink silk stockings, the summer bonnet in winter, and the sunken face, where a dab of rouge only serves as an index to the ravages of squandered health never to be regained, and lost happiness never to be restored, and where the practised smile is a wretched mockery of the misery of the heart, cannot be mistaken.

This woman is made to think, through catching a glimpse of a genteel and beautiful impoverished young girl trying to pawn some trinkets, of her own earlier self before she 'fell'; and when the girl and her mother 'involuntarily shrink from her' she sinks down in a fit of remorseful weeping. It is axiomatic with Dickens that every prostitute, however brazen and flaunting she may appear, is, sooner or later, tormented by shame and remorse and secretly yearns for restoration to society as a good (i.e., domestic) woman.

The first encounter we have with a prostitute figure in Dickens's fiction is with Nancy in *Oliver Twist*, who is essentially developed from the sketch just quoted (combined with the dying girl, murdered by her pimp, in another sketch, 'The Hospital Patient'). We see her first, through Oliver's innocent gaze, 'remarkably free and agreeable' in her manners, but her secret misery comes violently to the surface in the scene with Fagin after Oliver's recapture. Thereafter, however, she is really presented as a tragic heroine and more as a suffering wife than as an agonized prostitute. We see her only in connection with Sikes, pathetically trying to create some sort of home around him, nursing him in his sickness, and so on, and are not meant to speculate about when or how she actually plies her trade. 'The girl is a prostitute', Dickens roundly asserts in his preface to the 1846 edition of the novel (these words are dropped from later prefaces) and Nancy tells Rose that she is 'the infamous creature you have heard of, that lives among the thieves', but whilst reading the book we forget about her profession. She ascends the spiritual ladder that suffering is to erect for so many later Dickens heroines and he would surely have felt it bathetic for her to be shown as finally longing for a life of decent domesticity (quite apart from the unpromising nature of Sikes as a prospective partner in such an existence). The new life for which she desperately pleads as Sikes is about to murder her seems to be that of a sort of lay anchoress (an idea which would normally be quite abhorrent to Dickens – we shall see how he modifies it in the case of Little Em'ly):

> 'Bill,' cried the girl, striving to lay her head upon his breast, 'the gentleman and that dear lady, told me to-night of a home in some foreign country where I could end my days in solitude and peace. Let me see them again, and beg them, on my knees, to show the same mercy and goodness to you; and let us both leave this dreadful place, and far apart lead better lives, and forget how we have lived, except in prayers, and never see each other more.'[88]

Nancy, we might say, altogether transcends the role of prostitute in Dickens's imagination and the idea of redemption through domesticity simply does not apply in the exalted state into which she has moved.

The next time that Dickens touches on prostitution is in his Christmas Book for 1844, *The Chimes*, in which the hero, Trotty Veck, is shown a horrendous vision of what may become of his daughter Meg and her pretty little protégée, Lilian, through economic hardship. Despairing of earning enough as a sempstress to ward off starvation, Lilian goes on the streets but is tormented by remorse and returns to die (of shame, presumably) in Meg's arms, murmuring about Christ's compassion to Mary Magdalen. Then, in the last of the Christmas Books, *The Haunted Man* (1848), Redlaw encounters what we might call the quintessential Dickensian prostitute, haggardly brooding on a dark staircase:

> 'I am come here to give relief, if I can,' he said. 'Are you thinking of any wrong?'
> She frowned at him, and then laughed; and then her laugh prolonged itself into a shivering sigh, as she dropped her head again, and hid her fingers in her hair.
> 'Are you thinking of a wrong?' he asked, once more.
> 'I am thinking of my life,' she said, with a momentary look at him.
> He had a perception that she was one of many, and that he saw the type of thousands, when he saw her, drooping at his feet.
> 'What are your parents?' he demanded.
> 'I had a good home once. My father was a gardener, far away, in the country.'
> 'Is he dead?'
> 'He's dead to me. All such things are dead to me. You a gentleman, and not know that!' She raised her eyes again, and laughed at him.

By the time he wrote this melodramatic episode Dickens had been for two years playing a leading part in a particular effort to reclaim prostitutes. He had, in May 1846, eagerly responded to Miss Coutts's[89] plan of establishing an asylum for prostitutes discharged from prison who wanted to make a new start in life, and were prepared to go overseas to find it. In the course of a long letter to Miss Coutts he outlined a whole scheme of organization for the asylum and offered himself as ready to participate actively in its supervision and direction. He is quite clear that the prospect of their one day ending 'by God's blessing, in happy homes of their own' must be prominently set before the asylum's prospective inmates as they are being trained in 'Order, punctuality, cleanliness, the whole routine of household duties – as washing, mending, cooking' and he tries hard to convey to Miss Coutts one difficulty that she might not anticipate (showing that he is realistic enough not to expect that the promise of a domestic existence will invariably work like a charm on the class of women being addressed):

> . . . many of them would go on well for some time, and would then be seized with a violent fit of the most extraordinary passion, apparently quite motiveless, and insist on going away. There seems to be something inherent in their course of life, which engenders and awakens a sudden restlessness and recklessness which may be long suppressed, but breaks

out like Madness; and which all people who have had opportunities of observation in Penitentiaries and elsewhere, must have contemplated with astonishment and pity.

He urges that *'one, or two, or three, or four, or six departures from the Establishment'* should not be held a binding reason against re-admitting a girl *'being again penitent'*.[90]

Miss Coutts evidently demurred about the idea of encouraging the asylum's inmates to look forward to being decently married one day, albeit in a far-off country, but Dickens defended it stoutly. 'In the generality of cases,' he wrote, 'it is almost impossible to produce a penitence which shall stand the wear and tear of this rough world, without Hope – worldly hope – the hope of at one time or other recovering something like the lost station.'[91] A year later he backs this up with the evidence of a prison matron and he prominently features the hope of a home of their own in the leaflet, 'An Appeal to Fallen Women', that he wrote to be distributed in prisons to potential inmates of Miss Coutts's asylum:

> There is a lady in this town, who, from the windows of her house [Miss Coutts lived in Stratton Street, Piccadilly], has seen such as you going past at night, and has felt her heart bleed at the sight. She is what is called a great lady; but she has looked after you with compassion, as being of her own sex and nature; and the thought of such fallen women has troubled her in her bed. She has resolved to open, at her own expense, a place of refuge very near London, for a small number of females, who, without such help, are lost for ever: and to make it HOME for them. In this Home they will be taught all household work that would be useful to them in a home of their own, and enable them to make it comfortable and happy. . . . And because it is not the lady's wish that these young women should be shut out from the world, after they have repented and have learned how to do their duty there . . . they will be supplied with every means, when some time shall have elapsed, and their conduct shall have fully proved their earnestness and reformation, to go abroad, where, in a distant country, they may become the faithful wives of honest men, and live and die in peace.[92]

We notice Dickens's emphasis on the word 'Home' in describing the asylum. He it was who settled on this word for the place and perhaps chose the name of Urania Cottage for it (Philip Collins points out the contrast this name makes, however quaint it may seem to us, with the forbidding names of other institutions dedicated to the same end, like the British Penitent Female Refuge and so on). His object was, he wrote to Miss Coutts, 'to render [the inmates] an innocently cheerful Family while they live together there' and he kept this very much in view when settling how the house should be furnished and arranged, how the girls should be dressed (he rejected the idea of a drab uniform and chose dresses 'as cheerful in appearance as they reasonably could be – at the same time very neat and modest') and, above all, in selecting staff to run the place. He mocked Mrs Chisholm (whose scheme for assisting poor people to emigrate to Australia was publicized in *Household Words*) for being critical of the extent to which it was sought to create a domestic atmosphere at Urania Cottage. She asked him if it were true that the girls 'had *Pianos*' and, he wrote to Miss Coutts, 'I shall always regret that I didn't answer yes – each girl a grand, downstairs – and a cottage in her bedroom – besides a small guitar in the wash-house'.[93]

Although the Home was originally intended only for prostitutes there seems, as Philip Collins notes, 'to have been a change of policy, unnoticed or unrecorded'. It is clear from his anonymous article on the Home that Dickens published in *Household Words* in 1853, when the place had been in existence for five years, that many other kinds of girl were admitted such as

> starving needlewomen of good character, poor needlewomen who have robbed their furnished lodgings, violent girls committed to prison for disturbances in ill-conducted workhouses, poor girls from Ragged Schools . . . domestic servants who have been seduced, and two young women held to bail for attempting suicide.

Many of these, one suspects, were more susceptible to the sort of appeal Dickens made to them than prostitutes who, according to one of Dickens's chief allies in this project, G.L. Chesterton, Governor of Coldbath Fields Prison, all shrank from 'the irksomeness of quiet domesticity'. But a number of the girls who were admitted, and who may or may not have been prostitutes, failed to conform to expectations, such as 'that very bad and false subject, Jemima Hiscock' who 'forced open the door of the little beer cellar with knives, and drank until she was dead drunk; when she used the most horrible language and made a very repulsive exhibition of herself', or another girl called Sesina, 'the pertest, vainest . . . and most deceitful little minx in this town' who had to be sent away ('I think she would corrupt a Nunnery in a fortnight').[94]

It has often been noted that girls like these do not find their way into Dickens's subsequent fiction (Noah Claypole's hoydenish companion, Charlotte, might be considered an anticipation of them) and that his presentation of prostitutes in particular did not essentially change as a result of his ten-year involvement with Miss Coutts's Home. Of course, such prostitutes as did come into the Home would have been likely to conform to Dickens's idea of them as inwardly tormented by shame and remorse and it is not difficult to find evidence of very different attitudes elsewhere, for example in some of the women interviewed by Bracebridge Hemyng for the fourth volume of Mayhew's *London Labour* ('she became [a prostitute] from necessity; she did not on the whole dislike her way of living; she didn't think about the sin of it; a poor girl must live; she wouldn't be a servant for anything; this was much better'). And the vivacious ladies, many of them listed as being 'in genteel keeping', who appear in *The Bachelor's Pocket-Book and Man of Pleasure's Night Guide* for 1851 certainly do not sound very Dickensian (but then as one of their more celebrated modern successors might have put it, they wouldn't, would they?). One of them, a Miss Godlington of Dean Street, Soho, is described as having deliberately rejected the 'negative happiness' of marriage to an adoring husband whose feelings she did not reciprocate in order to 'taste the sweets of love blended with variety':

> She is ever lively, merry and cheerful; and in bed will give you such evincing proofs of her attachment to love's games, that although you leave a sovereign behind, you will be frequently tempted to renew your visit.[95]

The fact is, I think, that Dickens, a Christian Romantic and a man for whom domesticity was a real passion, was, unlike Zola, incapable of imaginatively comprehending such a woman as this. When he looked at prostitutes he imposed his own conceptions on them; either they were so far 'fallen' as to have become quite devilish in his eyes or else they were haunted by unhappiness. This emerges very clearly in a description he wrote in a letter to Wilkie Collins of the women he observed in a louche dance-hall in Paris in 1855:

> On Saturday night I paid three francs at the door of that place where we saw the wrestling, and went in, at 11 o'clock, to a Ball. Much the same as our own National Argyll Rooms. Some pretty faces, but all of two classes – wicked and coldly calculating, or haggard and wretched in their worn beauty. Among the latter was a woman of thirty or so, in an Indian shawl, who never stirred from a seat in a corner all the time I was there. Handsome, regardless, brooding, and yet with some nobler qualities in her forehead. I mean to walk about to-night and look for her. I didn't speak to her there, but I have a fancy that I should like to know more about her. Never shall, I suppose.[96]

The two prostitutes, Alice Marwood and Martha Endell, whom he had earlier introduced into his fiction were products of this kind of perception of such women as well as being strongly propagandist in the way they were conceived and developed. Alice Marwood in *Dombey*, written as Urania Cottage was being set up, is 'handsome, regardless, brooding' like the woman in Paris. She broods on having been exploited for gain by her mother when she was young and pretty, 'made a short-lived toy' of by Carker and then flung aside to sink in 'wretchedness and ruin' until she is 'concerned in a robbery' and sentenced to a term of transportation. She is reclaimed by the gentle kindness of Carker's pure and saintly sister, Harriet, who 'did not turn away with a delicate indignation – too many of her own compassionate and tender sex too often do – but pitied her'. Like Nancy, however, Alice has to die, having developed into too loftily tragic a figure for any other destiny. She tells Harriet, 'Evil courses, and remorse, travel, want, and weather, storm within, and storm without, have worn my life away' and dies in a sort of holy ecstasy after hearing Harriet read to her from the Bible 'the blessed history, in which the blind lame palsied beggar, the criminal, the woman stained with shame, the shunned of all our dainty clay, has each a portion'.[97]

Alice, like Nancy before her, is presented as a woman who had no chance of avoiding becoming involved in prostitution ('wretchedness and ruin') because of the sordid circumstances of her childhood. Dickens may make her speech implausibly histrionic but her history is, like Nancy's, an entirely credible one. Dickens came across a real-life case of a young girl who had been exploited by her parents, 'sent to evil courses for their gain', very shortly after creating Alice and commented to Miss Coutts,

> hers is, like some other cases that we have, a case in which it was next to impossible but that she must have gone, in youth, the way she has gone. It is dreadful to think how some of these doomed women have no chance or choice . . .[98]

By keeping this aspect of Alice's life before the reader Dickens can present her as an irresistible object of compassion from whom only a prude or a Podsnap could turn away in virtuous disdain. He goes a stage further, however, in creating Martha Endell two years later. The circumstances under which Martha became a prostitute are left wholly vague; we are told nothing of her earlier existence in Yarmouth except that she was employed by the benign undertaker Mr Omer. The implication would seem to be that she was not driven to prostitution by desperate poverty or social predestination but, presumably, fell into 'evil courses' after being seduced and then deserted by some local libertine. Dickens bases his appeal to the reader's compassion for her not on the circumstances of her fall but on her present state of social outcast (Ham Peggotty calls her 'a poor wurem as is trod under foot by all the town') and on her agonized remorse ('Making the same low, dreary, wretched moaning in her shawl, she went away').

Martha Endell is created by Dickens as a type of the penitent prostitute who will end in despair and suicide if someone does not intervene to give her a practical means of demonstrating her penitence allied to the hope of one day living a very different life – the model inmate for Urania Cottage, in other words. He does not invite the reader to consider her as an individual woman torn by conflicting emotions and involved in various relationships as in the case of Nancy or Alice. Mr Peggotty is brought into contact with her just in time to save her from throwing herself into the river and he gives her a virtuous mission for which she is peculiarly fitted, namely the seeking out of his lost Em'ly and rescuing her from the brothel into which she has been decoyed. Martha's reward is to be taken by Mr Peggotty, with Em'ly, to Australia where she is eventually sought in marriage by a good man and settles down as a pioneering farmer's wife in the Bush – through the voice of Mr Peggotty Dickens seeks to throw a pastoral charm over this destiny, which must have been rugged enough in reality: 'They was married, and they live fower hundred mile away from any voices but their own and the singing birds'.[99]

Em'ly is Martha's link to the plot of *Copperfield*. The two girls have been workmates at Mr Omer's and Em'ly pities and tries to help Martha before she herself falls. Em'ly's potential future is dramatically embodied by the figure of Martha, as the young girl's in the 'Pawnbroker's Shop' sketch had been by the tawdry prostitute hovering nearby. Dickens ironically causes Martha's sudden appearance, dogging Em'ly, to give Steerforth, who has begun to plot the latter's seduction, a sudden shock: 'That is a black shadow to be following the girl,' said Steerforth, standing still; 'what does it mean?'[100]

Em'ly is a character Dickens was proud of having created, telling Forster that he had a great hope to be remembered by her 'a good many years to come', and he tried to individualize her in a way that he did not individualize Martha. The story of the seduction and betrayal of a young simple girl by a sophisticated philanderer obviously fits in well with one of the grand unifying themes of *Copperfield*, the loss and betrayal of innocence, and Dickens saw in it an opportunity to put the plight of fallen women 'before the thoughts of people in a new and pathetic way, and perhaps to do some good'. The result is peculiar in a very Dickensian fashion. In his anxiety to present Em'ly and her fall as sympathetically as possible Dickens emphasizes her filial devotion to her uncle and adopted

346

father, Mr Peggotty – the role of devoted daughter being for him, as all his work shows, far and away the most sympathetic and moving female role conceivable. As a result Em'ly's fall seems primarily caused by an excess of 'daughterly' devotion and Steerforth and his charms appear almost incidental. When Em'ly is first presented as a child she tells David that she would like to be a lady so that she could show her love for Mr Peggotty in some dramatic fashion: '. . . I'd give him a sky-blue coat with diamond buttons, nankeen trousers, a red velvet waistcoat, a cocked hat, a large gold watch, a silver pipe, and a box of money'. This seems to remain her leading motive in life and when Dickens starts building up towards the climax of her elopement with Steerforth he emphasizes the ever-increasing intensity of her devotion to Mr Peggotty:

> 'To see the clinging of that pretty little thing to her uncle,' said Mr Omer; 'to see the way she holds on to him, tighter and tighter, and closer and closer, every day, is to see a sight.'[101]

Em'ly seems, in fact, to be nerving herself for some supreme sacrifice to enhance the well-being of her beloved father by adoption – to run the risk, that is, of becoming a Martha, a fallen woman, if Steerforth should not 'bring her back a lady'. Her farewell letter to her deserted fiancé, Ham, barely mentions Steerforth but is all about her love for Mr Peggotty ('Pray Heaven that I am going away from, have compassion on my uncle! Tell him that I never loved him half so dear. . . .'). As she subsequently seems to spend most of her time with Steerforth sending money (which is, of course, untouched) to Mr Peggotty or lamenting that she ever left him, it seems hardly surprising that Steerforth soon tires of her (Sylvère Monod comments, 'on imaginerait difficilement plus lugubre compagne d'un escapade galante') and tries to palm her off on his manservant. When she reappears after Martha's rescue of her and Dickens stokes up more sympathy for her during Rosa Dartle's cruel taunting scene, we hardly know whether we are to admire and love Em'ly as a daughter suffering as a result of her exceptional devotion or to pity her as a fallen woman. In the strange heroine/victim role which Dickens gives her she can clearly meet no ordinary fate such as marriage (there is no suggestion that Ham, who still loves her, might marry her when she returns). She ends up devoting herself to Mr Peggotty and a life of unobtrusive good works in the Australian outback – thereby undermining, as Philip Collins points out, the whole idea behind Urania Cottage since we are clearly meant to be more moved by her saintly ending than by Martha's pastoral domesticity.[102]

*

347

That Dickens continued to see prostitutes in Magdalen terms is shown by an episode in *Little Dorrit*, written seven years after *Copperfield*. A woman approaches Little Dorrit in the street at night, thinking that she is a child and Maggy is her irresponsible mother. The woman tries to warm little Dorrit's chilled hands:

> 'Kiss a poor lost creature, dear,' she said, bending her face, 'and tell me where she's taking you.'
> Little Dorrit turned towards her.
> 'Why, my God!' she said, recoiling, 'you're a woman!'
> 'Don't mind that!' said Little Dorrit, clasping one of her hands that had suddenly released hers. 'I am not afraid of you.'
> 'Then you had better be,' she answered. 'Have you no mother?'
> 'No.'
> 'No father?'
> 'Yes, a very dear one.'
> 'Go home to him, and be afraid of me. Let me go. Good-night!'
> 'I must thank you first; let me speak to you as if I really were a child.'
> 'You can't do it,' said the woman. 'You are kind and innocent; but you can't look at me out of a child's eyes. I never should have touched you, but I thought that you were a child.' And with a strange, wild cry, she went away.[103]

Once more we have the stark opposition between the domestically orientated woman with her 'very dear' father and the woman hopelessly exiled from all that yet pathetically yearning for some contact, however fleeting, with it and with her own lost innocence. No matter how many Jemima Hiscocks and Sesinas might pass through Urania Cottage, nothing would move Dickens from his conviction that prostitutes must be the most miserable of women, above all because of this exclusion from those domestic cares and joys for which female nature was created.

viii

We have seen that Dickens's presentation of the domestic ideal ruined by male brutality such as Jonas Chuzzlewit's or male weakness such as Richard Carstone's is invariably melodramatic and pathetic. When, however, the ideal is shown as unachieved because of female self-assertiveness such as Mrs Varden's or female inadequacy such as Mrs Pocket's, the subject is always presented comically even when, as with David Copperfield and Dora, the comedy is strongly tinged with pathos. One can say, of course, that in portraying comically the discomfort caused by nagging, querulous or domineering women Dickens is simply following a long-established literary tradition reaching back beyond Shakespeare's *Taming of the Shrew* to Chaucer's Wife of Bath and Noah's wife in medieval miracle plays; and we need look no farther than Trollope's Mrs Proudie to see that he was not alone among Victorian novelists in doing so.[104] But this subject is so omnipresent in Dickens's work from first to last and so clearly forms part of a wider pattern of humour directed against women as exploiters and oppressors of men — what we might call his 'Great Female Conspiracy' joke – that it is hard to resist seeing it as something personal to Dickens as well as traditional in literature. We may feel, too, that his relentless jocularity on this subject is just as much the product of a certain nervousness or anxiety about women as is his relentless punishing of his passionate anti-heroines like Edith Dombey.

We get some indication of how he might have handled in a non-comic way the subject of a wife wrecking the domestic ideal from his intensely admiring response to a story to which we have already alluded by a young lady called Emily Jolly, which he accepted for serial publication in *Household Words* during 1855. Miss Jolly's narrative, written in the first person, is entitled 'The Wife's Story'. The narrator is a cultured and sensitive woman with a passionate love for poetry and music. She relates how she found herself married to a good but limited man who loved her truly but could neither share her artistic interests nor respond to her as a person in the way she longed for him to do. She felt (with some justification, the modern reader might think) that he increasingly treated her as a temperamental and difficult child, and the more she showed her resentment at this the unhappier their life became. After one painful scene in which she obliquely accused him of being unfaithful to her he stormed out, met with a riding accident and was brought home for dead. The wife tells how she thereupon went mad with grief and remorse, recovering only to nurse their sick son. The child, however, died and the wife was again plunged into remorse until eventually it was revealed to her that the husband had not died after all. He returned to her and she submitted joyfully to him, conquering all her old self-assertiveness and becoming a model angelic wife.

Dickens was vastly impressed by this would-be harrowing tale, declaring it the work of 'a very remarkable woman' which showed 'a surprising knowledge of one dark phase of human nature'. He was responsible for one modification, however – in Miss Jolly's original version the husband was actually killed in his accident. Urging her to soften the story by preserving the husband's life, Dickens wrote:

> Let her suppose [him] dead . . . lose nothing of the progress of her mental suffering . . . but bring her round at last to the blessed surprise that her husband is still living, and that a repentance which can be worked out, *in the way of atonement for the misery she has occasioned to the man whom she so ill repaid for his love, and made so miserable,* lies before her.

As Angus Easson notes in his discussion of Dickens's editing of this story, both author and editor see the wife as very culpable and the husband as quite blameless, even heroic: 'any modern reader might well baulk at the idea of the wife needing to repent, since it seems rather that the husband has ill repaid her love and been pretty successful in making *her* miserable'.[105] Such a viewpoint would have been quite inconceivable for Dickens, however. He would undoubtedly have endorsed every word of the family doctor's reproach of the wife in Miss Jolly's story:

> Your husband is not a man of genius – not even a man of great depth or sensitiveness of feeling; but he has a true heart and a patient soul. He is infinitely your superior. You might well fall at his feet and pray his forgiveness. . . . [Your marriage] was a mistake, no doubt; but you, and you alone, have made it a fatal one.

Readers of Miss Jolly's strident propaganda for what would today be called male chauvinism can only be relieved that Dickens always chose to handle the subject of self-assertive wives in the comic mode; although we may still be made somewhat uneasy by the patriarchal assumptions underlying such humour we are so beguiled by the comic vitality of his shrews and scolds (also of ladies like Mrs Weller or Mrs Jellyby whose extramural enthusiasms are equally destructive of domestic bliss) that we need to be as fiercely feminist as John Stuart Mill in order to find them simply insults to women.[106]

Such characters form, as I have suggested, part of a larger pattern of revealing humour in Dickens's work along with his predatory spinsters and man-hungry widows. At its crudest this humour appears in such things as the facetious preface headed 'An Urgent Remonstrance, &c., to the Gentlemen of England, (being Bachelors or Widowers)' that Dickens wrote for a potboiler he produced in 1840 entitled *Sketches of Young Couples*. This warns that Queen Victoria's having announced her intention to 'ally herself in marriage' with Prince Albert may lead, especially in a Leap Year, to large numbers of hapless men finding themselves forcibly married:

> . . . a very distressing case, has occurred at Tottenham, in which a young lady not only stated her intention of allying herself in marriage with her

cousin John, but, taking violent possession of her said cousin, actually married him.

... similar outrages are of constant occurrence ... and ... unless the excited female populace be speedily checked and restrained in their lawless proceedings, most deplorable results must ensue therefrom. ...

... there is strong reason to suspect the existence of a most extensive plot, conspiracy, or design, secretly contrived by vast numbers of single ladies in the United Kingdom ... the object and intent of which plainly appears to be the holding and solemnising of an enormous and unprecedented number of marriages, on the day on which the nuptials of Her said Most Gracious Majesty are performed.

Four years earlier, in *Pickwick*, Dickens had evolved some genuinely humorous comedy (and, indeed, a central plot for the book) from the determined pursuit of his elderly bachelor hero by his matrimonially minded landlady, an experience which leaves Mr Pickwick justifiably apprehensive of all agreeable females such as Ben Allen's aunt with her 'evidently increasing admiration' for him – 'every glance of the old lady's eyes threw him into a cold perspiration'. The newly widowed Tony Weller also has cause for apprehension as a buxom neighbour seeks to comfort him. He confides to his son, ' Sammy, if I wos to stop here alone vun veek – only vun veek, my boy – that 'ere 'ooman 'ud marry me by force and wiolence afore it was over.' He relates the harrowing persecution he has undergone:

> The breath was scarcely out o' your poor mother-in-law's body, ven vun old 'ooman sends me a pot o' jam, and another a pot o' jelly, and another brews a blessed large jug o' camomile-tea, vich she brings in vith her own hands ... They wos all widders, Sammy, all on 'em, 'cept the camomile-tea vun, as wos a single young lady o' fifty-three.

The man who is not as vigilant as the chastened Tony is likely, in Dickens's comic world, to find himself undergoing the fate of Captain Cuttle's oracle, Bunsby, frog-marched to the altar. Bunsby is captured by the formidable Mrs MacStinger whose young daughter, moreover, shows 'a fatal concentration of her faculties' in observing the proceedings – she is a 'man-trap' in the making. The whole episode is jocosely presented as militant Woman's triumph over Man, Mrs MacStinger being supported by two lieutenants one of whom

> kept her eyes steadily on the bridegroom, and ... whenever they came near a court or other narrow turning which appeared favourable for flight, she was on the alert to cut him off if he attempted escape.[107]

351

Childbirth, too, provides an occasion for women to domineer over men in this comic world. When Little Dorrit is born in the Marshalsea the female prisoners take over the yard: 'the gentlemen prisoners, feeling themselves at a disadvantage, had for the most part retired, not to say sneaked, to their rooms'. In a private household the mother's female friends and relations rally round; they take over the house and formidable professional auxiliaries from the Gamp tribe are summoned up. Mr Meek finds himself driven from his own dining-room by his mother-in-law and a Mrs Prodgit ('Oh git along with you, Sir, if *you* please; me and Mrs Bigby don't want no male parties here!'). At a very early age Dickens himself had had, apparently, the uncomfortable experience of striking a jarring note in the midst of such a female triumph (here of a somewhat macabre kind). His nurse, he recalled, took him to visit a friend of hers 'who had four children . . . at a birth' and 'held quite a reception in her room on the morning when I was introduced there'. The stillborn babies were exhibited on a chest of drawers (putting the young Dickens in mind of 'pigs' feet as they are usually displayed at a neat tripe-shop') and the visitors began collecting money as a testimonial to this 'meritorious woman'. Dickens's refusal to contribute his pocket-money disgusted the company and he was sharply told that he 'must dismiss all expectations of going to Heaven'.[108]

Moreover, a woman could go on producing babies, it would seem, without any regard to the desires or financial anxieties of her husband. Even that paragon of husbands, Mr Harris, is reported by Mrs Gamp as saying of his ninth child that 'it was one too many, if not two'. Dickens's own mother's production of a fifth and sixth child (Alfred, born 1822, and Augustus, born 1827) after the family had got into difficulties perhaps seemed to her eldest son striking evidence of the maternal uncontrollability of women, and we have previously noted his rather extraordinary attitude towards his poor wife's fecundity, the rueful jokes in letters to his friends about her being in 'an *un*interesting condition', 'favouring me (I think I could have dispensed with the compliment) with No 10', and so forth. He must have editorially relished Wilkie Collins's joke in an 1858 *Household Words* sketch describing Mrs Bullwinkle, another of the Gamp tribe: 'About a month since, my wife advanced me one step nearer to the Court for the Relief of Insolvent Debtors, by presenting me with another child'.[109]

Special prerogatives in the matter of weddings and childbirths are only two of the weapons, albeit the strongest, in the armoury of that 'monstrous regiment of women' that is the source of so much Dickensian comedy. The most regularly used of these weapons are hysterics and fainting-fits, and any woman availing herself of these is sure to have the eager assistance of others of her sex. Dickens refers in *Dombey* to 'that freemasonry in fainting, by which [women] are generally bound together in a mysterious bond of sisterhood'. When Miss Wardle in *Pickwick* goes off into hysterics at an inn,

> the landlady, assisted by a chamber-maid, proceeded to vinegar the forehead, beat the hands, titillate the nose, and unlace the stays of the spinster aunt, and to administer such other restoratives as are usually applied by compassionate females to ladies who are endeavouring to ferment themselves into hysterics.

Later on in *Pickwick* we see Mrs Pott, ably seconded by her maidservant, turning the tables on her presumptuous husband with a formidable display of hysterics, and she has many successors in the novels, from Mrs Sowerberry in *Oliver Twist* through to Mrs Joe in *Great Expectations*. Prudent girls get some practice in during their maiden years: when a suitable occasion offers itself Miss Morleena Kenwigs 'fell, all stiff and rigid, into the baby's chair, as she had seen her mother fall when she fainted away'; and Miss Lavinia Wilfer, who 'hysterically speaking, was only just come of age', falls at an appropriate moment 'into a highly creditable crisis'. But perhaps Dickens's most elaborate example of the domestically tyrannical female is Mrs Varden in *Barnaby Rudge* since she can use not only hysterics but all other moods against her bewildered husband, being

> of such a capricious nature, that she not only attained a higher pitch of genius than Macbeth, in respect of her ability to be wise, amazed, temperate and furious, loyal and neutral in an instant, but would sometimes ring the changes backwards and forwards on all possible moods and flights in one short quarter of an hour; performing, as it were, a kind of triple bob major on the peal of instruments in the female belfry, with a skilfulness and rapidity of execution that astonished all who heard her.

She has also a powerful lieutenant in the bony shape of Miggs, her servant, who 'held the male sex to be utterly contemptible and unworthy of notice', and 'was accustomed to wish with great emphasis that the whole race of women could but die off, in order that the men might be brought to know the real value of the blessings by which they set so little store'.[110]
Only one male in the comic world of Dickens is a match, and more than a match, for this army of embattled females and that is the superbly anarchic dwarf, Quilp (contrast the hapless Mr Raddle in chapter 46

of *Pickwick*). It has often been suggested that this demonic character expresses and embodies his creator's repressed aggressiveness and enacts his deepest secret desires. Through him alone, we might add, Dickens can triumphantly overthrow that great and alarming female conspiracy which is such a prominent feature of his comic vision. In Quilp's absence the neighbourhood Amazons, under the generalship of his mother-in-law, invest his house and seek to stir up his submissive little wife to rebellion, telling her that 'if she had no respect for herself she ought to have some for other women, all of whom she compromised by her meekness'. They proceeded to swap stories of successful husband-subjugation: 'Another lady recounted her own personal struggle and final triumph, in the course whereof she had found it necessary to call in her mother and two aunts, and to weep incessantly night and day for six weeks'.[111] At the height of their excitement, however, Quilp suddenly appears among them, and, within minutes, he has utterly routed them by the sheer force of his comic/sinister personality.

*

Women banded together for any purpose are always presented as alarming by Dickens, even when the object of their association is essentially a good one and not simply the oppression of hapless males. He makes Esther Summerson note of all-female philanthropic societies:

> The ladies were as desperate as the gentlemen [philanthropists]; indeed, I think they were even more so. They threw themselves into committees in the most impassioned manner, and collected subscriptions with a vehemence quite extraordinary. . . . They wanted everything . . . they were going to get up everything . . . from five hundred thousand tracts to an annuity, and from a marble monument to a silver teapot. They took a multitude of titles. They were the Women of England, the Daughters of Britain, the Sisters of all the Cardinal Virtues separately, the Females of America, the Ladies of a hundred denominations. They appeared to be always excited about canvassing and electing.

Female energy, and the potential for passion in women's nature which he evidently believes is far greater than it is in men's, seems to make Dickens distinctly apprehensive. (Witnessing a powerful performance of *The Bacchae* would, one feels, have been altogether too much for him.) The 'rapacious benevolence' of the female philanthropists may still be seen as essentially comic, though the reader is meant to be disturbed as well as amused by the episode of Mrs Pardiggle's moral commandeering of the brickmaker's cottage. But the ferocity shown by women who are driven too far against their own nature, whose maternal or loving instincts are too grossly outraged, is no laughing matter. Even such 'out-and-outers' as Fagin and Sikes are daunted by Nancy's rage because, Dickens says, 'There is something about a roused woman: especially if she add to all her other strong passions, the fierce impulses of recklessness and despair: which few men like to provoke'. In his account of Mary, Queen of Scots, in his *Child's History* he makes a point of telling us that, while all her subjects were outraged by her marriage with Bothwell after her husband's murder, it was 'the women particularly' who 'are described as having been quite frantic against the Queen, and to have hooted and cried after her in the streets with terrific vehemence'.[112]

It is in *A Tale of Two Cities* that we find his most elaborate and horrified depiction of the bursting-forth of the fearful power that is latent in female nature, the diabolic energy into which all women's deep devotion to their families may be converted when they have been driven desperate by years of hopeless struggle to fulfil their natural role. When the news of old Foulon's capture spreads among the populace of Revolutionary Paris there is tremendous excitement. Dickens writes:

> The men were terrible, in the bloody-minded anger with which they looked from windows, caught up what arms they had, and came pouring down into the streets; but, the women were a sight to chill the boldest. From such household occupations as their bare poverty yielded . . . they ran out with streaming hair, urging one another, and themselves, to madness with the wildest cries and actions. Villain Foulon taken, my sister! Old Foulon taken, my mother! Miscreant Foulon taken, my daughter! Then, a score of others ran into the midst of these, beating their breasts, tearing their hair, and screaming, Foulon alive! Foulon who told the starving people they might eat grass! Foulon who told my old father he might eat grass, when I had no bread to give him! Foulon who told my baby it might suck grass when these breasts were dry with want! O mother of God, this Foulon! . . . Husbands, and brothers and young men, Give us the blood of Foulon, Give us the head of Foulon, Give us the heart of Foulon . . . ! With these cries, numbers of the women, lashed into blind frenzy, whirled about, striking and tearing at their own friends until they dropped into a passionate swoon, and were only saved by the men belonging to them from being trampled under foot.[113]

This horrific unleashing of female passion is part of Dickens's presentation of the evil consequences of the *ancien régime*, the crushing of humanity out of shape making it 'twist itself' into 'tortured forms'. Woman's apparently endless capacity for devotion to those she loves is made to turn into devotion to revenge, devotion not to life but to death, and she becomes then fearful indeed. She can be defeated only by equal and opposite female devotion as is demonstrated by Miss Pross's victory over Madame Defarge when Miss Pross finds that she must act to cover her 'darling's' escape from Paris with her husband and child:

> It was in vain for Madame Defarge to struggle and to strike; Miss Pross, with the vigorous tenacity of love, always so much stronger than hate, clasped her tight, and even lifted her from the floor in the struggle that they had. The two hands of Madame Defarge buffeted and tore her face; but Miss Pross, with her head down, held her round the waist, and clung to her with more than the hold of a drowning woman.

Madame Defarge may seem to be a far cry from Mrs Varden and Mrs MacStinger but she, like all the comic scolds and viragos, is an expression of Dickens's deep-seated fear of the terrible power that he sensed to be buried in female nature, a power that could be released by over-indulgent or timid husbands as much as by cruelty and injustice. And once it is released women will often seem to take pleasure in intensifying it to the point of hysteria, as happens with the female lynch-mob in *A Tale of Two Cities* or with Mrs Joe, of whom Pip says:

> ... I must remark of my sister, what is equally true of all the violent women I have ever seen, that passion was no excuse for her, because it is undeniable that instead of lapsing into passion, she consciously and deliberately took extraordinary pains to force herself into it, and became blindly furious by regular stages.[114]

ix

Dickens's apparent nervousness about any manifestation of aggressive female passion (as opposed to passive female devotion) may be linked to an equally detectable nervousness about his own strong sexual responsiveness to women. Both these things involved seeing women as adult human beings rather than as children or as angels, and this plainly worried him. The domestic setting as Dickens and his age idealized it – a haven of serenity and a spiritual powerhouse – could accommodate both children and angels but not the turbulence and sensuous delights of sexuality. The following passage from *A Christmas Carol* seems to illustrate the dilemma very clearly:

> They [i.e. Scrooge and the Ghost of Christmas Past] were in another scene and place; a room, not very large or handsome, but full of comfort. Near to the winter fire sat a beautiful young girl, so like that last that Scrooge believed it was the same, until he saw *her*, now a comely matron,

sitting opposite her daughter. The noise in this room was perfectly tumultuous, for there were more children there, than Scrooge in his agitated state of mind could count; and, unlike the celebrated herd in the poem, they were not forty children conducting themselves like one, but every child was conducting itself like forty. The consequences were uproarious beyond belief; but no one seemed to care; on the contrary, the mother and daughter laughed heartily, and enjoyed it very much; and the latter, soon beginning to mingle in the sports, got pillaged by the young brigands most ruthlessly. What would I not have given to be one of them! Though I never could have been so rude, no, no! I wouldn't for the wealth of all the world have crushed that braided hair, and torn it down; and for the precious little shoe, I wouldn't have plucked it off, God bless my soul! to save my life. As to measuring her waist in sport, as they did, bold young brood, I couldn't have done it; I should have expected my arm to have grown round it for a punishment, and never come straight again. And yet I should have dearly liked, I own, to have touched her lips; to have questioned her, that she might have opened them; to have looked upon the lashes of her downcast eyes, and never raised a blush; to have let loose waves of hair, an inch of which would be a keepsake beyond price: in short, I should have liked, I do confess, to have had the lightest licence of a child, and yet to have been man enough to know its value.[115]

Here is an intensely domestic setting and the only way in which sexuality could be admitted into it would be through an adult being allowed to play like a child, to be 'innocent' and yet at the same time sexually appreciative, an impossible combination. As we saw in an earlier chapter, Dickens had a fondness, that probably related closely to his memories of his own childish love for Lucy Stroughill, for depicting children as lovers. This was one obvious way in which his yearning to somehow 'purify' sexuality and yet at the same time retain all its delicious intensity found literary expression. Master Harry Walmers kisses and embraces his little Norah but because they are both infants there is no question of a sexual relationship. By the same token, however, there is no question of their being able to continue long in this idyll, hence the wistful wish of their adult protector, Cobbs, that 'there was any impossible place where those two babies could make an impossible marriage, and live impossibly happy ever afterwards'.[116]

Another way in which Dickens seems to be seeking to domesticate or neutralize sexual responsiveness to women is through writing about those he finds, or wishes to picture as, sexually stimulating as though they were really just playful little children, full of what he calls 'nature's own coquettishness'.[117] Thus a flirtatious encounter with a 'bright brown plump little' Italian chambermaid is presented as follows:

I smile at the brisk little woman in perfect satisfaction with her briskness; and the brisk little woman, amiably pleased with me because I am pleased with her, claps her hands and laughs delightfully. . . . As the little woman's bright eyes sparkle on the cigarette I am smoking, I make bold to offer her one; she accepts it none the less merrily, because I touch a most charming little dimple in her fat cheek, with its light paper end. . . . the little woman then puts her two little dimpled arms a-kimbo, and stands on tiptoe to light her cigarette at mine. 'And now, dear little sir,' says she, puffing out smoke in a most innocent and cherubic manner. . . .[118]

A 'thin bat-squeak of sexuality' (to borrow a famous phrase from Evelyn Waugh's description of another man-woman-and-cigarette encounter in his *Brideshead Revisited*) may be heard in this passage, but the impression Dickens is obviously seeking to create is of an affectionately teasing paternal or avuncular response to the woman rather than a sexual one.

Often it is as a wonderfully ingenious and pretty toy that the woman is presented rather than as a child, so that the idea of a full sexual response to her is made even more impossible. 'Neat' is a favourite adjective with Dickens when he is doing this. We have a particularly concentrated example in his description of being conducted round a Parisian abattoir (of all places) by 'a neat little woman with neat little eyes, and a neat little voice, who picks her neat little way among the bullocks in a very neat little pair of shoes and stockings',[119] and one might also cite the narrator's description of a lady's maid in the Christmas Story, 'The Perils of Certain English Prisoners':

> . . . a little saucy woman, with a bright pair of eyes, rather a neat little foot and figure, and rather a neat little turned-up nose. The sort of young woman . . . who appeared to invite you to give her a kiss, and who would have slapped your face if you accepted the invitation. . . . Being the kind of neat little woman it was natural to make a toy of – I never saw a woman so like a toy in my life – she had got the plaything name of Belltott.

It is fair to argue, I think, that the insistent presentation in Dickens of attractive young women as children or toys is not only a strategy for minimizing the element of sexuality: it probably reflected his own preferences too. It is worth noting that it was the fourteen-year-old Juliet not the mature Cleopatra whom he picked out as Shakespeare's 'ideal embodiment of woman's passionate love' and we may recall also his friend Maclise's complaint, 'I'm never up to his young girls – he is so very fond of the age of "Nell" when they are most insipid'. The kind of woman Dickens evidently found irresistible was the kind who seemed like a very young girl either in her virginal sweetness or in her kittenish vivacity.

358

Maturely beautiful women he might admire aesthetically but could not feel the same enthusiasm for: he once startled a Boston dinner-party when it was being discussed whether the Duchess of Sunderland or Mrs Norton was the more beautiful by interjecting ('expanding himself in his green velvet waistcoat'), 'Mrs Norton perhaps is the most beautiful; but the duchess, to my mind, is the more kissable'.[120]

The virtual absence in Dickens's fiction of any descriptions of female beauty below neck-level (Angus Wilson comments that we are jarred by having our attention drawn to Esther's smallpox-spoilt face 'because she has no body upon which a head could rest') also connects with his preference for women who are childlike in appearance because there is, of course, much less difference between the facial features of a young girl and those of a young woman than there is between their bodies. So with regard to Dickens's heroines we generally hear plenty about their beautiful eyes, hair, brows, etc., and, in the case of such secondary heroines as Dolly Varden or Dora, also about ringlets, dimples and perhaps even a 'neat' little ankle (it would of course be unsuitable to ascribe such more earthly charms to representatives of the feminine ideal such as Emma Haredale or Agnes). It is only with Little Nell that we hear a rather more comprehensive catalogue of physical charms through the gloating voice of Quilp: 'such a chubby, rosy, cosy, little Nell! . . . so small, so compact, so beautifully modelled, so fair, with such blue veins and such a transparent skin, and such little feet'. But even this is still pretty vague, and Nell would be too young for 'beautifully modelled' to be understood as referring to her breasts. These features, which most sharply distinguish women from girls, seem only to evoke a facetious response in Dickens – as, for example, in his description of the portrait in the Dedlock gallery, of a maid of honour of Charles II's time possessed of 'large round eyes (and other charms to correspond)'. The most famous bosom in Dickens, Mrs Merdle's, appears to lead an independent comic life of its own:

> It was not a bosom to repose upon, but it was a capital bosom to hang jewels upon. Mr Merdle wanted something to hang jewels upon, and he bought it for the purpose. . . . Like all his other speculations, it was sound and successful. . . . The bosom moving in Society with the jewels displayed upon it, attracted general admiration.[121]

For any suggestion in Dickens that a bosom might actually be attractive rather than a subject for joking we may look in vain.

*

Anyone familiar with Dickens's writings can easily assemble identikit portraits of three types of young womanhood to which he is always responsive. There is first the Fairy or Angel, the ethereally beautiful young girl with blue eyes and golden hair like Em'ly or Ada Clare or Lucy Manette; next there is the Good Sister, usually brown-haired, neat in her dress and modestly retiring in disposition but with great strength of character beneath her placid manner – this is a type represented above all by Agnes; and lastly there is the Kitten, bright-eyed, plump, merry, dimpled, 'fresh and healthful', usually appearing as a minor character except in the case of Dolly Varden. Dora, I think, combines the Fairy and the Kitten – more successfully, perhaps, than Ruth Pinch combines the Good Sister and the Kitten in one of Dickens's earlier blendings. Of the three types it is only the Kitten that evokes anything that could be called sexual response: in the other two cases one or other aspect of the domestic ideal has successfully blotted out any such idea. Dickens clearly delighted to see little girls in terms of budding Fairy or budding Good Sister – see, for example, his description of two children seen in a Christmas fireside circle:

> Around this little head on which the sunny curls lie heaped, the graces sport, as prettily, as airily, as when there was no scythe within the reach of Time to shear away the curls of our first-love. Upon another girl's face near it – placider but smiling bright – a quiet and contented little face, we see Home fairly written.

He might aesthetically admire bolder, more exotic types of feminine beauty such as Madame Victor Hugo's, with her 'flashing black eyes' and the look of a woman who 'might poison [her husband's] breakfast any morning when the humour seized her', or that of the young Boulogne fisherwomen ('the finest legs ever carved by Nature in the brightest mahogany, and they walk like Juno') and even concede its seductiveness (in the panther-like behaviour of Rosa Dartle there was, David says, 'yet something feminine and alluring') but it is not a style of beauty permitted to his heroines being, as it is, quite irreconcilable with the domestic ideal in any shape or form.[122]

When we turn from what Dickens finds attractive in young women to what he finds attractive in older ones we find ourselves confronted by the indisputably domestic figure of the Good Provider. One of his highest terms of praise for middle-aged women is 'comfortable', and they appear at their most desirable, appropriately enough, in the role of landlady, preferably widowed, of a snug inn. Mrs Lupin, the 'buxom, blooming hostess' of the Blue Dragon in *Martin Chuzzlewit*, is presented succu-

lently enough (she is 'comely, dimpled, plump, and tight as a gooseberry')
to make us credit Mark Tapley's enthusiasm for her, and we have met the
type before, in *Pickwick*, in the story told by the Bagman:

> . . . as Tom sat with his slippered feet on the fender . . . he saw a charming
> prospect of the bar reflected in the glass over the chimney-piece, with
> delightful rows of green bottles and gold labels, together with jars of
> pickles and preserves, and cheeses and boiled hams, and rounds of beef,
> arranged on shelves in the most tempting and delicious array. Well, this
> was comfortable too; but even this was not all – for in the bar, seated at
> tea at the nicest possible little table, drawn close up before the brightest
> possible little fire, was a buxom widow of somewhere about eight and
> forty or thereabouts, with a face as comfortable as the bar, who was
> evidently the landlady of the house, and the supreme ruler over all these
> agreeable possessions.

The actual woman is virtually merged in all the delicious eatables and
her ownership of them does indeed constitute her charm.[123] Peggotty's
appearance on Barkis's cart for the journey to Yarmouth with a basket of
refreshments on her knee, which, David records, 'would have lasted us
out handsomely, if we had been going to London', is enough to enrapture
Barkis ('Are you pretty comfortable?' is his lover's refrain). Having been
assured by David that it is indeed she who makes 'all the apple parsties,
and doos all the cooking' in the Copperfield household, he utters his
memorable announcement relative to his willingness.

Peggotty is not, in fact, a landlady but she is emphatically a Good
Provider; it is natural that her appearance in David's lodgings in London
should affront his landlady there, Mrs Crupp, who pretends to be a Good
Provider ('Mrs Crupp said, thank Heaven she had now found summun
she could care for!') but whose ample nankeen bosom proves to be a mere
cheat. When David boldly decides to throw a dinner-party it appears that
her kitchen fireplace is 'capable of cooking nothing but chops and
mashed potatoes' and she advises him to buy everything ready-prepared
from the pastry-cooks, leaving her 'at full liberty to concentrate her mind
on the potatoes, and to serve up the cheese and celery as she could wish to
see it done'.[124] Attentive students of Dickens's diction would have been
alerted to this Bad Provider by the use of the word 'stout', rather than
'buxom', in his initial description of her.

For buxomness seems to be a *sine qua non* for agreeable middle-aged
females in Dickens. His gallantry with the 'immensely fat' landlady of a
Yorkshire inn to which he refers in a letter of 1857 must have come easily
to him.[125] By contrast, disagreeable Mrs Spottletoe in *Chuzzlewit* is
described as 'much too thin for her years'. She also labours, however,

under the disadvantage of not being a landlady or a servant, or even a working-class wife and mother, like the 'healthy, wholesome and bright-eyed' Mrs Bagnet in *Bleak House*, who is celebrated for being always engaged in the preparation of meals. I can think of no middle-aged woman in Dickens, outside these categories, who is presented as attractive in a specifically physical sense. In general, they are presented as grotesquely *un*attractive and those such as Rachel Wardle or Volumnia Dedlock who presume to affect the charms of youth are ruthlessly caricatured. Although he was occasionally astonished, in real life, to find that middle-aged women like Lady Blessington ('she wears brilliantly, and has the gloss upon her, yet') and Madame Scribe ('her eldest son must be thirty, and she has the figure of five-and-twenty, and is strikingly handsome') could genuinely be as physically attractive as their juniors, in his fiction he will only ever offer a picture of attractive middle age in 'Good Provider' terms, as with Mrs Lupin, regarding whom,

> though she was not exactly what the world calls young, you may make an affidavit ... that there are a great many young ladies in the world (blessings on them, one and all!) whom you wouldn't like half as well, or admire half as much, as the beaming hostess of the Blue Dragon.[126]

Dickens's hostile portraits of middle-aged women who tried to remain attractive by artificial prolongation of such physical charms as youth had given them rather than by becoming Good Providers seem quite good-humoured, however, when set beside the sustained Swiftian savagery of his depiction of old Mrs Skewton and her ghastly 'Cleopatra' masquerade:

> ... Mrs Skewton's maid appeared, according to custom, to prepare her gradually for night. At night, she should have been a skeleton, with dart and hour-glass, rather than a woman, this attendant; for her touch was as the touch of Death. The painted object shrivelled underneath her hand; the form collapsed, the hair dropped off, the arched dark eyebrows changed to scanty tufts of grey; the pale lips shrunk, the skin became cadaverous and loose; an old, worn, yellow, nodding woman, with red eyes, alone remained in Cleopatra's place, huddled up, like a slovenly bundle, in a greasy flannel gown.

Granted that Mrs Skewton is meant to be a very unpleasant character, there still seems present in this passage, which reduces the old woman to a bundle of rubbish, a ferocity of disgust that is not found in the presentation of her nearest male equivalent in Dickens's work, the superannuated old beau, Mr Turveydrop in *Bleak House*. The source of the extra venom, I would suggest, lies in a basic hostility towards women asserting themselves as sexual beings. The older they are the worse it is, Dickens would seem to feel. The kind of old woman he approves of is the kind that fulfils the role of charming household ornament like 'that pretty old piece of china', the mother of Canon Crisparkle, who moves Dickens to the following eulogy:

> What is prettier than an old lady – except a young lady – when her eyes are bright, when her figure is trim and compact, when her face is cheerful and calm, when her dress is as the dress of a china shepherdess: so dainty in its colours, so individually assorted to herself, so neatly moulded on her?[127]

Household ornament, guardian angel, playful kitten, Good Sister, Good Provider – in Dickens a young girl or a woman may, according to age, represent any of these types, or a blend of more than one of them, for the benefit, comfort or pleasure of the men in her domestic grouping. Any assertion of herself as a person, however, with her own needs, demands and desires is invariably presented by him as something grotesque.

*

Given Dickens's nervousness about seeing women as possessed of a sexual responsiveness equivalent to men's, it is not surprising that he should be so fond, as we have already noted, of presenting wives as though they were children so that we seem to be reading about fathers and daughters rather than husbands and wives. This may seem no more than somewhat cloying to us when it is done in terms of sentimental comedy as with Dot Peerybingle, or as in Dickens's real-life description of the wife ('such an artless little creature') he delightedly observed aboard an American steamboat as she looked forward with childlike glee to being reunited with her husband after being away nursing her sick mother.[128] But we become uneasy when we are solemnly urged to admire, and even revere, such a situation, as in the case of old Dr Strong and his much younger and very beautiful wife, who spends most of her time sitting devotedly at his feet and addresses him as 'my husband and my father'. We note with disapproval, as Mrs Leavis says, 'Dickens's determination to believe that Annie is really fulfilled in such a marriage' (they are childless and the absentminded old Doctor is wholly absorbed in his Greek dictionary project, which is presented by Dickens as a piece of amiable futility).[129]

Dickens's fondness for depicting brother/sister ménages such as that of Tom and Ruth Pinch may also be seen as reflecting a tendency to avoid illustrating the domestic ideal in any straightforward husband/wife terms, and it is certainly quite striking, in the case of the example cited, how much suggestion of a sexual relationship does get into Dickens's description of the household once he has formally banished the very thought of such a thing by bringing the man and the woman together domestically as brother and sister. His account of the Pinches' settling into their home reads as though he were writing about a couple of self-conscious newly-weds:

> . . . there was a coyness about her very way of pouring out the tea, which Tom quite revelled in. . . .
>
> . . . she discovered, all in a moment, that Tom's shirt-collar was frayed at the edge . . . and set it right with wonderful expertness; never once sticking the needle into his face, although she was humming his pet tune from first to last, and beating time with the fingers of her left hand upon his neck-cloth.
>
> . . . off they trotted, arm-in-arm, as nimbly as you please; saying to each other what a quiet street it was to lodge in, and how very cheap . . .
>
> . . . during the whole of these preparations [for cooking] she looked demurely every now and then at Tom, from under her dark eye-lashes, as if they were all a part of the pudding and indispensable to its composition.
>
> . . . It was a perfect treat to Tom to see her with her brows knit, and her rosy lips pursed up, kneading away at the crust . . .[130]

It is just as well, one might feel, that Tom's friend, John Westlock, enters when he does to provide another target for Ruth's demure looks.

How little woman as wife moved Dickens, or was important to him compared with woman as sister or woman as daughter, is revealed, I think, in that strange fantasy-piece we have had occasion to look at before, 'A Child's Dream of a Star'. It will be remembered that this tells the story of a boy whose beloved little sister dies and goes to be an angel on a bright star that they had wondered at together before her death. The child yearns to join her but continues to live. First a baby brother and then the mother dies and they go to join the sister on the star but the child still remains on earth. Then we read:

> He grew to be a man, whose hair was turning grey, and he was sitting in his chair by the fireside, heavy with grief, and with his face bedewed with tears, when the star opened once again.
>
> Said his sister's angel to the leader: 'Is my brother come?'
>
> And he said, 'Nay, but his maiden daughter.'
>
> And the man who had been the child saw his daughter, newly lost to him, a celestial creature among those three, and he said, 'My daughter's head is on my sister's bosom, and her arm is around my mother's neck,

and at her feet there is the baby of old time, and I can bear the parting from her, GOD be praised!'[131]

There is no mention whatever of a wife, we notice. The two all-important relationships for the child and for the man he becomes are with his sister and with his daughter.

X

Woman as wife seldom stirred Dickens's imagination unless she could be seen essentially in sisterly or daughterly terms in that role. Towards woman as mother he had a rather more complex reaction, reflecting, no doubt, the complexity of his feelings towards his own mother. In his earlier fiction the maternal aspect of woman receives short shrift. The nearest that he can bring himself to portraying it naturalistically is in the thumbnail sketch of Mrs Bedwin (admittedly the only one of the 'good' characters in *Oliver Twist* who is quite convincing) and she is *grand-* motherly rather than motherly in her fussing and doting over little Oliver. Apart from her, motherly feelings in the early fiction are either a matter for laughter (Mrs Kenwigs overcome by the thought that her little daughters are 'too beautiful to live') – even for gross travesty as in the case of Mrs Gamp – or for the sentimental reminiscing of the highly implausible Cheeryble brothers, or for melodramatic exclamation as in Trotty Veck's horrific vision of his starving daughter and her baby:

> . . . he saw it harass her, and tire her out, and when she slumbered in exhaustion, drag her back to consciousness, and hold her with its little hands upon the rack; but she was constant to it, gentle with it, patient with it. Patient! Was its loving mother in her inmost heart and soul, and had its Being knitted up with hers as when she carried it unborn.[132]

Motherhood *in extremis*, like this, may move him to strike out a fine and powerful image ('hold her with its little hands upon the rack') but it is not until the latter half of the 1840s that he seemed able successfully to dramatize actual motherhood or motherliness seen under more normal conditions. This may perhaps have been partly the result of his ever-sharp remembrance of maternal 'betrayal' in childhood having gradually become overlain (though far from buried) by more recent, and happier, observation of woman as mother – Catherine Dickens had had six children by the end of 1845.

Although the majority of actual mothers in the novels continue to be shown as at best inadequate, like Mrs Copperfield or Mrs Gradgrind, a few honourable exceptions such as Mrs Bagnet begin to appear in the

365

humbler ranks of society. With the exception of Polly Toodle, however, they are really successors to Mrs Cratchit in the *Carol* where the essential focus is on the woman's being a devoted housekeeper, a Good Provider within strict financial limits, rather than on her actual mothering of her children. (It is worth noting how the parental anguish associated with Tiny Tim is focused on Bob Cratchit rather than on his wife and we can see the same thing with the Meagleses in *Little Dorrit*.) As to that heroic lady Mrs Micawber, her mothering activities are deliberately presented in such a fashion that we can only find them farcical: 'I hardly ever', writes David, 'in all my experience of the family, saw both the twins detached from Mrs Micawber at the same time. One of them was always taking refreshment.'

In the case of Polly Toodle, her motherly aspect (F.R. Leavis thought her 'perfectly done' as 'the natural motherly woman')[133] is emphasized because it is so important for the development of the story – both her longing to see her own children again which precipitates the second catastrophe in Paul's young life and her nourishing (physical and emotional) of Paul which makes his sudden deprivation of her such a calamity for him. So we see quite a bit of Polly as mother to her own children and, in particular, her anxious and loving concern for her graceless eldest child, Rob the Grinder, whom she seeks to defend against his father's growing unease about him: this is all very delicately and convincingly sketched in by Dickens. Even when about to introduce Polly as his motherly ideal, however, Dickens cannot wholly suppress his tendency to see woman in her most basic maternal aspect as a joke: Mr Chick, Mr Dombey's brother-in-law, wonders if instead of hiring a wetnurse for the orphaned baby, 'something temporary' might not be done 'with a teapot?'.

It is perhaps not without significance that the warmest and most memorable image of motherhood that Dickens created was David's nurse, Peggotty, who is not actually a mother at all. Her midnight expedition to comfort the confused and frightened little boy imprisoned by the Murdstones in his own home, whispering her loving reassurances through the keyhole, marks for David the beginning of a kind of filial emotional dependence on her:

> She did not replace my mother; no one could do that; but she came into a vacancy in my heart, which closed upon her, and I felt towards her something I have never felt for any other human being. It was a sort of comical affection, too; and yet if she had died, I cannot think what I should have done, or how I should have acted out the tragedy it would have been to me.

Her loving care and concern for him after his mother's death is very convincingly conveyed in chapters 9 and 10 of the novel – for example, in the anxious talk she has with the little boy about whether or not she should respond to Barkis's 'willingness':

> 'Davy dear, what should you think if I was to think of being married?'
> 'Why – I suppose you would like me as much then, Peggotty, as you do now?' I returned, after a little consideration.
> Greatly to the astonishment of the passengers in the street . . . the good soul was obliged to stop and embrace me on the spot, with many protestations of her unalterable love. . . .
> ' . . . I wouldn't so much as give it another thought,' said Peggotty, cheerily, 'if my Davy was anyways against it – not if I had been asked in church thirty times three times over, and was wearing out the ring in my pocket.'[134]

What, I think, Dickens has achieved so well in creating Peggotty through David's descriptions is the dramatization of that combination of emotional dependence with a certain admixture of comic appreciation that children as they begin to grow up – boys more than girls, perhaps – often feel towards their mothers. The comic appreciation Dickens had already dramatized in Mrs Nickleby (though Nicholas is generally more exasperated than amused by her), but with David and Peggotty he has for the first time succeeded in fusing it with a strong, earned affection for the woman, so creating a very human, believable mother-figure.

The motherly woman recurs many times in Dickens's fiction after Polly Toodle and Peggotty – in such characters as Mrs Meagles (always referred to as 'mother' by her husband) and Mrs Boffin, for example – but always with rather a soft focus and in a minor role. By comparison with his career-long preoccupation with sisters and daughters his positive response as an artist to woman as mother may be fairly described as minimal; his negative response to her, on the other hand, was a continuing fertile source for comic creativity.

xi

The final emphasis in this survey of Dickens's beliefs about and attitudes towards woman should fall, I think, on his evident preoccupation with the idea of natural sisterhood, or female-bonding as it might be more fashionable to call it nowadays. The actual sister-sister relationship always seems to have charmed him (if Catherine Hogarth had been sisterless would that have diminished her attractiveness in his eyes, one wonders?) and there is a delightful little comic extravaganza on the theme to be found in *Sketches by Boz* entitled 'The Four Sisters'. The Miss Willises

> seemed to have no separate existence, but to have made up their minds just to winter through life together. They were three long graces in drapery, with the addition, like a school-dinner, of another long grace afterwards – the three fates with another sister – the Siamese twins multiplied by two.

When one of them marries they all go to church together, kneel down at the communion-table together, repeat the responses together and all go into hysterics together at the end of the ceremony. And afterwards they continue all to live together with the bridegroom so that the neighbours cannot discover which one of the sisters he has married until one of them has a baby.

This kind of *jeu d'esprit* is certainly preferable to the attempt, which we have already looked at, in *The Battle of Life* to make sisterhood a theme for high seriousness. The latter story might seem to have been inspired by Mrs Ellis's eulogies of the sisterly relationship in her *Women of England*: 'there is sometimes a bond existing between sisters, the most endearing, the most pure and disinterested of any description of affection which this world affords . . . where a sister is a sister's friend there can be none so tender, and none so true'.[135] The heroine of Dickens's story, Marion, detects that her elder sister, Grace, is heroically suppressing her secret love for Alfred, Marion's fiancé (they have all been brought up together, incidentally, another instance of the compulsion Dickens seems to feel to present courtship and marriage in brother/sister terms as much as possible). Marion, we may remember, stages a five-year disappearance so that she should be presumed dead, or worse, thus clearing the way for Alfred to transfer his affections to Grace and marry her. Marion loves Alfred and he loves her, but her love for her secretly suffering sister is paramount. This very peculiar story was felt to be impossibly strained and far-fetched, even by Dickens's contemporaries: 'Even sisters', wrote one reviewer, 'are not always hanging on one another's necks and talking boarding-school sentiment to one another'.[136]

It is the extension of sisterhood beyond the family that figures most prominently in Dickens, however, and this might be seen as the reverse side of the 'Great Female Conspiracy' medal. His imagination is infallibly stirred – though seldom with satisfactory artistic results – by the succouring by women of women who really are victims of male brutality, or of male-dominated society (as opposed to comfortably situated women who, from sheer perversity and boredom, pretend to be). Rose Maylie's compassion for Nancy in chapter 40 of *Oliver Twist* is echoed again and again in succeeding novels. Ruth Pinch and Mercy Pecksniff, Harriet Carker and Alice, Florence and Edith Dombey, Meg and Lilian in *The Chimes*, Em'ly and Martha, Agnes and Dora, Agnes and Em'ly, Esther and Ada, Sissy Jupe and Louisa Gradgrind, Bella and Lizzie Hexam, Lizzie and Jenny Wren, Helena and Rosa in *Edwin Drood* – this list of examples of sisterly sympathy poured out for women who have been betrayed, exploited, brutalized or terrified by men might be made much longer. Even the harassed boarding-house keeper, Mrs Todgers, with her temper tried by 'commercial gentlemen and gravy', proves a true woman in this respect: 'in some odd nook in Mrs Todgers's breast, up a great many steps, and in a corner easy to be overlooked, there was a secret door, with "Woman" written on the spring, which, at a touch from Mercy's hand, had flown wide open, and admitted her for shelter'.[137]

It is indeed an absolute hallmark of a good womanly woman in Dickens that she should form emotional attachments to other women and aid and comfort them even when she herself may also be suffering. Miss Coleshaw, in *The Wreck of the Golden Mary*, ignores her own wretchedness in the drifting longboat after the shipwreck, in order to tend the frail and angelic Mrs Atherstone whose beautiful hair 'would have been now all tangled with dirt and wet, but that Miss Coleshaw was careful of it long after she was herself and would sometimes smooth it down with her weak thin hands'. In real life he observes that one of the prisoners remaining voluntarily in Coldbath Fields pending transfer to Urania Cottage was devoted to a fellow-inmate and bitterly distressed when the latter took herself off ('she really had hoped to reform, with this companion, and had thought they would become like sisters') and is convinced by this that the woman is redeemable: 'If she remain, I have no doubt of her, and hope we may count upon her reclamation as almost certain'. He greatly hopes too that the girls in the Home may 'form strong attachments among themselves' which would be 'a beautiful thing'.[138]

It is a mark of real evil for Dickens when a woman shows no sympathy, or even downright hostility, towards 'fallen' members of her own sex (when, as in the case of the suggestively named Miss Barbary, it is actually a matter of real sisters the evil is intensified, of course). 'That too many women are dreadfully cruel to their sister-women who have illegitimate children is painfully true,' he wrote to a female correspondent in 1863. 'But I presented this very point in an early Number of the present series of the Uncommercial Traveller; and then by no means for the first time.' He is referring to the essay entitled ' Some Recollections of

Mortality' in which he describes serving as juryman at the trial of a young servant accused of murdering her illegitimate baby. He recalls 'the un-sympathetic nurse who attended [the prisoner] and who might have been the figure-head of a pauper-ship, and how she [the prisoner] hid her face and sobs and tears upon that wooden shoulder', also 'how hard her mistress was upon her' in giving evidence, the 'cruel pertinacity' of that 'piece of Virtue'. The same essay also contains another description, written with a very personal intensity of horror, of an example of woman's inhumanity to woman. Dickens remembers how he was looking at the body of a young woman just fished out of the Regent's Canal when

> A barge came up . . . and a woman steered it. The man with the horse that towed it, cared so little for the body, that the stumbling hoofs had been among the hair, and the tow-rope had caught and turned the head, before our cry of horror took him to the bridle. At which sound the steering woman looked up at us on the bridge, with contempt unutterable, and then looking down at the body with a similar expression – as if it were made in another likeness from herself, had been informed with other passions, had been lost by other chances, had had another nature dragged down to perdition – steered a spurning streak of mud at it, and passed on.

In the novels Rosa Dartle's vindictive taunting of Em'ly, alluded to earlier, is perhaps the most strident example of Dickens's dramatizing what he saw as something horribly unnatural, the rejection of sisterhood. Em'ly's pleas to Rosa for mercy in the name of their common woman-hood only rouse Rosa to greater fury. Similarly, it is a measure of the degree to which Madame Defarge's woman's nature has been perverted (as a result, we might note, of her passionate reaction against the out-rage perpetrated on her sister long ago) that she is impervious to Lucy Manette's desperate appeal to her ('O sister-woman, think of me') on behalf of Darnay.

Still more horrific for Dickens than the rejector of sisterhood however, is the procuress figure, the woman who seems deliberately to ruin others, or to connive at their ruin. This is the role that Miss Mowcher was evidently intended to play in *Copperfield* before Dickens had to change her character totally after hearing from Mrs Hill and her solici-tor,[139] and it is the role Mrs Sparsit seeks to play in her relations with Louisa, Bounderby and Harthouse, doing all she can to facilitate Louisa's descent of the allegorical staircase she constructs in her fantasy, a descent leading step by step down to a 'dark pit of shame' at the bottom. Relevant here, too, is the following gloomy suggestion for a character found in

Dickens's Memorandum Book: 'I am a common woman – fallen. Is it devilry in me – is it a wicked comfort – what is it – that induces me to be always tempting other women down, while I hate myself!'[140] The nearest character to this actually created by Dickens is Miss Wade – a woman neither 'common' nor 'fallen' but bitterly twisted – who seduces the Meagles's orphaned maidservant, Tattycoram, into her own private hell. Whether, as some critics have alleged, Dickens intended his more sophisticated readers to understand that Miss Wade is actually a lesbian – and there is no reason to suppose that he was as innocent as Queen Victoria in such matters – is really of little moment. For Dickens her essential evil is sufficiently expressed by Mr Meagles when he tells her, 'I am not so innocent but that I have heard of such women as you who delight in making their sister-women as miserable as yourselves'. A different but related case is that of Miss Havisham, whose crazy vindictiveness towards men causes her to blight her young protégée's life. Miss Havisham repents too late, but another betrayer of her own sex, Mrs Lammle in *Our Mutual Friend*, repents just in time to save the hapless young Georgiana Podsnap from the terrible marriage into which the mercenary Lammles are seeking to entrap her. Dickens endows Mrs Lammle, like Mrs Todgers, with that 'secret door with "Woman" written on the spring' and she cannot keep it shut to betray one of her own sex.

*

This consideration of Dickens's fascination with the idea of natural sisterhood between women returns us to our starting-point in this survey of his attitudes towards, and beliefs about, Woman. For it is undoubtedly one of the things he would have cited had he been called upon to supply evidence of his belief in the emotional and moral superiority of female nature, 'so much quicker to feel . . . all tenderness and pity . . . than the nature of men'. Sisterhood between women naturally features prominently in his most elaborate presentation of the feminine ideal in *Copperfield*, the most overtly personal of all his novels. Agnes and Dora, the Angel/Sister and the Fairy/Kitten, avatars of Mary Hogarth and Maria Beadnell, between them incorporate everything that Dickens found exciting, lovable, fascinating, admirable and inspiring in Woman; and their instant mutual affection ('such well-associated friends, each adorning the other so much!') forms the crown of David's joy in them:

> I never was so happy. I never was so pleased as when I saw those two sit
> down together, side by side. As when I saw my little darling looking up so
> naturally to those cordial eyes. As when I saw the tender, beautiful regard
> which Agnes cast upon her.[141]

The modern reader's contemplation of this glowing vignette tends to be a good deal less ecstatic than David's. And, although the subtlety and delicacy of Dickens's art as seen in the creation of Dora is coming more and more to be recognized, the disastrously *voulu* nature of the presentation of Agnes remains a rock ahead, even for the most ardent Dickensians. Given the central position that Agnes occupies in Dickens's work, it is not surprising that this rock casts such a shadow over discussion of his presentation of women. The second part of this book has tried to indicate how much variety, power and subtlety Agnes's shadow tends to obscure in this aspect of Dickens's art. Not to end with her in the sort of survey we have been undertaking in this part, however, would surely be wrong. For better or worse, it is she who expresses most fully Dickens's conception of the feminine ideal – not everything he knew or felt or understood about women but everything he believed female nature, at its finest and purest, to be.

Appendix A

The 'Violated Letter'

TAVISTOCK HOUSE, TAVISTOCK SQUARE, LONDON, W.C.

Tuesday, 25th May, 1858

MY DEAR ARTHUR, – You have not only my full permission to show this, but I beg you to show, to any one who wishes to do me right, or to any one who may have been misled into doing me wrong.
Faithfully yours.

TAVISTOCK HOUSE, TAVISTOCK SQUARE, LONDON, W.C.

[Enclosure]
Tuesday, May 25, 1858

Mrs Dickens and I have lived unhappily together for many years. Hardly any one who has known us intimately can fail to have known that we are, in all respects of character and temperament, wonderfully unsuited to each other. I suppose that no two people, not vicious in themselves, were ever joined together, who had a greater difficulty in understanding one another, or who had less in common. An attached woman servant (more friend to both of us than a servant), who lived with us sixteen years, and is now married, and who was, and still is in Mrs Dickens's confidence and in mine, who had the closest familiar experience of this unhappiness, in London, in the country, in France, in Italy, wherever we have been, year after year, month after month, week after week, day after day, will bear testimony to this.

Nothing has, on many occasions, stood between us and a separation but Mrs Dickens's sister, Georgina Hogarth. From the age of fifteen, she has devoted herself to our house and our children. She has been their playmate, nurse, instructress, friend, protectress, adviser and companion. In the manly consideration toward Mrs Dickens which I owe to my wife, I will merely remark of her that the peculiarity of her character has thrown all the children on some one else. I do not know – I cannot by any stretch of fancy imagine – what would have become of them but for this aunt, who has grown up with them, to whom they are devoted, and who has sacrificed the best part of her youth and life to them.

She has remonstrated, reasoned, suffered and toiled, again and again to prevent a separation between Mrs Dickens and me. Mrs Dickens has often expressed to her her sense of her affectionate care and devotion in the house – never more strongly than within the last twelve months.

373

For some years past Mrs Dickens has been in the habit of representing to me that it would be better for her to go away and live apart; that her always increasing estrangement made a mental disorder under which she sometimes labors — more, that she felt herself unfit for the life she had to lead as my wife, and that she would be better far away. I have uniformly replied that we must bear our misfortune, and fight the fight out to the end; that the children were the first consideration, and that I feared they must bind us together 'in appearance'.

At length, within these three weeks, it was suggested to me by Forster that even for their sakes, it would surely be better to reconstruct and rearrange their unhappy home. I empowered him to treat with Mrs Dickens, as the friend of both of us for one and twenty years. Mrs Dickens wished to add on her part, Mark Lemon, and did so. On Saturday last Lemon wrote to Forster that Mrs Dickens 'gratefully and thankfully accepted' the terms I proposed to her.

Of the pecuniary part of them, I will only say that I believe they are as generous as if Mrs Dickens were a lady of distinction and I a man of fortune. The remaining parts of them are easily described — my eldest boy to live with Mrs Dickens and take care of her; my eldest girl to keep my house; both my girls, and all my children but the eldest son, to live with me, in the continued companionship of their aunt Georgina, for whom they have all the tenderest affection that I have ever seen among young people, and who has a higher claim (as I have often declared for many years) upon my affection, respect and gratitude than anybody in this world.

I hope that no one who may become acquainted with what I write here, can possibly be so cruel and unjust, as to put any misconstruction on our separation, so far. My elder children all understand it perfectly, and all accept it as inevitable. There is not a shadow of doubt or concealment among us — my eldest son and I are one, as to it all.

Two wicked persons who should have spoken very differently of me, in consideration of earned respect and gratitude, have (as I am told, and indeed to my personal knowledge) coupled with this separation the name of a young lady for whom I have a great attachment and regard. I will not repeat her name — I honor it too much. Upon my soul and honor, there is not on this earth a more virtuous and spotless creature than that young lady. I know her to be innocent and pure, and as good as my own dear daughters. Further, I am quite sure that Mrs Dickens, having received this assurance from me, must now believe it, in the respect I know her to have for me, and in the perfect confidence I know her in her better moments to repose in my truthfulness.

On this head, again, there is not a shadow of doubt or concealment between my children and me. All is open and plain among us, as though we were brothers and sisters. They are perfectly certain that I would not deceive them, and the confidence among us is without a fear.

29th May, 1858

It having been stated to us that in reference to the differences which have resulted in the separation of Mr and Mrs Charles Dickens, certain statements have been circulated that such differences are occasioned by circumstances deeply affecting the moral character of Mr Dickens and compromising the reputation and good name of others, we solemnly declare that we now disbelieve such statements. We know that they are not believed by Mrs Dickens, and we pledge ourselves on all occasions to contradict them, as entirely destitute of foundation.

[*Here follow the signatures of Mrs Hogarth and her youngest daughter.*]

The text is from Nonesuch *Letters*, vol. 3, pp. 21-3.

Appendix B

Dickens and Ellen Ternan: A Chronological Record of the 'Evidence'

The subject of Dickens's relationship with Ellen Ternan is still one of lively debate, and my purpose here is to present only an outline history of the controversy. As we have seen in chapters 5 and 10, rumours of Dickens's involvement with the young actress had begun to circulate from the time he and Catherine separated, and several years after Dickens's death some of these stories began to appear in print, retold in books of reminiscences. In one such book, *Keeping off the Shelf* (1928) Mrs Thomas Whiffen told a version of the misdirected jewels story and, in addition, claimed that Ellen (whom she refers to as Dickens's god-daughter) and Mrs Ternan were Dickens's travelling companions in the Staplehurst railway accident. Mrs Whiffen's statements were roundly refuted in *The Dickensian* (1930) by J.W.T. Ley who quoted Sir Henry Dickens's assertion that he had no knowledge of Ellen being his father's god-daughter, and that the involvement of the Ternans in the railway accident was 'pure invention'.

In 1928 'Ephesian' (C.E. Bechhofer Roberts) published the life of Dickens up to his separation from Catherine, told in the form of a novel. This aroused a storm of indignation, since the novel concludes with an account of Dickens's growing infatuation with Ellen Ternan and Catherine's jealous command to Dickens to 'Go to your actress'. In the Foreword to the 1946 edition Bechhofer Roberts felt able to conclude that time had shown him to be right.

Andrew de Ternant wrote to *Notes and Queries* in 1933 stating that his friend, the composer Francesco Berger, had recalled spending evenings at the Ternan household in Ampthill Square during the 1860s, playing the piano while Dickens and Ellen sang duets.

It was in an article in the *Daily Express* (3 April 1934) entitled '98 Years Ago To-Day Charles Dickens Began His Honeymoon' that the ardent Dickensian Thomas Wright first proclaimed that Ellen had become Dickens's mistress, naming Canon Benham as the source of his information. In his *Life of Charles Dickens* which appeared the following year, Wright elaborated on the story of the liaison and again, using 'facts supplied by Canon Benham', stated that Dickens took a house for Ellen in

Ampthill Square (in her mother's name) and visited her there 'two or three times a week'. According to this version Ellen was a reluctant mistress who made Dickens miserable, and this misery could be found reflected in his later novels.

In 1876, Ellen had married George Wharton Robinson. It was while they were living at Margate, where Robinson ran a school, that Ellen first became friendly with the Anglican clergyman, William Benham, then vicar of Margate, and joined with him in giving Dickens recitations. According to Wright, she was still tormented with guilt about her affair with Dickens, and eventually 'disburdened her mind' to Benham. Benham died in 1910, Ellen in 1914, and Dickens's last surviving child, Sir Henry Dickens, in 1933. It was not until after their deaths that Wright felt able to publish the story, a fact which his detractors took to be suspicious rather than tactful. Warmly challenged by the Dickens Fellowship and others, Wright set out to collect additional evidence of the affair. His uncompleted autobiography, *Thomas Wright of Olney* (published posthumously in 1936) gives an account of his first meeting with Benham in 1893 and includes a reproduction of the letter Benham had written to him in 1897 mentioning that he possessed the pen Dickens had used to write *Edwin Drood*, and that it 'was given to me by the lady concerning whom [Dickens] quarrelled with his wife. This between ourselves.' Wright went to interview Benham and, he claims, 'I took down Canon Benham's words on this occasion. The original sheets of paper lie before me at the present moment.' These 'sheets of paper' seem now to have disappeared: they are not to be found among Wright's known surviving papers which are all now at The Dickens House Museum, London.

In the last chapter of his autobiography, Wright claimed that from 1867 Dickens, using the name Tringham, had been living *sub rosâ* with Ellen at Windsor Lodge, Linden Grove, Peckham. This assertion was based largely on second- or third-hand local gossip, and the evidence of the Peckham ratebooks which showed that in July 1867 the rates for Windsor Lodge had been paid by 'Frances Turnham' (presumably the rate-collector's misspelling of Frances Ternan, i.e. Mrs Ternan), the following year by 'Thomas Tringham' and from 1869 to 1870 by 'Charles Tringham'. Unfortunately, the Peckham ratebooks for the period were sent for pulping during World War II, so there is no way of verifying Wright's findings. Wright died before he could fully assemble his case, and he may have acquired some other evidence. At any rate, in a private letter to J.W.T. Ley and Walter Dexter he claimed that 'There were children'. (This letter is now in the possession of The Dickens House

Museum, London.) No evidence has yet come to light to substantiate this claim.

In 1939 the publication of Gladys Storey's *Dickens and Daughter* appeared to give independent confirmation of Wright's findings. Gladys Storey had been the close companion of Kate Perugini in her later years (Kate died in 1929), and had made notes of Kate's reminiscences. Claiming that Wright's work was unknown to her Miss Storey had recorded Kate's memories of her father's affair with Ellen. Kate had stated, apparently, that Dickens had set Ellen up in an establishment in Peckham, and referred to their 'resultant son (who died in infancy)'.

Ada Nisbet's *Dickens and Ellen Ternan* (1952) surveyed all the evidence factual and conjectural to date. In addition, she was able to publish (with the help of infra-red photography) passages which had been obliterated from Dickens's letters and which contained personal references to Ellen in Dickens's own hand (see above p. 209).

In *Dickens Incognito* (1959) Felix Aylmer produced a reading of the cryptographic entries in Dickens's pocket diary for 1867 which led him to discover that prior to Peckham Dickens and Ellen may have lived in Slough. Adopting the pseudonym 'John Tringham' Dickens became the tenant of a cottage in Slough High Street; the diary entries prove that Ellen did go to Slough, but do not confirm that she actually lived there.

Edward Wagenknecht's *Dickens and the Scandalmongers* (1965) contained a summary and consideration of the evidence and the interpretations made of it. Wagenknecht argued strongly that the evidence produced to date could not be regarded as amounting to proof positive that Ellen was Dickens's mistress. In an article in *The Dickensian* (1966) W.J. Carlton suggested that Ellen may have sometimes accompanied Dickens to his hideaway in Condette, France, during the 1860s, and this would account for the deliberate vagueness in his letters about his movements in France. In 1968 J.C. Reid wrote to *The Dickensian* quoting Gerald Dunn, an elderly resident of New Zealand, whose father Henry had worked as a carpenter in Slough. He remembered his father telling him that in about 1866 he had done some work for Mr Tringham, tenant of a house in Slough. Local residents had told Henry Dunn that Tringham was, in fact, Charles Dickens.

The most recent evidence to add to this catalogue is the discovery of the Gladys Storey papers. Gladys Storey died in 1978 and her papers are now in the possession of The Dickens House Museum, London. An account of them appeared in *The Dickensian* (1980). These papers include the original notes Miss Storey made for her book *Dickens and Daughter* and contain notes of Kate's recollections which were not included in the published version. Kate had apparently told Miss Storey that Ellen's son Geoffrey had gone to Sir Henry Dickens and asked him outright if his mother had been Dickens's mistress. Sir Henry had admitted that this had indeed been the case, and to this note Miss Storey had added the marginal note, 'Henry F. Dickens told me this . . . on Sunday September 8 1928'. If such a conversation between Geoffrey and Sir Henry did take place, it would explain why Geoffrey maintained a strict silence over the Wright revelations. On a separate piece of paper Miss Storey had recorded, 'Sir Henry and I . . . talked about Ellen Ternan – there was a boy but it died . . .'. Also amongst the Gladys Storey papers is a copy of a letter of January 1934 from C.E.S. Chambers to Walter Dexter concerning letters, once in his possession, from Dickens to W.H. Wills, his sub-editor on *Household Words* and *All The Year Round* and his confidential man of business. (Chambers was the great-nephew of Wills's wife.) These letters contained 'instructions to Wills written from America during Dickens's second visit, regarding the welfare of a certain lady, then apparently sickening for her confinement'. Chambers had sent these letters to Sir Henry Dickens and nothing was heard of them again. In the same edition of *The Dickensian*, in a letter to the editor, Katharine M. Longley points out that at the time of Dickens's second visit to America, Ellen was in Florence, and suggests that the lady 'sickening for her confinement' may have been Dickens's daughter-in-law Bessie, whose child was born on 7 February 1868. Concerning the baby boy who died, Katharine Longley suggests that Sir Henry may have found a reference in the Chambers letters and perhaps leapt to the wrong conclusion. Such a reference might have been to Ellen's cousin's boy, born January 1867 and died September the same year.

In the 1981 volume of *The Dickensian* Katharine Longley shed some more light on the subject of Dickens and Slough. In an article entitled 'Dickens Incognito' she pointed out that Dickens's lifelong obsession with adopting pseudonyms was made all the more necessary in later years when, as a public figure, he required privacy and solitude. She added, in a letter to the editor later in the same volume, that her search of the ratebooks showed there was a second cottage in Church Street, Slough, held at first by 'Tringham' and later by 'Turnan' in 1866. Early in the following year, Ellen's sister Fanny had joined Ellen and her mother in Slough and Katharine Longley draws the conclusion that one cottage was the home of the Ternans, the other a retreat of Dickens's.

Abbreviations

ATYR	*All The Year Round*
CP	*Collected Papers*, 2 vols., The Nonesuch Press (1938)
Dksn	*The Dickensian*
DNB	*Dictionary of National Biography*
Forster	John Forster's *The Life of Charles Dickens*, ed. J.W.T. Ley (1928)
HW	*Household Words*
	Edgar Johnson's *Charles Dickens. His Tragedy and Triumph*, 2 vols. (1952)
MP	*Miscellaneous Papers*, ed. B.W. Matz
Nonesuch	Nonesuch Edition of *The Letters of Charles Dickens*, 3 vols. (1938)
Pilgrim	Pilgrim Edition of *The Letters of Charles Dickens*, 5 vols. (1965-81)
Storey	Gladys Storey's *Dickens and Daughter* (1939)
TLS	*Times Literary Supplement*
Wright	Thomas Wright's *The Life of Charles Dickens* (1935)

Novels and Stories

[*References are to volumes of the Oxford Illustrated Dickens*]

AN	*American Notes* (1842)
BH	*Bleak House* (1852-3)
BR	*Barnaby Rudge* (1841)
CB	*Christmas Books* (1843-8)
CHE	*A Child's History of England* (1852-4). (Bound with *Master Humphrey's Clock*)
CS	*Christmas Stories* (1850-67). (This volume includes 'The Lazy Tour of Two Idle Apprentices')

DC	*David Copperfield* (1849-50)
DS	*Dombey and Son* (1846-8)
HT	*Hard Times* (1854)
LD	*Little Dorrit* (1855-7)
MC	*Martin Chuzzlewit* (1843-4)
MED	*The Mystery of Edwin Drood* (1870)
MHC	*Master Humphrey's Clock* (1840-1)
NN	*Nicholas Nickleby* (1838-9)
OCS	*The Old Curiosity Shop* (1840-1)
OMF	*Our Mutual Friend* (1864-5)
PP	*Pickwick Papers* (1836-7)
RP	See *UT & RP*
SB	*Sketches by Boz* (1833-9). (This volume includes *Sketches of Young Gentlemen* and *Sketches of Young Couples*)
TTC	*A Tale of Two Cities* (1859)
UT & RP	*The Uncommercial Traveller and Reprinted Pieces* (1860-9). (This volume includes *To Be Read at Dusk*, *Hunted Down*, *Holiday Romance* and *George Silverman's Explanation*)

Fuller details of other works cited are given in the Select Bibliography.

Notes

Introduction

1 'They are . . . from their own constitution, and from the station they occupy in the world, strictly speaking, relative creatures' (Sarah Stickney Ellis, *The Women of England*, ch. 6).
2 Gladys Storey, *Dickens and Daughter*, p.100.
3 In Lionel Trilling's introduction to *LD* (Oxford Illustrated Dickens, p. xvi), for example, he refers to Amy as 'the Paraclete in female form'.

I Experience into Art

Chapter 1: Mother and Son

1 *TTC*, Book II, ch. 21.

2 Carlton papers, shorthand notebook commenced 1 March 1949, p. 7. In the possession of The Dickens House Museum.

3 For most of the information in this and the next two paragraphs I have drawn on the following sources: Storey, pp. 31 ff.; Leslie C. Staples, 'The Dickens Ancestry: Some New Discoveries. II', *Dksn*, vol. 45 (1949), pp. 179-88; Angus Easson, 'John Dickens and the Navy Pay Office', *Dksn*, vol. 70 (1974), pp. 35-45.

4 Pilgrim, vol. 1, p. 16, note. The Pilgrim Editors are quoting Thomas Powell's 'Leaves from My Life', *Frank Leslie's Sunday Magazine*, Aug. 1886.

5 Storey, p. 25. Recent research has shown that there was in fact no ball at Portsea on the night of 6 February 1812 according to the local newspapers, but there was one on 3 February, and it was perhaps this that Elizabeth attended. See Michael Allen, 'The Dickens Family at Portsmouth, 1807-1814', *Dksn*, vol. 77 (1981), pp. 131-43.

6 For Elizabeth's calling her husband 'D' see Storey, p. 109; her letter to Samuel Haydon, undated but written from 33 Ampthill Square, Mornington Place, Hampstead Road, is in The Dickens House Museum and is quoted here by permission of the Trustees. Elizabeth's devoted loyalty to John is all the more impressive if we consider the implications of what Dickens wrote about his father, in the autumn of 1835, to his solicitor friend, Mitton. The family were about to be turned out of their Bentinck Street lodgings for non-payment of rent. Dickens wrote: ' . . . my father went out yesterday accompanied by Alfred, to endeavour to get some money. . . . He sent the boy home to say he had been unsuccessful, and has not made his appearance all night, or forwarded a message of any kind./I own that at present his absence does not give me any very great uneasiness, knowing how apt he is to get out of the way when anything goes wrong. . . .' (Pilgrim, vol. 1, pp. 43-4).

7 Robert Langton, *The Childhood and Youth of Charles Dickens*, p. 26.

8 First published in *ATYR* (8 Sept. 1860) and reprinted in *UT*. It is, as Angus Wilson comments *(The World of Charles Dickens*, p. 28), somewhat difficult to reconcile the nurse remembered in 'Nurse's Stories' with Mary Weller as we learn about her from Langton (who interviewed her in 1888, shortly before her death at the age of 84). The nurse of the essay ('Her name was Mercy, though she had none on me') is remembered as having had a 'fiendish enjoyment' in terrifying her young charge with her macabre tales, defying him to disbelieve them by always pretending that they were about things that had actually happened to her own relations. Five years earlier, in 'The Holly Tree' (*CS*), Dickens (the narrator of the story is clearly the

thinnest of disguises for the author himself) had recalled his childhood self 'at the knee of a sallow woman with a fishy eye, an aquiline nose and a green gown,' whose speciality was 'a dismal narrative' of a landlord with Sweeney Todd-like proclivities. This woman, too, had taken 'a Ghoulish pleasure . . . in terrifying me to the utmost confines of my reason' and would assert that either she herself or her close relations had actually undergone the hair-raising experiences she related. Making all due allowance for humorous exaggeration and fantastication, I believe that the repetition in such close detail of this character points to her having had a real-life original in Dickens's childhood. But Mary Weller was only eight years older than Dickens and it sounds in these passages as though he is recalling someone decidedly adult with himself as very young indeed ('at her knee'), not the schoolboy remembered by Mary as running downstairs to her with his friend George Stroughill and saying, 'Now, Mary, clear the kitchen, we are going to have such a game . . .' (Langton, op. cit, p. 25). Against this, however, it could, I suppose, be argued that he was apparently not too old, when she had charge of him, for her to lull him to sleep by humming the Evening Hymn (Langton, op. cit, p. 29). The strongest argument, it seems to me, against Mary Weller's having been the story-telling nursemaid is that she said nothing at all about such activity to Langton when she was reminiscing about her time with the Dickens family. I think Mary probably did not enter Elizabeth Dickens's service until she was fourteen or fifteen, Charles being then six or seven, and that it was a predecessor, perhaps really named Mercy, who used to stimulate and terrorize the imaginative little boy with her ghosts and marvels.

9   Forster, p. 4; *DC*, ch. 4.
10 Reprinted in part in Philip Collins (ed.), *Dickens: Interviews and Recollections*, vol. 1, pp. 129-31.
11 Forster, p. 32.
12 Forster, p. 3.
13 Eleanor E. Christian, 'Recollections of Charles Dickens, His Family and Friends', *Temple Bar*, vol. 82 (1888), p. 483. An earlier version, 'Reminiscences of Charles Dickens: From a Young Lady's Diary', had appeared in *The Englishwoman's Domestic Magazine* in 1871. Passages from both versions are reprinted in Philip Collins (ed.), op. cit., vol. 1, pp. 33-44.
14 Forster, p. 25.
15 Marcus Stone, Autograph Notes concerning Dickens (MS, The Dickens House). First printed in Michael Slater (ed.), *Catalogue of the Suzannet Charles Dickens Collection*, 1975, p. 157. A slightly differently worded version of the incident appears in Stone's 'Some Recollections of Dickens', *Dksn*, vol. 61 (1910), p. 63.
16 Forster pp. 13, 12. For details about Huffam see 'The Huffams, the Barrows and the Admiralty' by 'Ephesian' (C.E. Bechhofer Roberts), *Dksn*, vol. 24 (1928), pp. 263-6.

17 Letter to Ellen Nussey, 14 Oct. 1846 *(The Brontës. Their Lives, Friend-ships and Correspondence*, ed. T.J. Wise and J.A. Symington, 1932, p. 115).

18 Forster, p. 13.

19 op. cit., p. 51.

20 Forster, p. 20. John and Elizabeth Dickens must have read *David Copper-field*, one assumes, and, if so, could not have failed to recognize the source of David's outrage when he is sent to work at Murdstone and Grinby's. But they were no doubt only too happy to suppress all memories of the Marshalsea and that difficult period in the family's life for their own sakes as much as for Dickens's.

21 Forster, pp. 25, 27, 28.

22 *OT*, ch. 18.

23 See p. 53 of his discussion of *OT* in *Dickens and the Twentieth Century*, ed. Gross and Pearson.

24 According to Charles Dickens, Junior, in his preface to the 1892 'Bio-graphical' edition of *Copperfield*, Catherine Dickens, having had the auto-biographical fragment read to her 'in strict confidence', besought Dickens not to publish it 'on the ground that he had spoken with undue harshness of his father, and, especially, of his mother'.

25 Forster, pp. 25, 35. Philip Collins has drawn my attention to the fact that apart from this reference in the autobiography there is no other evidence that Dickens ever had any yearning to become 'learned' or 'distinguished at a grammar-school, and going to Cambridge'. He suggests that such dreams might be appropriate for an eminent writer to say that his younger self had had, but that even in *David Copperfield* and *Great Expectations* there is no suggestion of scholarly ambitions. See also Philip Collins's essay 'Pip the Obscure' *(Critical Quarterly*, vol. 19, no. 4), an interesting comparison of Pip with Hardy's Jude, in which he observes that 'neither David nor his creator showed any ambition to become, when circumstances changed, a "learned man" in any sense that Jude would have recognized. Rather, like Pip and other Dickens heroes, they had that more commonplace ambition "to get on in life" ' (p. 32).

26 Matthew Arnold, *Culture and Anarchy*, 1869, ch. 2. Arnold calls Mrs Gooch's exhortation 'the Divine Injunction "Be ye Perfect" done into British'.

27 Forster, p. 35. Wilkie Collins told the American diplomat John Bigelow that he thought Forster was 'very injudicious in publishing what Dickens says about his mother, who after all, behaved quite sensibly in insisting that this boy should contribute toward the family support by sticking labels on blacking bottles so long as that was the best remunerated work he could do' (quoted by Arthur A. Adrian from Bigelow's diary in *Georgina Hogarth and the Dickens Circle*, p. 185). Forster's 'injudiciousness', if such it was,

certainly played into the hands of anyone who, like Dr John Brown, author of *Rab and his Friends,* was bent on denigrating Dickens: justifying to Ruskin his description of Dickens as 'one of the hardest hearted of men', Brown pointed to the evidence Forster had provided of Dickens's anger 'obviously cherished through life at his struggling, starving mother' (quoted by Tom Johnstone in 'Decidedly This Side Idolatry: Dr John Brown and Dickens', *Dksn,* vol. 74, 1978, p. 101).

28 F.G. Kitton, *Charles Dickens by Pen and Pencil,* vol. 1, p. 129 ('Mr Edward Blackmore's Recollections').
29 See Pilgrim, vol. 1, pp. 124, 137, 518, 524-5.
30 Pilgrim, vol. 1, p. 521; for quotations from Mrs Davey and Powell see notes 10 and 4, above.
31 Alfred Dickens to Mrs John Dickens, Derwent Cottage, Sunday Morning (MS, The Dickens House Museum, quoted by permission of the Trustees). The strong family affection that centred on Elizabeth is further illustrated by a letter she wrote on 12 April 1851 to a former schoolfellow of Dickens's who had written to express condolences on John Dickens's death. Elizabeth explains that she is staying with her younger daughter, Letitia Austin, whose 'affectionate kindness, and unceasing solicitude during the short weeks of my dear Husband's illness is and has been a great solace to me'. After a while, she continues, she has promised to go to Alfred's and mentions his '3 darling Children always a great source of happiness to me' (quoted by W.J. Carlton in his 'A Friend of Dickens's Boyhood', *Dksn,* vol. 66, 1970, p. 12).
32 Pilgrim, vol. 1, pp. 528 and 560.
33 Eleanor E. Christian, op. cit., pp. 483-4.
34 Nonesuch, vol. 2, p. 626.
35 Pilgrim, vol. 4, p. 313 (the letters and words within square brackets are conjectural, having been supplied by the Pilgrim Editors, the original MS being torn).
36 Pilgrim, vol. 1, p. 85.
37 My quotations from Johnson's *Life of Savage* are taken from *Lives of the English Poets,* ed. G. Birkbeck Hill, 1905, vol. 2.
38 There were other aspects of Savage's story, too, such as his ending in a debtor's prison, which must have stirred Dickens as well as the account of a mother's cruelty. See my article, 'How Dickens "Told" Catherine about His Past', *Dksn,* vol. 75 (1979), pp. 3-6.
39 Nonesuch, vol. 3, pp. 154, 156, 172, 192-3.
40 To W.H. Wills, 14 Sept. 1863 (unpublished).
41 Forster, p. 10.
42 Forster, p. 552.
43 Quoted in *The Evening News,* 27 Sept. 1910.
44 Pilgrim, vol. 4, p. 5.
45 Forster, p. 551.

46 In a letter to C.R. Rideal, quoted by Wright, p. 219.
47 Introduction to the Penguin English Library edition of *NN*, 1978, pp. 26-7.
48 Forster, p. 497.
49 cf. Nina Burgis's Introduction to the Clarendon Edition of *DC* (1981), p. xxxiv: 'David's feckless "family" could be laughed at and enjoyed because they were not in fact his family or responsible for his plight'.
50 *DC*, ch. 11.
51 *DC*, ch. 2.
52 *NN*, ch. 19.
53 *DC*, ch. 12.
54 Dickens actually puts Elizabeth's phrase about exerting herself into Mrs Micawber's mouth in connection with her academic enterprise. (*DC*, ch. 11): 'Poor Mrs Micawber! She said she had tried to exert herself; and so, I have no doubt, she had. The centre of the street door was perfectly covered with a great brass-plate, on which was engraved "Mrs Micawber's Boarding Establishment for Young Ladies"....' The second echo of Elizabeth's abortive school in Dickens's fiction occurs in *OMF*, Book I, ch. 4, when Mrs Wilfer (who is not otherwise connected with Elizabeth) reports to her husband that the 'Ladies' School' plate on their front-door has been removed in consequence of never having been paid for.
55 *DC*, ch. 11.
56 *DC*, ch. 12.
57 See below, p. 35.
58 Forster, p. 29.
59 Deborah Thomas, 'Dickens's Mrs Lirriper and the Evolution of a Feminine Stereotype', *Dickens Studies Annual*, vol. 6 (1977), pp. 154-66.
60 'George Silverman's Explanation', ch. 3. This story is included in the *UT & RP* vol. of the Oxford Illustrated Dickens.

Chapter 2: Brother and Sister

1 Forster, p. 2.
2 'Our School', *HW*, 11 Oct. 1851; collected in *RP*. Dickens surely had this objectionable little dog in mind when he described the end of the magic fishbone in Part II of his *Holiday Romance* (1868), a series of tales supposedly written by schoolchildren: ' "It only remains," said Grandmaria in conclusion, "to make an end of the fish-bone."/So she took it from the hand of the Princess Alicia, and it instantly flew down the throat of the dreadful little snapping pug-dog next door, and choked him, and he expired in convulsions'. (I am grateful to Mrs Hazel Shepherd for drawing my attention to this passage.)
3 'New Year's Day', *HW*, 1 Jan. 1859; collected in *MP*. 'On what other early New Year's Day can I possibly have been an innocent accomplice in the secreting – in a coal cellar too – of a man with a wooden leg! There was no man with a wooden leg, in the circle of my acknowledged and lawful

relations and friends. Yet, I clearly remember that we stealthily conducted the man with the wooden leg – whom we knew intimately – into the coal cellar, and that, in getting him over the coals to hide him behind some partition that was beyond, his wooden leg bored itself in among the small coals, and his hat flew off, and he fell backward and lay prone: a spectacle of helplessness. . . . I have not the least idea who "we" were, except that I had a little sister for another innocent accomplice, and that there must have been a servant girl for principal. . . .'

4 Forster, p. 514.
5 Robert Langton, *The Childhood and Youth of Dickens*, p. 34.
6 'Birthday Celebrations', *ATYR*, 6 June 1863; collected in *UT*.
7 Forster, p. 10.
8 See William J. Carlton, 'Fanny Dickens: Pianist and Vocalist', *Dksn*, vol. 53 (1957), pp. 133-43. I have drawn widely on Carlton's article for details of Fanny's musical career.
9 Dickens is probably making an affectionately teasing allusion to Fanny (using his other sister's name) in his short story, 'Sentiment', specially written for *SB* First Series (1836), when he writes of 'the brilliant execution of Miss Laetitia Parsons, whose performance of "The Recollections of Ireland" was universally declared to be almost equal to that of Moscheles himself'. Mr Carlton points out, in his *Dksn* article already cited (p. 135), that the playbill for a benefit concert for the actor John Pritt Harley at Drury Lane Theatre on 29 May 1827 includes the announcement, 'Miss Dickens (of the Royal Academy of Music), the celebrated pupil of Mr Moscheles, will perform her master's "Recollections of Ireland".'
10 Forster, p. 10.
11 Forster, p. 34.
12 Carlton, op. cit. p. 135.
13 *DC*, ch. 38.
14 Forster, p. 60.
15 Pilgrim, vol. 1, p. 25.
16 Storey, p. 107.
17 Nonesuch, vol. 2, p. 633.
18 Quoted by Carlton, op. cit., p. 138.
19 Frances R. Hullah, *Life of John Hullah*, 1886, p. 13. Quoted by Carlton, op. cit., p. 136.
20 His younger sister, Letitia, married a friend of his, Henry Austin, just two months before Fanny married Burnett (1837). Dickens's feelings towards Letitia seem always to have been those of an affectionate brother and a large collection of letters from him to her, mostly as yet unpublished, in the Pierpont Morgan Library, New York, show how greatly he concerned himself about her welfare after the death of Austin in 1861, successfully exerting himself to obtain a government pension for her on the grounds of Austin's public services as an engineer. Although Eleanor Christian (*Temple*

Bar, vol. 82, p. 483) thought Letitia 'not so full of fun as the rest of the family', a long obituary of her in *The Illustrated London News*, 8 April 1893 (drawn to my attention by Professor Kathleen Tillotson) notes that 'she had all the quickness and energy characteristic of the family, and her sense of humour remained keen and bright throughout'. Dickens's son, Henry, recalled her as 'A dear, good soul . . . Betsey Trotwood all over, both in looks and manner. She loved to be amused and, I am afraid, on the occasion of her visits I made a bit of a mountebank of myself in order to give her pleasure' (Sir Henry Dickens, *Recollections*, 1934, p. 28f.). She was clearly an exemplary daughter and sister. Her brother Frederick wrote to her after their father's death, '. . . such unwearying and unselfish devotion as yours in the hour of such painful trial I could hardly have imagined' and, before that, she had been a wonderful nurse to the dying Fanny: 'Believe me', Frederick told her, 'that the recollection of what you went through for poor dear Fanny and the consolation and comfort you must have afforded poor dear Father, will never be forgotten by me . . .'. (MS, The Dickens House, quoted here by permission of the Trustees.) Admirable as Letitia was and affectionately as Dickens regarded her, she was not, however, central to his early emotional history in the way that Fanny was. She was four years his junior and that in childhood is a very big gap.

21   F.G. Kitton, *Charles Dickens: By Pen and Pencil,* vol. 1, p. 137.
22   Pilgrim, vol. 3, p. 148; Pilgrim, vol. 4, p. 52; unpublished letter to Georgina Hogarth, 15 Oct, 1861; Nonesuch, vol. 3, p. 252. It should be added that, although Dickens thus allowed some serio-comic exasperation with Burnett to appear in writing to Catherine and Georgina he seems always to have been kind and affectionate about him in letters to Fanny or to Burnett himself. This can be seen from some recently discovered transcripts of letters from Dickens to Fanny and to Burnett now at The Dickens House. Writing to Fanny on 31 March 1848 he suggests that Burnett should attend the dinner to celebrate the completion of the publication of *DS* as it might help to promote subscriptions for some songs he is publishing (he could sing them at the dinner): he sends £5 to cover Burnett's expenses and expresses himself very warmly about his brother-in-law. Writing to Burnett on 5 Sept. 1848 after Fanny's death, Dickens refers to his promise to his sister to help Burnett and the children and says that he 'never can forget the patience gentleness and endurance of your affection for her'. He does allude, however, to their difference in religion and begs Burnett not to let his sons fall into the hands of very *bigoted* Dissenters. Another letter of 18 Sept. 1858 reassures Burnett that he (Dickens) is not upset by the news of Burnett's remarriage (Burnett was evidently embarrassed about not having told Dickens personally about this): 'Believe me', Dickens writes, 'I have never had an unkind thought of you. I was very glad to hear of your marrying again – thought it most natural and right . . .'.
23   In his *Memories of the Past: Records of Ministerial Life* (1883) James

Griffin writes: 'He [Burnett] was blessed with the instruction and influence of a pious grandmother and aunt, who inculcated on him the duty and importance of daily reading the Bible, for which he always expressed in later life his deep gratitude to God. When he was a mere child he was sent to live for a while with his grandmother at Gosport. . . . That remarkable man, Richard Knill [1787-1857; a very celebrated and energetic Noncon-formist missionary who worked in both India and Russia, founding a Protestant Bible Society in St Petersburg], was then . . . lodging at the house of Henry's grandmother. Little Henry was not overlooked by the loving-hearted and fervid missionary . . .'.

24 Griffin, op. cit., p. 171.
25 Letter from S. Patton in *The British Weekly,* 4 Jan. 1911: ' . . . from conversations I had with [Burnett] I gathered that Dickens never forgave him for leaving the stage'.
26 Griffin, op. cit., pp. 177-8, 200.
27 *PP,* ch. 22.
28 Griffin, op. cit., pp. 197-8.
29 Pilgrim, vol. 3, pp. 188-9.
30 The letter is printed in an appendix to Pilgrim, vol. 3 (p. 629).
31 'Recollections of Charles Dickens', *Temple Bar,* vol. 2 (1888), p. 483.
32 Forster, p. 522.
33 'New Year's Day', *HW,* 1 Jan. 1859; collected in *MP.*
34 Forster, p. 34.
35 *CB, The Haunted Man,* ch. 1.
36 As pointed out by Kathleen Tillotson in her lecture, 'The Middle Years: from the *Carol* to *Copperfield*' (*Dickens Memorial Lectures,* 1970, p. 13).
37 *CB, A Christmas Carol,* Stave 2.
38 Griffin, op. cit., p. 209. According to his father, little Harry was 'happy as a bird' on his sick-bed and 'insisted on having his little much-thumbed Bible placed ready to his hand. The Four Gospels seemed to him a kind of picnic-feast . . .' (Kitton, op. cit., pp. 136-7).
39 *DS,* end of ch. 8.
40 Forster, p. 27.
41 It seems likely, as Professor Alan Horsman suggests in his Introduction to the Clarendon Edition of *DS* (1974), p. xxv, that, despite the naming of Mrs Roylance in connection with Mrs Pipchin in Dickens's plan for the third monthly number of *DS,* Mrs Pipchin 'is not a portrait of one person only' since Dickens later told his American friend and publisher, James T. Fields that, 'When he was delineating the character of Mrs Pipchin, he had in his mind an old lodging-house keeper in an English watering-place where he was living with his father and mother when he was but two years old. After the book was written he sent it to his sister, who wrote back at once: "Good heavens! what does this mean? you have painted our lodging-house keeper, and you were but two years old at that time!" ' (James T. Fields,

Yesterdays with Authors, 1872, pp. 233-4). In 1814, when Dickens was two, the family resided briefly at 39 Wish Street (now King's Road) in Southsea (see *Dksn,* vol. 58, 1962, p. 89, and vol. 73, 1977, pp. 55-6). Mrs Roylance is not recorded as having lived there and it may be that some of the more unamiable features of Mrs Pipchin derived from whomever the Dickens's Southsea landlady was rather than from her. Her grand-daughter's husband wrote to Forster, after the publication of the first volume of his *Life of Dickens,* protesting vehemently against the identification of Mrs Pipchin with Mrs Roylance who was 'a lady in every sense of the word, a true Christian, and brimful of the milk of human kindness' (quoted by W.J. Carlton in his 'Postscripts to Forster', *Dksn,* vol. 58, 1962, pp. 87-92). Mrs Pipchin, however, appears again by name in one of Dickens's essays for *HW,* 'New Year's Day' (published 1 Jan. 1859; collected in *MP).* She is described there as a 'grim and unsympathetic old personage of the female gender, flavoured with musty dry lavender, dressed in black crape' who took him when he was a small boy to buy a present in a toy bazaar in Soho Square, London. This must relate to 1816/17 when the Dickens family were living in London and Charles was five, and the old lady in question does seem likely to have been Mrs Roylance who had been 'long known' to the family when she received Charles as a lodger seven years later, so perhaps the identification with Mrs Pipchin need not rest entirely on that character as presented in *DS.*

42 Forster, p. 479.
43 Forster, pp. 28, 32.
44 *DS,* ch. 12.
45 Forster, pp. 513-14.
46 Jack Lindsay, *Charles Dickens. A Biographical and Critical Study,* p. 301.
47 *LD,* Book I, ch. 5.
48 *LD,* Book I, ch. 20.
49 See above, p. 9.

Chapter 3: Lucy

1 'Dullborough Town', *ATYR,* 30 June 1860; reprinted in *UT.*
2 Forster, pp. 8-9.
3 Langton, *The Childhood and Youth of Dickens,* pp. 23-4.
4 Johnson, p. 13.
5 'Birthday Celebrations', *ATYR,* 6 June 1863; reprinted in *UT.*
6 Langton, p. 23. Langton asserts that 'some characteristics' of George 'are reproduced as Steerforth in *David Copperfield,* but this seems to me to be a rather desperate instance of hunting for originals of Dickens's characters.
7 It has been claimed that the Joe Specks of the Dullborough essay is identifiable as Dr John Dan Brown, a Rochester doctor who was the son of the Government Medical Officer in charge of the convicts in the 'hulks'

(prison-ships) on the Medway. See Henry Smetham, 'John Dan Brown. A Boyhood Friend of Dickens', *Dksn*, vol. 53 (1937), pp. 52-3.

8 'A Christmas Tree', *HW* Christmas Number for 1850; reprinted in *CS*.

9 *DC*, ch. 3.

10 *SB*, *Sketches of Young Couples*, 'The Young Couple' and 'The Old Couple'.

11 *DC*, ch. 3.

12 ibid.

13 See Philip Collins (ed.), *Charles Dickens: the Public Readings*, 1975, pp. 168-9. Professor Collins reported in the *Dksn* (vol. 67, 1971, p. 42) that he had found modern audiences before whom he had performed Dickens's reading version of the story surprisingly appreciative of it. One of his auditors believed the story to be 'a remarkable demonstration of Dickens's artistic control – precisely because what might otherwise be a nauseatingly sentimental story was made acceptable, indeed delightful, through his technique of having it told by Boots, a Sam-Wellerish character whose wit and tone undercut the sentiment'. My own view is that Boots as Dickens presents him serves only to intensify the sentimentality.

14 Another reminiscence of his childhood that Dickens weaves into this story is the singing of the Evening Hymn (see note 8 to ch. 1, above) which Lucy's mother sings every evening to cheer and console her fellow-survivors in the boats.

15 'New Year's Day', *HW*, 1 Jan. 1859 (reprinted in *MP*); and 'Birthday Celebrations', *ATYR*, 6 June 1863 (reprinted in *UT*).

16 See his marvellously detailed evocation in 'A Christmas Tree' *(CS)* of the impact that *The Arabian Nights* had had on his childish imagination and experience.

17 It is perhaps relevant to note that the school to which Dickens went after the blacking-factory period was in the Hampstead Road (which figures as the promenade for the school in this story). Dickens would have drawn a sharp distinction between his 'innocent' Chatham school self and his 'experienced' Hampstead Road school self. The latter would certainly have had a more knowing attitude towards seraglios.

18 This is all a striking example of a somewhat uncomfortable aspect of Dickens's art fiercely attacked by John Carey – the construction of fictional children purely as 'an adult amenity': 'Dickens is pretending that children are small adults. Their thoughts, he makes out, are like those of adults, only purer. They still believe the things which adults would find it comforting to believe, if only they could bring themselves to be fatuous enough. Such plastic children bring tears to the grown-up eye, because they represent an innocence which the grown-up wrongly imagines he once possessed himself. Tears of this kind are especially enjoyable because they are tears of self-pity without seeming to be so.' (*The Violent Effigy*, p. 136).

19 *CS*, 'The Haunted House', last para. of 'The Ghost in Master B's Room'.

20   See below, pp. 210-11.
21   *CS*, 'A Christmas Tree'.
22   Storey, p. 93 (quoting Dickens's daughter, Kate Perugini).

Chapter 4: Maria

1   Pilgrim, vol. 4, p. 346.
2   G.L. Du Cann, *The Love Lives of Charles Dickens*, p. 34.
3   Nonesuch, vol. 2, p. 634.
4   See pp. 12-14 of *Two Centuries. The Story of David Lloyd Piggot and Company of London, Tea and Coffee Merchants 1760-1960*, Harley Publishing Co., London, 1960.
5   'Birthday Celebrations', *ATYR*, 6 June 1863: reprinted in *UT*.
6   'The Bill of Fare' was first printed in Walter Dexter's *The Love Romance of Dickens*, pp. 23-40. It was subsequently included in vol. 2 of the *Collected Papers* in the Nonesuch Dickens, 1938 (pp. 284-93).
7   Johnson, p. 72; Pilgrim, vol. 1, p. 16, note 2.
8   A letter to Maria dated 28 April 1830 from her brother Alfred is addressed to her 'à Madame Martinez, 14 Rue de Berry, Paris'; cited in *Piccadilly Notes* (No. 5, p. 5), ed. J. Stonehouse and published by Henry Sotheran, Ltd.
9   Nonesuch, vol. 2, p. 627.
10 Dickens's contributions to Maria's album were first printed by Comte Alain de Suzannet in his 'Maria Beadnell's Album', *Dksn*, vol. 31 (1935), pp. 161-8. The album itself is now in The Dickens House Museum, London, and quotations from all the verses in it, by Dickens and by others, are here made by permission of the Trustees of the Museum.
11 *DC*, ch. 26.
12 ibid.
13 *GE*, ch. 38.
14 First published in *Dksn*, vol. 68 (1972), pp. 162-3.
15 This business about gloves must be what Dickens was referring to when he wrote to Maria twenty-four years later after she had commissioned him to make some purchases for her in Paris: 'I need not tell you', he wrote, 'that it [the commission] shall be executed to the letter – with as much interest as I once matched a little pair of gloves for you which I recollect were blue ones. (I wonder whether people generally wore blue gloves when I was nineteen or whether it was only you!)' (Nonesuch, vol. 2, p. 628.)
16 Nonesuch, vol. 2, p. 627.
17 We can get, I believe, a pretty fair idea of young Dickens's standing as a guest in the eyes of Mr and Mrs Beadnell from the sketch, 'The New Year' in *SB*. Young Mr Tupple energetically renders himself useful and agreeable to his self-satisfied hosts, Mr and Mrs Dobble, by his entertaining qualities ('. . .Ma says he shall be asked to every future dinner-party, if it's only to

talk to people between the courses, and distract their attention when there's any unexpected delay in the kitchen').

18 Pilgrim, vol. 1, p. 14.

19 J.H. Stonehouse in the second no. of his *Green Leaves. New Chapters in the Life of Charles Dickens* states (p. 31), 'There is a certain amount of evidence to prove that it was the mothers of the two lovers, rather than the fathers, who were averse to the continuance of the engagement between the two young people' but he does not tell us what this 'evidence' is. Possibly Stonehouse found it in the diary of Maria's elder sister, Margaret, to which he had been given access by Margaret's grand-daughter.

20 Pilgrim, vol. 1, p. 8.

21 Nonesuch vol. 2, p. 628.

22 Nonesuch, vol. 2, p. 635.

23 *DC*, ch. 38 (Oxford Illustrated Dickens text corrected here by reference to the Clarendon Ed. of *DC*).

24 *GE*, ch. 8.

25 Pilgrim, vol. 1, pp. 16-17.

26 Pilgrim, vol. 1, p. 25.

27 See above, p. 28. Dickens had described Mary Anne in 'The Bill of Fare' as 'the greatest tormenter, that I e'er knew' who 'On every flirtation . . . kept a sharp eye': 'She to each little secret always held the candle,/And I think she liked a small bit of scandal'. Beneath some lines of Moore's that Mary Anne copied into Maria's album someone has rather pointedly written, 'What is better than the art of pleasing? Pleasing without art'. She was evidently quite as accomplished a flirt as Maria and between the two of them they must have had great fun with the goaded and bewildered young Dickens.

28 Pilgrim, vol. 1, p. 29.

29 Nonesuch, vol. 2, p. 633.

30 Pilgrim, vol. 4, p. 346.

31 Autograph note signed 'M.S. Knox' and dated 9 Dec. 1933, now in the Humanities Research Center, University of Texas at Austin, and quoted here by permission of the University of Texas. Miss Knox, a grand-niece of Georgina Ross, wrote this memorandum for the Comte de Suzannet who had purchased Georgina's album at Sotheby's, 14 Nov. 1933. Suzannet published the gist of it in a letter to the *Dksn* (vol. 30, 1934, p. 151). See also W.J. Carlton, 'Dickens and the Ross Family', *Dksn*, vol. 51 (1955), pp. 58-66.

32 Wright, p. 53.

33 *NN*, ch. 9.

34 Elsewhere in *SB* Dickens notes, 'The word "dear" among girls is frequently synonymous with "wretch" ' ('The Steam Excursion').

35 *SB*, 'Sentiment'.

36 *NN*, ch. 17.

37 *NN*, ch. 23.

38   Pilgrim, vol. 1, p. 615.
39   Pilgrim, vol. 4, p. 462.
40   MS, The Dickens House Museum, quoted by permission of the Trustees. This memorandum was formerly in the possession of Lady Marie Dickens, widow of Sir Henry Fielding Dickens; she allowed Walter Dexter to quote from it in his *The Love Romance of Charles Dickens*, pp. 79 and 115-16. Dexter, however, both misreads the date of the memorandum and transcribes it very carelessly. Nor does he seem to have appreciated the significance of the document as evidence that Dickens did see Maria at least once between the end of their affair in 1833 and her re-entry into his life in 1855.
41   Nonesuch, vol. 2, p. 633.
42   Arthur Adrian indicates (*Georgina Hogarth and the Dickens Circle*, p. 238) what it was that must have prompted Georgina early in 1906 to make a memorandum for the family's information of her authoritative version of the story of Dickens and Maria, viz., the sale in 1905 of Dickens's letters to Maria by Maria's daughter, Ella. The letters were bought by an American collector and soon appeared (1908) in a volume published by the Boston Bibliophile Society, a book which Georgina succeeded in having banned in England. She must have seen herself as arming the family with the truth in anticipation of unwelcome publicity being given to this episode of Dickens's life. Being an old lady of seventy-nine, Georgina, not surprisingly, was a little vague in her recollections. Dickens and his wife returned from America in 1842, as she says, but the Winters did not marry until 1845 so there must have been more of a gap than she seems to suggest between the return and the visit. Moreover, there was no such street in London as 'Finsbury Crescent'; Georgina was perhaps confusedly remembering the Winters' later address, Artillery Place, off Finsbury Square.
43   All quotations in this paragraph up to this point are taken from Dickens's 1855 letters to Maria. See Nonesuch, vol. 2, pp. 627-33.
44   Forster, p. 35.
45   *DC*, ch. 21.
46   Kate Douglas Wiggin, *A Child's Journey with Dickens*, p. 31.
47   Nonesuch, vol. 2, p. 629.
48   Nonesuch, vol. 2, p. 634.
49   *DC*, ch. 26.
50   In 'The Bill of Fare' Dickens had described Maria's Daphne as 'the little dog that/Would eat mutton-chops if you cut off the fat'. In *DC* Dora declares (ch. 37) that Jip 'must have a mutton-chop every day at twelve, or he'll die'.
51   Forster, pp. 638-9.
52   Nonesuch, vol. 2, pp. 625-7.
53   Nonesuch, vol. 2, pp. 628-9.
54   Autograph memorandum at Dickens House, already cited.
55   Nonesuch, vol. 2, pp. 633-4.

56   Autograph memorandum at Dickens House, already cited.
57   Nonesuch, vol. 2, pp. 649-50.
58   See below, p. 76.
59   *LD*, Book I, ch. 13.
60   It is interesting to compare with the description of Clennam's meeting his old love again a similar episode in ch. 2 of 'Mugby Junction' (*CS*) when the melancholy middle-aged bachelor, 'Barbox Brothers', finds himself face to face with the woman whom he had passionately loved as a girl but who had married his friend instead of him. She now comes, 'a careworn woman . . . with her hair turned grey', to beseech him to forgive her. Dickens writes: 'Before him were the ashes of a dead fire that had once burned bright. This was the woman he had loved. This was the woman he had lost. Such had been the constancy of his imagination to her, so had Time spared her under its withholding, that now, seeing how roughly the inexorable hand had struck her, his soul was filled with pity and amazement.' Behind this seems to lie a sort of fantasy about punishing the girl who betrayed him; she must suffer, feel guilt and remorse and come, bearing all the signs of her suffering, to beg his forgiveness. Had Maria taken this line instead of both defying 'the inexorable hand' of Time as she clearly did and also re-presenting herself with all her old self-confidence, Dickens would not have been nearly so disconcerted. But then we should have had no Flora.
61   Autograph memorandum at Dickens House, already cited.
62   In her diary for 1884 she notes on one day, 'in the evening read some of dear Charles Dickens's letters to George [her brother]'. See Sotheran's *Piccadilly Notes*, 1933, J.H. Stonehouse (ed.), No.5, (3), p. 265; published by Henry Sotheran Ltd.
63   Wright, p. 231. Wright gives no authority for this assertion, nor does Johnson (p. 838) who seems at this point to be following Wright. So it may be that Dickens scholars have been traducing Mrs Winter in this respect; Mrs Warren's testimony about her mistress's 'addiction to nips of drinking' cited later must also be borne in mind, however.
64   Nonesuch, vol. 2, p. 785.
65   *TTC*, Book II, ch. 21.
66   Nonesuch, vol. 2, p. 739.
67   Nonesuch, vol. 3, p. 72.
68   'City of London Churches', *ATYR*, 5 May 1860; reprinted in *UT*.
69   Forster, p. 49.
70   *GE*, ch. 29; Forster, p. 49; *GE*, ch. 29; *GE*, ch. 33.
71   *GE*, ch. 38.
72   Pilgrim, vol. 1, p. 17.
73   There is, perhaps, a trace of the experience of loving Maria, though not of Maria herself, in 'George Silverman's Explanation' (1867). George, the slum boy from a rat-infested Preston cellar (the last image of the blacking-factory in Dickens's fiction?) is tainted with poverty and also ambition for a

better life, for which he is reproached as 'a worldly little devil', to his deep shame. He tries to conceal these things from the girl he loves, Sylvia, the pretty daughter of a prosperous farmer, so that she will not be 'hurt' (= offended) by them. She misunderstands him and treats him disdainfully which causes him bitter grief. George records, 'It was in these ways that I began to form a shy disposition; to be of a timidly silent character . . .'. Compare with this what Dickens wrote to Maria in 1855: 'My entire devotion to you, and the wasted tenderness of those hard years . . . made so deep an impression on me that I refer to it a habit of suppression which now belongs to me . . . which makes me chary of showing my affections, even to my children, except when they are very young' (Nonesuch, vol. 2, p. 633).

74 Arthur Adrian, op. cit., p. 100.
75 I am grateful to Miss Katharine M. Longley for drawing my attention to this coincidence and guiding me in a visit to the cemetery.

Chapter 5: Mary

1 Pilgrim, vol. 1, p. 144.
2 For details of Hogarth's career see ch. 1 of Arthur Adrian's *Georgina Hogarth and the Dickens Circle*.
3 Quoted by Adrian, op. cit., p. 130.
4 Quoted in Pilgrim, vol. 1, p. 129, note 1.
5 *Dksn*, vol. 63 (1967), p. 76.
6 Pilgrim, vol. 1, p. 65.
7 Jack Lindsay, *Charles Dickens*, p. 129.
8 Extracts from this letter were first published in the *Times Literary Supplement*, 23 Dec. 1960, in an article entitled 'A Letter from Mary Hogarth' by Kathleen Tillotson; the letter is published in full in Pilgrim, vol. 1, pp. 689-91.
9 Professor Tillotson comments, in her article just cited, 'what most strikes the reader of Mary's letter is the entire lack of any parade of herself, and the warmth of her interest in other people; she was perhaps one of those rare beings who really participate in the happiness of those around them, and whose radiance may be mistaken for beauty'.
10 Pilgrim, vol. 1, p. 630.
11 *Dksn*, vol. 63 (1967), p. 77.
12 Mary's handwriting is, in fact, good and legible but she 'crossed' her letter as many women did at that time (i.e., she wrote from left to right and then turned the sheet sideways and continued the letter, crossing the earlier lines at right angles). This saved space and expense as postage costs increased sharply if more than one sheet of paper were used.
13 Pilgrim, vol. 1, p. 263.
14 Pilgrim, vol. 3, p. 483.
15 'Recollections of Charles Dickens', *Temple Bar*, vol. 82 (1888), p. 502.

16   Quoted in Pilgrim, vol. 1, p. 65, note 3.
17   Quoted in Pilgrim, vol. 1, p. 253, note 2.
18   Robert Story, *Love and Literature*, 1842, pp. 217-18. Quoted by W.J. Carlton in his 'The Death of Mary Hogarth – Before and After', *Dksn*, vol. 63 (1967), pp. 73-4.
19   To Richard Johns [31 May, 1837], Pilgrim, vol. 1, p. 263.
20   See Pilgrim, vol. 4, p. 670. Writing to Forster in November 1846 Dickens said that he had been very worried about his health during the summer, 'Yet I had little pain in my side; excepting that time at Genoa I have had hardly any since poor Mary died, when it came on so badly'.
21   Pilgrim, vol. 1, pp. 260, 257, 259, 263, 629, 266 note 4, 323, 630.
22   *MC*, ch. 37. In a letter written to Lady Holland when he was finishing this novel Dickens referred to Tom and Ruth Pinch as 'two of the greatest favorites I have ever had' (Pilgrim, vol. 4, p. 145).
23   *DC*, ch. 59. *The Arabian Nights* story alluded to here is the one entitled 'The Story of Two Sisters who envied their Younger Sister'. Subtle readers may feel that Dickens intended his readers to note the contrast between the happy sorority in Traddles's chambers and the spite and envy of the two wicked sisters in the story towards their younger sister, the Sultan's bride, but this seems very doubtful to me. The point of the allusion to this particular tale is to introduce the three wondrous and beautiful objects that figure so prominently in it; they function as a more striking and arresting image for the effect of these lively, pretty girls in such a setting than the preceding conventional roses image.
24   Quoted by W.J. Carlton, op. cit., p. 73.
25   Forster, p. 199.
26   Pilgrim, vol. 1, p. 516 (letter of March 1839).
27   *Dksn*, vol. 17 (1921), p. 152.
28   *Dksn*, vol. 73 (1977), p. 178.
29   Pilgrim, vol. 3, p. 52
30   Pilgrim, vol. 1, p. 632; Forster, pp. 206, 270.
31   Pilgrim, vol. 3, pp. 483-4.
32   Forster, p. 349.
33   cf. Lindsay, op. cit., p. 255. Noting that Mariolatry or 'mother-worship' would have been one of the most striking features of Italian Catholicism for Dickens, Lindsay observes that the suggestion in the dream that this was the best religion for him, a suggestion which 'runs counter to every moral and intellectual bias of his waking life', 'comes from his feeling that there is inside him some mysterious force, a deep, unsatisfied yearning for union, which the terms of his waking life cannot meet'.
34   Nonesuch, vol. 3, p. 454.
35   Pilgrim, vol. 1, p. 516.
36   Albert J. Guerard, *The Triumph of the Novel: Dickens, Dostoevsky, Faulkner*, p. 71. Guerard defines 'forbidden games' as 'tabooed acts and

relationships, strong "anti-social" attractions or repugnances, threatening obsessions', and comments that Dickens's 'fondest forbidden game would appear to be imagined marriage with an idealized virgin: all the more forbidden because she might be daughter or sister or sister-in-law. Is there any way, a number of plots seem to ask, to legitimize these longings?' Guerard's detailed discussion of the way in which 'the *conscious fantasy* and enduring daydream of reunion with the lost Mary' enters Dickens's fiction 'with little disguise' seems to me to be an example of psychoanalytical criticism at its most lucid and persuasive.

37 Pilgrim, vol. 4, p. 55.
38 David H. Paroissien, 'Charles Dickens and the Weller Family', *Dickens Studies Annual,* Southern Illinois University Press, vol. 2 (1972), p. 7. Professor Paroissien anticipates me in noting the significance of Dickens's saying that he believed Christiana to be 'destined to an early death': 'his curious aside . . . suggest[s] that Dickens may have subconsciously associated Christiana with Mary Hogarth'. I think it more probable, however, that it was quite a *conscious* association, especially if Christiana bore such a close physical resemblance to Mary.
39 Pilgrim, vol. 4, pp. 58 (to Mr Weller) and 69 (to Thompson).
40 op. cit., p. 70.
41 op. cit., p. 89.
42 op. cit., pp. 99, 100.
43 op. cit., p. 400.
44 op. cit., p. 604.
45 This connection is suggested by Jack Lindsay, op. cit., pp. 121-3. See also Guerard, op. cit., pp. 72-3.
46 Reprinted in *RP.*
47 Forster, p. 514.
48 Edwin M. Eigner interestingly comments (in his *The Metaphysical Novel in England and America,* 1978, p. 129, note 36) that Rose Maylie's names 'both first and last, suggest that Dickens may have intended her as an anniversary tribute' to Mary.
49 *OT,* ch. 29.
50 The Clarendon Edition of *OT,* ed. Kathleen Tillotson, 1966, p. 187.
51 *OT,* ch. 32.
52 *OT,* ch. 51.
53 Forster, p. 150.
54 Vol. 2, p. 182, note 2.
55 Dickens does, however, make use of his experience of his persistent vivid dreams of Mary after her death in ch. 70 of *OCS* in order to heighten the pathos of Nell's death. Her 'little favourite and friend', the village child who had had some Wordsworthian conversation with her in the graveyard in ch. 53, dreams of her every night: ' " . . . all tonight, and last night too, it was the same. I never fall asleep, but that cruel dream comes back."/"Try

to sleep again . . . It will go in time."/"No, no, I would rather that it stayed – cruel as it is, I would rather that it stayed," rejoined the child. "I am not afraid to have it in my sleep, but I am so sad – so very, very sad." '

56   *LD*, Book I, ch. 14.

57   Pilgrim, vol. 3, p. 483.

58   Steven Marcus, *Dickens: from Pickwick to Dombey*, p. 289. I am much indebted in what follows to Marcus's detailed and illuminating discussion of *The Battle of Life*. See also Guerard, op. cit., pp. 73-4.

59   *CB, The Battle of Life*, Part the Second.

60   op. cit., Part the Third.

61   See last paragraph of *The Battle of Life* which begins, 'TIME – from whom I had the latter portion of this story, and with whom I have had the pleasure of a personal acquaintance of some five-and-thirty years' duration – informed me . . .'. Kathleen Tillotson notes this 'unusually personal coda' in her lecture, 'The Middle Years: from the *Carol* to *Copperfield*' (*Dickens Memorial Lectures*, 1970, p. 17).

62   Marcus, op. cit., p. 292. A crude and tactless early attempt to explicate *The Battle of Life* in terms of Dickens's biography, and specifically in terms of his relationship with Mary, was made by the irrepressible Percy Fitzgerald in 1902. Claiming that Mary 'had always secretly loved' Dickens, Fitzgerald speculated that she had hidden her affection, knowing that her sister Catherine also loved him, and that Dickens was portraying this directly in the story of Marion. See Arthur Adrian, op. cit., p. 236.

63   See page 368 below.

64   Forster, p. 437. See also p. 426.

65   See above, pp. 32-3.

66   See Nina Burgis's Introduction to the Clarendon Edition of *DC*, 1981, pp. xv-xxi.

67   See *DC*, ch. 15: 'I cannot call to mind where or when, in my childhood, I had seen a stained glass window in a church. Nor do I recollect its subject. But I know that when I saw her turn round, in the grave light of the old staircase . . . I though of that window; and that I associated something of its tranquil brightness with Agnes Wickfield ever afterwards'. The manuscript reads, after 'its subject', 'though I think there was an angel in it' (Clarendon Edition of *DC*, p. 191).

68   cf. Philip Collins, *Charles Dickens: David Copperfield* (*Studies in English Literature*, no. 67) p. 48f.: 'At [Agnes's] first introduction, nearly all her attributes are mentioned and they are repeated at most subsequent re-entries. . . . "Then come and see my little housekeeper", says Mr Wickfield, and there she is with her keys and her adjectives – *placid, sweet, tranquil, bright, happy, quiet, good, calm, grave* – and with her religiose associations . . .'.

69   *DC*, ch. 34.

70 See Alexander Welsh, *The City of Dickens*, pp.180-3.
71 See below, p. 161.

Chapter 6: Catherine

1   Dickens is quoting from, and summarizing, Swift's *Letter to a Young Lady on Her Marriage* (1723). See H. Davis (ed.), *Prose Works of Swift*, vol. 9, p. 89.

2   Nonesuch, vol. 3, p. 22 f. The so-called 'Violated Letter' (see Appendix A, above) is, in fact, a statement about the break-up of his marriage which Dickens gave to Arthur Smith who was to act as business-manager for the forthcoming public Readings. In an accompanying note Dickens wrote, 'My dear Arthur – You have not only my full permission to show this, but I beg of you to show it to anyone who wishes to do me right, or to anyone who may have been misled into doing me wrong.' By some unknown means the statement was given to a New York newspaper, the *Tribune* and appeared in its columns on 16 Aug. 1858. From there it was copied by many other journals both in America and England. Dickens announced that this publication was against his wishes, calling it a violation of confidence (hence the custom of referring to the document as the 'violated letter'), but his continued regard and friendship for Smith give rise to the suspicion that he may have connived at its publication. See Ada Nisbet, *Dickens and Ellen Ternan*, pp. 16-17.

3   Memorandum by Shaw dated Dec. 1897. BM. Add. MSS. 50546. Quoted by permission of the British Library and the Society of Authors.

4   See Pilgrim, vol. 1, p. 100.

5   op. cit., p. 95.

6   *DC*, ch. 37.

7   Pilgrim, vol. 1, p. 104. In a review of this volume in the *Dksn* (vol. 61, 1965, p. 75) Geoffrey Best comments interestingly if unsympathetically on Dickens's letters to Catherine before their marriage: '[they] are an uneasy mixture of pomposity, touchiness, affection, and baby-talk; they show that with whatever regard he had for her as she really was, there was mixed some obsession with an idea to which he was trying to make her correspond: the idea of that busy, blushing, simple, cheerful, bright, fecund, long-suffering and, above all, *loving* little woman who is already fully formed in *Sketches by Boz* and who was to remain a stock character for the next thirty years'.

8   [Nathaniel Beard], 'Some Recollections of Yesterday', *Temple Bar*, vol. 102 (1894), p. 320. Quoted by W.J. Carlton in his ' "Boz" and the Beards', *Dksn*, vol. 58 (1962) p. 13.

9   Letter to Jane Welsh, 2 April 1826. *The Love Letters of Thomas Carlyle and Jane Welsh*, ed. Alexander Carlyle, 1909, vol. 2, p. 262.

10 The *TLS* reviewer of Pilgrim, vol. 1 remarked (11 Feb. 1965) that Dickens 'appears to have been more fluent when he had something to reproach a mistress with than when the course of love was running smooth'.

11 Pilgrim, vol. 1, p. 110.

12 Forster, p. 39.

13 Pilgrim, vol. 1, p. 120.

14 It is even harder to credit the idea that he deliberately chose to marry Catherine 'because she was a goose' as, according to Mrs Andrew Cross (*Red-Letter Days of My Life*, 1892, vol. 2, p. 51) he was reported as having said he did. (I am indebted to Professor Philip Collins for this reference.)

15 Pilgrim, vol. 1, pp. 119, 120, 118, 128–9.

16 op. cit., pp. 133–4.

17 op. cit., p. 61.

18 op. cit., p. 95.

19 op. cit., p. 139.

20 Catherine appears to have become a great favourite with Braham. When he and his wife were visiting their friend, the Governor-General of Canada, in 1842, 'The Charles Dickenses arrived and . . . though neither Braham nor his wife much cared for him, they found Mrs Dickens delightful, and, for the sake of her company, had to lead the same flamboyant life that the young novelist favoured' (W. Hewett, *Strawberry Fair*, 1956, p. 43 – I am indebted to Miss M.E. Pillers for this reference).

21 F.G. Kitton, *Supplement to Charles Dickens by Pen and Pencil*, p. 11.

22 [Eleanor Christian], 'Reminiscences of Charles Dickens. From a Young Lady's Diary', *The Englishwoman's Domestic Magazine*, vol. 10 (1871), p. 336. Mrs Christian qualified her praise of Catherine's charms by commenting on 'the sleepy look of the slow-moving eyes' and her chin 'which melted too suddenly into the throat'.

23 See E.W.F. Tomlin, 'Newly Discovered Dickens Letters', *TLS*, 22 Feb. 1974, p. 183f.

24 Storey, p. 22.

25 [Eleanor Christian], op. cit., p. 337.

26 *Dksn*, vol. 63 (1967), p. 76; Pilgrim, vol. 1, p. 68, note 2.

27 Arthur A. Adrian, *Mark Lemon. First Editor of Punch*, 1966, p. 117; Storey, p. 103.

28 *The World of Charles Dickens*, p.105.

29 See Harriet Beecher Stowe, *Sunny Memories of Foreign Lands*, 1854, vol. 1, p. 266. Describing a meeting with Dickens and his wife at a Mansion House Banquet the previous year, Mrs Stowe writes: 'Mrs Dickens is a good specimen of a truly English woman; tall, large and well developed, with fine, healthy colour, and an air of frankness, cheerfulness, and reliability. A friend whispered to me that she was as observing, and fond of humour, as her husband.'

30 Pilgrim, vol. 1, p. 365.

31 Walter Dexter (ed.), *Mr and Mrs Charles Dickens. His Letters to Her*, pp. 241-2.
32 Edgar Johnson (ed.), *Letters from Charles Dickens to Angela Burdett Coutts 1841-1865*, p. 355 (letter of 9 May 1858).
33 'Recollections of Charles Dickens, His Family and Friends', *Temple Bar*, vol. 82 (1888), p. 502.
34 *Dksn*, vol. 63 (1967), pp. 79-80.
35 Pilgrim, vol. 3, p. 211.
36 Pilgrim, vol. 1, p. xvi.
37 Forster, p. 640.
38 Pilgrim, vol. 1, p. xvii.
39 [Eleanor Christian], op. cit., *The Englishwoman's Domestic Magazine*, vol. 10 (1871), p. 343.
40 Pilgrim, vol. 3, p. 155, note 1; K.J. Fielding, 'Two Sketches by Maclise', *Dickens Studies*, vol. 2 (1966), p. 13. Maclise's letter accompanied a sketch of the occasion which he had done for Catherine.
41 Pilgrim, vol. 3, p. 9, note 3.
42 Forster, p. 640.
43 See Pilgrim, vol. 1, p. 392.
44 *GE*, end of ch. 9.
45 A phrase Dickens wrote in the Memorandum Book he began keeping in January 1855. Quoted by Arthur Adrian, *Georgina Hogarth and the Dickens Circle*, p. 44.
46 Johnson, p. 266 (p. 170 of the revised one-volume edition of Johnson's *Charles Dickens* published in 1978).
47 For example, Johnson claims (p. 266) that towards Catherine herself Dickens's letters in the late 1830s 'begin to reveal a trace of something that only half disguises itself in jest' but the only piece of evidence he cites to back this up is a letter to Forster (see Pilgrim, vol. 1, p. 608) in which, far from 'making a game of Catherine's blunders' as Johnson asserts, Dickens is clearly praising her 'accustomed cleverness' which has helped him to decipher an illegible name.
48 Samuel Longfellow to Mrs James Greenleaf, 8 Feb. 1842, reporting Dickens's conversation at a breakfast given for him by Henry Longfellow in Cambridge, Mass. First published by Edward Wagenknecht in 'Dickens in Longfellow's Letters and Journals', *Dksn*, vol. 52 (1956), p. 9.
49 *OCS*, ch. 4.
50 Hesketh Pearson (*Charles Dickens, His Character, Comedy and Career*, p. 31) detected this quality in Catherine's portraits by Maclise.
51 Pilgrim, vol. 3, p. 291; Nonesuch, vol. 2, p. 553; ibid., p. 263.
52 [Eleanor Christian], op. cit., *The Englishwoman's Domestic Magazine*, vol. 10 (1871), p. 339.
53 *AN*, ch. 2. Hesketh Pearson (op. cit., p.101) notes that this 'recalls Quilp's pleasantries at his wife's expense: "I'm glad you're wet, I'm glad you're cold . . ." '.

54 Quoted by Philip Collins in his *Dickens. Interviews and Recollections*, p. 89.
55 Pilgrim, vol. 2, pp. 381; 390, note 4; 398, note 5; 393, note 1.
56 'Reminiscence of Charles Dickens's First Visit to America. By a Fellow Passenger.' Reprinted in Noel C. Peyrouton's 'Re: Memoir of an *American Notes* Original', *Dickens Studies*, vol. 4 (March 1968), p. 28.
57 Letter from Mrs J.L. Motley to her husband quoted in S. and H. St John Mildmay (eds.), *J.L. Motley and His Family*, 1910, p. 25.
58 Pilgrim, vol. 3, pp. 161; 202; 154; 196.
59 George Putnam, 'Four months with Charles Dickens, during his First Visit to America (in 1842): By His Secretary', *Atlantic Monthly*, vol. 26 (1870), p. 479; Pilgrim, vol. 3, p. 155, note 1; *Quebec Gazette*, 28 May 1842, quoted in *Dksn*, vol. 38 (1942), p. 142. Dickens considered 'heroic' Catherine's waiting on one occasion until he returned home late from a public engagement before opening some letters from home which had arrived that evening, having been much delayed in crossing the Atlantic (Pilgrim, vol. 3, p. 132).
60 The New York press: *The Spirit of the Times*, 19 Feb. 1842, quoted in *Dksn*, vol. 4 (1908), p. 204; for Longfellow's comments see E. Wagenknecht, op. cit., p. 7f.; for the Pittsburgh lawyer's (Charles B. Scully) see Marilyn P. Hollinshead, 'Dickens in Pittsburgh: a Stereoscopic View', *Dksn*, vol. 74 (1978), p. 37; for the Boston lady's (Caroline Weston) see N.C. Peyrouton, 'Some Boston Abolitionists on Boz', *Dksn*, vol. 60 (1964), p. 23; for Dana's see Pilgrim, vol. 3, p. xi; for the Southern senator's (John Caldwell Calhoun) see Pilgrim, vol. 3, p. 132, note 7; for John Quincy Adams's see Pilgrim, vol. 3, p. 113, note 1; for Putnam's see Putnam, op. cit., p. 478.
61 Johnson, p. 332; 'The wife of one of Dickens's Barrow cousins described Catherine Dickens as a complaining woman, and suspected that the novelist was nagged in his home'. The witness here was a Mrs John Barrow, daughter-in-law of Thomas Culliford Barrow, Dickens's uncle; her son communicated the tradition orally to Johnson. For the similar tradition in the Macready family see Philip Collins, 'W.C. Macready and Dickens: Some Family Recollections', *Dickens Studies*, vol. 2 (May 1966), p. 54.
62 'A Girl's Recollections of Dickens', *Lippincott's Monthly Magazine*, vol. 52 (Sept. 1893), pp. 338-9.
63 Forster, pp. 265-6.
64 Pilgrim, vol. 3, p. xii. Johnson assumes (p. 414) that Dickens's praise of Catherine's 'gameness' must be overcompensation for exasperation at her clumsiness, an exasperation which he has endeavoured to suppress by treating her accident-proneness in a comic manner.
65 *BH*, ch. 59.
66 *The Times*, second leader, 14 May 1934.
67 Quoted by J.A. and O. Banks, *Feminism and Family Planning in Victorian England*, p. 6.

68 Pilgrim, vol. 5, p. 487.

69 Unpublished letter of 17 Aug. 1850.

70 Pilgrim, vol. 4, p. 3.

71 Dickens fiercely attacked the Malthusians in his caricature of the political economist, Mr Filer, in *The Chimes* (1844). One of the dummy book-backs in his study bore the title *Malthus's Nursery Songs*.

72 Nonesuch, vol. 2, pp. 416-17.

73 Typescript copy of letter of 1 March 1840, now at The Dickens House Museum. Quoted by permission of the Trustees.

74 Pilgrim, vol. 3, p. 220 (letter of 29 April 1842). Another, and closer, friend with whom Dickens sustained a mock-amorous correspondence over many years was the petite and charming Mary Boyle, two years his junior, whom he met at the home of her distant relatives, the Watsons, in 1850 and who remained on affectionately friendly terms with him until his death. She fully shared his passion for amateur theatricals and acted opposite to him in the farce *Used Up* in which his role was that of her lover. He made great play with this in his letters to his 'Dearest Meery' as he called her, signing himself 'Joe' (the character's name). See Ada Nisbet, *Dickens and Ellen Ternan*, p. 81f.

75 Fred Kaplan, *Dickens and Mesmerism*, p. 77.

76 Pilgrim, vol. 3, p. 180.

77 Pilgrim, vol. 4, p. 243.

78 Nonesuch, vol. 3, p. 753 (letter dated 24 Nov. 1869).

79 Letter to Miss Coutts, 5 April 1860 (Edgar Johnson (ed.), *Letters from Charles Dickens to Angela Burdett Coutts 1841-1865*, p. 369).

80 Pilgrim, vol. 4, p. 249

81 op.cit., p. xi.

82 op. cit., p. 250.

83 W. Dexter (ed.), op. cit., p. 227.

84 Kaplan, op. cit., p. 82.

85 Included in the *UT & RP* vol. of the Oxford Illustrated Dickens.

86 Pilgrim, vol. 4, p. 219.

87 E. Davey, 'The Parents of Charles Dickens', *Lippincott's Magazine*, vol. 13 (1874), p. 773.

88 See K.J. Fielding, 'Dickens as J.T. Danson knew him', *Dksn*, vol. 68 (1972), pp. 151-61. Reprinted in Philip Collins, op. cit., pp. 76-9.

89 Letter to his wife of April 1855. First published by Susan Chitty in her *The Beast and the Monk*, 1974, p. 174.

90 Pilgrim, vol. 4, p. 612, note 1.

91 Quoted by Philip Collins, op. cit., p. 191.

92 H.S. Solly, *The Life of Henry Morley*, 1898, p. 201. (I am indebted to Professor Collins for bringing this passage to my attention.)

93 See his chapter on 'Charles Dickens' in *Victorian Fiction. A Second Guide to Research*, ed. George H. Ford, 1978, p. 50.

94 Johnson, p. 905.

95 Johnson (1978), p. 721.

96 ibid.

97 Nonesuch, vol. 2, p. 243.

98 *Dksn*, vol. 38 (1942), p. 162.

99 Johnson, p. 906.

100 Still more distorting is Arthur Adrian's handling of this letter *(Georgina Hogarth and the Dickens Circle*, p. 31) as he misquotes it so that Dickens is represented as joking about Catherine 'gradually falling into fits of imbecility'.

101 Johnson, p. 906.

102 R. Stewart (ed.), *Nathaniel Hawthorne's English Notebooks*, 1941, p. 379.

103 Johnson, p. 907

104 Forster, p. 835. cf. also his daughter Mamie's testimony: '. . . there was not a corner in any of his homes, from kitchen to garret, which was not constantly inspected by him, and which did not boast of some of his neat and orderly contrivances. We used to laugh at him sometimes and say we believed that he was personally acquainted with every nail in the house.' ('Charles Dickens at Home. By His Eldest Daughter', *Cornhill Magazine*, note 5, vol. 4, Jan. 1885, p. 39.)

105 Pilgrim, vol. 3, p. 276. (Did Mr Groves, one wonders, model for the butcher in *MC*, ch. 39, who 'had a sentiment for his business' and reproved Tom Pinch for awkwardly pushing into his pocket a steak he has just bought? The butcher 'begged to be allowed to do it for him; "for meat", he said with some emotion, "must be humoured, not drove" '.)

106 Nonesuch, vol. 2, pp. 823-4.

107 Adrian, op. cit., p. 25.

108 Letter of 9 March 1851 quoted in *Dksn*, vol. 38 (1942), p. 123.

109 Nonesuch, vol. 2, p. 278 (to Dr Wilson, 8 March 1851).

110 ibid.

111 W. Dexter (ed.), op. cit., p. 154.

112 G.M. Young, 'Mr and Mrs Dickens', *Victorian Essays*, ed. W.D. Handcock, 1962, p. 83.

113 Nonesuch, vol. 2, p. 297f.

114 op. cit., pp. 299, 300.

115 op. cit., p. 358.

116 Jane Welsh Carlyle, *Letters to Her Family, 1839-1863*, ed. Leonard Huxley, 1924, p. 326.

117 Margaret Lane, 'Mrs Beeton and Mrs Dickens', *Purely for Pleasure*, 1966, p. 184f.

118 op. cit., p. 185.

119 *The World of Charles Dickens*, p. 253. Wilson adds, 'It is some balance against the fact that his marriage did not waken in him a sufficient

understanding of women to give reality to the central emotional relationships of most of his great novels.'

120 Edgar Johnson (ed.), *Letters of Charles Dickens to Angela Burdett Coutts
1841-1865*, p. 254.

Chapter 7: Catherine: The End of the Marriage

1 See W. Dexter (ed.), *Mr and Mrs Charles Dickens. His Letters to Her*,
pp. 266-8.

2 Forster, p. 635.

3 Forster, p. 636. Supporting evidence for Forster's assertion here can be
found in the fact that Dickens began, in early 1855, to keep a Memorandum Book (now in the Berg Collection, New York Public Library) in
which he jotted down notions for characters, plots, etc. (see Forster,
p. 747). Hitherto he had not felt the need of such a thing.

4 Nonesuch, vol. 2, pp. 566 (letter of 12 July 1854), 623 (letter to F. Régnier
of 3 Feb. 1855) and 848 (letter of 22 May 1857).

5 op. cit., p. 838 (letter of 4 March 1857): '*I cannot tell you* what pleasure I
had in the receipt of your letter. . . . I immediately arose (like the desponding
Princes in the Arabian Nights, when the old woman – Procuress evidently,
and probably of French extraction – comes to whisper about the Princesses
they love) . . .'.

6 A rather improbable-sounding story about a dinner-party at Judge Talfourd's showing Catherine in a poor light, is related on Collins's authority
by Wybert Reeve *(From Life*, 1892, p. 110): 'The conversation turned on
Dickens's last book. Some of the characters were highly praised. Mrs
Dickens joined in the conversation, and said she could not understand what
people could see in his writings to talk so much about them. The face of
Dickens betrayed his feelings. Again the book was referred to, and a lady
present said she wondered when and how many strange thoughts came into
his head. "Oh," replied Dickens, "I don't know. They come at odd times,
sometimes in the night, when I jump out of bed, and dot them down, for
fear I should have lost them by the morning." "That is true," said Mrs
Dickens. "I have reason to know it, jumping out of bed and getting in again,
with his feet as cold as a stone." Dickens left the table, and was afterwards
found sitting alone in a small room off the hall – silent and angry. It was a
long time before they could induce him to join the circle again.' Several
things in this anecdote ring false (no Victorian lady of Catherine's type
would make such an intimate reference to her marriage bed in mixed
company) but it may well be a mangled version of an actual incident related
by Collins to show Catherine's obtuseness or naivety or, in general, what
Dickens had to put up with.

7 *Edmund Yates: His Recollections and Experiences*, 1884, vol. 2, p. 96.

8   Elias Bredsdorff, *Hans Andersen and Charles Dickens. A Friendship and Its Dissolution*, p. 128.

9   From a forthcoming volume, *Harriet Martineau's Letters to Fanny Wedgwood 1837-1871*, edited by Elisabeth Arbuckle, to be published by Stanford University Press, 1982. I am grateful to Professor Arbuckle for making the text of this letter available to me and to Dr Norris Pope for alerting me to its existence.

10 Evans seems to have been repeating every malicious rumour about Dickens he had heard, no matter how preposterous it might be. Thus Miss Martineau also tells her correspondent, on Evans's authority, the following bit of gossip: 'One thing which looks like a craze in Dickens is his being bent on purchasing the Rochester Theatre, in order to act there, *with his daughters*, on alternate nights with the company! His nearest friends had the utmost difficulty in dissuading him from this.'

11 'The Ruffian', first published in *ATYR*, 10 Oct. 1868.

12 Forster, p. 639.

13 ibid.

14 It has been argued (by those who accept Dickens's statements of 1857/8 that he had long been unhappy with Catherine) that the pathetic comedy of Dora's wifely inadequacy in *Copperfield* was inspired by Catherine's alleged domestic incompetence but this seems to me very questionable. See below, p. 160.

15 *LD*, Book II, ch. 15.

16 Storey, p. 96. The working notes on which Miss Storey drew for *Dickens and Daughter* contain two variants on this anecdote about Catherine's being ordered by Dickens to call on Ellen. One version has Catherine refusing to comply with Dickens's request, and the other stated that it was *Mrs* Ternan, not Ellen, on whom Dickens asked Catherine to call and that she wept but obeyed, as in the printed version. It does seem more probable that Mrs Ternan would have been, officially, the person on whom a call would have been made by another married lady, rather than her youngest daughter. See David Parker and Michael Slater, 'The Gladys Storey Papers', *Dksn*, vol. 76 (1980) p. 4 and note 2 (p. 16).

17 Nonesuch, vol. 2, p. 873.

18 Forster, p. 640.

19 Storey, p. 99.

20 Edgar Johnson (ed.), *Letters from Charles Dickens to Angela Burdett Coutts*, pp. 355-6.

21 *MED*, ch. 4.

22 Forster, p. 641.

23 Johnson, p. 909.

24 *Lazy Tour*, ch. 4 (the *Lazy Tour* is included in the CS volume of the Oxford Illustrated Dickens).

25 Attention was first drawn to the biographical interest of this story by

Professor Harry Stone on p. 127 of his 'The Genesis of a Novel: *Great Expectations*', in *Charles Dickens 1812-1870. A Centenary Volume,* ed. E.W.F. Tomlin, 1969.

26   Nonesuch, vol. 2, p. 890 (letter of 11 Oct. 1857 to Anne Cornelius, a confidential maidservant in the Dickens family for many years – she had accompanied Dickens and Catherine on their American tour in 1842).

27   Letter of 20 Aug. 1858 from Helen Thomson to Mrs Stark, first printed in full by Professor K.J. Fielding in his 'Charles Dickens and his Wife: Fact or Forgery?' (*Etudes Anglaises*, vol. 8 (1955), pp. 212-22. The authenticity of this letter which exists only in copies, the original having disappeared, was denied by earlier Dickens scholars, including Edgar Johnson, but has now been established beyond reasonable doubt (see W.J. Carlton, 'Mr and Mrs Dickens: the Thomson-Stark Letter', *Notes and Queries,* vol. 205 (April 1960), pp. 145-7). The 'various absurd proposals' that Dickens made to Catherine in order to keep up a public façade of continuing happy marriage were, in fact, just such as he himself was to castigate many years later in a letter to his friend, Frances Elliot, who was unhappily married to the Dean of Bristol: '. . . the monstrous absurdity of your repudiating your marriage on the one hand, and requiring that the Dean shall live with you at such and such times to keep up appearances, on the other, is fatal' (Nonesuch, vol. 3, p. 737; letter of 14 Aug. 1869).

28   Nonesuch, vol. 3, p. 21.

29   Storey, p. 94. We get a glimpse of the seething frustration Dickens was experiencing at the time in his report to Macready in March of a nightmare he has had: 'I was bent upon getting over a perspective of barriers, with my hands and feet bound'. He adds, 'Pretty much what we are all about, waking, I think?' (Nonesuch, vol. 3, p. 11).

30   Johnson (ed.), op. cit., pp. 352-3.

31   See quotation from John Bigelow below, p. 152.

32   Johnson (ed.), op. cit., pp. 354-5.

33   W. Dexter (ed.), op. cit., pp. 146-7.

34   Letter of 11 Aug. 1870, quoted in Philip Collins (ed.) *Dickens: Interviews and Recollections,* p. 155.

35   Quoted in Miss Thomson's letter to Mrs Stark (see above, note 27).

36   Dr W.H. Bowen notes in his *Charles Dickens and His Family,* p. 112, that when Sydney died in 1872 he left all his money, 'quite a considerable sum', to his mother.

37   See note 2 to chapter 6, above.

38   Johnson (ed.), op. cit., p. 361.

39   *DS,* ch. 2.

40   Forster, p. 39.

41   W. Dexter (ed.), op. cit., p. 277.

42   A letter of 21 May 1858 from Forster to Dickens's solicitor, Frederic Ouvry, seeks urgent clarification about 'the operation and requirements of

the New Act' and it seems reasonable to assume, in the context, that the 'New Act' referred to is the Matrimonial Causes Act of 1857. Forster begs Ouvry to *'assure* [himself] *with certainty'* on some points 'between this and 3 o'clock' and then to meet later in the day with Dickens and Forster himself. This may well have been in response to rumours that Catherine was being urged by her mother and sister to explore the possibility of divorce proceedings. Forster's letter was first published by Professor K.J. Fielding in his 'Dickens and the Hogarth Scandal', *Nineteenth Century Fiction*, vol. 10 (1955-6), pp. 64-74.

43   Dickens had attacked the cumbersomeness and great social injustice of the divorce laws in 1854 (when the first abortive attempt was made to introduce new legislation) in *Hard Times*. See John D. Baird, ' "Divorce and Matrimonial Causes": an Aspect of *Hard Times*', *Victorian Studies*, vol. 20 (Summer 1977), pp. 401-12. I have drawn on Professor Baird's article for many of the details in this paragraph.

44   Johnson (ed.), op. cit., p. 357.

45   W. Dexter (ed.), op. cit., p. 278.

46   K.J. Fielding, op. cit., p. 67.

47   For the full text of the 'Violated Letter' see Appendix A.

48   Unpublished letter.

49   See K.J. Fielding, 'Charles Dickens and Colin Rae Brown', *Nineteenth Century Fiction*, vol. 7 (1952), pp. 103-10.

50   Quoted by Tom Johnstone in his 'Decidedly This Side Idolatry: Dr John Brown and Dickens', *Dksn*, vol. 74 (1978), pp. 96-102.

51   W. Dexter (ed.) op. cit., pp. 257-8.

52   *Dksn*, vol. 50 (1954), p. 32.

53   W. Dexter (ed.), op. cit., p. 280.

54   On one occasion she did find herself in the same theatre as Dickens and was unable to control her distress. See [Jane Ellen Panton], *Leaves from a Life*, p. 143.

55   Johnson (ed.), op. cit., p. 360-1.

56   John Bigelow, *Retrospections of an Active Life*, 1909, vol. 1, p. 264. Bigelow thought Catherine 'not a handsome woman, though stout, hearty and matronly; there was something a little doubtful about her eye, and I thought her endowed with a temper that might be very violent when roused, though not easily rousable'. For a variant version of the misdirected jewels story, heard by Andersen, see Bredsdorff, op. cit., p. 128.

57   Johnson (ed.), op. cit., p. 369.

58   op. cit., p. 372.

59   op. cit., p. 376. Professor Ada Nisbet quotes *(Dickens and Ellen Ternan*, pp. 41-2) a close friend of Catherine's, Sir William Hardman, as writing that her grief over Walter's death was 'much enhanced by the fact that her husband has not taken any notice of the event to her, either by letter or otherwise. If anything were wanting to sink Charles Dickens to the lowest

depths of my esteem, *this* fills up the measure of his iniquity. As a writer, I admire him; as a man, I despise him.'

60 W. Dexter (ed.), op. cit., p. 264.

61 op. cit., p. 265.

62 Forster, p. 859.

63 Letter quoted by Alfred Dickens in his letter to G.W. Rusden (see above, note 34).

64 Letter from William Farren, *The Daily Mail*, 12 Sept. 1928: ' . . .The last time I met Mrs Dickens was when I sat beside her and her sister [Helen], then Mrs Roney, in the stalls of the Globe Theatre, at the first night of 'Dombey and Son' [i.e., *Heart's Delight,* by Andrew Halliday, first produced at the Globe, 17 Dec. 1873]. Mrs Dickens was greatly moved and the tears were falling. During the intervals she told me of the greatness of her husband, and one could see how great was her pride in him. . . .' Farren wrote again on the subject to *The Times* on 14 May 1933 (see Adrian, op. cit., p. 276, note 45).

65 [Jane Ellen Panton], op. cit., p. 145.

66 Letter of 5 Aug., 1872. Quoted by Adrian, op. cit., p. 172.

67 Rumours that Catherine drank persist into this century, the latest instance being the Mackenzies' assertion *(Dickens. A Life,* p. 246) that 'as the years passed and she became more isolated and neglected, Catherine took little exercise and indulged herself in food and drink'. Professor Wagenknecht remarks *(Dickens and the Scandalmongers,* p. 11) that he first heard allegations of Catherine's drinking in 1928 but has never found anything to confirm it. Annie Fields's surmise (quoted by Wagenknecht), 'He is a man who has suffered evidently', after recording that Dickens told her husband 'that nine out of ten cases of disagreement in marriage came from drink, he believed' *is* merely surmise. and, moreover, surmise by someone who adored Dickens and would want to excuse as much as possible his behaviour over the marriage breakdown.

68 Letter of 24 June 1858 quoted in Sotheby's Sale Catalogue for 21 May 1968. I am grateful to Professor R.S. Speck, the present owner of the manuscript, for supplying me with a photocopy of the full text and answering queries.

69 J.G. Millais, *Life and Letters of John Everett Millais,* 1899, vol. 1, p. 352. I am indebted to Professor Kathleen Tillotson for drawing my attention to the passage. She comments in a private note, 'What strikes me about this is that it counters the impression one gets from some biographers that Mrs D. lived a secluded life after the separation and didn't meet C.D.'s friends. And there's no suggestion that Leech (or the others named) sided with her against him, is there? I suspect that far more people than one knows simply took an independent line and continued to see both when it suited them.'

70 Two unpublished letters to Catherine now in the Humanities Research Center, University of Texas at Austin, illustrate her continuing enthusiasm

for things theatrical. One is a very friendly note of 9 Feb. 1866 from the actor Edward Sothern (celebrated for his Lord Dundreary), sending her his autograph as requested. The other is an amusing letter from Shirley Brooks regretting that he is powerless to get her a box for 'the Idden And' (i.e., Tom Taylor's historical melodrama, *The Hidden Hand*, 1864) but promising to ask the 'omnipotent' 'Uncle Mark' (i.e., Mark Lemon) to try to get one for her.

71   The departure of the youngest boy, Edward ('Plorn'), to Australia in 1868, aged sixteen, was a great trial to her. She lost no time in writing to him 'since she was desirous that he should find a letter from her on his arrival at Melbourne. He was much in her thoughts. . . . He had promised to send her a long account of his experiences on board; the smallest details, she declared, would be greatly interesting to her. "I miss you most sadly, my own darling Plorn," she could not refrain from telling him, and hoped, "please God", that he and "dearest Alfred" [already in Australia] had happy and prosperous futures before them. Harry . . . had been with her a great deal during the past week and had cheered her up.' (Storey, p. 125.)

72   Extract from Shirley Brooks's diary quoted by W. Teignmouth Shore in his *Charles Dickens and His Friends*, 1909, p. 262.

73   There is a nice glimpse of them playing with her at Gad's Hill after 1870 in an article by 'J.G.' (i.e., J. Gibbs) in his 'How I First Met Charles Dickens' *(Press News*, Dec. 1905): 'A few minutes later I had to smile. The youngsters had got Gran'ma in a swing, and the more she begged of them to stop it, the more they did nothing of the sort.'

74   See Elizabeth Dickens's comment on her quoted above, p. 125.

75   Nonesuch, vol. 2, p. 750.

76   Storey, p. 163.

77   The only other evidence we have that Catherine may have spoken out in private about her sufferings is a 'sad little note', as Johnson calls it, from her to Miss Coutts of 19 May 1858 which says, 'One day though not now I may be able to tell you how hardly I have been used' (Johnson, ed., op. cit., p. 357).

78   Unpublished letter from Kate Perugini to George Bernard Shaw, late Dec. 1897, now in the British Library (Add. MSS. 50546 79ff.). Quoted here by permission of The Trustees of the British Library.

79   I quote from a typescript transcript of Catherine Dickens's will at The Dickens House Museum, London.

80   Storey, p. 164.

81   N. and G. MacKenzie, *Dickens. A Life*, p. 305f. This judgment derives principally from Storey's words (pp. 22-3): 'Mrs Dickens's "faults" appear to have been principally due to her negativeness and anxiety in regard to her husband's health, especially concerning his meals, which, when he was engrossed in writing would, for hours, remain untouched; and her anxiety over the safety of her children. If one of them tumbled downstairs and set

up a howl in consequence, she would immediately fly to the conclusion that he or she had broken an arm or a leg.' Miss Storey is reporting Mrs Perugini whom she has quoted immediately before this as saying, 'There was nothing wrong with my mother; she had her faults, of course, as we all have – but she was a sweet, kind, peace-loving woman . . .'. 'Negativeness' is presumably Miss Storey's gloss, and the difficulty over mealtimes seems hard to credit as a serious persisting problem, given Dickens's well-documented habits of rigid routine in arranging his day. But Mrs Perugini's variously reported remarks about her parents are often contradictory: here is Miss Storey reporting her as saying Catherine was over-anxious about her children, but to Mrs Fields she once described her mother as 'heavy and unregardful' of them (quoted by Adrian, op. cit., p. 111).

82 Nonesuch, vol. 2, p. 264 (letter to the Hon. Mrs Richard Watson of 24 Jan. 1851). Dr Bowen comments (op. cit., p. 107), 'This honest revelation of his mental state illuminates the whole domestic tragedy'. Bowen's well-documented study of Catherine Dickens is, I think, the most sensitive and fair-minded account of her yet published.

83 Pilgrim, vol. 4, p. 253 (letter to Emile de la Rue of 27 Jan. 1845).

84 Charles Dickens, Junior, 'Reminiscences of My Father', Christmas Supplement to *The Windsor Magazine*, 1934, p. 21.

85 Notably Johnson who writes (p. 688), 'without ceasing to be the artless, childish creature that Dickens's memory painted Maria Beadnell as having been, Dora acquires after her marriage more and more of a colouring derived from Kate [i.e. Catherine]'. Arthur Adrian, too, writes (op. cit., p. 24), 'Like Dora . . . Catherine did not share her husband's intellectual interests, his efforts at improving her mind resulting only in nervousness'. So far as I know, no evidence exists for any such connubial pedagogic campaign and one wonders, in any case, if Dickens can properly be said to have *had* 'intellectual interests'. What he did have was a tremendous fascination with people and especially with the odder manifestations of their individual and social selves. Closely connected with this was his lifelong passion for the theatre. In both of these interests Catherine seems to have shared very fully.

86 Pilgrim, vol. 4, p. 161.

87 Letter to Henry Arthur Bright, 24 June 1858. Quoted in Sotheby's 1968 Sale Catalogue, see above, note 69.

88 *Harriet Martineau's Autobiography*, 1877, vol. 2, p. 379. Professor Speck informs me in a letter of 2 Oct. 1980 that the *Autobiography* 'was written in 1855, essentially at one sitting. It was immediately set into type, proof-read and printed in full. The *printed sheets* were then stored by the printer and Windermere publisher to be issued at her death . . . thus the text was frozen for the twenty-two years between its writing and printing and its publishing in 1877. . . .' He adds, à propos her comments on Dickens in 1855 and 1858, 'The mercurial change of opinion, of course, is not infrequent with HM'.

89 'A Visit to Charles Dickens by Hans Christian Andersen', *The Eclectic Magazine*, vol. 62 (May 1864), p. 111. Andersen's article originally appeared in *Bentley's Miscellany*, vol. 48, pp. 181-5. Andersen had taken to Catherine many years before, in 1847, when he first met Dickens: '*Mistress Dickens*', he wrote, had 'such an intensely good face that one at once felt confidence in her' (Bredsdorff, op. cit., pp. 26-7).

Chapter 8: Georgina

1 cf. Arthur Adrian, *Georgina Hogarth and the Dickens Circle*, p. 10: 'During the Dickenses' absence Georgina saw much of her little nieces and nephews. They in turn grew so fond of her that they babbled constantly of "Aunt Georgy" when their parents returned in June.' No source is given, however, for this account of the children's enthusiasm for their young aunt.
2 Pilgrim, vol. 4, p. 267 (letter to Emile de la Rue of 14 Feb. 1845).
3 See Adrian, op. cit., p. 28. Adrian quotes (p. 192) Georgina's letter to Annie Fields expressing her grief at Lytton's death in 1873: 'I sincerely loved Lord Lytton . . . he shewed a never failing regard for me – from the time I first knew him when I was quite a girl to the time of his death'.
4 Pilgrim, vol. 4, pp. 645, 215, 231.
5 See above, p. 97.
6 Thackeray's phrase. See his letter to Mrs Brookfield of 24 July 1849, describing his accidental meeting on the pier at Ryde of 'the great Dickens with his wife his children his Miss Hogarth all looking abominably coarse vulgar and happy . . .' (G.N. Ray, ed., *Letters and Private Papers of W.M. Thackeray*, vol. 2, p. 569).
7 Henry Morley's description of her as seen by him at a Tavistock House soirée in 1851 (H.S. Solly, *Life of Henry Morley*, p. 200).
8 Nonesuch, vol. 2, p. 395 (letter to William de Cerjat of 8 May 1852). According to Henrietta Ward (*Memories of Ninety Years*, 1924, pp. 283-4) the 'gentle and attractive' painter, William Mulready, seemed at one time likely to marry Georgina but nothing came of it; and Gladys Storey's records of her conversations with Kate Perugini include the statement that Georgina refused a proposal from Forster (D. Parker and M. Slater, 'The Gladys Storey Papers', *Dksn*, vol. 76, 1980, p. 4).
9 Nonesuch, vol. 2, p. 513 (letter to Georgina of 13 Nov. 1853).
10 W. Dexter (ed.), *Mr and Mrs Charles Dickens* (letter of 16 Oct. 1853), pp. 184-5.
11 Nonesuch, vol.2, p. 500.
12 Johnson (ed.), *Letters from Charles Dickens to Angela Burdett Coutts 1841-1865*, p. 239.
13 Esther's obsession with making herself useful to others and striving to 'win some love' for herself is made psychologically very plausible by giving her a fearsome childhood. An illegitimate child, she is brought up by a harsh

Calvinist aunt who pretends to be only her godmother and who tells her that it would have been better if she had never been born, exhorting her to 'submission, self-denial, diligent work' as the only suitable approach to 'a life begun with such a shadow on it'. Needless to say, this is fiction, not an account of Georgina's childhood!

14 *BH*, ch. 44.
15 *BH*, ch. 61.
16 *BH*, ch. 64.
17 Nonesuch, vol. 2, p. 569.
18 *LD,* Book I, ch. 22.
19 See above, pp. 37-8.
20 Adrian, op. cit., p. 77.
21 The Dickens family resided in Paris, October 1855 – May 1856. In March 1856 we find Dickens (writing from London where he has gone on *Household Words* business) to Georgina rather than to Catherine with instructions about the negotiations to be conducted with their French landlady. This seems to be the first evidence – surviving evidence, anyway – of Dickens's treating Georgina as the manager of his domestic affairs. A reference to her as 'my little housekeeper' (possibly an in-joke referring to Mr Wickfield's phrase for Agnes in *Copperfield*) in August 1850 relates to her running the family's summer-holiday home at Broadstairs while Catherine remained in their London home, awaiting the birth of the ill-fated little Dora.
22 Storey, p. 24.
23 *DC*, ch. 34.
24 See Appendix A.
25 She had taken down, at his dictation, much of his *Child's History of England* (serialized in *HW* 1851-3) whilst he was engaged in writing *BH*.
26 Miss Thomson to Mrs Stark. See note 26 to ch. 7, above.
27 Mrs Perugini, as reported by Gladys Storey, apparently believed that Georgina's interventions, like Forster's, were the reverse of helpful in settling disagreements between Dickens and Catherine: 'Miss H. & Mr F. were always called in over their quarrells [*sic*], & instead of allowing them to settle misunderstandings between themselves these two did nothing but muddle the situation' (D. Parker and M. Slater, op. cit., p. 4).
28 W. Dexter (ed.), op. cit., pp. 290-1.
29 Ray (ed.), op. cit., vol. 4, p. 86.
30 Hogarth's statement and Ouvry's letter quoted from K.J. Fielding's 'Dickens and the Hogarth Scandal', *Nineteenth Century Fiction*, vol. 10 (1955-6), pp. 64-73.
31 Unpublished letter.
32 K.J. Fielding, 'Charles Dickens and Colin Rae Brown', *Nineteenth Century Fiction*, vol. 7 (Sept. 1952), p. 104.
33 In his 'Dickens and the Hogarth Scandal' Fielding quotes from *The Court*

Circular, an entirely unofficial weekly publication, and from *Reynolds's Weekly Newspaper. The Court Circular* repeated the worst rumours about why Dickens's wife had left her home, i.e., 'on account of that talented gentleman's preference of his wife's sister to herself, a preference which has assumed a very definite and tangible shape'. *Reynolds's Weekly Newspaper* remarked, 'Let Mr Dickens remember that the odious – and we might almost add unnatural – profligacy of which he has been accused, would brand him with lifelong infamy . . .'.

34   According to Walter Dexter (letter to Comte de Suzannet of 22 February 1939, MS, The Dickens House) Gladys Storey had a note of a conversation with Henry Fielding Dickens in which the latter stated that the family possessed this certificate. Dexter adds that he had earlier heard this from another source, his predecessor as Editor of *The Dickensian,* B.W. Matz. If such a certificate was, in fact, obtained the embarrassment and humiliation its obtaining must have meant for Georgina would have added still more to her heroic stature in Dickens's eyes.

35   G. Ray (ed.), op. cit., vol. 4, p. 131.

36   W. Dexter (ed.), op. cit., p. xi. Ironically, it is Mrs Perugini, as reported by the late Miss Gladys Storey, who has been for modern biographers the strongest witness against Georgina's disinterestedness: 'Aunty was not quite straight', she is said to have exclaimed angrily after discovering that Georgina had once referred to her as 'intolerant', 'and I often stood up to her; *that* is why she called me "intolerant" ' (Storey, p. 212).

37   F.D. Finlay, an Ulster journalist, quoted in *Dksn,* vol. 29 (1933), p. 100.

38   Adrian, op. cit., pp. 131, 161.

39   *My Father as I Recall Him,* p. 12.

40   Dickens's enthusiasm for London social life seems to have been less than his daughter's. On 21 May 1863, for example, he writes to his Swiss friend, de Cerjat, that a certain City ball in honour of the Prince and Princess of Wales was to be 'a tremendously gorgeous business, and Mary is highly excited by her father's being invited, and she with him', and adds, 'Meantime the unworthy parent is devising all kinds of subterfuges for sending her and getting out of it himself' (Nonesuch, vol. 3, p. 353).

41   Nonesuch, vol. 3, p. 210.

42   Adrian quotes (op. cit., p. 104) a letter of 10 Aug. 1867 in which Dickens, in London, writes to Georgina at Gad's Hill, 'Last evening I missed you so much that I was obliged to go to the Olympic [Theatre]'.

43   *The Evening News,* 9 Nov. 1909.

44   Nonesuch, vol. 3, p. 160.

45   Forster, pp. 292-3.

46   Betsey married a man who turned out to be a scoundrel but her bitter disillusionment only gives her the more love to lavish on her hapless great-nephew, David.

47   I owe the identification of Halliday as the author of this essay to Professor

Philip Collins who informs me that the piece is reprinted in Halliday's *Sunnyside Papers* (1866).

48   Lady Pansy Lamb puts the matter well in her review of Adrian's *Georgina Hogarth (Dksn,* vol. 54, 1958, p. 24): 'To her, [Dickens] was clearly a glamorous hero, completely filling her horizon but as he had become her brother-in-law when she was nine years old, she never thought of him in any other relationship'. Such, it must be added, was not apparently the view of Thackeray's daughter, Lady Ritchie. Her daughter, Hester Fuller, wrote to Gladys Storey on 16 July 1939 after reading *Dickens and Daughter:* 'How *wicked* it was of Miss Hogarth not to withdraw – but my mother said she was in love with C.D. & was always charming & well & beautifully dressed, while Mrs C.D. was a weak and overwhelmed woman never out of having a child' (D. Parker and M. Slater, op. cit., p. 11).

49   Walter Dexter, reporting his conversation with Gladys Storey to the Comte de Suzannet in the letter already cited (note 33, above), writes that Miss Storey told him on Mrs Perugini's authority that 'Ellen was called to Gad's Hill (presumably by Georgina) on the death. Mrs P.[erugini] said she would never have allowed it had she been there.'

50   Mamie Dickens, op. cit., p. 15.

51   See 'Some Early Memories of the Dickens Fellowship' by Leslie C. Staples, *Dksn,* vol. 73 (1977) p. 134. Describing his visit as an autograph-hunting schoolboy to Georgina Hogarth, Mr Staples writes: '. . . she answered all my questions patiently . . . One question did arouse a little asperity. Would she agree that the character of Agnes Wickfield was in part founded upon her? "No, no, no," she replied, "not Agnes. Possibly there is something of me in Esther Summerson, but certainly not Agnes." '

52   See, for example, Angus Wilson, *The World of Charles Dickens,* p. 173. Wilson considers Georgina partly responsible for the presence in Dickens's fiction of the 'ideal of the passive, obedient, bright helpmeet who gives men spiritual and physical support in life's journey while asking nothing in return . . . a serious blemish in works of genius'.

Chapter 9: Father and Daughters

1   She was, in fact, christened Catherine Elizabeth Macready Dickens but never used those names. She told a friend in later life that this was because they were 'such a mouthful', adding, 'My Father always used to call me "Katie", but my brothers always called me "Kitty", and, eventually, so did my father. I like "Kitty" best of all – my friends call me that. I have dropped the three names with the approval of my solicitors – my signature is confined to Kate Perugini [she had become Mrs Perugini in 1874]'. (Gwladys Cox, 'Chelsea Memories of Mrs Perugini', *Chambers's Journal,*

vol. 6 (March 1937), p. 181.) As Dickens always spelled his name for her 'Katey' not 'Katie' I have used this form throughout this book.

2 Mamie Dickens, *My Father as I Recall Him*, p. 115.

3 Mamie Dickens, 'Charles Dickens at Home', *The Cornhill Magazine*, N.S., vol. 4 (Jan. 1885), p. 33. She makes the same point in *My Father as I Recall Him*, (pp. 14-15).

4 *My Father as I Recall Him*, p. 15. cf. Storey, p. 76.

5 In her *Cornhill* article already cited Mamie recalls a particular one of these songs 'about an old man who caught cold and rheumatism while sitting in an omnibus' which 'was a great favourite, and as it was accompanied by sneezes, coughs, and gesticulations, it had to be sung over and over again before the small audience was satisfied'.

6 Thackeray's elder daughter, Anne, who became Lady Ritchie, recalling the Dickens children's parties in her *Chapters from Some Memoirs* (1894), says that they 'were shining facts in our early London days – nothing came in the least near them. There were other parties, and they were very nice, but nothing to compare to these; not nearly so light, not nearly so shining, not nearly so going round and round.' Quoted by Philip Collins in his *Dickens: Interviews and Recollections* (p. 177).

7 Pilgrim, vol. 4, p. 177.

8 Lady Ritchie, *From the Porch*, p. 42.

9 Hans Christian Andersen visiting at Gad's Hill in 1857 noted in his diary, 'Of Dickens' daughters, *Marry* [sic] is like her mother, *Kate* very like her father's portrait in the early editions' (Elias Bredsdorff, *Hans Andersen and Charles Dickens*, p. 49).

10 Mrs Perugini to G.B. Shaw, 25 April 1889 (MS British Library [Add. MSS. 50546 79ff.]). This and all subsequent quotations from the unpublished correspondence of Mrs Perugini and Miss Storey with Shaw are made by permission of the Trustees of the British Library.

11 Storey, p. 76.

12 op. cit., pp. 77-8.

13 Storey Papers (blue and black notebook, p. 3) at Dickens House. Quoted by permission of the Trustees and Mr Charles Monteith.

14 *MED*, ch. 3.

15 His one deviation from this seems to have been in the matter of handwriting. Mamie in an interview for the 1895 Christmas Number of *'The Young Man'* and *'The Young Woman'*, having mentioned that 'my father was always much interested about our lessons, looking over our copybooks, slates, etc., pointing out where we were wrong, taking the greatest pains to impress upon us the why and wherefore of any faults he had to find', continues: 'He had a curious dislike for the very large roundhand writing copies which were set us in those days. . . . He stopped them entirely at last, considering them a waste of time, and of no use whatever in forming a child's handwriting.' In her *Cornhill* article she writes that Dickens would

give prizes to his children 'for industry, for punctuality, for neat and unblotted copy-books' – these things, David Copperfield's 'habits of punctuality, order, diligence', seem to have been what mattered to Dickens in developing a child rather than academic attainments.

16   Dickens was acquainted with Mrs Elisabeth Reid who founded the College in 1849 – see Pilgrim, vol. 4, p. 287, note 2. Margaret Tuke's *History of Bedford College for Women 1849-1937* (1939) records (p. 282) 'Catherine (later Mrs Perugini), daughter of Charles Dickens' as having been a student at the Ladies' College (as it was then called) in 1852, her twelfth year. The original registers for this period have not survived but a later transcript of them shows Katey as down for a drawing class. When the College was founded in 1849 it was for 'ladies above the age of twelve' but in January 1853 a 'junior department', or school, was started and the College age raised. It may have been after this that Katey was enrolled. Her teacher would have been Francis Stephen Cary, son of the Dante translator, and Head of the Bloomsbury School of Art. He exhibited regularly at the Royal Academy and the Society of British Artists between 1837/8 and 1876 and in 1854 showed a painting entitled *The Cricket on the Hearth* at the Society. (I am indebted to Professor Kathleen Tillotson for many of these details.)

17   Lady Ritchie, op. cit., p. 40.

18   See Storey Papers at The Dickens House.

19   Interview cited in note 15 above.

20   Johnson (ed.), *Letters from Charles Dickens to Angela Burdett Coutts 1841-1865*, p. 331.

21   'On Women Old and New', *Dksn*, vol. 14 (1918), pp. 313–15.

22   Storey, p. 14; 'Lady Mathews would relate, with a twinkle, that Kitty, at one time, was referred to as "The fast Miss Kate Dickens!" '.

23   In *My Father as I Recall Him* Mamie writes (p.8): 'My love for my father has never been touched or approached by any other love. I hold him in my heart of hearts as a man apart from all other men, as one apart from all other beings.'

24   Letter to Henry Arthur Bright, 24 June 1858. Quoted from Sotheby's Sale Catalogue of Books and Manuscripts, 21 May 1968, lot 403.

25   Storey, pp. 95-6. See above, p. 140.

26   op. cit., p. 94. New evidence (ostensibly records of Mrs Perugini's fireside talk) in the Storey Papers at The Dickens House suggests that Katey did brave her father's displeasure by keeping in touch with her mother: 'for nearly two years [after the separation] C.D. would scarcely speak to K.P. because she visited her mother' (D. Parker and M. Slater, 'The Gladys Storey Papers', *Dksn,* vol. 76, 1980, p. 4).

27   For the Thomson/Stark letter see above (note 27 to ch. 7).

28   Quoted by Philip Collins, op. cit., pp. 154-5.

29   See Wilkie Collins's account of his brother's life written for the *DNB*.

30 Just at this time (spring 1860) Millais, struck by Katey's beauty, asked Dickens's permission to use her as the model for the female figure in the painting, 'The Black Brunswicker', on which he was then working. Millais's son notes that Katey was 'a handsome girl, with a particularly sweet expression and beautiful auburn hair that contrasted well with the sheen of her white satin dress' in the painting. The picture shows an officer of the Brunswicker Regiment in full regalia parting from his wife who leans upon his breast and holds the handle of the door behind her as if to prevent his going. Katey gave Millais's son her reminiscences of the sittings, describing herself as having been 'very shy and quiet in those days' – something that we must, I think, find difficult to believe! See J.G. Millais, *The Life and Letters of Sir John Everett Millais*, 1899, vol. 1, pp. 353-5 (I am indebted to Professor Kathleen Tillotson for this reference).

31 Storey, pp. 105, 106.

32 Nonesuch, vol. 3, pp. 160, 173. In the letter to De Cerjat Dickens continues, 'My eldest daughter has not yet started any conveyance on the road to matrimony (that I know of); but it is likely enough that she will, as she is very agreeable and intelligent. They [Mamie and Katey] are both very pretty.' If it is true that, as Storey says (p. 104), Mamie was in love at this time 'but Dickens did not approve of the match, so that was the end of it', this would seem to be a singularly heartless way of writing about her.

33 These letters are now in the Pierpont Morgan Library, New York, and I am grateful to Mr Peter Caracciolo for drawing my attention to them. They are quoted here by permission of the Library's Trustees.

34 See Storey Papers (The Dickens House), blue and black notebook, p. 105: 'She was in love with Edmund Yates who was married to a lovely wife (the affair made K.P. [Kate Perugini] quite ill [)].' Miss Storey adds to this a footnote: 'he was not aware of her feelings for him'.

35 She does record one lapse back into reading however: 'The other day for a treat Charlie got me La petite Comtesse [by Octave Feuillet], to read. I never was more delighted with any story, it is so beautifully and pathetically written but so sad that it made me miserable. I shan't read any more books, for a whole day after I had finished my charming petite Comtesse, I found I took not the faintest interest in any of my household duties, and wanted only to sit by the fire and read, read, read all through my life.' She adds, 'Oh don't be frightened, I am all right again'.

36 According to S.M. Ellis who includes a sympathetic study of Collins in his *Wilkie Collins, Le Fanu and Others* (1931), the second of these novels, *Strathcairn* (1864), is 'a remarkable and delicately told story of frustrated love and resulting suicide, with picturesque scenic descriptions of the Highlands' and the third and last, *At the Bar* (1866), serialized in *ATYR*, 'is a tragic tale of poisoning'.

37 Ellis, op. cit., p. 72. (Ellis does not name the source from which he is quoting.)

38   See M. Veronica Stokes, 'Charles Dickens: A Customer of Coutts & Co.',
      Dksn, vol. 68 (1972), p. 26.
39   Nonesuch, vol. 3, p. 402; unpublished letter to Fields of 7 July 1868;
      Fechter's comments recorded in Annie Fields's diary for 3 Aug. 1870 as
      quoted by Adrian *(Georgina Hogarth and the Dickens Circle,* p. 130);
      unpublished letter to Fields of 14 Dec. 1868.
40   Walter Dexter to Comte Alain de Suzannet, 22 Feb. 1939 (MS, The
      Dickens House). Quoted here by permission of the Trustees and of Mr
      Richard Dexter. Some support for Storey's assertion might be adduced
      from Frederick Lehmann's dark hints about the 'infamy' of Collins's
      marrying anyone (see J. Lehmann, *Ancestors and Friends,* 1962, p. 210).
      We might note also that Collins told his mother six months after marrying
      Katey, 'We sleep in two beds like sensible people' (MS, Pierpont Morgan
      Library, quoted by permission of the Trustees).
41   Lehmann, op. cit., p. 211. Frederick Lehmann was a good friend of
      Dickens's by this date. His wife, Nina, was the niece of Janet Wills, wife of
      Dickens's sub-editor and confidential man of business. Other letters of
      Frederick's indicate, John Lehmann states, that Katey was 'discontented,
      and . . . intensely eager . . . to find other lovers'.
42   Unpublished letters of 2 Feb. and 13 Dec. 1866.
43   Quoted by Adrian, op. cit., pp. 124-5.
44   For the full poem (which is subtitled 'Written in a Lady's Album') see p. 105
      of vol. 13 *(Ballads and Miscellanies)* of the Biographical Edition of
      Thackeray's works (Smith, Elder & Co., 1899), edited by his daughter
      Lady Ritchie. See also Gordon Ray (ed.), *Letters and Private Papers of
      W.M. Thackeray,* vol. 4, p. 278.
45   Quoted by Adrian, op. cit., p. 177. Perugini (1839-1918), whom Georgina
      describes as 'a most sensible, good, honourable and upright man and
      devotedly attached to Katey', came to London in 1863 and began exhibit-
      ing at the Royal Academy that year. He was given encouragement and
      financial help by Lord Leighton. His paintings have titles such as 'Silken
      Tresses' or 'A Siesta' and are 'mostly of elegant ladies in interiors, some-
      times with a romantic or humorous theme' (Wood, *Dictionary of
      Victorian Painters).*
46   Nonesuch, vol. 3, p. 478.
47   Percy Fitzgerald, *Memories of Charles Dickens,* 1913, p. 54.
48   John Lehmann, op. cit., p. 167.
49   Nonesuch, vol. 3, p. 430. For Mamie's relations with the Humphery family
      see William J. Carlton's article, 'Dickens' Family Links with Penton', in
      The Andover Advertiser, 25 July 1969.
50   Nonesuch, vol. 3, p. 755.
51   Diary entry for 11 July 1870 by the *Punch* journalist Shirley Brooks;
      quoted by W. Teignmouth Shore in his *Charles Dickens and his Friends,*
      1909, p. 262.

52   See note 32 above.
53   MS, The British Library.
54   Adrian, op. cit., pp. 124, 119, 158.
55   'The Novelist of Christmas Time. Recollections of Charles Dickens. An Interview with his Eldest Daughter', Christmas Number of *'The Young Man'* and *'The Young Woman'*, 1895, pp. 55-8.
56   John Harwood, 'What I Owe Charles Dickens', *Dksn*, vol. 20 (1924), p. 89.
57   Mrs Perugini to Florence Dickens, 2 June 1906 (MS, The Dickens House, Kitton Papers; quoted by permission of the Trustees).
58   'Some Early Memories of the Dickens Fellowship', *Dksn*, vol. 73 (1977), pp. 132-7.
59   Mrs Perugini to George Bernard Shaw, 17 April 1889 and 10 May 1898 (MSS, The British Library).
60   *My Father as I Recall Him*, pp. 114-15 and 20.
61   Quoted by Philip Collins, op. cit., p. 288.
62   Storey, pp. 133-4.
63   Autograph note (not signed) by Shaw, dated Dec. 1897 (MS, The British Library).
64   Mrs Perugini to G.B. Shaw [Dec. 1897] (MS, The British Library).
65   Gladys Storey wrote to Shaw on 23 July 1939 (MS, The British Library) that Katey 'retained in the Chelsea flat some most incriminating letters written by Dickens to somebody; which letters were destroyed by Henry Dickens after Kate's death'. But if these had been to Ellen, whom Miss Storey has just been discussing in her letter, why does she not name her? And since Ellen survived until 1914 and left children to inherit her property why should Katey, who seems, unlike Georgina and Mamie, not to have remained friendly with Ellen, have come into possession of Dickens's letters to her?
66   Mrs Perugini to G.B. Shaw, 11 Dec. 1897 (MS, The British Library).
67   Nonesuch, vol. 2, p. 633.
68   See Adrian, op. cit., p. 125.
69   Bella is wearing mourning for a fiancé she has never met, John Harmon. He has been, so everyone believes, drowned just after his return to England from the Cape, having returned to claim a rich inheritance which his malicious father has made conditional on his marrying Bella whom old Harmon once saw having tantrums in the street when she was a little girl. Bella was dreading the meeting – 'how *could* I like him, left to him in a will, like a dozen of spoons . . .?' – but believed his money would 'smooth away' the ridiculousness of their arranged marriage. But now, she laments, 'here I am left with all the ridiculous parts of the situation remaining and added to them all this ridiculous dress!' (*OMF*, Book I, ch. 4).
70   *OMF*, Book IV, ch. 4.
71   Storey, p. 106.

72   *OMF*, Book IV, ch. 5.
73   'Mrs Perugini said that she could sum up the mistakes in her father's life on one half-sheet of notepaper, and that she would commence with the words: "What could you expect from such an uncanny genius?" ' (Storey, p. 91).
74   Quoted by Adrian, op. cit., p. 126.
75   Storey, p. 219.
76   op. cit., p. 91.
77   See Mrs Perugini's letter to M.H. Spielmann of 22 Sept. 1903, first published by David Parker in his 'The Gladys Storey Papers. A Footnote', *Dksn*, vol. 76 (1980), pp. 158-9.
78   Mrs Perugini to G.B. Shaw, 19 Dec. 1897 (MS, The British Library).

Chapter 10: Ellen

1   First published by Franklin P. Rolfe in his 'More Letters to the Watsons', *Dksn*, vol. 38 (1942), p. 190.
2   Newspaper review of 1857 quoted (p. 38) by Malcolm Morley in his 'The Theatrical Ternans Part IV', *Dksn*, vol. 55 (1959), pp. 36-44.
3   W.H. Bowen (*Charles Dickens and His Family*, p. 117) quotes a notice in an Edinburgh paper in which Mrs Ternan's virtues (with those of two other actresses) are thus summed up, 'all as much respected for their virtues in private life as they are for their genius on the stage'.
4   W. Toynbee (ed.), *The Diaries of William Charles Macready 1833-1851*, vol. 1, p. 111. Macready was kind to Mrs Ternan, however, when she was left a widow. In his diary for 21 Oct. 1846 (op. cit., vol. 2, p. 347) he notes: 'Letter from Mrs Ternan accepting with much feeling my offer of ten pounds, and wishing it to be considered as a loan. I wrote to her, enclosing a cheque for the amount; but unwilling to hamper her with the sense of a *debt*, requested, if the surplus of her labours offered it, to transfer it as a gift from me to her little girl.'
5   See, for example, Thomas Wright in his *Life of Charles Dickens*, pp. 244-5: 'An intimate friendship between the famous author and the young actress soon followed, a friendship that daily threatened to become more than friendship. She was often in his house and he liked to have her in his study when he was writing. How perilous is the rock named Beauty! What havoc may result from a smile, a whiff of scent, a touch — even a tear! Especially when mingled with the sob of violins!' Wright's authority for these assertions was presumably Ellen's former friend, Canon Benham (see Appendix B). Dame Una Pope-Hennessy, a far more soberly responsible scholar than Wright, nevertheless treated her readers to this flight of fancy about the *Frozen Deep* rehearsals in her *Charles Dickens* (1945): 'Little, fair-haired Ellen Ternan, with her sympathetic blue eyes, took up such a worshipping attitude and seemed so pathetically anxious to interpret every line and gesture according to Dickens's wishes that she completely captivated him.

The rehearsals took place at Tavistock House and the more its owner coached his team, the more his infatuation for Ellen grew. Both the Miss Ternans were charming and both ran in and out of the study, but only one sat on the arm of the manager's chair, sang duets with him at the school-room piano and seemed, to the family, to take possession of the house' (pp. 370-1).

6   This rather improbable-sounding incident seems to have been invented by C. Bechhoffer Roberts ('Ephesian') for his anti-Dickens novel, *This Side Idolatry* (1928). It was next presented (as having been told to him by Canon Benham) by Wright in his *Daily Express* article of 3 April 1934, '98 Years Ago To-Day – Charles Dickens Began His Honeymoon', and then used again by him (dropping the specific attribution to Benham) in his biography of Dickens the following year.

7   Storey, pp. 93-4.

8   Nonesuch, vol. 2, p. 873.

9   Mrs Perugini's description of Ellen, according to Gladys Storey (p. 93).

10   See Malcolm Morley, op. cit., p. 36.

11   A humorous account of their adventures, written jointly by Dickens and Wilkie Collins and published in weekly instalments in *HW* during Oct. 1857. Reprinted in the *CS* volume of the Oxford Illustrated Dickens.

12   These letters to Wills were first published by Ada Nisbet in her *Dickens and Ellen Ternan*, p. 57.

13   Unpublished letter.

14   This seems borne out by the letter he wrote to Wills on 25 Oct. 1858 asking him to inquire at Scotland Yard about the behaviour of a policeman who had apparently been embarrassing or annoying Maria and Ellen ('our two little friends'), who were living in unfurnished lodgings in Berners Street, off Oxford Street, whilst Mrs Ternan was temporarily away in Italy, getting Fanny settled there to pursue her musical training. 'My suspicion is,' Dickens writes, 'that the Policeman in question has been suborned to find out all about their domesticity by some "Swell". If so, there can be no doubt that the man ought to be dismissed' (letter first published by Franklin P. Rolfe in his 'Dickens and the Ternans', *Nineteenth Century Fiction*, vol. 4, 1949-50, pp. 243-4; quoted in part by Johnson, p. 940). Dickens also confides to Wills in this letter the information that it is he who has 'sent the eldest sister to Italy, to complete a musical education'. Whether or not he actually paid for Fanny's Italian venture, he certainly gave her letters of introduction like the (as yet unpublished) one of 12 Sept. 1858 to Mrs Frances Trollope to be found in the Humanities Research Center, University of Texas at Austin.

15   Johnson, p. 909. See above, p. 142.

16   The fantasy reappeared in a letter to another woman friend, Lady Duff Gordon, on 23 Jan. 1858: 'Nothing would satisfy me at this present writing, but the having to go up a tremendous mountain, magic spell in one

hand and sword in the other, to find the girl of my heart (whom I never *did* find), surrounded by fifty Dragons – kill them all – and bear her off triumphant . . .' (Sotheby's Sale Catalogue, 24 July 1979, lot 196).

17   Attention has already been drawn to the biographical significance of this story by Harry Stone in his 'The Genesis of a Novel: *Great Expectations*' (in E.W.F. Tomlin (ed.), *Charles Dickens 1812-1870. A Centenary Volume*, pp. 109-31).

18   For a summary of this controversy and the principal sources for it see Appendix B.

19   Dickens no doubt burned Ellen's letters along with hundreds of others in the regular bonfires of his correspondence that he began having in 1860. As to his letters to her, the Dickensian collector, W.R. Hughes, told Thomas Wright that someone had privately offered them to him for sale in London in 1893. Hughes, according to Wright (*Life of Charles Dickens*, p. 282) refused to buy them, saying that they could not have been acquired honestly; he advised the vendor to go home and burn them – curious advice, surely, as the proper course would have been to restore them to Ellen who was still living at the time.

20   For example, the famous letter of 4 July 1867 to one of his closer women friends, Frances Elliot, née Dickinson, who acted with him in *The Frozen Deep*. The letter was printed in Nonesuch (vol. 3, pp. 475-6) but misdated (see note 75 to Part X, chap. 1 of Johnson). Mrs Elliot, who was later to bother Dickens a great deal about her marital difficulties, seems accidentally to have discovered some secret about Ellen's past and evidently wished to send her some supportive message or perhaps even meet her. Dickens replied: 'I feel your affectionate letter truly and deeply, but it would be inexpressibly painful to N to think that you knew her history. She has no suspicion that your assertion of your friend against the opposite powers, ever brought you to the knowledge of it. She would not believe that you could see her with my eyes, or know her with my mind. Such a presentation is impossible. It would distress her for the rest of her life. I thank you none the less, but it is quite out of the question. If she could hear that, she could not have the pride and self reliance which (mingled with the gentlest nature) has borne her, alone, through so much.' I cannot agree with Johnson that the meaning of this is 'perfectly clear'. He believes it shows that Mrs Elliot 'in defending [Dickens] against his accusers, had learned the truth [i.e., that Ellen was his mistress] and assured him of her sympathy and support, even voiced a desire to meet "N" (Nelly) and be her friend. That plea, out of regard for Ellen's feelings, Dickens felt obliged to reject' (Johnson, p. 1060). We cannot be sure what Dickens means himself by 'your friend', for one thing; and somehow the letter seems to read very oddly if we are to suppose Dickens is writing to an old and intimate friend, a woman, who has just discovered he is keeping a young mistress. He seems to be totally unembarrassed on his own behalf, feeling no need whatever to explain or justify

himself (yet no man was ever more willing to justify himself than Dickens) and the reference to Ellen's 'pride and self reliance' is decidedly odd if he is, in fact, referring to her having agreed to become a kept woman. It seems to me far more likely that Mrs Elliot had stumbled upon some knowledge of a painful episode in Ellen's past which had been cruelly misconstrued by others at the time but in which Dickens fervently believed her to have played a wholly innocent part. In the preceding paragraph in the letter Dickens wrote: 'The "magic circle" consists of but one member. I don't in the least care for Mrs T.T. except that her share in the story is (as far as *I* am concerned) a remembrance impossible to swallow. Therefore, and for the magic sake [*sic*], I scrupulously try to do her justice, and not to see her – out of my path – with a jaundiced vision.' It is usually assumed that 'Mrs. T.T.' refers to Fanny Ternan who had married Thomas Trollope in October 1866 and whom he makes a clear reference to at the end of the letter, but it might equally refer to Ellen's mother, Mrs Thomas Ternan. We simply do not know. But, again, the phrasing ('her share in the story') suggests to me a reference to an episode in the past which caused Ellen suffering rather than to a current situation.

21 These extracts, and others similar, were first published by Ada Nisbet, op. cit., pp. 55-6.
22 In a long letter to his friend Thomas Mitton describing the accident (Nonesuch, vol. 3, pp. 425-6) he says, 'Two ladies were my fellow-passengers, an old one and a young one'. The young one can certainly be identified as Ellen through Dickens's letter to the stationmaster at Charing Cross of 12 June 1865 inquiring about some trinkets, including 'a gold seal engraved Ellen', lost by the young lady (Johnson, p. 1020) and it seems quite plausible, therefore, that the older lady should have been her mother.
23 Nonesuch, vol. 3, p. 429.
24 Nisbet, op. cit., p. 57. He seems to have made elaborate arrangements for her to be helped, if she should need help, by Wills. Among the Memoranda, pertaining to *HW*, etc., which he drew up for Wills's guidance during his absence, occurs one headed 'NELLY' which states, 'If she needs any help will come to you' and tells him that Forster, who holds Dickens's power of attorney, 'knows Nelly as you do, and will do anything for her if you want anything done' (Nisbet, p. 53; Johnson, p. 1076).
25 See Nisbet, op. cit., pp. 52-4.
26 [Julia Clara Byrne], *Gossip of the Century*, 1892, vol. 1, p. 225. Quoted by Nisbet, op. cit., p. 22.
27 Ellen retired from acting in 1859, and in 1860 acquired a four-storey terrace house (built 1847), with basement area, No. 2 Houghton Place, Ampthill Square, which stood just north of Euston Station (the terrace was destroyed in World War II air raids). An Assignment of the Lease of the property dated 2 July 1901 is at The Dickens House and shows that Ellen, by that time Mrs G.W. Robinson, sold the leasehold to a Mrs Day at that

date. Together with the document is a declaration by Ellen dated 19 June 1901 which states, 'In the month of March 1860 I in my then name of Ellen Lawless Ternan, Spinster, purchased from my sisters Frances Eleanor Ternan and Maria Susannah Ternan the leasehold premises No. 2 Houghton Place Ampthill Square in the Parish of St. Pancras . . ./Since my said purchase I have had quiet enjoyment of the said premises and have received the rents and profits thereof. . . .' The archives of the Bedford Estate show Mrs Ternan as paying the ground rent of the house from Lady Day (25 March) 1859. The ground rent continued to be paid in her name up to 1901 (she actually died in 1873) when Mrs Day became the lease-holder. I am indebted to Mrs Draper, Archivist of the Bedford Estate, for assistance in elucidating this matter.

28   See M. Veronica Stokes, 'Charles Dickens: A Customer of Coutts & Co.', *Dksn*, vol. 68 (1972), p. 26. Johnson calls attention to some large payments made to Wills from America during Dickens's 1867/8 Reading tour and remarks, 'In view of Dickens's parting memorandum to Wills about Ellen, and Dickens's decision not to have her join him in America, the reader may give these payments . . .what significance he wishes . . .'. As he is at pains to emphasize, there is no evidence to support the view that these payments relate in any way to Ellen (Johnson, note 45, to Part X, chap. 2). It does seem, however, that Dickens did pay Ellen's rent, under a pseudonym, when she was living at Peckham during the last two years of his life (see Appendix B).

29   *TTC*, Book I, ch. 4.

30   J. Foster, *Alumni Oxoniensis 1715-1886* (1888).

31   Morley, op. cit., Parts VIII, IX and X (*Dksn*, vol. 56 (1960), pp. 76-83 and 153-7; vol. 57 (1961), pp. 29-35). Morley derived much of his information from conversations with Ellen's daughter, Mrs Gladys Reece.

32   As testified by Mrs Reece in her correspondence with J.W.T. Ley, Aug-Dec. 1935 (these letters are now in The Dickens House archives).

33   These letters are now in the possession of The Dickens House Museum, London. For copyright reasons I am unable to quote them directly.

34   'Ellen Ternan – Some Letters', *Dksn*, vol. 61 (1965), pp. 30-5.

35   Thomas Wright, *The Life of Charles Dickens*, pp. 280-1.

36   Hugh Kingsmill (i.e., Hugh Kingsmill Lunn), *The Sentimental Journey. A Life of Charles Dickens*, pp. 196, 197, 195.

37   Two recent illustrations of the unquestioning acceptance of Kingsmill's identifications and consequent interpretation of Ellen's character may be found in Philip Hobsbaum's *Reader's Guide to Charles Dickens* where we read that Estella is 'based upon the Irish actress, Ellen Ternan, who eventu-ally became Dickens's mistress' (p. 277) and in Albert J. Guerard's *The Triumph of the Novel* where he remarks (p. 78) that Dickens may at first have tried to see Ellen as a new Mary Hogarth until 'she actually became his mistress, and . . . revealed certain unangelic mercenary traits'.

38   As demonstrated by Barbara Hardy in chapter 3 of her *Moral Art of Dickens*.

39   See the Clarendon Edition of *The Mystery of Edwin Drood*, ed. Margaret Cardwell, p. 41.

40   His relationship with Ellen was, of course, known to most of his intimate friends though they may not have known the exact nature of it. The hints dropped in later life by Dickens's protégés, G.A. Sala and Edmund Yates (see Nisbet, op. cit., pp. 27-8), suggest that they certainly assumed it was a lover/mistress relationship. The only friend of whom we have clear evidence as having discussed the relationship with Dickens himself is his American hostess, Annie Fields, who wrote in her diary on 2 May 1868 (the day after Dickens reached Liverpool, returning from his American tour): 'I cannot help rehearsing in my mind the intense joy of his beloved. Yet I know today to be the day and these hours, *his hours*. Tomorrow Gad's hill.' (Quoted by Arthur Adrian, *Georgina Hogarth and the Dickens Circle*, p. 114.)

41   Nonesuch, vol. 3, pp. 342-3.

42   Johnson, p. 1008.

43   Entry in Dickens's pocket-diary for 1867 quoted by Felix Aylmer in his *Dickens Incognito*, p. 95.

44   'George Silverman's Explanation' is included in the *UT & RP* volume of the Oxford Illustrated Dickens.

45   Nonesuch, vol. 3, p. 533.

46   It is certainly a most extraordinary coincidence that the man Ellen did eventually marry was called George *Wharton* Robinson. As she did not meet him, it seems, until after Dickens's death, and there is no evidence that Dickens knew of his existence (he would have been a boy of sixteen when Dickens wrote 'George Silverman') the thing really would appear to be pure coincidence, however.

47   Wilson writes *(The Wound and the Bow*, 1941, p. 72): 'This episode of Ellen Ternan has been hushed up so systematically, and the information about it is still so meagre, that it is difficult to get an impression of Ellen. We do, however, know something about what Dickens thought of her from the heroines in his last books who are derived from her. Estella is frigid and indifferent . . . she marries a man she does not love for his money. Bella Wilfer . . . is equally intent upon money – which was certainly one of the things that Ellen got out of her liaison with Dickens.' Later, he refers to Helena as the 'Ellen Ternan heroine' of *MED* and comments that she 'is here frankly made an actress'.

II The Women of the Novels

Epigraphs. In R.R. Madden, *The Literary Life and Correspondence of the Countess of Blessington*, vol. 2, p. 386; *A Woman's Story*, vol. 3, p. 12.

Chapter 11: 'Sketches by Boz' to 'Martin Chuzzlewit'

1   'Wilkie Collins about Charles Dickens (From a marked copy of Forster's "Dickens")', *Pall Mall Gazette,* 20 January 1890.

2   This distinction evidently survives adaptation of the novel. Victoria Radin, reviewing a revival of the musical *Oliver!* in *The Observer,* 1 Jan. 1978, wrote, 'In its fashion it is our 'Threepenny Opera' – but what a limp-wristed and anti-woman model it is. The undertaker's wife and Bumble's new widow-bride are music hall burlesques who could have been played easily in drag: the only woman of the piece is Nancy whose involvement with Sikes is literally the death of her.'

3   'On Going to See a Man Hanged' *(Fraser's Magazine,* August, 1840; Biographical Edition of Thackeray's Works, 1898, vol. 3, p. 643). At her initial appearance in the novel (ch. 9) Nancy is described by means of some rather arch irony which nevertheless intimates very clearly that she is slatternly, rouged and boisterous, and Cruikshank's illustrations of her certainly do not make her into a 'Gesner shepherdess' (see Michael Steig, 'Cruikshank's Nancy', *Dksn,* vol. 72, 1976, pp. 87-92). But Dickens soon begins to tone down these aspects of Nancy's appearance and manners until she is almost indistinguishable in these respects from a conventional heroine, hence Thackeray's objection.

4   *OT,* ch. 16.

5   F.R. Leavis will allow no Blakean excuses for the stylization of Little Nell, however. In his 'Dickens and Blake: *Little Dorrit*' he observes that 'to suggest taking Little Nell seriously would be absurd: there's nothing there. She doesn't derive from any perception of the real; she's a contrived unreality, the function of which is to facilitate in the reader a gross and virtuous self-indulgence' *(Dickens the Novelist,* 1970, pp. 225-6).

6   *MC,* ch. 29.

7   See ch. 11 of his *The City of Dickens.*

8   *MC,* ch. 29.

9   *MC,* ch. 40.

10   *OT,* ch. 37.

11   *OCS,* ch. 36.

12   The passage in the proof-sheets of *OCS* in which Sally states that she is the Marchioness's mother was first published by Gerald G. Grubb in his 'Dickens's Marchioness Identified' *(Modern Language Notes,* vol. 68, 1953, pp. 162-5). Grubb speculated that the passage was suppressed by Dickens because he feared that the Marchioness might be taking too much

of the reader's interest away from Nell but Angus Easson's explanation ('Dickens's Marchioness Again', *Modern Language Review*, vol. 65, 1970, pp. 516-18), which is the one I follow above, seems far more persuasive.

13   *AN*, ch. 3.

14   ' "You are quite a philosopher, Sam," said Mr Pickwick. "It runs in the family, I b'lieve, sir," replied Mr Weller. "My father's wery much in that line, now. If my mother-in-law [i.e., stepmother] blows him up, he whistles. She flies in a passion, and breaks his pipe; he steps out, and gets another. Then she screams wery loud, and falls into 'sterics: and he smokes wery comfortably 'till she comes to agin. That's philosophy, sir, an't it?" ' (*PP*, ch. 16.)

15   *PP*, ch. 52.

16   *BR*, ch. 80.

17   Mrs Porter of Clapham whose genius for 'scandal and sarcasm' terrorizes her neighbours is supposed to have been based on Mrs Leigh of Clapton, mother of Mary Anne, the friend of Maria Beadnell's who made mischief between Maria and Dickens (see above, p. 28). Mrs Leigh's liking for scandal is touched on in 'The Bill of Fare'.

18   *NN*, ch. 16.

19   When writing as an essayist rather than a novelist he seems to have been more fairminded, witness his comment in 'The Young Couple' (*Sketches of Young Couples*, 1840; included in the *SB* volume of the Oxford Illustrated Dickens) about the unmarried aunt of the bride at a wedding: 'People may call her an old maid, and so she may be, but she is neither cross nor ugly for all that; on the contrary, she is very cheerful and pleasant-looking, and very kind and tender-hearted: which is no matter of surprise except to those who yield to popular prejudices without thinking why, and will never grow wiser and never know better'.

20   *SB*, 'The Boarding-House'.

21   The nearest he comes to creating such a figure is with the actress Henrietta Perowker who succeeds in bewitching into marriage prosperous old Mr Lillyvick (*NN*, ch. 25) but later deserts him for a 'half-pay [i.e., retired] captain'.

22   *BR*, ch.9

23   *NN*, ch. 46.

24   *BR*, ch. 31.

25   *BR*, ch. 59.

26   *CB*, *The Cricket on the Hearth*, 'Chirp the First'.

27   *MC*, ch. 39.

28   *MC*, ch. 45.

29   See note 22 to ch. 5, above.

30   Jemima Evans in 'Miss Evans and the Eagle' (*SB*) is also a culpable 'Maria' but a good deal further down the social scale. Her flirtatious behaviour, and that of her friend, at the Eagle Tavern eventually provokes a breach of

the peace in which their escorts get beaten up: 'Miss J'mima Ivins and friend being conscious that the affray was in no slight degree attributable to themselves, of course went into hysterics forthwith; declared themselves the most injured of women; exclaimed, in incoherent ravings, that they had been suspected – wrongly suspected – oh! that they should ever have lived to see the day – and so forth . . .'.

31 *MC*, ch. 2.

32 'And she, poor creater', continues the indignant neighbour, 'won't swear the peace agin him, nor do nothin', because she likes the wretch arter all – worse luck!' Later in the sketch the wife herself appears, pathetically attempting to get her drunken husband to come home, only to be knocked 'flying out of the shop'.

33 *PP*, ch. 6.

34 The Marchioness is generally agreed to be a good and convincing portrait of a shrewd little girl made precocious through the difficulties she has to contend with, and the fact that Dickens was, as Forster tells us, using a real-life model for the character may have something to do with his success. The Marchioness was based, apparently, upon 'a sharp little worldly and also kindly' maid-of-all-work from Chatham workhouse who waited on the Dickens family in the bad days of young Charles's childhood, when the family were living in reduced circumstances in Camden Town and then in the Marshalsea Prison. Some mornings when the two children were waiting by London Bridge for the prison gates to open Charles would entrance the little servant-girl by 'telling her quite astonishing fictions about the wharves and the tower' (Forster, p. 30). From this remembrance – half pitying, half amused – of this Dickens creates the extraordinarily effective idyll of Dick Swiveller's enchantment of the little Marchioness by awakening her imagination.

35 *MC*, ch. 19.

36 *The Violent Effigy*, p. 163.

37 *Novels of the Eighteen-Forties*, Oxford Paperbacks ed., 1954, p. 157.

Chapter 12: 'Dombey and Son' to 'Little Dorrit'

1 My figures are based on the character-lists given at the beginning of each novel in the Oxford Illustrated Dickens series. These lists include many, though by no means all, minor characters (some of whom make only the most fleeting of appearances), but as this applies to both male and female characters it does not affect my point.

2 Esther's case is more complicated than the other two in that she has to be released from silence about her love not only by her lover but also by her guardian, Mr Jarndyce.

3 Kate Millett, *Sexual Politics*, 1970, pp. 89-90.

4 *DC*, ch. 51.

5   *LD,* Book II, ch. 34.
6   *DC,* ch. 64.
7   Barbara Hardy comments that this response is 'one of the many small details that make Dora's character more subtle than most critical accounts of it admit'. *(The Moral Art of Dickens,* p. 135.)
8   G. Orwell, 'Charles Dickens' *(Collected Essays, Journalism and Letters of George Orwell,* ed. Sonia Orwell and Ian Angus, Penguin ed., vol. 1, p. 503); Forster p. 557.
9   Philip Collins, *Charles Dickens: David Copperfield,* p. 48.
10 *DC,* ch. 39.
11 John Carey pretends to believe that the saintly tears Agnes does weep are, in fact, those of sexual frustration: 'David's obtuseness is enough to make any girl weep. For Agnes has perfectly normal instincts, in fact, and is pointing not upwards but towards the bedroom' *(The Violent Effigy,* p. 171). But this must be regarded as an instance of critical waggishness.
12 *DC.* ch. 25.
13 Collins, op. cit., p. 48.
14 *BH,* ch. 59.
15 *CB, The Battle of Life,* Part 3.
16 *LD,* Book I, ch. 24.
17 *DS,* ch. 47; *BH,* ch. 44.
18 Grace Greenwood, writing, over the initials 'GG', in *The New York Daily Tribune,* 5 July 1870, p. 6. Dickens confided in her, she reports, that 'he was about to get Esther in love, and hardly knew how he should be able to manage the delicate difficulties of the case'. I am indebted to Professor Philip Collins for bringing this item to my attention.
19 Letter to the publisher George Smith of 11 March 1852, written after reading the first monthly number of *BH (The Brontës: Their Lives, Friendships and Correspondence,* ed. T.J. Wise and J.A. Symington, 1932, vol. 3, p. 322).
20 *The Spectator,* 24 Sept. 1853.
21 Among the most illuminating of the many subtle, detailed and persuasive studies of Dickens's presentation of Esther published during the last twenty years are: William Axton's 'The Trouble with Esther' *(Modern Language Quarterly,* vol. 26, 1965); Martha Rosso's 'Dickens and Esther' *(Dksn,* vol. 65, 1969); Q.D. Leavis's discussion in *Dickens the Novelist,* pp. 155ff. (1970); Alex Zwerdling's 'Esther Summerson Rehabilitated' *(PMLA,* vol. 88, 1973); Crawford Kilian's 'In Defence of Esther Summerson' *(Dalhousie Review,* vol. 54, 1974/5); Lawrence Frank's ' "Through a Glass Darkly". Esther Summerson and *Bleak House' (Dickens Studies Annual,* vol. 4, 1975); and Paul Eggert's 'The Real Esther Summerson' *(Dickens Studies Newsletter,* vol. 11, 1980).
22 *LD,* Book I, ch. 24.
23 *LD,* Book II, ch. 3.
24 *LD,* Book I, ch. 14.

25 *LD*, Book I, ch. 19.
26 F.R. Leavis, 'Dickens and Blake: *Little Dorrit'*, in F.R. and Q.D. Leavis, *Dickens the Novelist* (p. 250). Leavis's whole discussion of Little Dorrit and how she is 'unquestionably "there" for us' should be read.
27 The famous closing words of *LD*.
28 Nancy instructs Rose: 'When ladies as young, and good, and beautiful as you are . . . give away your hearts, love will carry you all lengths – even such as you, who have home, friends, other admirers, everything, to fill them. When such as I, who have no certain roof but the coffin-lid, and no friend in sickness or death but the hospital nurse, set our rotten hearts on any man, and let him fill the place that has been a blank through all our wretched lives, who can hope to cure us?' *(OT*, ch. 40.)
29 *MC*, ch. 4.
30 Kathleen Tillotson *(Novels of the Eighteen-Forties*, Oxford Paperbacks ed., 1961, pp. 177-9) sees her as a complexly conceived character who is 'drawn into a sphere which distorts her effect', the sphere being that of the melodrama centred on the villainous Carker; so Edith strikes us as 'not a tragic heroine, but a tragedy queen'. F.R. Leavis (op. cit., pp. 23-4) is more severe, seeing Edith as taking Dickens 'into a realm where he *knows* nothing', the theme of the Bought Bride, so causing him to fall back on the 'theatrical clichés and sentimental banalities of the high-life novelette . . .'; her attitude towards Dombey is 'unreal' and 'it is impossible to make moral sense of her attitude towards her marriage'. Barbara Hardy (op. cit., p. 60 ff.) sees Edith as a character 'whose detachment, self-analysis, and insight are important, conscious and fundamental and, far from being implausible, most co-herent and sustained'; Dickens 'over-produces' her, however, and there seems to be a dichotomy between the 'mercenary heartlessness' of her actions (her two marriages) and her consistently moral 'reasoning and quality of feeling'. Particularly illuminating, I think, is the way in which Professor Hardy 'reads' some of Edith's big melodramatic scenes as successful dramatizations of more intimate conflicts that Dickens cannot present directly to his public, e.g. the boudoir scene between her and Dombey in chapter 40.
31 *DS*, ch. 30.
32 *DS*, ch. 40.
33 Here is a significant difference from Nancy, for if the latter had survived Sikes's enraged assault she would not, we may be sure, have devoted herself like Edith to getting vengeance, because Nancy loved Sikes whereas Edith has no such feelings for Dombey. It seems to have been axiomatic with Dickens that once a woman had given a man her love she could never subsequently, no matter how badly he treated her, really forsake him in her heart, still less persist in willing his destruction – witness Betsey Trot-wood's continued concern for her worthless husband. So Edith's double in *DS*, her illegitimate cousin, Alice Marwood, who had been sold by her

mother to Carker when she was young, kept by him for a while and then abandoned, thirsts for vengeance yet becomes desperate to save him as soon as she has actually helped to set that vengeance in motion: 'I relent towards him without reason,' she says, but the reason, the reader is clearly meant to understand, is that Alice cannot forget that Carker once had her love, no matter how sordidly.

34 Barbara Hardy (op. cit., ch. 3) sees Edith as the prototype of Louisa Gradgrind, Estella and Bella Wilfer but overlooks Lady Dedlock. Kathleen Tillotson (op. cit., p. 181) implies in a footnote that she finds Lady Dedlock and Tulkinghorn a great deal more naturalistic than Edith and Carker but does not develop any detailed comparison and contrast of the two pairs.

35 Carey, op. cit., p. 60.

36 An example of this 'protection' of Edith may be found in chapter 21 of *DS* where Dickens is mocking the expensive fashionable but miniscule lodgings she and her mother take at Leamington: ' ... the Honourable Mrs Skewton, being in bed, had her feet in the window and her head in the fireplace, while the Honourable Mrs Skewton's maid was quartered in a closet ... so extremely small, that ... she was obliged to writhe in and out of the door like a beautiful serpent'. About how the statuesque Edith disposed of herself in these narrow lodgings we hear nothing at all.

37 *BH*, ch. 2.

38 *DS*, ch. 27.

39 *HT*, Book II, ch. 12.

40 Carey, op. cit., p. 165.

41 *DC*, ch. 20.

42 *DC*, ch. 56.

43 Dickens evidently thought better of his first idea of specifying the song. In the manuscript of *DC* it is named as 'The Last Rose of Summer' but this detail was cancelled before proof (see Clarendon Edition of *DC*, ed. Nina Burgis, p. 372).

44 F.R. and Q.D. Leavis, op. cit., p. 83.

45 It is curious that Françoise Basch, who dismisses Rosa as 'nothing more than a monstrous puppet', should say (*Relative Creatures*, p. 150) that her rage is directed against Em'ly 'for no apparent reason'.

46 *DC*, ch. 50.

47 *LD*, Book II, chs. 21, 20.

48 *LD*, Book II, ch. 31.

49 *BH*, ch. 14.

50 *BH*, ch. 50.

51 For a perceptive early account of the psychological realism of Dickens's presentation of Betsey Trotwood see E.A. Fraser, 'The Psychology of Betsey Trotwood', *Dksn*, vol. 16 (1920), pp. 127-9.

52 *DC*, chs. 13, 19.

53 cf. Mrs Leavis's illuminating discussion of Betsey, 'created to play the

complex and inevitably ridiculous part of Reason or systematic rationality' but who is sympathetic 'because she can admit she has been misguided' (*Dickens the Novelist*, pp. 61-4).

54 *DC*, ch. 44.
55 Anna Maria Hall (Mrs Samuel Carter Hall), *A Woman's Story*, 1857 vol. 3, p. 11. Mrs Hall, who was a champion of women's rights among other causes, pays tribute to Dickens as 'the greatest genius of our time', but expresses the belief that he 'with all his liberality has done more than any other writer to lower us women in the intellectual scale'.
56 Forster, p. 639.

Chapter 13: 'A Tale of Two Cities' to 'Edwin Drood'

1 Lovelorn young Joe Willet in *BR* might be considered an earlier example. But the reader is quickly made to understand that Dolly Varden, for all her coquettish behaviour, does love him, and to expect that he will eventually win her.
2 The last of all is the comically named Mr Venus whose trade – he is a taxidermist and articulator of human skeletons – is obnoxious to the object of his passion, Pleasant Riderhood. 'She does not', she tells him, 'wish to regard herself, nor yet to be regarded, in that boney light' *(OMF*, Book I, ch. 7).
3 The lower-class Davis's love-trials anticipate Pip's in *GE*. He tells us: 'I well knew that she was as high above my reach as the sky over my head; and yet I loved her. What put it in my low heart to be so daring . . . I am unable to say; still, the suffering to me was just as great as if I had been a gentleman. I suffered agony – agony. I suffered hard and I suffered long, (*CS*, 'Perils', ch. 3).
4 *LD*, Book I, ch. 2.
5 *LD*, Book I, ch. 17.
6 *LD*, Book II, ch. 11.
7 See above, pp. 210–11.
8 *TTC*, Book II, ch. 21.
9 *GE*, ch. 44.
10 *GE*, ch. 38.
11 *The Moral Art of Dickens*, p. 75.
12 Returning home to inherit his dead father's considerable fortune, which under the terms of the old man's will he may only have if he marries Bella Wilfer (whom he has never seen), Harmon is attacked and thrown for dead into the river. He manages to save himself and then finds that he is presumed to have drowned or been murdered. He resolves to keep his identity secret for a while so that he may have time to observe and test the character of the girl his father had destined to be his bride. Under the assumed named of Rokesmith he takes lodgings at her father's house and

secures the post of secretary to Mr Boffin, Bella's patron. When Boffin and his wife recognize who he really is, he enlists their help in keeping up his alias so that his testing of Bella's character and her self-proclaimed mercenary attitude to life may continue.

13 *OMF*, Book I, ch. 4.

14 It is instructive to contrast the way in which Estella announces to Pip that she has no heart ('condescending to me as a brilliant and beautiful woman might' – *GE*, 29) with Bella's assertion of the same thing to Mrs Lammle (*OMF*, III, 5). Whereas Estella's little lecture seems forced and unnatural, Bella's affected chatter ('I don't mind telling you, Sophronia, that I am convinced I have no heart, as people call it; and that I think that sort of thing is nonsense') seems to arise very naturally out of the circumstances and of the cynical tone in which Mrs Lammle has encouraged her to talk.

15 *OMF*, Book III, ch. 9.

16 It has been persuasively argued by Julian Moynahan (in 'The Hero's Guilt: the Case of *Great Expectations*', *Essays in Criticism*, vol. 10, 1960, pp. 60-79) that Pip has already made this move, the characters of Orlick and Drummle being merely his alter egos.

17 Norman Page in his *Speech in the English Novel* (1973), pp. 97-105, calls attention to the way in which Dickens does make a gesture towards plausibility by making Lizzie utter one or two colloquialisms in her early scenes, before she has had any education, but this *is* only a gesture – mainly she uses very literate phrases even in these scenes, e.g. 'through some fortunate chance' – and Professor Page concludes that the 'important point' is that Lizzie 'belongs to the class of fairy-tale heroines . . . on whose lips realistic speech would be disconcertingly out of place'.

18 *OMF*, Book II, ch. 11.

19 I think it quite likely that Dickens had Grace Darling, a real-life heroine whom he admired, somewhere at the back of his mind when creating Lizzie Hexam.

20 Sylvia Manning, in her article, 'Dickens, January, and May' (*Dksn*, vol. 71, 1975, pp. 67-74) interestingly compares with Lizzie's rescue of Wrayburn a similar event in Dickens's Christmas Story for 1867, 'No Thoroughfare' (written jointly with Wilkie Collins): 'The young Swiss peasant girl Marguerite can rescue her dying lover because she has known how to get up to the Alpine peak where he lies dying and knows further how to be lowered on to the melting ice shelf and finally how to tie the rope into the necessary harness so that he can be hauled up. The chapter of the story in which this was described was written by Dickens, not Collins.'

21 In her *Dksn* article just cited.

22 *MED*, ch. 3.

23 *MED*, ch. 9.

24 *MED*, ch. 3.

25 For an interesting variant on this picture see *OMF*, Book II, ch. 11, where

the dark-haired Lizzie, calm and beautiful, is ostensibly comforting the crippled, gold-haired Jenny though it is actually the latter who is doing the pitying and seeking to comfort.

26 *MED*, ch. 7.
27 *MED*, ch. 6.
28 *MED*, ch. 7.
29 ibid.
30 *TTC*, Book II, ch. 15.
31 *GE*, ch. 26.
32 *GE*, ch. 8.
33 *Charles Dickens*, p. 129.
34 cf. Françoise Basch (*Relative Creatures*, p. 151) who sees Miss Havisham as 'the purest symbol of death in life' and says that she 'embodies the tragic echo of a betrayed and solitary woman'.
35 *GE*, ch. 29.
36 *GE*, ch. 49.
37 By J. Hillis Miller speaking in a seminar on 'Women in Dickens' at the Modern Languages Association Convention in Chicago, Dec. 1973. The seminar was reported in *The Dickens Studies Newsletter*, vol. 5, no. 1 (March 1974), pp. 4-7.
38 *OMF*, Book II, ch. 1.
39 *OMF*, Book II, ch. 2.
40 It is worth noting that Mrs Lammle conforms to the pattern set in Nancy and repeated in Edith Dombey in that her one good act is essentially motivated by self-pity. She decides to save Georgiana Podsnap from the hideous marriage in which the Lammles are trying to involve her, for their own profit, and tells Twemlow, 'I scarcely know why I turned traitress to my husband in the matter, for the girl is a poor little fool. I was a poor little fool once myself; I can find no better reason' (*OMF*, Book III, ch. 17).
41 *MED*, ch. 22.
42 *OMF*, Book III, ch. 4.
43 *Charles Dickens: A Critical Study*, p. 133. cf. Note 106 to ch. 14, below.

III Dickens and Woman

Chapter 14: The Womanly Ideal

1 *Dickens and Education*, p. 128.
2 Tennyson, *The Princess*, Section 7, 259-60; Virginia Woolf, 'David Copperfield' in *The Moment and Other Essays*; J.S. Mill, *The Subjection of Women* (Everyman's Library ed.), p. 238.
3 Tennyson, *The Princess*, Section 7, 275; Nonesuch, vol. 2, p. 768.
4 *The Princess*, Section 7, 268. Charlotte Brontë's Shirley might well have been thinking of this phrase of Tennyson's when she said, 'Men, I believe,

fancy women's minds something like those of children. Now, that is a mistake' *(Shirley,* ch. 20).

5 *Yeast,* ch. 10; Pilgrim, vol. 4, p. 324; *LD,* Book II, ch. 27.
6 Nonesuch, vol. 3, p. 229 (letter to Wilkie Collins of 12 July 1861); *A Strange Story,* ch. 7.
7 *DC,* ch. 60; *OMF,* Book III, ch. 17; *LD,* Book I, ch. 11; *Twelfth Night,* Act II, Scene ii.
8 *MED,* ch. 10; *OMF,* Book I, ch. 9.
9 *PP,* ch. 29; *CS,* 'The Wreck of the Golden Mary'.
10 See the opening of 'The Wife' in Washington Irving's *The Sketch Book of Geoffrey Crayon, Gent.*: 'Those disasters which break down the spirit of a man . . . seem to call forth all the energies of the softer sex, and give such intrepidity and elevation to their character, that at times it approaches to sublimity'.
11 *AN,* ch. 15; *AN,* ch. 7.
12 *DS,* ch. 3; *DS,* ch. 48; *UT & RP,* 'The Long Voyage'.
13 *OCS,* ch. 15; *OMF,* Book III, ch. 3; *OCS,* ch. 64. Dickens describes the Marchioness propping Dick up with his pillows 'if not as skilfully as if she had been a professional nurse all her life, at least as tenderly . . .' and beginning 'to work away at the concoction of some cooling drink, with the address of a score of chemists'.
14 *MC,* ch. 46; Nonesuch, vol. 3, pp. 387-8; *BR,* ch. 51.
15 *The City of Dickens,* pp. 184 ff.
16 [Mrs Edward Thomas], 'Woman', *The Metropolitan,* vol. 36 (1843), p. 319. cf. An article (author as yet unidentified), 'The Female Character', published in *Fraser's Magazine* ten years earlier (vol. 7, p. 600): '. . . death is disarmed of half its terrors when our last moments are hallowed by [a woman's] prayers'.
17 *OCS,* ch. 69; Pilgrim, vol. 5, pp. 448, 446.
18 *CS,* 'Mugby Junction', ch. 2. Another example of spiritual regeneration stemming from contact with a beautiful little girl appears in *CS,* 'Somebody's Luggage', ch. 2. The most famous instance of this in Victorian literature is not to be found in Dickens, however, but in George Eliot *(Silas Marner).*
19 *CHE,* chs. 22, 18; 'Sucking Pigs', *HW,* vol. 4, pp. 145-7 (8 Nov. 1851), reprinted in *MP.* The title 'Sucking Pigs' refers playfully back to an earlier article in *HW* entitled 'Whole Hogs' (23 Aug. 1851) in which Dickens had attacked fanatical 'whole-hog' extremism in such matters as temperance, pacificism and vegetarianism. Bloomerism is seen as potentially extremist but as yet only a 'sucking pig'.
20 Pilgrim, vol. 5, p. 542.
21 cf. his description of Pet Meagles *(LD,* Book I, ch. 2): '. . . there was in Pet an air of timidity and dependence which was the best weakness in the world, and gave her the only crowning charm a girl so pretty and pleasant

could have been without'. According to Georgina Hogarth, Dickens observed when he met the fifty-one-year-old Queen Victoria in 1870 that she had 'a girlish sort of timidity which was very engaging' (quoted by Adrian, *Georgina Hogarth and the Dickens Circle,* p. 133).

22 Pilgrim, vol. 4, p. 583. He was not always so charmed by this aspect of femininity, however. In 1854 he wrote with humorous indignation to Wills that, 'All the women and girls' in his house were 'stark mad' about a neighbour's wedding: 'Despotic conjugal influence exerted to keep Mrs Dickens out of the church', he reported; 'Caught putting on bonnet for that purpose, and sternly commanded to renounce idiotic intentions' (Nonesuch, vol. 2, pp. 553-4).

23 *DS,* ch. 31; Nonesuch, vol. 3, pp. 253, 340, 603; *CS,* 'The Holly Tree', ch. 2.

24 *CS,* 'The Poor Relation's Story'; *DC,* ch. 28.

25 In his Diary, under the date of 10 March 1848, Thackeray recorded a visit to the Streatham area and noted: 'All sorts of recollections of my youth came back to me: dark and sad and painful with my dear good mother as a gentle angel interposing between me and misery' *(The Letters and Private Papers of William Makepeace Thackeray,* ed. Gordon N. Ray, vol. 2, p. 361).

26 *SB, Sketches of Young Couples,* 'The Nice Little Couple'.

27 *DS,* ch. 18. Dickens's little grand-daughter, Mary Angela, was, Kate Perugini tells us, 'a great favourite of his' and the child's evident ability to be 'as staid and pleasantly demure . . . as a woman' particularly charmed him. Mrs Perugini recalled seeing her father rambling in the grounds at Gad's Hill with Mary Angela and her little brother. The little boy fell asleep and Dickens carried him in his arms 'and then the little girl . . . feeling, perhaps, that the weight of conversation would now rest upon her shoulders — began talking to her companion in the grave and earnest manner that had at first endeared her to him, and he walked slowly on, she trotting by his side; and they came to a seat under the great mulberry tree in the kitchen-garden, and there they rested . . . and the little boy dreamed his dreams — and my father, no doubt, dreamed his — while the little girl, like the sensible little woman she was, endeavoured to make herself agreeable.' (Kate Perugini, 'My Father's Love for Children', *Dksn,* vol. 7 (1911), pp. 117-19.)

28 *DS,* ch. 49.

29 Pilgrim, vol. 4, pp. 374-5.

30 See *Letters from Charles Dickens to Angela Burdett Coutts 1841-1865,* ed. Edgar Johnson, pp. 274 ff.

31 Nonesuch, vol. 3, p. 528; Pilgrim, vol. 2, p. 236; *BH,* chs. 51, 60, 65.

32 *MP,* 'Sucking Pigs'; J.S. Mill quoted in *Charles Dickens: the Critical Heritage,* ed. Philip Collins, p. 95; *BH,* ch. 4.

33 Queen Victoria to Sir Theodore Martin, 29 May 1870 (quoted in his

Queen Victoria as I knew Her, 1890, pp. 69-70); 'Frauds on the Fairies', *HW,* vol. 8, pp. 97-100 (1 Oct. 1853), reprinted in *MP.*

34   For example, we find him writing on 4 June 1868 (Nonesuch, vol. 3, pp. 652-3) to J.C. Parkinson, 'There is a little Bill before Parliament . . . for enabling a married woman to possess her own earnings. I should much like to champion the sex – reasonably – and to dwell upon the hardship inflicted by the present ban on a woman who finds herself bound to a drunken, profligate, and spendthrift husband – who is willing to support him – does so – but has her little savings bullied out of her continually. . . . Would you like to take this subject?' Parkinson's article, 'Slaves of the Ring', duly appeared in *ATYR* in July (vol. 20, pp. 85-8) and was reprinted in his *Places and People* (1869). Over twenty years earlier we find Dickens urging Forster to follow up an article in *The Examiner* about 'the defective state of the law in reference to women' by an attack on the scandalously inadequate sentence (seven years' transportation) passed on a notorious bigamist who had married three women in order to obtain their property and caused the death of one of them by cruelty. 'My opinion is', wrote Dickens, 'that in any well-ordered state of society . . . he would have been flogged more than once (privately), and certainly sentenced to transportation for no less a term than the rest of his life' (Pilgrim, vol. 4, pp. 609-10). The prolonged persecution of the great heiress Angela Burdett Coutts by an impudent bankrupt who claimed that she had promised to marry him and who knew how to manipulate the law so as to cause her maximum harassment and distress moved Dickens to write a ferociously ironic article, 'Things That Cannot Be Done', in *HW* (vol. 8, pp. 121-3, 8 Oct. 1853; reprinted in *MP).* In it he remarks that an 'ill-conditioned friend' of his called Common Sense is by no means satisfied with 'the determination of the Law to prevent by severe punishment the oppression and ill-treatment of Women': '. . . he says to me, "Will you look at these cases of brutality, and tell me whether you consider six years of the hardest prison task-work (instead of six months) punishment enough for such enormous cruelty? Will you read the increasing record of these violences from day to day, as more and more sufferers are gradually encouraged by a law of six months' standing to disclose their long endurance, and will you consider what a legal system that must be which only now applies an imperfect remedy to such a giant evil? . . .".' He moves on from this general indictment to satirize the law's failure to protect a woman in Miss Coutts's situation and, indeed, its apparent favouring of her persecutors. The injustices to women that resulted from the law's assumption that man and wife were one, dramatically exemplified by the sufferings of Caroline Norton, were the subject of quite a sustained campaign in *HW:* Eliza Lynn's 'One of Our Legal Fictions' appeared in April 1854 (vol. 9, pp. 257-60) followed by 'A Legal Fiction' by Wills in 1855 (vol. 11, pp. 598-9) and a second article by Eliza Lynn, 'Marriage Gaolers', in 1856 (vol. 13, pp. 583-5). Another *HW*

campaign relating to women protested against the dreadful and demoralizing conditions in which soldiers' wives were forced to live: see 'Soldiers' Wives' by Wills, vol. 3, pp. 561-2, 'The Soldier's Wife' by Wills and Henry Morley, vol. 11, pp. 278-80, and 'Women at Aldershot' by Marianne Young, vol. 13, pp. 319-20.

35 Mrs Lynn Lynton quoted in J.A. and Olive Banks, *Feminism and Family Planning in Victorian England*, p. 55; George Eliot to Emily Davies, 8 Aug. 1868 (*The George Eliot Letters*, ed. Gordon S. Haight, vol. 4, p. 468); Dickens's remarks to Elwin quoted in Warwick Elwin's 'Prefatory Memoir' to Elwin's *Some XVIII Century Men of Letters*, 1902, vol. 1, p. 249 (I am indebted to Philip Collins for this reference); Percy Fitzgerald, *Life of Dickens*, vol. 1, p. 207; *MC*, ch. 16; *BH*, ch. 30; Annie Fields's diary quoted in M.A. DeWolfe Howe's *Memories of a Hostess*, 1922, p. 186.

36 Pilgrim, vol. 2, p. 292.

37 [John Neal], 'Men and Women', *Blackwood's Edinburgh Magazine*, vol. 16 (1824), p. 390; Kingsley, *Yeast*, ch. 10; Masson, *British Novelists and Their Styles*, 1859, p. 181; [W.C. Roscoe], 'Woman', *The National Review*, vol. 7 (1858), p. 347.

38 Dickens to Mrs Gore, 27 Jan. 1853 (unpublished); Pilgrim, vol. 4, p. 548; Nonesuch, vol. 3, p. 86.

39 Pilgrim, vol. 4, p. 110; Johnson (ed.), op. cit., p. 291.

40 Nonesuch, vol. 3, p. 4.

41 Letter first published by Mrs G. Porter in her *Annals of a Publishing House. William Blackwood and his Sons*, 1897, vol. 3, pp. 44-5; reprinted in *The George Eliot Letters*, ed. cit., vol. 2, pp. 427-8.

42 Nonesuch, vol. 3, p. 111. According to W.P. Frith's recollections of Dickens, published in ch. 10 of F.G. Kitton, *Charles Dickens: by Pen and Pencil* Dickens told him that it was 'something in the soliloquy of Hetty Sorrel when she is trying on finery in her own room' that convinced him that *Adam Bede* was the work of a woman. Frith's account is somewhat hazy, however.

43 See below, pp. 349-50.

44 Forster, p. 613; Jerome Meckier, 'Some Household Words: Two New Accounts of Dickens's Conversation', *Dksn*, vol. 71 (1975), p. 5; Rosina Bulwer Lytton, *Very Successful*, vol. 1, p. 286 (quoted by Myron Brightfield in *Victorian England in Its Novels 1840-1870*, vol. 1, pp. 168-9.)

45 Dickens's Memoir of Adelaide Anne Procter was reprinted in *MP*.

46 See above, p. 255.

47 Dickens to Mary Boyle, 25 Dec. 1852 (unpublished); Nonesuch, vol. 2, p. 438; *BH*, ch. 35.

48 Eliza Stephenson, *Janita's Cross*, 1864, vol. 1, p. 242; quoted by Myron Brightfield, op. cit., vol. 1, p. 151.

49 Witness his remarks about Christiana Thompson, née Weller, whom he

had once been so strongly stirred by (see above, ch. 4), when he visited the Thompsons in Italy. He wrote to Georgina Hogarth from Genoa on 28 Oct. 1853, 'We had disturbed her at her painting in Oils; and I rather received an impression that what with that, and what with music, the household affairs went a little to the wall' (Nonesuch, vol. 2, p. 504). (One of Christiana's daughters, later Lady Butler, became a very celebrated painter of military subjects, exhibiting regularly at the Royal Academy from 1873 onwards.)

50 W.J. Carlton, 'Janet Barrow's Portrait Miniatures. An Australian Epilogue', *Dksn,* vol. 68 (1972), pp. 100-3.

51 *NN,* ch. 10.

52 Nonesuch, vol. 3, p. 101; Georgina Hogarth quoted by Adrian, op. cit., p. 189.

53 See his letter to Edmund Yates on the death of Yates's mother who had been a distinguished actress (Nonesuch, vol. 3, p. 179): 'All the womanly goodness, grace, and beauty of my drama went out with her. To the last I never could hear her voice without emotion. I think of her as of a beautiful part of my own youth . . .'.

54 Nonesuch, vol. 2, pp. 270-1.

55 Mrs Gaskell, *Life of Charlotte Brontë,* ch. 3; Tennyson, *The Princess,* Sect. 7, 299; [W.H. Wills], 'A Good Plain Cook', *HW,* vol. 1, pp. 139-41 (4 May 1850); *SB,* 'A Passage in the Life of Mr Watkins Tottle', ch. 1; *GE,* ch. 23; *SB,* 'London Recreations'.

56 cf. Rosamond Vincy in George Eliot's *Middlemarch* (Book I, ch. 11) who 'was admitted to be the flower of Mrs Lemon's school, the chief school in the county, where the teaching included all that was demanded in the accomplished female – even to extras, such as the getting in and out of a carriage'.

57 *MED,* ch. 3.

58 'My Girls', *ATYR,* vol. 2, pp. 370-4 (11 Feb. 1860).

59 Sarah Stickney Ellis, *The Women of England,* ch. 1; *SB.*

60 See *The Mill on the Floss,* Book IV, ch. 3: '. . . [Maggie] was as lonely in her trouble as if she had been the only girl in the civilised world of that day who had come out of her school-life with a soul untrained for inevitable struggles – with no other part of her inherited share in the hard-won treasures of thought, which generations of painful toil have laid up for the race of men, than shreds and patches of feeble literature and false history – with much futile information about Saxon and other kings of doubtful example – but unhappily quite without knowledge of the irreversible laws within and without her, which, governing the habits, becomes morality, and, developing the feelings of submission and dependence, becomes religion . . . .'

61 Dickens to Miss Coutts, 11 July 1856 (Johnson, ed., op. cit., p. 321). The movement for the teaching of 'Common Things' was launched by Lord Ashburton in 1853 and aimed to replace the system prevalent in elementary

schools of making children learn arid lists of names and 'nauseating facts', by a method of teaching them the elementary principles of science, for example, by reference to 'common things' that they were familiar with. For Miss Coutts's involvement in the movement and assistance given to her by Dickens see K.J. Fielding, '*Hard Times* and Common Things' in *Imagined Worlds. Essays on Some English Novels and Novelists in Honour of John Butt* (1968), ed. Maynard Mack and Ian Gregor.

62 *OMF*, Book II, ch. 1.

63 *BR*, ch. 7; *DS*, ch. 11; *UT & RP*, 'Our English Watering-Place'; *LD*, Book I, ch. 16.

64 *BH*, ch. 3.

65 *AN*, ch. 3; *MC*, ch. 17; *UT & RP*, 'Out of the Season'.

66 *UT & RP*, 'On an Amateur Beat'; Kate Perugini speaking at a Lyceum Club Dinner in honour of Dickens, reported in *Dksn*, vol. 6 (1910), p. 132; Percy Fitzgerald, *Memories of Charles Dickens*, p. 271.

67 Pilgrim, vol. 3, p. 282; *UT & RP*, 'The Calais Night Mail'.

68 [Edmund Dixon], 'The Rights of French Women', *HW*, vol. 5, pp. 218-21 (22 May 1852) and 'More Work for the Ladies', *HW*, vol. 6, pp. 18-22 (18 Sept. 1852).

69 *NN*, ch. 46 (Madeline Bray had had to submit as a daily governess 'to such caprices and injuries as women (with daughters too) too often love to inflict upon their own sex when they serve in such capacities, as though in jealousy of the superior intelligence which they are necessitated to employ . . .'); *MC*, chs. 9 and 36; *LD*, Book II, ch. 21. For an excellent discussion of the Victorian governess in fact and fiction see Patricia Thomson, *The Victorian Heroine. A Changing Ideal 1837-73*, ch. 2. Philip Collins observes *(Dickens and Education,* p. 40) that 'despite his satire on the unsociable superiority of the employers of governesses . . . Dickens and his household do not appear to have been very intimate with theirs, for I have never noticed the girls' governesses being named, and very rarely even mentioned, in his letters or the family's memoirs'.

70 *The Speeches of Charles Dickens*, ed. K.J. Fielding, pp. 65-6; [Harriet Parr], 'Two Pence an Hour', *HW*, vol. 15, pp. 138-40 (23 Aug. 1856); [Florence Wilson], 'Only a Governess', *HW*, vol. 19, pp. 546-9 (7 May 1859).

71 See Thomson, op. cit., p. 38. F.D. Maurice and Charles Kingsley began a series of 'Lectures to Ladies' in London in 1847 with a committee of professors from King's College set up to issue certificates of proficiency and this met with such an enthusiastic reponse that Queens College for Women was founded the following year and Bedford College in 1849.

72 *OMF*, Book II, ch. 1; *DC*, ch. 60; *CS*, 'Mugby Junction', ch. 1.

73 [Henry Morley], 'The Nurse in Leading Strings', *HW*, vol. 17, pp. 602-6 (12 June 1858); 'Bedside Experiments', *ATYR*, vol. 2, pp. 537-42 (31 March 1860).

74   Harriet Martineau quoted by Thomson, op. cit., p. 68; *NN*, ch. 3; *MC*, ch. 30; *NN*, ch. 17.

75   *CB, The Chimes*, 'Third Quarter'. This part of *The Chimes* was probably partly inspired by Thomas Hood's powerful poem, 'The Song of the Shirt' (first anonymously published in *Punch* in 1843), which dramatized the wretched plight of starving needlewomen, and also by the notorious case of Mary Furley in April 1844. Unable to earn enough money by sewing to keep herself and her child alive, Mary Furley desperately attempted to drown herself and the baby in the Thames. She was rescued but the child was dead; she was tried for murder and condemned to death, the sentence being commuted to seven years' transportation after a public outcry. See *The Christmas Books*, ed. Michael Slater (Penguin English Library ed.), vol. 1, p. 264.

76   For example: [Henry Morley], 'Day-Workers at Home', *HW*, vol. 13, pp. 77-8; [Henry Morley], 'Many Needles in One Housewife', *HW*, vol. 15, pp. 234-6; 'Needlewoman's Hall', *ATYR*, vol. 3, pp. 427-8; 'No. 7 Brown's-Lane' (about a sewing-school set up by Miss Coutts where women were trained and then employed in shirt-making on government contract for the army and navy), *ATYR*, vol. 12, pp. 304-8.

77   'In Great Britain in 1851 there were 2,765,000 single women aged fifteen and over. By 1861 this figure had risen to 2,956,000 and by 1871 to 3,228,700 – an increase of 16.8 per cent over the twenty years' (J.A. and Olive Banks, op. cit., p. 27).

78   J.A. and Olive Banks, op. cit., p. 33.

79   *CS*, 'The Haunted House', ch. 1.

80   George Dolby, *Charles Dickens as I Knew Him*, (1885), p. 244.

81   One exception to this is the Cruncher ménage in *TTC* (Book II, ch. 1) where Dickens seems to be writing with what he once called 'determined jocularity'.

82   *PP*, ch. 6; *MC*, ch. 28.

83   *BH*, ch. 67.

84   *Vanity Fair*, ch. 35; *SB*, 'Meditations in Monmouth Street'; *DC*, ch. 32.

85   Harry Stone, 'The Love Pattern in Dickens's Novels' in *Dickens the Craftsman*, ed. Robert B. Partlow (1970), pp. 2-20; Anne Marsh, *Emilia Wyndham* (1846), vol. 1, p. 59; *CS*, 'Mrs Lirriper's Legacy', ch. 1, 'Gaslight Fairies', *HW*, vol. 11, p. 505 (10 Feb. 1855), reprinted in *MP*.

86   Author's Preface to the Third Edition of *OT* (1841); Pilgrim, vol. 5, p. 183; *CB, The Haunted Man*, ch. 2.

87   For the American Emerson's comments on the brazenness of prostitution in the streets of London and Liverpool see Pilgrim, vol. 4, p. 276 (note 9); see also Dostoyevsky's comments ('In the Haymarket I saw mothers who had brought their young daughters still in their teens, to be sold to men') quoted in Angus Wilson's 'Dickens and Dostoyevsky', *Dickens Memorial Lectures*, pp. 54-5.

88   *OT*, ch. 47.

89 Dickens became a kind of 'unofficial almoner' to Miss Coutts during the 1840s and worked closely with her, notably in respect of her Home for Fallen Women, until the break-up of his marriage distanced them from one another. A distance was always there, however, created by Miss Coutts's enormous wealth, her unique status in Victorian society and her involvement in the grandest circles of that society; her narrowly Anglican piety also presented difficulties for Dickens from time to time. His many surviving letters to her, about the Home and other matters, are sometimes moving, often highly entertaining, but they seem very different in tone from his letters to other women friends. For all their occasional archness, they seem to have a conscious *de bas en haut* tone which can become 'almost fawning', as one of Miss Coutts's recent biographers, Diana Orton, has observed. His sincerity, though, cannot be doubted. He certainly admired and revered Miss Coutts for her dedication of her wealth to good works and for her personal qualities of retiring modesty, concern for others, and dignified firmness of purpose. He was also properly appreciative of her generosity towards his eldest son whose education at Eton she paid for. (See also Diana Orton's biography, *Made of Gold.*)

90 Pilgrim, vol. 4, pp. 552-60.

91 op. cit., p. 588.

92 Pilgrim, vol. 5, pp. 698-9 (Appendix D).

93 Philip Collins, *Dickens and Crime* (1962), p. 104; Pilgrim, vol. 5, pp. 179, 185; Johnson (ed.), op. cit., p. 166.

94 Collins, op. cit., p. 98; 'Home for Homeless Women', *HW*, vol. 7, pp. 169-75 (23 April 1853), reprinted in *MP*; G.L. Chesterton quoted by the Pilgrim Editors (vol. 5, p. 152, note 1); Johnson (ed.), op. cit., pp. 169, 153, 155.

95 Henry Mayhew, *London Labour and the London Poor*, vol. 4 (1862): 'Prostitution in London' by Bracebridge Hemyng, pp. 219-20; *The Bachelor's Pocket Book; or, Man of Pleasure's Night Guide to All That is Worth Seeing in 'This Little Village', forming the most Complete Directory to Casinos, Saloons, Theatres, Concerts, Night-Houses, &c.*, published by W. Ward's Parisian Repository, 67 Strand, 1851 (this volume is discussed and quoted by Ronald Pearsall in his *The Worm in the Bud. The World of Victorian Sexuality*, Pelican Books, 1971, pp. 321-24).

96 Nonesuch, vol. 2, p. 763.

97 *DS*, chs. 43, 33. 48.

98 Pilgrim, vol. 5, pp. 178, 185.

99 *DC*, ch. 63.

100 *DC*, ch. 22.

101 *DC*, chs. 3, 30.

102 *DC*, ch. 31; Sylvère Monod, 'James Steerforth ou le problème du mal dans *David Copperfield*', *Les Annales de l'Université de Paris*, 1967, no. 2, p. 7; Philip Collins, *Dickens and Crime*, p. 114.

103 *LD*, Book I, ch. 14. Gissing wondered how 'the same man who penned this shocking rubbish could have written in the same volume pages of a truthfulness beyond all eulogy' *(Charles Dickens*, p. 159).

104 It is the Victorian *women* novelists who present in a non-comic fashion the domestic unhappiness and discomfort caused by self-assertive or inadequate wives, e.g. Lydgate's marriage in George Eliot's *Middlemarch*, or Mr Gibson's marriage to Mrs Kirkpatrick in Mrs Gaskell's *Wives and Daughters*.

105 Nonesuch, vol. 2, pp. 679–80; Angus Easson, 'Dickens, *Household Words* and a Double Standard', *Dksn*, vol. 60 (1964), p. 111.

106 For one major Dickens critic, Gissing, they are, indeed, to be seen as triumphs of strict realism: 'Wonderful as fact, and admirable as art, are the numberless pictures of more or less detestable widows, wives, and spinsters which appear throughout his books. Beyond dispute, they must be held among his finest work; this portraiture alone would establish his claim to greatness. And I think it might be forcibly argued that, for incontestable proof of Dickens's fidelity in reproducing the life he knew, one should turn in the first place to his gallery of foolish ridiculous, or offensive women' (op. cit., p. 133). This emphatic judgment undoubtedly had a strong subjective element resulting from Gissing's bitter experience of two wretched marriages.

107 *PP*, chs. 48, 52; *DS*, ch. 60.

108 *LD*, Book I, ch. 6; *UT & RP*, 'Births. Mrs Meek, of a Son'; *UT & RP*, 'Dullborough Town'.

109 [Wilkie Collins], 'Mrs Bullwinkle', *HW*, vol. 17, p. 409 (17 April 1858).

110 *DS*, ch. 29; *PP*, ch. 10; *NN*, ch. 36; *OMF*, Book IV, ch. 5; *BR*, ch. 7.

111 *OCS*, ch. 4.

112 *BH*, ch. 8; *OT*, ch. 16; *CHE*, ch. 31.

113 *TTC*, Book II, ch. 22.

114 *TTC*, Book III, ch. 14; *GE*, ch. 15.

115 *CB*, *A Christmas Carol*, Stave 2.

116 *CS*, 'The Holly-Tree', ch. 2. It is worth noting that this story became one of Dickens's most popular readings. cf. Note 13 to ch. 3, above.

117 *SB*, *Sketches of Young Couples*, 'The Young Couple'.

118 *UT & RP*, 'The Italian Prisoner'.

119 *UT & RP*, 'A Monument of French Folly'.

120 For Dickens's reference to Shakespeare's Juliet see Philip Collins, 'Some Uncollected Speeches by Dickens', *Dksn*, vol. 73 (1977), p. 93; for Maclise's comment see Pilgrim, vol. 4, p. 599, note 1; for the Boston dinnerparty anecdote see Elizabeth Latimer, 'A Girl's Recollections of Charles Dickens', *Lippincott's Monthly Magazine*, Sept, 1893 (quoted by Johnson, p. 371).

121 Angus Wilson, 'The Heroes and Heroines of Dickens' in *Dickens and the Twentieth Century*, ed. J. Gross and G. Pearson, p. 8; *OCS*, ch. 9; *LD*, Book I, ch. 21.

122 *CS*, 'What Christmas Is as We Grow Older'; Pilgrim, vol. 5, p. 15; *UT &
RP*, 'Our French Watering-Place'; *DC*, ch. 46.
123 cf. the description of Mrs Varden in *BR*, ch. 80, quoted above, p. 229.
124 *DC*, ch. 24.
125 'The landlady of the little inn at Allonby lived at Greta Bridge, in Yorkshire, when I went down there before Nickleby, and was smuggled into the
room to see me. . . . She is an immensely fat woman now. "But I could tuck
my arm round her waist then, Mr Dickens," the landlord said when she
told me the story. . . . "And can't you do it now," I said, "you insensible
dog? Look at me! Here's a picture!" Accordingly, I got round as much of
her as I could; and this gallant action was the most successful I have ever
performed, on the whole.' (Nonesuch, vol. 2, p. 883 [Dickens to Georgina
Hogarth, 12 Sept. 1857].)
126 For Dickens on Lady Blessington see Pilgrim, vol. 3, p. 298; on Mme
Scribe, Nonesuch, vol. 2, p. 703; for Mrs Lupin see *MC*, ch. 3.
127 *DS*, ch. 27; *MED*, ch. 6.
128 *AN*, ch.12.
129 F.R. and Q.D. Leavis, *Dickens the Novelist*, p. 67.
130 *MC*, ch. 39.
131 *UT & RP*, 'A Child's Dream of a Star'.
132 *CB, The Chimes*, 'Third Quarter'.
133 F.R. and Q.D. Leavis, op. cit., p. 8.
134 *DC*, ch. 4; ch. 10.
135 *The Women of England*, ch. 8.
136 *The Weekly Chronicle*, 26 Dec. 1846.
137 *MC*, ch. 37.
138 *CS*, 'The Wreck of the Golden Mary'; Johnson (ed.), op. cit., pp. 105,108.
139 Mrs Seymour Hill was a diminutive chiropodist and manicurist whom
Dickens knew (she was a close neighbour of his in London and had
attended Catherine Dickens). When the Dec. 1849 number of *DC*
appeared, introducing Miss Mowcher in ch. 22, Mrs Hill and her friends
were convinced that the character was intended to represent her. She wrote
to Dickens to complain ('All know you have drawn my Portrait – I admit it
but the vulgar slang of language I *deny*') and he sent her a mollifying
answer, admitting to her that he had 'yielded to several little recollections
of your general manner' in creating the character and offering to 'alter the
whole design' of it if she would like him to do so. Mrs Hill's solicitor replied
accepting this offer and urging Dickens to effect the 'work of reparation' as
quickly as possible. See Pilgrim, vol. 5, pp. 674-7; also *DC*, Clarendon
Edition, ed. Nina Burgis, p. xli.
140 Forster, p. 753.
141 *DC*, ch. 42. We might note that the ideal offered for our exalted delight is,
as so often in Dickens, here juxtaposed with a comic parody of it. Presiding
over this meeting and instant 'sistering' of Agnes and Dora are Dora's two

little birdlike spinster aunts, Clarissa and Lavinia, who also exemplify complementary sisterhood but in a comical way.

Select Bibliography

[*Place of publication is London, unless otherwise stated*]

Works

New Oxford Illustrated Dickens 21 vols., Oxford (1947-58)
Oliver Twist ed. Kathleen Tillotson, Oxford (1966)
The Mystery of Edwin Drood ed. Margaret Cardwell, Oxford (1972)
Dombey and Son ed. Alan Horsman, Oxford (1974)
Little Dorrit ed. Harvey Peter Sucksmith, Oxford (1979)
David Copperfield ed. Nina Burgis, Oxford (1981)

Miscellaneous Papers Gadshill Edition, ed. B.W. Matz (1908)
Collected Papers Nonesuch Edition, 2 vols. (1937)

Mr and Mrs Charles Dickens: His Letters to Her ed. Walter Dexter (1935)
The Letters of Charles Dickens Nonesuch Edition, ed. Walter Dexter, 3 vols.
(1938)
Letters from Dickens to Angela Burdett Coutts 1841-1865 ed. Edgar Johnson,
(1953). (Published New York (1952) as *The Heart of Charles Dickens*)
The Letters of Charles Dickens Pilgrim Edition, vols. 1 (1820-39) and 2
(1840-1) edd. Madeline House and Graham Storey; vol. 3 (1842-3) edd.
Madeline House, Graham Storey and Kathleen Tillotson; vol. 4 (1844-6) ed.
Kathleen Tillotson; vol. 5 (1847-9) edd. Graham Storey and K.J. Fielding.
5 vols. to date, Oxford (1965, 1969, 1974, 1977, 1981)

The Speeches of Charles Dickens ed. K.J. Fielding, Oxford (1960)

Household Words 30 March 1850-28 May 1859. Bound, 19 vols.
All The Year Round 30 April 1859-18 June 1870. Bound, 20 vols. 1859-68; NS
vols. 1-3, 1868-70

Biography and Criticism

Adrian, Arthur A., *Georgina Hogarth and the Dickens Circle*, 1957
—— *Mark Lemon. First Editor of Punch*, 1966
Allen, Michael, 'The Dickens Family at Portsmouth', *Dksn*, vol. 77, 1981
Andersen, Hans Christian, 'A Visit to Charles Dickens', *Bentley's Miscellany*,

vol. 48, 1860 (Also published in the *Eclectic Magazine,* New York, vol. 62, 1864)

[anon.], 'The Female Character', *Fraser's Magazine,* vol. 7, 1833

Arbuckle, Elisabeth (ed.), *Harriet Martineau's Letters to Fanny Wedgwood,* Stanford, 1982

Aylmer, Felix, *Dickens Incognito,* 1959

Banks, J.A. and O., *Feminism and Family Planning in Victorian England,* Liverpool, 1964

Basch, Françoise, *Relative Creatures. Victorian Women in Society and the Novel 1837-67,* transl. Anthony Rudolf, 1974

[Beard, Nathaniel], 'Some Recollections of Yesterday', *Temple Bar Magazine,* vol. 102, 1894

Bigelow, John, *Retrospections of an Active Life,* 3 vols., New York, 1909

Bowen, W.H., *Charles Dickens and His Family,* Cambridge, 1956

Bredsdorff, Elias, *Hans Andersen and Charles Dickens. A Friendship and Its Dissolution,* Cambridge, 1956

Brightfield, Myron, *Victorian England in Its Novels 1800-1870,* 4 vols., Berkeley, 1968

[Byrne, Julia Clara], *Gossip of the Century,* 2 vols., 1892

Carey, John, *The Violent Effigy. A Study of Dickens' Imagination,* 1973

Carlton, William J., 'Dickens and the Ross Family', *Dksn,* vol. 51, 1955

—— 'Fanny Dickens: Pianist and Vocalist', *Dksn,* vol. 53, 1957

—— 'Mr and Mrs Dickens: the Thomson-Stark Letter', *Notes and Queries,* vol. 205, 1960

—— ' "Boz" and the Beards', *Dksn,* vol. 58, 1962

—— 'Postscripts to Forster', ibid.

—— 'Dickens's Forgotten Retreat in France', *Dksn,* vol. 62, 1966

—— 'The Death of Mary Hogarth – Before and After', *Dksn,* vol. 63, 1967

—— 'A Friend of Dickens's Boyhood', *Dksn,* vol. 66, 1970

—— 'Janet Barrow's Portrait Miniatures. An Australian Epilogue', *Dksn* vol. 68, 1972

[Christian, Eleanor E.], 'Reminiscences of Charles Dickens. From a Young Lady's Diary', *Englishwoman's Domestic Magazine,* vol. 10, 1871

Christian, Eleanor E., 'Recollections of Charles Dickens, His Family and Friends', *Temple Bar Magazine,* vol. 82, 1888

Collins, Philip, *Dickens and Crime,* 1962

—— *Dickens and Education,* 1963

—— 'W.C. Macready and Dickens: Some Family Recollections', *Dickens Studies,* Boston, Mass., vol. 2, 1966

—— *A Dickens Bibliography,* Cambridge, 1970

—— 'Charles Dickens: *David Copperfield*', *Studies in English Literature,* no. 67, 1977

—— 'Some Uncollected Speeches by Dickens', *Dksn,* vol. 73, 1977

—— 'Charles Dickens', *Victorian Fiction. A Second Guide to Research,* ed.

George H. Ford, New York, 1978

Collins, Philip (ed.), *Charles Dickens: the Critical Heritage,* 1971
—— *Charles Dickens: the Public Readings,* Oxford, 1975
—— *Charles Dickens: Interviews and Recollections,* 2 vols., 1982

Cox, Gwladys, 'Chelsea Memories of Mrs Perugini', *Chambers Journal,* vol. 6, 1937

Davey, E., 'The Parents of Charles Dickens', *Lippincott's Magazine,* Philadelphia, vol. 13, 1874

Dexter, Walter, *The Love Romance of Charles Dickens,* 1936

Dickens, Charles D., 'Reminiscences of my Father', Christmas Supplement to *Windsor Magazine,* 1934

Dickens, Henry F., *Memories of My Father,* 1928
—— *Recollections,* 1934

Dickens, Mary, 'Charles Dickens at Home', *Cornhill Magazine,* NS vol. 4, 1885
—— *Charles Dickens by His Eldest Daughter,* 1885, 1911
—— 'The Novelist of Christmas Time. Recollections of Charles Dickens', *The Young Man and The Young Woman,* Christmas no., 1895
—— *My Father as I Recall Him,* [1897]
—— 'My Father in His Home Life', *Ladies Home Journal,* vol. 29, 1912

Dolby, George, *Charles Dickens as I Knew Him,* 1885

Du Cann, C.G.L., *The Love-Lives of Charles Dickens,* 1961

Easson, Angus, 'Dickens, *Household Words* and a Double Standard', *Dksn,* vol. 60, 1964
—— 'John Dickens and the Navy Pay Office', *Dksn,* vol. 70, 1974
—— 'Dickens's Marchioness Again', *Modern Language Review,* vol. 65, 1970

Ellis, Sarah Stickney, *The Women of England. Their Social Duties and Domestic Habits,* [1839]

Fielding, K.J., 'Charles Dickens and Colin Rae Brown', *Nineteenth Century Fiction,* Berkeley, vol. 7, 1952
—— 'Charles Dickens and His Wife: Fact or Forgery?', *Etudes Anglaises,* Paris, vol. 8, 1955
—— 'Dickens and the Hogarth Scandal', *Nineteenth Century Fiction,* Berkeley, vol. 10, 1955
—— 'Two Sketches by Maclise', *Dickens Studies,* Boston, Mass., vol. 2, 1966
—— 'Hard Times and Common Things', *Imagined Worlds. Essays on Some English Novels and Novelists in Honour of John Butt,* edd. Maynard Mack and Ian Gregor, 1968
—— 'Dickens as J.T. Danson Knew Him', *Dksn,* vol. 68, 1972

Fields, James T., *Yesterdays with Authors,* 1872

Fitzgerald, Percy, *The Life of Charles Dickens as Revealed in His Writings,* 1905

Forster, John, *The Life of Charles Dickens,* ed. J.W.T. Ley, 1928

Gissing, George, *Charles Dickens: A Critical Study,* 1898

Griffin, James, *Memories of the Past: Records of Ministerial Life,* 1883

Gross, John and Pearson, G. (edd.), *Dickens and the Twentieth Century,* 1962

Guerard, Albert, J., *The Triumph of the Novel: Dickens, Dostoyevsky, Faulkner,* New York, 1976

Hall, Anna Maria, *A Woman's Story,* 3 vols., 1857

Hardy, Barbara, *The Moral Art of Dickens,* 1970

Hemyng, Bracebridge, Henry Mayhew's *London Labour and the London Poor,* vol. 4, 1862

Hobsbaum, Philip, *A Reader's Guide to Charles Dickens,* 1972

Howe, M.A. DeWolfe, *Memories of a Hostess,* Boston, Mass., 1922

Johnson, Edgar, *Charles Dickens. His Tragedy and Triumph,* 2 vols., New York, 1952. Revised ed., 1977.

[Jolly, Emily], 'A Wife's Story', *Household Words,* vol. 12, 1855

Kaplan, Fred, *Dickens and Mesmerism. The Hidden Springs of Fiction,* Princeton, 1975

Kingsmill, Hugh, *The Sentimental Journey. A Life of Charles Dickens,* 1934

Kitton, F.G., *Charles Dickens by Pen and Pencil,* 1890

—— *Supplement to Charles Dickens by Pen and Pencil,* 1890

Lane, Margaret, *Purely for Pleasure,* 1966

Langton, Robert, *The Childhood and Youth of Charles Dickens,* enlarged and revised ed., 1891

Latimer, Elizabeth, 'A Girl's Recollections of Dickens', *Lippincott's Monthly Magazine,* vol. 52, 1893

Lehmann, J., *Ancestors and Friends,* 1962

Lindsay, Jack, *Charles Dickens. A Biographical and Critical Study,* 1950

Mackenzie, N. and G., *Dickens. A Life,* 1979

Manning, Sylvia, 'Dickens, January and May', *Dksn,* vol. 71, 1975

Marcus, Steven, *Dickens: from Pickwick to Dombey,* 1965

Martineau, Harriet, *Autobiography,* 3 vols., 1877

Masson, David, *British Novelists and Their Styles,* Cambridge, 1859

Meckier, Jerome, 'Some Household Words: Two New Accounts of Dickens's Conversation', *Dksn,* vol. 71, 1975

Morley, Malcolm, 'The Theatrical Ternans', *Dksn,* vols. 54-7, 1958-61

[Neal, John], 'Men and Women', *Blackwood's Edinburgh Magazine',* Edinburgh, vol. 16, 1824

Nisbet, Ada, *Dickens and Ellen Ternan,* Berkeley, 1952

—— 'Charles Dickens', *Victorian Fiction. A Guide to Research,* ed. Lionel Stevenson, Cambridge, Mass., 1964

Orton, Diana, *Made of Gold: A Biography of Angela Burdett Coutts,* 1980

[Panton, Jane Ellen], *Leaves from a Life,* 1908

Parker, David and Slater, Michael, 'The Gladys Storey Papers', *Dksn,* vol. 76, 1980

Paroissien, David H., 'Charles Dickens and the Weller Family', *Dickens Studies Annual,* Carbondale, Illinois, vol. 2, 1972

Pearson, Hesketh, *Charles Dickens. His Character, Comedy and Career,* 1949

Perugini, Kate, 'Edwin Drood and the Last Days of Dickens', *Pall Mall Magazine,* vol. 36, 1906

—— 'A Dickens Dinner at the Lyceum Club', *Dksn,* vol. 6, 1910

—— 'My Father's Love for Children', *Dksn,* vol. 7, 1911

—— 'On Women Old and New', *Dksn,* vol. 14, 1918

Ritchie, Anne, *From the Porch,* 1913

Rolfe, Franklin P., 'Dickens and the Ternans', *Nineteenth Century Fiction,* Berkeley, vol. 4, 1949-50

—— 'More Letters to the Watsons', *Dksn,* vol. 38, 1942

[Roscoe, W.C.], 'Woman', *National Review,* vol. 7, 1858

Solly, Henry S., *The Life of Henry Morley,* 1898

Staples, Leslie C., 'The Dickens Ancestry: Some New Discoveries II', *Dksn,* vol. 45, 1949

—— 'Some Early Memories of the Dickens Fellowship', *Dksn,* vol. 73, 1977

Stokes, Veronica, 'Charles Dickens: A Customer of Coutts and Co.', *Dksn,* vol. 68, 1972

Stone, Harry, 'The Genesis of a Novel: *Great Expectations', Charles Dickens 1812-1870. A Centenary Volume,* ed. E.W.F. Tomlin, [1969]

—— 'The Love Pattern in Dickens' Novels', *Dickens the Craftsman: Strategies of Presentation,* ed. Robert B. Partlow, Carbondale, Illinois, 1970

Stone, Marcus, 'Some Recollections of Dickens', *Dksn,* vol. 6, 1910

Stonehouse, John H., *Green Leaves: New Chapters in the Life of Charles Dickens,* 1931

Storey, Gladys, *Dickens and Daughter,* 1939

Suzannet, Comte Alain de, 'Maria Beadnell's Album', *Dksn,* vol. 31, 1935

Thomas, Deborah, 'Dickens' Mrs Lirriper and the Evolution of a Feminine Stereotype', *Dickens Studies Annual,* Carbondale, Illinois, vol. 6, 1977

[Thomas, Mrs Edward], 'Woman', *Metropolitan,* vol. 36, 1843

Thomson, Patricia, *The Victorian Heroine. A Changing Ideal 1837-1873,* 1956

Tillotson, Kathleen, *Novels of the Eighteen-Forties,* 1954

—— 'A Letter from Mary Hogarth', *Times Literary Supplement,* 23 Dec. 1960

—— 'The Middle Years from the "Carol" to "Copperfield"', *Dickens Memorial Lectures,* 1970

Tomlin, E.W.F., 'Newly Discovered Dickens Letters', *Times Literary Supplement,* 22 Feb. 1974

Toynbee, W. (ed.), *The Diaries of William Charles Macready,* 2 vols., 1912

Wagenknecht, Edward, 'Dickens in Longfellow's Letters and Journals', *Dksn,* vol. 52, 1956

—— *Dickens and the Scandalmongers. Essays in Criticism,* Norman, Oklahoma, 1965

Ward, Henrietta, *Memories of Ninety Years,* ed. Isabel McAllister, [1924]

Welsh, Alexander, *The City of Dickens,* 1971

Whipple, Edwin, 'The Shadow on Dickens's Life', *Atlantic Monthly,* Boston, Mass., vol. 40, 1877

Wiggin, Kate Douglas, *A Child's Journey with Dickens*, Boston, Mass. [1912]
Wilson, Angus, *The World of Charles Dickens,* 1970
—— 'Dickens and Dostoevsky', *Dickens Memorial Lectures,* 1970
Wright, Thomas, *The Life of Charles Dickens*, 1935
—— *Thomas Wright of Olney,* 1936
Yates, Edmund, *His Recollections and Experiences,* 2 vols., 1884
Young, G.M., 'Mr and Mrs Dickens', *Victorian Essays,* ed. W.D. Handcock, 1962

Index of Female Characters

General Index

[*Dickens's works (novels, sketches, essays etc.) are indexed under their titles. Dickens himself is not indexed.*]

Buss, Frances, 181

Carey, John, 241, 261, 265–6, 391,
431
Carey, Francis Stephen, 416
Carlton, W.J., 26, 378, 385, 387, 393,
397, 400
Carlyle, Thomas, 105, 132, 245, 400
Carlyle, Jane, 105, 132, 133
Chambers, C.E.S., 379
Chesterton, G.K., 292
Chesterton, G.L., 343
'Child's Dream of a Star, A' (*RP*), 25,
36, 92, 192, 364–5
Child's History of England, A, 16,
309, 414
'Child's Story, The' (*CS*), 36–7
Chimes, The (*CB*), 340, 404
Chisholm, Caroline, 343
Chorley, H.F., 188
Christian, Eleanor, 13, 16, 21, 32, 81,
111, 115–16, 122, 387–8, 401
Christmas Carol, A (*CB*), 33–4, 133,
356–7
Cinderella, 316
Clari, 28
Colden, Frances, 122
Collins, Charles Allston, 184–8, 189,
420
Collins, Philip, 126, 161–2, 251, 301,
342, 343, 347, 384, 391, 399
Collins, Wilkie, 65, 66, 133, 136, 140,
142, 165, 182, 184, 204, 205, 221,
325, 352, 384, 404
Compton, Emmeline, 126
Cornelius, Anne – *see* Brown, Anne
Coutts, Angela Burdett, 134, 144,
145, 151, 152, 153, 297, 306, 310,
314, 327, 341–3, 439, 444
Crivelli, Domenico, 27
Cubitt, William, 190

Dallas, Eneas Sweetland, 184
Dana, R.H., 118
Danson, J.T., 125
Darling, Grace, 309, 435

Davey, Mrs, 5, 6–7, 12, 16
Defoe, Daniel, 302
David Copperfield, 9, 19, 43, 44, 47,
62, 66, 73, 100, 157, 243, 253, 275,
346; Copperfield, David, 4, 9,
19–20, 21–2, 25, 35, 42, 44, 52, 54,
57, 62, 64; Dick, Mr, 272; Heep,
Uriah, 17, 251; Jip, 63–4, 392;
Micawber, Mr, 17, 19, 251, 311;
Murdstone, Mr, 19, 20; Peggotty,
Mr, 225; Quinion, 9; Steerforth,
62–3, 64, 75, 251, 266–7, 268,
275; Traddles, 83–4; Wickfield,
Mr, 252
de la Rue, Emile, 122–5, 142
de la Rue, Madame, 122–5, 142, 149,
303
Dexter, Walter, 15, 188, 195, 377,
394, 415
Dickens, Alfred Lamert, 12, 14, 34,
146, 352, 385
Dickens, Mrs Alfred Lamert, 15
Dickens, Alfred Tennyson, 16, 145,
146, 159, 409
Dickens, Augustus, 34, 352
Dickens, Catherine, 14, 29, 31, 47, 61,
77, 78, 79–80, 101–2, **103–62**,
163, 164, 168–71, 173, 177, 183,
191, 195, 204, 207, 208, 365,
373–5, 376, 384, 400, 401, 402,
403, 406, 407, 409, 410–13, 414,
415
Dickens, Charles, Jr., 134, 146, 153,
156, 157, 160, 384
Dickens, Dora, 130–1, 179
Dickens, Edward, 138–9, 159, 411
Dickens, Fanny (*later* Burnett), 3, 17,
25–39, 54, 92, 99, 122, 177, 296,
387–8
Dickens, Frank, 159
Dickens, Frederick, 4, 29, 34, 91, 388
Dickens, Henry Fielding, 139, 164,
376, 379, 388, 415
Dickens, John, 3–12, 15–16, 18, 21,
22, 25, 26, 27, 37, 51, 130, 174,
382, 384